Rewind and Search
Conversations with the Makers and Decision-Makers of
CBC Television Drama

Taking the reader behind the cameras, Mary Jane Miller traces the history of four decades of television drama on the Canadian Broadcasting Corporation (CBC) English network. She combines interviews with forty CBC personnel with her own commentary to explore how these programs were made and why.

The first half of *Rewind and Search* looks at the makers – the producers, directors, writers, story editors, and actors – while the second half deals with the decision-makers, issues, policy, and ethos that affect the production of CBC television, including drama. Miller pays particular attention to the ways in which programs were influenced by evolving audience expectations, technological advances, and changes in policy, personnel, and the corporate structure of the CBC.

With more cutbacks and a change of mandate looming on the horizon, the CBC is at a crossroads. *Rewind and Search* reveals the value of television drama as an important part of our Canadian heritage, a part that should not be overlooked.

MARY JANE MILLER is professor of film studies, dramatic and visual arts, Brock University.

Rewind and Search

*Conversations with the Makers
and Decision-Makers of CBC
Television Drama*

MARY JANE MILLER

McGill-Queen's University Press
Montreal & Kingston • Buffalo • London

© McGill-Queen's University Press 1996
ISBN 0-7735-1365-5

Legal deposit first quarter 1996
Bibliothèque nationale du Québec

Printed in Canada on acid-free paper

This book has been published with the help
of a grant from the Social Science Federation
of Canada, using funds provided by the Social
Sciences and Humanities Research Council of
Canada.

McGill-Queen's University Press is grateful
to the Canada Council for support of its
publishing program.

Canadian Cataloguing in Publication Data

Miller, Mary Jane, 1941–
  Rewind and search: conversations with the makers
  and decision-makers of CBC television drama

  Includes bibliographical references and index.
  ISBN 0-7735-1365-5

  1. Canadian Broadcasting Corporation – History.
  2. Television plays, Canadian (English) – History
  and criticism. I. Title.

  PN1992.65.M54 1996   791.45'0971   C95-920823-2

Contents

Acknowledgments

My deepest debt is to the many people I interviewed during my fifteen-year research into Canadian television drama. Those who spoke for the record and willingly took time to check facts and correct transcripts are Robert Allen, Paul Almond, David Barlow, Ivan Fecan, David Gardner, Hugh Gauntlett, Bill Gough, Nada Harcourt, Denis Harvey, Philip Keatley, Martin Kinch, Sam Levene, Jeannine Locke, Maryke McEwen, Trina McQueen, Mavor Moore, Sidney Newman, Joe Partington, Mario Prizek, Herb Roland, Anna Sandor, Alice Sinclair, R.H. Thomson, Eric Till, Kate Trotter, Ed Vincent, Hugh Webster, Ron Weyman, Don S. Williams, and Grahame Woods. John Kennedy's *carte blanche* and his willingness to share ideas over several years were crucial to the writing of this book, as well as to my previous book, *Turn Up the Contrast*.

Others who helped me understand how television dramas get to air are producers Douglas Lamb and Martin Weiner, director George Mc-Gowan, directors of photography Nick Evdemon, Brian Hebb, and Ed Long, designers Rudi Dorn and Dan Yarhi, composer Phil Schriebman, editor Vincent Kent, head of audience research Brian Stewart, and researchers Dennis O'Neill, Oly Iwanyshan, and Philip Savage of CBC Enterprises. I would also like to thank Ernie Dick, wearing his old hat at the National Archives and his more recent hat as CBC corporate archivist. It all began with Sam Kula, who in 1979 was director of the National Film Television and Sound Division. He gave me access to the then uncatalogued drama kines in his care. Professor Ross Eamon shared his oral history tapes of interviews with Ron Weyman and Robert Allen. Professor Malcolm Page recognized that inside an unshapely and lengthy manuscript two books were lurking. This is the second.

I would also like to acknowledge those faithful members of the Association for the Study of Canadian Radio and Television/AERTC for their encouragement over many years, their comments, and their devotion to this particularly fruitful tree which we have grafted from the various disciplines that study radio and television: Howard Fink, John Jackson, Renée Legris, Sylvie Robitaille, Paul Rutherford, John Twomey, and many others, both academics and archivists.

Andrew Borkowski and other officers at *SCAN* put me on their mailing list, and articles from *SCAN* are quoted throughout this book. They give glimpses into the world of CBC producers, and provide both intelligent and timely interviews and analysis of changes in technology and the broadcasting environment from the point of view of the makers and decision-makers.

This book would not have been written without the thirteen years of support I received from the Social Sciences and Humanities Research Council or the two sabbaticals I received from Brock University. The support of members of the Department of Film Studies and Dramatic and Visual Arts is also much appreciated.

Christine Fraser has been with this project since its first draft. Over the years she has transcribed tapes, kept track of people, talked over ideas and organization, carried out research, and been indispensable to its success. At the publication stage, I would like to thank Rosemary Shipton for her sympathetic and knowledgeable copy editing and her helpful conversations, and Katya Davison for proofreading – again.

As ever, I owe much to my companion, partner, critic, expert in the field of computers, information manager, and husband, Jack Miller.

Finally, I dedicate this book to my late father, Larry Miller, and Elizabeth Miller, my mother.

Introduction

When I began formal work on CBC television drama eleven years ago, I was drawn to two questions: Was there a golden age of television drama? And where did contemporary television drama stand in relation to that rumoured golden age? *Turn Up the Contrast: CBC Television Drama since 1952* charted that unknown country and came up with some answers – now open to revision as we continue to explore the cultural memory and broadcasting heritage in greater depth. Since the processes that shaped those materials are not generally found in books or periodicals, or even in the CBC collection of reports and memoranda in the National Archives of Canada, but are locked up in the memories of those who were there, I had to rely on interviews with both the pioneers and the current practitioners to help me understand how and why the ways of making television drama changed.

In the early 1980s I began to interview people, learning what questions to ask as I went along. I also learned the perils of oral history, adding the fallible memories of my sources to my own fallibility. Still, certain broad themes and attitudes about the early history of CBC television drama as contrasted with the attitudes and focus of the late 1980s and early 1990s became apparent. Behind the story I was telling and the programs I analysed lay another story. It seemed to me this narrative might also be of interest to the same mixed readership – scholars, archivists, students, critics of the media, people inside the CBC, and general readers who found my first book useful. To make sense of this process over a forty year period I have drawn on the multiple perspectives of a selection of the producers, directors, writers, story editor, actors, and the executives who set policy – using a multivocal approach. I have provided whatever additional explanation and interpretation I thought essential. Other books written in the United States have used this approach with varying degrees of success, but my research has not turned up any such publications in Canada.[1]

Mythology does infuse some of the memories of those interviewed, but as the interviews demonstrate, the mythology developed remarkably consistently in the 1950s and 1960s. The mythology, and the underlying corporate culture then changed direction significantly in the 1970s and early 1980s. It has changed again in recent years, with some serious consequences. The mythology is one of the elements in this complex story which I seek to uncover and to document in greater depth than journalists can do.[2]

The protocols used for interviewing most of these people (the very early ones excepted) were identical. I pointed out to each person the disagreements, amplifications, multiple and occasionally contradictory perspectives that editing and juxtaposition would create. Every interviewee after 1984 was told before my tape recorder went on that the interviews would be organized and presented by topic and theme, not in sequence or in one place. Being involved in the dramatic arts, for the most part, the interviewees thought that a dialogue or symposium would be a useful and challenging way of presenting the material. When contacted later for formal permission to use quotations from the edited material (which was always sent to them for approval), I explained again how the book would be organized. In all but one interview (which I did not use), no one objected either to the contents of the raw transcripts or to my edited drafts. Several people offered amplifications, which were incorporated into the raw transcripts and used in this book. Only two people among the forty I approached refused to be interviewed.

Some of these interviews are remarkably candid. I offered every interviewee a chance to go on the record for the National Archives of Canada (NA), as well as basic editorial control over what I would publish. Trina McQueen, excellent television journalist as she has been, found this control rather odd. I felt, however, that candour was of the utmost importance for the archival record and that people interviewed should have an opportunity to reflect on and to clarify what they said. All interviewees saw a full transcript of their interview to determine whether they wished it to be deposited in the National Archives of Canada, and all had a chance to elaborate on or to explain what they had said both for that record and for this book. Each person who is quoted approved of my editing, although R.H. Thomson was the only one to see a draft chapter. The material chosen in many cases represents about a fifth to a tenth of the often lengthy conversations we had. In each chapter, the date of my interview with each person is included with the first excerpt.

No one refused permission to use the abbreviated material on the grounds that I had somehow compromised any intellectual and artistic integrity.[3] A few warned me that the process of interweaving would be difficult and time-consuming. Many thought the idea a stimulating way to hold the reader's attention and to explain complex processes. It is the people who generously shared their time with me in interviews, on the sets of productions, during the breaks in sound mixes, and in editing suites who made this book possible.[4]

One purpose of this book is to reveal the praxis of making television drama on the CBC English network through the years using the words of the makers and decision-makers of CBC television drama themselves. My emphasis in *Rewind and Search* is on how those programs were made and why, rather than on the programs themselves (many of which have been discussed in *Turn Up the Contrast*). I also focus on how the programs[5] were influenced by the evolution of the technology and the changes in personnel and policy. There is a tradition of oral history and published interviews about production in popular cultural studies, but no book of any kind exists on the practical side of Canadian television drama. The title *Rewind and Search* suggests an opportunity to reflect on what has been recorded. The reader will find that the interviews and my own comments are both intertextual and contextual; intertextual in that they will cast new light on specific programs within the same network, and contextual in that they may help to explain why as Canadians we have the television drama we have.

This book is also a record of the early days of CBC television drama when the processes and the issues of what to make and how to do it were relatively straightforward. For this period (1952–68, broadly speaking), the various perspectives on what happened and how converge. I then record and analyse the transition through the first of the hard times, 1968–73, a task made easier because the documents exist, memories are fresher (and in some agreement), and the evidence of the programs that resulted were visible to the viewers and to the corporation. The era of John Hirsch (1974–78) is already well documented because Hirsch was an articulate and outspoken man who told journalists in some detail what he wanted to do and why, and because his internal reports are very detailed. Again, people's memories of him and of that period are both vivid and convergent.

I was given generous access to John Kennedy's Drama Department during the 1980s, and the observations of others about his period of leadership are augmented by the fact that I was able to see so much more of the material as it was broadcast. The year 1985, in which the already relentless squeeze on funds turned into the first severe round of cutbacks, is also the year I set to work finishing *Turn Up the Contrast:*

CBC Televisoin Drama since 1982 filing away for a future book my analysis of the drama programs that continued to pour out of the television set. I picked up the threads of *Rewind and Search* just as Kennedy's tenure as head of tv drama was ending. Major changes both in the direction of the department and in personnel were in the wind.

Another factor that motivated my continuing research in this area was unexpected, but inevitable in the light of the ever-increasing external constraints on the CBC and the changing technology and broadcasting climate. I was ready to return to my work on this book in 1988, just as CBC drama was overtaken by a profound structural reorganization and an indisputable internal crisis. Many of those more senior producers and writers I spoke to were deeply shaken in their confidence in the CBC. Several have since retired or turned to other pursuits. Yet CBC English television has also managed to produce and telecast more drama in 1990–94 than it telecast in the 1960s–80. Unwittingly, I had resumed research at a cusp in the CBC's history. My own interpretation of what is happening does not appear in detail until the "wrapup" of chapter 12, so readers will have a chance to judge for themselves among the sometimes conflicting, even contradictory points of view about this reshaping.

It is never easy to assess history on the run. Unlike *Turn Up the Contrast*, this book is not primarily an evaluation of CBC television drama, but it does provide a context for a later assessment of the programs made in this decade of rapid change in the technology of recording and transmission, the organization of delivery systems, and the fragmentation of the audience. Indeed, sociologists, historians, and cultural studies experts may well be more interested in these conversations than in any analysis I might do on the aesthetics of the dramas themselves.

This is not a comprehensive set of interviews of CBC personnel. That would be impossible, given the limits of time and normal book length and the vast size and geographical scope of the corporation (10,000 employees before the last round of cuts, and with hundreds more who have left). The effect of hundreds of voices would be babble. Even though television is a collective art form, there have been literally hundreds of producers, directors, writers and actors, cinematographers, designers and other crafts people who have set their imprint on CBC television drama. Inevitably, key figures from all periods of CBC drama are missing from this study.

I chose instead to introduce the reader to a small number of voices – about forty directly or in paraphrase. Various factors influenced my selection; in some instances, I sought people out because of my respect for and familiarity with their work; or simply because they had been with the corporation for a significant length of time; or because they were senior management with the responsibility of making the crucial decisions about the kinds of drama we see and hear; or because I got to know them in the course of observing productions. In all cases the people who appear in this book do so because they were articulate. A very few would not talk to me because they feared that being quoted would have an impact on their careers or because they were too angry to discuss the CBC of the 1990s.

In *Rewind and Search* there are also three explicit personae of the author. One is MJM, who is the interviewer asking questions in a specific context on a particular day. The second is expository – the authorial voice that explains or amplifies or comments, and is signified by square brackets within an interview. The third voice is analytical, represented both by the editorial process itself and the reflective and analytical passages.

The first half of the book is a study of the makers or the creative people – directors, writers, producers and actors, with two chapters on other crafts and changing technology. The second half is a study of the decision-makers, along with the issues, the policy, and the CBC ethos as they affect the making of television drama. Multiple, sometimes contradictory, and sometimes complementary views are expressed on a variety of topics in both parts.

Those readers interested in the full transcripts or tapes will find most, though not all, at the Moving and Sound Image division of the National Archives. I hope that the collection can serve as a research tool for other scholars who have different skills and different questions to ask of the material recorded. Scholars who wish to consult the raw transcripts and tapes will find they have access to some interviews as soon as I have published this book, and that others have been sealed for a variable length of time by the interviewees themselves to protect their reputations or their jobs – their interpretation of their circumstances, not mine. Many of the programs cited here and in *Turn Up the Contrast* are available for viewing in the archives. It is true they are not easily accessible – nor are the programs analysed by my colleagues in the United States and Britain, or the films analysed for the past eighty years by film scholars. Nevertheless the analysis of these artifacts continues. Indeed, the proliferation of television materials in video stores may eventually catch up with the scholarship,

I would like to conclude with an example provided by my colleague and friend Ernie Dick, a former archivist with the Sound and Moving Images branch of the National Archives and now the official CBC archivist. At the 1991 Learned Societies conference he presented a paper to the Association for the Study of Canadian Radio and Television in which he pointed out that the English division of the CBC seldom celebrates its accomplishments, and then does it far too modestly. The contrast between the CBC and Radio-Canada, and between the regions and the English Network, became apparent from the clips he presented. A local Montreal station, CBMT, for example, opens every broadcast day with an eleven minute montage of its city and province – the station's heritage. Regional programs like Newfoundland's *Land and Sea* observed their 25th anniversary with pride and confidence. Yet the equally long-lived national program *The Nature of Things* was far more reticent about its anniversary. In painful contrast to Radio-Canada's hours of retrospective, CBC English television celebrated the network's fiftieth anniversary with a modest and somewhat disjointed one-hour tribute.

These examples demonstrated to me once again that, too often, the CBC hides or throws away its accomplishments, downgrades its practitioners, suffers from cultural amnesia about its own past, and then wonders why Canadians are less committed to public broadcasting than they used to be and why internal morale is so often low. These are by no means the only reasons for the sense of crisis dogging the CBC, but they are factors over which the CBC could exercise some control if it would. The corporation itself needs to sit down, rewind, and search its own history and its ethos. The fact is that cultural amnesia can be fatal unless memory and reflection, however selective or flawed, reverse the deterioration of the body politic. *Je me souviens – I Remember* is, as Quebeckers already know, the only way for a culture and a country to survive.

Rewind and Search

1 Directing

> A lot of directors today have not had the opportunity, or do not even care, to build into their fabric at least a passing knowledge of theatre and all aspects of dance, opera, or music. You should have a continuing curiosity, if not a deep interest in all those things. You must go and see them. On the other hand, Elia Kazan said: "You may now be exhausted from all that you have to learn. You may well ask me how it is that I made so many lousy films in my time – it still comes down to instinct!" You've still got to have that spark that makes it work. You can have all the knowledge, yet you can make a clinker of a film because something is missing and you have failed to put it there or it wasn't there in the first place; you have misread it, and no amount of background will save you. But you'd better have that background. ERIC TILL

Television is a collective art, but what we see on our living-room sets, no matter how edited and rearranged, is, frame by frame, what the director chose to show us. That was true in 1952 when the CBC first went on air. It is still true. Thus we start our probe into the process of making television with the role of the director. The director's sensibility controls the vision of and often mediates between the writer and the designer, the director of photography and the sound and lighting people, and the thirty or forty others who work on the show. The relationship of the director and the producer in the first season of a series and in most anthologies and movies is complex. As the key to the whole enterprise, this relationship is addressed in the first two chapters of this book. In contemporary practice, what we see on the television screen is the *gestalt* of the producer's overall vision as well as the work of many others. But as viewers we see the material using, first of all, the director's "eyes."

THE EARLY DAYS: "LIVE" AND "LIVE TO TAPE"

Robert Allen began as a producer/director in the early 1950s, replaced Sydney Newman as supervising producer in 1957, was executive producer of the various electronic forms of drama developed in the 1960s and 1970s including *Folio* and *Festival*, and was executive producer of many anthologies and series on tape and film from *The Way We Are* to *Seeing Things* until his retirement in 1991. I began the research for both my previous book, *Turn Up the Contrast*, and this book by interviewing him.

ALLEN [1981]: In 1952, when television started, the CBC brought in a handful of people from various places, some more experienced than others. Some had been working in the theatre for one or two years. They all gathered here and began to learn how to do it. It is not easy for a director to learn to cope with the machinery of television. Moreover, he has to face a group of between thirty and fifty people in addition to the cast. We had at least three (sometimes four) cameras at the same time which you had to move from one place to another as the action shifted. The director had no chance to stop. When I think of the actual broadcast, the director was performing as much as the actors. Unlike film, with live television it was the director who determined everything. No retakes, no stopping to change reels. Just start and go.

MJM: The directors learned by doing it?

ALLEN: By doing it, yes. And there was the small group who continued to do it, until we all dropped dead, practically.

MJM: I can't get over the number of productions each of you did, one every two or three weeks. It must have been mad.

ALLEN: I was doing a ninety-minute show every three weeks. And the next morning I had to find another topic. Which meant reading, asking people, and in two or three days deciding what to do. I was also doing a half-hour of *Sunshine Sketches* every week. We were able to do stage plays on live television, because we cut the play. (There was no real adaptation.) We were on a treadmill, we were running fast enough not to worry about whether we were going to be shot down or not. [As far as censorship is concerned, always an issue in television, it was more difficult, because it went out live, for sponsors, politicians, or CBC brass to stop a show.]

PAUL ALMOND, television producer/director and film-maker [1991]: When I started at the CBC, the Drama Department was, I think, on the fifth floor. You got out of the elevator and you turned left and there was this big room with eight desks for script assistants outside eight offices where the television director/producers were: Arthur Hiller, Leo Orenstein, Murray Chercover, and David Greene (who didn't do the half-hours), and soon Ronny Weyman. The four of us were doing half-hours, *Ford Theatre* and *On Camera.*

MJM: *GM Presents?*

ALMOND: No, *GM* came a year or two later. *Ford Theatre* is a little half-hour thing that Arthur Hiller was doing with Murray for a year in 1954. And then there was David Greene, Sylvio Narazzanno, and Henry Kaplan – they were the big dudes and eventually they did *General Motors Theatre.* Just this little group of people were turning out two half-hours a week and one hour a week. Then some of them were borrowed by *Folio,* so we were turning out a ninety-minute program, and an hour, and a half-hour. That's three hours of television drama a week, just the seven of us. Every two weeks I did one and every two weeks Arthur Hiller did one, and so on.

But we had a tremendous sense of camaraderie and of obligation (I'm sure it's not there now, I hear it's just terrible). We felt we were being paid to do what we loved, which was, to me, totally astonishing, to be paid and to be given an office and told you could direct whatever you liked! So we all watched each others' shows and the next morning we would drop into each others' office and discuss what we liked and what we didn't like about them. We were very open with each other. [With the scattering of producers all over and the use of directors on short-term contracts, this seldom happened by the 1980s in either a professional or a social context. Although the many scattered operators of the CBC have been gathered under one roof in Toronto at last, the 1990s have brought further decentralization because of the increased emphasis on independent productions.]

Sylvio Narazzanno worked with designer Nicolai Soloviov, but mainly I did my big shows with designer Rudi Dorn.

MJM: Other people tell me you were a team.

ALMOND: It was really exciting. In those days of live television the most important thing was to catch the moment of drama – not at a dress rehearsal but on the air. You had to catch that elusive spark. Getting that live performance was quite different, you did it once. The art of trying to direct actors in those days was somehow to bring the performance to a peak at the right point – on the air. Just as the performances varied through the rough dress rehearsal (the first time, cast and crew did the drama "at speed"), the dress rehearsal, and the show, so the camera would vary, it wouldn't just hit fixed marks. If a person was being tremendous on air we'd go in much closer, I'd say "closer, closer, she's terrific, closer!" and then suddenly "OK, pull back, wait a minute." So everything happened spontaneously. The camera work was spontaneous with the acting because your shots reflected the intensity of the minute – which is impossible in film.

MJM: Producer/director Mario Prizek told me that when it was really going well a cameraman would offer a shot that hadn't been on the original plot.

ALMOND: Oh, of course, all the time. During rehearsals they'd frame shots one never thought of, sometimes actually on air.

MJM: And if it were a better idea, then Prizek would simply pick it up.

ALMOND: Of course, because you are editing at the same time. We had shot lists. Each shot was marked with the camera number (we always had three or four cameras). The camera turret contained four lenses: a 2-inch, 3-inch, 5-inch, and an 8-inch – a good cameraman could rack over from one lens to another and focus in two seconds with one hand. For example, shot 42 would be on camera 4. (Everyone wrote scripts in a different way.) When you were going through, the script assistant would say "Ready shot 42 on 4," and she readied the cameras. Now what happened when you startled to go off the shot list is you said "I'm flying" – that was the key word. When you said "I'm flying," everyone held their shots and then you could switch to whatever camera you wanted, regardless of the shot list. I'd say "Take 2," then I would call the other camera to flip over to a tighter shot: "3 flip to an 8! OK, take 3! OK, now we're back on script!" and then she'd say "Ready shot 43 on camera 2" and then I'd take 2. So that's what Mario was talking about. That's the way it was done. Editing at the moment, it's very exciting, very exciting!

Some directors like Eric Till, David Gardner, Ron Weyman, and Phil Keatley directed both electronic (live-to-tape) and film drama with equal facility and pleasure.[1] Paul Almond was one of the few to become primarily a feature film-maker – and yet in our discussion he started me by his observation that live television was in some ways more technically impressive than tape or film.

ALMOND: Live television had a kind of fluidity and spontaneity that allowed it to do things that feature film could never do. It seems to me that it starts with the black-and-white camera on those pedestals. Do you remember seeing them?

MJM: Yes. I do, indeed.

ALMOND: There was a ring that the cameraman held with one hand that controlled the direction and the up and down. He had his other hand on the focus so that the camera could move in and out, up and down, very fluidly. In film, when the camera moves, you put marks on a floor and the dolly pusher has to hit the mark because somebody else is doing the focus. At least three guys are manipulating the camera: one man is looking through the camera, the focus puller is on focus, and the dolly pusher is controlling the movement. In television this was all done by one man. As he's going in, he adjusts his focus. He goes up and down exactly as he feels and the action moves at that moment. As in no other medium, the camera becomes a tool for reflecting art.

MJM: The script assistant was always a woman, wasn't she?

ALMOND: Yes, of course.

MJM: Then they were called "script assistants." Now, an assistant producer would be a more accurate title, would it not? Because she was, at that time, a combination of assistant director, assistant producer, and time-keeper.

ALMOND: That's true.

MJM to RON WEYMAN, executive producer in the 1960s of *The Serial, Wojeck, Quentin Durgens MP, McQueen the Actioneer*, and many drama specials [1987]: So, in effect, your script assistant had to stay detached enough to stay on the timing and keep that particular rhythm rolling.

WEYMAN: It was a period where that particular person was thoroughly taken for granted. But it was a wedding, it was the kind of relationship that you took for granted.

MJM: Did you try to work with the same person all the time? Did teams of that kind form?

WEYMAN: Oh, yes, it went on for years. I can remember being told that my script assistant, Anne Weldon, was going to be shifted around, and I asked the executive why. "Oh, just because I feel like it," he replied. And I said, "No way."

MJM to ALMOND: Being a script assistant would be a darn good start, I would think, to being a producer.

ALMOND: What you said in your book and what I have to keep emphasizing is that England had a big film tradition and also a certain television tradition. America had a film tradition. We were the only country that had no tradition – so television was our beginning. We did things in television that they didn't do in England or America. When Sydney Newman went over to England, he brought some of those theories of how to make television with him. Several Canadians followed – Sylvio Narazzanno, Hank Kaplan, and Ted Kotcheff.

I remember I went over to do my own play *The Hill*, which had won a few awards.[2] In those days the British cameras were working exactly as in film. When you set the camera position in rehearsal they'd mark it on the floor with chalk and give it a number. But I'd say, "Maybe the actors are being slightly different this time so maybe it should be over here," and they'd say, "Well, no, I go on my marks." I'd say, "There's no such thing as "marks" in television, you don't have marks!" But I got them to do it by the end, since I had three days of camera rehearsals.

MJM: It was a good, innovative play.

ALMOND: That process broke traditions at the BBC and it began a kind of new way of working, because I wanted things to be fluid. I mean, that's television.

I wrote *The Hill* for the television medium. It starts with the narrator saying, "This is a television studio and these are actors. Tonight, they are going to perform for you the crucifixion of Our Lord." You saw the people standing around, you saw the set, which was just a huge cyclorama and some risers (flat plywood platforms). Then suddenly, on a cue, the actors rushed into a tight throng yelling "Crucify Him!" and the camera dollied in to exclude everything but the faces, and there you were, right in Jerusalem – much more realistic than having a painted set, because there were these real, frenzied faces. You see, at that time Rudi Dorn and I were working on theories about what TV should be. We were against "realistic sets" because we had this theory about the only real thing being the emotion expressed on the face of a really good actor. Film could take you to the actual place, TV couldn't – we were locked into a studio. That's how we evolved the idea of a plain cyclorama and no set for *The Hill*. When you have a face crying in closeup, we said, you don't need a set. So this was kind of a seminal drama in the sense that the set is the face or faces against a plain background and that's the drama, the emotion. Rudi was instrumental in doing that.

MJM: You're talking about television as if the medium itself were fluid. Your work has itself been characterized by the fluidity of camera.

ALMOND: Oh really? Well, that may be. But I think a lot of us were using this fluidity, because the cameras were so mobile and often the sets were quite stylized.

MJM: Yes, they were, weren't they? But television adapted to stylized sets before location shooting and the drive for narrative realism narrowed the range of possibilities.

ALMOND: Exactly, and that's why it was so wonderful because it was like really good theatre. I did *Under Milkwood*, a radio play by poet Dylan Thomas, with Rudi Dorn. We had, all over the studio, the odd bits of wall, a fragment of a house, a window. On a wide shot of the whole studio, it was almost Dali-esque. Then the camera moving in would catch a face in the window, and it would be perfectly realistic. As you broke away it would suddenly become non-realistic (the window floating by itself), and then, suddenly, you would move in and you'd get caught by another moment of realism. Those television cameras could do that. In film that would be so clunky it wouldn't feel right.

MJM: You were all around the same age, too, weren't you?

ALMOND: Yes, we were. I was actually younger than anybody at the time, but nobody knew that. I was twenty-two. You see, Bob Allen is the one who hired me in 1953, because for a brief stint he was the supervisory program director. He hired me and put me with Sydney Newman, supervising producer of the sponsored drama.

MJM: So you worked on the commercial drama for a while?

ALMOND: Yes, before I got to Allen's *Folio/Festival*. That was the big thing and I couldn't get there for a year or so.

TRAINING

ALMOND: First I followed David Greene around doing *The Portrait of Dorian Grey*, with Lloyd Bochner playing the lead. So I was in ten days' rehearsal with him. A week later Sydney called me and said, "Paul, I've got half an hour next Wednesday." He said I'd better do what's now called a dry run, not going on the air. So I said, "OK, Sydney," and he said "Here's this script ..." I said, "Sydney, if it's a dry run, I don't want anything you hand me. I'll find my own thing." So I found T.S. Eliot's *Sweeny Agonistes* and I did that as a half-hour. I thought, I'm not going on the air and I'll learn, and I used every trick I could find. I used prism shots, upside-down shots, everything in the book. People were coming into the control room to see it, so it got me a bit of a reputation. I was really only in training for three weeks.

I did my first show on the air before they knew I was hired. After about two months I saw them giving out paycheques. It was a Friday and I thought, "I've been here a while now (two months), maybe I could get one." So I went to Sydney Newman and said, "Shouldn't I get a paycheque, too? I mean they're all getting it." He said, "Let me call up." And you know, they had no record of me! The employment office at the CBC, large probably even in those days, was furious that I'd been hired without its knowledge. But I'd done a show on the air, so I wasn't really afraid. They made me come in and fill out forms for a whole day. I only did it because I was needing my paycheque. After all, it was the first paycheque I had ever gotten in my life. I'd only been out of college (Balliol, Oxford) for about two years, I think.

DAVID GARDNER, producer/director in the 1960s and actor from the 1950s to the 1990s [1983]: In 1959 I had just come back from the Old Vic Company on tour. There was no training school, but for three months we were turned loose at the CBC. The first month you observed and asked questions. The second month, you sat in the producer's "hot seat" for the first time and you cut your teeth on *Mr Fix-It*, a short how-to show. In the third month you were given a half-hour drama to produce. You cast it and did everything that would be expected – and then you saw what happened. So the first month you went around asking, "What is a camera, what does it do, how low can you "pedestal" down?" [The old, heavy cameras were mounted on "pedestals," and could not point straight down to the floor or angle up from a lower position.][3]

Then there came the horrible day when for the first time you sat in the hot seat. I say "horrible" because many people didn't get past this moment. Peter Boretski came out in hives the first day he sat in the control room. He eventually beat it and did a fair amount of television work, but the first time it hit him that way. It required a certain kind of coolness, a capacity to time things and feel things out, and eye/hand coordination (except your hand never touches anything) to be able to time music coming in and rolling film. You've got to roll the film three seconds in advance to make it come up on camera on cue. I did *Mr Fix-It* and for my sins, *The News*, which was very hard and technically very difficult because you were constantly cueing film and telecine, but it was good training. Then you graduated to *Scope* and *Folio* and the "biggies."

The CBC saw half-hour drama in the 1960s as a training ground for producers. If you came to Bob Allen with an idea, you also had a slot to do it in. *Q for Quest* and others, which were the experimental slot, were the trial-balloon place. And a lot of interesting, very controversial things happened. If you really hated abortion, then you would do a sharp little drama on it. There were taboos, of course, about what you could do (and abortion was probably one of them). But to me this was closer to the [American] *Studio One* kind of experimentation. We often used the bare studio. I can remember doing shows with just a few stylized trees in them and the studio in black limbo.

The first three waves of producer/directors experienced the rough-and-ready days of apprenticeship described by Almond. By the 1970s, however, the roles of producing and directing had been separated. John Hirsch, the new head of TV drama, had a mandate to develop new directors for the drama department.

PHILIP KEATLEY, producer/director of *Cariboo Country*, the *Beach-combers*, and drama specials [1985]: When CBC TV came into existence [1950–57], it had a training program for producers and directors. In fact, the BBC said that their training system was based on what they had learned from the Canadians in the 1950s. Then in 1974–75, in response to the senior management's recommendations in the drama report,[4] they gave the neophyte directors a studio and said, "Everything in television is so bad, we do not want you to be taught all the terrible things we've been doing with it. Here's a studio and technicians who know how to use it and are transparent as far as opinions and technique are concerned. They can do what you want." [That didn't work either because what the directors selected, for the most part, came from the innovative but technically rudimentary stages of the alternative theatre. They ran into all kinds of barriers – union rules, a complex technology, and a corporation wary of formal experiment.]

In 1977 I was asked to set up a training program for directors because things had gone sour. The idea was that we would talk to the BBC and do something with them because they had always had training for the producers. Leonard Chase, who is the head of training for the BBC, personally came over and we ran four-week courses – BBC style. I was supposed to learn how to do it, and then do it continually for the department. We picked nine people, all theatrical people.

This time anybody who got into the course was to be, in effect, sponsored by departments in the corporation. The guarantee was that at the end of the training (four weeks), the department had to hire the trainee. We got several good directors out of it, but not in drama. The only people I can think of who stuck with it and went through in drama didn't stay in the CBC. I would say that our success rate with more formal training was 3 per cent more effective than the unreliable training that happened before.

In the 1980s John Kennedy and Herb Roland tried this scheme again. They brought the BBC people back for the anthology *Judge*. Kennedy had said, "You have to find a way for them to be in this chair in Studio 7 at the end of the year and, if not, we aren't getting anywhere." I replied, "Then you have to provide the programming opportunity," and he did. They brought the BBC people back and did a training session with them, then had them direct a show for *Judge*. The only thing that I didn't like about it was that *Judge* was too much a "shooting pattern" formula [because of a very restricted studio space, one or two sets, and three tape cameras] to be really useful for letting a director learn his trade.

After producing the 1970s hit series *A Gift to Last*, Herbert Roland went on to produce *Judge*, a series that was in reruns in 1990 on YTV

– a children's specialty channel, even though it was often a challenging program for adults about contemporary social issues.[5]

ROLAND [1989]: I'm very proud of some of those episodes.

MJM: My favourite one among those I've managed to see was about the Jehovah's Witnesses. That was a very difficult subject.

ROLAND: Yes, Danielle Suissa directed that one. There are some lovely things in that. We got David Gardner back to direct a program on abortion, which George Allen wrote and I found very good. [It was good. It examined the conflicting rights of husbands and wives over a fetus.] He was the only guest director we had because *Judge* was meant for new directors, but he hadn't directed for fifteen or so years. It was well ahead of its time. Was that the one I put an "adult audience" or some kind of framing on?

MJM: Yes, presumably because by that time the schedulers had moved you to a family time slot – 7:00 or 7:30 on a weekend.

ROLAND: When *Judge* began it was the first year of *The Journal*, and that program went off the air for the summer, so they put us on at 10:30. We got a million-and-a-half viewers. Then it was just unbelievable what they did to us. After the first year they weren't going to let us go on, yet we got those fantastic ratings during that summer. John Kennedy, head of TV Drama (1978–89), resurrected the show with a new set. John was a great help, a great supporter right from the beginning. I didn't feel strongly at that time about the lack of writers, but I was really concerned about directors. I didn't foresee the death of multi-camera [tape/studio drama]. I thought that the rule would always be that the corporation would include at least one "tape" drama in the schedule, as it had been in the 1970s to the mid-1980s, such as *Gift to Last* and *The Great Detective*. So I wanted to train directors for the multi-camera setup. The directors also had to learn to work with actors. I came up with this idea of *Judge*. What a challenge it was, for new directors to learn how to handle it. It was set in one room, mostly in the court room, so it was not easy to make it really interesting or exciting visually. But I also found these limitations a wonderful way to get performances. Performances are what drama is all about.

Eventually I came up with four scripts. They got the money to bring the BBC course over here. In fact, at the end of the four weeks, each new director did a sort of a bastardized script of *Judge*, a short fifteen-minute one. But I always said that "this series is to bring new directors along, but we are not flashing on the screen something that says 'New directors.' I want *Judge* to stand on its own."

Since *Judge* was cancelled, the opportunity to learn has been provided not by in-house training but by the half-hour anthologies originating in the regions, *The Way We Are* [1987–89] and the independent half-hour regional productions of *Inside Stories* (1990–91).

David Gardner, who successfully pursued a doctorate in the 1980s at the Drama Centre at the University of Toronto while acting full time, was the first director I interviewed. His memory in television spans the period from 1954, when he played Rosencrantz, to a continuing role on *Homefires*, when I spoke with him in 1983. He continues to make many dramatic appearances and many commercials, even in his "retirement."

GARDNER: I was a graduate in art and archaeology. I worked with Leo Rampen, who is the producer of the religious series *Man Alive*. (Leo is a superb connoisseur.) We did a show called *The Face of God*, a look at the portrayal of Christ in art from the beginning of the earlier art scratchings to Brancussi. It was really a very beautiful show and got a lot of notice. I don't know if it won an award or something. It was a half-hour live, using maybe 150 graphics, with the camera panning over, moving, and dissolving from one to the other. It was a very beautiful show with music.

People thought that *For the Record* was a new kind of series. And really it was not. The CBC was being very controversial in the 1950s, tackling programs that were extremely risky. However, the one-hour slot tended to be commercial anthology, *GM Presents* and so on. Because it was sponsored, you had to be careful. There was one very controversial episode about showing a hanging, *Shadow of a Pale Horse.*

I was assigned to most of my shows or I was asked to do something. Then Ron Weyman [who was developing filmed drama in Toronto, while Phil Keatley in Vancouver stretched the form in *Cariboo Country*] said, "Would you like to work with me on this?" We did *Mr Member of Parliament* [which became *Quentin Durgens MP*]. Then I became the executive producer of that series, as Ronny had been of *The Serial*. These things all evolved. Bob Allen would say, "David, I would like you to do a Bernard Shaw." I think the first one I did was *Village Wooing*. I loved Shaw because of my theatre training and background. So I did *Doctor's Dilemma*, *The Apple Cart*, and *Dear Liar*, and shows like that. I was asked to do a lot of the plays that were adapted for television.

MJM: Were you involved in the adaptation, in the sense of getting the play down to television proportions or adapting something intended for the theatre to television conventions?

GARDNER: Very much so. As a producer/director you shaped your
script.

MJM: You had the actor and the author in one person with Gratien
Gélinas in *Yesterday the Children Were Dancing,* a drama about
separatism first staged in an English translation in 1967.

GARDNER: Yes, but it is not a good television adaptation. There was
no great money involved. Instead of just one set, we had two extra
rooms, so that you had a little more movement, and we did one
car ride in the beginning of the show, but essentially it was a
televised stage play.

George McGowan pioneered taking tape cameras on location for
George Ryga's 1963 *Q for Quest* production of *Two Soldiers.* I really
developed the technique. We would take three tape cameras on *Mr
Member of Parliament,* set them up, and do scenes with three cameras. We would have Gordon Pinsent running down the street of
New Hamburg to an ambulance, a long shot from a hotel window
across the street from one camera, and two cameras down at the
ambulance so that we could intercut dialogue back and forth.
Sometimes five minutes, even ten minutes, would be taped as a
sequence.

MORE ON THE FORMATIVE 1950S

The days of directors learning on the job after a short hands-on
apprenticeship are long gone. But when the CBC was moving into
television in 1951, few producer/directors had any experience. They
came into television from radio, the theatre, and the National Film
Board. In 1990 I interviewed another veteran of the very early days,
the first supervising producer of CBC television, Mavor Moore, who
was responsible for finding people and training them in the United
States (1950–51), then after 1952 on the spot.

MJM: Somebody, I think it was Mario Prizek, said that first generation of producer/directors was distinctly cosmopolitan European in
flavour and that a second generation came along about five years
later.

MAVOR MOORE, writer/actor/producer [1990]: I don't think there
was a particularly European flavour, but I'll tell you what there was
that the CBC had never had before: a considerably Jewish flavour.
This I remember well because when Stuart Griffiths and I had
drawn up our list of proposed appointments, we brought it into
Fergus Mutrie, director of television, who was an extremely fair-
minded man. Fergus looked at the list and his first comment was:

"A lot of Jewish names on that list." (Now this was a time when there was a great deal of anti-Semitism at the CBC, as the very few Jews in there would have told you; Lorne Greene had a difficult time, John Adaskin had a difficult time. I know of deliberate instances of anti-Semitism in the CBC.) Fergus saw this list and I said, "Yes, Fergus, a lot of Scottish names there, too!" And he smiled and said nothing. Then Stuart said very quietly, "Fergus, do you want to make anything of this?" And Fergus said, "No." And that was the end of it, we got our list through. But there in one swoop were half a dozen very able young Jewish men and women, and the reason was enormously simple: they hadn't been given a chance before. They were bright, they were talented, some of them had experience in film or theatre or whatever. Sydney Newman was one of them. There was nothing wrong with the proportion; what was wrong was that it startled the CBC.

MJM: So there is a strong sense of improvisation at this period, making it up as you go along.

MOORE: Oh, yes. There is a funny story that director David Greene [who won Emmy awards, directed live and taped television, movies and mini-series] still tells. David had been in New York with the Olivier Old Vic Company, and he decided he rather liked it in North America and wanted to stay. He thought it would be easier to get a job in Canada with his British passport. So he came up to Toronto looking for a job as an actor.

I kept him waiting two hours, apparently, and he says he was livid with fury at the end of this. No one kept him waiting for two hours, especially in a hick town like Toronto. He says he came into my office, fuming, and I said to him immediately, "Sit down Mr Greene. I've looked at your letter of reference and I'd like to ask what you want to do here?" And he said, "I want to act." I said, "I really think that with all the experience you've had in the classical theatre, you should be directing. Would you like a director's job?" The fact of the matter was that I had been hunting for some months for someone with experience in film and a background in classical theatre, and then this guy walked into my office. So that is how David Greene became a director; he had no thought of it before I mentioned it.

As Greene says, "In Toronto I found myself in just the right place at the right time. They badly needed TV directing talent and since my credits were great ... and the credits that sprang from my imagination even greater, they signed me to a contract with the Canadian Broadcasting Corporation. I'll always love Canada because they gave me a chance to show what I could do. Finally I returned to New York with my precious green immigration card."[6]

MOORE: But that sort of thing was happening all the time. We had, in that period, a lot of Americans coming up who were caught in the McCarthy era. One was of particular interest to me because he had done variety at NBC. Variety was the thing we were quite weak in. We had really only one experienced producer, the late Don Hudson, a talented, difficult man, very insistent on having his own way. Norman Jewison who had floor managed some of our variety shows was coming along, but was not yet very experienced. So we hired this guy from New York. And he did produce several variety shows, but found it enormously difficult to work with so few staff. He was used to a large staff, as most Americans were.

MJM: And probably a bigger studio, too.

MOORE: Well, it was largely that the money was sloshed around down there and we had none to lose.

Within a year or two, CBC TV drama had progressed from adaptations of early CBC radio-plays to scripts written specifically for television. Sydney Newman came on board from the NFB to become, in 1954, the supervising producer of sponsored drama. In 1957 he left to become the head of drama at ABC (U.K.) and then head of drama at the BBC in the early 1960s. During this period he gave contemporary British playwrights a major place in television's bill of fare and created a climate in which new playwrights could flourish.[7]

NEWMAN [1984]: *First Performance* [an anthology of four plays broadcast in October in the 1950s to sell Canadian Savings Bonds] was a very good thing because I had a lot of fun with the Bank of Canada. I knew a man named Herb Richardson, who was the secretary of the Bank of Canada, a dollar-a-year man, in charge of the annual Savings Bonds campaigns. I was in charge of drama, and he insisted on working with me instead of the Bob Allen *Festival* group.

MJM: I wondered about that, because it was a very prestigious series, all original Canadian scripts in the second, third, and fourth years.

NEWMAN: I insisted on that, and Herb backed me. He was a great Canadian nationalist. He also trusted me. The will of the sponsor is very important.

MJM: The dramas were presented with considerable panache.

NEWMAN: He had a big mind. We brought in international stars. Herb had a great sense of showmanship.

MJM: But he had the confidence, as you did, in the Canadian playwrights?

NEWMAN: After a great deal of work. We went crazy getting it.

MJM: Len Peterson's *Fire and Ice* ended up being very visual. One
by Arthur Hailey, *The Seeds of Power* (directed by Paul Almond),
was about sabotaging a nuclear power plant in India. It was very
visual, the camera was all over the place – lots of suspense. *Panic
at Parth Bay* by Lester Powell, directed by Harvey Hart, dealt with
a nuclear accident and the contamination of the technicians.

NEWMAN: No, that had nothing to do with me.

MJM: [Consulting a printout] *First Performance*, 7 October 1958,
starring Esse Ljungh, Fran Hyland, and Hugh Webster.

NEWMAN: Was I supervising producer?

MJM: Yes.

NEWMAN: I don't even remember it. Isn't that amazing?

MJM: Not really, not given everything that has happened since.

NEWMAN: Do you know how many shows we were doing at the
BBC each year that I was responsible for? Seven hundred and
twenty separate dramas, including twice-weekly soap operas,
twenty-six episodes of *The Forsyte Saga*, single plays, and children's
serials. I can't remember them all.

THE "GOLDEN" 1960S:
ADAPTATIONS AND ORIGINALS

Sydney Newman and others left the CBC in 1957–58 to seek wider
horizons. There was another exodus in the mid to late 1960s. I asked
actor/writer Hugh Webster about the loss of many of the experienced
producer/directors to the United Kingdom and the United States at
that time.

WEBSTER [1984]: I know lots of directors who fought battles, but
most of them lost and made way for the people to take over who
were less likely to fight. There was a point where they just got
tired of bucking the setup. A lot of it had to do with the fact that
they had to look south, because the facilities and the money were
there. Also they felt they were wanted.

MJM: But the Canadian talent often didn't have the same freedom
in the States as they had on the CBC in the 1960s.

WEBSTER: No, but they had the money. When we were all starting,
we were all pretty well of the same age. We were all trying to have
a family, we were all trying to buy a house. And there's no point
in saying, "Oh well. Money's not important." Damn right, it's

important. It's as important to a TV producer or an actor or a
writer as it is to anybody else.

ELIZABETH WEBSTER [Hugh's wife]: There was quite a lot of good
stuff being done in the States. All those E.G. Marshall [*The
Defenders*] programs and so on, which one could switch to.

WEBSTER: In that earlier period, there was a lot of good American
television: *Camera Three, Studio One, Playhouse 90* – just great!

MJM: But they all appeared in a decade of American television
anthology that stops in 1960.

WEBSTER: There's something about New York, the hard-hitting
New York show-business Broadway tradition. But in the late 1950s
when television went to the soft California climes ...

MJM: ... it became predictable.

I interviewed Eric Till early in my research, a producer/director who
chose to stay with directing and who has given us some of our best
television drama, from *Pale Horse, Pale Rider* and *The Offshore Island*
to the 1970s tape studio dramas *Bethune* and *Freedom of the City* and
the 1980s filmed mini-series *Glory Enough for All*. We started with
production conditions in the early 1960s.

MJM: You had a three-week rehearsal and one week to do it?

TILL [1983]: No, sometimes only three days to do it. Something like
Offshore Island was done in three days.

MJM: That may explain its edge, though the script itself was very
intense.

TILL: We just had to be enormously organized.

MJM: You would perform in sequence?

TILL: Yes, you would.

MJM: But by that time, being "live-to-tape," there would be some
editing capacity?

TILL: Just a little. From scene to scene, not within the scene, that
was all.

MJM: Directors chose the designers they wanted to work with, did
they not? [These creative partnerships often made the difference
between pedestrian and imaginative television.]

TILL: Yes, we did. More often than not we got the person we
wanted.

MJM: And I see pairings occurring in the credits.

TILL: Yes, Rudi Dorn and Paul Almond were inseparable.

MJM: Did you have any particular favourites?

TILL: Trevor Williams, and then Rudi, from time to time. I would
ask for Rudi on special programs. *The Dream of Peter Mann* [a

highly stylized 1960s anti-war play for the theatre by British writer Bernard Kops] was pure Rudi Dorn.

MJM: Certainly, the last effect is. Presumably it was your idea, but what an extraordinary thing.

TILL: What, the coffins? I remember people gasped when they walked by the studio and saw all of those coffins.

MJM: Yes. And you went to a negative, somehow, and then back to the positive as an analogy to a nuclear flash.

TILL: Some little technical gimmick. I can't remember now why I did that.[8]

In the 1960s dozens of plays from the classical and the contemporary European repertoire were produced on the CBC. Canadian plays adapted for television diminished in number, though Canadian scripts for television did continue to appear.

GARDNER: One of the questions you asked was the relationship between television and theatre. Well, in the 1960s there really wasn't a relationship between the theatre and television. There was a fair amount of theatre, but there wasn't much Canadian theatre yet. So, if you were a Canadian writer, you still wrote for television and radio. Only with the 1970s do we get the explosion on stage with the alternative theatre movement. At the same time, with the new emphasis in the 1970s and 1980s on television, we didn't need stage plays any more. Bob Allen, in particular, was the executive producer of tape drama in the 1970s, finding stage plays and having them adapted for television.

MJM: The resurgence of Canadian theatre in the 1970s finally broke into television briefly in the Hirsch period.

GARDNER: *1837* and ...

MJM: *Ten Lost Years, Red Emma, You're Alright Jamie Boy*, and *One Night Stand* – there is a whole flood of them. And then it stops.

GARDNER: Yes, but since the mid 1970s everything that the CBC has produced is original, a fact that people forget, and shouldn't.

Newman has little regard for the idea that the CBC should be a window on world theatre or on Canadian theatre.

NEWMAN [1984]: They did a lot of stage material. Bob Allen did many, many dramas, Ibsen and stuff like that, which I could not stand.

MJM: You have been quoted before as saying that, despite what many people think, Ibsen is not a logical choice for television.

NEWMAN: The point is that he was hot stuff in his day, but his stage characters talk too much. I'll put it another way. I actually had an aversion to doing stage plays on television, an absolute, strong aversion, because they are two totally different mediums.

GARDNER: Now, with the 1980s, we return to the theatre via the medium of pay television. Director Robin Phillips's version of *Waiting for the Parade* began on stage and was then adapted for pay television. Because of pay television's need to eat up material, a new liaison is happening between the theatre and television [and continues in the United States]. Hirsch goes to Stratford, and suddenly we get *The Taming of the Shrew* and *As You Like It* and *The Mikado* being televised for the CBC as well as specials. The economy is dictating that we recycle material, but they have now become specials. Also, it is a shame if a production like *The Mikado* is not recorded. So these theatre productions for television become either pay television or CBC specials.

This was before c channel, a pay channel, collapsed and seven years before a few independent stations started at irregular intervals to show taped versions of plays by contemporary Canadian playwrights. In the early days of 1995, Bravo, the newest pay arts channel, and Showcase, the "fiction" channel, where, for the first time ever, reruns of Canadian drama programs appeared on a regular basis in prime time, both launched their services. However, their success or failure may be determined by circumstances over which they have no control. An unprecedented consumer revolt erupted over the cable companies' decision to reshuffle the "bundles" for which subscribers pay. Rogers and some of the other large cable monopolies rearranged the channels, with the result that consumers had to pay more for their old favourites because these services were paired (by order of the CRTC) with the new channels. Worse still, they used a "negative" option marketing technique (except where it is illegal, in Quebec and Nova Scotia), which meant that consumers who did not say no were billed automatically for the new services. In reaction, Rogers, now the biggest company, cut Bravo, Showcase, and the other four new services loose and restored the status quo – but retained the negative marketing option. Subscribers were angry with cable companies, with the CRTC that approved the strategy, and with the new and worthwhile services that had nothing to do with it. With potentially much less guaranteed income, the chance to see theatre adapted for television one night a week (Bravo), or past television successes from the CBC and other networks (Showcase), may well not survive.

STRATFORD ON TELEVISION

After a decade with very little adaptation of theatre to television, the CBC decided in the mid-1980s that it had a duty to a cultural icon – Stratford. Producing recreations for television of theatre productions directed and designed for the stage was quite a challenge. Sam Levene, whose roots were in documentary, current affairs, and topical drama in film, took on the task of capturing the fluid Stratford productions on tape.

MJM: You told me that, rather than going for the open stage environment, you were more satisfied with recreating an enclosed studio setup.

LEVENE, producer, executive producer [1988]: The first year we made it very clear that we were observers at a typical Stratford performance with an audience. We called it *An Evening at Stratford*, subtitled *The Taming of the Shrew*. Norman Campbell [best known for his early television musicals as well as Gilbert and Sullivan, ballet, and opera] would still argue that is the best way to direct it. As I did more of them, I felt that the acting performances were too stagey, too artificial, loud, and hard to sit through.

MJM: The attempt to recreate the stage production ignored the advantages of television?

LEVENE: Yes. I don't think it makes for bearable viewing of the two to three hours of a Shakespearean comedy. It is just too long to sit there. You have to make it more intimate, quieter, more realistic.

MJM: Is that why you thought that Molière's *Tartuffe* might work better than the average Shakespearean tragedy? Because *Tartuffe* was written for a seventeenth-century theatre shaped like a shoebox, it is an intimate play.

LEVENE: It also has a real set because the whole thing takes place inside somebody's house. A Shakespearean play goes all over the place! *Tartuffe* was much more manageable. Our job as TV producers is clearly to be as faithful as we can to the director's concept. We have no intention (or time within the week available) to change the concept. If we hadn't liked the concept, we wouldn't have chosen that play. We alter it to the extent it needs to be for the medium.

MJM: It seems self-evident that the CBC is going to choose a play that is accessible to a large audience. They are not going to pick the less accessible plays of Shakespeare.

LEVENE: No. It is asking a lot of the audience to sit through two-and-a-half hours of classical drama on television. So you had better give them something that they know, that they have studied at school, preferably a famous play like *Macbeth*. Otherwise you are limiting the audience too much. Stratford did an interesting *Measure for Measure* a few years ago; I was really tempted to push for that one. [It was a controversial and very contemporary production superbly directed by Michael Bogdanev]. But I guess you want somebody to watch. A lot of people walked out on it. I wish we had done it, but I would like to have done two shows that year. It becomes a financial and economic issue.

In 1993 Norman Campbell produced the CBC's version of *Romeo and Juliet*, another safe choice of play. But in this instance the play was shot as it was performed for audiences at Stratford. This meant that the acting, the vocal pitch, and the gestures were geared for the theatre, not television. The result defeated even a director of Campbell's long experience. Even with a fresh start – a decision to do Shakespeare specifically for television and with innovative expert directors like Jonathan Miller – the results can be problematic. As someone who teaches Shakespeare and has seen most of the BBC productions of Shakespeare's canon, I can say that the overall result was wildly uneven – worth trying, usually worth watching, but unpredictable.

In the early 1990s the independent stations are filling their Canadian content quotas with plays adapted for television, and so the wheel comes full circle again. The economics of television has always been part of the presence or absence of stage plays on television. But technical advances also shaped audience expectations. When television moved outside the studios, using both film and tape, the studio conventions of television which resembled theatre both in rhythms of performance and in choice of camera shots yielded to the rhythms and conventions of film. Adapting stage plays for a more filmic or flexibly electronic medium took much more time and effort.

There are two ways in which television could reconnect to the superb writing skills now evident in a mature Canadian theatre scene. One would be if the drama returned to the more flexible conventions of the studio, as in Pierre Berton's simple and highly stylized *Heritage Theatre* (1986). The other would be if television directors, producers, and writers applied the self-reflexive conventions of sketch comedies like *Codco* to the wider spectrum of drama as a whole. Instead, Hugh Webster's summary in 1984 is still valid for most television drama in the 1990s.

WEBSTER: The style has become realistic cinematics, following the American tradition of destroying German impressionism and all the adventurous film-makers. For television made in Hollywood, what they present is real. Their fantasy land is real.

Yet American Hollywood reality is not ours. Compare the CBC's late 1980s gritty teen drama *Northwood* with the wildly successful analogue *Beverly Hills 90210*. The puzzle for me is why during the late 1980s on the CBC such energizing particularity was to be found only in television series for adolescents. Perhaps infusing the spectrum of TV drama with some adaptations from our theatre would further regenerate television drama for adults in English Canada.

THE FRANCOPHONE FACT

In the 1950s and 1960s producer/directors had the opportunity to do dramas that meant a lot to them, that excited them, because often they proposed as well as produced and directed the program.

MJM: You did a selection of French-Canadian plays which seems to have been a conscious way to introduce to the rest of the country plays that they had never heard of, that they would never have seen in translation.

ALLEN: There was a period where we were scratching our heads and wracking our brains to find some way of making English Canada more aware of French Canada, and vice versa. And there were many meetings between people from Montreal and Radio-Canada. There was some possibility of exchanging musical programs, but we really couldn't find a way of sending to the French network one of our productions either with subtitles or with dubbing. Mainly, people in the 1950s and 1960s were very suspicious about subtitles. They didn't think they could be read on the little screen, which is nonsense, because there is a way of subtitling. Certainly, nobody was enthusiastic about dubbing. Dubbing is a horror. So that kind of exchange didn't get very far. But some of our producers were very interested in French-Canadian things, although most of them couldn't read them in the original. Some of the plays were being translated (not very many), but we thought it was the mandate of the CBC to reflect something about French Canada to the rest of Canada. I don't think we succeeded in doing enough about Quebec. You wouldn't know, of course, that the script editors read an enormous volume of French-Canadian scripts looking for material that we could translate or have translated or adapted, or whatever had to be done. The ones you did see were all stage plays.

The script editors, however, reported that while they read many, many scripts, a lot of them were not really appropriate to being done in English because they were so regional. They rested on so many cultural assumptions that the English audience were not aware of that they needed to be explained.

So we find at the heart of the CBC Drama Department, in its formative years and with its hold over Canadian imagination, a self-imposed vicious circle. The audience didn't know enough about Quebec to enjoy drama that would help them know more about Quebec. One of the four exceptions (now lost to us – the kine has disappeared from the can in which the film was kept) was Paul Almond's *Puppet Caravan*.

ALMOND: *The Puppet Caravan* was the first drama ever done at the CBC in both English and French [since *The Plouffes*, and the first time in an anthology]. Geneviève Bujold, François Tasse, and Jean Doyon were bilingual. We did the English production in Toronto, and we shot the French production a couple of days later in Montreal. But the interesting thing about that production is that when the actors spoke French, their moves were quite different and the shots were different. The change in rhythms of how you behave when you're being French from when you're being English made the whole production different.

DIRECTORS' CHOICE

One of the pleasures of interviewing these directors was hearing them articulate what satisfied, even thrilled them. I asked them which were their favourites among the dozens of dramas they directed. Mario Prizek, who left his mark on our television history with his sophisticated sensibility, his willingness to experiment, and his interest in Quebec drama, is one of the most articulate of the directors I encountered.

MJM: You didn't find that anyone worried about controversy when you chose *Galileo* (1963). I'm surprised because that was a very strong, hard-hitting production.
PRIZEK [1983]: Helena Weigel, Brecht's widow, liked the kine of it so much that she asked for a copy for the Brecht archives, so it's at the Berliner Ensemble archives.
MJM: That's a compliment, isn't it?
PRIZEK: Yes. We had to fight so hard to get the rights from Weigel to do *Galileo* on television because of Brecht's disappointment, his

hatred of the earlier film production of *Drei Groschen Oper*. He
didn't want his things done anywhere except the stage.

MJM: She might also have feared that during the height of the Cold
War there would be all kinds of distortions.

PRIZEK: Well, of course, I did add one thing to it and that was the
atom-bomb blast at the end. When Galileo with his back to the
window says to his daughter: "What's the evening like?" and she
says, looking out at the image of the atom bomb, "Lovely." That
Helena Weigel loved because she said it gave the total metaphor of
the meaning of the play.

MJM: You'd also prepared for it with shots of the Canadian Nuclear
Disarmament posters, and so forth.

PRIZEK: On the stage you would have suspended printed legends
over each scene. At the beginning of each scene I used Hugh
Webster (who looked so much like Brecht himself) to take the
place of the printed legend cards.

MJM: Did you ever identify him as "Brecht"?

PRIZEK: No, never. I said: "Let it just speak for itself. He's the
narrator."

TILL: *Offshore Island* (1963) is another painful 1960s anti-war piece
about a mother, son, daughter, and older male friend who survive
a nuclear holocaust. I can remember an incident in the shooting,
where one of our executives realized what I was doing at the end
of the piece, which puts a knife in [because it is Americans who
"rescue" the family and who share responsibility very explicitly for
that nuclear holocaust]. This executive said: "Eric, that is a bit
much and somewhat powerful," and I said: "Well, it stays there.
This is the way it was written and nobody is going to change
anything." The corporation was terrified.

MJM: Why?

TILL: I suppose because people at the time were afraid that it was
anti-American. I remember we had one actor, American-born,
walk out on it. He said: "Eric, you will never work in the U.S.A.
after what you have done." And I said: "I don't consider this an
anti-American film, it's an anti-war film," even though the Americans do come off badly, instead of the Russians.

MJM: Indeed they do, but it is pretty even-handed!

TILL: I remember the night it was transmitted, I was with some
dear friends. We sat and watched it and then he and his wife got
up and left the room, my wife left the room, and I sat there alone.
I thought, "My God, it is so bad that they are embarrassed." So I
went to pour myself a drink and I found one lady on the bed just
racked with tears, crying. The gentleman had gone out to the back

and stood looking at the sky. He couldn't control his emotions. And then people began to phone and say – "the power." Even the author Marghanita Laski, when she saw it, said: "I never thought I would cry over that."

MJM: She saw your production?"

TILL: Yes. She wanted it to be even rougher on the Americans.

MJM: But then, she lives in Britain and we live in Canada. Sometimes, we see things in a more even-handed way.

TILL: I am constantly asked to make a film of it and I just will not, because you can't do that story today.

I just want to remember now the power of Irene Worth, who played the protagonist, and what it was that everybody was feeling at that time, with Kennedy, the 1962 October missile crisis, and all of that nonsense going on. I had come across this play and I said, "That's the damned thing we should do right now."

Eric Till, often identified as an "actor's director," also enjoyed doing the classics.

TILL: I remember being outrageous and telling the actor who was playing Jean in *Miss Julie* that during his famous long speech I wasn't going to put the camera on him. I was going to put it on Shirley Knight, playing Miss Julie. He said: "Why?" Because, if you think about it, the whole speech is done to create an effect upon this woman. You are going to admit later in the play that it is all rubbish, that all you were doing was manipulating her. Therefore, you ought to be able to do that with your voice and I ought to see that this woman is succumbing to everything that you talk about. So we'll put the camera on her!" He was mortified. He did forgive me, but he was furious. I remember that after we had done it, after we had stuck it all together, I thought, "Well, that's quite interesting." Shirley was brilliant. But I remember Nathan Cohen [theatre and occasional television critic] just tore me to shreds. He just loathed it.

MJM: He was wrong about a great many things, including a lot of our television drama. *Private Memories and Confessions of a Justified Sinner* [1964, based on a novel about seventeenth-century Scottish Presbyterian obsessions] was a remarkable thing for you to have chosen to do. It was as obscure a choice as you could have made, although it was fascinating.

TILL: I have never repeated anything. I have never done anything twice in my life, ever. For years I was asked to make a film out of *Pale Horse, Pale Rider* (1963), and I said: "No, I couldn't do it better now, I would just do it differently." I couldn't do *Offshore Island*. The only thing I would like to do again is *Private Memories*. When I read the book again, five or six years later, I found new things in it that I had never seen before.

One day, it must have been in the mid-1970s, I received a telephone call from Scotland, asking if I would like to make a film of it. I went across there but, unfortunately, it was just too costly. Eventually the Scots made a film of it. The one thing that my production doesn't have (which I didn't recognize at that time) is that the book is staggeringly funny, naughtily funny, in a good, Scotch way, and I kick myself for not having seen it. It would have been an entirely different production, but it is wickedly funny.

MJM: I did discover, from a close Scottish friend, how central that book has been over the centuries to the Scots' psyche.

TILL: They even have an opera of it!

MJM: Well, I am a Presbyterian, so I have a particular feel for the dilemma, the trap of the doctrine of Predestination, which is the framework of this drama.

TILL: Somewhere at home there is a copy of the *Scottish Daily Express* with an article in it about the fact that Canadians had done "our work"! At that time, it was just known as a piece of literature. No one had written a play about it, no one had written an opera.

MJM: Did somebody come to you with a script, or did you read the novel and say: "Oh, my gosh!"

TILL: I read the novel. It is just an amazing book. It is a story told twice, but it is so complex, so evil.

MJM: I had a feeling that much was escaping me on a first viewing. There is a great deal to be seen in your production.

TILL: Yes, you really have to look and you really have to listen to it. It is incredibly complex.

MJM to ALMOND: Who did you think your audience was?

ALMOND: I never thought about it, never had the slightest interest at the time. We did what we thought was good, we used our own sensibilities. We would get phone calls that night. Even when the credits were on, the phone would start ringing.

MJM: People cared.

ALMOND: I guess nowadays, nobody phones. You're right. We were divorced from the audience, and yet when you did a show and there weren't twenty-five calls right away, you'd know instantly while still on the air that it wasn't too good. But if it was a good show you were flooded.

MJM: Did you get people phoning up and saying, "What do you mean doing this horrible thing?"

ALMOND: No, but you got letters. I used to get a lot of hate letters with all my Pinter plays.

MJM: Then why were you doing Pinter? Because you liked him specially? Because Bob Allen asked you to?

ALMOND: No. I did them because in those days Pinter was the leading playwright. Our mandate was to give Canadians the best material we could get. Christopher Fry at that time was a major playwright and Clive Exton, Jean Anouilh – all those guys were important, so you had an obligation to do their works.

MJM: You also did one of the *First Performances.*

ALMOND: Yes, I did, with one of Arthur Hailey's plays.

MJM: That's right, *Seeds of Power* [about the research centre for atomic energy in Canada at Chalk River].

ALMOND: I did a couple more, I did one of his called *Time Lock.* Those were exciting days, getting kids twelve years old to perform on air.

MJM: Kids and dogs – what a horror!

ALMOND: I also did Shakespeare, always with Rudi Dorn. With *Julius Caesar,* his whole set was the base of a huge 12-foot decorative column at one end of the studio. *Macbeth* was simply a flight of steps and a huge throne. We had Sean Connery, and Zoë Caldwell as Lady Macbeth.

EXPERIMENTING WITH TECHNOLOGY

GARDNER: Have you ever seen *With His Head Tucked Underneath His Arm?*[9]

MJM: No, what was that?

GARDNER: It was a Len Peterson original, about Evariste Galloise, a famous French child prodigy, a mathematical genius. It was the first television show that introduced Richard Monette as a young boy of nineteen whom I had just seen at a drama festival. It was a real experimental show because of the techniques I used. It was filled with comic transformations. Somebody would walk behind a tree and come out in a new outfit. Powys Thomas was Evariste Galloise's nemesis, continually hunting him down. He played twenty roles in the piece as a teacher, as a kind of villain, and as a devil figure, and kept reappearing in a new disguise. So we had to use all sorts of disappearance techniques – for example, locking a camera in position onto a tree and stopping tape while the actor changed into another costume and then walked back out from behind the tree. We were then able to "marry" the two shots together. The first videotape editing was done physically with a razor blade. You had to cut through and join it again with something very like Scotch tape. You could see the "edits" all over the place. However, a really good edit went through without any sparkles (little electric sparkles coming off). Finally, you had an edited tape. Then you took another generation [dub] off the whole edited tape, so at least it didn't go on air with the Scotch tape. (Otherwise it might come unravelled on air.) A show like *With His Head Tucked Underneath His Arm* had something like fifty or sixty of these physical edits.

The trouble was that you only got two hours of tape time to record a show – from 10 to midnight. The whole process was wrong. We had two or three days in the studio just to rehearse the action, but you were not able to tape it. We should have rehearsed and taped throughout the whole day. Then all of this would have been done within the three-day slot. But instead, the system was that you "dry-rehearsed" for three days. Then you had two hours of recording time and you had to fit everything in. This show was an all-night thing. There were bets being made as to what time it would finish. It was a notorious show because it went to 4:30 in the morning. But when I look back at it now, I am astounded that between 10 o'clock at night and 4:30 in the morning we were able to tape a show of this complexity. It created a great storm inside the Drama Department. I was gently raked over the coals and had to write extensive memos and so on.

The principle of re-editing also developed in the 1970s, as the CBC got more and more into film. Because when you can edit and re-edit, the product gets better. Yet the program may lose some of the impetus of a live show or tape. Hirsch insisted on many re-edits of shows, and the budgets went sky-high.

George McGowan was one of several directors from the 1960s who left for Hollywood in the early 1970s, becoming well known as a director of action/adventure series. He then returned for a while to do every episode of *Seeing Things*, the quirky 1980s CBC hit show. An actor who worked with George McGowan in the 1980s describes him as an extremely intelligent director, a poet, and a wonderful audience who knows "bullshit" when he sees it. Not only was he the first to take the clumsy tape cameras out of doors with *Two Soldiers*, he also experimented with film. Ron Weyman used him to direct an episode of his filmed series *Wojeck*.

WEYMAN: There was a party sequence. McGowan (who at his best is phenomenal) decided that he was going to shoot this party scene, which is six minutes and fifty-four seconds long, in one shot, which he does. I asked him: "Where is your coverage?" He says: "There *is* no coverage! It works by itself." And I say: "Sure it does, but when you get to the fine cut [the last edit], I think you are probably going to find it too long, and what are you going to cut to?" He said: "Well, I'll go back and get a couple of inserts." And indeed, he needed them. But it was a beautiful film.

Weyman, a key person in the development of CBC film and drama, teamed up with writer Philip Hersch to create *Wojeck*, which was the first true series drama at the CBC and one of the very best. The level of audience engagement with *Wojeck* has never been matched. I asked him about how his work on *The Serial*, *Quentin Durgens MP*, and *Wojeck* fitted into the drama department of the mid to late 1960s.

WEYMAN: Well, curiously enough, I felt pretty lonely half the time. The only time I saw a boss was when I would go up and say this is my plan, this is my budget, this is what I want, and this is what I'll deliver! He would say fine, and that would be that. This is partly because we were on a roll, we knew what we wanted, and I had good people working with me.

MJM to cameraman (then writer) GRAHAME WOODS [1989]: You had a whole succession of different directors on *Wojeck*. What was it like to work with different directors? Because, as cameraman, you did have some of the best.

WOODS: Weyman picked his directors extremely well. George Mc-Gowan did one and I was very nervous because George had this incredible reputation. He'd done a lot of good stuff for *Festival* and he'd done a lot of big stuff down in the States. And here was I going to be shooting for George McGowan, who was at this point a real nail-biter in terms of television drama, but a wonderful guy.

MJM: Paul Almond?

WOODS: Paul Almond, yes, that's an experience working for Paul.

MJM: Is it? I gather he has his own very strong ideas. Was it a little difficult as cameraman, since you had your own ideas, too.

WOODS: No, he's very responsive. He creates a lot of energy, but it was the first time I'd worked with him and he got me revved up. He had a passion for what he was doing and it was infectious.

ALMOND: Yes, I did *Wojecks*,[10] that's when we started to do film. People like Ron Weyman pioneered this *Wojeck* series on film. It didn't have all the trappings of a big American production.

Wojeck was clearly influenced by the documentary tradition of the NFB and the CBC. In the 1970s the CBC attempted to blend pure documentary and dramatized segments in their ambitious series on the nineteenth-century conquest of our geography by railroad.[11]

MJM to TILL: In *The National Dream*, the dramatized segments were knitted into the documentary sequences. How did that work? Such a hybrid must have been very difficult to create in terms of achieving a single vision.

TILL: I think it would have worked better if all the narration had been done *after* the drama had been assembled. What happened was that frequently there would emerge from the drama the very essence of what Pierre Berton was talking about as a narrator. So you would have the same information coming by the viewer again, which slows down a program and finally bores the audience. I suspect, initially, people were surprised at the amount of information that came through from the drama alone.

We were dealing with people who weren't enormously experienced. Pierre was concerned about everything being historically accurate. Once it began to emerge on the screen in the editing room downstairs, from both what was there and what could be done, I came to think that the drama probably should have been done differently.

MJM: In my view, the drama is what people carried away – as well as the breathtaking scenery and the sense of scale, which only filming on location could accomplish. But it is the drama that makes events real to people. It is the classic paradox – the fiction comes closer to the truth than pure documentary.

TILL: It is my favourite shoot of everything I have ever done.

MJM: Is it?

TILL: Yes. For week after week I was just absolutely astounded by the kinds of things we would find to do with that enormous film unit out west, shooting things I had never thought of, really, and having a wonderful time doing it. Some of that unquestionably comes through. We worked like demons. I would take crews up a mountainside and then decide I didn't like the shot. People would moan and groan, and back down we would go and find ourselves in some other breathtaking location. You just had to be a fool if you couldn't shoot them properly. And it was in so many segments. There was a winter, spring, summer, and then a fall shoot. Twice out west and then in Ottawa. It was wonderful stuff, the material was good, the people in it were good.

MJM: I think people felt good about watching it, too.

PERSONAL STYLE

From the early days, good television directors developed their own personal style, which involved both their choice of material and their way of telling the story. Even when series became the norm, some directors could infuse a given format with their own sensibility.

MJM to GARDNER: When you and Ron Weyman each directed five of the *Jake and the Kid* episodes, you would have to meld your styles, would you not?

GARDNER: We were supposed to meld our styles as much as possible. It is interesting that you say that because I just met W.O. Mitchell and, casually, in conversation, he said "Oh, in *Jake and the Kid* I always knew which were which." It is very true. There was a kind of *auteur* type of thing happening in the 1960s. There were the George Bloomfield productions. Eric Till carved out a niche for himself in the 1960s which he has changed considerably in the 1970s and the 1980s.

MJM: He and Paul Almond did a great deal of work that depended on creating an atmosphere.

GARDNER: Absolutely. And there were styles of shooting. Eric Till often created a very lonely shot. He liked more distance. Television is usually a closeup medium. I can remember from the very beginning Henry Kaplan, who did some of the early live dramas in the 1950s, would always say "T for television," meaning "tight for television." Put your head closer to somebody when you are talking to them because it is "t" for television, tight, tight, tight!" But someone like Eric Till explored the lonely shot, that is the figure sitting with space above and along the sides. This lonely figure was one of his stylistic trademarks. *Pale Horse, Pale Rider* was one of the early ones where he made that kind of atmospheric mark. He has since completely thrown that away. But then again, the storyline doesn't always call for that. Paul Almond's work was more moody, but the camera moved a great deal. He was a very volatile director, a tough director to work for because he kept performing himself and saying "No, no, it is impossible, darling" and that sort of thing. But once you got to know and like Paul, it was terrific.

I would describe my own style as eclectic.

MJM: From what I have seen of yours, so would I. You seem to adapt very much to the material.

GARDNER: That was my intention. In fact, almost every show I did looks slightly different from every other. There were certain distinctions in my work that I worked very hard for; interaction among players and characters, so that the scenes between people had an extra vitality. That was the way I worked as a director. Shooting film scared me a little bit more than it did some of the others. I only belatedly came to learn how to shoot better and better.[12]

MJM: Were you more comfortable with naturalism to begin with?

GARDNER: Yes, I would say so. Psychological naturalism.

MJM: And yet you did the N.F. Simpson ...

GARDNER: *Resounding Tinkle* ...

MJM: Yes, and you did that in a highly stylized way, adapting the absurdist stage conventions to television – and enjoyed it I would imagine.

GARDNER: Marvellous fun. I began to be a much more expressionistic director. I had started with a great deal of realism, but then I slowly moved towards expressionism. I still like that in my stage work now.

Prizek characterized his approach to directing this way:

PRIZEK: My aim in directing is always, "Don't include your own ego." Realize the *author's* intention, and if you can't understand the author's intention, don't do the play. This allowed me to do things like T.S. Eliot's plays, although I'm an agnostic. After we finished the first one, at the "after-the-show party" the cast were talking about a religious subject and they all stared in amazement when I told them I was an agnostic. They said: "We knew you were raised a Roman Catholic, but we thought you were religious because you were able to identify with all these things." And I said: "I was identifying with the author's intention."

Before I even presented a program idea, I would research the idea until I was very attached to it. I would research everything that writer had written, that I could get my hands on, so that, if I didn't have *all* the answers, I certainly knew a hell of a lot more answers than the performers would ever have questions to ask me. But you know there were times when they asked me questions I couldn't answer and I would say: "I don't know. Let's find out." And we would do it together. You see, I have a very omnivorous appetite in all the fields of science and art. I love mathematics. I'm interested in electronics. I'm interested in all the sciences. It was a debate with myself whether I would end up in the sciences or in languages or in humanities. I ended up in the humanities at university. If you were to look at my library, there is everything from sacred books of the East right through to science-fiction, mathematics, music and opera scores, so I've always been very flighty in my tastes.

MJM: I was going to say that I think you use a great many styles as a director. There are some directors, in the 1950s and 1960s particularly, whose work I can look at and say, "That is probably directed by x," but I don't find I can do that with you.

PRIZEK: Whenever I read a script or a play, I always read it in my mind's eye to see whether it was a fast-cutting show, whether it was a slow-moving show that needed fluid camera action, and so on. So I adapted my style to the author's intention, *always*. And I used a minimum of technical gimmickry because I know if I use an effect that's very clever and the audience looks at it and says, "How did you do that" or "My, that was clever" for three seconds, I've lost it.

MJM to TILL: You often get astonishing performances. You seem to be "an actors' director." Is that fair to say?

TILL: That is what a lot of people say, and it always baffles me. If you are not, what the hell are you? A bus conductor?

MJM: I notice that the human beings are in the foreground of your work. There are other visual metaphors and you work in various styles, but the human dilemmas are always the focus. And in television, too often the focus on the human interaction means closeup after closeup.

TILL: Television is absolutely sinful in the way it destroys the value of a closeup. Because someone has to shoot a one-hour film in five or six days, the fastest way to do it is to shoot it in closeup. But that takes away from the "colour" of that particular shot. It is also the greatest shot for performers because it is their closest contact with their audience. It is just them – their face, their eyes. Therefore it is the most wonderful, the most valuable shot you can possibly have, and it is destroyed on the box. Everything is a closeup.

MJM: The closeup has become a cliché beyond the point where anybody notices the shot, unless an extraordinary performance is taking place, or unless it is used selectively, which is seldom.

TILL: I have had discussions with people who say: "We must have this whole sequence in closeup." I did a play for pay TV recently which was like going back to the 1960s and doing a stage play on the box. There were some heavy discussions from time to time between the author, me, and one of the producers about why we should have that particular sequence or this text in closeup. I said: "No, if you have this in closeup you take away from there. Wait, hold back! And then, let the actor do it" – and in my opinion, it worked! But it is an overworked shot.

MJM: It excludes some of the body language too, as well as the context of the figure in the landscape.

TILL: Because the early shows were very studio-bound, they didn't teach us to have a sense of the great outdoors. We had no sense of an actor using a tree, a road, a piece of wood, or the wind, and letting it be part of the performance, which is what is so magical with a good film actor. We had to go out and watch others and find out for ourselves. An experienced director once said to me: "How do you feel about making your first film?" I said: "Terrified!" "Quite right. Will you do me a favour?" I said: "What is it?" He said: "Just tell me a simple story, don't show me how clever you are, just tell me a good story. You show me in your second film all the techniques you master, but first time out, will you just tell me a good story?"

I never forgot that. It came back most strongly many years later when I was teaching a credit course out of York in film. I had this group of young, energetic, often imaginative youngsters who were so full of film technique. I was terribly dismayed because all they could see was technique. They were just terrified of story. I guess, in many ways, that is what I have always tried to do (with the exception of things like *Private Memories* – there is a lot of technique in that), but technique should never hit you in the face. You should never try to make the audience aware of how clever the director is.

Eric Till does not often do episodic series television. As one of the most established and respected directors of both electronic drama and films of various lengths, he can be and is quite particular about what he does.

TILL: It is really so simple. The reason why there are some really magic programs is that people have a desire and a passion to do that particular program, they have a way in their head to do it, and they have a reason to do it. When John Hirsch came in as head of television drama in the mid-1970s, one of the first things he did was to phone me up and say: "Eric, what do you want to do? Tell me something you want to do!" I said: "I want to do a play called *Freedom of the City.*" He said: "Well, do it!"

Now, not all our programs were like those. In the 1960s I did go to Bob Allen and say: "I would really like to do this ..." but some of them I did because Bob would come and say: "Hey, we need a comedy, for crying out loud." This is not to say that I put less energy or less imagination into it. But the ones that really tended to surprise people were those that were done with immense passion, like *Offshore Island*. In the 1960s, television became series like the original *Alfred Hitchcock Presents*. People were astonished when I was asked to do one of those and I said "No, thank you." But I wouldn't be very good at doing that stuff. That is a producer's medium, not a director's medium. A director today going in to do that sort of nonsense is not allowed to change the script in any way because the script is approved by the network. By the time you finish shooting, half of it is edited anyway. And that is what they expect! That is why television is a producer's medium. Back then, and just occasionally today, television becomes a director's medium again. Just now and again, somebody is allowed to pick up and do something with passion and imagination.

DIRECTOR AND WRITER

The partnership between Eric Till and Hugh Webster is not a typical working relationship between producer/director and writer, but it produced some superb television drama from the mid-1960s to the late 1970s. In *Turn Up the Contrast* I analysed two of their many collaborations, *Kim* (1963) and *Freedom of the City* (1975).

MJM: Brian Friel's *Freedom of the City* is a wonderful piece of "televisual" television.

TILL: It is better on television than it is in the theatre.

MJM: I thought so, too.

TILL: It is a collaboration with Hugh Webster, who adapted *Kim*, *Offshore Island*, and *Night Must Fall*. Hughey first worked with *Kim* as a writer, and he seemed to bring an instinct. He was one of the first people to say, "You don't need that speech, Eric." I would ask, "Why in hell don't we need that speech?" "Because you can act it." He would bring that knowledge as an actor: "I can act that, I don't need to say that. I can project that quality." Hughey always seemed to understand what it was that was driving me, why I wanted to do a particular piece.

MJM: With something as intricate as *Freedom of the City*, surely the multiple time scheme doesn't come out of adapting the play. The way it is structured comes out of you as a director.

TILL: Hughey and I would argue about how one would shape this drama. I remember explaining to him what I wanted to do with the church at the funeral of the three protagonists and how I wanted to do those soliloquies that are in the middle and at the end of the play. I said: "I'll link it with the Fauré *Requiem*." He said: "What do you mean?" So I stuck on a record of the Fauré *Requiem*.

WEBSTER: Eric is very much influenced by music, because his first move into broadcasting was running a music library for the British Expeditionary Force radio station in Germany. His musical knowledge is immense. But he's not any kind of dry musicologist; music speaks to him in emotional terms. He'll find keys in music. I've listened to more records at Eric's place – with him getting across the sort of feeling that he wanted in a scene. That's why I say he's an absolute master at that sort of thing.

MJM: Using music as metaphor and counterpoint?

WEBSTER: Absolutely. Sometimes what he wants is sitting right in the Beethoven Ninth or a Bach chorale or whatever.

TILL: I was never surprised when Hughey went away and came back with all kinds of additions and ideas. But he knew what I wanted to do and he knew why I wanted to do it.

He had only one major question up front about *Freedom of the City*. He said: "Why, as an Englishman, do you want to do this play?" And I said: "Because it was a bastard of an Englishman who said what is in the Goddamned play, not Brian Friel. It was the Lord Chief Justice of England who said it. That is why I want to do the play." The horror story is that all the justice's lines are direct quotes from the Lord Chief Justice of England. The play upset a lot of Englishmen, but it needed to be said. And it was a very human story.

After we did that, John Hirsch asked me again what I would like to do. I said that I wanted to do something silly. And I ended up saying: "Do you mind if we do the first hour of *Pygmalion*?" Hughey Webster asked again: "What do you want to do that for?" I said: "I think it would be funny if we get the right people to do it, just one hour."

MJM: And it was funny, it was delightful.

TILL: It is a piece of English theatrical nonsense. Once again Hughey read it – he phoned me and said: "You don't want to do this!" I said: "Hughey, I think we'll have a ball with it and the audience will like it." And he said: "All right." He always wanted to know why I wanted to do things. Acts I and II of *Pygmalion* are all style, they are just nonsense. But there again, I was really in the mood to do it. What was wonderful about John was, he would literally phone and ask you what you wanted to do. And I suppose he *knew* that the best work from a director really comes when he has got that passion to do something – even when he makes a mess of it, it will be so passionate. It will have something going for it.

DIRECTOR AND ACTOR

One thing has not changed over the years. The director still determines what will go out live or on tape or film and how it will be performed. The director of photography may illuminate that vision with his or her own special composition for the telling images, but the director initially "calls the shots." Yet in this most collaborative of arts – in which a bad edit, ill-chosen music, inept costuming or lighting or makeup, terrible dialogue or bad staging can lessen the impact or even ruin a scene – the viewer will still focus above all on the actors. Characters, and what happens to them, is what television drama is all about. In the end, it is actors who must embody the vision of all the people off-camera.

As director David Greene said, "They're the ones who have to stick their faces in front of millions of people, and as a consequence they're sometimes scared stiff. They need tender loving care. And occasionally they need a kick in the ass ... Each actor needs different things from the director; this one needs support, this one needs to work at it harder ... this one needs help in letting go."[13]

MJM to RH THOMSON [1989]: Is it the director's job to give feedback to actors, among other things?

THOMSON: I'm not sure that it's feedback. It's to guide. He is not going to say "laugh or cry" or whatever. He is going to say, "Rob, you can do more," or "Tone that down there," or "Why don't we just throw in some stuff?"

MJM: Would you refuse a film on the basis of who was directing it?

THOMSON: It is conceivable, yes. If you look at the combination of script, producer, and director and realize that it is a lethal combination, that the chances of success for it are so tiny, you shouldn't do it.

If you are out of work and starving, then you do it, you don't have a choice. A director, for me, searches out and articulates perception and vision. Producers are for providing something for the market. When the director is reduced to a floor manager, you know you are in trouble.

MJM: You've seen this happen?

THOMSON: Too many times, especially in the episodics. A director is reduced to the floor manager, getting the actors to hit their mark. Television is one person's vision, the director's. He or she puts all the elements together, and when you take that away you change television and it becomes the producer's vision. They are finding a product to deliver to a market. If they only want scripts that fall within the series' bible,[14] then that is a response to the demands of the market. Gone is the vision.

MJM: But if Eric Till or Donald Brittain is the director, you know they are not going to manipulate you.

THOMSON: Absolutely, but they are the wild cards, the exceptions in the television industry. Such people are on the edge of the pond because of fashion.

Eric Till directed and Grahame Woods wrote the successful two-part mini-series about Banting and Best called *Glory Enough for All*, which starred R.H. Thomson and featured an actor much praised for her theatrical roles, Kate Trotter, as his estranged fiancée.

TROTTER [1989]: I don't think of something like *Glory Enough for All* as being typical TV. It's such an exception that it's neither film nor TV. It's a gift.

MJM: In what way?

TROTTER: Partly it has to do with the quality of the material.

MJM: The writing?

TROTTER: Yes. More time and effort and intelligence and experience and talent was spent on the writing. Partly it had to do with whose hands it was in. Eric Till is a man with so much experience and knowledge. I think it might have had to do with connections to the theatre as well. R.H. [who is her close friend] is not a typical TV performer.

MJM: How much preparation do you, as an actor, get beforehand?

TROTTER: *Glory Enough for All* is about the only one that actually springs to mind.

MJM: Where you had time to think and feel your way into it?

TROTTER: Yes, that's right.

MJM: You were working with Eric Till, who is an "actor's director" as well as a superb director in other respects.

TROTTER: Yes. I had three or four weeks with that script and then it was shot over a period of about three months, so I was in at various times. I had lots of time to let it sift down and think about it. I went in to do my toughest scene, the barn scene where Edith said good-bye to Banting. Apparently Eric had all sorts of shots organized, so we were to take the whole afternoon to shoot it. R.H. and I got ready and Eric said, "I would like you to just run the scene and we'll watch." I mean that is amazing, "We'll watch." He wanted to see what we wanted to do. He and the wonderful director of photography and the camera crew sat really respectfully and watched as R.H. and I felt our way through it. Eric didn't even give us any direction at that point. He knew that he wanted R.H. to go in the stable and for me not to be able to see him while I spoke. Other than that we could do as we pleased.

So we did the scene while he watched and he said, "Thank you, I'll be with you in a minute." Then there was this little chat. He set the cameras where he and the DOP had been standing and they did the necessary lighting. He said "Let's just shoot it." There was this atmosphere of calm and respect and we shot the scene. Eric came out and said, "Can you do it again, just for safety, just like that?" I said "Yes." I came in and we did the scene again. Again Eric said, "Now I want to do a closeup." Then we shot R.H.'s closeup in the stable and that seemed to be it! I said to the DOP, "When are we going to do it from the other direction?" And he said, "Oh no, that is all Eric is going to do." I said, "Why? I thought he had all these great shots planned." He said, "No, when he saw the scene he wanted to simply shoot it with no gimmicks." Now, you see, that is a rarity: that is a director who does look at what the actors are doing and holds it and treasures it and is flexible enough to alter his plans because of it.

Don't get me wrong. I'm sure Eric *could* have given us detailed directions, but he *chose* not to. For me he combines the best of the stage world and the film world. He makes one feel proud to be an actor. As essential as I think that is, not all directors would consider that a necessity. Donald Brittain did it, Ralph Thomas does it, and so does Tim Bond.

WEBSTER: In *Race for Heaven*, Chris Wiggins and I were two old-age pensioners, living in an attic, who have a falling out. It's a stupid little thing, but it was a very funny little piece. One of them says, "By geez, when I die, everybody's gonna know it when I die because I'm gonna have the finest funeral of all." The other says, "Ah no, nothing of the kind. I'll have the finest funeral." So they both set about lining up the funeral. Well, the fact is there's only one undertaker. Then one of them says, "But I'm gonna have it first." So then they go on in the funniest, most bizarre ways possible trying to catch contagious diseases. One guy takes a job carrying sacks of dynamite in a quarry trying to blow himself up. None of it works. It was written by an American writer, but American networks wouldn't touch it because it was "glorifying suicide." That's how the CBC got to put it on. For years afterwards, when I was touring with Canadian players, I'd have people coming up to me saying, "Weren't you in *Race for Heaven?* Yes, you were." Chris Wiggins, the very same. It was a very popular show.

ELIZABETH WEBSTER: In a way it was sort of avant-garde, wasn't it?

WEBSTER: It wasn't really avant-garde. This is the whole thing. It might have stood on a certain number of toes in the States, although I'm quite sure it wouldn't have. But anything that just might have offended would never appear on American television. Yet you could get it on up here. That sort of opportunity held producers here and directors here, because they could do stuff that they couldn't do down there. There still is something happening at the CBC every now and then, but not enough to hold the kind of people and the number of people we need.

TILL: When people ask me why I didn't go back to England or down to Los Angeles, I say: "Where in the world in one year could I have gone from doing the kind of plays that I did to working with Glenn Gould, to doing something with the Royal Winnipeg Ballet, to Beecham & the TSO? Where else in the world could I do that, but here? Why would anyone be such a fool to go anywhere else?" It was only when it all changed that I decided I wouldn't leave the country, but I would go and work elsewhere. I started to go back to Britain and to do a few films there. But that was all part of my development. I needed to be thrown in the deep end again, to be thrust up against people that made me afraid at first, to make me think that I'd better have my answers right.

Eric Till has never "left" this country permanently, nor did Mario Prizek, Ron Weyman, Robert Allen, Paul Almond, Allan King, René Bonnière, and a few others who held the creative centre together through good years and bad – in some cases up to the present time.

Directing television can often be a mechanical exercise of a well-practised craft. There are many competent directors who can get good competent work from series actors within the tight shooting schedule. They give the editors lots of "extra footage" to smooth the bumps and they plant the cameras where the action is. They pull in for lots of closeups to signal to an audience, who have only one eye on the scene, that a laugh, a plot point, or a "significant" emotional moment is at hand. Given the hours to be filled by two-and-a-half English networks (CBC, CTV, and increasingly CanWest/Global), plus the informal arrangements among independent stations, competence is what most Canadian viewers expect most of the time. Unfortunately, when they get it, they are likely to think the program originates in the United States.

But as we have just heard among these voices, there are directors who will take risks, break with television's conventions, challenge the cast, crew, and viewers, and thus make some memorable programs bearing their own personal stamp.

The complex relationship between a producer and a director depends, of course, on both the personalities involved and whether the project is a two-hour drama special or a half-hour episode in a long-running series. In the last two decades, television drama has become primarily a producer's medium.

2 Producing

Producers in CBC television start the project and they finish it. It takes almost a year, start to finish, to do a drama special or even a one-hour anthology. Although producers on *For the Record*, for example, had projects in various stages going simultaneously, you need somebody who is willing to stay there for the year, and directors aren't interested. Why should they be? Yes, it is producers who carry it through and directors who come in. MARYKE McEWEN

Passion – and adventure – often ran high in the 1950s and 1960s as directors, who were also producers, put out a vast quantity of both popular and prestige drama "live" or "live to tape." However, by the late 1960s, for reasons outlined below, the two functions were split, as they had been in Britain and the United States. When the functions split, some producer/directors decided to concentrate on producing, which in most contemporary television provides the controlling vision. Others (Harvey Hart, Daryl Duke, and most notably Eric Till) chose to stay with the essence of the enterprise – directing the action in front of the camera's eye – that is, the performances, composition, and internal rhythms of the drama. Television, unlike film, is not primarily a director's medium. But there are directors with the imagination, will, and experience to project their own vision on the drama they direct. They know how to get the best from actors. They are involved in pre- and post-production decisions, such as casting, music, and design. They shoot in such a way as to shape the editing. On the set, such men, and very recently a few women, create the atmosphere in which really good work can happen.

When a sensitive producer and a knowledgeable director meet, trust each other, and work together, when both have a passion for the project, whether full-length film, pilot, anthology, or episodes in a series, the result is more likely to be good television. Whether it succeeds or fails, it will certainly have a spark.

THE EVOLUTION OF THE PRODUCER

MJM: In the 1950s and early 1960s the producer had almost complete control over casting, some choice of designer within the constraints of scheduling, and, above all, was likely to initiate the project itself.

DAVID GARDNER [1983]: We were called producer/directors, with a little diagonal line between. "Produced and directed by ..." was the credit you got at the end of a show, and indeed you were a producer.

MJM: Why were those functions split?

GARDNER: Well, that is a good question. Until I left television in 1969, I was producing and directing, so it's more a question for the 1970s.

I would suggest it had to do with greater efficiency in the sense of "you are hired to direct, so just direct the players." A better answer to that question is the fact that, in the 1970s, there was no longer a stable of producer/directors employed by the CBC. In the 1960s (even though some of us had an annual contract) there was a stable of producers/directors. We were the Drama Department and therefore we were employees of the corporation in a direct sense. Certainly there was a camaraderie of working together, of knocking ideas back and forth and saying, "I saw your show last night and loved it or hated it" or what have you. But in terms of working, we tended to work in direct relationship with the executive producers above us. There would often be several executive producers. For instance, there would be Bob Allen, who was the head of TV drama in the 1960s, an unheralded man. It is very unfortunate that he did not receive the recognition I think he deserved. Underneath him would be a series of other executive producers, with slightly different labels; for example, Ron Weyman was in charge of *The Serial* and other filmed drama, so one worked directly with Ronnie.

As I discovered from these conversations early on, "the plant" – the support staff – had produced the programs. Then unit managers, who still run the day-to-day budgets, took more of the administrative responsibility. Finally, the position of producer was created to guard the cash box until, very slowly, with the delayed advent of film and the switch to contracting directors on a per-show basis, television drama became a producer's rather than a director's medium. Since the late 1960s, producers have increasingly made most of the key decisions.

I interviewed a few of the men who bring both insider and outsider perspectives about the evolution of the role of producer and the implications for television drama. Sydney Newman was a supervising producer who left the CBC in 1958 to become a powerful figure in television drama in the United Kingdom. He then returned to head the NFB in the 1970s until his retirement. Philip Keatley, who retired in 1990, produced drama on the West Coast for thirty years as well as supervising drama production there and being responsible for training programs for new directors. As someone working in middle management in a wide variety of roles, Hugh Gauntlett (who also retired in 1990) has seen people come and go, and programs succeed or fail, since the 1950s.

THE EVOLUTION OF THE ROLE OF PRODUCER

In the early days it was simple. Originally the same man (always a man, then) produced and directed the live drama program – kept track of the budget, cast the show, consulted the designers and technicians, rehearsed the show, and "called" it with the help of his invaluable "script assistant." He chose which camera shot would appear on the viewers' screens and when. Certain kinds of scripts went to producers with an aptitude for suspense, or surrealism, or song and dance, or whatever – although most drama producers did most kinds of drama at one time or another. Within the parameters of a given anthology – for example, *On Camera* (which seems to have been pretty eclectic), *GM Presents* (with its emphasis on popular Canadian subjects in the early years), or *Folio* (which became the showcase for "high" culture and for experiments in the medium) – producers could and did make suggestions about what script they would like to do. Program ideas came from all over. The supervising producer or the story editors would also come up with something and then, a decision having been made, a producer/director was assigned to do it.

When I talked to Sydney Newman he was on his way to England to work on projects for the independently owned, off-beat channel 4. He started out by sketching his early years with the CBC.

SYDNEY NEWMAN [1984]: I fell passionately in love with television during my year in New York, 1949–50. The CBC had read one of my reports on outside broadcasts or "remotes," so I first became supervising producer in charge of outside broadcasts. That meant that I put Foster Hewitt on television. The first two years I did *Hockey Night in Canada* and the first Grey Cup. I also did some live quasi-documentaries with Marshall McLuhan and Ted Carpenter called *Varsity Story*. After two years of this, I really became bored and fed up. When you do hockey it is so exciting at first, but after a while, like most sports, it is a crashing bore. The players have the fun. The people recording it don't.

By 1954 the head of drama, Bob Allen, was promoted. They couldn't find anyone else, so I went in and offered myself. Fergus Mutrie, who was the director of television, said, "What do you know about drama?" I said, "Nothing, but I know cameras and I'm intelligent and I've done stage sets. That is my only connection to the theatre." He tried me out and I cut the mustard. I was thirty-seven years old. I haven't looked back since.

When I took over drama I inherited Sylvio Narazzanno, a brilliant director called David Greene, and a chap called Henry Kaplan. I also inherited Murray Chercover [president of CTV until 1989].

MJM: Leo Orenstein?

NEWMAN: No, Leo was in the second wave. The second wave included Paul Almond, Ron Weyman (who had been a director for me at the NFB), Mel Breen, Arthur Hiller (now a top Hollywood director), Ted Kotcheff, and Charles Jarrott.

MJM: Eric Till? Harvey Hart?

NEWMAN: Harvey Hart did some work for me, way back. No, Eric Till never worked for me. The CBC was peculiarly organized. I was supervisor of drama, doing mainly commercially sponsored shows: *General Motors* and Proctor and Gamble's half-hour series called *On Camera*. Then there was this other section under Bob Allen called *Festival*.

MJM: *Scope/Folio/Festival*?

NEWMAN: That's right. They did opera, they did a whole range of things. I had the best directors, though.

MJM: Was there an interchange among some producer/directors between the commercial and the non-commercial drama?

NEWMAN: Some, yes. David Greene and Mario Prizek did the occasional *GM Presents*. But I didn't particularly like the style of that whole group. I felt they were slack, no pace, no tempo. I also thought their work rarely had a sense of urgency. In short, they didn't have McLaren's Advertising Agency for *General Motors Theatre* and a different agency handling Proctor and Gamble's *On Camera* as on their backs as I did.

MJM: They were a bit more theatrically oriented. Why did so many leave?

NEWMAN: Not everybody left during the first exodus of the late 1950s, not by a long shot. But we had flexed our muscles to capacity in Toronto. We wanted to flex our muscles internationally. We wanted competition of a bigger kind because we had no competition in Canada. The only one I know who left for money was Arthur Hiller. That was because of an insulting remark made to him during negotiations in which he asked for $300 a year more than Fergus Mutrie offered him. Arthur was so offended that he took a kinescope of his latest play down to New York and got a job. Now, he didn't go to get more money in the States. He left Canada because he was angry. I certainly did not go to England for money. I went to England for exactly the same money that I was getting in Toronto.

Paul Rutherford documents this period in his book *When Television Was Young*, which both complements and in some key places disputes the evaluation of 1950s and 1960s television drama that I made in *Turn Up the Contrast*. Rutherford's assessment of Newman seems to me to be apt. "More than anyone else he came to fulfill the role of drama impresario with the vision to push people to develop a high quality and popular style of drama ... a great champion of both realistic and Canadian drama ... Paul Almond, then a youthful producer, credited Newman with bringing him down to earth, making him realize the need 'to do the simple sort of homey show.'"[1]

MJM: When the first wave of producers left, they were not particularly dissatisfied with the way the place was being run? They just wanted a larger stage and a bigger challenge?
NEWMAN: Exactly. In the 1960s it was different. The tremendous shrinkage of drama took place around 1960, and it has been shrinking ever since. Consequently, with less opportunity for work, people had to leave. Canada forced them out.

E.A. Weir backs that up. In *The Struggle for National Broadcasting in Canada*, he wrote: "Drama [had] ... been decimated. According to ACTRA [the radio and television actors union], Canadian drama has been reduced by at least 50 percent from that of four or five years ago. The many fine dramas sponsored by *General Motors* and subsidized by the CBC have been replaced by *Bonanza*. During 1963–64, drama on *Festival* was cut about one-third, while *Playdate* was cut down by thirteen programs. Particularly hard-hit have been English programs out of Montreal." He also points out that the consequence was increasingly hard times for writers, performers, and producers, and he discusses the exodus of talent. The reasons were "slashed budgets, discontent with pressures [unspecified], indefinite policy, lack of leadership, the need to report to executives who, whatever their other virtues, have little or no record of accomplishment in production and little understanding of the creative mind."[2]

Yet during the previous fifteen years the CBC had offered a freedom to experiment that was unique compared with what was happening in both the United States and Britain. This, together with the technical excellence developing at the CBC and the hands-on experience of CBC personnel, meant that, in a steady trickle during the late 1950s, and then in the aftermath of the *This Country Has Seven Days* crisis, New York and Hollywood welcomed Norman Jewison, David Greene, Frank Peppiatt, Charles Aylesworth, Arthur Hiller, and Harvey Hart. The big exodus to England of producers, including Sylvio Narazzanno and Ted Allen, however, was triggered in part by the success in England of *Flight into Danger* in 1957, which brought Sydney Newman to the independent British company, ABC. Many writers like Stanley Mann and Arthur Hailey followed. Among the actors were Lorne Green, Lloyd Bochner, William Shatner, Toby Robins, Sharon Acker, Elaine Grand, Leslie Nielsen, James Doohan, John Vernon, and John Colicos.

PHILIP KEATLEY [1985]: We had a mechanism in Vancouver (which Toronto did not) called the Producers' Association. The association came into existence in Montreal in 1959 as a result of the producers' strike that sent René Lévesque into politics. They formed their own association in Montreal, and then they started branches across the country.

PAUL ALMOND, producer, director [1991]: The *This Hour Has Seven Days* furore had a tremendous impact on drama as well, even though it had nothing to do with it. It has no bearing, in a sense, in a book on drama, but it's something very important because we suddenly got a collective feeling of strength.

MJM: It's interesting that you would characterize it that way, because David Gardner characterizes it as being the "coup de grâce," the beginning of the end when people just got fed up and left.

ALMOND: People? Do you mean directors and so on?

MJM: Yes, specifically directors.

ALMOND: For me, personally, I went freelance around 1957, 1958.

For Toronto producers who had not actively supported the Radio-Canada producers' strike, it was *Seven Days* that stirred them to form their own separate association. Whatever the history, to an outsider this division between regional producers and Toronto producers seemed like pure folly, particularly in the current chilly climate. In 1991 the two associations finally moved to unite.

I asked Hugh Gauntlett, who laboured in the often stony fields of middle management for three decades, about the flow of Canadian talent out of the country in that period. I kept hearing stories of how certain programs became a ticket to jobs abroad.

HUGH GAUNTLETT [1985]: A few people went to the United States in the 1950s and many had gone to England. It seems to me that the exodus followed *Flight into Danger*, which really created a sensation in England and Sydney Newman's going there. He didn't take many people with him, but there was a Canadianization of English television drama.[3] *Flight into Danger* was significant because nobody over there had tried to do action drama. It was an action drama singularly well conceived within the limitations of live television and done with considerable panache. It was the first television masterwork of popular entertainment. I don't think that it had crossed anybody's mind at the BBC that you would even try that kind of stuff. [*Halliwell's Television Companion* says "it was one of the first dramatic entertainments to prove that what's on at home can keep the cinemas empty."][4]

HUGH WEBSTER, actor/writer [1984]: Nathan Cohen showed me the original script of *Flight into Danger*, the best play that had come across his desk. And he wanted my opinion on it before he went to bat for it. I read it and I said to Syd Newman, who was head of drama at the time: "That's a first-rate show. That is one of the best I've ever read."

MJM: He had a vision?

WEBSTER: Oh, yes.

MJM: Canadian. Populist. Both period and contemporary.

WEBSTER: Yes.

MJM: Trying a fair number of forms.

WEBSTER: Absolutely. Not afraid to go into battle with anybody.

NEWMAN: The reason I was offered a job by ABC television in England was because the BBC had run a series of dramas called *Canadian Television Theatre*. There was my name up on the screen every week for twenty-six weeks: "Sydney Newman, Supervising Producer." They were kinescopes of dreadful, dreadful technical quality, 16-mm grainy things. But they were dynamic, exciting. They were different from what the British were accustomed to seeing. The BBC also bought a lot of Canadian stuff during the 1960s.

MJM: I gather ABC and then the BBC gave you a relatively free hand.

NEWMAN: Totally. I have the sort of personality which is seemingly compliant. I am sensitive to my environment, but I work in that environment without losing my soul, or much of my soul. I am also a rather irreverent person in many ways. I like shocking people. You are aware that I created *The Avengers* and *Dr. Who*. There is a rather vulgar, easy to take, escapist side of me, although *Dr. Who* was never regarded as a piece of escape entertainment.

MJM: *The Avengers* [rerun on Arts and Entertainment pay channel as recently as 1991] had a good deal going for it, too.

NEWMAN: I am talking now about escapism.

MJM: But it was literate and allusive.

NEWMAN: I set out to prick the bubble of the hot passion that the Brits were experiencing for spies. I went on the air with *The Avengers* about nine months before James Bond hit the air. My central character, Pat MacNee, was, roughly speaking, my version of a James Bond type of person.

MJM: MacNee had appeared on CBC television in the 1950s.

NEWMAN: That is how Pat got the part. He was one of my staple actors in Toronto.

MJM: *Z-Cars* was another ...

NEWMAN: *Z-Cars* was created prior to my going to the BBC. The only time I did touch it was when the ratings (which for four years were about sixteen million a week) had dropped down to about twelve million. I called the producer in one day and I said, "David, I think we should kill it while it's at its peak." He said, "Oh, dear." I said, "Why not take the three central characters of *Z-Cars* and move them into another division of policing. We'll change the title, do it exactly the same way with that same nice, easy realism and rivalry." And so, he created *Softly, Softly*. The ratings immediately jumped up to sixteen million again.

MJM: There you have continuity. In British and American television, you often find continuity of television personae.

NEWMAN: Of course.

The CBC has not encouraged a Gordon Pinsent, Cynthia Dale, or Louis Del Grande[5] to choose and star in other series tailored to their own talents, as American networks did with Bill Cosby, Michael Landon, or James Garner. The lack of continuity in Canada is a major disadvantage for Canadian series. On the other hand, I would argue that the fact we had no television "stars," but rather a repertory company of superb television actors who demonstrated a marvellous range of abilities over television's first fifteen years, was one of the things that made our television anthology distinctive. Another was the range of talented producers. The same tolerance of diversity encouraged the contrasting talents of men like Newman, Prizek, and Till – with one odd omission.

MJM to MAVOR MOORE, the first producer of TV drama at the CBC and midwife to its early years [1990]: So having got CBC drama launched, you left to go on to the Stratford Festival. You didn't in fact leave the CBC, in that you continued as a writer and as an actor. Did you ever direct or produce in television again?

MOORE: No, I was never asked to.

MJM: You astound me.

MOORE: The only time that anything was ever said to me about coming back to the CBC was after Al Ouimet became president. He said to me once: "You must come back and join the corporation again." I said, "That would be very nice, Al," and I heard no more. That's the only time it was ever raised. I've been a consultant to them since and sat on various advisory committees and that sort of thing, but I've never directed for them again, no. In fact I've never directed television since. I've directed for radio, but not for television.

This polymath of a man wrote, directed, and acted in all kinds of radio and theatre, wrote and acted in reams of television, was a full professor and chair of York University's theatre department (founding their television drama script archive), and headed the Canada Council in one of its difficult periods, the early 1980s.[6]

Meanwhile a second generation of producer/directors from the 1950s, among them Mario Prizek, continued to flourish.

MARIO PRIZEK [1983]: In the late 1950s and 1960s I was producing and directing at least six to eight ninety-minute dramas a year. I did the first Edward Albee and the first Ionesco on television. I did the first Pinter ever done in North America on television. I also did plays by writers who have still not been performed in America. People like Arrabal [*Picnic on the Battlefield*]. Ionesco was barely heard of in North America when I did *Bedlam Galore for Two or More*.

MJM: That was a really interesting production.

PRIZEK: It was great fun to go from doing a Chekhov play to doing an Absurdist drama.

MJM: I remember one of your earliest productions. The CBC adaptation of Sartre's *The Unburied Dead* made a tremendous impression on me as a teenager.

PRIZEK: Lorne Greene's last Canadian role before he went to New York and Hollywood. Does it still stand up?

MJM: Beautifully.

PRIZEK: I'm always amazed when I see one of my old shows. I always approach it with great trepidation. They showed *The Duchess of Malfi* at Harbourfront one evening recently and asked me to be present to answer any questions. It was such a strange experience. You see, I had never seen the work performed in any form because I was sitting in the control room calling the shots.

MJM: You had never seen a kine of it? How eerie that must have been for you.

PRIZEK: It was. Very eerie. I was looking at it as if it were somebody else's work because I couldn't imagine how I had dared to try some of the things I tried. When you're younger you take on so much more, you think you can do so much more. In later years you question much more before you do it.

ALMOND [1991]: Television was still a cottage industry in the 1950s and early 1960s. You did it yourself, you'd go in and you'd make it yourself. As soon as it gets bigger, the more distant it gets, the further you get removed from what is really significant art, feeling art, a drama that speaks to people, arrests them and grabs them. Now it's just off there in that little box in the corner and it's not interesting. That's why I make my own films. Making your own films is not possible at the CBC any more. CBC TV drama is not interesting to do, and so you don't bother doing it.

RON WEYMAN, executive producer, producer/director [1987]: Times have changed. The opportunity to work intensively in a number of areas, because that is what one did, is gone. TV has become specialized now, and people have got assistants and assistants.

MJM: I don't know of anyone at the CBC who both produces and directs as a normal thing. It's happened occasionally when somebody got sick or something, but it just doesn't happen. Once those two functions were split, they stayed split.

ALMOND: That's terrible, there's no reason for the two of them to be split, there never has been. Unless it is like France, where the director is king and the producer is only there to take the money worries off him. But do you think Orson Welles, Stanley Kubrick, Sydney Lumet, Woody Allen, Stephen Spielberg, Ingmar Bergman, to name the greatest film-makers, are beholden to producers? Of course not. They are their own bosses. The only time we'll get decent films again in Canada is when someone recognizes that! Especially at the CBC. Even at Telefilm, when I started *The Dance Goes On*, some functionary, following orders, stopped the application for *two precious months* while I was waiting for word. When I finally found out, I went stomping in there with my big boots on. "What's happening?" "Oh, it's all a mistake, she was just following rules. You see, no director can be his own producer. But in your case ..." Yes, I guess since I'd been doing it for nearly forty years they had to admit I could still apply. But that shows even Telefilm sometimes doesn't get the message.

PRODUCERS AND MANAGEMENT: EARLY DAYS

As in every theatre, television, radio, or film organization in the world, there are conflicts between those who make the drama and those who make the overall decisions.

ERIC TILL [1983]: It seemed as though someone would send memos around about "things you cannot do" just after I had done them. I remember once, someone sent a memo around saying "you must constantly change the image on television," meaning the audiences will get bored looking at the same shot all the time. I had just done a whole scene of two people sitting side by side. I made the judgment that if the performances are interesting there was no need to change the camera, so I just left the camera on. After *Private Memories and Confessions* there was a report that came out about the sort of things they didn't want on television, specifically "big crowd scenes."

MJM: And you had that incredibly long and complicated crowd scene in *Private Memories*. Mind you, it was very surrealistically done.

TILL: But that seemed to be the way of things with me at that time. I, personally, felt saddest at the change in the nature of drama in the mid-1960s. That is principally why I left the corporation to become a freelance director. It became very obvious it was going to slip more and more into the American mould of programming – which is not interesting to me at all. Drama was also gradually changing to film through the early 1960s.

ALMOND: I'm the one who's had the most shows banned at the CBC. I did Anouilh's *Point of Departure* (1960) with Bill Shatner and Lloyd Bochner. Management was so afraid they cancelled it. I have the *Toronto Star* headline – "CBC Bans Sexy French Play." They ran it two months later, late at night. I did another *General*

Motors called *Shadow of a Pale Horse*, with a hanging they said was too explicit. They cancelled it and then put it on later.

MJM: They did put it on eventually? Or did they put it on during an hour that nobody would watch it, which is what happened with *Point of Departure?*

ALMOND: That was the second one, and there was another one we did. So I have done three plays that were banned.

MJM: What was the third one?

ALMOND: *Fellowship* by Michael Tait. It was based on a true event in Toronto, I think, and had a crucifixion in it which they said was too strong.

MJM: I don't know it.

ALMOND: It was in 1975. They played it late at night. [My colleague at Brock University, Jim Leach, who has a special interest in Paul Almond's cinematic work, remembers staying up late at night to see this film. Regrettably, it was broadcast before VCR was available.] Frankly, some people get all up in arms, but I never worried when my shows were put on late because it wasn't my job to say whether a show should run. I just did them. In fact, I probably liked the publicity I got from being a sort of daredevil.

Meanwhile, the second exodus of producers in the mid-to-late 1960s had not resulted in a fresh wave of talent joining the corporation. Some gifted producers remained, but even they were beginning to tire by the time John Hirsch had been appointed in 1974. Hirsch had virtually no television experience and certainly no extensive knowledge of the first twenty years of CBC TV drama when he said: "The whole tradition of producer has been grossly neglected in this country. We just don't have the talent at a stage of development that can be tapped immediately. We have been going to England and America to get talent. We are still a very colonial country. Instead of developing our own talent, it is easier to go outside for it. In the long run it's very costly, not cheaper at all."[7]

Fifteen years later, Paul Almond concurred:

ALMOND: A talent to bring people together is looked on as almost un-Canadian, too American. Above all, one must not be successful. If people are successful, you must ruin them in two days. The best way to get along in some institutions is to fail consistently. We don't know how to deal with people who are ambitious and difficult.

THE TELEVISION GENERATION
OF PRODUCERS

Producer Maryke McEwen came up through the CBC's informal but well-worn route to producer as a story editor, then co-producer in the late 1970s, then drama producer in the *For the Record* unit in the early 1980s. She moved from the anthology *For the Record* to the pilot, and was executive producer for the first two seasons of *Street Legal*, before moving on to drama specials like *The Diary of Evelyn Lau*. She holds a more contemporary point of view about the irreversible split between directors and producers.

MCEWEN [1984]: Directors really aren't producers. Directors are creative – even directors I know who have produced their own stuff. It drives them crazy. They have to split their heads. What directors should be able to do is be completely free to plan their work, work with the actors, and not worry about the money or the schedule. Somebody else should worry about that for them. If you stick directors with a producer's hat, you immediately hobble them. They become small and narrow in their focus, and they aren't going to do the job for you. I would rather have directors who are completely off the wall than those who are worrying about whether we are going into overtime because, then, they aren't doing their job with the actors.

MJM: It sounds as if you're saying that the two jobs appeal to two different kinds of people.

MCEWEN: I think they do. They are different people.

MJM: So the continuity in the development of a program comes from the producer?

MCEWEN: I think so. I think it is better for the show, however, if the director has a chance to get to know the script and to work with a producer early. Any pre-production you do pays in the long run, financially as well as creatively. Some people don't involve directors. With a series like *Seeing Things*, the director just comes on board. It is already cast and scripted, and they just shoot it. [Not in that particular case. George McGowan directed every episode of this series and left on it his own imprint of experience, ease, and willingness to use whatever he found in a setting or got from the performers.] That way of operating works for series. But there is always somebody who is going to give you that little thing that might just make it that much better. Why deny it to yourself? I'll take advice from the janitor, if he has a good idea.

Script editor Alice Sinclair, who died in 1990, was one of the first people I interviewed. I talked to her both on and off the record on several other occasions. She taught me a lot about television process because her sharp, sometimes sardonic eye and her three decades of television experience as a story editor gave her a unique perspective on the various roles of director, producer, writer, and actor, and on the policy-makers and the programs themselves.

SINCLAIR [1982]: Fifty years from now, when there's nobody to ask, scholars will spend time wondering why specific changes from script to final scene were made.
MJM: And it could simply be that there wasn't the money for a given special effect.
SINCLAIR: It could be that there wasn't the money. It could be that this particular character had been tailored to a specific actor, but he'd taken another job. A lot of decisions are made on a practical, not an artistic basis. Certainly, for the young and starry-eyed, that's always a surprise.

Writer/producer Bill Gough worked primarily on drama specials and anthology. He is married to writer Anna Sandor, who has her own views of how directors and producers can make or mar a program. Both write as a team for episodic television, and Sandor has written adaptations and original scripts for drama specials, notably her original script for *Charlie Grant's War* and *Two Men*. I talked to them in 1988, a year before they left for the United States, where they have since written movies of the week for American network television.

MJM: How does the relationship between producer and director work?
GOUGH: It is the same as the relationship with the writer. It is essential for the producer to know the director's craft and to know it well enough that their discussions are practical and meaningful. If you don't know that, then you waste the director's time and you never get a focused vision.
MJM: Some producers have been story editors rather than directors.
GOUGH: Yes. That is useful in terms of analysing story.
SANDOR: The psychological relationship that a director and a producer has is very important. Bill tends to work again and again with the same people, and I have heard it said that he gets the best work out of certain people. He has done wonderful work with director Martin Lavut.

GOUGH: Every time.

MJM: Indeed, he has.

SANDOR: Don Brittain did his first TV drama, *Running Man*, for Bill. Bill and Don got along really well. There are a lot of producers who don't know what they are doing. If I were a director I would go nuts thinking, "My God, I'm going to be in Taiwan at the time of the mix and this person who knows nothing is going to be there ruining my work!"

After working as a unit manager and as a writer on *King of Kensington*, David Barlow gained his experience as a producer in series television, specifically *Seeing Things*. Since then he has produced and co-directed two drama specials, *Trivial Pursuit* and *Sanity Clause*. He continues to write and produce for series.

MJM: On top of all the other things producers do, they must also possess a sense of story, because they have so much influence over the shaping of the program. I learned that from watching you work on various phases of *Seeing Things*.

BARLOW [1988]: Yes, producers have more influence in episodic television.

MJM: Would you agree that there are occasional directors who have more control over what they do because of their experience and background? I'm thinking primarily of people like Allan King or Eric Till. Wouldn't producers tend to trust their judgment?

BARLOW: They certainly do in single shots [movies or anthology drama]. This is not to denigrate their work, because they are obviously big creative talents, but I would suggest that if you put up episodes of a series which Eric has directed against those which somebody else has directed and try to find which is which, it would be tough to do.

MJM: Because the primary vision is the producer's.

BARLOW: The producer's, combined with the fellow who directed the pilot. Any of these guys when working as a series director will come in and say, "What is the style that I'm supposed to serve here?" They will also bring their own contributions, but within that context. I think you can tell the difference in episodes if you really study them, and a talent like Till's will obviously always show. You will say, "Well, why is that just that much better? The actors' performance in that was just that much better, the visuals were just that much better." It is a particular talent at work. But he doesn't go so crazy that he takes it outside the overall context of the series. He just does his thing, and it happens to be so much better than most people's that it shows. But it's a tough study to make that distinction. In contast, if you look at one of Eric's TV movies, you know it's Eric. He definitely brings a certain style and quality to it.

MJM: There is obviously a major distinction between producing a series of the kind we've been talking about and sitting down and producing a single project, where you do it, it goes out, it may get rerun once, but you're finished with it. You haven't done as many of these independent projects, such as *Trivial Pursuit* and *Sanity Clause*. How do they feel?

BARLOW: Oh, they are a lot better because of two things. One is you don't have to sustain your concentration over six or seven years. You have to sustain it over only two or three, because that's about how long it takes to do one of these single shots. It's easier on that level. The other thing is that, at least when I did a series, I found there wasn't a day when I didn't think about the previous episode, or the one that was being written, or the one that we should be writing, or the one that we'd shot which needed to be worked on. It never, ever goes away because no matter what you do, you have to progress towards making eight hours a year or twenty-two hours a year. The numbers of episodes expected doesn't really matter so much because the process is exactly the same. By these dates, I must achieve this objective. Every year, you've got to keep doing that.

MJM: Even when you're not shooting?

BARLOW: Yes. You still know that all you're doing is waiting to start it again. So, it's a tremendous treadmill and very demanding. Very lucrative, but very demanding. When *Seeing Things* stopped, the relief was extraordinary. [Star and co-producer] Louis Del Grande and I were so physically ill by the time we got to the end of *Seeing Things* that we were just relieved. Why do it again? Because work is like that. But there is that monkey-on-the-back quality of a series. You have made a contract with the box that eats programming, and you must feed it. With a "single" that's not the case. It's about "How can we develop, how can we make this better in the time that's available to us?" It's a much more attractive way to work, but it's hard to make a living at it.

MJM: You're a producer, though, who pretty well produces your own ideas.

BARLOW: Absolutely. Yes.

MJM: You really aren't interested in other people writing.

BARLOW: No, I am not, I am not a market for other people. I listen to stuff sometimes because I get browbeaten, cornered, or cajoled into listening to stuff. But that's not what I do. If I stay in this business for another twenty years, I won't get done all the stuff that I'd like to do and that Lou and I would like to do – either something we write or something that we like that we could get somebody else to write.

MJM to ALICE SINCLAIR [1988]: What happens when you have a producer with a basic vision of a series and then he or she leaves and another producer comes in. It must be very difficult to keep the continuity.

SINCLAIR: If the original producer has done enough shows for there to be a strong imprint, then the second producer goes along with that until he's sufficiently comfortable to put his own imprint on it and then it gradually changes. [This process is quite visible in the nineteen years of *The Beachcombers* and in the evolution of *Street Legal*.] Obviously if your main lead is a gay young bachelor, it's foolish to give him a wife and family who turn up in episode thirteen. Stan Colbert had put a strong imprint on *Side Street* [1975–79], and it survived longer than *The Collaborators* [1973–75]. *The Collaborators* fell apart with a change in producer.

MJM: The concept didn't change as much in *Side Street* as it did in *The Collaborators*, although there were significant cast changes between seasons.

SINCLAIR: *Side Street* was, from the start, a more formula kind of thing, whereas *The Collaborators*, though it was not entirely successful, could have been quite an innovative series.

MJM: *The Collaborators*, from this distance, anticipated by fifteen years nearly everything that everybody praised in *Hill Street Blues*. Canadians have a habit of anticipating major trends in television. We just don't notice when we do it.

SINCLAIR: Well, of the watchers of *Hill Street Blues*, who is going to remember *The Collaborators*?

MJM: Yes, that's one of our problems, isn't it? Not even the people who worked on the shows remember them.

SINCLAIR: That's right.

Despite the intermittent efforts at formally training people as producers or writers, directors or actors, the CBC has many talented people who learned on the job. As Hugh Gauntlett told me:

GAUNTLETT [1985]: You really learn producing or directing mostly by coming up the ladder and doing some simple kind of activity throughout.

MJM: Is there much active recruitment?

GAUNTLETT: Yes and no. Even when there is a surplus of people, there is always some kind of recruitment going on. Drama, in particular, or a new enterprise like *The Journal*, will suck in a whole bunch of people from radio, print, and other media. In the case of drama, since three-quarters of the working population is freelance and to some degree coming and going, there is always turnover and some (but not a big) opportunity for new people to get involved.

MJM: I was struck by the fact that Martin Kinch [artistic director of Toronto Free Theatre in its formative years] came in from the alternative theatre. He was simply given *Some Honourable Gentlemen* to produce.

GAUNTLETT: That's right. But he was nursed through a transition of learning the television business by people who took an interest in him.

McEWEN: I don't think anyone could learn to produce a film without the apprenticeship system. You can learn technique at a film or broadcasting school, but you have to start at the bottom to get the full understanding of film because it's very complicated. It's not just point A to point B, it's the people. What kind of person makes a grip? A good lighting guy? How do you talk to them? How do you schedule them? How do you get the best work you can out of them? What are individual directors like?

PRODUCERS AND MANAGEMENT: CONTEMPORARY PRACTICE

McEWEN: In England, they have the tradition of production people going up the ranks, so the top-level guy at the BBC can talk to you about shows. They haven't forgotten how. That is what they are there for: production value, scripts, and so on. Here, there is this huge chasm between "us" and "them." There are the production and backup units who think we are flaky (that's the nicest thing they can say about us) or genuinely a pain in the ass, and they wish we would go away. Then there are the bureaucrats. The bureaucrats are running one network, and we're running another network, and they don't mesh. It's the middle management where you really notice it because that is where the changeover happens. We have very little in common. They don't know who we are. They don't talk to us, unless we do something really good that they might notice, but then only for a little while.

MJM: You don't get a sense that they are engaged with what you are doing? You don't get feedback from them?

MCEWEN: No. You have two different companies and three or four different accounting systems going on in this corporation which just stymie production.[8]

Some reforms of the accounting system have since occurred (see chapter 11). In other respects, I have found from these and other conversations with CBC personnel that the sense of two corporations, one for those who make the programs and one for the rest, still exists. To some degree it is comparable with the front-office/backlot split in movies, or the company and artistic director vs management, marketing, and board of directors split in theatres. In other words, it has been part of the history of all performing arts since travelling players settled down and built themselves a permanent secular theatre in 1575. The issue, however, is not the inevitable tensions between creative people and managers. They do not have to agree, but they do have to understand one another. A succession of presidents – Al Johnson, Pierre Juneau, Gérard Veilleux, and, most unlikely of all, ex-Tory cabinet minister Perrin Beatty – with no broadcasting experience at all may be one of the roots of the problem. One of the bridges of communication between the two structures should be the executive producer.

ALMOND: I did another show for the CBC and it was awful. You know what I'm talking about? I went into this room with everyone talking to each other – a producer and a this and a that and a unit manager and so on, it was all bureaucracy. In the old days I was the producer/director and casting director. With my one script assistant we did everything. What's the big deal now? Why do you need fifteen people? You don't need them. So I was bugged by that and I've never gone back.

I haven't made a CBC show in eleven years. Here I am, with nearly forty years of experience, why wouldn't I be the first person they would want to come in and do some of their important dramas? I haven't forgotten anything. But they haven't asked me and I haven't wanted to do it. There's been some wonderful young guys. I know Martin Lavut. Some people do good things and they can function within that, but I personally don't think I could.

Also, in the 1950s one wasn't plagued by this thing of stars and ratings. In our day we just did the show. Your responsibility was to yourself, to your actors, and to the other guys in the drama department or on *Festival* to do a good show. It wasn't to sell anything or to do a "product" or to reach a wide audience, that was your last idea.

To some degree, even as the hours on the schedule available for drama shrank, that creative freedom continued up to the late 1980s.

MJM to executive producer SAM LEVENE [1988]: Your basic constraints as executive producer on *For the Record* were that it must be a topical Canadian drama anthology. Any other constraints other than the budget or the hour-long format?

LEVENE: That's it!

MJM: So there was a fair amount of freedom.

LEVENE: Lots of freedom in those years. John Kennedy gave us a lot of freedom. My job was to report to him and keep him fully informed. He would naturally have veto power, but he seldom exercised that. He never did in my four years.

GAUNTLETT, head of arts and science at the time: On the whole question of bailiwicks: obviously, one has got to have some concern about the relationship of the bits. When a head of drama gets into it too far, he begins demotivating the people who are doing it for him. You have to strike the balance. The producers are the ones who have to make sense of it all. There are some people in whom one has great confidence. You don't waste time and effort on them. There are others who you have less confidence in. You have to do a great deal of peering over their shoulder.

MJM to LEVENE: As an executive producer, what did you do?

LEVENE: The job was to do the best possible, most hard-hitting, topical Canadian drama. I believed we were there to be challenging and provocative, although the anthology was meant to be accessible to a wide audience.

The individual program could have humour in it, but the purpose was serious. We were not there to preach, but we were there to shed light on a topic. Now everything has changed. The Americans are into the "disease of the week" [in later years the "crime of the week"] and that has given topical drama a bad name. Ralph Thomas called them "journalistic dramas" – it was a nice phrase. But *For the Record* wasn't a recreation of reality; it was never a docudrama. It was topical, issue-oriented drama, and there is a big difference. We hardly ever did a recreation of a real event with the actual characters.[9]

We were also expected to get decent ratings for the show. Generally speaking, we didn't get enormous ratings, but they were respectable. It wasn't meant to be minority viewing; it was meant to be serious viewing for the largest possible audience.

MJM: You were the executive producer. Did you sit down at the beginning of planning a season and say, "Here are twelve topics I think we should be able to turn into shows."

LEVENE: It certainly can work that way, and sometimes it did.

MJM: Did it work that way for you?

LEVENE: I think it did for a couple of years. Then more and more the individual producers would propose their stories, and I would accept them or decline them. The three or four producers assigned to the unit and I would collaborate on the series. I did have lists of subjects or topics I thought were worth examining, some that I pushed hard for and some that I convinced one of the producers to run with.

MJM: Can you give me an example?

LEVENE: *The Winnings of Frankie Walls* was an unemployment story. When I took over the series in 1978, unemployment was high, a hot issue. That was one of the first stories I thought we should tackle. It was also the first script I commissioned, but it turned out not too well, so we never produced it. I think I commissioned a second one and probably a third one by the time we got Robert Forsyth to create what became *The Winnings of Frankie Walls*. Bill Gough had just come in from Newfoundland to be the producer on that show, and so it worked. It was one of the first ideas I brought to the series, but it was actually produced two years later.

MJM: You are describing a brokering situation there when you say that the topic was finally married to the appropriate writer who also clicked with a particular producer. Is that one of the major things an executive producer does – bring talents together?

LEVENE: First of all, an executive producer within the CBC is a producer. He is not a money man or a company administrator, but a producer who in particular situations develops a series with other producers working on it. An executive producer may still personally produce his own programs, as I often did.

MJM: As executive producer, you must have a hand in selecting directors as well as producers?

LEVENE: Yes, we have a hand in everything, selecting directors, cast, and script. But you develop your relationships with your producers. The first year I didn't know them very well. The second year I knew them better and the third year even better, and a couple of new ones came in. But you leave them more and more on their own. They want to be left alone, and they don't want you interfering. So you have this creative tension.

MJM: A producer either new to the concept of the series or new to producing would need more help from you.

LEVENE: That's right, and we had both. We had new producers or experienced producers who were new to drama or new to topical drama, so naturally I would be more involved with those shows.

BILL GOUGH [1988]: The whole setup has been traditionally producer driven ...

MJM: ... producer/director originally. Now, producer ...

GOUGH: The director has a part to play, but in television not as
important a role in originating the project as the producer or the
writer, as far as I am concerned.

MJM: How would you define the role of an executive producer?

GOUGH: I don't know. Drama is different from current affairs. I
used to be an executive producer in current affairs and it was very
much a "hands-on" job. The role of executive producer is important in getting the right people together, but it's actually not needed
in many projects. I haven't had an executive producer on anything
I've done in a long time. I've had associate producers or line
producers whose work is invaluable, because that is a clearly
defined function. An executive producer is for the most part an
administrative necessity more than a creative force.

MJM: And the selector of projects?

GOUGH: To a certain extent, yes. That is also important. But generally, that tends to be a "Let's do a show about unemployment."
That is not a dramatic statement. The statement "Let's do a show
about unemployment" is not "Oh, this is a great idea! Let's do *The
Winnings of Frankie Walls*." Or "Let's do a show about wife abuse"
is not the same as "Let's do *A Far Cry from Home*." They are
different categories of statement. The danger in bureaucracy is
that people can make general statements, and when they see a
show result because of the specific talents of those who did the
work, they are under the illusion that somehow they created it.
That isn't necessarily correct. On the other hand, without the
ultimate support for *Charlie Grant's War* that John Kennedy eventually gave, the show could not have been done. So the position of
head of drama is an absolutely vital one. You cannot get a show
done without a ...

MJM: ... gatekeeper?

GOUGH: Yes, I guess so.

MJM: Somebody who can then empower the whole thing at that
level ...

GOUGH: Yes, that's important.

MJM: Doing the fighting with the directors of programming.

GOUGH: There are far too many levels of bureaucracy, and most
aren't needed.

MJM: As a producer, do you have any control over the commercials,
– for example, whether a given commercial will be disruptive in its
content to the tone of your drama?

GOUGH: I actually do. For the first run of *Charlie Grant's War*, I wanted to know what the structure of the commercials would be and where they would appear. I tell them not to put voice-overs promoting other programs over the closing credits because I always have music in there that means something. I will also go in, at the time of assembly, and watch everything being put together. It's laziness if you don't.

The people in the commercial department resent it to a certain extent, but if you phone them up to point out potential difficulties, it's in their interest as well. For example, in *Mama's Going to Buy You a Mockingbird*, Geoff Bowes played the husband who dies of cancer. He was also in a series of commercials about life insurance. So I told them to keep those commercials out of there.

By moving into series and longer form and continuing to remain in longer form, there is a real problem with the ability of writers, producers, directors, and so on to gain the volume of experience. You only start picking up things through experience. With series, you've got the same three, four, five, leading characters every week. You've got a narrowing group of writers, because it is a specialized form of writing. When you don't have good writing, the series fails. But you also limit the number of producers and directors. In the United States that's irrelevant, because they have such a huge talent pool and such a volume of production that they should be doing series. Yet even there, because of the expansion of cable and of networks, you are getting weaker material because you don't have people who have to fight as hard to get to do it.

The question raised by Gough is fundamental. Do writers, producers, and directors learn from doing series and "graduate" to drama specials? Anna Sandor and the team of Louis Del Grande and David Barlow did. Ivan Fecan, former director of entertainment programming and later vice-president of English networks, Nada Harcourt, former creative head of series drama, and other decision-makers I talked to, argue that episodic series and soaps are the place people learn to write, direct, and produce. In the 1950s and 1960s people learned on fifteen-minute shows and then on half-hour anthologies. In the 1980s the directors' training ground for three years was *Judge*. Producers have apprenticed on series like *King of Kensington, Seeing Things*, and *Street Legal*. The issue is not how you get to be a full-fledged creator of programs in one of these capacities, but whether the CBC allows (or can afford) the diversity of formats and "one-off" specials in the 1990s which would continue to provide the opportunities found in the 1970s and 1980s for the richly diverse talent now making television drama in Canada – or too often – in the United States.

For example, producer/director, executive producer Don Williams got regional drama on the air in Winnipeg throughout the 1960s and early 1970s and went on to be the executive producer for *The Beachcombers*. His television versions of the Royal Winnipeg Ballet's adaptation of *The Ecstasy of Rita Joe* and his own adaptation of Morris Panych's *Last Call* are extraordinary television. Both were innovative, surrealistic, and in the latter case self-reflexive. Even so, as he said in 1985: "I also get a kick out of recreating something that really happened to human beings. By that I mean something that had more to do with the human beings than the fact that they happened to be on the first ship that reached the West Coast. I prefer a story about a real person who is still alive. For example, in *Death of a Nobody* (1967 Wilderness Award), a young person was killed and the people who killed him got away with it."[10]

Up to the 1980s it was possible for an executive producer to get a program on fast and for a head of drama to find a slot in the schedule. This meant that television drama could respond quickly and accurately to a developing story. Sam Levene managed it with *Final Edition*.

MJM: Did you personally produce *Final Edition*?

LEVENE: Yes, *Final Edition* was one that I cared a lot about. It was also one that was very topical because two newspapers folded in August of that year. We got it out within six months. It was really fast. We commissioned a script from Tony Sheer in August or September and we got it on air on 22 March 1981.

MJM: Commissioning Tony Sheer meant that you commissioned somebody who has a lot of experience in writing television.

LEVENE: I wanted somebody with anger, and Tony always wrote with feeling. I called him and he jumped at it (and was available, luckily), so we did it fast.

Producers and directors do not always agree. *The Newcomers* [1978–9] was a series of seven television films commissioned by Imperial Oil about waves of immigrants from pre-Confederation times to 1978. Eric Till directed three of them, including *The Prologue*, which dealt with the Git'Ksan of British Columbia.

TILL [1983]: There is a dilemma in docudrama. Very often one is asked not to be as strong with the drama because it will overpower the documentary. But while you are directing it, you can't do that; you have to go for the blood and guts and the emotions. Yet frequently it will be edited with restraint. Therefore, to me it doesn't quite work. I am very fond of documentaries as such, because I think they have a way of telling a story and an emotion, which is different, but can be equally powerful.

I think that the policy in the 1980s and 1990s of doing only Canadian stories is not right, and that one should be doing some powerhouse international stories from a Canadian viewpoint. I also think that one loses out on the maturity of the writers and audience, if we are not doing our version of whoever or whatever. There is a brand new audience for international subjects now. It will work against us; we have got to be able to deal with these international stories. And the world having grown so small, you really cannot say "I won't do anything but Canadian stories about Canadians." These international stories will have our imprint on them. They will have "Made in Canada" on them, which is really what we want.

Till's critique of our narrowing range of subject matter is, even with the spreading impact of the collapse of the Cold War, a solitary one. No critic in a newspaper or periodical, no academic (other than myself), and no one within the corporation seems to have taken that point of view, as my interviews with John Kennedy[11] and Ivan Fecan[12] demonstrate.

Within the parameters of "Canada first," however, the CBC in the 1980s achieved a fairly wide range of tone and subject matter. Jeannine Locke made a major contribution to that spectrum. Until her retirement in 1991, Locke was a writer/producer of topical dramas like *You've Come a Long Way, Katie* and *The Greening of Ian Elliott*, historical dramas like *The Private Capitol* and *Chautauqua Girl*, and human interest stories like *Island Love Song* and *The Other Kingdom*. I talked to her in December 1989, as personnel and structural changes were hitting the old drama department.

MJM to LOCKE: You have a capacity that is relatively rare in Canadian television, although common in American television, to be the writer and the producer rather than just the generator of ideas. Somehow you find the time to do that while you're continuously producing programs that are already in the works. That must be difficult to do. How does it work?

LOCKE: I believe that it benefits a production to have a combination writer/producer on board from the beginning to the very end. I'm on set from morning to night during filming. Besides being handy when "wild" lines are needed to fill in the background sound, I happen to have the whole script in my head, so that if a scene isn't going in such a way that it allows for a payoff scene further down in the script, I'm there to complain and explain. For example, there is a scene midway through *The Private Capitol* where Amaryllis must demonstrate her delight at belonging to the inner circle of Ottawa society. Otherwise, her later refusal to leave Ottawa comes right out of left-field, so to speak. In that first scene, as originally filmed, the actor was much too cool – there was no sense of the society columnist loving her work. I explained to the director how and why it was going awry, and we reshot it. What worries me about television is that it seems to fall between the "end of the world" on the news and "taking valium time" in entertainment. Look at *Dallas*, with its free-floating characters: they've got no motivation, they're boring, they're hilarious; but live they never did. With those characters, there is at least escape, because in *Dallas* there is no reality. I mean, you rise from the dead in *Dallas*.

A two-hour drama takes a year to eighteen months from beginning to end of production. It's a tremendous satisfaction (and I repeat, an asset to the production) to have the kind of control that comes with the combined writer and producer roles. As for the stages that give me, personally, the greatest joy, there are two: that point in the writing where the characters are alive not only in my head but, I believe, on the paper; and the editing process, which is where you learn everything you must know to produce a drama. It's in editing that you confront your mistakes. I like to think that I don't make those mistakes the next time; I make new ones.

MJM: You really enjoy the editing?

LOCKE: I love it.

MJM: Day in, day out?

LOCKE: When I come to the point when the picture is cut, I always feel kind of sad. I always think "Ah, I've got to go back to the office."[13]

CHARTING THE EVOLUTION OF SERIES
OR MINI-SERIES

Projects originate in a variety of ways. Herb Roland, an experienced producer of drama series, outlines one way – going back to *Gift to Last* (1978 – a hybrid of series and serial conventions).

ROLAND [1989]: Gordon Pinsent was the writer of the original Christmas special *Gift to Last*. I just babbled on to John Hirsch, "Yes, well we can have this family and the young and the old, you know, going back in time, and the rest ..." and all of a sudden it started evolving. I remember driving down to see him. He was busy doing *Rowdy Man* in Charlottetown. But the minute he started putting things down on paper, they lived.

Many things changed in adapting a Christmas special into a series. The character of Sheila grew. She was never intended to be so important in the series originally.

MJM: Would the fact that Sheila's character expanded depend mostly on the on-screen chemistry between Dixie Seattle and Gordon Pinsent?

ROLAND: Yes. Do you remember that scene under the table in the Christmas show?

MJM: Yes I do. [Seattle and Pinsent have a comic flirtation while the party goes on above them.]

ROLAND: It created that kind of chemistry between them. Of course, we brought in the character Gerry Parks [who played the good, stay-at-home brother and foil to the restless protagonist Edgar]. In the Christmas special he was almost an extra [a minor character]. The character of Edgar was Gordie's idea. He saw him originally as a big guy, a Santa Claus figure. When we started casting, he was shooting *Who Has Seen the Wind* in Saskatchewan. But we didn't get anywhere with casting. I think we had Melvin Douglas lined up by then [the American star of the original special], but we still did not have an Edgar. I was talking to Pinsent on the phone one evening with no preconceived ideas or anything and he was going on about this character. I said, "I'm sorry Gordon, everybody struck out on this." Suddenly out of the blue (I'd not thought about this really) I said, "Gordon, if we have some special makeup or something for you, how would you like to play Edgar?" He paused: "I'd be honoured to."

MJM: Well!

ROLAND: That's how that happened.

MJM: So he had been seen all along as basically the writer and yet there is so much of his acting *persona* in the character of Edgar.

ROLAND: Once we started, who else could have played it?

MJM: You were not then thinking about a series, were you?

ROLAND: I did not think of it as a series because it was a Christmas show. I must say it was Hirsch ...

MJM: ... who said, "Why don't we do more with this?"

ROLAND: "Do three more" – and I said, "Wonderful, I've always wanted to do a series." But Alan Scarfe [who had played the father of Clement and Jane] was at Stratford. Again, we sat here and I said, "Gordie, let's kill him off in episode one, maybe we can get him for a couple of days," and that's exactly what happened. He died at the end of act one. What a theme, dealing with death, which was really what that show was about. It was one of those things that just fell into place. It was wonderful.

MJM: Isn't that Canadian? L.A. doesn't normally start something that might become a series with a show dealing with death.

ROLAND: We did five episodes, I think, the first year (1978). It was ludicrous, the money we had. I don't know if you remember episode five, which was the "big ball." The audience is hoping that Sheila and Edgar will get together, and he chickens out?

MJM: I remember that the writing on that episode was one of the finest in the whole series.[14]

ROLAND: Yes. I wanted to do it at St Lawrence Hall.

MJM: Logical. It was a regimental ball, wasn't it?

ROLAND: Yes. But for the size of it you would have needed at least fifty couples. Nowadays, of course, you would do it. Then, even though we did the dance off-camera, we still had about twenty people. We had to send to England to get the uniforms. But we were still lacking the money to do it fully.

MJM: Obviously, *Gift to Last* was crafted with a lot of love from a lot of people.

ROLAND: A lot of people. The design was based on that village we built up in Kleinburg. You know, one of my happiest moments in the whole thing was at lunch time when everybody was gone. I just sat in that street and lapped it up. Yet, Gavin Mitchell [the designer] built the village for very little money.

MJM: It must have been a designer's dream, because of the beautiful period costumes.

ROLAND: Jim Swan also contributed enormously. He started directing with the "Catholics" episode.

MJM: The one that began with the Orange Parade. It is the best episode as far as I'm concerned.

ROLAND: Yes, it was heartbreaking.[15] The whole thing was difficult for Dixie to do.

Then Gordon Pinsent said "No more," even though I had been fighting with John Kennedy to try and get more episodes. (A few months ago Gordon and I had lunch and he said, "By the way, I owe you an apology. I was wrong, we should have carried on.") During our discussion about how to end the series I said, "Gor-

don, I don't want big sentimental slush, but I want something.
Give us Pinsent at his best. A little speech, I don't want to call it
an aria, but just something to the future." He gave it to Gerry, not
himself. All he did say, I think, was a few lines, "Happy New Year
to all of us" or something very simple.

MJM: Well, the camera looks around at the various characters during that speech. Because the speech is given to Parks, there is a
certain amount of rotund cliché that fits his character. But there is
also the counterpoint of the camera doing a little reprise of various
relationships, noticing things. The final toast is "to the future,"
and thus the viewers are included in the family circle.

ROLAND: But I just wanted something from Gordon. My point is
that he never hogged.

MJM: No, he didn't. There were whole episodes where he was not
the focus at all.

In other instances, the circumstances surrounding the birth of a
mini-series or serial are not so favourable.

MJM to LEVENE: What is it like to work with the mini-series form
like *Vanderberg*? Would it have certain kinds of satisfaction,
because you would have a longer form to work with?

LEVENE: Yes. We were, unfortunately, not set up to do a series
properly, because we were asked to do a three-hour mini-series,
and that's a bit short. We had barely finished post-production
when we were asked to do three more parts. It was a little hard
connecting part 3 with part 4, because months had elapsed in
between, with no thought of doing more. We got most of the
same actors back, but we had to make some shifts. We also
improved it because there was a little time to rethink. Nevertheless, it wasn't conceived the way a mini-series ought to be.

Producers also experience a very special form of frustration in that
they can spend months, sometimes years, in contemporary television
developing projects that never make it to the screen. For example,
Levene worked long and hard on a *Wojeck* special, "*Wojeck* after 20
years," a project suspended for more than two years after shooting
had started and then completed by another producer. Herb Roland
outlines the evolution from a producer's point of view of *Riverpark*, a
project that was not produced.

ROLAND: I went to John Kennedy in August 1987 and I said, "I
want to do this serial." He said, "Yes, develop, go." We did some

research and he was all for it. Originally I wanted to get two half-hours a week, and they said, "No, we don't want two half-hours, make it an hour."

MJM: A serial based in Toronto?

ROLAND: Yes, an inner-city neighbourhood, but also somewhere very much in transition: yuppies moving in, the bums being moved out. So you have a real mixture. I wanted to do this multicamera on tape. I said, "You know, this is going to be a big logistics problem," and Kennedy said, "Screw the logistics, we'll forget about that."

MJM: Why would it have been a logistics problem?

ROLAND: Well, because I didn't see a small thing, I saw a lot of people, a big ensemble work, therefore a lot of sets. It would cost money and require a big studio and a big setup, because there would be so many different families, but obviously it wouldn't need that all at once. Amortized over many months it wouldn't be that expensive either, but initially it would be very big. I remember him saying, "Don't worry about that now, let's get going." The emphasis would be on a feeling of neighbourhood ...

MJM: With no specific protagonist?

ROLAND: No. Exactly. He okayed the research and I chose George Allen, the writer who'd worked with me on *To Serve and Protect* and a few episodes of *Judge* (because I felt we had a good rapport), to go around exploring areas for several days. We settled on Broadview and Queen. I was going on holiday. George was being paid to do research and he had written episodes. I came back and you know what happened? Everything was changed. I reported not to John but to Nada Harcourt [the new head of series in the reorganization instituted by Ivan Fecan]. She liked it very much, but that was two years ago. Nine months after that, I was told, "We don't want a serial, we want episodic." When we turned episodic, "You don't really want to do this on tape do you?" So the whole thing had also changed to film. George and I then put our heads together and made some adjustments. A year ago exactly, we presented the first really detailed outline, structured as episodic drama. We created a new character who was a lady of ethnic, Greek background who ran for city councillor. Without telling me, Harcourt had showed the outline to Fecan, and he adored it. I said to myself, "Well, that's it, we are simply doing it."

However, in August of 1989, they were asking, "Why don't you shoot it in Vancouver? Politically, it's right to keep Vancouver busy." [*Mom PI, Max Glick,* and *Northwood,* which appeared in the 1990–91 and 1991–92 seasons, were all made in Vancouver.]

MJM: So now you are doing film on location and not tape in a studio?
ROLAND: No, we were to have a sound stage setup, like 9-B or
  Street Legal, but with a lot of location shooting. So this version is
  what I call mark 3. Mark 1 was the serial, which my heart was in
  and it worked beautifully, so much better than House of Pride[16]
  [one of Roland's earliest projects]. There was much more meat to
  it and the characters were wonderful. We had retained most of
  those characters for mark 2. It was episodic [which requires con-
  ventionally a single protagonist or occasionally three or four leads,
  not an ensemble, and consists of one-hour units in which the plot
  complications are usually resolved]. For mark 2 we created the
  new character, the councillor and her family, so it was episodic
  with strong continuing elements.
MJM: That means you are now emphasizing a "star," and putting in
  the background all the subsidiary characters ...
ROLAND: This is what I fought desperately. I even came to a point
  in July where I said, "This means an enormous amount to me,
  but maybe we just better forget the whole thing," because I did
  not want a knight with shining armour as focus. Besides, a city
  councillor doesn't have too many dramatic stories in her job. She
  is only one voice.
MJM: Sewers are not very exciting.
ROLAND: No, and neither is getting a cross-walk or whatever. We
  came to a kind of understanding. I said, "Yes, we can make her
  the most featured player, but the others must be equally important, except they are not on as often." I had written five episodes in
  this format by July. Then we had a disagreement because we
  didn't know who the star would be. Within a couple of weeks,
  George Allen and I found ourselves in Vancouver talking to Phil
  Keatley, who was extremely helpful. He liked the script very much.
  We had good vibes. The only thing Phil said was, "You know I've
  never read anything that smacked so much of southern Ontario or
  Toronto." George spent three weeks in Vancouver in September
  and did an enormous amount of research, and learned a hell of a
  lot of things.

The story ends after our interview because, at that time, Roland was
still waiting to hear what would happen. Riverpark was killed in
January 1990 after two years in development. The reason given to
Roland was that there was no money for a one-hour pilot that year.
Shortly after, Herb Roland left the CBC.

In the collective work that is television drama, some personalities
and talents mesh together better than others. When those people

work well together, the odds of success improve significantly, although as with all performing arts there are no guarantees of success even within the most rigid of formula drama.

MJM to GOUGH: Has the way the corporation works, at least in the past, militated against good teams who develop rapport?
GOUGH: Two things have worked against the development of the team. The main thing has been scheduling backwards, getting what I would like to do after the current project analysed at the treatment stage, then getting it analysed at first draft: "Yes, No, Yes, No, Maybe, Maybe, Maybe," then years later doing it. I have lost assistant directors who would work with me under any circumstance because of that kind of scheduling. If you have a certain track record, the CBC should say, "What would you like to do next?" If I then screw up, fire me. The key to the power of producing is the ability to assemble and then reassemble things, so that you do get a pattern, working together, evolving. You don't need a series to get that. One of my reasons for leaving the corporation is that there isn't enough work there for me. It bores me. I can't sit around and wait between projects or develop them because I am too busy doing them for real. Yet, you can put teams together. If you look through the years you will find that I have certain teams that I've worked with: the same sound man, the same editor who plays a vital role.
ALMOND: For myself I must say that I love the CBC. I would have done anything for it, but often I'd just go work somewhere else. I was trying to get a feature film on for years. Once I managed to get my first motion picture made (*Isabel* for Paramount), I still came back to the CBC because I have always liked it. But on the last couple of shows the whole atmosphere was so different from anything I had ever known or dreamed of, I just never wanted to go back again.
MJM: You did a powerful film, and won a Genie in 1980 for a film called *Every Person Is Guilty*.
ALMOND: Well, it was just a film.
MJM: It was on *For the Record*, and it was a really good one!
ALMOND: But when I was on set, they said, "If you change one word it has to be phoned back to executive producer Ralph Thomas to get his approval." On the first day an actor said "Hello" instead of "Hi," and everything stopped. It was like working in a straightjacket. It was fun to do, but it wasn't like what I'm used to – I run my own films. I mean if there is a producer there, I feel

he is there to help me, not to say, "Well, you have to ..." I do what I like! But it was OK, and I was pleased to get that award.

The fact that of all the people quoted in this chapter, only director Eric Till and producers Sam Levene and David Barlow (a writer as well) still do work for the CBC (among other clients) is due, in part, to a natural flow of people moving on. But it is also due, in part, to a widely perceived change in the ethos of the Drama Department which is affecting the 1980s generation as well as those with longer experience. I will discuss this change more fully in chapter 10 on the CBC ethos and in the conclusion.

3 Writing

The fact of the matter is, the lot of the television writer in this country is a miserable one and unless there is a radical change in the nature of the medium and the nature of the craft as it is practised in Canada, you will find yourself producing unsatisfactory work and, incidentally, starving.
JOHN HIRSCH[1]

Lack of money is one of the reasons that the CBC has been chronically short of good writers. Not all the blame, however, rests on parsimony, misplaced priorities, and underfunding, three favourite ways of explaining a situation that stretches back to the golden age of CBC radio. Nevertheless, throughout its history, too many of the decision-makers at the CBC have refused to recognize the worth of good writing, which means they do not put enough of the scarce dollars available into scripts – the most fundamental element of any good television drama. In the first fifteen years, one may argue that this constraint was largely internal, not external.

Many television writers in the 1950s and 1960s could not make a living from what the CBC paid them, so they left for England or the United States. Stanley Mann became a fine screenwriter for both Hollywood film and for American television. Ted Allen wrote novels and screenplays, as did Arthur Hailey, whose novels now number in the millions of copies. Bernard Slade went first to Hollywood to write sitcoms and then became a successful Broadway playwright, and Stan Daniels wrote and produced three seasons of *Mary Tyler Moore*, *Phyllis*, and *Taxi*, as well as television movies and films.

Dennis Braithwaite reported in the *Globe and Mail* in the early 1960s on a CBC hunt for scripts.[2] The CBC received 16,000 scripts of all kinds, and bought 600. The going fee then was said to be $350 for a half-hour, $850 for an hour, and $1000 for a ninety-minute play. In 1970 Paddy Sampson, producer of the experimental *Program X*, complained to Blaik Kirby of the same newspaper that he couldn't find scripts, even though he paid $1000 for a half-hour script, one-fifth of his total weekly budget for the program.

As early as 1963 Robert Allen addressed the problem in an internal report (9 July). A special report on the Drama Department, commissioned in 1973, also highlighted scriptwriting as a major problem for the CBC.[3] Writing came up again at the CBC think-tank on drama at Fern in October 1983 and at a similar gathering at Deerhurst in 1987. From all this internal evidence, one pattern is clear. Whenever the developmental series disappear – the short-lived anthologies like *Q for Quest, Program X,* and *Peepshow,* or even a more formulaic series like *Judge* – CBC scriptwriting suffers. On the other hand, the half-hour anthologies in the 1980s, *Where We Are, Inside Stories,* and *Family Pictures,* helped to ensure some development opportunity for new-comers to learn how television drama works.

It is just as difficult to make a living writing TV drama today as it was in the 1950s and 1960s. Yet it does not matter whether television drama is live, taped, or filmed, it is fundamentally dependent on good scripts – a fact widely recognized in Britain, where the audience sometimes chooses to watch a program just because it is written by Dennis Potter, Alan Plater, Harold Pinter, Tom Stoppard, or Trevor Griffiths. Collections of television scripts and studies of playwrights have been published in Britain since the early 1960s. Together with reasonable access to scripts (until Thatcher's Philistine economic policies prevailed at the BBC library and archives), and with the advent of VCRs, British scholars had been able to produce several books on specific television dramas, on particular series or playwrights, and dozens of articles in both scholarly periodicals like *Screen* and more accessible periodicals like *The Listener.* In the United States, scholars are also finally paying serious attention to writers. As Richard Collins in his chapter "The Intellectuals, Television and the Two Solitudes"[4] discusses in considerable detail (and Paul Rutherford[5] and I note more briefly), producers, directors, and writers of drama in Canada, for the most part, work in a critical vacuum. If serious scholarship is rare, so is conscientious, informed, and balanced criticism in newspapers and periodicals. Neither the medium nor the disciplines of television criticism have been taken seriously by most of our newspaper editors or by the academic community. Yet, as writer Grahame Woods pointed out to me, the makers of television do read the critics, though they say they don't.

WOODS [1989]: It's a sadomasochistic line of work. In television generally you get into something where you set yourself up to get knocked down by critics or by the audience. It's fine when the critics are nice, but it can be devastating at times.

MJM: You know, you are one of the few people who's admitted to me that newspaper and magazine critics matter.

WOODS: Oh yes. I think if anyone says the critics don't matter they're lying through their teeth. It's important to a very small group of people what the critics say. For example, at 1255 Bay [then the CBC English Television head office] everybody reads the critics.

More to the point, there has been no consistent or original dialogue between specialists in popular culture, informal and interested general critics, or spectators in the performing arts, including those who make drama programs or programming decisions. Such mutual self-depreciation leads to silences, amnesia, and the undervaluing of what is accomplished.

Mavor Moore was the first head of CBC drama. Fortunately, he has written a memoir,[6] a book eagerly awaited by people interested in radio, television, theatre, musical comedy, theatre history, and the inner workings of the Canada Council, which Moore guided through some rough years. One of the battles he waged resulted in John Hirsch becoming artistic director of Stratford for the second time. Unfortunately, the book stops with the early 1970s. Moore on our cultural amnesia:

MOORE [1990]: Quite early on, for instance, I did a production for CBC television of Morley Callaghan's *To Tell the Truth* [*CBC Theatre*, 23 October 1952, adapted by Mavor Moore], which I had done on the stage. And we did some of the Robertson Davies stage plays at that time [for example, *Fortune My Foe*, 7 May 1953]. I was flabbergasted when, not so long ago, the CBC announced, "At long last Robertson Davies is going to reach the screen!" They were going to do a television adaptation of one of the novels. This was thirty-nine years after we did his plays.[7]

MJM: They did that in a more recent instance with Margaret Atwood. I gather she doesn't want to remember her *Purple Playhouse*, but she did write one. But that doesn't appear in any press release.

MOORE: She did, yes. We don't remember our history very well. The *Toronto Star* recently phoned me in Vancouver to say it was publishing a piece saying that the transfer of George Walker's *Love and Anger* from a small alternative playhouse to the St Lawrence Centre was the first instance of the transfer of a non-commercial show into a commercial theatre. The reporter said, "Somebody has written me a letter saying this isn't so, that you did it with *To Tell the Truth* in 1949." I said, "To tell the truth, we did." And he said, "Well, that wasn't really a commercial show, was it?" and I said, "Oh, yes, we made $47." There was a long pause and he said, "Oh, I guess I'm wrong," and I said, "I guess you are."

MJM: My first question to those who were there at the time was, "How did someone learn to write for television? Where did the scripts come from?" Were you stockpiling scripts in 1950 before the CBC went on the air in 1952?

MOORE: Not at the beginning. But we must have started that quite early on. Remember that two years is not a long time when you are starting from scratch to learn all the technical stuff necessary. The producers, the script assistants, the floor managers (as we called them then – now studio directors) all had to master the technology too. Meanwhile the technicians were trying to master other things than merely how to run a camera.

Story editor Alice Sinclair commented on the problems of doing plays on television that originate as a stage production:

SINCLAIR [1988]: One of the difficulties about remounting a stage production in the studio is that the actors find it hard to remember cuts. And to scale down, because their performance has been set in the theatre. For the writer, adapting a play is just as hard as writing an original play. The writer has to be true to the spirit of the book, and at the same time effectively structure it into a proper television drama. In some senses, adaptations are harder. On the other hand, you do have a finished body of work that you feel is worth doing. In that sense they're easier.

MJM: To some extent, viewers who watch Ibsen don't have to be concerned about the quality of the dialogue. We can settle down and look for other things. In those cases you can take a certain level of quality for granted.

SINCLAIR: That's right. We did a lot of Ibsen.

MJM: Ibsen and Chekhov were supposedly the natural choice for television, although what interests me is that there was a lot of expressionist absurdist drama being done as well.

SINCLAIR: We did people like Ionesco, didn't we?

MJM: And most of the absurdists, at length, in fascinating ways.

SINCLAIR: That sounds to me like treason.

In the late 1980s and 1990s, with shrinking budgets and battles for advertising dollars, proposals for adaptations from the world of theatre would have been seen, as Alice ironically termed it, as "treason."

EARLY WRITERS

As one might expect, many early television dramas were adapted from radio scripts already broadcast. I documented the transition briefly in "Canadian Television Drama 1952–1970: Canada's National Theatre of the Air."[8] Paul Rutherford also points out that "a viewer could only have enjoyed such plays as *Markheim* or even the simpler *Ikon of Elijah* [in the anthology *The Unforeseen*, 1958–60], to name but two cases, if he or she paid close attention to what was said – the teleplay wasn't really an assault on the importance of verbal language."[9]

SYDNEY NEWMAN, 1950s CBC supervising producer [1984]: My own experience with the writers who were prominent in the *Stage* series [the CBC's flagship radio drama anthology, which had huge audiences in the 1940s and early 1950s] was that they had enormous difficulty in relating the spoken word to the power of the image.[10] Their dialogue tended to be redundant to what was so visually clear because the audience could see the action and the face of the actor. Marvellous writers like Len Peterson, Allan King, Lister Sinclair, and people like that had problems writing for television. Lister was in a better position because he had done some theatre work, but generally the best writers were unable to make a smooth transition into television. Len was a personal friend of mine. He had written a lot of stuff for me when I was at the Film Board: commentary, narration, or general scripting. I worked very hard with Len and he did, in fact, write two fairly good plays for me, one very, very good one, but it was like pulling teeth. It was tragic.

MJM: *Ice on Fire?*

NEWMAN: That's right. Ted Kotcheff directed that play.

MJM: I think that was one of the very best from that period [1957].

NEWMAN: Most of the writers began in radio, but a lot of them couldn't make visual what worked superbly on the air. For instance, a great radio documentary/drama writer was Tommy Tweed. But something like *The Brass Pounder from Illinois* is photographed radio. It is not very good television. *With His Head Tucked underneath His Arm* is by Len Petersen. A most unusual and evocative little drama about Evariste Galloise, whom nobody has ever heard of, a mathematical French genius.[11] Yet rarely did Len's plays work on television – something to do, perhaps, with his social conscience, but very much to do with his sense of absurdist drama. His plays were tougher to adapt to the psycho-realistic medium [which television became]. Expressionistic plays were always a problem.

Would you like to know about Arthur Hailey? He had never written a drama in his life. He was English, but was in Canada during the war in the Air Commonwealth Training Scheme, teaching navigation. After the war he said he hated that class-ridden country, and returned to Canada. He got a job as a technical writer for a road magazine. He told me that his bureau drawers were filled with blue and pink rejection slips.

One day, flying to Montreal on a business trip (when the food was being served), he got an idea about what would happen if the food was poisoned. He looked up his old buddies and found out the latest techniques of landing planes. Then he rented a typewriter and literally vomited out the play in twenty-four hours. Like any good Canadian, he sent his play to NBC in New York. They rejected it. He then sent it to CBS in New York, and they rejected it. Then he sent it to the CBC script pool, because he didn't know who to send it to. They read it and said, "This guy has possibilities." So they passed it across to my story editor, Nathan Cohen. Nat reads it, he comes running into my office with this sheaf of papers, saying, "Sydney, at last I've found a writer!" I said "Wonderful!" because he was really exhilarated, "Let me read it." "Oh no," he replied, "you don't want this. Nothing can be done with this. It's too complicated, we can't do it." I tore it out of his hands, went home, and read it. It was the most gripping thing I had read in my life, up to that point. I came in on Monday and I said, "What do you mean we can't do it? Of course we'll do it." Cohen didn't know anything then about the technical side of production. But I had the good wit to give it to my most proficient director, David Greene. David did a magnificent job. It was a very complicated show for us to do at that stage of our technical development (1956), because it involved twenty-one film inserts into live action. All the film inserts showed the plane flying or the plane taxiing on the ground. Cueing from live to film was always a hazardous thing, but he did it perfectly.

The Americans heard about this play and I got a letter saying that CBS had bought it from Arthur Hailey. They wanted to do it and would I sell them my film inserts? I gave them to CBS, because I thought it was such a great honour for a Canadian writer to appear over the American network. We were not going to see the production in Canada, so Arthur erected a great big aerial to get the cleanest signal from Buffalo. He invited the whole gang of us, including Jimmy Doohan [Scotty from *Star Trek*, who played the protagonist], Corrinne Conley [the stewardess], David Greene and his wife Katherine Blake, my wife and me, and a few others. We were fed a great dinner, and then the hushed moment came and the play was on. We watched it and I had a vague feeling of dismay, that it wasn't really good. I kept my mouth shut, being diplomatic. David kept saying, "Ah, this is no good. Who directed this? This is no good." When it was over, Arthur was very upset about what David had said. He thought the show was terrific. Arthur pulled me aside and said, "Sydney, what do you really think? You'll tell me honestly." I said, "If you want to know the truth, I think they did it beautifully. It was professionally done, it was slick, it was neat. But it lacked a sort of freshness. Why did you let them change your script?" He said, "What do you mean, 'change my script.'" I said, "That line, remember when the stewardess is talking to the doctor and she says, 'The only hope for this plane is if one of the passengers who isn't sick can fly it,' and then the doctor says, 'Wait a minute, I was sitting next to a chap who said he flew a Spitfire in the war, but he was probably boasting.' Why did you let them cut the line, 'he was probably boasting'"? He said, "They didn't cut that line. That was never in the play. David put that line in."

That line was the key line: "Maybe he was boasting." It was what set the doubt that he couldn't land the plane. It says a lot about Arthur as he was at that time. He wouldn't miss out on a thing like that today.

MJM: Effectively, they remounted the script down there.

NEWMAN: They did their own show, but they used our twenty-one film inserts.

MJM: But our kine version was the one shown in Britain.

NEWMAN: That is right. We repeated it in Canada on *General Motors* and it got an even bigger audience the second time, as I recall. Then Arthur sold it to Hollywood, and they made a Hollywood movie out of it. He got himself an American agent. He did about five or six plays for me here in Canada and he was gone.

MJM: The same with Bernard Slade?

NEWMAN: Well, Bernie was both an actor and a writer. I don't remember him much as a writer, oddly enough. I remember him as an actor.

MJM: He was not a memorable writer at that time. I've seen the television plays and they are competent.

PAUL ALMOND, producer/director [1991]: In the early days Nathan

Cohen and George Salverson were story editors and their main job was to try to persuade producer/directors, who hated the scripts they kept forcing on us, to go and do them. They rewrote a lot. George rewrote a couple of scripts I'd written. They were both very useful because in those days we had a sense of what would be exciting television, but I don't think any of us had a real sense of how to construct a story. We were all struggling, and we knew how to be flashy and exciting, but I'm not sure I had a great story sense at that time.

MJM: Would it have been easier to deal with stage plays? You did quite a few of them.

ALMOND: I did a lot of them, but that was for *Festival* under Bob Allen – a whole different ballgame.

MJM: Some of that "story" work would be done for you. I mean you did some masters like Giraudoux, Anouilh, and Pinter.

ALMOND: Yes, and I did a lot of Christopher Fry – I loved Christopher Fry. I used to be a poet. Those stage plays were not really television, though; you always felt doing a stage play that it wasn't television. Though I must say my most enjoyable shows were modern plays on *Festival* – Fry's *Sleep of Prisoners* and so on.

MJM: What about writers?

ALMOND: Writers? Forget it. No writers, nobody paid any attention to writers; we never met a writer, nobody knew what a writer was. This is the early days 1953–55 [*On Camera*]. Sydney Newman found these sort of "deadbeat" scripts somewhere in America, second hand, gave them to us and said, "Try your luck, you got to make it work." We'd say, "I can't do this Sydney, it's full of shit!" and he'd say "Goddammit, we got to get something on the air. I don't care what you do! Make it work!" We would argue and fight, and we'd say to each other, "That Sydney, did you see the script he gave me last week?" "Yes, I refused to do it!" We'd talk to each other about it. Most of the scripts were terrible, though some were good. But there was no thought of developing a body of writers to work in those days, not the slightest thought. I'm telling you the truth.

Canadian writers were being used on *GM Presents* and *Folio*. Many more wrote for the half-hour network anthologies, and many wrote for the regions in Vancouver, Winnipeg, and Montreal. Douglas Bowie (*Chasing Rainbows*, 1988), who also wrote the very successful mini-series *Empire Inc.*, first wrote half-hour scripts for Montreal's *Teleplay* in the 1960s.[12]

ALMOND: Later, around 1960, it suddenly became, "Where are we going to get our scripts?" Somebody would say, "Writers! What an idea! Let's try to get ourselves some writers." Then we started to work with writers. I started working with Chuck Israel. Our first was "Ruth," which introduced Sharon Acker, who became a TV star. We got on very well, so we started to work on several things. But I must say if you, as a producer, got a writer and you two thought up an idea you wanted to do, it was like a heresy or underground activity. In the later years of the 1960s it was as if we were somehow betraying the management or something, "a director and a writer are getting together to make a film – what is this?"

Chapter 2 on producing, demonstrated the many ways an idea for a script could be generated. I wondered about the priorities in the United Kingdom, where the author has some status and a tradition of playwriting that goes back 700 years.

MJM to NEWMAN: Ideas were not thrown at Clive Exton, Harold Pinter, Alun Owen, or David Mercer. It appears they brought ideas to you.

NEWMAN: Yes and no. I always felt it was my responsibility, with my story editor, to go to the writer with the idea. What would sometimes happen is that they wouldn't like the idea, but in the subsequent discussion they would come up with something of their own. It was always a positive thing, an aggressive, marvellous thing. I felt that was really my job. How does that marvellous, beautiful public out there want to be raped tonight? People like Owen, who had developed his own style, or Pinter wrote for me. They knew the type of thing I wanted. The initiative really was ours – not that everything they wrote was what I had asked them to write.

MJM: You prompted them to think in a given direction?

NEWMAN: That's right, initially. Once the relationship was established, there was no necessity for that. I'll give you one instance. I was a great reader of *The New Scientist*, a very popular but genuine science magazine. I read about the Geophysical Year, in which they were going to put a satellite up. I said, "You know, there's going to be a man in one of those satellites one of these days." So I called on Donald Giltiman to write a story about a man in a satellite. We went on the Sunday night and, honest to God, on Tuesday morning we learned that the Russian Gagarin had circled the globe! Kate Blake was in that play and it was directed by Charles Jarrott, whom I had trained in Canada. There are other instances, dozens in fact, of my prompting a play.

Newman developed in Canada and later in Britain the functions of a television story editor. The story editor is just that – an editor, whose job is to serve the script and thus the writer's interests.

SINCLAIR: It is not unknown, of course, for actors, producers, and directors to alter a script on the floor, but in my opinion, they rarely alter it for the better.

MJM: In Canada they have this right though, contractually? This is understood by the writer, unless the result is so bad that he wants to take his name off the show or raise a fuss.

SINCLAIR: Minor adjustments, yes. If an actor finds a line extraordinarily difficult to say, if it doesn't roll out, then he will often say: "Could I say it this way?" And if that doesn't alter the meaning or the intention or anything else, the writer will not raise a fuss.

ANNA SANDOR, writer [1988]: I am forever grateful that I was an actor. Particularly in television, the actors have such a hard time of it. You want to make it easier for them. I know what it is like to read a script by someone who writes on paper and doesn't consider, for example, transitions. I have had more story meetings where the producer has said, "We will do this," and I will say, "You can't act that." And I have had more actors say to me that they love doing my stuff.

MJM: You write speakable dialogue.

SANDOR: Yes, I write speakable dialogue and I try to keep in mind how an actor gets from point A to point W, and that you can't skip B, C, and D.

MJM to SINCLAIR [1982]: What happens when the director or producer want to cut a scene?

SINCLAIR: We always have the right to cut for production or to alter.

MJM: Well, of course, a scene can be cut anyway in the edit. Will a writer rewrite if circumstances demand it?

SINCLAIR: If a writer has set a scene in the Toronto Stock Exchange and we know, as we do, that the Toronto Stock Exchange will not allow us in, then he has to set it somewhere else.

JEANNINE LOCKE, writer, producer [1989]: I never think about fulfilling anybody's expectations. When I sit down to write, after I have decided what the situation is, then I live with those characters until they are so lively that I find I'm interested in accompanying them for that period of time. It makes sense to me that the characters are everything. *The Greening of Ian Elliott* certainly isn't going to give universal satisfaction. [It had a double focus: a controversial projected dam and homosexuality in the United Church Ministry.] But (except when I put a disclaimer at the bottom) I don't think about how the government of Saskatchewan is going to react. You know, you just get involved in the doing.

MJM: You are also telling me why your dramas are not overburdened with didacticism, which is always the temptation when television deals with new territory in documentary or topical drama. You told me that the letters you got about *The Other Kingdom* included phrases like "I didn't know this ... you've saved my life ... I lost my fear ... I felt better." But if you had set out to say, "That's what I'm going to do," you probably would have turned out something that was very didactic, emphasizing the issues instead of the characters.

LOCKE: Certainly one thing one doesn't want to do is produce a training film.

First I had approval to put *The Greening of Ian Elliott* into development. I had the treatment go-ahead, so I guess it was 12 April 1989 that I started actually writing the first draft. I write quite quickly, only because it's been boiling around in my head for so long. In May, although I hadn't got a response to the first draft, I went out on a research survey. Then I went back at it on my own and did a second draft. Then I got comments from Ivan Fecan and comments from Jim Burt [in charge of movies and miniseries], some of which I disagreed with violently. Then I wrote a third draft that was ready in July.

The Private Capitol took longer than that. It was a bugger because there were the constraints of "this is history, this is an adaptation of an element of a book." At the CBC it's not impractical – as it might be outside – to both write and produce. As a CBC producer I have certain advantages. The obvious one is that I don't have to spend time and energy getting the funding for a project. But equally important is the existence of an in-house, talented, and experienced support staff right at the CBC. So I can concentrate on script development. Script development comes in three stages: proposal and treatment (a detailed outline scene by scene), first-draft script, and final draft script. At any of these stages a project can be killed. During these stages, I'm preoccupied with writing (having done most of the research preliminary to a proposal).

It's when the second-draft script is approved that I start functioning as a producer; meeting with casting, design, and wardrobe and organizing a survey of locations. (The writing, from proposal to approved draft, usually takes about three months.) I invariably write a third draft, concurrent with my producer duties, because there may be changes to the script to accommodate shooting locations and also because I benefit from hearing dialogue by the actors who come in to audition for parts. I should add that I usually have in mind certain actors when I start to write; it's helpful to have their voices with me when I'm writing lines.

CENSORSHIP

MJM to SYDNEY NEWMAN: You did run into censorship in the United Kingdom as well as in Canada, didn't you?

NEWMAN: *Three on a Gas Ring* for *Armchair Theatre*. It's about three girls who live on a boat on the Thames and they are easy, relaxed people, sort of an artsy-craftsy crowd. The third girl is seduced by a sculptor (Alan Bates). She becomes pregnant and she is going to bring the baby up herself, helped by the other two women. It was regarded as immoral, as "destroying the family."

MJM: It did get out?

NEWMAN: No, it never did! I was pretty censorious myself, in a funny way. For example, I was always personally opposed to any blasphemy in my shows. No characters in *Armchair Theatre* ever used the word "damn," or said, "Jesus Christ." The writers used to say, "We don't want to be blasphemous either, but we need an expletive," and I would say, "Make up your own." Excretive words like "shit" weren't used. I was ahead of my time, but I didn't want to be so far ahead that I would lose or offend audiences.

ALMOND: There was another script that Rudi and I did with executive producer Ed Moser called *The Broken Sky*, which was about Rudi's war experiences. We had to fight so hard to get it on. They really hated it. I think I have that somewhere in the National Archives. It was a lovely TV drama and it gave the first chance for three very important performers in Canada: Donnelly Rhodes, Heath Lamberts, and Diane Leblanc. The ending of *The Broken Sky* (if you can imagine this little TV studio) was set on a bridge outside a German village at the end of the war, when hundreds of villagers were rushing across to greet the Allies. Diane was crying out trying to get to Heath, and Heath was being pushed back by the villagers shouting and crying out, and in the general mayhem they separate, never presumably to meet again. Looking back on it, it was madness to attempt, but somehow, I think, we brought it off. I loved working with Rudi. He had been in the German army, being Viennese – had I been born earlier, we would have been trying to kill each other instead of making great TV shows together. High points in my life, I must say.

DAVID GARDNER, actor/producer [1983]: About the commissioning of plays and so on, it is probably better to speak to the story editors. For instance, with *The Paper People*, Doris Gauntlett and I liked Timothy Findley very much, as an actor first. He was just beginning as a writer, but he would bring in material that was haunting and unusual, so we encouraged him. *The Paper People* came out of that. But there was a mixture of commissioning things and assignments.

MJM: A whole pool of playwrights from the 1960s write and write and then disappear.

GARDNER: You are absolutely right. The 1952–64 writing stable was developed because we were turning out a lot of television drama.

MJM: Four or five times the amount produced for the late 1970s to mid 1980s.

GARDNER: Four or five times the amount! Everybody who had written was encouraged to bring the plays in and get them adapted for television.

MJM: Have you any theories about the fact that most of the pool of writers seemed to have evaporated by the mid 1970s.

GARDNER: I would say it is simply the coming of age. Television is a tough medium to write for. Many of the plays of that period were also very indulgent and heavy handed.

MJM: Also, the first wave of writers trained in radio [Mac Shoub, Charles Israel, Lister Sinclair, Tommy Tweed, and Len Peterson] were all from the same generation.

GARDNER: They were all about thirty. But by the time you hit the 1960s, they would be fifty. And as you know, television eats up material, this medium. It requires very good, precise, delicate material. Joe Schull was one who made the transition.

Anyway, maybe the radio dramatists did hit the male menopause at that period, but a new batch of writers started to come in. Also, by this time, in Ken Gass's famous phrase, "all of the apples that had fallen off the tree had been scooped up and used." In other words, we had to cultivate the orchard and write new stuff. But a new generation replaced the old in the mid 1960s in all the media. New writers were happening in the theatre as well: Michel Tremblay,[13] David French.[14] As a producer, I read many plays by French, a young Newfoundland actor, who would bring in little half-hour TV dramas in the beginning. We were all encouraging him as a television writer. [And French could learn the craft by seeing his early efforts on Montreal's *Shoestring Theatre*.]

WRITERS WANTED

After his term as head of drama, John Hirsch wrote an article in 1978 for the *Globe and Mail's* column Mermaid Inn entitled "Dear writer, TV drama needs your energy. But beware monsters." In many ways, it is still relevant to the 1990s.

HIRSCH: "Take the last point first, money. You are provided with an absurdly limited market, less than eighty hours a year to write for. That is all the CBC drama department can afford to produce. That's approximately three days worth out of 365, roughly seven hours per province per year. Compared with the BBC's 500 hours and the literally thousands of hours from the U.S. networks, our programming opportunities amount to a very small spit in a very large ocean. This is a brutal reality: it is highly improbable that you will earn a living wage in Canada as a television drama writer, even if you're highly gifted. And if you are good and the American wolf comes knocking on your door to offer more goodies – what will you do? Our fees are certainly not competitive.

"Canada lacks an indigenous tradition of popular entertainment.[15] And in the past few years of growing nationalistic striving, the mood of our writers' search for a Canadian voice is, like all radicalizations, thoroughly earnest and somber. That might make good polemics – but at times pretty boring entertainment. We can't forge our identity solely through well-meaning but vastly dull 'problem plays.' Nor is anyone interested in watching a frustrated novel trying to make it as a teleplay. No one watches television out of patriotic duty. You have to learn how to grab wandering attention and hold it for an hour or so. We have to bear in mind what the public wants. We are too uptight about what we feel it needs."[16]

Six years later, actor/writer Hugh Webster made it clear to me that little had changed.

MJM: Were American scriptwriters as underpaid as Canadian?
WEBSTER [1984]: No. You could write two scripts in the States, and you'd be sitting pretty for the year.
MJM: The average price for a script remains very low. Is that the reason why TV drama is in such straits?
WEBSTER: Sure. If you started breaking the amount of time you have to spend on a script down to an hourly wage, aaah – you're down to about twenty-five cents. It's shocking, it really is. What it

does, of course, is it militates against being able to write full time. There's only a few that can really do that. Now writers are taking their example from the crud that's being churned out from the States. This is the stuff that sells, obviously.

ELIZABETH WEBSTER [1984]: Special effects make more money than anything else because they can make a big bang when they can't say it.

In the United States, script ideas are generated by heads of entertainment, producers (who are sometimes writers), and writers with a track record. New writers can break in through the soaps – or very occasionally by interesting an agent in their scripts. The pool of available scripts is enormous. There is also the very American, extrovert way of assuming that an event which grips the nation's attention – the long suspense over the rescue of a little girl from a well or the Anita Hill/Judge Thomas confrontation – should become a television movie. Indeed, in an interview, one of the panel testifying for Judge Thomas was asked why Hill would put herself through the public ordeal of testifying, to which she replied, "First the book, then the movie." No one in Canada would automatically assume that the horrors of the Montreal massacre or the backroom deals during the fall of Meech Lake would be fodder for docudrama. Despite our successes with topical collective theatre in the 1970s and 1980s, as a culture we do not habitually frame our crises as if reality existed to serve television or movies.[7]

PRODUCERS AND WRITERS

Bill Gough and Anna Sandor, both very successful writers, agree that although the art is collective, the focus has to be on the writer's script as realized by the production team.

GOUGH [1988]: You are working in a partnership in every aspect. But it comes back to centralized control in one area which has to be grouped around producer and project. Every element of it is important. There is absolutely nothing that is unimportant, at any place or at any time, which is connected with a film. Nothing.

MJM: I have heard that an idea for a program can come from just about anybody who is plugged into the system. It can come from a writer, a producer, an executive producer. It can come from what used to be the head of CBC drama, or just about anywhere.

GOUGH: There is a substantial difference, however, in the proposals that don't come from the writer or a writer-connected person. The suggestion will be so general in form that it is practically meaning-less other than saying "you get to Vancouver by heading west." You don't get your road mapped out in the way that a writer's proposal does. So many people who are in the creative fields are under the illusion that they have actually proposed story ideas, and they haven't.

SANDOR: Actually, there are very few story ideas that haven't been proposed.

GOUGH: "We're going to do a series on business." That is not a proposal. That is not an idea.

MJM: However, that may represent a policy decision.

GOUGH: That represents a decision in a broad area. That's "we'll go west to get to Vancouver." *The Winnings of Frankie Walls* is Rob Forsyth's because of his creation of Frankie Walls. The production evolved in response to the material, but Rob Forsyth, the writer, is at the centre of it. No matter what the reaction or the interaction with the writer, that's where it comes from. And that's where I'd love to see control moving.

MJM: Is that more true of anthology than it is of series program-ming – where the writer is given a set of characters, location, and the format?

GOUGH: You can tell our episodes of *Seeing Things* from everybody else's *Seeing Things*.

Martin Kinch, a producer in the Drama Department for a few years in the 1980s, left to become artistic director of Toronto Free Theatre in its formative years, artistic director at Theatre Calgary, and a play-wright. I have known him since the 1960s as a thoughtful and arti-culate observer, capable of an outsider's view as he works.

KINCH [1984]: Another problem in television is that most drama on the CBC is initiated by producers. However, they aren't the ones who are going to write these shows. There's a real danger in that system. The writing, the analysis, and the level of thought tend to be less committed, less rooted, and less strong because the actual impetus hasn't come from the person or persons who are going to write the scripts.

Levison and Link, who created the American hit series *Columbo* and *Murder She Wrote*, point out that in the United States, "the writer-producer calls the shots – subject to much backseat driving from an ever expanding bureaucracy of network executives who march under a banner that reads: 'It's our money.'" Steve Bochco, co-creator and executive producer of *Hill Street Blues*, is more succinct: "Television is a writer's medium, which is why writers become producers."[18]

In contrast to American practice, Jeannine Locke's combination of writing and producing her own script is the exception, not the rule.

LOCKE: When did I start thinking about *The Greening of Ian Elliot*? I know exactly when it was. It was in May 1987, I was listening to CBC radio's "Sunday Morning," and they were talking about the Rafferty–Alameda Dam project in Saskatchewan. I thought, "Isn't that interesting?" So I started collecting a file, because I was still in post-production with *The Private Capitol*. Then I thought, I need a character who is an outsider, someone to come in and be involved, like society reporter Amaryllis in *The Private Capitol*, who is also an outsider.

MJM: The Chautauqua Girl was also an outsider in a small community she didn't understand. These characters act as bridges to the audience, who are also outsiders.

LOCKE: So I thought, "Who is going to lead them?" Concurrently I was reading about the great dustup in the United Church over the ordination of homosexuals. Then I went out west, just about a year ago. A rancher took me the length of the valley. CBC Regina gave me their whole file on the dam, which was very useful. I had real problems, because I knew it was highly unlikely that they were going to win the court battle, that they were going to save the valley. But at the same time they had come together and fought this fight. Then of course the decision in federal court stated that the government must undertake environmental impact studies. So I thought, "That's their triumph, whatever happens," having got together and having accomplished this. Then I was trying to figure out how to explain the valley and how to get it in my own head.

I wrote my Master's thesis on Thomas Hardy. Hardy talks about how the rivers change, the villages change, the people change, but the land remains [Locke's dialogue quotes Hardy in *The Private Capitol* and refers to Hardy in *The Greening of Ian Elliot*].

MJM: It's also a very Canadian/Brit thing to do, to trust the audience and quote Thomas Hardy. I'm sure you didn't sit around explaining the reference for five minutes. You just assumed, if the viewer understood it, fine, and if she didn't, the allusion wouldn't be utterly crucial to what else was going on.

Conservative premier Grant Devine delayed the environmental assessment through his court battles, so the dam was virtually completed before that court decision. The valley was about to be flooded by the time the program actually aired. The United Church had also, by then, affirmed at its General Council the right of homosexuals to be ordained in places willing to do so. Unfortunately, the CBC delayed broadcast until June 1990. By then, the fact that most of the congregation accepts Ian Elliott's sexual preference and that the coalition against the dam which he leads wins a moral victory had lost much of its savour. The dispute over the timing of its air date (June is also a month when fewer people watch television) was one of the factors in Locke's resignation from the CBC.

STRUCTURING THE SCRIPT

Anna Sandor's scripts, like Jeannine Locke's, have their own unique flavour.

SANDOR: I always try to put humour into my scripts. I think that people without humour are boring. So I try to write characters, unless they are really hateful, who have humour. It enhances the situation to inject humour either through the situation or through the character.

MJM: Even in something as formidable as *Charlie Grant's War*, which could have been unrelieved tragedy?

SANDOR: Yes. My favourite example of that is *Running Man* [*For the Record* (1980), about a homosexual married teacher who eventually declares his orientation]. That is now totally dated because of AIDS, but there is a very tense scene when the protagonist's wife confronts him. She says something like, "Were you thinking of Cowboy Bob when you were making love to me?" I love being with an audience when they are looking at that. There is this sort of gasp, this enormous laugh of relief because how could you put something funny in this scene and get it right?

The longer the piece is the more I like it. Yet in a way I hate it more because it never seems to end. I just wrote an adaptation of *The Stone Angel*. The first draft was almost longer than the book, although the film is supposed to take about an hour and a half. But it was really fun. Unfortunately, with the CBC these days, they have nine breaks in TV movies. Now that's really unnatural. That almost makes it harder than a sitcom, because in a sitcom you've got basically one break in the middle.

MJM: In sitcoms you have the teaser, commercial, Act I, commercial, Act II, commercial, and then possibly ...

SANDOR: The tag. It's a much more natural structure. Nine acts gives a drama a really artificial kind of structure.

A film is obviously not a novel. To tell a story filmically is different from telling a story on paper. When you are looking at the
treatment, at the outline stage, you have to *see* what is going to be
there. Then to go one step beyond that, when you are looking at a
script, you have to *see* what is there. I've got a lot of experience in
story editing. Some scripts read wonderfully, but you know they
are going to be garbage. With other scripts there is almost nothing
there; yet if you know how to read a script, you know that there is
a lot there. Then you need that sense of knowing how to get from
A to B. There is a very pedestrian way of getting from one point to
the other, or there is an interesting way. How do you keep the
audience intrigued, and how do you make sure that they come
back after the commercials?

Bill Gough addresses the one problem common to writing, directing, producing, and acting.

GOUGH: You have to be able to hold the entire structure in your
head simultaneously, otherwise you cannot see the ramifications
of moving a scene further up or further down in the middle. You
can't see what a changed line would mean.
SANDOR: So often someone will say to you, "We're going to take
out this character." And you'll say that if they take out the character, what that does is "x." But they will just stare at you.
MJM: As writers, have you ever had something changed, not in
direction, or casting, or design, or whatever, but simply in the
editing stage, to the point that you thought the film had been
fundamentally restructured?
GOUGH: *Dying Hard* was totally restructured in the editing and was
working so poorly that I told Ralph Thomas, executive producer of
For the Record, I wanted to see it. He agreed, and then I essentially
took over the editing for a while and managed to approximate its
original structure. I wrote a number of songs with Joe Byrne for it
that were added afterwards to patch up rocky sections within it.
There are good sections within the film.
MJM: But writers who don't have your skills, your background, and
(more to the point) your presence around the place might write a
script that had been shot as they wrote it, yet in the editing it
could be fundamentally changed.
SANDOR: *Population of One.* In those days I had power but I didn't
know it, so I just kind of stayed away because I assumed that was
what I had to do. The whole front section of the movie leads up to
this romantic confrontation between R.H. Thomson and Dixie

Seatle. She is a twenty-five-year-old virgin, he is a handsome young professor, they have a few dates, and this and that. It's all very chaste, and then finally they go to bed. It's her first time and he can't perform. It turns out he is chronically impotent. He somehow thought it would be different with her because he had such a good, close relationship with her. Anyway, it's a very sad, dramatic situation. (There was a whole section that wasn't accepted because they thought it was a little too raw, but I wasn't shocked because I knew that wasn't going to be used.) They go to bed. He tries and he tries and he can't, and there is a kind of dissolve. Then we cut to the morning and there is this very tense breakfast scene where, as women tend to do, she takes it upon herself. She says that maybe she did something, and he tells her that he thought it would be different with her. Then he gets angry and leaves.

What this came down to in the film was this: she is waiting for him, he comes out of the bathroom and gets into the bed, goes hump, hump, hump, and turns over. Then you see them in the morning. She looks kind of confused. He goes to the fridge, takes out a bowl of yogurt, throws it at the wall, and leaves. I have had more people say to me that they didn't know what happened there. It's not even a question that it wasn't the way I saw it. Apparently, what was shot of them in bed was so bad it couldn't be edited properly. I suppose the actors and the director had the misguided feeling that by throwing the yogurt, it would tell us everything we needed to know.

GOUGH: Sometimes a thousand words are worth a picture.

WRITER AND STORY EDITOR

The relationship of the writer and the story editor varies both formally and informally, depending on the mesh of the personalities involved.

MJM: When there were these great numbers of live productions going out, presumably there was much less time to work with writers than there is now, or does it work that way?

SINCLAIR [1982]: There must have been less time, but I don't actually remember that, oddly.

NEWMAN: In England, I had the role of story editor codified. I was paying the story editor to protect the writer against my other staff. That is what gave a writer dignity and made him really say, "I'm going to stand or fall by what I'm saying." That is why I got the best writers in the country and developed them.

The story editor rarely had the time to go to rehearsals. If the director made any line changes, the production assistant at the end of the day would have to take the master copy of the script and note the changes on the face of the script. The first thing the story editor did when he arrived in the morning was to read the changes. If he thought the changes offended the writer or changed the writer's intention, or if he had a doubt about the change, he would get in touch with the director and say, "Why did you make the change?" The director would often give him a good reason. Then the story editor would call the writer and say, "Please, we would like to make this change and here is the reason why." If the writer said no, the story editor would try to convince him. If he couldn't, the line went back in as the writer wrote it. Every story editor I had at ABC Television and then at the BBC followed those rules.

SANDOR: I think the story editor serves an extremely important function. Jim Osborne is a wonderful story editor as well as being a writer. Jim was story editor, or "story consultant" as he is called, on *Charlie Grant's War*, *A Marriage Bed*, and *Mama's Going to Buy You a Mockingbird*. He's been story editor on a number of Bill's things that I didn't write. He is terrific.

First of all, I think a story editor has to be able to write. I don't think it is enough for a person to have analytical powers. Its very important, but I think the ideal story editor is someone like Jim, who is a writer and who has good analytical powers. They don't try to make the script theirs. There also has to be a real rapport between the writer and the story editor, because so many writers think the story editor is going to destroy their work. However, I wouldn't let a story editor do some things. For example, I've worked with one who wanted to throw out some of the most important stuff that was in the film, just to tamper with it. The danger occurs when story editors feel that they are actually writing. It is not the same as writing. There is nothing like writing except writing. You can produce the film, direct it, edit it, whatever you want, but if you haven't done the writing you haven't done the film. Everything flows out from that.

The ideal story editor/writing relationship is where the story editor works with the writer all the way through, from first reaction to the outline on. But it wouldn't occur to Jim to rewrite a word of my stuff. Nor would he be in a situation in Bill's production where he would. We talk about it and I write it. I've had instances, we all have, where story editors rewrite material, and its just silly.

SINCLAIR [1988]: A story editor who suggests just that it needs to be solved is not a proper story editor. But the story editor who comes up with an absolutely brilliant solution that nobody else has ever thought of probably should be a writer.

I was struck by the parallel between what Sandor thought a writer needed to experience and Eric Till's description of the whole range in the arts which the director needs to experience (see epigraph, chapter 1).

SANDOR: It's so alarming that today so many young writers have a background of having seen only film and television. All their movies and all their ideas are about films and television. (Some of the New Wave stuff about film-making, I like.) Storytelling can transcend experience, but it has got a better chance if you have the experience behind it as well. What is occurring right now in the sort of "NBC North" that the CBC is becoming is narrowing down the accessibility of the corporation for more people. That's despite a healthy, growing trend towards independent production. You are still going to end up with fewer people doing programming, and I think there is something wrong with that.

MJM to SINCLAIR: How about the constraint of the commercials interrupting the flow? You don't think that distorts the drama too badly, on the whole?

SINCLAIR: No, because I think it is good to have many climaxes as you go along. Also, there is the thoroughly convenient fact that, if you want to, say, change seasons, you can do it between acts.

When you get the first draft, you count the number of pages in each act just to see if they're fairly equal. Now they don't have to be equal to the minute, but you can't have a fourteen-minute act followed by a two-minute act.

MJM: Some people say that the audience attention span is getting shorter. The five-minute scene is unusual now in series drama. In American as well as Canadian television drama in the 1960s, the five-minute or even ten-minute scene was perfectly acceptable. You can see that with *Wojeck*, even with all that rapid cutting.

SINCLAIR: It would be interesting to see what we would do with a play like Ibsen's *Ghosts* if we were to remount it. Would we have cutaways and things? I don't know.

MJM: I find that some of the current television drama is very "busy."

SINCLAIR: Well, I think that goes with the territory, because as you work on something and become thoroughly familiar with it, you tend to think, "God, is this going to hold?" You've been over it so many times, its so "old hat" to you. You wonder if its going to grip the viewer when it really isn't gripping you anymore, and I think there's a tendency to beef it up. One of the things that a writer has to find a way to do is to end the show, not just stop. That's how you can sometimes get trapped into very neat endings, at least at first. The other thing that writers quite often do is come with an absolutely splendid set of characters and splendid situation and a marvellous solution, but with no ideas about the middle. In the three-act structure, the second act is notoriously the hardest one – developing the situation in an interesting way. But it often just meanders and doesn't lead you anywhere.

There are two things that enrage me. When, in an early scene, you have a baby or a dog for background and colour. Then the people go their merry way and the dog or the baby never come in again. Look at Olivier's film of *Hamlet*. They never seem to have an arras hanging on the wall unless Polonius is going to hide behind it.

LEARNING THE CRAFT

SANDOR: I have had this label placed on me, in Canada, that I am a "CBC writer." I have had people call me in the past and say, "We were going to ask you to do such and such, but we know you are a CBC writer." First of all, there is no such thing, unless you are working in the documentary section. But obviously, as I think most people who work in television in this country know, there are not many places to work. Therefore, I have done the main body of my work for the CBC, but I have also worked for a great many other people.

MJM: You started in electronic drama, in sitcom. Do you find that writing for a one-off film special is different because tape and film are produced differently?

SANDOR: I read Constance Beresford Howe's *Population of One* on my holiday from *King of Kensington*. I showed it to someone at the CBC because I thought it would make a really good TV movie. The next thing I knew the CBC had bought it. Then they said, "Here it is, do you know how to write film?" I said "Sure!" So I went to the CBC library and took out a couple of scripts. One was a *For the Record*. I looked at them just to see the format. Again, ignorance is bliss, because I love movies. I grew up on movies. Since I have that kind of visual imagination, I think in those terms. So I thought all I'd need was to know the format, and I copied that.

Actually, my first draft of *Population of One* was too funny because I was so used to writing sitcoms. I didn't have jokes in it per se (it wasn't quite that silly), but I did have to be pulled back from that.

Producer David Barlow's experience includes working on *King of Kensington* as well as co-producing *Seeing Things* with Louis Del Grande.

MJM: I've been told that there's a dearth of comic writers in this country.

BARLOW [1988]: I don't think there is. I hope there isn't or we're going to be in serious trouble. Finding good writers, comedy or serious or whatever, is hard, because it's a developmental thing.

MJM: Robert Allen emphasized the need to develop writers in 1963.

BARLOW: Exactly. You can't train writers in isolation. You have to have programs and, at the same time that you're producing product, you have to commit to development. Now all of us, once we get into production, become very selfish and are only interested in getting it done because it's such an onerous task. When we're in production, we don't want to develop. We just want tremendously talented people to come through the door, write the script, collect the cheque, go home, and we'll shoot the script. But that doesn't always happen. You have to commit to development, you have to find people, and if they're good they'll get better if we keep giving them material. Most writers do improve with time.

MJM: Is it easier for writers once the actors are cast?

BARLOW: When they can see the pilot. It'll walk, it'll talk, and so we can say "Yes, we want to do more of that, less of this," or "We want that character to go this way, or that." The fact that you have a pilot before you go to series makes it a lot easier to write. If writers want to pitch stories to a series, they usually come in and take a look at the pilot. If the series is running, they look at a couple of the episodes that the producers think are the best examples of what they want to do, and then the writer talks to the producer.

It's hard to find good writers because we haven't given good writers enough chance to work. It's a craft. [Few people in Canada will use the term "art" if the context is popular culture.] You learn it only by doing it and doing it and doing it. We've been exporting writers for years. There's no reason to think that somehow they stop growing, that somehow pollution killed them off. It didn't – they're there. They just have to be developed. I was at a comedy seminar yesterday. There were 125 people in the room, and I would venture to suggest that at least half of them wanted to be comedy writers.

MJM: Series can change after awhile. When some other producer takes over, they can start edging it in a different direction, which is one of the prerequisites for longevity in a successful series.

BARLOW: It's organic, that's right. It should grow. It should develop.

MJM: And the writers will both reflect and sometimes originate those incremental changes.

BARLOW: Yes.

IVAN FECAN, director of entertainment [1989] (eventually vice-president of English television and now thinking about programming as a vice-president for Baton, the biggest shareholder at CTV): Every month we publish our list of potential projects and 90 per cent of it will die. It's supposed to die. Only 10 per cent of it will make it as a pilot, and maybe a few per cent of that will make it to series. We need writer/producers in this country. We have made it so difficult that all our producers have turned into businessmen/producers. In the 1970s the story was that you brought a lawyer and an accountant together, and you got a Canadian movie. I am not saying that it is like that in television, but everyone is far too concerned with the business of television, and not enough people are paying attention to the screen, to the writers, to the only reason that this medium exists – the creative side. That is why I have a lot of respect for Sonny Grosso [*Night Heat* and *Top Cops*]. He does the final polish. He can rewrite a line while they are shooting. He can supervise the cast. He is a really creative writer/producer. That is wonderful.

MJM to BARLOW: Part of the policy of Canadianization is going to be "more" Canadian drama, isn't it?

BARLOW: That's right.

MJM: The eight or ten episode season will not exist.

BARLOW: It'll be twenty, or perhaps they will start with thirteen. There will be opportunity because producers will be scrambling to get anybody who's got promise on board so that they can continue to feed this mill.

MJM: When I analysed the first two years of *Beachcombers*,[19] it became clear to me that three or four early writers who had not been writing series television before contributed elements that subsequently became distinctive to the series. Keatley's input as producer was a major factor, but the writers he worked with developed a collective feel for the series. They each had their own different interests and emphasis, but together they created the shape of the series in its most successful years.

BARLOW: The writers will write to the form, but the best of them will bring qualities that will help to develop that series.

SANDOR: In the United States there is a sausage factory, but there is a sausage factory here too. The people I have talked to in the States, network executives and so on, have known "story" because they have had a lot of experience at it ...

BILL GOUGH: They're better at it.

SANDOR: ... the particular executive you are dealing with has thirty movies of the week on his desk. I went into these meetings thinking, "Oh ya, here we go." I was astonished by the incredible amount of respect for the writer and by the fact that these people knew exactly where the weak points of the story were. It was never "this is what you do now." It was, "Well, how about going in this direction?" Even if they specifically could not put their finger on what to do to make it better, they always knew what was wrong. I was just amazed. There wasn't one thing that got by them. It was all story, story, story. They'd point out that this was weak and that was weak and say, "Let's work together to make it better." Very few people here know story ...

GOUGH: ... know film story at all ...

SANDOR: ... or know film.

American series writer Stephen Kandel: "The craft which, given talent, is learnable – consists of applying workable and adequate solutions to dramatic problems, usually with the use of melodrama. Quick and easy. It becomes second nature, an automatic response ... To write serious drama [for series] means to deny the audience what most of the audience wants, which is relaxation, relatively painless entertainment."[20]

Reflecting on the comments of Gough and Sandor, I realized that what they defined as a good focus in television drama is what I would identify as a specifically American weakness. In my view, the primary difference between most American movies of the week and the best Canadian drama specials is exactly the American emphasis on *story*. In those dramas the viewer is buried in plot, excitement, peril, suspense, melodrama, incident piled on incident, too often at the expense of the character development, subtext, and nuance, which have characterized more of our television drama, including Sandor's own full-length scripts.

TEAMS DO WORK

WOODS: Historically, when you go back over the CBC's television series, the successful ones have been those that have either origi-

nated with a writer or the writer has been in from the very beginning working one-to-one with the producer: *Quenten Durgens*
[Weyman/George Robertson]; *Wojeck*, which was a Weyman/Philip
Hersch; *Seeing Things* [Barlow/Del Grande], *Gift to Last* [Roland/
Pinsent], *Empire Inc.* [Marc Blandford/Douglas Bowie]. For some
reason, they don't learn at the CBC that you've got to have this
kind of team work.

Another very successful team that worked together for a decade was
the creative partnership of writer Paul St Pierre and producer Philip
Keatley in the anthology *Cariboo Country*. The longer drama specials
The Education of Phyllistine, How to Break a Quarter Horse, and *Sister
Balonika* were also the result.

KEATLEY [1985]: There's a story in *Cariboo County* called "The
   Strong People." We went ahead and did it. It was one of the episodes that made us decide to get out of the half-hour.
MJM: You felt it had been squeezed?
KEATLEY: Yes. There are such major mythic themes in that story
   that we didn't want to leave it like that. It's the story of the founder,
   the successor, the usurper, and civilization corrupting the perfect
   society. These four major mythic themes are all in there. I think we
   could do it in feature-length in a way that would be quite nice.[21]
MJM: The most striking thing about *Cariboo Country* is that it
   assumes that the audience is capable of intelligently sorting things
   out for itself. The fact that the subtextual nuances are not available
   to everybody all the time makes it rich and worth watching more
   than once.
KEATLEY: Also, it's gawky. It's meant to look as though maybe it
   wasn't made by professionals.
MJM: And it's open-ended. I just watched "The Hunt on the Happy
   Anne." The technician who ran the film said, "What happened?" I
   said, "It's open-ended. You figure out what happened." She was
   conditioned by the standard TV convention of narrative closure to
   want a wrapup.
KEATLEY: I think that's very unfortunate. In the original writing of
   The Education of Phyllistine, there was a narration. [This is before
   Ryga's influential play *The Ecstasy of Rita Joe.*] The last shot of the
   film is a little girl, very straight backed, walking away down the
   dirt road. Paul had written a lovely narration which went as it did
   up to the point that you see it in the film, but then continued –
   about the fact that at the age of sixteen she was picked up on a
   drunk and disorderly charge and was put in the local hoosegow.

Three months later she was picked up a second time and sent down to the women's prison. At that time, there were no holding prisons outside, so kids picked up on drunk charges the second time around were all shipped down here to Vancouver. When they were turned out at the gate, they got a couple of dollars and were on their own. They'd come out the back door and go down to Gastown. That's it – the end of it. The narration said, "She did six months, came out and became a prostitute on skid row, and a year later she died in her own vomit." We looked at it and knew it was too much. Maybe that's what happens to the Phyllistine we see in that story and maybe it isn't.

"Gawkiness" – the refusal to be explicit, an insistence on visual and verbal metaphor – still enriches television on occasion. The hybrid of series/anthology that was *Cariboo Country* developed the collaboration between writer and producer.

KEATLEY: I was interested in actors and performance and scripts that were character pieces. I loved the studio work. I was dead wrong about *Cariboo Country* at the beginning. The first script was "The Window at Namko" [in *Spectrum*, a regional drama anthology, 5 June 1958]. I read it and was very disdainful of it because it didn't seem to me to have any dramatic construction. The script actually had things like "Somebody says and somebody else says ..." But producer/director Frank Goodship liked it very much and we did it. The audience response was immediate. They recognized what was in it right away.

We commissioned another called "Justice on the Jawbone," which I directed.[22] "Jawbone" is a local word in the Cariboo that means credit. You put it on a cheque or put it "on the jawbone." I didn't understand the plot at all. (I don't think anyone understood the plot.) During the dress rehearsal I was sitting in the control room and I suddenly said, "Of course, that's what happened! That's what he did!" There was great joy on the floor as I told the cast that I finally figured out the plot.

At the beginning of doing *Cariboo Country* as an anthology with continuing characters, I got together about six scripts in very rough form. They were scrawls on two sheets of paper. There was money to buy first-draft scripts, but there was no commitment yet whether we would do this because the rule still existed that the CBC wasn't meant to be in fiction film. By then, St Pierre and I knew each other well enough that we knew which were good ones. I had started to tell my bosses that sometime in the future we should put this together. I was going to get another thirteen of these shows, but they were going to have to go to film.

Keatley and St Pierre did projects together for many years, most of them on film. Actor/writer Hugh Webster told me about writer/producer partnerships from the writer's point of view.

WEBSTER: Coming up with an adaptation for Eric Till's *Kim* [1963], I really was serving his central idea. Eric gave me the book *The Heroic Heart*. I read it and I was very moved. I was also struck with the central idea, which is of a young man finding a spiritual peace while his body is being broken. As he says in his diaries, at the very point when the clubs are landing, he has managed to move his mind onto another plane where he doesn't feel the pain. So we wanted to counterpoint the brutal reality of what his body was going through and, at the same time, try to get the fact that – for lack of a better word – his soul was moving on a completely different level. For instance, when the machine-gun that executes Kim started, the sound was a bouncing ball coming down the stairs (that was my daughter dropping that ball down the stairs), bang, bang, bang ... It was an attempt to heighten the impact by doing the very opposite.

I was really struggling with the piece, knowing we wanted to do something very special with this little half-hour. One night in New York we sat around and talked about it. I told Eric, "I've only been able to write one shot, but I think it's the one that will enable me to get going on the whole thing, and it's the last shot." (That was the way I always wanted to work in those days, to get that very last shot.) That was the sand pouring out of the sand bags and covering Kim's face as he sank down to the bottom of the post after he was executed. I told Eric what the shot was and he said, "That's great. That's great."

MJM: These powerful visual metaphors are characteristic of Till. Here, it's a result of the interplay between you as writer and Till as director.

WEBSTER: Oh yes. Have a look and see the stuff that's on the screen now. Run cars in a car chase across the screen for two-and-a-half minutes and that's two and a half minutes you don't have to write. Two-and-a-half minutes is a lot of writing.

At the CBC the transition to full-scale series in 1966 was eased by the interconnections of the *Cariboo Country* anthology and Ron Weyman's work on *The Serial*.

WEYMAN producer, discussing the impact of *The Serial* format on writers [1987]: People who had been hanging around for years, scratching their heads saying "What am I going to do?" suddenly, in that new context, had brilliant ideas. In that third year of *The Serial* we developed *Wojeck*, which was purely on film. I was also in the business of getting home-town writers to write films which in fact would be feature pictures. They could then break through the artificial relationship (as I saw it, at that time anyway) between television and the screen.

WOODS: When the first season of *Wojeck* was coming to an end, I was passing Ron Weyman's office one day and he said, "How would you like to try your hand at a script?" I thought he had some other project he was talking about, and I said "Which program?" "*Wojeck*." It was the kind of moment that, as a cameraman, I didn't expect, because I was all caught up in what I was doing. So I came up with an idea in twenty-four hours based on the knowledge that I had gained as a cameraman doing a documentary film on homosexuality with Ron Kelley. I thought of a story about a man who had a homosexual past and was blackmailed ["Who's Art Morrison?"].

One of the problems with *Wojeck* was that there always had to be a body. So many of these series are hung up on something that you have to have.

MJM: At least the plot could turn on a disease or other forms of death rather than repetitively on murder. But you're right, there had to be a corpse.

WOODS: The experience was very exciting, because I shot it as well. When veteran crews get their scripts for the next production, they read it and they often say "It's garbage, what a pile of shit this is." I didn't particularly want to sit there while they said that, so the crew had no idea who wrote the script. We were shooting a scene between Wojeck and crown attorney Arnie Bateman in Ron Weyman's living room. I'm at the camera, lining up a shot and Ron said, "Well, let me see if I can get the writer on the phone." So he goes into the kitchen, has a cup of coffee, comes back out, and says, "That's fine, no problems, the writer agrees with me." It was only at the "wrap" party that it was announced that I wrote the script. I was very pleased with it, of course. I saw it when it was in reruns. You know, one of the wonderful things about *Wojeck* was that it was so far ahead of its time in subject material.

MJM: I'm still wrestling with that myself. I wonder why it is that sometimes fiction threatens an audience far more acutely than reality unclothed. Perhaps this is why *Wojeck* had such an impact on viewers – plus the fact that Weyman was allowed to exercise his own judgment about subject matter.

WOODS: The three people concerned with every script of *Wojeck* were the writer, the director, and the producer. So you had this team work, you had this control and understanding of not only what this script was about but also what you were going to be doing down the road.

MJM: What is it like to write within the limitations of a given set of characters and character relationships? Is that frustrating?

WOODS: I guess in hindsight I was very happy to have that frame-work, because it took a lot of the load off me. Later on while writing for other series it was difficult. I pretty well created *The Collaborators* so I was able to have some control. I don't think it was the best thing in the world, and there were some bad casting choices. It was supposed to be Paul Harding's series, as the foren-sic scientist. But Michael Kane, the policeman, being the superb actor he is, stole it right from under Harding. A lot of actors don't realize that you've got to work every moment you're on the screen, and Michael worked. He's always been considered trouble at the CBC, but it is part of his act. When it gets down to it, he delivers. He has a wonderful, bawdy sense of humour.

As another example of television's narrative conventions creating structural problems, Paul could never get into the sequence of the show until he had a body. As a writer, I got stuck in this damn autopsy room. In the States, of course, the medical examiner comes out to the scene of the crime and investigates. Here they don't, they wait for the body to be brought to them, they do their thing, and home to mother.

In part, I was responsible a little bit, unconsciously, for Paul becoming very dissatisfied, because the medical examiner was his part. I came up with a script that I think, finally, was the opening of the season for the series and I created a character whom I fell in love with (it's a danger), who was the cop.

MJM: You wrote one of my favourite scripts, though, for the second season of *The Collaborators*.

WOODS: Which was that?

MJM: It was the one about the young woman who had suppressed the memory of a murder.

WOODS: That was based on a true story.

MJM: That was a very good piece of work, because there were mul-tiple ambivalences.

WOODS: And within the series format that kind of thing is difficult. That was one of the nice things about CBC's *For the Record*. It gave you an opportunity to get into the head of the character.

MJM to producer HERB ROLAND [1989]: You developed a lot of good writers on *Judge*. Some of them were new to the craft at the time, weren't they?

ROLAND: Yes. That is our biggest problem.

MJM: Finding writers?

ROLAND: Yes.

MJM: There have been, in the past, series that developed some writers, your own *Judge*, for example, or *Beachcombers*. How is it that we continue to scramble for writers? Mind you, I understand that a half-hour is not the same as writing a two-hour movie.

ROLAND: Well, you had to be one hell of a craftsman to do *Judge*. To get a beginning, a middle, and an end in twenty-three minutes is not easy.

Any series that survives longer than a season or two evolves. Producers and broadcast executives plan that evolution and prepare "bibles," detailed accounts of what has happened and what general direction the show will take for the next season. Writers are given copies of the bible and are asked to produce outlines or drafts that put flesh on these bones. Yet the process is not rigidly controlled. If a character (introduced to supply a minor plot line) is a hit with the audience, the character will reappear and the whole shape of the series may change. Nevertheless, every series starts its next season with a bible, a set of continuing characters, a format, and an executive producer's sensibility as reference points for the scripts.

WRITERS AND MANAGEMENT INITIATIVES

MJM to IVAN FECAN then director of entertainment [1989]: In what ways would you say *Street Legal* "improved"? I realize that's a loaded question.

FECAN: It virtually wins its Friday night time period against every show, Canadian or American, which is pretty amazing. I moved it to Friday at eight and we added a lot more of the "relationship" kind of material to it. We structured the stories differently. There is more of a format to it, and we tried to introduce more conflict to it.

MJM: Interpersonal conflict?

FECAN: Interpersonal and subject conflict and fights about issues among the partners of the law firm. One of the problems I had with it in its first two seasons was that it was hard to distinguish one character from another. Everybody was very nice and there was little conflict. Without conflict I don't really understand how you can have drama. I personally believe the show also looks better. We introduced a few new people and made other changes.

MJM: You experimented?

FECAN: Yes. It wins its time period every week pretty well as of January 1989. The actors are being recognized in the street, and I get a strong sense that it is a living, breathing thing now.

MJM: The street recognition is a good indicator that it has become part of people's lives?

FECAN: It's usually the best indicator.

At that time (1988–89), Fecan was also trying to find and develop a set of reliably funny, audience-building sitcoms.

FECAN: In a sitcom, character is more important than incident.

MJM: So we are not going to see a comedy that is primarily physical slapstick?

FECAN: The decade for that passed a while ago.

MJM: Sitcoms are notoriously difficult to originate in Canada. Nevertheless, I'm amused that the critics have very short memories about what we have already accomplished in the form [*King of Kensington, Hangin' In, Airwaves*].

FECAN: Sitcom is a form we have allowed the Americans to do, and for ten years since *King of Kensington* we have given up on. *Hangin' In* was a sitcom, but not one of our better ones. I think it was okay, but it was very soft. I don't think sitcom is an American form at all. We have as much right to it as the Americans and the British. Moreover, many of our Canadian writers are responsible for the sitcoms in American television because they couldn't get a job here. We have not provided the opportunity to work.

MJM: Sketch comedies like *Codco* and *Kids in the Hall* are not going to pay the bills for the comedy writers.

FECAN: Yes they are, because the number one source of writers for situation comedies comes out of sketch ... what I'm saying is that out of *Kids in the Hall* and *Codco* you will get a generation of television/film stars. You'll also get a generation of writers who choose to work in another form. As you look at American and British comedies you'll find that most of the writers and performers come from standup or sketch. You have to have development, and we didn't have it before. In every country that has development, you might do a hundred pilots and ninety-nine will fail. There is no shame in that.

Nada Harcourt, then head of development for dramatic series at the CBC, talked to me in 1991:

HARCOURT: A developmental series can be a regional series like *Family Pictures*, and this year it is *Inside Stories*. Through various workshops across the country by people brought in to lecture (Paul Hagus of *Thirtysomething* and executive story editors who work in the business), participants have gone on to work in series that are not only on the CBC but on other networks as well. *ENG*'s Wayne Grigsby and Barbara Samuels are graduates of "Collaborative Vision";[23] Rick Shiomi, who did a half-hour for *Family Pictures*, is now a writer on *ENG*. There's an enormous amount of cross-fertilization that goes on. So the CBC has attempted, even with its limited resources, to feed that development. We were the ones who developed *ENG*, and then at the last minute we couldn't afford to do it and it went to CTV. We benefit by their work on other series, and they benefit much more frequently from us. I'm in a very favoured position because I know what they're all doing and I can say, "This writer is just finishing, grab him before somebody else does." That's a luxury I have that perhaps an executive producer might not have, or a director. I can say, "They're doing three in Vancouver and they're coming to do one in Toronto – let's grab him for this in Toronto while he's here." I have all the production schedules, and we're very competitive for good people.

MJM: From what you say, "Collaborative Vision" was a set of workshops done across the country for people who applied successfully to be able to take them. These are fundamental, first-level training exercises.

HARCOURT: Yes, first-draft series story, advanced series story, master classes – we've had a master class in movies with only five participants. Our intention is also to try to do something for executive story editors on the conceptualization of series. A great many of them have fallen into series that already exist. I feel that the next stage is the most critical stage of all – creating, conceptualizing parameters, operating principles, all of that.

The beauty of being a head is that you have writers on a series whose sensibilities you've explored, and you are able to proffer suggestions about who might be good to explore. What becomes crucial is to try to get the best people. There is a lot of competition for them.

COLLABORATION

Many writers prefer to write the more prestigious full-length drama specials. But each television form requires specialized skills.

SANDOR: I find writing full-length films much easier than writing sitcoms. To do sitcom well is the hardest thing in the world. Back in the old days of *King of Kensington* it was three jokes per page, double spaced. (People always say that you put the laughs in after, but you don't. It's a state of mind.)

As *King of Kensington* went on, that went by the wayside, but when it started that was the rule of thumb. You have to have situation, character development, jokes, and everything within a twenty-four-minute script [now twenty-two].

MJM: Plus your resolution.

SANDOR: Exactly. So for me it was a great pleasure to be able to write something with a longer format where you had a little more time, where you didn't have to worry about laughs.

JOE PARTINGTON, producer [1989]: This is the way we used to do *King of Kensington* (when I say "we" I mean producer Jack Humphrey and Anna Sandor for a long time, and then Carol Commisso). If we had regular writers we would have them in and we would talk about what happened the previous year; about possible ways to go, areas of weakness, and so on, and try collectively to come up with ideas. Often, people who are excellent writers are not good in a group environment at all. Writers in general tend to be highly competitive. They tend to think that their work is the only work that is any good, and they don't like their work being rewritten. I think that has something to do with people who have a need to express themselves. But Anna was very good and Carol Commisso, too, so there was more of a group environment. Jack Humphrey would have the last word, as the executive producer. If he had to recast leads or whatever, he would probably talk with whoever was head of drama, otherwise he was on his own. Today, it is a little different in that it's tighter.

JOHN HIRSCH, head of drama (1974–78), wrote at the beginning of his tenure: "Our writers have trod solitary paths and done fine work. But television is a collaborative medium. Until you allow yourself to open up to the process of collaboration, until you stop feeling threatened when your scripts are worked with, until you can stop looking at collaboration as an impurity in the medium instead of its very essence, you will not develop your skills quickly or efficiently enough."[24]

MJM to PARTINGTON [1989]: Sitcom requires many episodes every year. It may have a run of four, five, or six years if it's good, or if everyone is happy with it. Is the temptation to become more topical? To pick stuff up from the headlines from the current working situation, from whatever is a trend?
PARTINGTON: Yes.

I asked him whether topical references made problems for reruns and sales abroad. "Stripping" is the term used when the whole run of the series is sold to individual stations or networks. Episodes are then shown daily, usually but not always in their original broadcast order. Some episodes may be dropped or edited in rerun.[25] To sell any series for reruns, a minimum of sixty episodes is required. Therefore, the series must have had a successful run of several seasons to create that amount of "product." It is a fact of life in North America that few series make money for their originating companies until they are sold for reruns.

MJM: How does the topicality work for resale? For stripping?
PARTINGTON: I don't know. Some people are concerned about costumes, because the fashions will be dated next year, or they want to make sure that we don't have Canadian references. It's not to avoid Canadian references on principle, but just so, wherever it's shown, people can feel comfortable with it. So period and place are masked in trying to protect the foreign sales right off the bat, because we are talking hundreds of thousands, if not millions of dollars for the creators over ten years. Yet I think every show, whether it is successful or not, has to have its own identity.
SINCLAIR [1982]: What makes things interesting is people, characters. Everybody is interested in other people.
MJM: When a producer initiates script ideas, who brings it to life?
SINCLAIR: I would think it's about fifty-fifty, whether the idea for the script is generated by the writer or a producer. In For the Record, for example, they have an active story editor who generates a number of ideas, and they hire research people to go and see if this is a general subject. Then a producer who has already been interested in the form of it, the story editor, and probably the executive producer will sit around and say: "Who do you think would like to write this? Who do you think would be good for this?" They come up with a writer and offer it to him or her. Sometimes they have been wrong. The writer has not been interested, although the hungrier they get, the more likely they are going to be interested. Occasionally they have asked the wrong writer.

Another way is for a writer to come in with an idea. He has sat at home and thought: "I wonder what producer would like this?" and he's tried to raise the producer's interest.

We get a great deal of unsolicited stuff because we are a public corporation. Anybody who has a piece of paper and can type a grocery list thinks he or she can write.

MJM: Do you read it?

SINCLAIR: Yes, we have to.

MJM: Do you ever turn up somebody?

SINCLAIR: Yes. What we almost never turn up is a script, or only very occasionally, because unless you work on the fifth floor it's difficult to know what we want from day to day.

MJM: Perhaps you could tell me why it was in the early 1970s there was this notion that novelists should write television scripts for the anthology *The Play's the Thing*. [Atwood, Richler, and Robertson Davies among others.]

SINCLAIR: I remember struggling with Margaret Atwood. What happened was that Fletcher Markle, who was at the time the head of drama, got a bee in his bonnet that he would get all his novelists to do television scripts. He had that awful insulting thing by Mordecai Richler.[26] So Markle contacted the novelists and paid them vast sums of money to try and write a television program, but I don't think they were terribly interested. I think it's unfair to ask somebody to leap from one medium to another. It's totally different.

MJM: The story editor must have been very important for those scripts.

SINCLAIR: That was George Jonas, who's a good writer himself.

MJM: There's a lot of adaptation of non-dramatic material now, but not plays for the theatre or radio material.

SINCLAIR: Very little.

MJM: There never were many television scripts adapted for the stage but there are even less now than there used to be. Once in a while in the 1950s and 1960s a television play would become a stage play. W.O. Mitchell's *The Devil's Instrument*, *The Black Bonspiel of Wullie Macrimmon*, and *Back to Beulah*, Gordon Pinsent's *A Gift to Last*, and a few others. [Mavor Moore quite consciously wrote scripts intended to be performed in all three media – radio, television, and film.]

SINCLAIR: Sometimes writers become so entranced with an idea that they don't feel they have mined it fully, so they go back to it again in some slightly different form. We have one writer who started out with a television play [Bill Gough's *Maud's House*] who has a publisher who is interested in publishing it as a novel [and did]. It's a subject that has been on his mind for a long time.

MJM: Television writing is a craft, and I know it's possible to churn out scripts of good quality for a series. But surely it can also be an art, particularly a script that focuses on something the writer really wanted to write about.

SINCLAIR: Yes, but you can intrigue a writer with a subject if you don't give him a plot. I'll give you an example. I wanted very much to do a show about somebody who was about to retire, and was looking forward to it enormously, had all sorts of plans and did retire, and it all went to pot. The character just didn't like it, and what do you do then? Well, put in no more specific terms than that, I was able to interest a writer.

MJM: Would you ask a writer to work on an idea unless you thought that a producer would want it, that the head of drama might accept it and find a place on the schedule for it?

SINCLAIR: Even a producer will go out and get a writer without checking with John Kennedy [then head of TV drama]. And Kennedy is pretty catholic in his tastes and pretty generous in giving people free reign.

MJM: How many of the scripts that reach the second- or third-draft stage reach production?

SINCLAIR: Scripts are written in three stages: outline, first-draft, final script. That is an unfortunate provision of the ACTRA agreement, because that's not how it works. We frequently have to go to revisions. Three stages are not enough. But that's the way it's supposed to be. *Hanging In*, which is doing twenty episodes, had five scripts that were started but not finished.

MJM: It seems like a reasonable proportion.

SINCLAIR: Out of about eight productions so far of *Seeing Things*, one or two may have to be rescued. Moreover, scripts have a shelf-life.

MJM: You mean aside from their topicality?

SINCLAIR: You may be working hard on a show that you know has to be produced in the summer because it all takes place on the beach, but if you don't have a production date, you put it aside, and you go on to other things; you and the writer lose your enthusiasm for it. And it's hard to revive.

MARIO PRIZEK producer/director [1983]: I have drawers full of still-born ideas.

MJM: I suppose the time comes and goes. There are so many factors, are there not?

PRIZEK: Your availability, the availability of the talent, availability of

the equipment and studios, of your like or dislike of the assignment, what other assignment you are working on simultaneously,
whether they can be meshed ...

SINCLAIR [1982]: We demand of our television that everything be
structured. Documentaries are structured. The news is structured.

MJM: Structured to tell stories?

SINCLAIR: Yes, that's right. So in that sense, everything has been
dramatized.[27]

MJM: Indeed. I think that's so. And oddly enough, I think there's a
spill in the other direction. There's a trend, certainly at the present, towards the factual or the historical rather than the domestic
and the intimate, or the provocative or the lyrical. We're very into
documentaries as drama specials as a general mode in the 1980s
[although *The Great Escape* and *Flappers* also found a home in the
CBC in that period].

SINCLAIR: We're also very much into escape.

Backstretch, about harness racing on a "B" track, was one of the
1980s series that should have been a blend of "escape," with its
unusual location and the excitement and suspense of racing, and
"realism," with its range of marginal characters and their down-to-
earth problems. Alice Sinclair talked very frankly about the problems
with the series. It did get off to a promising start, and did have some
interesting episodes, but it became melodramatic too quickly without
being exciting.

SINCLAIR: Part of the reason we lost our way was that none of the
writers (and none of the rest of us really) knew much about harness racing. The best scripts we had were from one of the guys
down at the track who was an aspiring writer. He came up with
story lines that we would never have thought of. We did have a
consultant from the track, but he wasn't very helpful because we
had a lot of letters from harness-racing people pointing out errors
of plot and errors of fact.

MJM: Those mistakes will really jar some viewers, while others who
also know better won't care at all.

SINCLAIR: So much of television is so formulaic that it often seems
as if the people who make television are not connected to the lives
people lead. I can't tell you how many scripts come in that are
based on old movies. I don't mean they're plagiarized, but they are
based on what people have seen on television or in the movies.
They are not based on the lives people lead. I think we let

Backstretch down in that respect and I'm sorry, because it was an awfully good idea.

THE WRITER'S VISION

WOODS: Characters become a part of your life and you inject a lot of your personality into them. When writing *Glory Enough for All*, I empathized very much with Banting. I knew what he was going through and I was able to transfer my feelings into that character. I think I was dead on in terms of his personality.

MJM: First you do a lot of research and then you develop your own personal empathy?

WOODS: Yes. Michael Bliss placed little snippits in his books on Banting to give you an indication of the kind of man he was. From that you have to expand it. As a writer, you're always in different roles. You have to be a little bit of an actor, because you've got to hear the way the dialogue is being spoken and you've got to make sure that the next character who speaks doesn't have the same speech pattern. I had a big discussion, not argument, with Michael Bliss. He had read the first draft and he didn't like my dialogue because he comes from an academic world. He didn't like the way that I had Banting (a) be a little bit ungrammatical and (b) drop his g's. But Banting is a man from Alliston [a small Ontario town] in the 1920s and he speaks like a man from rural Canada.

After Bliss had seen the first screening, he phoned me up and he said, "You are absolutely dead right." He was on cloud nine. That was one of the most gratifying calls. When you are adapting or using somebody else's material that they put all their hard-earned energy into it, you want to do it justice.

MJM: It must be jarring even after all your years of experience to create that ideal world, then to get the words on the page, and finally to see it put on the screen.

WOODS: Most of the time it's disappointing, particularly with me. I write very visually, so in my head I see it. I see the location, I see the shots, and more often than not it doesn't come out that way. I write in a very visual sense. I even suggest the length of lens sometimes.

Two of the best television scripts ever seen on the CBC were broadcast when CBC television drama in general was going through a very bad patch. Grahame Woods's *Twelve and a Half Cents* [1970], and his sequel *Vicky* [1973], both directed by René Bonnière, reminded viewers of what the CBC could still do in a basically dry period. Wife and child abuse were unfamiliar subjects in the 1960s and 1970s.

WOODS: David Peddie said, "Would you be interested in doing a show on child abuse? We've had a couple of goes at it and it hasn't worked." I said I'd be delighted to do it. At the time, I was still a cameraman, so I wound up writing these things on aircraft and in coffee shops. I couldn't possibly do it that way now, but in those days it was the only way.

MJM: What are the chances, then or now, of your saying, "I want to write about this; here is my script," and getting it on?

WOODS: It's very risky, but I have been to the CBC and said I have this idea that I'd very much like to do, I think it is important and should be done, and I've been given the go-ahead. That was *Anne's Story* (1981) [which focused on an incestuous assault on Anne as a child as it affected her adult life]. It was not something I like to talk about, because it ended up, as far as I was concerned, as a disaster. I don't go on location very often because there is nothing worse for actors, or for the director, than knowing that the writers are hanging around.

One of the critical scenes in the whole play in terms of the message was something I had talked about to a lot of psychiatrists and people at rape crisis centres. Anne's family come back for the grandmother's funeral. They're closing up the house and everybody's saying goodbye to each other. The guy who had raped Anne, who is now married with kids, comes up and goes to say hello. She freaks out and has the confrontation scene. The producer cut it. His argument was that the actor who played Anne couldn't handle it and it didn't work. He shot it and then didn't include it in the film without even consulting me, going directly against all these reports from the story editor that the rushes of the scene were electric. My God, it should have been, because it was a very powerful scene and it was essential to the script. I complained, and it got me nowhere.

The song at the end of the movie [Anne is a country and western singer] also gives it a real Hollywood ending that goes totally against the whole point of the film.

MJM: Yes, I remember that struck me as a weakness.

WOODS: I had no idea until it was mixed, finished, printed.

MJM: At the BBC the writer, through custom, has more control over that kind of major surgery.

WOODS: Well, contractually in the ACTRA agreement they also post a consultant to provide or offer changes. Ethically they should, but in most cases they don't.

MJM: It's a matter of trust. At the BBC, all hell breaks loose if you don't consult.

WOODS: While that show was being mixed and cut, I was doing another show on *For the Record*. I didn't notice at the time, but as fast as I was writing the script the director was in there rewriting it. Because it was getting close to shooting time, I was doing it right there at 790 Bay. And four or five doors down they were rewriting it.

MJM: What do you do in a situation like that?

WOODS: Again I raised the roof, and I had my name taken off it. But you get this reputation. It's a very incestuous group down there. If you're a trouble-maker they want to know about you. I think this is one of the reasons why writers are traditionally quite paranoid.

It probably started with John Hirsch's reign, the idea that everybody can write except the writer. They have more series now written by a committee. It's getting to be "get anybody to do it." Since after *Wojeck* and *Twelve and a Half Cents*, the writer has been considered a necessary nuisance. When they did the anthology series, it was an opportunity for writers to write. But there is no way in this country a Dennis Potter or a John Mortimer would somehow materialize. There just aren't the opportunities, and they do not give the writers the clout. If Dennis Potter had come with that brilliant series of *Singing Detective* to the CBC, they would have freaked out!

MJM: But is the message to the writers right now, "Stay with these very 'nitty gritty' subjects. We'll be documentary in flavour, documentary in tone?"

WOODS: No, I don't think it's a conscious message. I think they've been thrashing around for years trying to find a series that will hold the audience, and so far they haven't. *Gift to Last* was an exception.

MJM: It had the variety of tone and style of anthology.

After twenty years, Grahame Woods has left writing television drama to become a marriage counsellor. In the CBC of the 1990s he thinks there is no place for his values and his talent.

In a 1994 conversation with me for the *Canadian Theatre Review*, David Barlow, speaking then as writer and story editor for *North of*

60, gave me some visionary ideas about new opportunities for writers for television when it converges with CD-Rom.

MJM: I think the next phase will be hypertext dramas.

BARLOW: That's right. They're talking about everybody writing 900-page screenplays. There will be all sorts of choices, and we'll have to work in four and five dimensions.

MJM: Won't it be fun, though?

BARLOW: It will certainly be challenging. It will be fun and hopefully it will not be something that makes your head hurt for a long time. Writers always complain that in television drama, for instance, all the characters are not well rounded. If you're having to do three or four different versions of the same story, you're going to find that a lot of those supporting players will be much more fleshed-out human beings or characters than they were.

MJM: Sure, and writers might be able to have a little hypertext flag, so you could footnote and explain instead of having to do it all in the exposition. That would have come in handy on *North of 60* when the audience had to get used to a whole new culture.

BARLOW: Yes, absolutely.

Without question, there is still good writing, the backbone of all good television drama at the CBC in the 1990s. What I wonder is whether we will continue to see and hear scripts that reflect experience in the medium and, more important, experience in living such as Anna Sandor, Jeannine Locke, Grahame Woods, and Louis Del Grande brought to movies and mini-series. All four have left the CBC. Suzette Couture, Rob Forsyth, Don Truckey, and Doug Bowie, to name a few other writers with some writing credits in the more demanding forms of television drama, remain. The question is, Will their best scripts appear on CTV or on the CBC in the 1990s? Much more important to TV drama, Will they appear at all?

4 Acting

> I made an incredible discovery which had never occurred to me before in my life. I always thought that drama was low-angle shots, high-angle shots, scenics, and panoramics. I had to learn that the actor was the key thing in the drama. The actor was even more important than the writer. I have been the greatest exponent of writing. But it is the actor who brings it to life. I have produced dozens of plays where the script is tawdry, but the performance (and of course the director helps the performer) is what made the play. There have been a lot of marvellous plays which were ruined by actors. I had to learn that. SYDNEY NEWMAN

Before we begin to assess Newman's words, let us have a few comments on how actors and directors interact.

MARIO PRIZEK, producer/director [1983]: I direct different actors in different ways. Kate Reid I directed more by inadvertence than by advertence;[1] I didn't direct her by telling her "do this, do that" or "what's your motivation here" in front of the other people. After we were in a coffee break, I'd take her to the side and quietly speak to her. I'd say: "Why did you do that? You don't feel comfortable with that 'sit' at that point, do you? Don't do it if you don't feel comfortable." "How did you know I wasn't comfortable?" "Because I saw you hesitate." This is how we worked well together.

MJM: I'm sure, though, with an actor like William Hutt, you had to be very much more intellectual.

PRIZEK: Oh, with Bill it was right out. He wasn't embarrassed to be told to do something, he wasn't embarrassed to tell you he wasn't going to do something. You talked it out to find out who was right. In some cases we might both have misconceived a dramatic moment. We couldn't figure out why a scene wasn't building properly, and then one of us would come the next morning and say, "I got it! I got it!" You'd have seen Kate Reid in something that somebody else had done and you'd say, "Kate, I loved what you did but I don't think that was the right vehicle for you," or something like that. You could be perfectly frank and there was marvellous camaraderie and cooperation and feedback.

MJM: You obviously value the contributions you got from actors.

PRIZEK: I loved that. I hate doing any acting myself. I only appeared on the stage in order to find out what acting was all about, so I could become a director. Even acting badly, you discover the mechanics, the psychological, emotional mechanisms, the devices by which things are created, how the psychology of a character is uncovered, how the subtext runs, and so on. Even if you do it badly yourself, you already have an advantage over a director who's never acted.

PAUL ALMOND, producer/director [1991]: I want to say a bit about acting styles too, because we worked in different ways with actors. Around the middle 1950s I worked with Miriam Karlin, who was a member of the New York Actors' Studio. When we did a Charles Israel play called *The Doll*, a psycho-drama, Miriam came in and said, "What's the intent of the scene, what's my action?" and all this studio stuff I didn't really know about. I had been a bit British; I'd been to Oxford for three years, where I read Modern Greats (philosophy, politics, and economics). I used to go down to London every chance I had and watch the great theatre of the time: Gielgud, Redgrave, Richardson, Peggy Ashcroft. Peter Brooke was in his heyday, and Stratford-on-Avon was only a short distance away. I had an old ex-army Royal Enfield motorcycle, which let me get to a lot of things, even in term time. I also acted with the Oxford University Dramatic Society and the Experimental Theatre Company, I was directed by Tony Richardson, and I even won a best-actor award under William Gaskill [both influential directors in London's theatres in the 1960s]. So I was influenced by the classical training in Britain of the time. But the Actors' Studio in those days was almost entirely based on unlocking the emotions (they had devices like "sense memory"), which is why so many of the very great television performances of the 1950s, with directors like Lumet and Frankenheimer, used actors from there. I went down to New York, attended a few of the Studio sessions, and became a fanatic: "Everything's got to be free and I don't want a script, just improvise." These poor British actors would be confused. I'd say, "What is this? You said what's in the script!" and they'd say, "Well, I thought I was supposed to!" So I went through this awkward phase before it became incorporated into my directing style.

Of course, the phase wore off, but Karlin did teach me the virtues of improvisation, which meant that something could be entirely fresh, entirely new, *on the air*. With the control I'd developed and the rapport with the cameramen, it could lead to some pretty extraordinary moments. Of course, this was all before "improv" became the rage in theatres and standup comics.[2]

ACTING "LIVE"

Acting in the early days of television was a very different experience from the technically polished "product" which is the aim of television production today. There is a real gap between veterans of live television – who learn their lines and want to complete a scene as one unit – and some young actors who want take after take, so *their* performance looks good, regardless of how the rhythms work and how the scene as a whole may be affected by breaks and repetitions.

DAVID GARDNER, actor/producer [1983]: I played Rosencrantz in David Greene's production of *Hamlet*. You should realize that *Hamlet* was live, three or four hours at least, in Studio 1, the little studio.

MJM: Why that little studio? That's insanity!

GARDNER: I don't think Studio 7 was built then.

MJM: No wonder they used so many overhead shots in that production – out of sheer desperation, I guess.

GARDNER: Out of sheer desperation and also because they needed a five-camera setup. They would have one camera, the gondola camera as it was called, hanging up in the air. Gertrude, played by Katherine Blake, fainted in the middle of the live production.

MJM: It must have been terribly hot with the lights and those heavy costumes.

GARDNER: I would say a combination of heat, live shooting, and heavy costumes – also that her stays were very tight. She was quite a well-built lady. It happened when she came to report that Ophelia had drowned. Then with great woe and weeping she sank gently out of the camera shot – and she sank for real. We found her and undid her. Luckily, there was enough time before she had to come back and drink the poison. But this sort of thing was happening all the time. This was part of live television.

It was also one of the reasons why people watched. Live television is now only to be seen in sports and during elections, wars, or other catastrophes. We still watch riveted, waiting for mistakes, admiring the risks, the danger, the energy created by the much less mediated and controlled event. When the cameras can't watch, a hundred thousand casualties of the Iraq War slip from our view and from our version of the war. When we can watch, and the mixture is as volatile as sex, politics, and race, a live broadcast in prime time of Judge Thomas's testimony in the U.S. Senate subcommittee hearings can and does get higher ratings than the Pennant playoffs of the American League. The positioning of Professor Anita Hill's testimony about Thomas's sexual harassment in the afternoon and the Judge's testimony in prime time was the only (though very crucial) intervention the medium made between viewer and event.

Television or radio drama broadcast live has an edge that no prerecorded show can possibly have. In this chapter most actors discuss modern performance conditions, but the original live performance of *Flight into Danger*, for example, has a real difference in energy and immediacy from the Hollywood film.

An American television film director and self-described "television cat" points out how much actors on live television controlled their own performances: "You could rehearse them as much as you wanted ... but they could, if they wanted to be nasty about it, change the performance totally ... In film, of course, we have the total control because we can go into the cutting room and change a performance eight different ways."[3]

HUGH WEBSTER, actor/writer [1984]: Where live television was concerned, I haven't the faintest idea how a lot of the scripts got to air.

MJM: They were so accident prone?

WEBSTER: It was almost an impossible feat, but you had to do it and it was done.

MJM: In a lot of them, it doesn't show. The plays are not sloppy.

WEBSTER: No, we tried not to make them sloppy. But there was only one way we knew how to do it. You see, when I started there was no television – because I started in radio. But with radio, your face isn't on there. There was a small group, known as "the clique," of very fine radio actors working for radio producer Andrew Allan – people like John Drainie, Bud Knapp, Tommy Tweed, Frank Peddie, Ruthie Springford, Jane Mallet, and Grace Webster – all those people were absolutely first rate at their work. They were so versatile that they could come up with some old doddery character one week on stage, and then next week be playing an urbane man about town, and they were never mixed up. I produced and wrote the radio memorial for John Drainie.

MJM: He was versatile as a television actor, too.

WEBSTER: He didn't do badly. He wasn't quite able to come up with the magic he was able to come up with on radio, but he came awfully close. He was a fine actor. [He played Wullie Mac-

Crimmon in W.O. Mitchell's *The Black Bonspiel of Wullie Mac-Crimmon*, which had two live productions. The script began on radio, went to television, and is still produced in theatres.] Lloyd Bochner played old Cloutie, and Frank Peddie played Wullie in the first. I wasn't in the first one, I was in the second.

MJM: A few scripts have a life of their own. There have been so many productions of it.

WEBSTER: Yes. I've done it on stage; I've played Wullie on stage five times – Lennoxville, Calgary, and Edmonton. So the country's had its share of the theatre version, too.

ALMOND: If an actor was having a hard time, somebody would say, "By the way, so and so hasn't worked in six weeks, he's really starving, can somebody do something?" You'd say, "Yeah, okay, I'll give him an extra on tomorrow's show." We took responsibility for our community – that's true – so if an actor had been out of work for a while and had a family, we would hire him and actors would know that. The actors were also a small community in 1954–56. We, the producers, were public servants with an obligation to feed our actors and entertain our viewers.

CONTEMPORARY ACTORS ON ACTING

Film, television, and respected theatre star Kate Trotter, a member of the television generation, defined for me how live theatre, film, and television are experienced by the actor.

TROTTER [1989]: For me, it is like being a long-distance runner, and theatre is the training. Theatre is where you practise your sprints, your knee bends, and you get your body in shape. Then the sprint is the television show. You've got to be able, sometimes, just to toss it off and go. The long-distance run is the film work. It's only by doing the work on the stage that I can actually do that long-distance run and/or sprint. [An aside from director ERIC TILL [1983]: I think one should acknowledge from time to time where one's limitations are, but I think it is absolutely essential that performers move about and not just get stuck doing theatre; they get bad habits, just as they get bad habits if they work only in television or film.]

American television series writer Stephen Kandel comments that "Actors in television are mostly very competent but rarely more than that. And yet you see the same actors doing Little Theatre and they're terrific ... you see performances. The nature of television inhibits good performances. It inhibits good writing and good performances feed on good writing."4 We still have some actors who move back and forth: R.H. Thomson, Eric Peterson, Kate Trotter, David Ferry, Brent Carver, Booth Savage, Colm Feore, Janet Amos, Miles Potter, Sonia Smits, to name a few in the Toronto area. Yet the fact is that it is very difficult to make a living in acting. Becoming a "star" – or Canada's equivalent, which is to be recognized on the street – has happened to perhaps twenty actors consistently in Canadian television history.

Actor R.H. Thomson talked to me in 1989 about the hazards of doing only television.

MJM: The 1980s and 1990s actors may star in film or television only. They may even become "personalities," which has not been the "Canadian way," has it?

THOMSON: As television production is a greater and greater percentage of the work, a significant part of the acting community knows how to do that.

MJM: And doesn't connect to the theatre?

THOMSON: No.

MJM: It's a commonplace in England that actors work in film and television, sometimes because they love it and sometimes because it butters the bread. The theatre, however, is their "reviver." Is that your experience?

THOMSON: Pretty well. Television and film is the provider, though one can also be offered a television project that is interesting to work with. Theatre is interesting and real. I have been very lucky, because I have been offered projects in theatre that are satisfying. Sometimes you also get paid a theatre salary on which you can live – that's quite a change from the ground-breaking small alternative theatres of the 1970s.

MJM: The actors and the directors have been subsidizing our theatre for many a long day.

THOMSON: Something like the salary at the Royal Alex for *The Real Thing* – my eyes just fell out of my head.

MJM: Toronto has grown up.

THOMSON: But then you go back and work for $400 a week in the alternative theatres.

It was interesting in the free-trade debate in the 1988 election. A number of us were working quite hard to keep the debate going from a cultural point of view. We needed money to buy space in the newspapers. Suddenly I thought, "Put your money where your mouth is." Someone said to me, "You've got three days to raise ten thousand dollars," and I thought, "Why not phone all the people I know who'd done really well in television?" For the first time one could think of phoning a circle of people who actually had some cash.

But success in finding work as an actor in television often depends on having "the look" of the day. Television viewing is not as easily defined as film is in the Laura Mulvey sense of spectatorship and the "gaze."[5] Like film, however, it is a medium very much of and for its time.

Actors usually have a sense of their own potential acting range and persona, if they have one. "Stars" by definition have persona; actors may or may not.

THOMSON: I have been doing a film for a producer who doesn't have any money, so he's not hiring a casting person. I thought I'd suggest some people to him and I started flipping through "Face to Face" [a book of pictures of available actors, which he had on his kitchen table]. There is the "in the swim" activity in the centre of the pond, and the outside gets quieter and quieter. Whether you've been away or whether you just happen not to have work that kept you "in the swim" as it were, somehow you can, through no fault of your own, drift to the outside and sit there, unnoticed. It's really strange, and it takes an extra "umph" for somebody to rediscover you in a tiny way. Take someone like me. I've started feeling old-fashioned. I expected to be out of fashion when I was sixty-five, yet now, suddenly, I feel that the things I hold to be important (priorities, the angle I approach the work from) seem to be slightly out of fashion. You feel yourself drifting towards the outside of the pond. Age is a factor, especially with women. It has nothing to do with talent.

MJM: Could I put that in a different way? You are not a "sitcom" actor. If sitcoms dominate the CBC or CTV, then there is less work for you. As long as the CBC is doing relatively challenging and serious (probably long-form) television and as long as there isn't a perpetual turnover of casting directors and producers, you will continue to be cast for television roles.

THOMSON: There is also a certain way that people look at each other on the street. I don't mean just straight teeth and glossy hair. It's hard to describe. The psychological portrait is not in fashion any more. Personality and the charming presence or magnetic presence is.[6]

THE STAR SYSTEM

MJM to NADA HARCOURT, then head of development for dramatic series. [1991]: I did an interesting interview with R.H. Thomson about a year ago. His sense is that, because the series is the basis for survival of CBC drama, actors like him are becoming more and more peripheral; they are not series leads, they are character actors. That pool of versatile actors simply may not be able to work very much in Canada.

HARCOURT: I disagree. I think it's his free choice. He's a very talented actor, but generally speaking I think what he's speaking of is a consequence of the choices he's made for himself as an actor. Megan Follows has made the same decisions. She doesn't really want to do series [in fact, she played Juliet at Stratford in 1992]. She's a very sought-after actress with an enormous audience appeal. Her choice is that she would prefer to explore a character in long form.

MJM: Thomson was talking about a structural change of emphasis within the CBC. I'm not sure he would disagree with you; that is, if he doesn't want to do series, there may very well be less for him to do.

HARCOURT: Eric Peterson is an actor similar to R.H. Thomson, enormously skilled as an actor. But he has chosen to act in a series as Leon Robinovitch in *Street Legal* and exerts a considerable weight because of his skill in that series. So I do think it's free choice. There are stars that carry with them their personas, the Bea Arthurs who have been in three series and who have played the same part, and Bill Cosby who has virtually developed (over twenty-five years) his family-schtick comedy and then taken that into *The Cosby Show*. There are so many examples of that.

MJM: We have a few in Canada. I think Gordon Pinsent is one who has a persona. He is a good enough actor to leave it behind in different dramatic contexts, but it is a persona that people warm to in this county.

HARCOURT: Absolutely.

MJM: But we have fewer of them. I think our actors excel at losing themselves rather than presenting ...

HARCOURT: A fixed persona. It's simply because there hasn't been a sufficient number of series to carry that persona through. Louis Del Grande is certainly one about whom you would say, even if he isn't playing the character in *Seeing Things*, there is so much appeal in his individual persona that you can take that and build another series on it. [You could say the same about Paul Mastroianni in *Liberty Street* in 1994–95.] You have a wonderful actor who's fourteen years old playing the reckless and likeable Joey in *Degrassi* – there's an emerging actor's persona that he can take into other series – but how many other series can you take it into?

Do you look at an ensemble of such characters and build a series on them? Yes, you could, if it could be financed.

MJM to TRINA McQUEEN, then program director of English Television Network [1988]: It has been a fact of CBC life that there was no "star system." Instead there was an emphasis on the collective performance, the acting "company." I see that changing over the past few years. There's a new sense of building personalities, based, I presume, on the fact that part of the formula for television success is audience identification with individual actors.

McQUEEN: The program director [Fecan] should be heavily involved in making sure that people who have performed wonderfully should be brought back on the air right away.

MJM: To catch that momentum with the audience.

McQUEEN: To catch that momentum, so that they don't to have to spend two years in Hollywood in B-movies and then playing regional theatre in Muskoka.

MJM: At least now we have enough theatre around that there can be some interplay.

McQUEEN: Sure.

MJM: And that seems to be better for the performers. They get a different kind of stretch.

McQUEEN: Yes. But I think of Kenneth Welsh and how wonderful he was in *Empire*. He's been used intermittently. I think the Americans or the British would have found a series for him.

We do lose people. John Colicos, an immensely talented actor who did a superb *King Lear* at Stratford in 1963, went south after *Get Volopchi*. He's been back to do the odd thing, but not much. Both Colicos and Kenneth Welsh appeared in the 1989 TV film *Love and Hate*, Welsh in the leading role of Colin Thatcher, Colicos as the successful prosecutor. Yet for steady work, Welsh had to take a role in later episodes of the American cult favourite *Twin Peaks* in 1990–91. Grahame Woods added another name to those Canadian actors who have a strong television persona and who went south.

WOODS, writer [1989]: John Vernon is one of the few actors we've had who has this great on-screen presence. They let him go. He's done some good things down there, but I think he would come back at the drop of a hat if he had been given the right vehicle. [Vernon shone in Sandor's script *Two Men*, then (after two decades) picked up his role as Wojeck in the drama special *Wojeck: The Fire Next Time*, 1992.]

ENSEMBLES

We have also had actors who carried successful series: Al Waxman in *King of Kensington*, Lally Cadeau in *Hangin' In*, Donnelly Rhodes in *Danger Bay*, Louis Del Grande and Martha Gibson in *Seeing Things*, and ensembles such as Sonia Smits, Eric Peterson, Cynthia Dale, and C. David Johnson in *Street Legal*, Sara Botsford, Mark Humphrey, and Art Hindle in *ENG*, and Bruno Gerussi, Pat Johns, and Robert Clothier in *The Beachcombers*.

Joe Partington has observed and worked with actors in a variety of roles – as a unit manager, story editor, line producer, producer, and executive producer since the mid 1970s.

MJM: When you have something like *King of Kensington* or *Hangin' In*, where you've got, in effect, a trio of characters who carry things, do they have to get along week after week as people as well as on screen?

PARTINGTON, producer [1989]: It certainly helps. That particular trio got along well and went out of their way to be sensitive to one another's needs. If one was in a bad mood, it was dealt with. It was very much a nurturing environment among the three of them. The producers, I assure you, were grateful for that because it took a lot of stress off upstairs. It's not always that way. I'm sure you've read about *Laverne and Shirley*, where Cindy Williams would have her agent on the set counting the lines and timing the air time given to her.

The stars tend to feel that they are personally responsible for the success of the show. They may have forgotten that they weren't even in the pilot or that the show wasn't written for them. All that will be remembered is that they are carrying the show. They demand an enormous amount of attention and respect, which they are entitled to.

MJM: Do they try to shape a story line as opposed to a line of dialogue? I know they say, "Look, my character wouldn't say that," and they may very well be right, having worked with the character so long.

PARTINGTON: The *Kensington* cast, in particular Al Waxman, used to say that they were the "custodians" of the characters. Actors will use this to try and influence a great many things. Steven Bochco [*Hill Street Blues*] said, "When you cast for a play, the actor will become the character that is written. But when you cast for a series, cast very carefully because the character will become the actor." That is right. Actors, like the rest of us, want to be loved.

They want to be larger than life, they want to be wonderful. If their character has aspects that are evil or mean or promiscuous, whatever, they will often try and change that character. You can imagine what would happen on *Golden Girls*, for example, if the actor playing the character who is so interested in sex didn't want to do that anymore. If that happens, the show goes away. I think it must be human nature, because I've seen numerous variations of actors trying to change the character to make him or her more lovable. Under the guise of being the custodian of a character, they try to eliminate personal characteristics or actions or situations they don't want to do.

CASTING: A KEY ELEMENT

Casting is one of the key elements that determines success or failure in television drama. Before the script is in its final (or sometimes first) stage, before designs are conceived, sets built, or crew scheduled, the producer, sometimes the director, and while Fecan was director of entertainment several other people including Fecan himself, start the search for the key actors for the movie or series. The CBC may be moving towards creating "vehicles" for a few stars; they may start with the actor and *then* assemble script, producer, and so on. Though common in the United States and the United Kingdom, this process has been virtually unknown here. Adding Donnelly Rhodes (already well known as the star of *Danger Bay*) to *Street Legal* for a season, even as a very different character type, used the recognition factor and the "star" quality to refresh the look of and character interaction on *Street Legal*.

The issue of casting by nationality is a vexed one. The demand for all-Canadian casts can occasionally be a real constraint. Very few roles demand a specific nationality, particularly if the focus is on individual dramas, not series, which are by definition completely dependent on the personality of the leading actors. John Colicos, Christopher Plummer, William Shatner, Donald Sutherland and Kate Nelligan (who appeared in Eric Till's successful electronic drama *Bethune* in 1975), and Leslie Nielsen are all Canadians who returned for a specific show or series without difficulty, yet they also carry the cachet of "foreign stars."

The CBC record for "colour-blind casting" – casting parts that are not race specific with actors from any visible minority who happen to fit the role – is mixed and until recently inadequate. The indisputable fact is that the leading roles in recent series (*Street Legal's* crown attorney Dillon is a notable exception) – *Mom PI, Material World,*

Urban Angel, Road to Avonlea, and *Max Glick* – are all white. *North-wood* is not as representational of Vancouver's ethnic mix as the *Degrassi* triad was of Toronto's. *Inside Stories* was an anthology foregrounding a different minority every week – sometimes with considerable complexity, sometimes with an embarrassing dependence on stereotype.

However, colour-blind casting is slowly developing as a norm, too slowly according to Ivan Fecan [see chapter 11]. There will come a day when an actor from a visible minority is featured without fuss among the protagonists in a series. The CBC does have a better record using Native people for Aboriginal characters and has launched a major series, *North of 60*, which stars Aboriginal actors as well as whites [1992–]. In the 1994–95 season Tina Keeper was the only Mountie and the only continuing lead actor, the white male Mountie having been written out in the first episode of the third season. Another was later introduced, but is clearly a secondary character. Yet as recently as 1989 the producers of *Divided Loyalties* (CTV) felt free to cast a white actor as Mohawk protagonist Joseph Brant. The issue has not disappeared.

In the early 1970s, ACTRA, faced with ever-eroding drama schedules, became more public in its protests about the casting of American guest "stars." They picked a sympathetic cause in 1975 when they successfully blocked the casting of American actress Kathleen Widdoes as Nellie McClung (a major figure in the Canadian drive to obtain votes for women). Ironically, the play was intended to recognize 1975 as International Women's Year. Kate Reid eventually played the part, yet casting actors from the United States or abroad was commonplace from the 1950s on into the mid 1970s.

MJM to ROBERT ALLEN, producer, supervising producer [1981]:
   Did you encounter problems in the 1960s when you decided on occasion that you wanted a good American actor for a lead role?
ALLEN: No problem at all. We brought people in from America and from England on the theory (in which I still believe) that it benefits Canadian actors to work with performers who have had much more experience, who are better trained, who are superior in their profession. I know this is true. I remember once that Dame Edith Evans came and did (for the nine thousandth time) *The Importance of Being Ernest*, which she loved, after she thought she'd never do it again. But the people working with her had an experience that they had no other way of getting.

Casting Canadians became the rule in the late 1970s to mid 1980s. Now international casting is coming back into fashion with international co-productions in which the cast must include actors in leading roles from each of the producing countries. CTV's long-running *Bordertown* was one example with one American male, one Canadian male and one woman from France. *Counterstrike*, also a CTV series (1991–94), uses one each of "Canadian" (Christopher Plummer), English, French, and American co-stars.

American producer of sitcoms, Gary Goldberg, calls casting his most important job: "The success of a television series is ninety percent casting ... if you don't have this x factor ... if you don't have people they like, you're not going to get the chance to let those other elements work."[7] As Sydney Newman said in the epigraph to this chapter, casting makes or breaks even the best of scripts.

PRIZEK: Kate Reid was into kitchen-sink drama on TV. Everyone was casting her as a housewife. When I did *Queen after Death*, I cast Kate. She read the script and she said, "This is a marvellous play, Mario, but I can't do this. This is period drama" (even though it was written in the twentieth century). I said, "You *can* and you *will*. Just put yourself in my hands." And I supervised her makeup, her hair-do, her costuming. Afterwards, she screened the kine and she came out of the screening room with tears in her eyes. I thought, "Oh God, she hated it." I walked up to her and said, "Katie, are you all right?" and she said, "Mario, I'm beautiful" [and she was].

PHILIP KEATLEY, producer [1985]: *Sister Balonika* was the only film we were able to make that year because somebody had blown the budget back east. *Sister Balonika* was a problem, mainly because of a piece of miscasting. The second thing was the anecdotal structure of the story, with no increase in dramatic tension, which didn't work over ninety minutes. But there was a subtext in that story which could have overcome that and become the plot, if I hadn't miscast.

MJM to THOMSON [1989]: If you find yourself with somebody with whom you normally work well but they have been miscast, is there anything you can do to retrieve that?

THOMSON: No.

MJM: Not a thing?

THOMSON: They don't know they are miscast, so you don't think too much about it. You just get on with it and try to make whatever works work. I can't react to what other actors should be doing. I must respond entirely and only to what they are actually doing, even if it's wholly inadequate. I have to play right into it. Otherwise, there is no reality for the camera.

Not all actors are professionally trained. The ensemble of *The Kids of Degrassi* grew up on camera and was "trained" by workshops run by the creative team of Linda Schuyler and Kit Hood. Several docudramas on the CBC used a mix of professional actors and amateurs. For *Rough Justice*, the casting process was typical of some dramas in the *For the Record* anthology. Ten-year-old Jennifer was a thirteen-year-old who had never done television before. Her mother, also not a professional actor, played the non-speaking role of a policewoman who sits with the crown attorney while he gets the child's statement. Most of the crowds in the corridors were real lawyers or court employees. Garrick Hagon, who played the crown attorney, was available for a short period between Stratford and England, where he now lives. (Twenty years ago Hagon had played Kim, the central role in Eric Till's superb half-hour about a Danish resistance fighter.) Alan Royal, subsequently familiar to many viewers as the reporter in *Night Heat*, badly wanted to play the molester – a demanding role – and got the part. Peter Dvorsky as the father is now regularly seen on television as well as on stage.

Casting depends on a complex, often instinctive set of choices. Producers have a major, sometimes deciding vote on who will be right for a part. The "casting couch" rumours so common in Hollywood don't seem to be a major part of CBC gossip or actors' paranoia, though "looking available" does seem to be a factor in casting women, particularly for series.[8] That factor is also visible to women watching most TV series. The interchangeability of the young, bouncy blondes in sitcoms and the thin, waif-like blondes in primetime soaps is sad – the facelessness of it all. Woman as commodity was never more visible than in the 1990s, whatever the dialogue or the plot. That specific phenomenon is not as visible in Canadian television drama – but even here, one need look no further than local news, much of the sports coverage, and above all the commercials.

MJM to BILL GOUGH, producer [1988]: You would see the casting director as somebody who presents you with all sorts of ideas, but you are the decision-maker.

GOUGH: In every show ...

MJM: ... with the director's input?

GOUGH: ... with the director. But the final choice is up to the producer. If that is removed from the producer and the director combined (with the appropriate casting officer), you are enforcing a kind of sameness, one person's taste on everything.

MJM to writer ANNA SANDOR [1988]: When you are writing for a series, you may have the actors in mind. You'd know how particular actors will deliver a line, you'd hear their voice, their body moving in space, and so on. But with your first full-length adaptation *Population of One* or your own *Charlie Grant's War*, you didn't have that luxury. Have you ever written with the actor in mind?

SANDOR: It depends. In certain instances, yes, you have someone in mind. For example, in *Charlie Grant's War*, fairly early on in the writing, R.H. Thomson was in our minds. There are not, unfortunately, many young Canadian leading men who have that kind of charisma and range. There are lots of wonderful actors, but in that instance you are casting very physically. R.H. was also thin enough to be believable in a concentration camp. That was a bonus. It was after the second draft that he accepted. R.H. is very ethical about what he will accept. He and I had a long talk, because he had some very good suggestions. So he actually had a certain amount of input. That doesn't happen very often – although some of his suggestions wound up on the cutting-room floor because of things like time.

At other times, you really don't know who is going to play the part. For example, *Two Men*, which we have just finished shooting, was actually written about two years ago. There were various problems with getting it done. But there was a role in it for an older, wisecracking Jewish woman who was dying. Bill and I met Lila Kedrova ...

GOUGH: ... thanks to Dorothy Gardner [the head of casting at CBC for over a decade, now gone].

SANDOR: I said to Lila that I had a part that I was going to rewrite, so that if we ever got the show done she would have a role. Then I rewrote the part for her. When we got the go-ahead she was cast, and she was wonderful, incredible. That is an instance of changing the part for the actor. I wrote something recently [*Martha, Ruth and Edie*]. But I had absolutely no input other than the writing. The person cast in the lead is unlike anything I ever imagined the character to be. It just totally changes the character.

One of the main reasons I like working with Bill is because there is a lot of input from the writer, rightly so. I think the person who knows the most about what is on the paper and what comes off the paper is the writer. Not every suggestion I give Bill is heeded, but, when I say that I can see so-and-so in this part, I've never had Bill say that he wasn't going to audition that person because they were wrong.

GOUGH: But you are better at it. Some writers are hopeless.

SANDOR: That's my acting background.

GOUGH: Their idea of casting would work against what they wrote.

But if it helps them to visualize a specific person while writing, that is fine.

Casting can even become a political football. Those who attacked the Bomber Command segment of *The Valour and the Horror* roundly objected to the character actor cast as Bomber Harris because he had played villains. Yet one of his last roles had been the lively inn-keeper in the stage hit *Les Misérables*. This was not an instance of a star persona colouring a character, but one of "mnemonic irrelevance" – connotations drawn from personal memories unrelated to the role or the context. Such *ad hominem* attacks on the casting and on the age of the producer/writers, both too young to have served in the Second World War, weakened the arguments of the veterans who opposed the series.

American (and some British) actors have a television persona that combines elements of their "look," their personality, and even a particular genre. There is a James Garner or Lindsay Wagner or Alan Alda or Bea Arthur "type" of character. Type-casting makes for stardom and steady work. It can also be the bane of an actor's existence. On the other hand, the actor's range may indeed be confined to that of his or her television persona. Some actors can act in a variety of roles; others flourish playing consistently one aspect of their own personality. Executives like Ivan Fecan have ideas about our system and the American system of developing acting talent.

IVAN FECAN, then director of entertainment [1989]: If you look at the new crop of theatrical and television actors, you see a lot of them tracing their careers back to soaps. Soaps are ...

MJM: ... a training ground?

FECAN: They really are. They're the workshops where you learn your craft. Now, we're trying to repatriate a lot of the Canadians working abroad. We find people who are doing soaps or working on different continuing series and we say, "How would you like to do a prime-time series?"

HOW AN ACTOR CAN INFLUENCE CHARACTERS AND STORY LINES

David Gardner, who got his start in theatre,[9] has acted on television since its early days, from Rosencrantz in *Hamlet* to a continuing role in a series.

MJM to GARDNER: You played Larry, a continuing character in *Home Fires* (1980–84), and have been able to watch it develop. I was thinking about the interplay between the actors and the roles they play. Would Gerard Parkes [Dr Lowe – the male lead] have much to say about where his character was going?

GARDNER: I would think, being Gerard Parkes, a great deal. Almost every episode is rewritten in the rehearsal period, sometimes totally. If you look over your right shoulder you'll see *Home Fires'* scripts. The pink and the blue pages are rewrites. On the top is the last episode we just did, and you can see it is almost totally rewritten. The storyline is plotted, roughly, where it is going, what's happening to the characters. But when you get to the actual dialogue of scenes, people just say, "Why do we have to say this?" So a lot of cutting and rewriting is also happening.

Home Fires was always meant to be a kind of wartime soap opera, but it takes place in Canada, not overseas. There is no war footage. It is about a family at home in Canada and how they responded to the war, and it touched a lot of people.

MJM: It would seem to have a natural shape then.

GARDNER: The shape of the war. They didn't expect *Home Fires* to "go." It began as a six- or eight-episode series. Would it catch on or not? But it developed a loyal, not immense, but consistent audience. There are several hundred thousand viewers who tune in regularly and really are concerned. They write in and say, "Will Larry marry Marge?" I get stopped on the street by people who want to know.

MJM: Your character [Larry] has been there for almost its whole run, hasn't he?

GARDNER: Yes, since the beginning. I don't consider the character really developed, however.

MJM: No, I'm glad you said that, because I don't either. That happens to some characters, and not to others.

GARDNER: The potential for romance wasn't originally planned, but Sheila Moore, who plays Marge, and I said, "Here we are, why don't we do something about this?" And so, slowly, our relationship just became one of the minor plot lines. It gets resolved in the final episode – Marge catches the wedding corsage and we look at each other and all that. That is how a series develops.

People also grow older in the series. The young boy who plays Sydney has matured and is suddenly no longer a gangling teenager. He has girlfriends and so on. All of these things have been built into the script. Gerard Parkes began with his hair tinted dark and a moustache. Now he has no moustache and his hair is grey. He just couldn't be bothered doing it every time, so they let him age.

MJM to PHILIP KEATLEY, producer of *Cariboo Country* [1985]: I watched "The Infant Bonaparte" and "Strong Medicine," in which the character of Bonaparte John died. But he comes back later in the series, perfectly hale and hearty. What was your assumption? That the audience wouldn't remember? Or were you deciding that the story, in which he reappears, happened before that point?

KEATLEY: That's right. Originally we had a storyteller in the anthology – Arch MacGregor, the local storekeeper who could make jumps in time.

MJM: The series was not intended to be chronological?

KEATLEY: No, it wasn't. These were a bag of stories, and some of them happened and some of them didn't happen. Some of them should have happened.

MJM: That is also why you could change actors? "Frenchie" is played by two different actors.

KEATLEY: Frenchie changed only between the studio series and the film series.

MJM: So you really didn't play fast and loose with the players?

KEATLEY: No. Originally in the studio we had people like Eric Vale, an English actor, who played Ol' Antoine. He had done the first two shows. At the last moment, when we became a series, he said, "I'm too old. I'm going to fail you in a series. I'm not going to be able to remember the words for thirteen shows." That is when we panicked and found Chief Dan George. There was an absolutely glorious actor, Frank Vyvyan, who played Morton Dilloughby. Frank got emphysema. He was just wonderful, but he was too sick. He was replaced by a man named Buck Kindt who was not an actor. He was a southern Alberta rancher.

Acting is a difficult, insecure, vulnerable profession – a tough way to make a living. Few of the thousands who throng the agencies and send in résumés earn enough in a year to stay above the poverty line, and many of those who do end up writing or directing. Appearances in commercials with their residuals are basic financial security for many actors in every industrialized country. But in the 1990s, American and European actors are being hired for commercials intended for Canadian markets because the business executives have hired American advertising agencies. The comments among Canadian actors when viewers were bombarded in 1990 with deprecating, self-consciously Canadian jokes on behalf of Canadian Airlines by a character actor from the American sitcom *Barney Miller* may well be imagined. Canadian Airlines should have been renamed Colonial Airlines for that ad campaign, but it has not been the only culprit.

ACTING FOR TELEVISION

Television acting is its own skill, analogous in some ways to acting for film and in others to theatre. But the days of "red light on – here we go!" live television have gone. Then the performers, hampered as they were by huge cameras, cables, hot lights, and flying scenery, at least did the play from beginning to end in real time and real (if cramped) space. For the actor of the 1980s and 1990s, television on tape or on film presents different challenges. The constraints are enormous – but the challenge of bending these constraints to the service of the character never leaves the mind of those actors, particularly those who see the medium as an art as well as a living.

Story editor Alice Sinclair, on shooting out of sequence:

SINCLAIR [1982]: It changes the performances. You would be unwise, for example, to start your first day of shooting with the big climactic scene.

MJM: Directors try to give the actors some kind of build?

SINCLAIR: And of course the actors have the whole script.

MJM: That's true. They can see where each detail fits, and as professionals they can reach for it. I was on the set during the latter end of the shooting of *Ready for Slaughter* and it was clear that Diane Belshaw, who played Gordon Pinsent's wife, had had two weeks to observe very closely the family whose farm was being used. In other words, she had taken the opportunity to do instant research.

SINCLAIR: Another thing we also do occasionally is "block shooting." If you have a two- or three-parter, you will do scenes from each of the three parts on a single day. That, of course, is a money saver.

MJM: Perhaps that would also pull the mini-series form together for an actor because she would be thinking of the three episodes at once. I would think it would depend on how experienced the actor was.

Sydney Newman has the advantage of double-vision – the U.K. and Canadian experience over many years:

NEWMAN [1984]: One of the benefits of Canada is that the possibilities for creative expression have been so limited that our artists have had to be multi-faceted, multi-techniqued. You take a John Drainie, who was a brilliant radio actor, and put him in front of a camera, and he knew exactly how to scale down his voice and his face. He was very good. We inherited a lot of very good actors and actresses from the *Stage* series.

MJM: And we kept some of them, too.

NEWMAN: Most of them, yes. We didn't keep Kate Reid [who went to New York for a long while] and we lost Lorne Greene.

MJM: William Shatner [Captain Kirk] and Lloyd Bochner [a wide range of parts, often the villains, since his confidence, courtly demeanour, and suave good looks simply read "villain" to American viewers].

R.H. THOMSON AND KATE TROTTER ON ACTING

Three very articulate men, well known to Canadian audiences, highly regarded as performers, and as different as New Brunswick, North Bay, and New York, talked to me about their perceptions of acting styles in this country. That only one would allow me to quote him directly, because of the fear of repercussions, suggests a serious malaise in the CBC in the late 1980s and early 1990s, a question I will explore further in chapter 10 on ethos and in the conclusion.

One argued that the acting in this country had improved enormously because he thought it now resembled extroverted or method acting. I disputed his point of view, since the acting of Frances Hyland, William Hutt, Douglas Rain, Martha Henry, Frank Peddie, Lloyd Bochner, and dozens of others was superb in the challenging dramas of the 1950s and 1960s. His point, however, was that any method or approach to television acting was legitimate if it resembled truth. To paraphrase, he said something like "Close-ups in television and film are not the place for huffing and puffing artificiality. They make us feel lonely, but they are not true. You must tell the truth." The second well-loved and versatile actor in the profession would not be interviewed for this book because he feels displaced by the current regime at the CBC, his talent and history devalued by the kinds of television product now being made.

R.H. Thomson was the third. His early acting experience was in small alternative Canadian theatres. He has played protagonists in Renaissance tragedies, a farmer/soldier in the War of 1812, a rebel martyr in the 1837 Rebellion, a principled labour lawyer, a businessman turned Second World War hero, Frederick Banting, the shy Jasper Dale, and a very convincing psychopathic second-in-command to Hal Banks. He has also worked in American television throughout his career. Thomson shared his sense of how American television stardom and production systems operated.

THOMSON: The "stars" have input. They say, "I do it this way and I say it that way." I've watched Lindsay Wagner and others do it. They go to the director and say, "It says here that I cry and I think it would be better if I didn't cry; I'd like to tone that down." They often take the guts out of scenes, yet end up looking very good themselves in the style they know so well and do very well. But, too often, this approach distorts scenes as they go along. However, stars are so high in "pecking order" there is no question of disagreeing. And, to confound opinion, there are exceptions.

I shot a scene once with Lindsay Wagner and Armand Assante. After the scene was shot I sat and thought, "Why did this go so strangely?" It occurred to me that there were three distinct acting styles going on in that scene. There was Lindsay Wagner, totally confident, very good, doing Los Angeles–style acting – "looking good." I don't just mean hair and teeth, I actually mean the delivery, the placement, the degree and edge of emotional experience, the playing with the camera. You package "moments" in a good-looking reality. Everything looks good.

Armand Assante was doing a New York–style, basically what I call "bouncing." Everything is bounced off the walls: everything is scattered – dialogue, intentions, beats, movements. It's a very frenetic and captivating style and has a truth to it in its time and place. Then there was me doing "Canadian acting." I had got past the stage where I thought my performance was just bad. Now I recognize that it is not bad, just different. That scene had three totally different styles.

MJM: What would you say is "Canadian acting"? Maybe that isn't a fair question.

THOMSON: No, but it is worth trying to answer, and I don't know if I can answer it. For every answer you will get, fourteen people would rise from their seats and say, "You smug Canadian, how dare you say these things. The Americans do that too and the Brits do it."

I saw 1949, David French's show about the Mercers, on closing night with a Canadian cast and one expatriate. It worked very well. The only difference I saw was that the expatriate was far more direct at playing his moments, explicit, extrovert. His moments were like primary colours: good primary colours, honest primary colours, well-built primary colours. He was a little apart, and not quite as involved with the rest of the company, who had worked together for so long. They were not as explicit in variety and focus, as in "That's what is happening, now let's move on to the next direct moment." It was a more subtle, more indirect, and a more communal (I don't want to say better) acting style. These differences imply a degree of self-effacement that carries the story better. The Canadian actors were there simply to deliver a more implicit version of the story, as opposed to a style that telegraphs the focus from moment to moment with no shame, no complexity, little puzzle, no enigma, no incompleteness, nothing implicit. A dense accumulation of explicit moments need not assure complexity!

MJM: Would you say that we have a style based on ensemble acting?

THOMSON: As soon as you say, "What do we have?" you think of all these exceptions. There are many actors in the States who have all the stuff that I'm describing. We are trying to identify the Bell curve, and yes, I agree.

There are a couple of other things about Canadian style. I think we have a wider range of people who we will consider as "leads." The Dustin Hoffmans are the exception to the rule in the United States. Here the definition for the acceptance of who is a leading player is wider, as it is in Europe.[10] Very few actors retain a degree of innocence or naiveté or vulnerability. Most who achieve that dollar figure or a degree of notoriety or "profile" start becoming "who they are."

MJM: Public figures.

THOMSON: Public figures. So I include that vulnerability in a very general way as a component of the Canadian acting style. I think we should acknowledge it so we can maintain it.

MJM: So the CBC has been right in refusing to build up a star system?

THOMSON: I happen to agree with that. But it is very embittering for me to say that because I also ask, "Why isn't the CBC offering me another big project now? How come they don't pick up the momentum from *Glory Enough for All* or *Charlie Grant's War?*" Right, actors do that kind of thing.

It gets very expensive to be selective in your choice of job, especially if one hasn't worked for a while. It's also expensive in the long term in that I think I could have had a much higher profile as an actor if I'd played a lot of different games, some outside the country, whatever.

MJM: You could probably play the personality game if you wanted to. There is a persona I associate with you, which you seem to be able to leave behind when a completely different character is needed, as with Jasper Dale.

THOMSON: I fail whenever I try to project an on-screen personality. I've tried to do that in a number of American TV movies where one plays the "doctor this" or the "boyfriend that." Unless I have paints to paint with and I'm busy painting, I get so self-conscious I get stiff. So I will look at the work and think, "That's bullshit, that's not me, I mean there is nothing really coming through." I come through when I'm actually painting as hard as I can go. So I don't think I could play that game. I've tried, and I get very broken up about it.

MJM: So there is no such thing as "an R.H. Thomson" kind of role?

THOMSON: I hope not. In my more depressed moments, when I thought it was close to being all over, I would say to myself, "No, I've had some wonderful chances. I should be grateful that I've actually had a whack at *Charlie Grant's War* or *Glory Enough for All* or *Hal Banks*, or the peak of them all, *Hamlet* [in the theatre]. I've been so lucky to have had a shot at those things."

That for me is "pay," and I can deal with periods of being turned down because I've been paid in another currency – opportunity. However, it doesn't make me feel very secure.

MJM: By definition you are not going to feel secure, are you, as an actor?

THOMSON: No, I'm an employee who works on short terms, I'm self-employed, and I'm subject to pressure ...

MJM: I don't mean just that. Of all the roles on the creative side of television, I think acting is the most difficult – also the most vulnerable to criticism and abuse.

THOMSON: Look at those people who want fame. You can watch their hopes and dreams fade. I watch talented friends who aren't working, what is happening to all their dreams?

MJM: But despite all that, you choose to take risks, don't you?

THOMSON: Yes. Michael Gibson came out with an interesting phrase. He said he wasn't interested in actors who have "gone to seed." And I thought that is actually quite frank. A plant that has not gone to seed is continuing to reach, to reach, to reach ... I think television does this to actors. It is an interesting image because the forms of television go to seed so quickly. That is what formula television implies, a severe truncation of creative reaching.

Kate Trotter, like R.H. Thomson, has played in everything from Shakespeare and Brian Friel to films like *Joshua, Then and Now*, and series like *Street Legal* and *The Campbells*. She also starred in the *For the Record* ninety-minute special *Kate Morris VP*. Not unexpectedly, she has a different though equally articulate and thoughtful point of view on acting for television.[11]

MJM: Clearly, acting schools don't do a lot of "this is how you act for television, beginning at zero."

TROTTER [1989]: Oh no, none. I don't think that is necessarily bad. I think the notion of teaching anybody they can even begin to act for the stage in three years is a bit of a joke. At the age of sixty, if you survive, you can call yourself an actor. That is the problem of being an actor. You learn only by doing.

MJM: A series presents the audience (and the actors) with sets of characters and familiar types of situations. You, as actor, walk in. You are a fresh face from the audience's perspective, so viewers spend energy getting to know your character because they know the others. Are they going to identify emotionally with you in the twenty-two or fifty-eight minutes available?

TROTTER: Often you end up fighting. You are fighting for the character, you're fighting for your integrity, you are fighting for someone to believe that you have got a brain. There is definitely a feeling that actors "get in the way." After all, the producers have a format, and it seems to be working. I sometimes think they grit their teeth and really wish that you would "just do *your* job." For them, that means saying the lines and hitting the marks [standing where you are supposed to].

MJM: What is it like walking into a series where the relationships are all established among the continuing players?

TROTTER: It's tough, actually, very tough. But it helps if you have worked with the other actors before – if you know one another. The show benefits and, as an actor, you feel that you have a life-line of a sort. I have done a stint on almost all of them. I did a *Philip Marlowe*, I did a *Night Heat*, I've done a *Campbells, ENG, Street Legal, Diamonds* ... you desperately try to juggle it all!

[An aside from DAVID GARDNER: The trouble with series is that you eventually become straight-man for the adventure that is conceived this week. In come the characters to whom something happens or who are going through a crisis of some sort. They get the "acting" parts. The lead characters or the sustaining characters just have to respond.]

TROTTER: I had a very difficult time on *The Campbells* [about pioneer life in Ontario in the 1830s] because I felt strongly that my character would not be trapped into a period dress code. She was very independent and, more importantly, practical. I know the regular cast members agreed with me, but they had given up the fight long ago. I think wardrobe found me "very difficult," and possibly so did the producers. But I felt I had to be true to the character as I perceived her. For instance, I played a scene where I was sitting out in the woods by myself sketching a bird. Not even the wagon is in sight. I took off my jacket and rolled up my sleeves. The response was "Oh, I couldn't do this. This was period costume!" The opening shot was me falling into the shot from a tree. So what I did was, I hooked my dress in my belt loops. "Oh, but now her bloomers are going to show and you can't ..." so I said "Well, you show me how you jump out of a tree in a full skirt!" But I felt I could take my skirt down when I got out of the tree, and when someone comes on shot I could roll down my sleeves. It makes no sense to sit in the baking hot sun with a coat on and a hat to paint birds! The series actors all laughed and said "Go to it!" because they had been through their fights. You have those kinds of fights because you come in with a fresh energy and a kind of conviction about what is right. The people who have done battle all year just want to shoot the sucker. They say, "You want me to wear the hat? I'll wear the hat!" I regretted making life difficult on set – but I felt very caught between a sense of personal responsibility and taking the line of least resistance.

I think, finally, you cannot be completely objective about the result of a piece of theatre or film or TV. I don't think the performers or the directors can be objective. It's a cake batter and everything goes in. You just pray you'll get a well-balanced cake.

MJM: It's good to hear someone who cares and says, "They could be so much better!"

TROTTER: But there are a slew of Canadian actors who say that all the time, every day, we scream it to the heavens! There is a whole generation of us!

Why do they do it? They all call theatre/film/television "the business." Yet, for the best of them, a television role isn't a "product," another "bit," a line in a résumé. It certainly isn't a nine-to-five job. This is clear to any observer on a set. I first discovered this as a graduate student in 1963 when I observed the Stratford Company in rehearsal, from first read-through to technical dress rehearsal. When you put some of Canada's best actors and a director like Michael Langham under the same roof and give them time to work, the process is utterly absorbing to watch. Most of those actors were also the actors who did such admirable work for Mario Prizek, Paul Almond, or Eric Till at the CBC in the late 1950s and early 1960s. Many of the actors who succeed (and many who are good at the craft do not end up making a living) love to perform. They were born to do this, and nothing else will do. Yet each one approaches acting differently.

MJM to THOMSON: Could we take a look at the process for a moment? When you're in the theatre, you can study the script ahead of time. You have a set rehearsal period working with the other actors. Then you open with an audience, and you get to do the whole play every night for its run. Almost none of that is the same even for full-length television or film. How soon do you get a script?

THOMSON: It depends. Sometimes you get them a couple days beforehand. For *Glory Enough for All* I had a year and a half before.

MJM: Grahame Woods said he had the incredible luxury of writing with you in mind, knowing you were going to play the lead. You had been cast before he got the script going.

THOMSON: Oh really? Is that true?

MJM: Did you not know that?

THOMSON: I know that Gordon Hinch, the producer, phoned me up three years earlier and said, "Read the books and are you interested?" I said, "Of course I'm interested." I thought the scripts were written.

GRAHAME WOODS, writer [1989]: If Gordon Hinch wanted to change one word, he would phone me. Eric Till, the director, read my script and said, "I see this and I see this," and followed it very closely most of the time. It was very rewarding. Then to get such fine actors and actresses in such small parts, like Kate Trotter [Banting's fiancée] and Martha Henry [the mother of the diabetic child] and to get screen time. That scene in the stable [see Trotter in chapter 2] must have gone on for ten minutes. In most other shows it would be gone, yet it really needed that time. R.H. Thomson's performance was superb!

THOMSON: I always want to know the source of the script. If it's a book, then I want to read the book. If it's about a person, I want to read the biography about the person. I want to explore their world. Recently I rushed out to the World's Biggest Book Store to try and find *The Chronicles of Avonlea* and *The Story Girl* [for Jasper Dale, a continuing character on *Road to Avonlea*].

Sometimes it even means writing. You read the scene and you go, "OK, now if I were like that and if I had to respond to this, what would I say?" So you write different versions, just so you arrive on set with a whole bunch of material, so you've got more on your palette than just what is written down.

I want the earliest draft I can get my hands on and, when different drafts come in, I keep the first. I always want more than what is in the script. Sometimes from an early draft you can understand the intention better, even though you see how it's been reduced and altered. You say, "Oh, I see the real intention," so you know how to place it. Or sometimes you say, "You wrote it far better in the first draft." I exercise some choice of what eventually arrives on screen.

MJM: When do you start talking to the director about the basic concept of character?

THOMSON: It depends on the difficulty or the scope of the project. If I'm playing a marginal doctor in a episodic story, I don't talk to the director at all. If it is *Charlie Grant's War*, which was demanding, I have to do a lot of the work on it. Donald Brittain was to direct that the first time I came to it. [Martin Lavut actually directed it.]

MJM: Do you get much chance to give some feedback to the producer or the director?

THOMSON: It depends on the project entirely; it depends on the people I work with. I guess it's safe to say most don't want feedback from anybody. They say, "We do want feedback," but really they don't. We were all assured with the film for TV *Samuel Lount* that we were going to rehearse and workshop. Yes, the dialogue wasn't there yet, "but we were going to fix it and that's why we are hiring all these theatre actors," and all this mouth-flapping went on. Push got to shove, and when we started working on it we had not so good results.

MJM: It wasn't awful, awful, awful, but it was "problematic."[12]

TROTTER: Often, producers don't have any idea how hard actors work. Good directors do, but, by and large, I'm not sure many producers do. There is nothing worse than not connecting with a director. You are dead in the water when that happens, be it theatre, television, or film.

THOMSON: Directors can certainly be very creative partners. There are different ways of giving feedback, though. There is the very correct and diplomatic way, which is by suggestion or request or offering, and there is the not quite so diplomatic form, which is painful. But sometimes, as in *Charlie Grant's War*, the stakes are very high. The story had many wonderful bits to it. The acting problem was that you cannot make cliché from Auschwitz and all that death and suffering. If you do, you are offending not only the people who suffered but also the people who are watching the program. So diplomacy is reluctantly left aside and it becomes "I'm sorry, but this is what I'm doing," or you resort to actors' tricks to bury the clichéd or the unplayable. You say your words, carry out the requisite intentions, but bury them so deeply under other things in the action that you in fact defuse, as it were, all the clichés. There are different ways to give feedback, depending on how difficult you want to be and depending on your ego. You get different feedback in the theatre. The audience is very involved. On the other hand, you never, ever see yourself. In film you actually get to see it and that is important, because you can sit there and think "that's junk, that's garbage," or you sit there and think "that works."

MJM: Do you go to rushes?

THOMSON: I can't, I get very self-conscious, so I can't go to rushes.

MJM: But when it's done you want to look at the finished piece?

THOMSON: Oh yes, I want to look at it. I want to see if the story worked. You actually get to decide whether you like it or what you will do next time or what you should stop doing as far as a different story is concerned. When you watch the scene you go, "I should have stuck to my guns, I should have fought that one through," or you see a half-intention and you think, "Robert, why didn't you have the courage of your convictions and keep on with it?"

That's one kind of feedback. Another is when people tell me they like it, that it works, that it affected them, or whatever. That doesn't happen in the theatre.

There is another kind of feedback I have noticed recently. Not often, but sometimes, people come up to me and say, "Thank you very much for staying here." When they say "Thank you for staying," you realize that you are doing something beyond the short span of doing individual programs or dramas; that you actually are contributing in a small way to building some counterweight to the conventional mass, that you are part of a developing landscape. The best kind of response is when a crew will become involved in a story, because television crews have seen a lot of television drama come and go. It takes a little while, but if it is going well, you know you are ahead of the game, because the crew is actually starting to become involved in how the story is unfolding and how it is getting shot.

MJM to TROTTER: Both television and theatrical film present the same problems in terms of not acting scenes in sequence, don't they?

TROTTER: Yes.

MJM: So, you try to hold the whole performance in your head: where it's going, where this particular bit fits. Presumably you are hoping for a director who helps you do that, as well as other actors who will give you some sort of consistency in performance. You don't have an audience either to energize you or to tell you where you are going off track. As an actor, who do you pick for an audience?

TROTTER: I've learned that if the crew is on your side they can give you so much, it is unbelievable. They will group around the camera and feed you, because they come to believe in the film. You are all part of a team. I am very thrown if I think someone on the crew doesn't like my work.

MJM: They give you the energy, the responses ...

TROTTER: And they give you their respect.

MJM to THOMSON: How do you keep track of your own performance when you have to play out of sequence? There are two things I don't understand about film acting: one is how you keep your sense of how the pieces fit together, and the other is how you keep your performance relatively on track when you have to repeat it over and over?

THOMSON: Now, let's imagine I'm on this scene and I have a feeling I want to do it this way. Ah, what's up there already? Oh, I see, there is that, that, that, and that. Well, I've got a lot of that there, I think it's important that the character do this now ... I'm going to shift this scene ... yes, that's OK ... what am I missing? ... Holy shit, I missed all that other stuff! Where can I put all that? There must be a scene when I can put that in. Yes, that is where I can show a particular colour, because I missed something else from the previous scene that is really important. [As if to director Eric Till]. "Eric can we put a moment in like that in this scene?" Shooting out of sequence allows you to do that kind of stuff. Do you see what I mean? Of course it is not as cold-blooded as that, but one can see what one has achieved already, a rhythm here and a rhythm there.

MJM: It seems to me that telegraphing emotions and ideas must be a major hazard for a film actor, because you are often playing the narrative backward. For example, you could be playing the climax very early in the shoot. Yet, the discoveries you make later can't feed into what has already been filmed.

THOMSON: Yes, it's true. And sometimes you suddenly find a scene (out of its own spontaneity for good or for bad) playing entirely differently than anyone ever intended, and there it is. It's on the film, and what are you going to do?

So you've got to reshuffle the whole deck to see how what you want to convey is going to go in. In the theatre I am used to working on the little spans of the moments of the characters. I am also used to working on the span of the play, the "build." You work on that span over time, you perfect it, and you get better during a run. All that experience comes in very handy when I am dealing with a film out of sequence over ten weeks. Now a lot of films don't require this craft at all. I mean, it is a little unfashionable to look for that kind of journey. So I mouse away and try to put a little of it in because I think any character in any film or any story should have a little journey. Everyone should have a journey, even my little marginal "doctor" part.

MJM to TROTTER: It must be very hard when you are switching media from theatre to television. How do you scale down your performance to fit into the box?

TROTTER: Instinct and the other actor. On stage you have more distance to throw the emotion, you put more power behind it. If you are doing a closeup, then the camera is about two feet from your nose and the person you are talking to is sitting with his head scrunched up against the lens. You are not going to get a whole lot of feeling of distance.

MJM: Do you find the technology intrusive?

TROTTER: Oh, you do. You have to fight it and fight it. You have hub-bub going on everywhere, people screaming and yelling and throwing cables. The last few seconds are "mikes in the shot, OK, mike up, OK, mike down, OK, there it is, now can you move one inch to your left, all right back, that's it, that's your spot. All right action!" All the time you are worrying about where things are, whether your hand is going too far into the shot, whether you are standing exactly right, how you are going to hit your mark. It's very hard. I'd say the concentration is harder than it is for the stage, because the stage encompasses your audience. You concentrate in a big swoop and you bring them all in. To do theatre you need a third eye on the audience, but in film and TV you have to have about fifteen different eyes on everything. Finally, your concentration has to be like locking a key in a door.

MJM: Do you find yourself walking through some of the "bread and butter" stuff? (In television, not in theatre.)

TROTTER: I don't think I ever have, actually. I hope that there never comes a day when I do.

MJM: But obviously it would be very easy just to say, "To heck with this, it is a half-hour of television that nobody will ever remember, it is gone, so what."

TROTTER: There have been some times when I wonder how on earth I'm going to get through. But I've yet to feel that I haven't done my absolute best. I've done three *Friday the Thirteenths*, all of them with wonderful directors. But television scripts are not always of a high quality, and sometimes you do panic and hope your parents won't be home the night it airs, or your children!

MJM: Is it still fun?

TROTTER: It depends who is directing it. I did one a couple of years ago which *People* magazine called the worst film of the year, *Murder in Space*. It was a gimmick for pay TV. Seven astronauts of various nationalities went into space, and only four came back. The audience had to guess who killed who, how, and why. Whoever got the right answers got a gift. Now, the horrifying thing was that the actors and the director did not know who had done the murders. Can you imagine doing the script where three people get knocked off and you don't know if you've done it? How do you play the script? How do you begin to do it? Well, the producers didn't want that secret out of the bag, because it was the gimmick that was important.

I did an *Alfred Hitchcock* called "Hunted." This was a two-hander, and it was a two-week episode, so it was a very big deal. This was typical TV. It was fast, down, and dirty. I memorized fifty-two pages of script, cold, before the first shoot, because I was doing a stage play and we were in rehearsal. I knew I was not going to have time to learn lines at night, and it had never occurred to me that there was an option. I had never met Edward Woodward [a British actor who starred in several seasons of an American action show], and it was all very intimidating. He was given a large Winnebago, and the Canadian press was only interested in him – our "American guest star"! I felt a lot of pressure at first to prove myself. I have never felt much support from the Canadian press; it is a great dilemma. We don't like to be arrogant or self-aggrandizing. But, on the other hand, we need to build our industry. We need to celebrate our success. Edward Woodward, as wonderful as he is, doesn't need our help! Luckily for my own ego, I was nominated for an American award for the performance.

MJM: How much rehearsal, if any, did you get on a thing like that?

TROTTER: None!

MJM: None. So you go in ...

TROTTER: And you do it. There is no time for anything else. You've got six or seven scenes to shoot in a day, plus the camera turnarounds. That's what takes the time. We would walk it through, mainly for the camera. What TV calls "rehearsal" often has got nothing to do with acting. They want to know approximately how loud you are going to be, because they want to know where to place the mikes, and they want to know where you are going to be, because they need to be organized technically.

The difference between that experience and working with R.H. Thomson is night and day. I don't ever have to prove myself with R.H., and you're working on something together. [R.H. and Kate are also good friends.] Perhaps the older you get, the less intimidated you get – I hope so.

SURVIVING

In 1985, during the first large round of cutbacks which decimated CBC Vancouver, Joy Coghill, a regional actor on the West Coast who starred in *Ma Murray* and many other CBC television dramas, said, according to Philip Keatley's paraphrase, "It's our fault. We thought when we came into this thirty-five years ago, it was always going to expand; there was always going to be more opportunity; there was always going to be an appreciation and love of the arts and the artists because that is what we have known all our lives. Now, here we are in our mid-fifties and we've discovered that our friends, brothers, and sisters who didn't come into the arts don't think we're that important. The ones who went into law or into business or politics are now telling us that we are not needed. It's our fault that we were so gratuitously self-centred and didn't have the sense to actually see what the 'real' world thinks. We thought we were being appreciated. We're going to have to do something about it ourselves."

It should not be necessary for artists and makers to lobby for the right of the arts to exist. Only in Reagan's United States, Mulroney's (Paul Martin/Jean Chrétien's?) Canada, and Thatcher's Britain would the centrality of the arts in civilized life even be questioned. On the other hand, my belief that the energies of artists should go primarily into the arts, not the politics of the media, is probably an English-Canadian viewpoint. In Quebec, Lise Payette can be a talk-show host, then a PQ cabinet minister, then a writer of several successful *téléromans*. Although, as we have seen, people can shift from cameraman to writer, actor to writer to producer, and director to producer, the world of English-Canadian television is separate from the world of politics – and distinct from pressure groups. In English Canada, culture is still a marginal activity, as Collins so aptly describes it in his introduction to *Culture, Communication and National Identity*.[13] Nevertheless, the CBC is, in itself, an often marginal corporate culture working within a mandate given by an Act of Parliament, and still accountable through the CRTC to its voter/viewers. In the 1990s the CBC's basic survival is in question. By 2000 we will know if it has moved back into or been recognized as part of the cente of our collective sense of self or whether it will have dropped off the edge of the map.

Measured by hours broadcast from 1973 to the mid-1990s, Canadian television drama was a marginal activity at the CBC. But we need to remember our cultural history. In the nineteenth century there were places in Canada haunted by Methodist, Baptist, and Presbyterian sensibilities where plays could only be performed if preceded by a lecture. The performance, according to the polite fiction maintained, was merely an illustration to the edifying words of the speaker. Moreover, this distrust of drama was characteristic of Franco-Catholic culture as well from the time of Frontenac.[14] But Shakespeare's actors were prevented from serving on a jury. Actor/playwright Molière was denied burial in sacred ground. With the exception of classical Greece and not excluding Renaissance England and seventeenth-century France, only a few performing artists have ever lived anything other than marginal lives. It is from the margins that what really matters now and for times to come becomes apparent. Like the prolific Elizabethan playwrights, the makers of television drama in the early years gave no thought to the permanent value of their work – or to the survival of the kines that bring them to life forty years later. Those who live and work on the margins build the bridges between our present and that of our grandchildren. We often say "only" a movie, a play, a sitcom, a docudrama. Yet those dramatic forms are often what we revisit (or revive) to re-enter a little of the past. Cultural histories and after-the-fact analyses merely supply the context for what really matters – the programs themselves.

5 Other Roles behind the Camera

The Drama Department ... issued objectives, and set artistic direction and strategies. But the scale of examination and planning required was impossible by a department alone. There was no integrated plan which recognized that production methods, industrial relations, audience strategy, recruitment and administrative methods were all inseparable. The consequences have been debilitating: The absence of a network strategy has confused and often demoralized the Drama staff. And the production methods and system have defied the efficient production of drama.[1]

As with most large corporate cultures, including those that blend the industrial and the artistic to produce what some practitioners call "programs" and others call "product," the CBC has had seasons of harvest, seasons of fallow, and seasons of drought. Through every season, those off-camera work to keep the machinery running, the workers fed and paid, the communication lines open, and the plans on paper ready for photographing, recording, editing, and play on the air.

UNIT MANAGER AND LINE PRODUCER

The chief facilitator behind the camera is the unit manager. Writer/producer David Barlow started as a unit manager (as did head of TV drama, then head of the western regions, John Kennedy).

BARLOW [1988]: At the CBC, a unit manager is similar to a production manager in an independent production and is responsible for all the contractual arrangements. You are actually a signing authority for the corporation. That's why it's a staff position. You have to go through the RCMP check and all that. You are responsible to the corporation for the budget for the program: for initialling or approving all expenditures related to the program; for making all locations agreements if you're going to film on location; for approving the rental of all equipment and facilities outside the corporation; for keeping track of the hours worked by the crew – that kind of thing. It's part manager, part accountant, part coordinator.

The casting people make the contractual arrangements for the actors.

There is some negotiation, because the way a show is budgeted in-house is that key personnel, particularly in the design area, will estimate costs for your production, and then, as part of the rest of the budget, they will submit the number of hours they need to do the job. So, there is sometimes some gentle negotiation there.

You serve two masters. You are a staff employee, and the producer is often a freelancer. You serve the CBC, because you have to report if it seems the production will go over estimates. You also have to report to the producer if he's embarked on a path that you know will take him over his budget. If it gets to be a problem, then the producer has to negotiate with middle management.

MJM: The unit manager couldn't say to the producer, "You can't spend any more money?"

BARLOW: You can't, really, because you're working for him as well. It's your responsibility diplomatically, without appearing to be a spy, to scurry over to the administrative director and say, "By the way, we're going to go over budget," so he can have a chat with the producer.

MJM: So, this is pretty good training, really, for ...

BARLOW: ... the foreign service!

MJM: That, too! For being a producer.

BARLOW: Yes, it certainly introduces you into the nuts and bolts of how to put together a production at the CBC. It's the business side. It has the management component of having to deal with all the personalities that work on a production. But there is no creative component.

Unit managers sometimes serve on series as "line producers" on the way to becoming "producers." And any producer may pitch in as a line producer, as Joe Partington did for Bill Gough on *Mama's Going to Buy You a Mockingbird* and *Two Men*, and for David Barlow on *Sanity Clause*. As someone experienced with the way the CBC operates, he also worked on the first episodes of *Material World*.

JOE PARTINGTON [1989]: I started in the summer of 1987 on *Material World* as a line producer. The script was done, but I was involved with everything else. I'm not quite sure what the function of the title is, but I think it's to distinguish the creative producer from the organizational producer.

Another person who keeps an eye on the whole story line is the story editor. There was some discussion of the role of story editor from the writer's point of view earlier. The evolution of the role of the story editor in cbc television is a tale going back thirty-five years.

SYDNEY NEWMAN, producer, supervising producer, head of drama, ABC (England), BBC [1984]: What a story editor did in the 1950s is now refined. His job was to go out and get the scripts. When I got to the cbc, there was a central script department. But the success of any play series is just like any magazine. It has to have a character or style of its own. No central department can handle that.

I said that I needed my own story editor and I hired Nathan Cohen [and later George Salverson specifically for *On Camera*]. Cohen knew nothing about television, but he was a man of taste with a very acerbic mind. I defined what I wanted for *General Motors* and I said, "You go out and get the material." He would wine and dine writers, keep them interested, pick their brains if they had any story ideas. If they didn't, Nathan and I would work out ideas that we wanted which were hot and we would commission a writer. I gave him quite a free rein. Then he would work with the writer, when the writer wanted help. When it reached the point where Nat thought the script was a workable proposition, he would come in and say, "I think you should read it now." I would read the script, make my criticisms (which I would then give to Nathan), and he would interpret my criticism to the writer, although sometimes I spoke to the writer myself. Basically, that is what the story editor did.

In fact, I defined the story editor as the protector of the writer – even against the cbc, and later in Britain at ABC and then the BBC.

STORY EDITORS ON SCRIPTS

Alice Sinclair was a story editer who also saw decades of changes before her retirement in 1989.

SINCLAIR [1982]: Doris Gauntlett, Doris Mosdell, and I [the three most influential story editors at the cbc] were known as "the three witches." Although its hard to believe now, the producers in those days were young sprouts, and we were older than any of them. Our nickname wasn't entirely affectionate, because we did have a fair amount of clout.
MJM: In terms of what was chosen, or in terms of what happened to it?

SINCLAIR: What happened to it.

MJM: Would you take a play or something that could be adapted and say what you thought about it?

SINCLAIR: From time to time.

MJM: Robert Allen said the plays were just cut for time, that there was no attempt to adapt them for television.

SINCLAIR: His perception is probably right, because most of the things we were doing were stage plays.

MJM: I asked Allen what might be rewritten, given that this was a different medium. His sense was that, with the pell-mell momentum of getting programs out every week, plays were simply cut to time.

SINCLAIR: I remember one of the most maddening things I ever had to cut was Norman Campbell's *The Merry Widow*, with Mario Bernardi conducting. Every time I came across a piece of expendable dialogue, Mario would say, "You can't cut that, that's over the intro to Maxim's," or something. Naturally, we all wanted to get in as much of the music as possible, but when you came to examine the play, it was one of those well-made plays, with oodles of plot that couldn't be cut.

MJM: When you've been working on a show as a story editor, do you see it through the post-production process?

SINCLAIR: No. The story editor goes up to what you might call the blueprint stage, and then you are not involved in the actual shooting or the post-production stage. But when there is a rough cut, you will be invited (as a courtesy) to that screening. You are free to give general comments about the editing.

MJM: Specifically about the clarity of exposition, the plot line?

SINCLAIR: Yes, and of course it would be only under the most extreme circumstances that we would reshoot at that stage. However, it would be possible to re-edit. The story editor is responsible to the producer and, to an extent, the writer for the script that is going to be shot. Part of the job is making sure that they both share the same vision.

MJM: Bridging between them, translating one to the other?

SINCLAIR: Sometimes, yes, and doing your best to have some creative ideas, about how best to bring out this vision. But the producer is top dog.

MJM: A story editor, then, would take the script to the point where it is going to be shot. Would there be time to consult a story editor on rewrites once the production reached the taping or filming stage?

SINCLAIR: Sometimes yes, sometimes no. When you're out in Saskatchewan with *Nest of Singing Birds*, no. In fact, you may not even be able to consult the writer. But that is all explained in advance to everybody.

MJM: The CBC has a different system from the British, where the writer has control over every line. Basically, they don't rewrite without his or her explicit consent, after the fundamental reorganization in the late 1980s of the BBC and ITV. This too is changing.

SINCLAIR: Certainly you would not make any major changes, particularly changes in construction, without a writer's permission, but if an actor continually "fell about" on a single line, you might alter it. However, performers are dangerous guides. If a performer has difficulty with a line, it is much better for the producer, the director, the story editor, or the writer to rewrite it for the performer. Performers, somehow, don't seem to be good at rewriting their own dialogue. Of course, they're good at getting comfortable dialogue from someone else. I'll tell you the place where changes do sometimes happen. Auditions for the performers take place before the final stage of the script, as a rule. The director and the producer, who have been present at the audition, will sometimes come in and say, "You know so and so gave a really interesting twist to that line. I think it would be a good idea for us to emphasize that twist," something none of us had thought of until that moment.

MJM: Would it be different for a series? Would a performer start to shape a character ...?

SINCLAIR: As Flo Patterson did in *Backstretch*, for example. Yes, but that would come with succeeding scripts. It would be the writer who had seen the performance responding to it. It would not be the performer overtly putting on any pressure. Series like that have their own particular problems in development because they are, in effect, serials. You can't write six at once, however strong your "bible" is, because there are invariably details that don't fit. What you may be able to do is start three with your "bible," get them to a certain stage, and then compare how they're going, so that adjustments can be made to later scripts.

MJM: And since they're likely to be by several different writers, the intermeshing would again be the story editor's problem. Does it make a story editor's job easier, or more difficult, to work with the constraints that series impose?

SINCLAIR: Both.

MJM: So out of the constraint comes creativity.[2]

SINCLAIR: We had an occasion doing *Jalna* in which the young actor who was required to be aged refused to appear in her aged makeup for a key scene. So we tried to figure out who else could be the recipient of that information, and came across somebody else who was just as satisfactory.

I don't know whose original idea it was to have the Whiteoaks in the present as well as in the past. But I know that Fletcher Markle, who was head of drama at the time, was very keen on it, and John Trent, the producer/director, was very keen on it, because early on as a story editor I went to John and said, "I don't think this is going to work."

MJM: Ron Weyman said the same thing ...

SINCLAIR: And John said to me categorically, "If it weren't for that, I wouldn't be interested." So I had a choice between going with it or resigning. John Trent was a super director, and I was very new to film. I thought I would learn more by going with it, so I stayed.

Unfortunately, Alice Sinclair's instincts about the problems of flashbacks and introducing scenes updated to the present were more accurate than those of Fletcher Markle or John Trent. When *Jalna* was sold abroad, it was re-edited in chronological sequence.[3]

SINCLAIR: One of the story editor's jobs for an adaptation is that you have to do a chapter-by-chapter summary, in this case of all the Jalna books. This is for reference, so that when somebody says, "Where the hell did she throw the slipper at Renny?" you can find it.

MJM: An early episode of *Street Legal* was shot with two endings, one much less evocative than the other. Producer Maryke Mc-Ewen's sense was that this second ending was not needed, that to hear from these two runaways, the real mother of the baby in question and her woman lover, to reassure us that they were doing OK, simply destroyed a lot of the resonance of the drama's ambiguities. She thought that all we needed was a scene where Carrington Barr comes in, sees that they have fled, and is absolutely shocked. That's where it ended, and that's where the episode should end – and in fact that was the version shown.

SINCLAIR: I can see it going both ways, that you start with the ambivalent ending, and then nervous brass get after you, so you shoot another one. Then you can show them the one they wanted and demonstrate that it doesn't work. New writers from time to time would ask me if they could see a script. Scripts are kept at the talent bank before going into the York University Archives. Writers could not take scripts out of the talent bank. They had to read them there because of the copyright copying law. We used to keep the script from the first faint notion, if it were written down, to the production script. I always thought that for students of drama that would be more interesting than just seeing the production scripts.

MJM: Absolutely. Access to the process is how you learn. Too often the scholars who are working on the material don't understand that there's process behind the scripts they read. In fact, archivists and especially librarians often want to keep the clean first draft rather than the battered, rewritten, and annotated versions.

As Alice said, the writing process is where the program takes a fundamental shape. I asked her who talked together about the script:

SINCLAIR: The story editor and the writer, and probably the producer, and in some cases the director. Eric Till, for example, is excellent on script, and very creative. We sit around the table brainstorming when something doesn't seem to be going well. The first step on the way to a solution is to ask the right question. It's not always easy to find what's wrong with it, but until you identify that, you're not too far ahead on getting it right. Then, if the session is working well, the wildest ideas will come out from anybody around the table and be picked up by somebody else. It's like a football game. By the time it has been kicked around and you have come across what you think of as a happy solution, it would really be impossible to say who had contributed what.

The first draft of the script of Rough Justice, about a middle-class married man who molests a young girl, and what the law and the court system do to her, was submitted by a court reporter for the Calgary Herald with years of experience.[4] Don Truckey had already written some things for local production (once again illustrating the importance of "farm teams" – opportunities for writers to learn their craft). Maryke McEwen wanted to explore the impersonal workings of our system of justice and asked him to rewrite the script around that focus, keeping his original characters. Later, when it became apparent that scenes between the father and mother were not working well (or as Peter Lower, the story editor, put it, "Nothing interesting was happening; they did not come to life off the page"), the character of the mother was dropped at the suggestion of director Peter Yalden-Thomas. Thus the program, quite appropriately given the subject matter, had an almost entirely male cast.

MJM to writer GRAHAME WOODS [1989]: A script goes in stages from idea to treatment, outline, draft, and so on. Are the story editors there as feedback for you? As question askers?

WOODS: They're there as all those things. Primarily their function is to sit down and say, "OK, this doesn't work. Why doesn't this work?" or "If we play it this way ..." It's a collaboration.

Much of the emphasis in television criticism falls on the image, with dialogue a distant second. Music and sound effects are essential to the creation of atmosphere and mood as well as to clarification of the narrative, yet they are usually ignored.[5]

MJM to writer/producer JEANNINE LOCKE [1989]: When you are thinking about music, how do you articulate what sort of thing you want from a music director or even a composer – in rare instances for special movies, and if the money's available?

LOCKE: *The Greening of Ian Elliot* has "found music" in the show [diagetic music motivated from within the frame]; for example, "This Is My Father's World." There is a scene in which a little song, a favourite of one of the women, "Softly and Tenderly, Jesus Is Calling," is used. With that small-town Saskatchewan setting and those people, the music has to be plain. The film ends with the congregation singing "Be Joyful," which is "Ode to Joy." We always put in some music, because it's almost impossible to do an opening credit sequence if you don't have some music. So I went to the library and got out, not a symphonic, but a very simple piano version of "Ode to Joy." The composer argued with me, but I think "Ode to Joy" works beautifully for us there.

MJM: Under the credits at the end or in the beginning?

LOCKE: At the beginning and the end, because you come out on a hymn which is "Be Joyful."

MJM: Rather than having your composer create something specifically for it.

LOCKE: With the exception of *You've Come a Long Way, Katie*, all my dramas have had music built into the script, and that sets the tone for the score. In *Chautauqua Girl*, based on musical acts used on the 1930s Chautauqua circuit, for example, there was the actual performance of music in the tent and, most effectively, by the Scots Concert Party, which takes its music to an old arthritic farm woman. This was a period piece. Obviously the score had to reinforce the sense of period, just as much as the wardrobe and the props. Same thing in *The Private Capitol*, set at the turn of the century. The patriotic songs sung in the context of enlistment for the Boer War are already there when the composer goes to work.
    Eric Robertson, a composer whose work I admire tremendously,

has done the score for my four most recent dramas: *The Other Kingdom, Island Love Song, The Private Capitol,* and *The Greening of Ian Elliot*. His talent is to use the music already there – the fiddle music of Cape Breton in *Island Love Song* and the hymns that are built into *The Greening of Ian Elliot* – and to integrate it into his score. I don't mean to suggest that his score is simply an adaptation – it's highly original – but it is inspired by the music already there, and you hear echoes in the score. In this way it reinforces the script most effectively – it's not what I call wallpaper music, which is there simply to cover up a weak performance or other flaws. Music is a great binder. It helps to create seamlessness and to advance the action. A strong score behind landscape can actually expand it beyond the size of the TV screen – it is thrilling to have that happen. But a powerful emotional scene is usually cheapened, I believe, by music. To sum up: I wish I were a musician instead of a drama producer – the satisfaction must be so immediate for musicians.

MJM: Talking about the setting, the people, that kind of bridging music and so forth, presumably Roberston had to come up with a score that embodies those qualities.

LOCKE: Yes.

MJM: Something that sounds plain and strong and appropriate to the prairies, sky-scrapers, and so on.

LOCKE: Our theme in *The Private Capitol* was "Minstrel Boy," which is what "our Bessie" sings just before the party for the soldiers. So "Minstrel Boy" keeps recurring. But there is one scene in the living-room of Bessie's parents after "our Bessie" (along with Mackenzie King's great friend, Bert Harper) drowned at a Government House skating party. At the very end of this scene, Mackenzie King talks about Harper, who died trying to save Bessie, and he says, "A chivalrous act, a chivalrous Knight, Bert, our Galahad." When we were doing the mix, Eric had written a music cue that started over Mackenzie King's lines, and I said to the editor, "Of course we are not going to use that cue. (The editor just puts in the cues because it is very useful to have them there for the mix.) As far as I'm concerned, it doesn't come in until the following scene." And he said, "Well I guess that's the big difference between this show and most of the shows I have mixed. In those, there would have been music over that entire scene."

MJM: Too often there is no trust in simple sound effects, no trust in the human voice.

LOCKE: And no trust in the audience – that the audience would care for Bessie and have some notion of who Bert Harper was.

MJM: One of my major irritations in television over the years has been the way that music is abused. Yet there are also some brilliant scores.

LOCKE: Oh yes, and music can bind together a sequence. We put music behind a scene in *The Greening* – and the music made it work. It had never worked before.

THE EVOLUTION OF TELEVISION SOUND EFFECTS AND MUSIC

Mixing sound on sixteen tracks in a modern studio is very different from trying to use music and sound effects in the days of live television. Now retired from the CBC, Ed Vincent was a sound technician from the days of radio and early television, and then a music consultant for many years.

MJM to VINCENT [1989]: There would be some relationship between creating sound effects in radio and the early days of live television. But they would not work in the same way, would they?

VINCENT: In radio, it was a different setup. You were in the studio with the actors and you worked with what they called a "cocktail bar," because you were able to mix records. (It seems very primitive today). There were doors and coconut shells [for horses' hooves] and things like that. I loved all that stuff. Well, in television it was different because they set you up in the control room rather than "on the floor." Although they had cocktail bars there at the beginning, too, most of the live sounds were done by the actors or stage people on the floor. So you wouldn't be required to knock on doors and do footsteps and things like that. This meant a whole new atmosphere. You're in a control room with twenty other people, and you're away from the actual action on the floor.

MJM: Could you see the performance? [In radio, live or live-to-disk or tape, sound-effects technicians shared the actors' space on the floor. The technicians who ran the "grams" or the turntables were up with the producers, and could see the floor from a booth.]

VINCENT: You could see it only on the monitor, unlike radio where you had an uninhibited view of the area of operation. You might have had a huge window, but it was probably blocked off with a flat or a set. At the beginning in CBC television in Toronto, sound effects in the television area were an afterthought. They had these control rooms built, and each control room seemed to have what they called an "observation gallery" for visitors. That lasted about three-and-a-half weeks before they realized, "Hey! We need this for operations." So they turned the visitors' gallery into an open sound-effects area, up above the control room. That was interesting in itself. Some people would still be allowed to come in, and that was really strange. Later, they realized that sound effects requires space of its own, so the studios incorporated a separate room for the sound-effects operation with a glass panel in between, always next to the audio man.

In sound effects we weren't responsible for the sound coming in from the floor. That was the audio man. We would feed him our signal. But he didn't want to "ride the pot" [potentiometer – volume control], as they say. We would do that ourselves. He had enough problems with the two booms [which held mikes in position tracking the actors when they moved]. If we needed his help, we would ask him (particularly when our levels seemed to go up and down), "Did you touch the pot?" "No, I didn't touch it." "Well, it's higher now." We still don't know to this day how it varied. I think it was a ghost. We would also be required to go down to the floor to do some live effects, but generally speaking they were done upstairs in the control room.

MJM: What kind of rehearsal did you have?

VINCENT: The days of live television were very long days. Usually the crew call was about 7:30 in the morning, and you probably would be on the air about 9 o'clock at night with a live show. You'd get your script in advance because you'd have to prepare the effects. You would go to a meeting with the other people. The director would discuss the play with the set designer and everyone else. For an hour-long show on Friday night, we'd have two days; on Thursday an all-day rehearsal, and Friday all day, then the show. Variety shows got just one day. They were probably a little less demanding for sound effects. But with the variety show in the earlier days, 1953–56, sound effects would involve things like audience reaction, that sort of thing. We'd be using "soft cuts" for that. A soft cut is a recording you have made on an acetate disk of applause and so on. This was before tape.

MJM: You had many disks spinning?

VINCENT: Oh yes! With the cocktail bar you could have three, or you could gang up two of them and have six. It wasn't sophisticated, but it was fun.

MJM: Music and sound-effects were created by the same person?

VINCENT: Yes. When we were dealing with drama, the sound–effects person would be responsible for all the sound effects as well as the "ambient" sounds [the sounds that create the acoustic environment that defines the space] that you might want to throw in; it was pretty well up to you to create that, unless the director had some specific thoughts. Then, if there was a film clip, you'd try to match up what was required.

As well as the sound effects, you would be required to play back (off the turntable) recorded music that was made especially for television. There would be a music consultant in your control room with you and he would give you the records. He would say, "Cut three, cut four," and you'd play that music along with your effects. We were pretty busy. Because of union jurisdiction, he wasn't allowed to play the music, but he would hand you the music, and if you were busy you'd really rely on his being right there. As I say, in live days there was no opportunity to stop and go again. It was wild. I don't think I would do it again, but I'm glad I had the experience. But this "10, 9, 8, 7, 6, 5, 4, 3, 2, 1! Ready!" holding a record, and everyone's waiting for this opening music. We would also be responsible for the fading in and the fading out, the mixing. It was immediate mixing in those days.

MJM: Who cued you?

VINCENT: In the case of music, generally the music consultant. The producer was on the same level, two rooms away. We could see him vaguely, but even though we had intercom, he was too busy with his pictures and actors and cameras. He pretty well left us alone. If he specifically wanted something from effects, he might cue us. But we were pretty well on our own with the music consultant.

When you did it live, the actors would often change their pace.

MJM: So you'd be glued to the monitor.

VINCENT: Right! We couldn't do anything about the drama running short or long if it was a background piece of music. We hoped it would work out well. For the most part, I think it did.

MJM: When I watched that material, I was surprised at how smooth some of the complex ninety-minute dramas were. There was specially composed music for some of them. Did it arrive on a disk, or how did that work?

VINCENT: Later, there would occasionally be specially composed music and we would play that off the quarter-inch tape as if it were a record. But in the earliest days of television, *General Motors Theatre* and those, we wouldn't be using original music. I'm talking about video drama now [live to kinescope or tape], not film. Occasionally, we used some music of Morris Surdin on *The Devil's Instrument*, for example.[6]

MJM: He was a great radio composer.

VINCENT: Yes. I worked with him later in television as a music consultant. I don't want to get ahead of what we're talking about here, but when we used original music later, it was done in a more sophisticated way because we had sixteen-track mixing, where it would be post-production as in film.

Some of the problems we had were due to the fact that we were fighting inadequate equipment. I was never one to complain, I just accepted what I had and did the best I could with it.[7] But it certainly was not state-of-the-art. Some of the radio equipment and most of the equipment in television audio was designed by CBC people. In Studio 7 and Studio 1, the equipment for sound effects was simply a couple of turntables. Then they got into remote buzzers and bells – that's what gave you trouble. I remember that one didn't work. Fortunately, we were into video tape at that time.

MJM: So you could stop and fix it?

VINCENT: Yes. That sort of thing happened. But we did the best we could with it, and seemed to get by for the most part. Playing the music and playing background music, voice-over, narration, and sound effects were our job. In the early days of variety, the union would not allow us to pre-record.

We got away with so much. When I think about it now, I get palpitations – which I did then, although there was a very good tight feeling at times. Every show seemed to have a particularly tough sequence. I would be thinking how "Act 2, Scenes 1 and 3" would go. And I'd hope I didn't do anything wrong or that it would work as well as I'd hoped. But never did I come away from any show thinking it was as good as it could have been. Instead, I was thinking, "Gosh, I hope people haven't noticed the problems."

During the broadcast, the producer/director was preoccupied, trusting the music consultants and the technician to get on with it. Ron Weyman talks about his reliance on them to achieve the effects he needed.

WEYMAN producer, executive producer [1987]: The music was being pumped in from records. Suppose the scene, which had been playing at a certain pace, in fact got quicker or slowed down. The actor would be looking at someone a moment longer. The poor guy with the music has put on the music, but it is running out! But the lady is still sort of making up her mind, or whatever it is. Well, you can't have the music running out, therefore he would have at least two disks running at the same time, so he could then switch and cover.

DAVID GARDNER, actor/producer [1983]: In drama, most of the music was recorded, which meant that it had to be cued; you had to time the music out carefully. You had music consultants, like Andy Duesbury (who is now dead) and Eddie Vincent, who hunted music for you to fit in particular bits. Say you needed twenty-six seconds of dark, moody music, when somebody goes up a set of stairs, then something for tripping down the street and dragging a piece of wood along a railing fence or something of that nature. Mostly, music was recorded. But Norman Campbell's big ballet productions had to have a live orchestra for the dancers to dance to.

VINCENT: You also had an opportunity to fill in with atmospheric sounds, and I enjoyed that – throwing in a dog bark somewhere. For a while that was my identification. There'd be no dog on the set, you'd never see it, but just for some atmosphere. That, per- haps, came from radio, too. But when I opened the door, went out on the street or in the country, I would have my sparrows going, crows and things. Of course we didn't see them. So it was import- ant, even in a locked-in, live, "studio-bound" show.

In the live days of television, there was no such thing as "post- production" or sound mixing. Most of the music was available on records from various libraries in England. Now it's a multimillion dollar business. When we first started, I think we had about fifty records from Boosey and Hawkes and from Chappell, the music publishers. That was it. And then some of these libraries slowly came on the market, and the music consultant had a wider range from which to choose. Before the sophisticated post-production techniques, we did occasionally use original music off a quarter- inch tape, played back directly into the show. But I don't remem- ber that as happening often. It was mainly recorded material.

MJM: People don't notice this kind of sound tapestry, but it makes the painted sets work. I'm thinking of Eric Till's *Offshore Island*. He was known for liking plays that took place outdoors and trying to get people to build sets that looked like outdoors. If it didn't sound like outdoors, all that illusion would fall apart.

You wouldn't have the radio problems of creating a three-dimen- sional space in the same way, because you'd have the studio itself and people would be moving to and from mikes already in place or moving with the actors. What would happen, for example, if an actor slammed a stage door. Was the sound heard the one the stage door made or was it one you supplied?

VINCENT: I worked on an early play Robert Allen produced called *Justice* on the problem of the cell door. We took the cell door from the old radio studio, across the parking lot, brought it into the television studio on the floor, and I set up a microphone. I clanked, closed the door, looking at a monitor. We did the stage cell door live, and I had to watch a monitor just like anyone watching, as if I were at home, to try to match it. It worked pretty well. That was one of the first of the dramas produced by Robert Allen. Sometimes there would be the luxury of having two sound effects men on the show, one in the booth and one on the floor, because some of the sound effects had to be augmented in this way. Car doors were the same, although they would probably have an actual car in a studio. A lot of it was quite good, but it could have been a lot better.

I remember one show where Barbara Hamilton played the part of a character who was clipping roses. They wanted the sound of the rose protesting. We worked on that and devised some kind of sound. A tree falling slowed to 78 rpm sounds quite different.

Video tape was a help because if something went wrong, we could always do it again. But still it took a long time, and they couldn't sync music or sound effects electronically all through the 1960s and 1970s. When I was working on shows such as *The Great Detective* [1979–81], it was taped, edited, and we could stop anywhere and go back. Nevertheless, in post-production the sound-effects technician had to start the music or the effect at the proper time manually, by looking at the monitor. We did have a device that gave us time and thirty frames to a second in video; for example, in 14½ seconds this music begins. But still it required the technician to play the music or the effect manually to the picture, looking at the monitor as you would at home.

In film, the technique is to take a piece of material and lock it up to that very frame, so you have $\frac{1}{24}$ of a second control [which made film sound tracks much easier to mix, another reason why many producers and directors preferred to work on film]. That's been true of film for years.[8]

MUSIC CONSULTANT

The job of the music consultant evolved along with the rest of the technology.

VINCENT: Producers like Mel Breen would come in to the record library where Andy Duesbury was working in the late 1950s. They didn't have time for music, but they knew they needed it. They'd go to the library and say, "Please help me." Andy was the one they'd ask for help. He was a nice guy, he was helpful, he knew music, and he had a dramatic flair. So they all cornered Andy. It got to the point where the record librarian said, "You either work with them or me." Sid Newman was smart, a very smart man. He could see this happening. He said, "My producers want this man, Andy Duesbury. Who the hell is he?" So he went and said, "Do you want to work for us?" "Oh, I guess so." "Come on over." That's how it started; that's how he became a music consultant for these producers.

MJM: After you were hired to help him, you worked out the assignments between you?

VINCENT: Pretty well. It sort of fell into place. Andy would do *For the Record* or something like that and some of the specials. The sound effects technicians worked separately.

MJM: From the music person?

VINCENT: Occasionally, we'd phone each other, and I'd say, "What are you doing in sequence so and so?" "Well, I've got a problem here and ..." And I'd say, "I've covered that with music." "Oh great!" That was not necessarily the way it was going to be in the final mix, because the producer had the final word. For the most part we went our individual ways on both tape and film. If the character went outdoors, the sound effects man would have to be concerned about the effects: the door closing and the footsteps and so on. But the decision would be made later at the mix as to the balance of both music and sound effects.

MJM: Would the other people working on the drama want more music?

VINCENT: Very often they would. I can't tell you how many times they'd say, "The show needs music; it needs help." There would be places where I would look at the scene and say, "I don't think you need it." "Oh yeah, we need it. Needs energy." "Energy," that was the favourite word of some people. As music consultants, we didn't throw music in just because we were music consultants. We tried to be judicious about it. But very often they would want a line of music somewhere. You'd think, "Really?" Usually those requirements were difficult because it wasn't an obvious place to put a line of music.

MJM: For *The Great Detective*, which is set in the nineteenth century, where would you find appropriate music for that?

VINCENT: I wish we could do it over again now, because there's more available. You always wish that. In the case of recorded music, material was coming in all the time. Every three or four weeks there would be a batch of music.

Usually you had finished a show and then a record would come in that would be just right. To give you an example, the theme for *The Great Detective* came off a ten-inch album dealing with the Victorian period. There were about six, eight cuts, four or five on each side. The composer was Paul Lewis, who seems to have specialized in Victorian music. (Andrew Duesbury was the music consultant.) We found this piece and called the executive producer and the producer at that time. They didn't jump at it right away; they wanted some alternatives, which we found. We didn't have too much from which to choose because the music has to be copyright clearable; you can't just throw on something because "it would be marvellous" without it costing you an arm and three legs. There are several libraries that produce this music. You buy it and you pay them for the use of it. It's $60 a minute or something. It sounds like a lot of money, but it isn't really in relative cost.

MJM: The theme was wonderful, energetic ...

VINCENT: It has character. I think it was like Dougie Campbell's character (he played the Great Detective). One interesting thing: the executive producer liked the piece, but he wanted a drum roll at the beginning, which wasn't on the cut – a snare drum. But we found a snare – brbrbrbr ... pum pumpum. So we added that. But then we had to put that in on every episode. Sometimes the credits were of different lengths, and that required editing.

MJM: The theme was also used in the bridges to commercials.

VINCENT: Oh yes, though very often we would use dramatic music to get into the break. If he's come across a dead body or something, there might be a "sting" to go into the commercial, because it wouldn't be appropriate to use the signature tune.

MJM: Was there more than one music consultant on a show?

VINCENT: No, but we worked together. We would look at each other's work very often and bounce ideas off each other.

MJM: After you'd seen the episode, were you allowed some leeway in choosing music?

VINCENT: Yes, quite a bit. As you went through it again, you made additions or changes. Then you were so bold as to have it transferred, without the director hearing it, onto quarter-inch tape in sequence. That meant simply taking records over to the sound-effects area and having them transferred to audio. Then we edited it into a sequence. Usually, in an hour show, there were about twenty-six cues of different pieces of music, perhaps more. I enjoyed editing. You took a bar out or lengthened it. It was fun. Then you called the director before you went to the mix, and you played it for him with the picture. You'd push the tape in and he'd look at it and say "Marvellous" or "Not sure of that." So then you made any changes that were necessary and you didn't see him again until the mix – the moment of truth. We called it the "mix down."

MJM: That's when everything is put together?

VINCENT: Yes. I take the tape to the mix day – it's usually one day to mix it. You give the sound-effects man the music track and you go through the film or tape with the time code [which allows everyone to cue the track to individual frames or sequences]. He has to push the button to cue and record at the right time. If it doesn't work, you have to stop and get it right. You've gone through the tape in a couple of hours and have to put those twenty-six pieces on a sixteen-track. Then you have a coffee while the sound-effects person does his bit. Next you're layering tracks. The sound-effects person might want two tracks for his sounds. I might want two tracks, too – to go from one music piece to another, or to do something fancy with that music track; for example, "source music" [film people call this kind of music diagetic, when the source is visible, as with a dance band, or when it can be inferred from the setting, as with a nightclub]. On *The Great Detective* we very seldom had "source." But if it was a contemporary setting, you might want a radio effect. Now you've got the sound on two tracks, the music perhaps on two tracks, and there are also a couple of dialogue tracks. At that point you start it all together, as in film, and you begin to "mix down," which I always enjoyed, because that was the moment of truth and of balance.

MJM: I've found in drama film specials, like those shown on *For the Record*, that the producers got involved in these final mixes. Did they not get as involved in electronic drama?

VINCENT: Yes, but in electronic drama the director always had a lot to say. A good example is *The Great Detective*. A director such as Jack Nixon Browne (bless him he's gone), would come in and sit very closely with us and we'd talk about the balance. Later on, they often would involve the producer. Sometimes it was very distressing, because you'd have three people sitting in there – director, producer, and (rarely) executive producer.

MJM: Would it be the same process for sitcoms as it was for the longer dramas?

VINCENT: No, sitcoms usually had original themes and very little music. And if they did, they would have the person who did the original music theme do some little playoffs [music transitions to commercials or station breaks] later. But we were never involved in sitcoms that way. Rather, in drama, electronic drama, and documentaries, *The Nature of Things*, things like that.

MJM: How did you carry all the music coming into the library in your head?

VINCENT: It wasn't a problem. As new material came in, we would listen to it. Our librarian would call us and we'd go over and listen. If you had a retentive memory, it was helpful. But now it's to the point where you can't possibly keep up. Yet I still know, even today, where to go for such themes as the Victorian music – the de Wolfe "library." Each library seemed to specialize in certain kinds of music. But you really had to go over there and just listen.

MJM: The process as you describe it is very creative, because you are in effect presenting choices, suggestions about where and how much music and what kind should be used in particular, or where it can be used as counterpoint. Would you make a decision, for example, that a scene might need a little ironic or other dramatic counterpoint?

VINCENT: Oh yes, I did that fairly often. We didn't always succeed, but we would try to do that.

MJM: Did you work on the filmed cop shows like *Side Street* and that kind of thing?

VINCENT: Yes.

MJM: What would be the difference between that and *The Great Detective*?

VINCENT: With the cop shows, you're working with a genre where you haven't got much scope. It's action. There could be dramatic moments, but it's either "subjective" music or it's "action." Action music is action music, although there were dramatic moments there too. The cop shows started out with recorded music and then went into original. There was a larger library of music for that kind of show than for *The Great Detective*. Some producers say they'd rather work with recorded music.

Whether it appears on the music charts or in the supermarket muzak, or simply remains a signature tune, title music is very important. Steven Bochco, co-creator and first executive producer of the much honoured 1980s American series *Hill Street Blues*, went so far as to say that he thought his title music was "a substantial reason for the series' ultimate success."[9] The off-hand theme for *M*A*S*H* is still heard as easy listening music, perhaps retaining its ironic tone for those who remember the series, pleasant for those who do not.

VINCENT: Apparently [director of entertainment] Thom Benson had some ideas about what the theme for *The Beachcombers* should sound like. After some discussion and some "nudge, nudge, wink, wink" sort of thing, it was decided that the music would be done out of Vancouver. Philip Keatley, the first producer, had Bobby Hales, a local jazz musician, in mind. He pretty well left the setup to us; he was good that way. He and I had given Bobby the piece I had previously selected from the recordings library to give him some guidelines. There were also a couple of phone calls from head of drama Fletcher Markle about what they would like the theme to include. By this time Bobby wondered why he got involved in this whole thing, but it worked out fairly well. We had a nice little Greek dance in that original *Beachcombers* theme which I think worked quite well for Bruno's character [Gerussi played Nick Adonidas, the protagonist]. I remember being at the recording studios when we did the actual recording of that theme. When I got back to Toronto I sent Thom Benson a copy, suggesting that he should listen to it and that he would come to love it. It worked for several years.

As a sideline to that story, some years later another show was developed out of Vancouver called *Ritter's Cove* (1979–81), a CBC co-production with West Germany. The producer of that series stipulated to Kerry MacIntyre, the music consultant in Vancouver, that he didn't want a Beachcomber's kind of feel for the theme. Just as a joke, I suppose, I let Kerry hear the same theme I had originally chosen for *Beachcombers* and he loved it! It became the theme for *Ritter's Cove*.

Sometimes an original score becomes a completely integral part of a good drama – memorable without being obtrusive. I watched a "mix-down" of the sound and tracks for Maryke McEwen's *Rough Justice* (1984), a piece written by Don Truckey on what happens when a child is forced to confront the justice system that protects her molester.[10]

The particular situation that provides the dramatic conflict is a case of sexual assault on a ten-year-old girl. With the changes to the law in the 1980s, which distinguished between various degrees of assault, and the dearth of case law as precedent in each category, the script posits that the Crown has decided to make this instance a test case of "sexual assault causing bodily harm." Ironically, as the drama demonstrates, the prosecution and the time in jail and in court taught the well-to-do molester how to get away with his crime. For the defence lawyer, the case is simply a further excuse for cynicism and a mildly troubling incident in a successful practice; for the police, just another frustration; and for the judge, the completion of an average morning's docket. But it is also an unforgettable trauma for the father and his daughter, who is the victim not only of the assault but also of the plea-bargaining and the career-oriented, clubby system of justice in Canada. Throughout the film, the facts are never in question in the mind of the viewer; the far more disturbing issue is the fairness of our justice system.

I watched one sequence of *Rough Justice* as it was mixed with the "fine cut" or last edit of the film. Given the subject matter and approach, the choice of electronic music was just right. The cold music on the synthesizer reflected the style of the camera work and the dramatic construction. In the three or four weeks after the film was shot, the composer looked at a rough work print of the film twice through with the producer, noting where the music would be appropriate. After the third run through, they discussed where the cues should come and what they should sound like. The composer met the producer three more times while he was writing the music, giving him an idea of what the music would sound like. After he had finished writing the music, the musicians and the composer got together to lay down the music tracks.

Finally, the sound track of dialogue and sound effects, additional sound effects, and the music were mixed, frame by frame, with the producer, the director, the editor, and the composer all there. During the mix, they listened for sound levels and quality, considering where the cues should come in, when they should be faded out, and whether there should be music under a scene. For example, during the plea-bargaining between the lawyers, the crown attorney removes his robes as he admits defeat, while the lawyer who is defending the molester dresses for court. The camera observes the defence lawyer negotiating with the image of the crown attorney in the mirror. As the defence lawyer wins his points, he takes over the centre of the mirror.

His random whistling, the footsteps casually overheard, and the cold resonance of the room itself make an effective accompaniment to this casual poker game with people's lives. The music seemed to undercut the carefully understated tone of the dialogue and the performances, and to overstate the shifts of emotion. After looking at it with and without the music, everyone agreed to omit that particular music cue. In theory, producer Maryke McEwen would be the arbiter in any disagreement, but in fact the director, Peter Yalden-Thomas, did much of the negotiating in this instance, and most of the minute but crucial decisions were arrived at collectively.

The music during the climactic preliminary hearing is not "music" but single tones, heart-beats, claps, echoes, electronic sounds in various perspectives and at various levels, building a sense of the child's growing fear and revulsion. When she breaks down at the trial, the scene disintegrates into a series of fragments, the father scooping up the child and rushing out of the court, the judge calling an adjournment, the officers lunging forward, the defence attorney muttering "You bastard" to the crown attorney. The sound effects and dialogue are mixed, so there is the right balance of the sounds of court confusion, the child's sobs, and the key lines. The music bridges the inside of the courtroom and the exchange between the father and the crown attorney on the huge staircase outside (including a change of the acoustic atmosphere and a cross-fade of the noise of the court with corridor sounds). Sound, music, and picture synchronize to an appropriately abrupt conclusion – to be followed immediately by a cut to the quiet sounds of ice-cubes clinking in a glass as the defence lawyer tells his partner about the day's events.

In most television drama, the music conventions come straight from Hollywood B films, formula radio drama, and ultimately from nineteenth-century melodrama. In mysteries and copshows, music is routinely used to pump up the emotions, signal suspense, pick up the pace, fill in with spurious romance or excitement when the action flags, and tell the viewer that it's all right to laugh. Music can fix mistakes. When we don't know who a character is because she moved too quickly, the music can tell us.[11]

A COMPOSER'S PERSPECTIVE

Phil Shriebman's music on *Seeing Things* performed some of those functions, but in many ways it was non-formulaic.[12] Consequently, it had its own following among the audience. People noticed and enjoyed it for its own sake, which was a real asset to the show as long as Shriebman avoided the danger of upstaging the program as a whole. Careful attention to the musical allusions in a show can be very rewarding; for example, in an early episode of *Seeing Things*, during a crucial speech in which a rabbi evoked the war and its anguish, the accompanying music sounded like a Kaddish (a prayer said as memorial for the dead).

Schreibman did not use standard repetitive cues for standard scenes, in part because there were very few formulaic scenes of the car chase, kiss, or "He's got a gun on me" type. All those incidents did occur in the series, but his fondness for the elements of comedy, satire, and parody, which was shared by co-producers David Barlow and Louis Del Grande, undercut the "insert cue 22 again" approach. Louis Ciccone, the protagonist, has been rescued by a slapshot that knocked the villain cold, by a cake thrown at the villain, and by a rabbi in a yeshiva. This kind of climax is not conducive to formula music writing. In fact, Schreibman wrote a complete score of fifty to eighty cues for every show – an unusually high number of music cues for any series.

His contribution began when he got a copy of the work print on cassette (often the script changed so much during the shoot that it was not of much use to him). With the help of a VCR, he made a list of cues, indicating where he thought music belonged in the episode. After consulting with Barlow, he sat down and wrote a full score for the show, which he tried out for timing and effect on a synthesizer connected to the VCR's stereo system. All this was accomplished in two weeks.

Next he rehearsed for two days with his musicians, using the same group every time plus extra people when required and when the budget allowed. The next day they recorded in an all-day session. Schreibman and sound editor Kevin Townshend then mixed the multiple sound tracks, enhancing this one and balancing that to produce one music track ready for the final sound-mixing session.

Successful sound is unobtrusive. As with design, sound effects should usually be what the audience might expect to hear, generally uncluttered and always subordinate to the dialogue. This was crucial to a comedy/action drama like *Seeing Things*, where one-liners were tossed off all the time. Often those lines were lost in the original recording of the take and had to be dubbed later in the studio. The sound editor could also remove extraneous sounds or add in a tire screech or birdsong missing from the actual take. Since *Seeing Things* often substituted the imaginative destruction of objects for shooting, maiming, and fist-fights, the series gave the sound effects' person a chance to play with all kinds of reverberation, electronic enhancement, and odd sounds to create the sound equivalent of an exploding telephone booth or a motor boat gone berserk.[13]

CAMERA: "WITHOUT WHICH ..."

Despite the preceding emphasis on the sound and music that support the performances, television drama should not be radio with pictures. One of the visual conventions for which CBC docudrama became known was the adaptation of the conventions of "direct" cinema – hand-held camera, quick movement, composition that seemed simply to catch the subject on the run, self-reflexive sequences acknowledging the camera as subject as well as observer. Ron Kelly's *The Open Grave* (1963) was an early and well-known example internationally.

WOODS: Producer Ron Kelly had a lot of clout. He said, "I want Grahame Woods," and so it came about that my name was synonymous with the hand-held camera.

By this time CBC had bought its own hand-held camera, and I was using that. I had worked mostly using that hand-held camera with one sound man and then another, Jerry King. The relationship between the camera and sound men is important. You have to know each other's movements and thoughts well, in terms of anticipating action, particularly on documentary where there are no scripts.

MJM: You mean to say, if you suddenly wanted to move to get that shot, the sound man has to be right with you.

WOODS: And make sure he doesn't get his microphone in the shot. Particularly when you're working in a hospital situation, as we were in a documentary. When somebody's rushing in for emergency surgery from a motorcycle accident, you've got to fade into the woodwork. So, it needs tremendous rapport. As a cameraman, you don't do a film and then have a break and do another one. The minute you finish one, literally the next day you're on another one. In 1964 I was also doing a film with Ron Kelly on Bruce Kidd, because he was our great hope for a medal at the Tokyo Olympics. This was one of the exciting things about working with Ron. He also had this idea about "what happened to a child of Hiroshima, twenty years later." So he got on the phone to Thom Benson (he was good friends with Thom) and said, "Look, we're here, we've got the footage, think of the money you're saving, why don't we do this film?" It was called *The Gift*.

From a photographer's standpoint, that has to be one of the highlights. Shooting this film was like one big high – again with a hand-held, a mimimum of equipment. We invented as we went along. I think it was one of the best things I have ever shot. We did it in something like seven days, which was unheard of. I felt if I stood on my head and pointed the camera I'd get a fantastic shot.

You've got the whole production going through your camera, and if you screw up, the first thing they jump on is either the lab or the cameraman, nobody else.

MJM: Tell me something. Do the directors set up the composition, or do they tell you roughly what they want? Is it their fault if it doesn't look right?

WOODS: I was lucky in that most directors let me do it. We'd talk, I'd say, "How do you see it?" and I would set up the shot for them.

MJM: They would block it, you would frame it.

WOODS: They would block it, yes, and I would say, "Why don't you shift this a little bit?"

MJM: Would that involve the actors as well?

WOODS: Yes.

MJM: You would suggest business to the director ...

WOODS: Let's talk about *Wojeck*. There are different characters. It's also the first time that CBC drama made a series (*Cariboo Country* excepted) on location. These directors have worked exclusively in studios. The Wojeck house was Ron Weyman's house. And the camera would be jammed up into a corner in that pokey little kitchen. But that first year it was a new experience for everybody involved in the whole production. It was exciting. If you're lucky, it happens to you once in your career. Since then, they've done a lot of dramas, a lot of series. But I don't think any of them had the same kind of momentum within the crew, and that translates onto the screen.

You have all these built-in hazards that you have to overcome. You've got to light the scene, but at the same time you've got to make sure you don't see the lights in the shot, the little things.

MJM: And it can't look "lit." Were there no sets at all for *Wojeck*? For example, his office and so on?

WOODS: The office was built in an old ambulance station on Davenport. But even the sets were built in actual locations, so you still had some of the restrictions. I did all but one of the first ten episodes, and I think all except two of the second ten.

MJM: So there was a particular personal visual style that was yours, an overview that was Ron Weyman's (who also selected the directors), and a writer who wrote all the scripts for the first season [Philip Hersch]. David Peddie was another of the key players in the *Wojeck* team, working with film and developing all the scripts.

WOODS: In studio drama you had your Eric Tills and your George McGowans and your Mario Prizeks who did shape the show and were responsible for it. Most of them called the shots. They sat in the control room: "tighten that shot, pan the light." The cameraman with the live camera was just a technician, he pointed it wherever. Now it's a technicians' union. They are not paid to be creative and they believe it, so they aren't creative. Obviously there have been some very good ones, particularly those who have worked on *Festival*. But producers, particularly in a series, are given a lot of power, and a lot of times they misuse it.

The freedom Grahame Woods enjoyed in the 1960s shooting film for Ron Weyman, or that the studio cameramen enjoyed working live with Paul Almond or Mario Prizek, has become rare. The "look" of a series, the visual conventions of a genre, and the weekly turnaround can restrict the creativity of those who actually shoot the scenes. Steve Bochco commented that *Hillstreet Blues*, with its "sloppy, messy, ragged" look that was different from the 1980s American (though not Canadian) television, posed a problem for director of photography Bill Cromager. Up to that point people had been fired "for not giving [producers] the kind of brightly lit, clean-looking film they wanted."[14]

In a 1991 conversation, producer Maryke McEwen talked about choosing both directors and directors of photography. She was looking for people who could understand the subject and script, and then find that "look" or "feel" the style she needed for a docudrama about street kids. In her view, continuous work on series television can blunt the sensibilities of both directors and directors of photography. Director George McGowan, however, could switch from the paint-by-number format of American copshows to the many quirks of *Seeing Things* with no apparent difficulty.

DIRECTOR OF PHOTOGRAPHY

Several years earlier, in 1984, Maryke McEwen talked about the collaboration between the producer/director and the director of photography.

MCEWEN: Brian Hebb [who did eight dramas on *For the Record*] reads the scripts. He gets involved in preparation, a lot more than some of the other guys. He thinks dramatically with his eyes, and some cameramen don't. They can make you a nice picture, but it is not necessarily the right picture for the scene or for the dramatic content. Brian has good drama sense and it works; it shows in his pictures.

MJM: I would presume that a director could block a scene so he couldn't do that. It's the collaborative thing again.

MCEWEN: Brian and director Peter Yalden-Thomson (*Rough Justice*) have a really good relationship. I think they complement each other. Each one is better for the other one. If Brian got a director who didn't have Peter's strong sense of visuals, he would waver as well. He would get bored and do a dolly shot where it doesn't belong, or light a scene not quite the way it should be. He needs somebody to work with, to feed on, but then we all do. Brian is better for Peter and Peter is better for Brian, because they have each other.

The reason Brian is leaving the CBC is that he needs more of a challenge. He needs to work in 35 mm and he needs to work for himself. He also needs to work in an environment where he's appreciated. He's appreciated by me and when he's working with me that's fine, but the minute he's finished my show they put him on a street interview or something because they don't have another cameraman available. That is not respecting his skills as a director of photography. On the plus side for Brian, he's been able to do all kinds of drama, work with all kinds of people, learn from some of the best lighting and cameramen, like Norman Allen, and do documentary when he felt like it. If he wants to do a documentary, there's lots of work for him. It's fun travelling, and you can meet different people.[15]

R.H. THOMSON, actor [1989]: If I am playing a small part it doesn't matter, but if I am actually carrying a fair bit of the story I try to understand what the director of photography is doing. I try to understand what he is looking for, and to see if I can either play into it or play with it. A creative DOP is up to something and you have to understand how he will see things. You can help him ...

MJM: How?

THOMPSON: Just by where a scene gets blocked. You see from the way he is lighting the set that he wants it to look a certain way. If he is a guy who likes deep shots, you play stuff in shadows. If a DOP couldn't ask for another take, he'd give me the look and I would ask for it. If I needed another take and just couldn't ask for it, he would say there was something wrong. Because good DOPS are up to something. I want to understand where and how I fit into the picture in the brain. I don't mean cold-heartedly or cold-bloodedly. It does affect how one places one's work.

Nick Evdemon, the director of photography for forty-two episodes of *Seeing Things*, echoed art director Dan Yarhi when he said that the overall style for this series was romantic and warm.[16] He characterized the normal style of mystery genre as "harsh, high contrast, flash." He was also cinematographer on the last year of the 1970s copshow *Sidestreet*. The shooting style he used was adapted somewhat to each episode, but the basic problem was to find an appropriate style. The demands of comedy are quite different from the shadowy world of mystery. For one thing, the jokes are often sight gags, thus more lighting is required. According to Evdemon, the equipment in the 1980s was better and more sensitive than it was for *Sidestreet*. Thus he could use far more sophisticated techniques.

With location shooting, particularly in the changeable weather of southern Ontario's temperate climate or Vancouver's "sunshine coast," too often a shot begins in sun and has to be continued in dull overcast light. It's the editor who tries to make the change disappear by cutting to a closeup of a character and hoping the audience will forget. In this, he is aided by the rules of Gestalt perception, which dictate that a human being tends to see what he/she expects or wants to see. Evdemon recalled for me a long sequence in a *Sidestreet* episode which was continuous time in the plot, but took three days to shoot. The first day was the last of a very dry spell. The next day it poured, so they added a line in the dialogue commenting on the rain. The third day, they had two feet of snow. That day the director reblocked to shoot under the trees, some of the crew shovelled away what they could, and then everyone hoped the editor could bluff it. It worked. Evdemon went on to win two Geminis for episodes of *Seeing Things* and one for *Glory Enough for All*. He has been director of photography for specials like Jeannine Locke's *The Private Capitol* and sitcoms like *Material World*.

THOMSON: I don't think producers want people to delve. I don't think they want a cinematographer to move outside the set style for the piece and to look for shots that say something beyond the immediate demands of drama. Same with directors. I've watched directors who have quite a bit of talent and who have done a few films fall back to the episodic stuff and fit within the formula and the expectations of those producers. They have truncated their creative abilities. I also think the same thing can happen with the actor. They don't particularly want actors who want to delve or want to draw certain colours out because (a) that's not the story board and (b) it's going to upset the expectations of the audience, who are used to a certain thing.

MJM: There is no doubt that with most series, viewers are tuning in primarily to enjoy the familiar elements, the conventions.

TRUST THE CREW

Whether series or drama specials, the drama is only as good as the people behind the cameras. TV is a collective effort, particularly in an artifact as complex as television drama. I asked writer/producer Jeannine Locke to explain how and why the crew was important.

MJM: Producers often speak about the "whole picture." How do they see the role of the crew? From what you've said, a bad crew can wreck all the best-laid plans.

LOCKE: A crew will quickly sense that the people in charge don't know the direction in which they are going. It's not that the crew works less hard, it's just that they don't make that extra effort! That's when they'll use that line, "I'm just a common old working man, it's not my job. I don't have the authority to question what's happening up there." Conversely, I don't think it's well enough understood that a great many people on a crew care very much what they are involved in. The assumption that they simply go out and do their thing and scarcely know whether they are in Pakistan or the wilds of Saskatchewan is absolutely untrue.

MJM: If the crew don't trust the people who are making the overall decisions, they would be much less likely to make their own suggestions?

LOCKE: Absolutely.

MJM: They would just take orders and do it.

LOCKE: On *The Greening of Ian Elliot*, in church basements and halls, I never heard any bad language from this crew because they had such a respect and affection for those prairie people, and because we had about three hundred local extras. Prairie people are rather open and trusting. They hadn't had a film in that particular region, so we were lucky. The crew responded to that. There is nothing unusual about this, because it goes all the way up. It's important that respect goes all the way up and allows for that involvement, that extra effort, that tremendous satisfaction that has to be a part of any production. The crew comes on at one stage. Not all the crew sees rushes – those fragments that are being produced during the production. Moreover, we shoot in blocks, which have nothing to do with the chronological order of the story. Unless you are quite involved, you lose track.

MJM: Do they get scripts of their own?

LOCKE: Absolutely.

Throughout the history of television drama, directors of photography and lighting directors have had to light and shoot what costume and set designers give them.

WEYMAN: In the days of live television the designer had a tremendous vision of his own. There were certain conventional ways to cover a square room, because you have problems when it comes to camera placements. You invent ways of getting cameras to the actors, such as shooting through a door. A designer who comes from the stage finds it difficult when you say, "I don't need the whole room; what I do need is that and that; I just need a fragment."

Rudi Dorn was astonishingly good – creative. He took a rope and said, "Let's make a set, we need three cameras here, we need the rooms." Then suddenly the blocking of the shot, the emotional content of the shot in relation to the people, is influenced by the set, which becomes dynamic. Not all designers work like that. I was mentioning the limitations of space in the drama studio. It is all very well if the script requires two rooms, living-room and dining-room. But if, in fact, you have a living-room, a dining-room, a kitchen, a railroad station, the deck of a ship, and a beach, before you get the script written you go to your designer and ask, "How can we do this?" He says, "We fly this in. There is the beach, which is long and narrow, seen from two angles. One angle looks like it goes on forever from this angle, with barbed wire in the foreground. But in fact, it occupies only a narrow strip down the wall, so you can fly in front of it, you could even drop in a sky." You discover that, by determining what it is you are going to shoot, by limiting your angles and saying this is the most effective angle, you can accommodate an extraordinary amount in a small space. In live television, while you are on one camera, a proscenium has floated in and by the time the camaraman comes back, it is another scene. You have redressed that set.

MJM: You have done it in motion.

WEYMAN: In motion, while you are on air.

MJM: Quietly, with luck.

WEYMAN: Well, it was a different standard of sound.

It is now possible, in the era of film and tape, to talk to the designers, soundmen, actors, director, producer, cinematographers, lighting designers, and others between takes if you are allowed on set as an observer. When things are going reasonably well, it is the ideal environment in which to ask questions, because people are on their own familiar territory, with the answers to questions arising from the production itself fresh in their minds. I did not observe on sets with a tape recorder in hand. I preferred to chat during breaks, which explains why, in this section, there are fewer direct quotations.

One of the first things that would strike any observer is the rigorously differentiated tasks of each person. A hairdresser tends the hair – not the actor. Only assistant directors talk to the extras, not the director. If the director talks to the non-speaking actors, it changes their status – and salary. The assistant director keeps discipline on the set, freeing the director to concentrate on the larger picture and on the speaking parts.

Senior designer Rudi Dorn suggested Dan Yarhi, a freelance

designer, to David Barlow for the pilot of *Seeing Things*.[17] When the series was given the go ahead, Barlow fought to keep Yarhi rather than work with a series of staff designers. He argued that for the special needs of a series like this, with its occasionally bizarre and fantastic scenes, "in-house CBC design is far too locked into realism, far too picky and hung up on detail, with very little imagination for the atmospheric, the stylized, the fun." He felt that few CBC designers knew how to design for film, because they were so used to tape. Eventually, because of union regulations, Yarhi would have had to join the staff. The financial penalty, which entailed giving up his freelance work, meant that Yarhi left after twenty-seven episodes. The 1984 cutbacks further eroded the potential for teamwork which had contributed so much to the success of *Seeing Things*.[18]

Dan Yarhi learned from his mentor, Rudi Dorn (who viewed unimaginative designers as people who designed from a "Sears catalogue)," that sets are "designed 80 per cent for the actors and 20 per cent for the viewers." Yarhi's view of the series was that each episode needed a different style: for example, the "Haunted House" episode required a look of fantasy about some of the scenes; in contrast, the story about an imported hockey player who is a spy had the hard-edged look of locker-rooms and arenas. The running subplot about the relationship of Marge and Louis gave the show its basic look of warm, textured, rounded edges, a comfortable, lived-in look. The newspaper offices where Louis works, however, are cold, linear, and harshly lit by fluorescent overheads, and Louis is always trying to get out of there.

Marge's townhouse started out as a real location owned by an architect with a wife who did pottery and loved primitive sculpture, wallhangings, and plants. However, the architect's neighbours complained about the traffic problems created by filming. When *Seeing Things* had to move, they recreated that original house. Walking around the set, I found that the stereo worked and that the books were appropriate to a thirteen-year-old boy, their son. "Marge's records" also represented stages in a life and changing tastes. The walls were decorated by a mix of sketches she might have done, reproductions, and a few good purchases. Most of this did not show up on the camera but, as Yarhi pointed out, it helped the actors give depth to the characters. In contrast, crown attorney Heather Redfern's apartment was tasteful, neutral, contemporary, but with carefully chosen Chinese and Oriental artwork and porcelains.

The early seasons of *Street Legal* had office sets for Chuck, Leon, and Carrie which showed a similar meticulous attention to detail, from the prints on the wall to the choice of plants, thus helping the viewers and the actors to differentiate among the three. For new characters, in settings unfamiliar to the audience, it is important to give both the actor and the audience information about the character, to make him or her feel at home. Much of an art director's time is spent finding interesting locations that serve the needs of the series, the blocking indicated by the script, the mood or atmosphere, yet is a place where there won't be logistics problems; for example, distance from the central plant or periodic bursts of deafening noise.

The climax of the *Seeing Things* episode that parodied *The Maltese Falcon* (and Sax Rohmer thrillers) is a good example. It was written to take place in the garden of a Chinese restaurant. When it turned out to be too small for the slapstick chase, the producers chose to stage the climax in the 1930s Art Deco of the Sunnyside Swimming Baths on a bright mid-winter day. New business and new lines developed related to the arches and the echoing spaces. Since Toronto has been the setting for most series filmed at the CBC, it was a point of pride to the *Seeing Things* unit that they found all kinds of new settings for the episodes.[19]

Yarhi also told me that set decorators, who concentrate on the detailed props and furnishings, are valued in direct proportion to their contacts and their ability to beg, borrow, scrounge, and dicker – as well as for their imaginative contributions. They pay for the use of the materials they find, but usually work within very limited budgets. Permanent sets are also good for art directors and set decorators, because they are then free to concentrate on smaller details. When *Seeing Things* had to use Studio 7, it took three days to get the sets up and to take them down. Giving them a space of their own for a studio (a converted warehouse) helped enormously. It has become the norm with other production units for series.

As in theatre, one function of successful design is to provide new information required in each episode, setting the scene with the lighting, period details, and individualized touches that tell the story in a glance. Yet the designer must also provide what people expect to see. For example, when they were about to shoot the haunted house episode of *Seeing Things*, which involves a scene at a construction site, all the available buildings under construction in Toronto at that time were reinforced concrete. However, most viewers associate "red steel girders" with high buildings. Therefore, a set was built four feet off the floor of the roof of the CBC's Sumac Street building where sets and props were built and stored. After the "stunt-double" was taped going up in the elevator on an actual high-rise construction site, the scene was intercut with appropriate footage of dizzying shots out of the elevator and master shots of the site from the point of view of the rising elevator (speeded up slightly, since the real elevators crawl). Thus the visual expectations and the time sense of the audience were both satisfied.

Location shooting can produce all kinds of problems, from where the unit sleeps and eats [*Ready for Slaughter* was shot in Lion's Head, population 600] to redesigning, on the spot, someone else's home or business. In *Out of Sight*, a drama about a controversial psychiatric treatment for the criminally insane, the setting chosen was the abandoned maximum security building at the Lakeshore Psychiatric Facility. Most of the rooms, halls, and common-rooms were painted bright yellow, even the wire mesh on the windows. The orange carpets were full of cigarette burns, the guards' stations were still in place, and notices were still tacked on the bulletin boards. Through the heavy wire mesh on the windows, the actors could see a large green park. In this instance, the ambiance, altered very judiciously by the art director, crept into the very bones of everyone who worked on the show. There were times when I thought the more interesting drama was off camera, in the reactions of everyone to the confined, falsely cheerful, eerily deserted, high-security building. In a Pirandellian sense, the play was in the playing, and the location definitely became a character in the plot.

THE EDITOR

Editing a film is a collaborative act which rests primarily in the skilled hands of a specialist. Vincent Kent, freelance editor of all but one of the episodes of *Seeing Things*, had, in the 1970s, edited *Police Surgeon*, *Matt and Jenny*, and *Swiss Family Robinson*, all shown on CTV or Global and sold abroad or to American syndication, and all made (if not financed) in Canada. He won a Gemini for *Seeing Things*, and edited David Barlow's production of *Sanity Clause* and *Breaking All the Rules*.

The editor's "work-print" is not colour balanced. He also works with the raw sound track, without the score and the sound effects that help the transitions and provide a context for the scene. As Kent noted, his job was made easier in *Seeing Things* because director George McGowan's Hollywood experience meant that he shot enough film for the editor to work with. The editor has the job of selecting the best shots from each take, juxtaposing master shot, action, and reaction shots in a rhythm appropriate to the particular dramatic situation, and trying to fix some of the inevitable fluffs that have occurred.

Suppose the editor and the producer decide that a plot point needs more emphasis; for example, they want to point up that Marge is impatiently waiting for Louis to leave Redfern's too upscale housewarming. The editor switches focus from a two-shot with dialogue between Heather and Louis to a mid-shot of Marge leaning on a door-frame away from them. Kent and Barlow decide to emphasize this slightly by post-synchronizing (adding on another sound track over the original sound) a sigh from Marge – a very tiny detail added to the scene after it has been shot. The editor also adds his or her own emphasis by directing the focus to the speaker or to the listener (action and reaction shots), choosing when the point of view changes (subjective or objective), and establishing the varied rhythms.

The next thing an editor is likely to do is cut the show down to the required minutes and seconds while looking for logical "act" breaks. *Seeing Things* had a set number of commercial breaks, but they did not have to occur at exactly the same time every week. In a mystery, the act break normally comes on a point of "jeopardy," to leave the audience in suspense, or on a plot twist, a surprise to bring viewers back from the fridge. This particular series often cut away to a commercial after a joke of some kind.

When the script is overwritten and overshot, cutting the film to fit a precise time slot is easy enough. But as a good series progresses, the writers are likely to come up with tighter and better scripts. As Kent told me, it is therefore more difficult for the editor to shave off the seconds. In eighteen working days the print goes through at least four or five cuts. The first might simply cut scenes to save ten or fifteen minutes and is called the rough-cut. Seven minutes could go on the second, two on the third, and the fourth or fifth will be on time. For a program like *Seeing Things*, which Kent called "pacey," there were often close to a thousand edits in a one-hour show. The average for a one-hour program is five hundred. By the third and fourth cut he was dealing with a few frames at a time. The producer, David Barlow, reviewed every stage in the editing. The star of the series and co-producer, Louis Del Grande, always attended at least one film-editing session. Robert Allen, as executive producer, would add his observations about the final cut.

Kent, who has seen a great many series come and go, volunteered the opinion that *Seeing Things* was of high quality. He admired the degree of professionalism, the sense of teamwork and mutual respect, and took pains to point out that a series like this was an invaluable training ground for people in all aspects of film-making.

In the late 1980s the old analogue technology of physically cutting film or tape changed. In an interview in *Canadian Theatre Review*, David Barlow sketched for me those changes as they affected *Sanity Clause*, one of the best of recent CBC dramas, co-written by and starring Louis Del Grande and directed by George McGowan.[20] I asked David Barlow if the director would use the master shot, shot reaction shot method of traditional film-making.

BARLOW [1994]: You shoot on film, but you shoot at thirty frames a second as opposed to twenty-four, just to make it compatible with the video tape. If you start with film negative, you're going to get film quality. Tape is not as sophisticated as film, but it will retain the quality of the film if it is duplicating a film. That's why it looks better on television than video. Vincent Kent's a wonderful editor. His challenge on that picture, aside from making it all work, was familiarizing himself with a new system. It was done with a whole bank of three-quarter-inch video tapes, so that each tape would be duplicated maybe three times so you could get speedy access to any individual take. There were two or three different ways the electronic machines could access that take, and it would go to the fastest one. These would playback to a computerized console. From the console you would select takes and assemble. You could literally store various takes, and then edit the scene in a different way and store that. Yet it was a hybrid system, in the sense that you were still dealing in a linear fashion with the material. It's just that by multiplying the versions, you could mix and match in fairly quick order. When you assemble a sequence, it too would be recorded on several machines, so you could get to it quickly. Now [in 1994] it's all done with random access systems. It's all computer work, so there is much greater speed and much greater ability to manipulate the information takes that you're getting. It also takes less time to dub off a digitized copy of any particular cut. Although it's not broadcast quality, it's certainly good enough to look at. Then, to get it back up to broadcast quality, the negatives of the film have been transferred to video. You can do great colour correction on tape. Also, you can take your film negative and transfer it to a positive video tape, so you never have to print the film. The video is in turn digitized onto computer disks. You edit on computer disks, and they not only provide the editor with an on-screen digitized image but they store all the information about the time codes and where the takes are on the original videotape. So, at the final cut, the editor prepares the disk, they put this disk in, then load the video tapes. They assemble a cut version on videotape that matches the digitized version, including overlapping sound, advanced sound or advanced picture, dissolves, and other special effects.

MJM: Digitizing the information is an exciting development from an archival point of view – cheaper, easier to store, and every "copy" is a master print.

BARLOW: Oh yes, sure. Eventually it will be on three-and-a-half-inch disks, so retrieving and looking at the film will be no problem. [Moreover, the newest tape technology will produce broadcast-quality digitized images.]

Two conclusions may be drawn from the process. One is obvious. Television drama is a collaborative art, with every member of the off-camera team contributing not only their hands and skills but also their imagination to what we see on our screens. The other conclusion is less obvious. Good, distinctive, popular television drama that speaks to its audiences, whether as a single event or as a series, depends on a personal vision that permeates the collaborative effort. This vision may come from the writers, but more often from the producer or the director. But it must be personal, particularized, and unified in its effect.

Sometimes it is the interplay of two people, the actor/writer Louis Del Grande, writer/producer David Barlow combination, or the teams of writer Philip Hersch and producer Ron Weyman (*Wojeck*), or writer Paul St. Pierre and producer Philip Keatley (*Cariboo Country*). Like those old favourites of Shakespeare's day, Beaumont and Fletcher, or Marston, Massinger, and Middleton, teams can create superb entertainment. Sometimes they create masterworks. Collaboration is as old as Greek tragedy and as necessary to television drama of quality today as it was to victory in the Dionysia in fifth-century Athens. These partnerships and their successes depend on all the others behind the camera who deserve respect. Such respect has been a rare commodity in some periods of CBC drama.

McEWEN: That happens to all the boys, every one of them. My staging crew from *Shellgame* [the two-hour special that was the pilot for *Street Legal*] finished Thursday night. They had a huge wrap-up Friday, and they were put to cleaning out a studio Sunday night, with no respect for the work they did. The dolly-pusher was fabulous. He had a lot of work. He is a dramatic camera dolly-pusher; he is not the garbage cleaner, and that is the way they treat them. No wonder they leave. Brian Hebb is not getting the operators he should have or the focus-pullers he should have. It takes a toll; you get tired.

You can have a makeup person who has done a wonderful job for you, but she's probably doing news today. They aren't looking at her and saying, "Hey, she's a fabulous artist for drama and we should keep her on drama." Nor are they looking at her and saying, "She's just come off a six-week shoot of long days and seven-day weeks and she must be absolutely exhausted." They stick her in news or an afternoon show or something. Their managers don't see them as human beings, but as interchangeable parts.

MJM: And they are part of the "service" section. They aren't really part of the drama department.

McEWEN: That's right, they won't assign them just to drama. They should, I think.

In the traditional hierarchies of the visual arts, *artists* make sculptures, paintings, watercolours, and photographs. *Craftsmen* (usually women) make quilts and pots. In the 1990s those barriers are slowly breaking down even in the national galleries. Hierarchy is also breaking down in radio and television. The term "crafts" in television is defined as those who contribute the "hands-on element" during the actual taping or filming. A look at the list of abbreviations in *Who's Who in Television* reveals at least 150 different roles.

WOMEN ARE CRAFTSPEOPLE TOO

Equity within the unions is also a problem. Women are seriously underrepresented in the technical roles. Pat Armstrong, writing in *Changing Focus*, reports: "A female sound technician explained, "It's real male dominated and continues to be ... People don't think a woman can hold a tape recorder or understand the camera or lift a light." Another woman sound recordist is convinced that if she had been a male she would have "made more money and would have gotten more work, just because there aren't any women out there doing it. I never met another woman recordist. I never met another woman who does boom ... I have worked with a woman grip once and I think that is the extent of the women I have worked with over the years as a technician ... I would say 99.9 per cent of the people doing the hiring have never heard of a woman doing that position. Then why would they have any great faith that that person could carry it off?"[21]

Margaret Visser adds, "Nowhere are women weaker in the field than at straight technology: at shooting film, maintaining equipment, managing machinery. Art directors are 29 per cent women; photography directors are only 1 per cent women. The job category in which women earn the least relative to men is 'shooting.' And things are getting worse in the 'professional,' 'semi-skilled manual' and 'manual' groups in the private sector. Technology remains a male preserve. Women are probably scared away from it from an early age; it just never becomes, for most of them, an option. This is in spite of the traditional view that women are good at finicky and precise rather than hefty work. It must be that women are *culturally* turned off, intimidated through socialization. They then become oddities if they try to enter fields of technological expertise."[22]

The old hierarchy of television suggests that the actors, writers, directors, editors, directors of photography, and designers may be thought of by the public as "artists," while the others on whom their work depends are "crafts people." The ideology implicit behind that designation troubles me. Bad makeup can ruin a scene, as can inept lighting, the wrong prop, a badly placed microphone. Perhaps the distinction, if any, is between the visible, the more-obvious-to-the-audience elements (semioticians would call them semantic codes), and the less visible elements, the organization of codes or syntax.

Yet the 1987 Drama Subcommittee Report found that "there was no integrated plan which recognized that production methods, industrial relations, audience strategy, recruitment and administrative methods were all inseparable." To get a show on air, there must certainly be a hierarchy of decision-making. But just as in theatre or an up-to-date factory, the productivity and the "product" are better when the organizational structure functions as a "company" (in its original sense of a working network of valued contributors), so too the company model may well work best for the production of drama. We see it at work unofficially in the 1950s and early 1960s. There is also a strong plea for just such a model in the 1987 report. It began by citing the detailed Drama Search Committee report made by Thom Benson, Peter Hernndorf, and Robert McGall in 1973: "The Drama Department has been particularly hampered by the inflexibility of its relationship with the television plant in Toronto, by the quality of personnel in a number of key jobs, and by the lack of training opportunities at the CBC." And continued:

There is no real acceptance of the fact that the responsibility for drama *production* (after a given idea has been accepted and funded) should be delegated *completely* to the Drama Department and its producers ... only in the most exceptional cases should the Director of Entertainment Programs or the Managing Director get involved ... At this moment, far too many people get involved in the process ...

The problem of production methods is simply a mess, with no redeeming virtues. Pick up any thread of the problem and follow it through the fabric and you will inevitably arrive at this conclusion: To solve the specific problem represented by this thread, you would have to reform the entire structure of the Corporation. The alienation, inefficiency and waste induced by the current production methods have been alluded to in the first chapter [of the report]. There are at least three, if not five "currencies" between "direct" and "overhead," all trading at a black market rate. No one can tell a civilian what a production actually cost the Canadian taxpayer and presume to go to church on the same day.

Some assumptions need to be addressed: There is an assumption held broadly that we can produce many of the productions we do much more cheaply. The answer is no, not in the current production environment.

The "direct" costs of a drama production are less than half the complete costs after "manpower," "departmental" and other "overhead" are applied. There are substantial variables based on repeat costs, and buyouts. In the end, the exercise of cutting out an actor here and there, or bargaining the writer down become secondary to the total bill, which has been actually trowelled on by various layers according to formulas, or according to interdepartmental billing.

The "direct" costs (actors, writers, etc.) of one episode of the proposed serial, would be $20,000 an episode. The "manpower" (basic crew/design requirements) are estimated at $40,000 an episode [in 1987 dollars]. The repeat cost of that one episode would be $9,000. On top of that, add "overhead," which can be calculated a number of ways, depending on whom you talk to, one being: add 90% of directs and manpower costs. "Overhead" defies simple definition, but comprises "departmental" and that episode's share of the cost of running the network.

It becomes quite absurd, in this context, to surgically diminish aspects of the episode. The majority of the savings will not be on the "direct" side, but on the side over which we have very little control. Therefore, it becomes impossible to scale down current Drama levels without reforming the manpower, departmental and overhead. i.e., without reforming the fundamental production methods of the network as a whole.

Undoubtedly, there is a plant side to this story which, upon examination, would be quite compelling too. No matter. We have a system which does not work and which is wasting the taxpayers' money without making anyone rich in the process ... We are convinced that efficient drama production is predicated on dedicated units: Maryke McEwen projects that further, describing a system of permanent teams, whose assignments would be scheduled back to back; this would allow the advantages of keeping efficient teams together, and planning drama production two years in advance.[23]

The "Drama Subcommittee" report included recommendations based on observations which are supported in many of the interviews I recorded. They make a logical conclusion to the first five chapters of this book.

RECOMMENDATIONS:
1 That the system of costing and describing the costs of a drama production be simplified, and that the confusions which allow differing claims of how much something costs be settled.

2 That a priority of any reform of Drama be a complete rethinking of the relationship between the Drama Department and Service Departments. The Drama Department should be, as far as humanly possible, in control of all the aspects required to produce its programs.

3 That the basic building block of efficient drama production be the dedicated production unit, emphasizing strong teams, under the producers' administration.[24]

As we shall see, the first recommendation was adopted. What happened to recommendations 2 and 3 are addressed in chapters 10 and 11.

6 Technology

Film, with its high visual definition, is a much more transportable medium. But film is so expensive there is less drama. And less drama means fewer writers and actors. And the quest for money means international partners, which lessens the unique character of place, of the country of origin. SYDNEY NEWMAN

The story of television technology, of how it has shaped television drama and now fragments audiences, is rooted in radio, a technology that existed before those who had invented it had figured out what to do with it. Radio signals were available in the 1900s, but no one realized that radio's apparent weakness of being heard by everyone was its greatest strength – that it could broadcast not just distress signals, but also songs, stories, and news that could be heard by anyone with a set.[1] Before we look at the complex story and multiple viewpoints on the evolving technology of television, Mavor Moore, the first person in charge of television drama, describes an event from the early days of television. A *Front Page Challenge* headline on this anecdote might read, "CBC Beats U.S. on Coronation Film Footage in 1953."

MOORE [1990]: It was an extraordinary experience. Oscar Burritt, our film expert, was on the plane. Stuart Griffiths, our program director, had experience as a radio technician; he put himself through college working as a radio repairman and had a rare combination of technical and program skills. It was Griffiths who had the idea of putting a hot film processor, as it was called, on the plane so the film could be processed on the way home. None of the other networks had thought of that. We were on the telephone with London and Montreal because the films were going to be put on the air from Montreal (it's closer to London than Toronto). We were out to beat the big networks.

The plane with the film aboard set out from London. We got word that the NBC plane had started ahead of us, heading for New

York. The CBS plane had not yet got off the ground in London. Then we heard that the NBC plane had developed trouble and had returned, while our little airforce plane was merrily coming across the Atlantic. It landed at Gander, and then we had a frantic phone call from Burritt. It was an American Air Force base, and the Americans would not let them through with the film. They were, of course, desperate and excited, because they were losing time. Our guess was that the base had already heard from the American networks saying, "If, by any chance, the Canadians come through, hold them up!" Anyway, there was a pause, and Griffiths on the phone said, "Oscar, how many of them are there?" Oscar said, "Two." Griffiths said, "How many are there of you?" Oscar said "Three." Griffiths said "Rush them!" and hung up. They did, they got through, and they got down to Montreal. Then they came on the air with the tail end of the film, because they hadn't rewound it. They had to take it out again and rewind it. But finally, when we went on the air, it was a very exciting moment. By that time we were feeding NBC. They had conceded that we were there first. They phoned us and said, "Can we take the feed from you?" We arranged to feed them through Buffalo – Montreal to Toronto to Buffalo to NBC.

When we saw the CBC signal go up on Buffalo, knowing that it was going to all the rest of the networks, this was quite a moment. But the feedback we got from that, which is the point of this long story, is that most of the Canadians watching the Coronation watched it off the Buffalo station, not the Canadian one.

Still, as Moore pointed out in *Reinventing Myself,* the Buffalo *Courier Express* saw the opening night of the English Television Network as "three hours of unusual, interesting and highly professional entertainment ... All in all, it looks as though Canadian talent is sure of a substantial U.S. audience."[2] I find myself bemused that, over four decades, Canadians have no real idea of how many U.S. viewers in border cities and towns, or by cable, the CBC has informed and entertained.

LIVE ON KINESCOPE: STUDIO DRAMA

Canada in the 1950s had no microwave transmissions, and broadcast satellites were unknown. Up to the late 1960s some remote communities[3] were sent kinescopes; black-and-white filmed records shot from the master television monitor. Some, not all, of those cans of 8-mm film survived, so a researcher can still see some of the "live" drama productions just as they went to air in Montreal, Toronto, or Vancouver.

MARIO PRIZEK, director [1983]: We had three weeks of rehearsal for a ninety-minute show, and three days in the studio. The third day in the studio included the actual telecast that evening after supper, live-to-air, so you had only two and three-quarter days, really.

We had marvellous camera teams on those shows. They were very artistically oriented engineers, two or three of them in particular. If you explained to them carefully, before your first camera blocking started, what your intentions were in each scene, what kind of mood you wanted to create, they would immediately grasp it. Sometimes while you were on the air they would discover a new shot that you hadn't even conceived of, that was so gorgeous and so perfect for the moment that you said: "Hold that shot, Tom. Take 3," right there. Then you'd cut right back into your regular planned pattern of shots.

If camera 3 had shot no. 20, and then didn't have another shot until shot no. 50 (and it wasn't a particularly rapid exchange of dialogue), he would shop around. I would be looking at all the monitors, because you always have to look at least one monitor ahead to be ready to prepare your switch for the next shot. In my later years, I never spoke any more than was necessary. The cameraman already has the encumbrance of the "program sound" feeding into one earphone and the "control-room sound" feeding into the other earphone, so I tried to keep it as quiet as possible. I didn't speak to the switcher. I held up my hand showing him the number of fingers corresponding to the numbers of the camera coming up; and then I'd snap my fingers at the point the shot was needed, "camera 5, take." I would warn the switcher of the fade. Then I'd give the rate of fade by moving my hand. Meanwhile, the cameramen were able to hear my script assistant saying what shot was coming up on what camera. This kept everything much calmer, and everything flowed much more rapidly.

Where there was movement within a shot, I talked the cameraman through it, saying, "Very, very good," "No, slower," or "Don't reach the tight closeup until such and such a point two bars from now. I'll tell you." Here is the original script for *The Duchess of Malfi*. See? "Shot 43, closeup John Drainie and Frances Hyland – the Duchess," "reverse angle of shot on camera 3."

MJM: One of the things that impressed me about *The Duchess of Malfi* was your sense of visual composition, the actors in relation to that incredibly varied background. Yet it was basically a unit set.

PRIZEK: Yes. There were two reasons why I had that particular kind of set in mind. I wanted very badly to do the play. It took a lot of talking to get the brass to approve anything at that period except Shakespeare. Shakespeare was acceptable, but Webster, Who's heard of Webster?[4] I finally talked them into letting me do it when I told them who I proposed as my cast[5] and they thought it was going to be a smashing performance. I said to myself, "Gee whiz, how do I get all these locations into one studio with no time for set changes? Well, I have to use a unit set of some kind." The primary inspiration for the setting in *The Duchess of Malfi* came from the magnificent set of engravings Piranesi made and titled, the *Carceri Prison* etchings. Escher has also made similar drawings of staircases and architectural mazes that produce feelings of claustrophobia, terror, and panic in the viewer; those huge, terrifying structures, fantastic structures, the staircases that lead nowhere, everywhere, arches and strange things that look like instruments of torture lying about – everything on a gigantic scale, dwarfing the people. Even though the spaces are vast, there's a feeling of claustrophobia. I showed them to my designer and I said: "That's my set. Just by putting in a throne and flying in a banner, this area becomes a throne room, whereas another moment it's just a passageway," so I could position my cameras all around and use each spot in several ways.

MJM: Also by changing the lighting of each scene?

PRIZEK: Yes. For *Queen after Death*, the four basic acting areas required represented a throne room, a prison courtyard, a small nunnery chapel, and an adjoining garden/courtyard. As our studio for dramatic productions was very small, it was exceedingly difficult to accommodate all four sets, let alone a large camera crane for those high, long shots the dramatic action seemed to call for. The designer, Rudi Dorn, came up with an ingenious solution to our problem. He ran a high, wide wall down the middle of the studio's length and placed two of the acting areas on either side of this wall; a couple of arches in the length of the wall permitted easier access to all four of the areas. He built camera tracks on top of this wall so the cameraman could give me both static and moving high-shots in each of the four areas. In addition, I located some of the action on the cameraman's access stairs, moving the prison guards and their prisoner, Inez de Castro (Kate Reid), up and down, to and from the prison courtyard, so I had dramatic exits and entrances from camera foreground to courtyard back and middle ground. Studio 1 was tiny. It had one dressing-room for both men and women, so they were changing behind sets, behind flats that were going to be thrown into the next scene.

When everyone is improvising solutions to problems under the "every night is opening night" conditions of television, each person behind the cameras has to be inventive.

RON WEYMAN, producer/director [1987]: We didn't think too much – we just said, "Well, we need such and such," and we went and did it. We were constantly pushing at the edge. You have probably seen some of the shows we did out of Studio 1, live. The engineers who constructed Studio 1 had been working within their imagination and their experience, but as soon as the producers went in there, they started figuring out ways to get the show on. There were two or three very good designers, who started doing odd things with the given space, so as to make it work. It was very tiny, and yet absolutely remarkable shows were done in it.

Constantly, you'd find someone saying, "Well, why can't we use the car outside?" or "Why can't we do this and that?" But the first impression I had was that not only the studio but the alley-ways, the cars, and a piece of the street were being used as a studio! There was no limit to one's invention or one's energy. Presently, they said, "We must have a new studio," so they built a new studio.

MJM: Would you ever find yourself improvising when there wasn't a disaster?

WEYMAN: Well, some people did, and they could bring upon themselves their own disaster!

MJM: Yes, I would think it would be a very risky thing to do; for example, if an actor didn't know a camera was going to move somewhere else ...

WEYMAN: Exactly. I saw Paul Almond do this a number of times and I have been guilty of it myself, too. When a scene is going well under the pressure of its being broadcast, there is a moment which is just absolutely beautiful, and you want to hang on to that. But then the script girl would give you a punch in your ribs and point to a little note that said, "You have got to detach that camera in order to get it over there." Now, if an actor's performance is such that it is absolutely riveting, and I as a producer say, "I've got to hold on to that," you can see what would happen. The cameraman who has worked out his passage between A and B, literally to the second, has suddenly discovered that he has three seconds less time than he thought he had.

In the late 1950s and early 1960s there would be myself as the producer/director and my assistant, Anne Weldon. Curiously, everyone else tends to fade away, because we were the center of the thing. But there would be a switcher, who worked pretty much from the master script. You were supposed to have had two run-throughs before going on air, but sometimes, if things got pretty ropy, you didn't get that.

When a live drama looked as if it would be too long to fit the time schedule, we would have a session with everybody involved, cameramen and so on. I would say, "We are going to lose page 73 of the script, camera 1 zap right through that and 74." The next cue would be so-and-so's entry. [The actors would have to cope with the change on the run, as well as the crew and the cameramen.]

MJM: What if the show ended too soon, by a minute or two?

WEYMAN: You tried to avoid that, but it did sometimes occur. You would do the credits slowly. There was no way that we could turn out a show every week, but we discovered we could. And very soon, you had tapes you could cut and start and stop. Anyway, that so-called golden era of live television came to an abrupt hold, when Hollywood demonstrated that it could turn out a film series every week. That magic of being in a closed space was, at its best, an astonishing magic; it was not stage, it was not film, it was television. Once you start you don't stop, and you shoot it all within this enclosed space – the studio. Television drama was created to quite a degree by the imposition of those limitations.

RADIO IS NOT TELEVISION

Actor/writer Hugh Webster describes the differences between radio and television in those early years:

WEBSTER [1984]: You take an issue like the *Hilda Morgan* controversy and you add the visual aspect to the radio version. The visual, the sense of seeing something, is overpowering. [Lister Sinclair's *Hilda Morgan* had been broadcast on the radio *Stage* series with somewhat less controversy than was generated by the television version. Hilda Morgan was an unwed mother/teacher protagonist and thus a problematic figure in the early 1950s].[6] When you see something take place, rather than when you hear something taking place, it affects you differently; if the audience is straight-laced or puritanical, they'll take it on radio because ...

MJM: They've got more control over this medium. The listener can choose whether to engage the imagination fully. On television, the viewer does not have to supply as much detail.

ELIZABETH WEBSTER, Hugh's wife [1984]: The visual is instantly memorable.

MJM: Yet television can distance the viewer from the story. If a radio play is good, it makes the listener imagine perfection. The visual makes all the choices for the viewer.

WEBSTER: You're right.

ELIZABETH: You can argue with the choices.

MJM: But on television the choices made are more difficult to ignore. It is more difficult to become as involved in good TV drama as in good radio drama.

ELIZABETH: One other thing that is a tremendous difference between the radio and the television worlds is that CBC radio is not broken for commercials.[7] An unbroken attention span makes a tremendous difference to how deeply involved you are. If every thirteen minutes, you're going to be released to go to the fridge, the rhythm is completely different.

LIVE-TO-TAPE

The late 1950s and early 1960s were a time of technological change, known by the ironic oxymoron of "live-to-tape." Producer and head of TV Drama, Robert Allen, summarized the evolution from "live-to-tape" to the divergence of electronic technologies and filming technologies.

ALLEN [1981]: There is no difference between slotting in a piece of film and a piece of tape in the production of a live show. In the beginning we did a ninety-minute show all at once in one day. Then there was a period when we acquired tape, when we had to use it as the need arrived. We weren't allowed to "stop tape," which meant there was no editing, so in effect we were still doing live shows. But now we were doing them at a more convenient time. It was a way of utilizing the studio facilities more economically, so we could do the show live-to-tape and transmit the tape at some other time.

Then they developed the possibility of stopping the tape once or twice in an hour or an hour and a half, usually at the end of an act. Producers were able to persuade the authorities that you could stop the tape once or twice, because there had to be a costume or a makeup change or some other change. Stopping the tape meant that those two pieces of tape on which there were pictures had to be put together. In the early days, the technician who was responsible used to cut the tape with a razor blade, using a microscope to look at the tape. Then he would join together the two pieces of tape with sticky tape! Sometimes the splice came apart.

Then some of us got thinking, we could make much better

shows if we had several costume changes using several "stop tapes," or if some of the actors could move from this set to that set. In live television, we had the device of ending a scene on a bowl of flowers and starting the next scene on another bowl of flowers. We got tired of doing that. So we used multiple stops. We got to the point where we did a lot of stops, and a lot of editing, and had to book the editing facilities for hours and then days.

MJM: But you were still doing the dramas in sequence?

ALLEN: Yes. Then we invented the technique of doing all the things in this set, and all the things in that set. It was more economical and it saved a lot of time. But we ended up with thirty, fifty, one hundred different scenes that we had to put together using multiple cameras. Then some of the directors said, "To hell with this multiple camera business," and started to use single camera. And that was pure film technique.

ENTER FILM

Ron Weyman fought for the use of film in television drama throughout the 1960s.

WEYMAN: There were any number of reasons why the old brigade wanted to be comfortable and not move from electronic studio drama to film. I can remember an amiable big guy in Studio 1 who was the union representative saying: "You are going to have trouble. Down the line I can see all the studio people being laid off." I said, "What is the alternative to it? Do you want us to continue to play to lesser and lesser audiences, ho-hum, people turning it off, or do you want a new galvanized drama? Which do you want?" "I want my job," he said. I said, "Well, you better figure out how your job can jump from the electronic studio to the film studio, because that is really what we are talking about. There are a lot of jobs and people in the studio; you just give them another name and they do it on film, so what the hell?" I didn't hear too much more about it, but there were people at the CBC who were against getting into film. The side arguments, with the Film Board, were purely invention. We were able to demonstrate that we could do something the Film Board was not undertaking, and we could do it within our own budget without disrupting or destroying the studio structure. Furthermore, people watched it and said: "Hey, this is terrific!" Also the CBC could sell the filmed drama in England and abroad. A new age was upon us, and all these arguments simply fell away.

At that point, 1964, I had been developing *The Serial*. I hadn't been shooting film because (1) we weren't supposed to be into drama film, (2) we didn't have the money, and (3) within the CBC, there was this investment in the studio and with all the people who worked in the studio. The whole business of film was in fact, *mystique*. We did go and shoot, and we did have experience in shooting news and features, but that was supposed to be quite different.

With *The Serial* I devised a system. It was the first serial we had. Each of them ran five, six, or seven episodes – a half-hour at 8 o'clock. They were first of all shot live in the studio. But one of the early episodes was set in Nova Scotia. Rather than hanging bits of seaweed about or having seagull noises, I would try to persuade them to let me take a crew of three people down to Nova Scotia for a period of ten days to shoot essential background stuff.

MJM: Without actors?

WEYMAN: With actors. But carefully structuring the whole thing, so there was no dialogue and we wouldn't have to worry about sound. We just flew them in and flew them out. If we could do that within our budget, no one was going to get upset. It was not a traditional form, but it didn't at that point invade anybody's area directly. Instead of having the sound of seagulls in the studio, we saw our hero coming along on the beach, or whatever. We were there! This sounds so incongruous today, but people literally had not seen the Nova Scotia beach (or whatever) as a setting for drama before.

MJM: People knew the difference, obviously. When they looked at that, they said: "Hey, that's Nova Scotia, that's not a set!"

WEYMAN: At the end of each story I would have the announcer say something like: "We would like to hear from you. How do you like this? Do you want more of it?" We got so many letters from across the country and the northern United States, from doctors to hard-rock miners, to Japanese farmers somewhere out west whose kids' bedtime had been shifted!

MJM: In the days of "live" drama you could respond relatively quickly to something topical. These days, thanks to the complex technology and the escalating costs, if you get it out in eighteen months, it's good going.

WEYMAN: Yes, live television was much more barometric. You were out there, and you could reflect at once on what was happening. Today, you say, "How is it going to fit in with what else we have got going, and is it going to be as timely if we shoot it six months from now?" It is a different world.

MJM: There are losses as well as gains. The general attitude is that, because the technology improves, the picture is sharper, and there are pretty colours, all aspects of the drama improve – or that the only good drama ever made disappeared in 1960. One or the other. But you have obvious losses and gains with technological change.

WEYMAN: The Drama Department was not uniquely attractive to the creative people off camera until we started using film. As soon as you have film, you have something which is exportable, which a director, designer, or cameraman can put under his or her arm and take anywhere in the world. And the game changes right then. You had to use film to keep up with the times, but in doing so, you inherited everything that goes with it – international competition, and so on.

Up until that time, 1964, the programming mix out of Studio 1 was about one original play out of five. It seemed to me that if I was going to be in this country at that stage, I was going to make Canadian stuff.

MJM: It was a time of great optimism and nationalism for one thing.

WEYMAN: It was the time to do it. And it happened. We did it, and we have been doing it ever since. Film House was pretty nice, but it meant that everything had to be done so swiftly. We needed forty-seven people for a crowd scene. Before, you couldn't have more than five people, because you had to pay them. The whole pay-scale was different. I needed these forty-seven people for just an hour and a half, which came under quite a different scale. The obvious thing was to have an office with about four people to administer film. That was the way it worked for about five years until it was decided, without talking with me or with any of my crowd, that we were all going to move from Film House to Bay Street. There we were, once again, in this big office, with people all over the place, most of whom were not related to our immediate needs. It meant a diffusion of energy.

Early television film technology was large, clumsy, heavy, and difficult to work with in studio or on location. Before he became a writer, Grahame Woods was a sought-after cameraman.

WOODS [1989]: When we went to Brazil, I had an enormous camera that had to be on a tripod and 1200-foot rolls of film. The sound men had this enormous bunch of antiquated sound equipment, which had to be lugged all over the country. Yet 90 per cent of the film wound up being shot on a little hand-held camera. The NFB did a film on Paul Anka, which was a real breakthrough.

MJM: *Lonely Boy.*

WOODS: And Don Pennebaker was doing his stuff down in the States. So Ron Kelly said, "Let's get a camera and do a film in Toronto General Hospital." We rented the equipment. This was the first time hand-held cameras had been used within the CBC. Somehow I got the reputation of being the cameraman who made this breakthrough. We were in the emergency ward for about three weeks and shot a very provocative film called *Such Is Life,* which was put in the vault because somebody in it had complained it was shot without his permission. It was a very moving film.

Ron Kelly was instrumental in a shift in television drama with *The Open Grave.*[8] Although the scenes were partially scripted in that the actors were given little descriptive paragraphs, much of it was "ad lib." It seemed to me as though I was sitting on the tail end of a rocket. Simultaneously, I was shooting a film with Doug Leiterman on Diefenbaker. I had this glorious week – the Diefenbaker film was broadcast back to back with *The Open Grave.*

MJM: You were also moving more and more into television drama.

WOODS: I've been called the man who shoots reflections and bolts and hubcaps. The aim of most cinematographers, and this again stems from the British tradition of feature films, is to get on television drama as the director of photography. So there was a lot of scuttlebutt as to who was going to get *Wojeck.* It was dramatic to go out of the studio into real locations, but the credit really lies with Phil Keatley. There was the story about the Indian girl.

MJM: *The Education of Phyllistine* on *Festival.*

WOODS: The Vancouver connection between Phil Keatley and executive producer for *Festival* Bob Allen helped. What Ron Weyman did was take Keatley's idea and run with it. A major breakthrough was what Ron did with *Wojeck.*

COLOUR

Readers over thirty-five will remember how startling it was when colour television became available. The colour on early sets resembled the neon colours in 1990s ski jackets, but transmission and sets steadily improved. Well after the Americans were broadcasting in colour, the CBC began in 1967 to transmit a few drama and other specials in colour. *Wojeck* began in black and white and moved to colour in the second season (1967–68).

WOODS: In the second series of *Wojeck* we went to colour, which was a whole new experience for any sustained use in drama. We were not working then on the kind of stock we work on today, which has tremendous latitude and allows you to light a scene with a match. We had horrendous stock – the first colour film I ever shot was a nightmare. And not only that, I screwed it up. The guy who oversaw all quality control saved my neck.

Colour-film stock has improved as the technology to broadcast it has steadily improved. Now black and white, not colour, is the signifier charged with meaning and nuance. Nevertheless, on rare occasions (for example, the many television adaptations of Sinclair Ross's *The Painted Door*), the climax will depend on the ability to *see* colour.

WHEN TECHNOLOGY DRIVES THE PROGRAM

In my two lengthy conversations with Hugh Gauntlett, an executive in middle management from the early 1960s to his retirement in 1989, we talked about television as a medium in the 1980s and how the technology used in other forms of television – news, sports, and so on – influenced the style narrative conventions of television drama.

MJM: People think that what we have on television in the mid-1980s is what viewers expect and, therefore, that this is what the CBC must give them. Stubbornly, as a person knowledgeable about forms of drama over the centuries, I do not buy that argument – that representational drama is the only form an audience will now accept.

GAUNTLETT [1983]: I don't wish to discourage you from not buying it, but there is something about television, something Trina McQueen was saying about it, by which the bad drives out the good. It is not directly a matter of cause and effect between the audience and the medium, but rather the effect on the medium itself. The need to emulate the competition seems to be irresistible. The law seems to be, "If a means of production is available, it will be used regardless of what it contributes to the effect."

I can give you one or two examples. I have been chairing a committee that deals with the development of computer systems. I am not really fond of it, but you have to sort it out. The coverage of the 1984 election depends on the computer system, which has got to be upgraded. Why does it have to be upgraded? Well, we don't want CTV to beat us. How are they going to beat us? They have been working on their computers. And in the end, it's whatever the computers want at the moment. There's a picture, and we have got stuff crawling across here, stuff crawling across there. I can see them wanting to do things with a database, so that you can get facts quicker. But that is only half of it. What they want is a machine for taking computer output and putting it on the screen [which of course is commonplace ten years later, but largely ignored by the viewers]. I don't really think the viewers can absorb what they are getting on the screen now, and I know that nobody ever does any research on it. However, I respect the skills of a younger generation of viewers.

This rapid growth of new technology is partly generated by the Sports Department, which is always on the leading edge of technology, using the latest gadgets because it is possible to do so: all of that "slow-mo," "replay," instant statistics, mini-profiles of the players, pan your camera down the bench. And it gets richer and richer. The curious thing is that in sports all that works. Playing the game – men running around with a ball in mud the way it used to be – is now irrelevant. There is no mud, and quite soon there won't be any ball – it'll all be electronic. [He made this comment before there were sophisticated electronic video games.]

If you watch *The Journal* being produced, you'll see the anchor ask a question of what in fact in the studio is a green hole in the wall, and bang! the guy answers the question. But that happened three days ago. We are doing eight seconds tonight, but the next two minutes we did yesterday. It is an electronic jigsaw puzzle in which you ask, "What is real here?"

I don't think the use of increasingly sophisticated technology is caused by a rational calculation of "this is what the audience wants." Shakespeare would never get on the CBC now, if it were not for our obligation to Stratford [an obligation that has already vanished like much else with the budget cuts].

MJM: Audiences no longer know about the choices of form and format they could have.

GAUNTLETT: No. Mind you, in some ways, television is increasingly narrowly addictive, as for "the jolts per minute." When I see Nancy Reagan on the front page of the *Globe and Mail* sitting on the knee of Mr T from *The A Team* as Santa Claus, it's a bizarre juxtaposition.

MJM: I still maintain that people will watch football *and* watch Ibsen. But clearly, mine is a minority point of view. Meanwhile the pressure is, as it was in the early 1950s, to get the program made and broadcast.

In the 1970s and 1980s the schedule itself came to revolve around a clearly defined proportionate mix of electronic and filmed drama. In 1988 I asked writer/producer David Barlow whether that informal arrangement of hours and resources still held after the arrival of Ivan Fecan and the reorganization of the Drama Department.

TAPE VS FILM

MJM: Are there still a certain number of hours assigned to tape and a certain number of hours assigned to film?

BARLOW: That's not the way it's working anymore. Tape fell into serious disuse here. Once *Hangin' In* shut down, there was no more three- or four-camera taping of drama done in the department, or in the CBC. They did some studio drama, but it was single-camera tape. *Not My Department* was done single-camera tape, *Chasing Rainbows* was done single-camera video tape. It was done high-definition television (HDTV) as well, but it was really single camera. Herb Roland would go and shoot Stratford on tape. But tape fell into disuse and everybody did film. Fecan's emphasis is, "Let's get the idea first and then we'll find the facilities." That really breaks down that assumption of "We gotta have another tape idea." However, he understands that the most economical form of half-hour drama is three to four cameras using videotape.

MJM: Why? What would film's advantages be for you in planning a pilot for a half-hour comedy program?

BARLOW: I should state my prejudice right off – I don't like tape. I'm not a big fan of the half-hour, four-camera format. In doing a half-hour, what we're trying to do is something that, while it fulfils the demands of the genre of the half-hour comedy format, will be like a little film – a little half-hour film. There will be more, shorter scenes, there will be some location work. Our series is set on a commuter train. A good portion of each show is on a commuter train, even though (if the pilot goes to series) we will build that train in the studio.

MJM: As a writer/conceiver of this pilot, why do you want to do many short scenes on film?

BARLOW: Just so you can juxtapose more stuff, do contrast between scenes, and set up conflict in the story between scenes as opposed to just within the scene. With live-for-camera tape, you're doing a one-act play. You'll have three or four sets. The obligation is to get the people in the room and have them talk.

MJM: And they move in real time.

BARLOW: Yes, and they make entrances and exits and there's often a live audience. So you're really doing something that's closer to a play than to a film. Lou Del Grande's preference and my preference is to do film. We're trying to get closer and closer to the people on the screen being recognizable as real people. That may sound strange from the people who did *Seeing Things*, but what we're both attracted to is getting realistic people up on that screen –

MJM: How very Canadian of you!

BARLOW: – that behave in a realistic way. A lot of sitcom is not like that. What we want to do is eavesdrop on two people, in an office, having a conversation about something. Either because we know these people or because of what they're talking about, we are fascinated by this and we are dying to eavesdrop. That quality, to me, is a film quality. I guess we're voyeurs. The short scenes are just how film happens to have evolved at the moment.

The only survivor among the sitcoms chosen for production that year (the Barlow/Del Grande submission was not produced) was *Material World* on tape. *Material World* mark II was shot, the next season, on film and became much more a series of mini-dramas than a sitcom. In my view the improvement did not come from the more "naturalistic" look of film, but from much more credible acting based in turn on more imaginative scripts.

Many sitcoms still have the flavour of live-to-tape. They are shot with a live audience at least twice, and then the best scenes are edited together. Mistakes can also be corrected on a "pickup" if necessary. The Fox network's *ROC* [1991–94] however, was actually broadcast live to the eastern United States. The show's edge was appropriate to the tough issues of class and race, and often made compelling viewing – but it did not get the ratings Fox demanded.

Producer Joe Partington recalled what an earlier four-camera, taped sitcom with a live audience was like:

PARTINGTON [1989]: With *King of Kensington* [1976–79] there was a show taped Thursday night and twice on Friday. When they didn't laugh on Thursday night, you'd go into a room with Jack Humphrey, Louis Del Grande, David Barlow, and Alec Barris (if he was the writer of the episode), and whoever else was around and you tried to make it funny.

MJM: You'd rewrite right then?

PARTINGTON: Yes, and that was very exciting.

MJM: It would keep everyone on their toes, but it would be very good for the show, I would think.

PARTINGTON: Usually they laughed a lot more the next night. The unknowables are things like, "Was it just a bad audience?" But "flop sweat" is an enormous motivator. I was new to it, too, so I was very excited. When an audience comes to a studio they are coming to be entertained, not to be critics. So when they don't laugh, that's a good indication that it's not funny.

On *Flappers* [1978–81] and *Hangin' In* [1981–87], it was left to the producers to decide whether it was funny. The crew would come in for the technical rehearsal, so you'd get some gauge, but it's not the same as an audience laughing.

MJM: You wouldn't do three tapings then?

PARTINGTON: No, we did *Hangin' In* over four days instead of five. It was segmented into Lally's story, David's and Ruth's, and it would evolve very quickly.[9] After three days a terrible thing can happen on a sitcom – the cast start examining the script. To avoid that, we pulled a day out. So it was two days of dry rehearsal and then the third day it was "on-camera" rehearsal. We would rehearse and record each scene, but only to half-inch tape. Then at night we would review the half-inch tape and do rewrites, costume changes, and the like. On the Friday, Alan Erlich (one of the directors) would again rehearse and record each scene, adding the changes. I would be on the floor. If we thought of anything on Friday we would put it in as well. You need a director like Erlich to cope spontaneously with changes like that.

Taping permits a sitcom or a variety special to be recorded in front of an audience. Filming does not – one of the reasons for the ever-present laugh tracks now used in either format.

PARTINGTON: *Material World*[10] is also recorded in front of an audience, but it is done on just one night. It's done in the afternoon without an audience. You try to get the whole show on tape for safety, and then you do it in front of the audience, with "pick-ups" afterwards if things go wrong. Performance changes in front of an audience. Kate Ford is co-creator, producer, and sometimes a writer of *Material World*. Her experience with *Family Ties* [a long running u.s. hit sitcom] was that, although they would tape the whole show in the afternoon without the audience, ninety-nine times out of a hundred the show that would go to air was the one that was taped in front of the audience. The actors came up for it.

We've got actors who are experienced, people like Linda Soren-son and Jayne Eastwood, but somehow we haven't got the acting experience in Canada that gives actors the confidence not to let their emotions run away with them in front of an audience. If I were told that *Family Ties* was done in the afternoon and that they added laughs, I would believe it, because it's always calm. Although you see them waiting for the audience to stop laughing, it's not heightened. The tempo and the voice pitch isn't up. So on *Material World* we have tended to use a lot from the afternoon show. Katie Ford is also after that naturalism she is used to from *Family Ties*.

In both performances, with and without audiences, the blocking tends to be the same and the shots tend to be the same, so you can go in and out using scenes or shots from each of the perform-ances. That's why it's important to have a director and a switcher who will keep the shows the same, and actors who will hit the marks. Then you have that flexibility to edit. It's amazing what can be done as long as you don't change the lighting. Things are technically quite stable these days, with computerized cameras and computerized lighting boards. You can go back and forth, and it's pretty seamless. We've done it a lot.

THE ADVANTAGES OF TAPE FOR SERIES

Herb Roland, another veteran producer, is an eloquent and persuasive defender of electronic drama.

ROLAND [1989]: If only I had done *To Serve and Protect*[11] on film, we might still be going.
MJM: Wrong medium? Was tape not in fashion at the time?
ROLAND: Portable video cameras are finally available, but much too late. They have been assigned to the arts and sciences and the sixth floor; six betacam units, those lovely small cameras, with a director of photography [DOP].
MJM: Why is it too late?
ROLAND: Because drama will never look at it. I'm using them for Veronica Tennant so she can do the introductions to *Sunday Arts* all around town. I prefer tapes for performances. I want runs at scenes, I want a flow, people talking, people communicating. Not that you can't do it on film, but it takes longer to get that kind of performance level.
MJM: And you don't get the immediate feedback using film?[12]

ROLAND: No. You have to trust your DOP more. It's television. We are not doing feature films. You can have some wonderful performances on film, but it takes much more time, which we can't afford. We've got to shoot an hour series in ten days, nine days, you can't afford that kind of time.

MJM: *Gift to Last* [1978–79] was ...?

ROLAND: ... taped with the odd remote film camera. The equipment we worked with! I used to come back to John Kennedy and say, "We can't go on with this." One day I actually threw the crew out. It was this ridiculous early portable camera and it kept breaking down. We had a week of nothing but trouble out on location and I finally said, "I've had it." I phoned up the office and said, "Get me a film crew here immediately," because everytime we would get going it would break down. So we ended up going out with these big studio cameras on location. On that one and a couple of others, we did the location stuff on film.

MJM: Your eye doesn't detect the transition – not on the average set with the average viewer.

ROLAND: I looked at one not long ago that didn't look so bad, technically. But they are nothing compared with what these new electronic cameras can do now. And if you take as much care as you do with film lighting, it's unbelievable what you can get. What I'm talking about is sacrilege. It's old-fashioned, nobody does that.

Nada Harcourt, creative head of dramatic series, looked at modern tape and film as aesthetically of equal quality.

HARCOURT [1991]: David Cronenberg just shot a couple of episodes of *Scales of Justice* on tape, and his creativity really energized the crews that were working with him in terms of his use of tape. It's always the same thing. Where does the creativity come from? Who has the vision and who has style? That can be done using tape as well as film.

MJM: But it's a longer process, isn't it? In actual shooting?

HARCOURT: Not really. All our film productions are post-produced on tape. There is amazing laser technology that we're using. It's all off-lined onto tape.

MJM: So that the master is a tape, not a film?

HARCOURT: Yes, absolutely, a one-inch tape, that's how we air it.

MJM: But you still get the nuances, because originally you shot it on film.

HARCOURT: Yes, so that you can control the lighting.

Clearly, David Barlow does not agree with Herb Roland and Nada Harcourt.

MJM: Do you think that film technology contributes to the possibilities of complex drama in a series as opposed to a more standard formula sitcom?

BARLOW: Yes. One of the first questions that Fecan asked Louis Del Grande and me when we pitched our idea of the commuters' sitcom was, "This is film, right?" He could tell from the idea. And then, when we conceived it, we thought of it as a filmed show, as we had with *Seeing Things*. It's like, "Am I going to type this or am I going to write it with a ball-point pen?" You make that distinction early. Both media bring certain qualities to them that dictate the entire look and tone and style. There are hybrids. Something like *Cheers* and *The Mary Tyler Moore Show* were always shot on film, but were actually done in a tape format. I think they look better.

George Schaefer, long associated with *Hallmark Hall of Fame*, finishes with a scene in no more than three takes if he is using tape. When filming, he does fourteen or fifteen, because "you spend forty-five minutes getting everything right for that forty seconds ... It's silly to settle for anything less than perfection in film."[13]
David described the limitations of tape technology in the 1980s.

BARLOW: Tape is – videotape. High-definition videotape from Japan notwithstanding, videotape cannot give you as much picture information in a frame as even 16-mm film can, and once you get to 35-mm film, forget it. The ratio is something like one to three for 16-mm film, and 35-mm is four times as detailed as 16-mm film. Also, the taped image cannot sustain as wide a contrast ratio, which is why it's flat. When you take a 16-mm film print and transfer it to videotape, the colour and the shadings shift – the electronic equipment can't handle the range of tone, shading, and contrast of 16-mm film. You have to fiddle your tape electronically so it looks like film. You have to make that adjustment because the equipment says, "Oh, my goodness, there's a one to thirty contrast range here and I can handle only a one to ten! Well, we'll pull down those whites," or "Those whites will all look really white and the oranges will look really orange." Tape doesn't have the contrast range and cannot operate in low light levels. Finally, it is not as flexible. You just have to follow a film cameraman around and see some of the places he gets to and most of the things he does. These things are not yet available in the dramatic form.

Yet since our conversation in 1988, videotape technology has made rapid advances. The single camera tape technique has already been mentioned. Producer Sam Levene was one of the first to use it in a series.

LEVENE [1988]: Traditionally, the sitcom is a taped show, a multi-camera taped show. *Not My Department* was an attempt to do a single-camera show with tape, shot to look like film, or at least taking a film approach. It would have been nice to have done it on film, but it was fine working on tape, using essentially a film-trained director of photography. I think we got some satisfactory looking pictures on it.

As Levene pointed out, single-tape camera technique affects the performances.

LEVENE: Traditional tape comedy is frequently performed in front of an audience, so you perform in a different, broader kind of way.
ALICE SINCLAIR, story editor [1988]: If an idea were presented for a show, and you knew it had to be on tape, you would have far more studio sets and interiors. Also, the whole look was different, because what you seldom have in film is a camera that moves. I don't mean that it's impossible, but mostly it is single shots. In tape, they're swooping around like ballet dancers all the time. If it's a tape show, the script assistant and the producer will have a script showing what camera and when. But in film, a director is rarely seen with a script in his hand. What the director is conscious of is that he is covering the scene in such a way that his editor has plenty of material to work with. The film editor isn't at a loss because he can't cut from here to there. The standard thing you take is a master shot, then a reverse master, and closeups of everybody, and, depending on the scene, maybe a two-shot or a long shot. That's the simplest.
MJM: What about something like *Backstretch* [two seasons in 1983–84], which had a lot of exterior work? Were the exteriors in Elmira at the racetrack shot on tape?
SINCLAIR: Some of them, but there was a good deal of chromakey in *Backstretch*, where actors perform in front of a blue screen. There are two tapes. One is shot with the actors in the studio. On another generation of the tape, the background is taped and the two are "married," so that the actor appears to be on the race-track. This happened because the actors were not good sulky drivers. When they had a bunch of real drivers thundering up

their backsides, they stopped acting and looked terrified. I must
say I don't blame them, because those sulkies are going thirty
miles an hour when they come out of the starting gate. What we
did was, we had the thundering horde of real drivers going around
the track, and the actors in the studio, with a couple of stage
hands shaking the shafts. They didn't show up (we hoped) and the
actors would act their little hearts out.[14]

PARTINGTON: Film people talk about themselves as though they
were genetically different. It involves a commitment, because
you're outside so much. Maybe that's why this myth of "special"
film people and "special" attitudes exist. I didn't find it so different. Today most of the films are done half in the studio, particularly the series.

MJM: In film and tape, producers have more direct control over the
image itself than they do on film alone. In film, producers control
some of the specifics of the edits, sound mix, and so on. But with
tape, particularly the weekly sitcoms, the producers are pretty well
at hand with the director, saying "How about this and how about
that," are they not?[15]

PARTINGTON: That tends to be true especially in sitcom, which is
practically all that's done on tape anymore. The producer or the
executive producer tends to be a writer, and it's often very hands
on, although you try to leave the directors alone and let them do
as much as possible on their own. However, the executive producers and the writers who may be around have very strong opinions about how the script should be realized – so that is different.

MJM: If the writers are around, that couldn't be more different
from film drama, particularly anthology and specials.

PARTINGTON: Yes, that's true.

MJM: Producers are involved directly in getting the image onto the
tape in a way that the producers of film are not.

PARTINGTON: Yes, although on film series today the producers are
a lot more "hands on." From what I know of Street Legal, for
example, the producers are right there overseeing everything. The
show has a look that they try to keep consistent, even though
directors change.

MJM: The producer's sensibility prevails and the directors come and
go.

PARTINGTON: Whereas when you do a film special, you hire a
specific director. Ideally, you are really giving the film to him.

MJM: Well, if it's Eric Till you had better, or he is not going to do
good work for you.

PARTINGTON: With Eric Till, if you were going to challenge anything he is doing, you better know what you are talking about and you better be able to present it in such a way that you are taking into account his experience. The same with people like George McCowan.

JOHN KENNEDY, head of television drama through the late 1970s and 1980s [1985]: It's amusing in a bizarre sort of way at the moment that the tape people (those who work with tape all the time, technicians and the management types) are quite concerned that we're turning to film. The film people are quite concerned that we're turning to tape. If you pick up a television technological magazine, it says, "Tape is the thing, folks. That's where it all is – it's lightweight, fast, and now the image quality is rapidly gaining on film." Our thrust from drama's standpoint – remember that drama is only one user of the technology – is to use both film and tape because they serve different purposes.[16]

David Barlow continues:

BARLOW: The great thing about using tape even for a film in post-production is that it's fast, the materials are reusable (because it's all computer related), and there is greater opportunity to manipulate. Once you've paid for the enormous capital costs of the equipment, to manipulate it quickly is an important factor.

MJM: When you post-produce using tape, you start with film and end with a tape, don't you?

BARLOW: Yes, that's right. They're working now on making sure that they can synchronize tape and film, because there is about a two-frame difference per second between video tape and film. There is a substantial quality loss when 16-mm film is transferred to tape.

MJM: The CBC uses 16-mm film.

BARLOW: That's right. When you do opticals and when you do successive prints, when you take a negative from your negative to do successive prints, you really do start to sustain loss in a far greater rate than you do in 35-mm film, where you can strike hundreds of prints and multi-negatives. You don't have the same problem, because the film itself is bigger. So, once we get to digital video to do multiple copies of something from 16-mm film, the post-production that follows the editing of the film itself is very attractive.

MJM: The editing of tape has always been more difficult. A producer does much more editing as he or she shoots.

BARLOW: That's right, and it requires an enormous capital investment to get tape editing equipment that is the equivalent of a Steenbeck and a Movieola.

MJM: The irony is that, originally, tape was supposed to be the money-saver. Yet, around the late 1960s, early 1970s, tape stopped being the money-saver because people used the time and money to get each scene better, and so on.

BARLOW: And it's not a money-saver when you start to roll in capital cost.

John Kennedy, in the middle of his term as head of TV Drama, put it this way: "The plant in Toronto is in sad shape and this will not improve in the near future ... Suffice it to say that neither producers nor directors nor technicians approach that place with any real confidence that it will work well on the day. This is a major barrier to any imaginative use of the videotape resource in Toronto."[17] Such a situation creates a self-fulfilling prophecy. Naturally tape falls into disuse by the 1990s.

BARLOW: No one ever factors in capital cost. They say, "Putting capital costs aside ..." Well, the reality is this. All of *Seeing Things* was cut by editor Vincent Kent in a little room next to a tailor's shop on the second floor of a building at the corner of Carlton and Yonge. There were a couple of wooden bins that I think Vince Kent had made himself, an air conditioner in the window, a Movieola that he'd had for 207 years, and a Steenbeck. In the forty-three episodes, there were 800 or 900 cuts an hour in the final versions. Thousands and thousands of feet of film went through there, were cut there, assembled, and shipped off. To do the equivalent on videotape, you would need four videotape machines and a climate-controlled room, because you've got to watch humidity and you've also got to watch the temperature, so it has to be a sealed, climate-controlled room. The machines are so sophisticated that you need a technician – not a screwdriver, which is what Vincent uses when the stuff goes bad. Those machines are worth about $250,000 each, maybe more. Then there are all sorts of support materials as well, if you want to do slow motion or the stuff we would send out to the lab in film. Yet nobody ever factors that in when they say tape's faster, cheaper, better, and quicker.

ACCELERATING CHANGE: HIGH DEFINITION

High-definition television is one of several recent technologies that may change television production substantially. What it provides is a much sharper picture on a screen that can be much bigger. HDTV uses digital technology. It allows the producer to create inexpensive special effects – for example, to place an actor on top of an inaccessible mountain without any of the crude "marrying" of the image of the actor and the chromokey image of the mountain. What HDTV requires, however, is a different recording system, a different transmission system, and a new receiver or TV set. None of this technology is in place in most countries except Japan. Refitting with this component would be very costly indeed, and the viewer would have to buy a new TV set to take advantage of the higher quality. As with current transmission signals, which differ in numbers of lines in North America and in Europe, arguments over HDTV standards based on excluding one country's technology and expertise from another's market are now raging in the technical journals and business sections of our newspapers and the Americans'.

The high-definition television used by the CBC was pioneered by the Japanese in the mid-1980s.[18] It was essentially an improvement on the analog technology used in our current North American recording and transmission system. When supplied to a set that could take advantage of it, however, HDTV provided double the resolution, so the screen could be much larger than the normal size. Yet this technology will almost certainly not be adopted by North America or Europe in the 90s for two reasons.

The first problem is whether the new and the old signal can be broadcast simultaneously on a single channel and be received by both the old low-resolution and very expensive high-resolution television sets. The second problem is whether the signal can be squeezed into an already overcrowded broadcast band. It may be that with the coming of high-frequency direct broadcast satellites, together with the already extensive use of cable in Canada, the channel crowding will not be as important. Thus, simultaneous broadcast of both standards on a single channel may not be critical. However, with this restriction lifted, the logical choice for new HDTV format will be digital – the video equivalent of CD audio technology. Gone will be the noise (snow). With fast digital compression/decompression computer chips, the integration of computer and video technologies will provide us with the HDTV of the future.

Such integrations of the two technologies are already in use with expensive video editing work stations. Later this decade, video editing software and chips will be mass produced at low cost for the general consumer market. Eventually, digital HDTV will be combined with video editing and other entertainment activities, some of them interactive in one home centre (see chapter 12).

When David Barlow was interviewed in 1988, analog HDTV was inferior to film in terms of definition and contrast, but this will not be the case with digital HDTV. Depending on the technology chosen, it may well be possible to use the same signal to display low, medium, or very high resolution images, depending on the cost of the receiving and display device. Resolution as high as that obtained from film stock is already possible; for example, it is well known that digital computer techniques were used to generate the high-quality special effects in the George Lucas *Star Wars* trilogy in the late 1970s and early 1980s.

In the last decade, these techniques have moved from the $30 million super-computers to the desktop graphics work stations costing $30,000. Barlow's $250,000 editing machine (1988) can be obtained for $25,000. Modern cartoons are currently generated on these graphics work stations. The 1992 hit movie *Beauty and the Beast* and Spielberg's 1993 blockbuster *Jurassic Park* had large portions done on work stations made by the 3D graphics pioneer Silicon Graphics. The late 1980s and early 1990s TV trend in science fiction depends on economical computerized special effects. *Star Trek: The Next Generation, Deep Space Nine,* the short-lived but spectacular series *VR5, Earth 2, Babylon 5,* and the mid-1990s hit *The X Files* depend on computerized camera work and graphics. With digital TV, it will also be possible to restore information lost in transmission or even to enhance the quality of old films that have deteriorated, just as the quality of pictures transmitted from satellites orbiting distant planets were clarified by computer enhancement.

DENIS HARVEY, vice-president of English Television throughout the 1980s [1988]: Doing *Chasing Rainbows* (1988) in HDTV was my decision. It was a difficult decision, because our engineering people strongly recommended against it. I also had trouble understanding what was the point of it. If it wasn't going to show as HDTV on a regular television screen, why do it? But the reason I was finally persuaded was that the matting allowed Marc Blandford, the executive producer, to get effects that gave a "shine" to the series at a low cost which he would never have got otherwise. I still don't know. I think that the whole idea about getting the market very excited about HDTV for its ability to create a better picture is all bullshit, because if it doesn't show on a normal television screen, what does it matter? "Well," said Blandford, "you develop the skills and someday there will be a HDTV."

MJM: You've got a period series that won't date, and there may be a market for the HDTV version ten years down the road.

HARVEY: Probably, but I didn't approve it on that basis.

Whatever the technological advances just over the horizon, and despite Thatcherism and its erosion of public broadcasting, the BBC is still the benchmark for drama production around the world. I asked Sydney Newman, who has worked on both sides of the Atlantic since 1954, about the BBC's facilities.

MJM: How flexible is the BBC technically? Something I was reading suggested that the BBC is so locked into a massive studio plant that it is not as free to make filmed drama as North American production centres are.

NEWMAN [1984]: That is relatively true, but you use the words "locked in." The fact is, the whole economics of the BBC is based on studio production. They have many studios, but they have learned how to exploit them spectacularly successfully. *The Forsyte Saga* was all studio.[19] People always said, "We have to work with film because every shot has to be individually lit." The fact is that our lighting technicians at the BBC were so brilliant (and in commercial television too) that you never felt the confinement of the studio. Now, of course, they are using more and more film, and they are really screwing up their economics in the BBC.

Some 1980s series like *The Jewel in the Crown* and *Brideshead Revisited* are too expensive to mount in the frugal 1990s. Moreover, the bidding war for private broadcasting licences in the United Kingdom left most companies strapped for cash and some of the most creative (Thames in particular) out in the cold. The appointment of a new head of the BBC in the late 1980s, who cut muscle as well as fat and shook up some of the most ossified of "Auntie BEEB's" practices, may have kept it from the privatizers of the Conservative caucus, but his policies also heated up the debate about the BBC's pre-eminence and how to maintain it. Quality broadcasting on TV in Britain is consequently much more difficult to make. As Newman pointed out, during the 1970s and 1980s the evolution of the technology sent up the costs, resulting in more visual quality. However, sometimes the result can be less distinctive programming.

I asked Trina McQueen, whose broadcasting experience has been chiefly in news and current affairs, about film and tape.

MJM: I wouldn't imagine it happens with current affairs, but drama has often been a house divided. Technologically I have found there was a tremendous cachet with film. It seems to have something to do with the fact that television was step-sister to the "real thing" – cinema. Despite the high-definition TV and single-camera tape, I'm still getting the sense that "if it's on film it's real," whether it's of high quality or not, and "if it's on tape it's not as worth-while."

MCQUEEN [1988]: You're absolutely right that there is an envy of film. The people who worked in 16-mm film desperately wish that they could work in 35-mm, and you see all kinds of cunning schemes by which people hope they can get their film shot in 35-mm. I don't know why people long to be in movies, long to do a movie so much, but everybody in television wants to do a feature. I do not find, as a viewer, that I'm as satisfied by something on tape as I am with film. Tape is just not as good. The colours are too bright and brassy.

MJM: It's flat and it doesn't get the depth of field. Still, you can have something as inventive as *Freedom of the City*[20] on tape, because Eric Till uses the medium of tape self-reflexively.

If many television producers and directors really want to make feature films, television's other step-sister, theatre, has become Cinderella to film and television. Yet Eric Till would recast the fable, with television as Cinderella.

MJM: Why in the 1980s is there no interplay between the theatre and television, as there is in Britain?

TILL [1983]: Part of it is snobbery. There is still a belief that television is a junior, bastard medium, and that television will never train anybody as an actor, whereas the theatre will. There is also a lack of maturity, because we don't move around as often as we should. I remember in the first feature film I directed in England, *Hot Millions*, we worked around Maggie Smith's television commitments. She was doing a play for the BBC, so we just had to work around her rehearsal schedule. You'll find all kinds of great film directors working in the theatre, yet also doing commercials in England. It is a much more intelligent attitude, and you have the same thing happening in the United States.

TELEVISION'S HIERARCHY OF FORMS
OF DRAMA

Similar to film's hierarchy of "drive-in" or "straight to video films," "modest" money makers, reasonable successes, blockbusters, and "art films," television also has a hierarchy based on the stars, resources, costs, producers, directors, and technology. I asked Ivan Fecan in 1989 how this worked.

MJM: There is a real hierarchy, it seems, with theatrical film considered to be aesthetically superior, followed by made-for-TV movies, then taped specials, and, last of all, series and sitcoms. I notice you are using film language, and other people do too: "movie," "film," "picture." That was one of the first lessons that I learned, everybody at the CBC aspires to doing movies.

FECAN: Sometimes I aspire to it.

Clearly, Nada Harcourt did not aspire to making "movies". Her frustrations with the hierarchy are palpable, but her point about a successful series being the "cash cow" is also valid.

HARCOURT: It's a cliché to say that making series, whether taped or filmed, is hard work. It is all consuming. The motivation for a producer doing a series is very strong financially, because you have something that has shelf-life and that you can sell internationally. If you want to explore an idea in a movie, it is easier to do.

Sometimes a creative person has a passion for one idea, and some people don't want to do series. There are a number of in-house producers who want to do movies, and who are developing movies, but there are very few who really want to commit to series. There are fewer who want to commit to conceptualizing and then working up series. The other thing about series is there is a different cultural recognition for films, a publicity process. The movie has been invited to Cannes, it's opening the Festival of Festivals, all of that wonderful sharing with your colleagues and celebrating of events – none of that pertains to series. Series is slogging it out on a day-to-day level in your work boots and your jeans, vying for audience ratings and awards, but that kind of recognition is not the carrot in series. By and large, it's more difficult for an executive working in series, because the stroking is not there on a day-to-day basis. You have to have a certain altruism, which is an enjoyment of the collaborative process, of the magic moments that occur in the daily rush prints you can build on, the magic moments that occur in the scripting. It is definitely a different kind of incentive, a kind of nurturing incentive.

MJM: That correlates with the viewer's experience of the thing itself, the intimacy and the weekliness of it.

HARCOURT: Absolutely.

MJM: And the willingness to say, "Well, I didn't like that episode, but I'll be back next week because I care very much about those people and what may happen two weeks down the road."

Whether for series or for drama specials, HDTV is not the only or even the most significant technological advance that will restructure our television. In 1985, producer Philip Keatley in Vancouver foresaw the impact of satellites, including direct broadcast satellites and the potential disappearance of regional stations as independent producers of programs.

KEATLEY: My favourite technological nightmare is what one could do with the technology that exists. One could take fifty national reporters, hook them up with one hundred researchers, give them two editors and two two-man sound/lighting crews for Beta-cams, a word-processor computer link, and access to a satellite, have them travel, and close this centre down. [In the late 1990s journalists will run their own cameras and edit the footage. In a downsized CBC, Vancouver could be closed down.]

CNN, thanks to cable, basically works that way, often substituting immediacy and length of coverage for analysis. Most viewers can now move between Newsworld (which regularly carries BBC World Service), CNN, CNN Headline service, and the CBC *Prime Time News* and *Sunday Report*, as well as a half-hour of national news at 11 PM on CTV or Global at will, for a price. Others simply aquire the signals on Earth dishes that are rapidly shrinking in size.

In the mid-1990s the debate is also about the disappearing role of regulators like the CRTC, as direct broadcast satellites bypass networks and cable to bring channels to small, relatively cheap satellite dishes that will be parked on window sills all over North America. When the delivery systems undergo radical change, the makers and decision-makers are directly affected.

McQUEEN: What we talk about in production strategy is that somehow, just as Canadians develop ways to run a railway, or to do other kinds of technology, some kind of research and development should be done on ways of creating faster production. There must be production innovations, all kinds of things that would allow us to reduce the cost of doing a Canadian program. If I had one government program that I could fund, it would be that. It would be a huge R&D into television production, designed to keep the cost down, which would not only help Canadian producers and make Canadian programs possible, but would also be instantly and universally exportable. Canadians could make billions, because the cost of production is major all over the world. Why we haven't turned our attention to making cheaper television programs that look good, the way that we've been able to make cheaper cars that look good, or cheaper TV sets that look good, is beyond me, because a lot of television is technology. It is machines and wires and electronic chips.

MJM: And expectations, obviously. I don't see much self-reflexivity in Canadian television drama, where it's conscious of its own form and it makes the viewer watch the form as well as the content critically.[21]

McQUEEN: But first, you can only do the basics. We've got to get our act together, so that we can have a few regular series on the air and some good movies. To me, to go into a mode of experiment or high art in television is necessary, but it comes after doing the kind of thing that people want from television, that they expect from television, that they spend 85 per cent of their time watching on television – unless you're going to say "the hell with all that." And you'd be wrong to do that in public broadcasting. I think you'd be wrong because there's still this hunger for stories about *us*. The form may be the same as the British or the American, but the stories, the content has to be distinctive. Maybe the first thing to do is to make sure that program content is different, and then move on to the different forms in which you can do it. Ideally, a large amount of volume would give you the opportunity to experiment, and the innovative technology to interact with the ideas of writers and producers, directors, designers, and directors of photography. And perhaps, once every two or three years, as John Kennedy did after a prolonged strike of the technical unions, the CBC might do a full-length "studio and film insert, live drama" that would recapture for makers and viewers alike the immediacy that is now one of television drama's neglected forms.

It remains to be seen whether such flexibility, such innovation, can survive the cash-strapped 1990s. One columnist in the *Globe and Mail*[22] foresaw a move to "more centralization, greater cooperation among the services, fewer commercials and greater use of such technological innovations as satellite transmissions," an increasingly credible projection that could bring us Keatley's vision of CBC television centred on two "superstations" in Montreal and Toronto. By 1995 the scheduling strategy called repositioning, anchored by the hour of *Prime Time News* at 9 o'clock, was abandoned.[23] However, certain kinds of cooperation among the services, together with major changes in process and in technology and who uses it (reporters with their own cameras, doing two or three jobs, for example), may preserve the standards set earlier. Possibilities for new forms of programming are opening up – and they include much more feedback from audiences. The new Discovery channel is already asking viewers which among several pilots they wish to see become a series – with votes by both e-mail or "snail mail." Other program have Web sites for internet users seeking more information or for feedback. Discovery also uses e-mail and Internet for elements of its nightly *at discovery.ca* science/information/quiz/speculation show. In fact, several of the news, education, and information services are offering weekly half-hour or hour programs that update viewers on new technologies of the information age. Viewers may well be frustrated, however, until it is easy to capture the information in writing from the screen. To *use* this information, a viewer cannot simply "go with the flow."

As we turn to chapters on policy and ethos, we should bear in mind the plans announced for changes in programming, journalistic accountability, management and production efficiency, corporate communications, and cooperative production with other broadcasters. But the following characterization of the CBC by Robert Patillo, then CBC vice-president of communications, is the most interesting self-perception offered by the CBC upper management in recent years: "We are very conscious of our absence of an image. The image of the CBC is very fragmented, very diffused."

The 1993 answer was to hire well-known public figures to proclaim that they "go public" – choosing CBC hockey or news or *Street Legal*. At every station break, the CBC reminded us that it is a public network with different programs. In 1994–95 we were offered tantalizing "behind-the scenes" vignettes. More useful were the cross-promotions: CBC Radio advertised and sometimes supplemented TV programs with context or interviews, and CBC TV put faces on the well-loved voices of CBC Radio. The policy-makers have the job of making sure that the differences are visible in the programs themselves as well as in the advertisements. New technology, and new uses for old technology, new cooperation between programs are only part of the answer to the problem of creating CBC services that are visible and distinctive.

Two voices from the magazine *Wired*, which exists in both online and in hard copy, put the technology and its uses into a mid-1990s context.[24] Nicholas Negroponte, director of the MIT Media Lab, wrote under the heading "HDTV. What's Wrong with This Picture":

As intelligence in the television system moves from the transmitter to the receiver, the difference between a TV and a personal computer will become negligible. As the television's intelligence increases, it will begin to select video and receive signals in "unreal time." For instance, an hour's worth of video – based on a consumer's profile or request – could be delivered over fiber [optic cable] to an intelligent TV in less than five seconds. All personal computer vendors are adding video capabilities, thereby creating the de facto TV set of the future. While this view is widely respected, it is not yet accepted worldwide. The biggest reason to be optimistic is that the digital world carries with it a great deal of tolerance for change. We will not be stuck with NTSC, PAL, and SECAM, but we will command a bit stream that can be easily translated from one format to another, scaled from one resolution to another, transcoded from one frame rate to another – independent of aspect ratio. Digital signals will carry information about themselves and tell your intelligent TV what to do with them. If your TV does not speak a particular dialect, you may have to visit your local bookstore and buy a digital decoder, just like you buy software for your PC today.

Michael Crichton, novelist and writer of the film scripts for *The Andromeda Strain, Rising Sun,* and Jurassic *Park,* and executive producer for the hit 1994 TV series *E.R.,* adapted a speech he gave to the National Press Club for *Wired.* Entitled "Media Sources: Today's Man's Media Is Tomorrow's Fossil Fuel," it is a detailed, persuasive attack on television news and information programming:

Once Al Gore gets the fiber optic highways in place, and the information capacity of the country is where it ought to be, I will be able, for example, to view any public meeting of Congress over the Net. And I will have artificial intelligence agents roaming the databases, downloading stuff I am interested in, and assembling for me a front page, or a nightly news show, that addresses my interests. I'll have the twelve top stories that I want, I'll have short summaries available, and I'll be able to double-click for more detail. How will Peter Jennings or MacNeil-Lehrer or a newspaper compete with that?

Good question – but what in this tailor-made-for-the-discriminating-and-computer-literate-consumer hard copy will happen to serendipity, to browsing, to stumbling over a biting cartoon or an infuriating editorial, a new columnist, or a bit of bird-watching that might start a new hobby?

What kind of roots and wings does the CBC possess, or remember that it once possessed, to take itself and us into the next century? The chapters on policy and ethos may supply some answers. But first the question confronting both a policy-maker in the 1950s, when we had little national theatre except radio, and more acutely in the 1990s, when we have less money and far more international entertainment available, is: Why make Canadian television drama?

7 Why Do Canadian Television Drama?

CBC drama has been a marginal activity up till now, even though somebody who's passionate and cunning can overcome the institutional bias
against drama. I think to a certain extent there has been an institutional
bias against drama on the CBC because it's troublesome, it's risky, and it's
expensive. TRINA McQUEEN

Why make Canadian television drama? The answers are as varied as
the individuals who make the programs or make the policy decisions.
What is television drama for? What is *Canadian* television drama for?
Many people have asked themselves both questions. When I focused
on Canadian television drama in my interviews, everyone admitted
that "Canadian" television drama is a term whose meaning is ultimately independent of the CRTC definitions of content and the pass-
ports of a specific quota of participants.

MJM: A nationalist thrust came to bear on *Festival* in the mid to late
1960s.
ROBERT ALLEN, producer and head of TV drama [1981]: Before that.
The *Festival* producers did Canadian plays at the time of the government's drive to sell Canada Savings Bonds.
MJM: *First Performance*, in the late 1950s.
ALLEN: The Bank of Canada wanted Canadian material, so we had a
stimulus to develop Canadian scripts. Having done so, we continued. For us, the emphasis on Canadian drama started with that.
But Canadian material was already being done by *General Motor's
Theatre* and so on [despite the constraints of half-hour or hour-
long time slots and the advertising agencies' active oversight of
scripts for the commercial anthologies].

What constitutes Canadian isn't simply defined as written by a
Canadian, directed, produced, photographed, post-produced, and

telecast in Canada. If it were, Telefilm and the CRTC would not need a very elaborate formula to define co-productions as Canadian. Does the internal perception of Canadian depend on what the program is about? I asked Denis Harvey, then vice-president of English television, about the Canadian content in the drive for Canadianization.

MJM: Suppose somebody wanted to do a two-hour movie special on the Vietnam War. We had a distinctly different cultural attitude towards that war. Would that subject constitute Canadian content?

HARVEY [1988]: If you are telling me that this script is set in the United States and it talks about the U.S. role in the Vietnam War, no, I wouldn't allow it to be done. If it is about the Vietnam War seen through Canadian eyes, or about people who fled the Vietnam War to come here, or the effect of the war on our views of war and international involvement and peacekeeping, or whatever, yes. It's got to be set in this country, and it has to be something about us as a people. Give me an example of what you mean?

MJM: *Two Soldiers* (1963), written by George Ryga and directed by George McGowan, was about two soldiers talking together on a country road, walking on their way home from nowhere to nowhere. Initially they talk about what it was like to be in the army, and by the end they talk very eloquently about nuclear war. It was just about that. It couldn't have been more Canadian, and yet it was not specifically Canadian.

HARVEY: That is a more difficult one to answer. I'm not sure how many times we have issued specific instructions. When I came into this job in 1984, I spent my first six months seeing independent producers, because they were puzzled about what exactly we wanted. Just at that time the independent market and Telefilm were starting. I told them I didn't want a story set outside Canada. Maybe we would have the luxury in three or four years of doing something that wasn't obviously Canadian, but at that time we were desperately in need of dramas that people could see were Canadian. I told them not to come in unless they had a Canadian story. I told John Kennedy, then head of TV drama, the same thing. I did not specifically get into things that were subtle, such as the example you were talking about.

MJM: Kennedy would be in sympathy with you.

HARVEY: Yes, he was, although not totally. He would argue that some stories were universal, that if a story was done in Canada by Canadian writers and so on, it would be Canadian. I could buy that, but at that time I'd have said we didn't have the luxury.

This book contains excerpts from conversations I had over several years with executives of diverse backgrounds whose jobs changed as the research progressed. Vice-president of English television, Denis Harvey, came up through the Sports Department and was in charge of Canadian television drama, among other things, throughout the 1980s (he resigned in 1991). Ivan Fecan, who was Harvey's hand-picked successor to Jack Craine, worked at City TV and at the CBC, and returned to Canada after a few years in Los Angeles as a protégé of Brandon Tartikoff, president of NBC Entertainment. He was for several years director of English television entertainment, then vice-president of entertainment and vice-president of English television. Fecan is now a vice-president of Baton Broadcasting. Trina McQueen, who came up through the News and Current Affairs division, was director of the Planning Department, then vice-president of news and current affairs, followed by eighteen months as vice-president of the regions. She left the CBC in 1993 to become president and general manager of Discovery, a new specialty channel. Each of them, like their successors, identifies as the primary goal of the CBC in the 1990s that leap of faith in the Canadianization of most of the remaining American hours on CBC prime time. One possible result of that process, if it continues, would be to transform drama from being a marginalized activity, an expensive luxury, into a necessity.

Yet Richard Collins claimed in *Culture, Communication and National Identity* that Canadians had created a postnationalist, postmodern country devoid of national myths and of the need for them.[1] To Collins, this made Canada a model for the new postmodern state. His book had been out less than a year when the Meech Lake storm broke – raising in a very concrete way the question of whether a country with few myths can survive as a political entity if it does not fully imagine itself in its national culture.

The questions of whether there is a distinctive Canadian popular culture and how to create and sustain it is often the site of a "contestation," a struggle between nationalists and those who see popular culture as a global phenomenon. The fact that "national" culture does not and cannot exclude popular culture here or anywhere else may offer hope in these troubled years, when the survival of Canada itself is in question. Another vital struggle is framed in terms of quantity versus quality. The numbers of hours given to drama are measured, defined, and evaluated by many at the CBC in terms of rating dollars spent and dollars earned. Others, fewer in number, evaluate the programs using criteria that more or less reflect the mandate as spelled out in the two broadcasting acts of 1968 and

1991. I talked with writer/producer Jeannine Locke in 1989 about what Canadianization should *not* mean.

MJM: I gather from what you are saying that the message in 1990 is that the bread and butter is series and mini-series. Movies really have to fight for resources.

LOCKE: That is certainly true for in-house movies. I think that *Small Sacrifices* (1989, starring Farah Fawcett) was a real object lesson. It had a big U.S. star, a grisly story, and it got huge ratings, yet it was "Canadian content" because it was filmed in Edmonton and had a lot of Canadian performers. The fact of the matter is that drama has to be paid for in some way. This in a season where in-house films are going "into inventory" because there is no money to put them on.[2] *Small Sacrifices* got something like three million viewers. It's the story of a woman described as a sociopath, a woman who kills her children. It was not about anything wrong in the system. She was one of those people who never ran into the system. She didn't knock off milk stores or anything like that; she simply tried to kill all her kids. That film really bothered me. At the end, the producers and writers sweep it all under the table and I thought, "What are we pandering to?"

MJM: It seems to be the American instinct to solve all the problems by narrative closure and to omit the context that creates the dramatic situation or that might complicate any resolution of it. Even if the larger problems aren't solved, it's all right, because the characters you've been identifying with are safe and sound.

LOCKE: And meanwhile you have had this delicious look at the dark side of human nature.

MJM: And it's been very safe for the viewer.

LOCKE: Perfectly safe.

MJM to producer SAM LEVENE [1988]: The word that keeps coming up as praise for the new CBC dramas of 1989 is "slick." I would take that as a pejorative.

LEVENE: Some people would say: "Slick is good!" Don't say "slick," say what it is – wonderful, terrific – because it is the way the Americans do it. I don't often hear the old saying, "I can always tell it's Canadian, there's something about the sound." Instead, I will often hear: "You are doing well, I can't tell anymore whether it is a CBC drama or an American drama!" Plus, on the box, viewers don't even know what they are watching half the time. They just press buttons. They may not know whether it is Canadian or American, CBC or CTV.

THE RELATIONSHIP OF CANADIAN AND
AMERICAN POPULAR CULTURE

MJM to producer DAVID BARLOW [1988]: Canadianization can be
defined several ways. It can be defined as "made here, but interchangeable" with the mid Atlantic or cross-border product. That's
very difficult to do, and, if we do it, it's self-destructive. But we
could call the network Canadianized and have seemingly endless
series like *Check It Out*, CTV's 1970s clone of American sitcom.
The other extreme would be television drama so constricted that
everything had to be sealed within our borders. What does Canadianization mean? How is that coming down the track to the people
who make the programs?

BARLOW: I think it means "Made in Canada," and "distinctively
Canadian." For the CBC, it means something different from what it
means for drama aired on CTV and Global. The sticking point is
that, more and more, we are not distinctively Canadian.[3] If you get
away from moose heads and beer and fish, and you start to reflect
this country, you reflect people who are North Americans. You are
going to be honest about where it's set, the cultural reference
points. For example, in *Street Legal*, they're not going to go to
court in business suits, they're going to wear robes. But we are
North Americanizing ourselves. We have adopted an enormous
amount of American popular culture. So, if we really "do" this
country, you're going to see a lot of that.

MJM: What we do is inflect American popular culture, though.

BARLOW: If you look at *Breaking All the Rules* [produced by Barlow]
about the Canadian inventors of Trivial Pursuit, it is a distinctly
Canadian production, but it is full of American reference points.
They end up going to New York City at the end.

MJM: Their ad hoc way of doing things was very Canadian, surely.

BARLOW: Absolutely. But I would venture to say that the majority of
Trivial Pursuit questions that are quoted in the program are American questions because the majority of the questions in the game
are American. That game represents where a lot of us stand as far
as popular culture is concerned. So, I think that Canadianization
means reflecting this country, but once you start reflecting this
country, you start to see a lot of American influence.

MJM: That's what we see when we look in our mirror.

BARLOW: And you've been there. If you look at 1950s CBC drama,
it's full of English accents, because that's what the country was
about in the 1940s and 1950s. Drama, in partiular, was about that
English orientation.

MJM: What makes you think that? Your memory?

BARLOW: Yes, my memory. It's not true?

MJM: No.

BARLOW: My memory of the big actors of the time is that they were either British, who'd come to Canada, or British trained.

MJM: But, in fact, there weren't many British actors – Tony Van Bridge and a few others. The faces you saw over and over again and the accents you heard in that time period were Canadian; Frances Hyland, Doug Rains, John Drainie, Norma Renault, and William Hutt.

BARLOW: Yes. It's just what we retain, isn't it?

MJM: Well, it's interesting what you do retain. I sometimes think that if Canadians remember a show as being good, it's perceived as having being rooted in somebody else's culture.

As a producer, when you are thinking about sales abroad, do the topical and Canadian elements prevent syndication? You and Louis Del Grande always do very topical stuff.

BARLOW: It's a false issue, and I've always felt so. It's something people say. It's like saying, "Snow doesn't sell in the south." It's a standard thing in the United States: "Series in snow don't go." But the topicality issue is just not true. *All in the Family* had topical references. You do have to be careful, but not a lot. We always had topical references on *Seeing Things*. You can't do a show with Lou, without him wanting to comment on what he feels about everything. It's the same with him as a writer and as a performer, so you just do it.

MJM: It becomes part of the distinctive flavour of his work – and yours.

BARLOW: I find the stuff that sits in limbo profoundly alienating. If it doesn't have any topical references, doesn't refer to brand names, it's like Cosby's New York brownstone. Where are the bars on the bottom window and the security system? *Seeing Things* had a fantastical quality to it, but it was rooted.

An aside to this serious debate comes from producer Mario Prizek, who commented on our "Canadian" sense of humour – aside from our considerable gifts for self-reflexive satire.

PRIZEK [1983]: In a funny way, Canadian people are dour. It does not matter from what ethnic group they come. If they've been born here, especially, they are dour people. We're rather like the Swiss. The comedy we're best at is quips within a slightly more serious framework, or out-and-out slapstick farce in short spurts, sketches.

That's why the *Royal Canadian Air Farce* is so much fun – we specialize in that kind of humour, but we cannot sustain it because we don't see life that way. We don't fantasize about life as much as the Americans, especially in the California area. Even our actors have that attitude that they would rather be doing serious drama.

The thing I like about Lally Cadeau's show *Hangin' In* is that the ingredients are very fresh and light, and you get that lovely flow between serious and light – the comic. If we produce a situation comedy in Canada it is going to be from that kind of line – from Louis's show. [*Seeing Things*, most of *Airwaves*, some of the episodes of *Material World* (marks II and III), and the better episodes of *Max Glick* also had this flow between the serious and the light.]

BARLOW: Another thing that will happen, just to get the volume of production up, is that more of Vancouver, the West, and Halifax will be seen on the screen. There's not enough capacity in Toronto to generate the volume of material Ivan needs to generate, so you'll see these other places. Writer Bill Thomas and I are working on the Reuben Ship story.

MJM: You know about Reuben?

BARLOW: He wrote *The Investigator* [a very controversial CBC radio drama which skewered Senator Joe McCarthy and, by inference, the House Un-American Activities Committee. Reuben Ship was one of the victims of the "red scare," who was deported in handcuffs for being a union organizer among writers in Hollywood. Speaking of "popular" culture, an estimated one million bootlegged copies of *The Investigator* found their way into every corner of the United States.][4]

MJM: Why did that particular subject interest you?

BARLOW: What is fascinating is that he is prototypical. He's a Canadian who dreamed the American dream, as a lot of us did growing up. He had the idea that if you want to make it in show business, you go to Hollywood.

MJM: Particularly in the 1940s and 1950s.

BARLOW: Reuben got caught up in the black side – that America has traditionally not tolerated the range of political activity that this country has. He wanted to live and dream the American dream, yet he did not want to give up his political activity to do so. It has a backside to it as well, in that research has indicated that he was on an official black list in Canada. Canada imitated the United States, even in those days: "We'd better do it here, but we won't do it officially."[5]

MJM: Alice Frick has written about the problems of getting *The Investigator* on the CBC.[6] This drama is a myth and a memory for a certain generation.

BARLOW: It is a very tough sell, and I don't know if the show will ever see the light of day. It's expensive, it's Montreal, it's Toronto in the 1950s, it's Los Angeles in the 1940s and 1950s, it's very difficult to do. Trivial Pursuit appealed to me because you can't do a TV movie about people who invented a board game. Nobody would ever do that.[7] As Lou said, your closest parallel is the *Young Thomas Edison story*. There was another reason why I was attracted to both the Trivial Pursuit story and the Reuben Ship story. I grew up in St Catharines, twelve miles from the border. All my formative life is about that relationship between Canada and the United States. Years and years ago when I first met Lou, he used to say, "the amazing thing about Canadian drama is it doesn't acknowledge that huge American influence."

MJM: It used to. In the 1950s and 1960s there were also dramas on *G.M. Presents* in which Canadian writers and Canadian actors did stories about Korea, Italy, the U.N. in Cyprus, or wherever. Now that element is gone.

BARLOW: I grew up with more American influences than Canadian influence. That's another reason why the Trivial Pursuit story and the Reuben Ship story appealed to me, because I'm interested in what happens when we journey into a relationship with America. There's always that tension and that interplay, which is fascinating to me. Obviously, since Lou is an expatriate American, it fascinates him too.

MJM: Canadians talk a lot about American politics and American social life, but you wouldn't mistake a Canadian conversation about the presidential election for an American conversation. Our perspectives on it are very different; for example, you say there's a much greater political range here.

BARLOW: I agree that recently we haven't dealt with that on Canadian television, yet it is such a big aspect of our society. We just don't acknowledge it to the extent that we should. Yet the English feel that *The Killing Fields* was a British picture, even though it's about an American and a Cambodian in Cambodia during the Khmer Rouge takeover. That film was developed, produced, directed, and financed by Brits and, as far as they're concerned, that is a British film. They have the cultural confidence to be able to say that. We haven't got to that point. We have to work through Canadianization, narrowly defined.

I'm very optimistic and I believe that there will be an explosion of drama. I feel that the only negative side of this drive to reclaim prime time is that it will have to be Canadianized or that's it. This is the last kick at the can for anything distinctive, or separate. In the next three or four years there'll be a tremendous amount of product, and some of it will be good and some of it will be dreadful, and some of the dreadful stuff will be extraordinarily popular.

As creative head of dramatic series, Nada Harcourt had to find and bring to the small screen the weekly fare, the bread and butter (and the occasional steak) of the schedule – one likely based on a framework derived from American popular culture, but inflected to reflect Canadian laws, mores, problems, and even Canadian popular culture.

HARCOURT [1991]: My job as head of series is the best job in the world; it's extremely character building and it's wonderful working with Ivan. He's deeply respectful of creative people, and we're trying to find more of them. Certainly mechanisms have been set in place to do that as fully as we possibly can, given the constraints. It's the art of the possible. On Canada's mosaic, it's difficult to be lectured to about minorities and to do everything all at the same time. It is our wish to reflect the specific multicultural facets of Canada, but that is a growth pattern. Of course, we respect ethnic voices. It would be wonderful to set a series within a visible minority family. One has to be ever vigilant not to tokenize, and to give a character a three-dimensionality that the issue really needs. I think *Degrassi*, with Lucy as a black leading character, has achieved that to a certain extent, but it's easier when you are dealing in the unevaluative world of children, who are altruistic. We're looking, we're always looking. We have a black lead on *Street Legal* [Carrie's love and very briefly husband, Dillon, a crown attorney], and yet someone in the press says "Yes, but he's café-au-lait."

MJM: You are trying to make television in a fractious time.

MYTHS FOR A COLD COUNTRY

Maryke McEwen, like David Barlow, came up through the corporation (he as a unit manager, she as a story editor) in the 1970s. Both are producers who supervised successful series in the 1980s and both love television. David writes scripts, Maryke does not, but both are tuned to contemporary television modes in the late 1980s and early 1990s. I asked her about making myths for our country, a role I perceive as part of the answer to why we do Canadian television drama.

MCEWEN [1984]: If you could take some of the subconscious mythology that has already built up about the west and transform it into a true Canadian mythology, without falling into the traps of the "shootout at the o.k. Corral," you'd have created a new art form. But if it's going to be Canadian, it has to be one of those pieces with big land and small people and huge spaces of silence. It would be really interesting.

MJM: So you think that television has a potential mythos? Would that be the antithesis of *For the Record*?

McEWEN: Not really. *For the Record* is just trying to dig a little further inside Canadian mythology.

MJM: But *For the Record* often demythologizes Canadian self-images. I'm not saying that just to be critical. That is a very important function of drama.

McEWEN: Some of the myth is just bullshit. *For the Record* is creating a new myth in a way. If you demythologize some of the garbage, such as John A. Macdonald as a hero because he built the railway, and you look at the man as a man ...

MJM: *The National Dream* did not really consciously demythologize. But what strikes me is that it does make myth from the landscape ...

McEWEN: ... rather than the people.

MJM: The landscape is the only constant. In eight episodes there was only one major hero other than Sir John – Cornelius Van Horne. They finally got to the personal, rather than emphasizing the machines or the landscape in the two episodes about him.

McEWEN: One of the strengths of Canada, to me, is diversity. The more people try to draw this country together as one, the more mushy it gets. The more you allow it to have its own voice, the specific voices of each province, each area, the more you get that strong sense of Canada – not as a whole, but as a collection of different people and different cultures. It's the diversity of Toronto that makes it interesting, not the fact that it is a big city, because it's not. It's a collection of neighbourhoods.

MJM: Are you saying that, because of our regional diversities, we can't create a national myth of any kind?

McEWEN: I don't think you can create a national myth that says, coast-to-coast, "this is the basic Canadian experience." You can give a recognizable Canadian experience in Newfoundland. Then, if you do it well and not just for Newfoundlanders, you can try to translate it to the rest of the country and say, "That is part of us" [as *Codco*'s television success demonstrates]. I could do a program, but please don't ask me to define the identity of Canada.

MJM: But that is exactly what you are doing.

McEWEN: By default.

MJM: By simply engaging with what you see around you, you are
defining the Canadian identity. Any really decent program that is
grounded here is doing that – some with greater insight or impact
than others.

IVAN FECAN, then director of entertainment [1989]: Quality is even
more attainable now as we're beginning to value our Canadianness
as the world shrinks, and America gets closer. The whole free
trade negotiation has been very interesting because I defy anyone,
in a sentence, to tell me what Canadian culture is. But I would
also say that, in the last eight or nine months, people have come
to value it more, whatever it is.

A common definition of a Canadian is a person who asks, "What is
a Canadian?" In 1990 I attended the Banff International Festival of
Television. I fell into conversation with a writer from France who had
been sent to the conference to get some ideas about dramas that
might express the new "European" identity expected to emerge from
the New Europe. What he did not want to write was "Euro-pud" – a
blancmange of everything for everyone. I suggested something that
only a Canadian would instinctively think of, "Why not write dramas
about the search for a European identity." He did not laugh – and it's
not a laughing matter. Cultural identity and cultural artifacts are
symbiotic. Without one, the other does not exist.

WHO IS A CANADIAN VIEWER?

I was particularly interested in the ideas of producers, directors,
writers, and management about the audience for Canadian television,
not what kind of audience actually watched the program, but what
sort of person they visualized as the viewer – and whether that
perception then shaped their decisions about the programs.[8] As one
might expect, one of the first answers, that of a creative producer/
director, was personal.

RON WEYMAN, executive producer (who also paints) [1989]: These
are very basic questions, which one is never really asked. Why
does one paint this, and who is it for? It is not for anybody. It is
something which comes out of one's environment, one's guts at
the moment. A painting and a film are quite different, of course.
Painting is a direct individual expression, and film is the individual's expression of a concept, with the help of a dozen, a score of
other people.

If one is living in this world, and has certain visions of right and wrong, a certain moral position, then one is attracted to a particular line of argument, of work. The whole field of what is possible in drama and film is limited obviously by the environment in which you live and by the people you share that environment with. If I were a producer at Twentieth Century Fox, I would be given a list of twenty or so names of writers and I would talk to all of them and get their ideas. Their ideas would be translated by me as a producer either to a formula, something already there, or to something new. But I would have to work within the limits of what was considered to be acceptable, and in good taste, and entertaining. In this country, chances are I *wouldn't* be given such a list, and I would know the half-dozen writers available to me, all of whom are scratching for ideas. I would be guided by my own inner compulsions to a degree, my own sense of what is important and what is not. I have been lucky in that respect. *Wojeck* throws a lot of things into question, instead of being just good entertainment, but first it is an examination of certain aspects of our society. The subject, if done elsewhere in the world, would have been so watered down that it would not have been worth doing – in which case, who knows, I might have been a painter or something else.

For Nada Harcourt, the answer is in cultural context and in a preference in Canada for family programming.

HARCOURT: Some critics believe that the CBC should be PBS north, as in "Why don't we do the *Singing Detective*?" Well, excuse me, programs like *Brideshead Revisited* and *The Jewel in the Crown*, which are universally praised, drew flies when they were broadcast on the CBC, partly because of their lack of Canadian cultural context. Our intention in our series is to be mainstream, to be entertaining, and to garner as many of the demographics in the audience as is possible for a Canadian audience. Consequently, we are not going to get very far if a large financial investment is made in foreign product, something that draws 250,000 viewers.

Family programming is not something I chose to do because I like it, but because the audience wants it, particularly in Canada. There's no question that the success of those programs is directly proportionate to an audience need. The fact that it's found universal and international acclaim speaks also to a universal need. It's very important to have a partnership with your audience, to gauge what they might be interested in, what their concerns are, what the economic concerns are. I'm very proud that I had some ability, as a woman, to gauge the public appetite and to say we should be doing more from the point of view of young people and of women. Women view more television. Because there will always be a large proportion of women between the ages of eighteen and forty-nine, that's a growth audience, an audience that advertisers are very interested in. If you can couple that with children, then you augment your audience with something that's very sophisticated. Teenagers aren't large viewers of television. The idea is always to try to maximize your audience. Family programming has really done that.[9]

With her roots in current affairs, Trina McQueen had a more detached perspective, an awareness of the ironies that attend the question. She is aware of the case I put in *Turn Up the Contrast* for CBC drama as a cultural activity essential to our national health.

MCQUEEN [1988]: CBC drama has been a marginal activity until now, even though somebody who's passionate and cunning can overcome the institutional bias against drama. To a certain extent, there has been an institutional bias against drama on the CBC, because it's troublesome and expensive. But it is also what the majority wants, in addition to news and current affairs. When we do a drama, there's always that terrible holding your breath to see what people are going to think. I hear that so much when we're talking about Canadianization. People say, "It sounds wonderful, but what if we do it wrong?" There is not as strong a belief in our ability to do drama as news and current affairs.

MJM: What an irony, from my perspective looking at nearly forty years of CBC drama.

MCQUEEN: But again, forty years of marginal activity. Therefore, it's got to be thought of as very high quality. If you're doing it as a marginal activity, and you have failures, then the public perception is that your failure rate is probably 50 per cent. Every problem that you talk about – people's lack of identification with it, people's perception of it as "not good" – results in part from its marginalization. You have to search so hard to find any Canadian TV drama, and then to find the treasures, you have to search even harder. I can remember as a kid (and I know it's not popular to say this), I hated *Don Messer's Jubilee* so much that it turned me against the entire CBC, against the notion of the CBC as an entertaining network. To me, the CBC was these fat, old people, and I did not want to watch because I didn't want to see myself in that. However, I can remember watching *Nightcap*, a late-night set of satirical sketches on the CBC, and saying, "That's me." One program that turns people off, in which they do not see themselves, can destroy their perception of CBC drama.

MJM: Would you buy the argument that when the CBC does eight episodes, it can keep the quality up, but with it's limited resources it can't do twenty episodes?

McQUEEN: I buy it, 100 per cent. But I look at the British experience, where they love to do eight *Monty Pythons* or eight *Fawlty Towers*. At the same time, they're giving the audience their *East Enders* two nights a week. If you've got the quantity, then you can have both – then you can have the superb little jewel that everybody looks forward to year after year. But if you've only got one *Seeing Things*, and if it's only on six times a year, you're in trouble.

MJM: What about reruns in all this Canadianization? Will there be more space for it?

McQUEEN: Yes, if you haven't bought American programs for fifty-two weeks a year, you have many more holes to fill up, presumably with Canadian reruns. You also have to do them for economic reasons. You have to write them off. Or are you talking about reruns of former programs?

MJM: I'm talking about reruns of good Canadian programs that may be more than a year old. This is the only country in the world that isn't "rerun heaven." Instead, Canada is rerun heaven for American and occasionally British TV. [In 1995, however, Showcase, a new specialty channel, reran *Wojeck, King of Kensington, Street Legal, Adentures in Rainbow Country, The Forest Rangers, Airwaves,* as well as CTV's *ENG* and the independent *SCTV* during the day and in prime time.]

McQUEEN: One of the reasons why we don't do it is that reruns are likely to be daytime fare, and generally our budgets for daytime fare are so much below what a Canadian rerun costs that it's difficult to schedule them. For instance, we might have $5000 available for a half-hour segment, but the *King of Kensington* is $7000 or more. So you can do it maybe once. To program a whole afternoon of Canadian reruns would be, economically, a challenge.

MJM: How about retrospectives? To give reruns a more pretentious title, and perhaps to imply more pride, more care, and more purpose.

McQUEEN: We regularly do that: this year with *Moments in Time* (reruns of *For the Record*), followed by *Wojeck*. We used to do it with *Rear View Mirror*.[10]

MJM: The BBC has done a retrospective of the writer Dennis Potter. They said: "Here's somebody whose work we like even when we've censored it or refused to show it. We'll do a formal, well-publicized retrospective of some of his dramas. We'll show some pride in it." I also know they have another channel to do that on, BBC-2, with no sponsors to persuade.

McQUEEN: And they also have a whole bunch of other stuff. We don't have the programs.

MJM: Suppose you did a retrospective of Eric Till's work as a director.

McQUEEN: That is a very interesting idea. It comes back to the fact that there hasn't been enough air time or enough money for it. There have never been enough resources. But, sure, we could and we should do that.

Ivan Fecan, with his roots in Canada, his most recent experience in the United States, and his global outlook, had a different view of "what CBC television drama is for." After all, he reorganized CBC drama so that many more of the crucial decisions landed on his desk. Yet he did have a clear set of parameters set for him by the mandate, the network itself, and his own intuition and sensibility.

MJM: You describe a vision of whatever comes out of the development process as different from what is next door, south of the border.

FECAN [1989]: I don't know that. I don't want to define what we are going to do as starting out by trying to be different from what is there. What we want to do is be truthful and meaningful.

MJM: Wouldn't that in itself make a difference?

FECAN: I don't think it would make a difference compared with the sitcom *The Wonder Years*. It would make a difference compared with *Growing Pains*.

MJM: I don't mean to characterize American popular culture as untruthful and us as truthful. What I meant was that our truth is different from their truth.[11]

FECAN: Some of our truths may be the same. We are all human. Some of our truths may be very different.

MJM: So Canadianization is not going to be "moose nose and maple leaf."

FECAN: You might do a satire on it.[12]

MJM: No, there is a real question here. I have noticed that there has been a continuous constriction of subject matter and of style over the years because there weren't many hours available and not much money.

FECAN: I don't know where the real responsibility is. But if you are beaten down by lack of money year after year after year, maybe you don't go out and try as hard.

MJM: My question is this: Is there going to be room on the schedule for the *Canadian* look at today's hijacking, tomorrow's famine relief in Africa, the next day's popular cultural trend, or the political situation in the United States? We don't even make programs about the United States which foreground that country from a Canadian perspective.

FECAN: Are these documentaries that you are talking about?

MJM: No, I am talking about drama: our fictional view of other people's problems and concerns.

FECAN: I think there are two ways of doing that. The cliché that the world is a small place is very true. The whole world is hooked into television. We are all watching stuff go down live. I think there is a way of introducing that kind of perspective either as a story line or as an element in an ongoing series. There is nothing wrong with that and, if it makes sense as a story, we will try to tell it.

I have given people targets. As the guy who has the schedule, who is the buyer, I guess (or whatever you want to call it), I must have some kind of vision that many kinds of visions can plug into. I also have some sense that there are things we will do and things we won't do. We won't do *Night Heat*; we will not run beauty pageants; we will do *Anne of Green Gables*.

MJM: Why won't you do *Night Heat*?

FECAN: Because it has nothing to do with this country. If the Americans want to come up here and take advantage of the lower dollar – wonderful. If they want to come up here and make Canadian content by the rules that the government has set up, that is wonderful, too. I don't object to their doing that. In fact, I have a lot of respect for Sonny Grosso, producer/writer of *Night Heat*, because he is a practitioner. He is something we don't have enough of in this country. We need more people who can do that kind of thing, but who also want to talk about things going on in Canada. I don't mean just whether Mayor Eggleton or Mulroney is re-elected. I mean things that Canadians care about.

Contrast Fecan's mentor at NBC, Brandon Tartikoff, then president of NBC Entertainment: "We have to make sure that we have the kind of shows that [ad agencies] feel will provide a compatible, comfortable medium for their commercials. If the shows are offensive ... morally outrageous ... too violent or too sexy, we could be getting twenty-eight ratings but our sales department would be selling them at half-sponsorship! As for NBC's 204 affiliates, they must feel the content is suitable and likely to win its time period."[13]

APPLIED CANADIANIZATION

MJM: What kind of vision have you painted for the people working on mini-series and the movies.

FECAN: I have targets, and they are so general you can drive a Mack truck through them. I really have to find a way of getting the small, independent film-makers involved so we can do a lot more. I can pick up a lot of shows or movies that are developed elsewhere and put them into the schedule.

Later, in a CBC press release of 6 August 1991, Fecan was quoted as saying:

"I believe in the importance of national cinema. The films we have selected are individualistic, quirky gems, not unlike the films Britain's Channel 4 has invested in, rather than big box office attempts."

The four films are:

Diplomatic Immunity, Sturla Gunnarsson's critical examination of Canada's foreign aid policy in Central America; *Clearcut*, Richard Bugajski's dramatic view of one native's chilling protest and armed hostage-taking; *Sam and Me*, Deepa Mehta's story about a Pakistani immigrant's first taste of Canada; *South of Wawa*, Robert Boyd's portrait of relationships in small-town Ontario.

"To say *Diplomatic Immunity* was hard to get financed would be an understatement," said the film's producer/director, Sturla Gunnarsson. "It's a hard-edged film that a lot of people find disturbing and it took us 10 years to get it made. From the time that Ivan Fecan read the script, we enjoyed the CBC's unconditional support. We couldn't have made the film without them," Gunnarsson added.

Deepa Mehta, producer/director of *Sam and Me* commented: "If Ivan Fecan at CBC had not read the script of *Sam and Me* overnight and made a commitment to buy it for TV the next day, the film quite simply would never have been made. The money sure helped, but the belief in an 'obscure immigrant script' is really what makes a film-maker grin with joy!"

The fact that these complimentary remarks appear in a press release does not undercut the argument that the CBC's patronage is as vital to small independent film-makers in Canada as Channel 4 is to the struggling British cinema.

FECAN: The objectives are very simple. I would like to do a couple of historical pictures. I want to do a number of things that focus on issues. We are developing the Colin Thatcher story [*Love and*

Hate, 1989–90] and the Marshall story [*Justice Denied*, 1989–90, with the NFB]. There are a lot of interesting things going on in this country that would make fascinating work. I want to do a number of "Disney-like family pictures," Disney/Touchstone, where there are strong characters that have to deal with problems but there is some kind of inner resolution. It may not be a happy one. It may be a bitter one, but there is some kind of growth. *Anne of Green Gables* is the obvious one. There are others that you can point to that fall into that category [*The Little Kidnappers* and *Princes in Exile* (1990–91), and *Jane of Lantern Hill* (1991–92), all rerun at least twice].

Those are the targets, because those are the kinds of pictures I would like to build a schedule with, unless someone comes in with passion who is better. We are going to want that, because it is the passion that is going to drive good TV drama. But when you leave home in the morning to go to work, you want to have targets. If you find something that is better, you go with what is better. The targets are there, but they are not exclusive. It not only depends on the passion, it also depends on the timing. If you have eight pictures and all the protagonists die of cancer, maybe you don't want to do a ninth one. Maybe you want to sit on the script for a year. It doesn't mean you throw it out. It just means that maybe that year you don't do it. I want to make sure that the pictures we do make have clarity of purpose, so that when we finally commit to shooting a picture, we know why we are doing it. If we decide we are doing something largely as an entertainment, we will do it as an entertainment and not try to make it a lot of other things as well, so that, in the end, it doesn't become a lot of nothing. It is that clarity of purpose that I am very concerned about.

DAVID BARLOW, producer [1988]: Instead of starting with how much material can the plant handle each year, how much crew do we have, and what does that translate to in hours of programs, Fecan's come the other way: What programs and how much programming do we want to do? What shows do we want? How many shows do we want to get on air? How much do we want to Canadianize this network? And, of that, what kinds of things do we want to do? What personnel do we need to do those kinds of things? What will that require in terms of production effort? How much will we be able to do within the corporation? How much will we farm out? How much will go to regionals? How much will be independent? What will be the mix? That was one of the major recommendations out of the Deerhurst Conference of CBC employees from across the country.

FECAN: The difference is that the departments don't exist anymore. They don't have any more money, they don't have any air time. There's a pool of money and there's a pool of air time, and I believe that the best idea gets the go ahead. That's the long and short of it. All the administration, the production management, is run by a group that reports to me separately to encourage the standards and quality.

MJM: You've got far more hours available to you than John Kennedy had in the late 1970s to the mid-1980s when he was told he could have only seventy hours of drama for the entire season.

FECAN: But the system is very different now internally. We have a lot of different creative heads, but none of them owns any air time and none of them has any production money; it's all pooled.

MJM: As I recall our conversation in 1988, your idea of breaking up this monolith of a single drama department was to get rid of the housekeeping element and to free people up to concentrate more on production. From your perspective nearly a year later, has it worked out that way?

FECAN: Yes, and it gets rid of the territorial aspect. There was a fair amount of territoriality. That happens in any organization that has evolved and has been around for a long time. The idea was that if you had twenty hours last year, you had to have twenty or twenty-one this year. My idea was that the best script gets the production money, and the best thing we can make gets the slot.

My sitcom department is an office about a quarter of the size of mine. It has one person in it, and he has to share a secretary. That's the whole department. The series drama department has four people and would fit into maybe twice the floor space of mine. Departments aren't what they used to be. They are buyers, buyers and developers. Their job is to come forward every two or three months and present what they have or what they have been able to find and want to develop further, as well as monitoring the shows they have on the air. I insist that somebody on the programming team actually reads every script, which previously was not possible. The way that people were distributed did not make it possible, because so much production was happening in one place and so little in another place. The people in charge of the majority of the production did not have the time to read every script and to make notes.

A different perspective on Fecan's reorganization, expressed to me by many experienced producers, is that during his tenure and after, much more influence, both on the choice of programs and on the process of making them, was exercised by people without much programming experience; that "committees" met over and over; that eight or nine people had to approve the casting rather than only the producer, the executive, and perhaps the head. MBA jargon for it would be "micro management." However, the creative heads were said to enjoy this hands-on "creative control" approach.

MJM: It must be quite exhausting. You are involved with script approval, in casting, in public relations.

FECAN: Yes, I'm involved in everything, in every area including sports, except for news and current affairs. I don't exercise any control there, but I schedule it.

MJM: And you are involved in arts and science?

FECAN: Absolutely.

Denis Harvey, vice-president of English television in the 1980s, had a vision of Canadianization congruent with Fecan's.

HARVEY: I have tremendous faith in Ivan. I worked for a year to get him back. He's the first director of programming in this corporation who's ever actually read scripts. He reads scripts, he meets actors, he's moved the casting director to his floor, he's got the head of comedy on his floor, he wants to move all his area heads to his floor if he can find the space. He reads scripts night, day, and weekends. He notes scripts and sends them back to people, and tells them what he thinks is right or wrong with them. He is being very active – which can be good or bad, depending on how good he is.

Given Fecan's promotion to vice-president of arts and entertainment and then, in 1992, to vice-president of the whole English network, the CBC president and Board of Governors seemed to have decided that the answer was "good." Yet by 1994 he had left for CTV, as had Trina McQueen for Discovery. Fecan did not publicly explain his decision. McQueen is quoted by Knowlton Nash as "'bone numbingly weary' at the prospect of more budget cuts."[14] Within a few weeks, CBC president Gérard Veilleux had resigned, and eighteen months later his successor, Tony Manera, also resigned, saying he had been lied to about the budget cuts ($350 million over the following three years).

Nada Harcourt, speaking in 1991, was familiar with budget constraints but could not foresee what lay ahead in 1995–98. She obviously enjoyed working on the series that were the backbone of CBC television drama.

HARCOURT: That overview, which comes early in the developmental process, is the most interesting creative time for the two of
us because it's when Fecan is so helpful in giving his feedback as
a neutral observer, saying, "This is working really well" or "I think
you should recast this actor or actress for the following reasons."
The search for brilliant writing in adult series is a large challenge,
because we sit next to the American giants. We do not have the
authentic crime, the mean streets. We have to find new and challenging ways of doing genre programming like *Crime Stories*
which have a Canadian spin on it that is completely believable. We
are not going to be doing *Miami Vice*. It is not our style.

MJM: If you did a *Miami Vice North*, everyone would laugh; they
simply wouldn't believe it represented us.

HARCOURT: *Mom PI* is more us, because what we're interested in
is the diversity of human nature. That concept allows for such
exploration.

MJM: One of the *Mom PI*'s I saw had an interesting, problematic,
non-formula ending. I'm thinking of the one about arson, where
the protagonist chooses a way in which his friend can restart his
business. But the price for that is to give up the prosecution of the
villain. That's not exactly your standard family programming.[15]

HARCOURT: I think that moral ambiguity is more reflective of real
life. Issues in the 1990s include biotechnology, the law, abortion,
all those issues where the public is split 55 to 45 per cent. That's
the area that makes interesting drama, not easy answers.

THE MAKERS ALSO THINK ABOUT "WHY DO CANADIAN TV DRAMA?"

Co-founder of Toronto Free Theatre, artistic director of Theatre
Calgary, and for four years a CBC television producer, Martin Kinch
spoke to me in 1984 about what Canadian television drama might be.

KINCH: One of the big problems is that nobody has given a great
deal of thought to television drama. What is it? What is it, if it's
not the adaptation of novels, if it's not the creation of compressed
history? All these things it is, but that can't be the centre of what
it is. The centre has to be the creation of a "drama for television":
and I don't think that is represented by *either The Duchess of Malfi*
or *Queen after Death*, or any of those shows I remember as a kid.

Ron Weyman had thought the same thing in the early 1960s, as he
told me in 1987.

WEYMAN: By then it was quite apparent to me that we should be writing our own shows in this country. We had not been inventive enough. The background of producers was mostly documentary and radio. There weren't enough of them to fill that studio with riveting drama week after week, particularly since, in the United States, live drama studios were simply gone. In Canada, we had not made that transition. We were in a ho-hum time with studio anthology, many of which were imported scripts or classics – all very worthy, but very ho-hum.

It was a period when something new had to occur. With my peculiar background in film I talked with various writers, who could not think themselves into the limits of the studio but could see themselves taking a novel and adapting it in seven sections to shoot partly on film. [From this came the *The Serial* on film and the human dimensions of the documentary subject in *Wojeck*.]

A writer sees the question from the vulnerable position of the person who must put the words, the backbone of the drama, on the page.

MJM to ANNA SANDOR [1988]: Why make Canadian television drama?

SANDOR: I think it is absolutely imperative to do it. We have a terrible view of culture in this country. Culture is something to be swept aside, it's a waste of money, and so on. Moreover, we are the only nation in the world that is overwhelmed by the culture of another nation. We accept this because we happen to have the same language and a mistaken notion that we are just like they are. Those two things coupled are very dangerous. So there has to be a place that gives people a sense of who we are collectively. Why do Americans have that sense of themselves? Its because they have had their movies and their stories –

MJM: – their popular culture –

SANDOR: – their popular culture. Exactly. There is a whole generation that fought in the Second World War, and a whole generation who didn't, yet they all have that feeling of being Americans. I'm not saying that there should be a propaganda machine at work here, but the good side of propaganda is popular culture, its heroes and villains. That's how you find out about yourself.

BILL GOUGH, producer [1988]: I define a grave danger which exists and which will thwart the ability of people to make good television drama. For a writer to get a project done, it requires anonymous readers in various bureaucracies to respond to projects. Give me a Samuel Goldwyn any day of the week, because then you've got a chance with someone who is reading out of their own life experience. What you've got otherwise is (typical of Canada) a turning of an essentially entrepreneurial enterprise, show business – and it is a business – into a land of bureaucracy, with forms, with readers, with researchers, who have got nothing to do with it.

My life was influenced a great deal by both CBC radio and CBC television. That's why I care so passionately about it and why I am so pissed off at what is going on with it right now. Without it, my life would have been completely different. That includes the ability to do world-class production work out of St John's, Newfoundland (which is almost impossible to do now because of budget restrictions). I was able to do a lot of work in Newfoundland, where I learned my craft.

SANDOR: There also used to be a kind of habit of watching TV. When I was a kid I got to work on CBC as an extra on television drama. I just took that for granted. I worked all the time doing little things on CBC, *Wojeck* and the anthology series, and *Festival*. People watched it.

GOUGH: I used to watch *Q for Quest*.

SANDOR: I don't know what happened between then and now, but everyone would talk about *Wojeck* the next day.

KINCH [1984]: We're spending more at the periphery than we are at the centre: more energy, more thought, more time and resources on the reactive side, where you say, "Oh God, is it novels this year or cop shows?" instead of really getting down to what is the centre of it all. But the most we can talk about is that television drama is usually something that has eight parts or even three parts. It has that kind of extension.[16]

HARCOURT: Good drama, in my opinion, always allows for an exploration of character that reveals why people's backgrounds make them think in a certain way. So it's very challenging to create characters. One of the best characters ever was the villain in *The Jewel and the Crown*. He became so clearly articulated that one ultimately felt both rage and pity, which is the essence of great drama.

MJM: The same thing happened with "Sir James" in *Empire Inc.* The long form gives writers and actor a chance to humanize those people. One of my problems with *Love and Hate* (I'm in a very small minority here) is that, in one sense, it wasn't long enough and in another it was too long. It wasn't quite long enough to get inside Colin Thatcher or Joann Thatcher, and it was too long as a straightforward story of the murder of an abused woman.

HARCOURT: Yes, a limited series would have explored those moments. But this film was based on a real event, which allowed the audience to relate to it in terms of a custody battle taken to its absolute, hellish ultimate, but only made possible through the examination of the *hubris* of that man's power.

MJM: As far as the battle for the children goes, fundamentally he wins. To me that's the most chilling aspect of the entire story, even more so than the murder.

HARCOURT: Well, it was a real life story.

MJM: Exactly, and that's why it's so scary.

HARCOURT: The more favoured parent is usually the successful parent, the parent who has more money, more power. It's more frequently the male, and that is what is so tragic.

Martin Kinch continued to discuss what is Canadian and what is television drama.

KINCH: I'm a great fan of *Seeing Things*. I've never seen *Cariboo Country*, but my sense of it is that *Seeing Things* and probably *Cariboo Country* and a great deal of what we do actually belongs in a light entertainment department. I'm not trying to be snotty about it, but what I'm saying is, "What's the centre?"

MJM: Where's the seriousness?

KINCH: Yes. Probably the most interesting TV series I ever saw was John Hopkins's *Talking to a Stranger*, the original one. What is interesting in the four connected plays could not have happened in the movies.

MJM: No, that's true.

KINCH: Even though you blow it up and look at it on screen, something like Ingmar Bergman's multi-part series *Scenes from a Marriage* is blatantly television.

MJM: As is *Cathy Come Home* and *Culloden* [two very influential BBC docudramas by Ken Loach and Peter Watkins in the mid-1960s, shown here on *Festival*].

KINCH: That sort of thing is what we give far too little thought to. When we get serious, we have a tendency to make scaled-down movies, rather than to make what is unique to that small screen with it's possibilities of extension.

MJM: Television can extend over time, but must contract space?

KINCH: You contract space and extend in time. German film-maker Rainer Fassbinder went off and made all these wonderful television movies that eventually got released over here as "movie" movies – and are influencing all the "movie" movie people. They seem to have no relation to the audience for whom they were actually made. The kind of appalling stylization that comes right out of the theatre, which somebody like Fassbinder could bring to television, combined with its limited resources, created those movies. You couldn't do those in 35 mm because no film producer would let you. That seems to me to be innovative, but we have not built on that perspective very much.

Working in television, I feel very cut off from the world. But when I look at something in the *Fanny and Alexander* class [directed by Ingmar Bergman, also made originally for television], I think, "This is what we should be doing. This is really crucial." Ultimately, we're either going to be a kind of palliative entertainment service, or we're going to be a service that is somewhat more disturbing in the way that any kind of drama is – the way Neil Simon is, if properly done.

Kinch and actor R.H. Thomson have their roots in the same milieu of serious experimental theatre.

THOMSON [1989]: The United States is the most extroverted nation on Earth. The flip side to that is the Scandinavian or Russian, which is deeply introverted. Because the States is such an extroverted country, and they amuse themselves and do all the things that one does in life in extrovert fashions, they have developed a form called episodic television, which is totally explicit drama. The nature in which they dramatically entertain you is not only explicit but, more accurately, it's extroverted. This is why the cars always blow up when they go over the cliff and hit the bottom. This is why beauty is always in the geography of the people rather than anything inside. That's the way that nation wants to do it. So episodic television builds plotlines and characters which, to me, look simplistic. But it's not simplistic. To them it's natural for their culture, because they live in an extrovert world.

MJM: And they demand closure. You have to know what happened, you have to know who was right and who was wrong, and preferably you have to have "poetic justice," although not always. One characteristic of Canadian television at its "best" is that it doesn't close. It tends to leave the plot or the character's motives open and ambiguous or ambivalent.

THOMSON: Yet continuity demands that you have to take your jacket off on screen. Otherwise, when they come back to you without your jacket on, you will confuse the audience. The same process works all the way through the art form, acting, writing, shooting, everything. You must make things so clear for the audience. That's the sand paper, as it were. One ends up making something that's mediocre because you've sanded off all the ambivalence or ambiguity or puzzles or jumps and leaps of imagination. Take the example of taking my jacket off. If I take off my jacket and I don't take my jacket off in the shot, as you cut from me with my jacket on to something with my jacket off, you are asking the audience to involve themselves and fill in the gap. That is symptomatic of what I would like to do all the time with shots. As it becomes more and more of an industry, a product, it is not in the interest of the people who make television to engage their audience.

MJM: But it's also true that our TV drama doesn't create larger-than-life, easily understood figures because our temperament is different. We tend to take a very different path, even in our episodic television. When we make something like the *Phoenix Team*, based on the idea "We've got impressive spy teams run out of Ottawa by Mavor Moore," the response is to laugh. I tell my students about that series and they invariably giggle.

THOMSON: Because we're trying to do something in a manner that is not true to us. The problem is we don't see that as "not us." We see what we make initially as "that's bad," because it doesn't fit all the previous examples that have been done so well in the States. We look at it and say, "That's bad, we can't do that, we make bad television, let me turn to another station that makes good television." So the nature of American television drama, it's explicitness and it's extrovert qualities, have become associated with what is good television. That's the assumption that has to be pulled apart. I wish we had more European programming coming into our living rooms to show us alternatives, so we could see that we actually are a slightly different race.

Martin Kinch defines another of those differences:

KINCH: We think that our TV is somehow, at bottom, primarily a news service. It's probably important to have issue-oriented drama, but the dangers are obvious. In most cases it's simply propaganda. What is the ideology we all have? I don't have one myself. But I do feel the necessity to say sometimes, "What are we not addressing?" We are not addressing ourselves to the mainstream of ordinary life in this country. We do a lot more than the Americans, who don't address it at all! But we don't do as well as the British, who do it considerably better. Issue-oriented drama like *For the Record* opens and wraps up the subject in a way that doesn't allow the program to be assertive or mysterious. On the other hand, the worst thing would be to compete with the Americans for the fragments they're going to have anyway. That's the danger; that's what might be coming.

Made in Britain, The Boys from the Blackstuff, and A Very British Coup are a few top-quality British hits from the 1980s. All three were also formally innovative and ranged from three to six hours in length. None of the subjects addressed (unemployment, delinquency, the potential for political subversion, class warfare, and personal disintegration and betrayal) were wrapped up for British audience into neat, "realistic" packages, and they were popular as well as critical successes.

Philip Keatley would not agree with Kinch that issue-oriented drama "wraps up a subject." His sense of documentary and Paul Saint Pierre's wry ambivalence created many gaps in *Cariboo Country* for the viewer to fill.

MJM: So you started to have interplay between the two forms of drama and documentary?

KEATLEY [1985]: We based everything in *Cariboo Country* on the fact that there was a Canadian documentary tradition. We thought, "Let's hang on to the stuff that is our strength; hang on to documentary quality."

MJM to program executive HUGH GAUNTLETT [1985]: I sense that people are distracted. They have stopped expecting the CBC to imagine Canada for them and, to some degree, the CBC *has* stopped. We do see things from Calgary, Edmonton, Vancouver, St John's, and there is a certain amount of showing ourselves to each other, but almost no myth-making.[17] One of the things that is very striking about early television drama is the very conscious sense, picked up from CBC radio, of making myths for ourselves. Now there is this continuous cutting down, not imagining simply or grandly, or even tapping into the archetypes that people perceive. Back in the 1960s, *Cariboo Country*, in a half-hour format with not a lot of money, was a myth-maker.

GAUNTLETT: Is there something in Canadian life that does not make myths?

MJM: Our theatrical renaissance in the 1970s and 1980s made myths: *Billy Bishop, Maggie and Pierre, The Donnellys, Zastrozzi,* the Mercers, Tremblay's characters from the Montreal Main demonstrate that we can and we do make myths. I don't think you can say that the country doesn't need that, because that is a human thing, not a Canadian thing.

GAUNTLETT: Maybe John Kennedy is not that kind of a guy.

MJM: It seems to me that John is the kind of person who would let somebody else be that kind of a person.

GAUNTLETT: There is another factor: all this pseudo-management science under which we labour and all the management practice based on producing more widgets. It may be that the kind of programming you are talking about may be alien to such thinking.

MJM: When you actually see the process of making television drama, it is reassuring how much chaos there still is. It is an art and not a science, despite the industrial models.

If Gauntlett is right, the CBC's upper management decision to initiate a million-dollar consultation with yet another firm of management consultants in 1995, intended to help them manage the 25 per cent downsizing, may do yet more damage to the creative side. The 1990s are even more obsessed with widgets than the 1980s.

Some years later we can look at a few of the newer myths made by television. The fictional Anne, Sara, Marilla, and Hetty from Avonlea do live in a past that was distinctly ours. Another group of characters who are larger than life for their young audiences are Joey, Wheels, Lucy, and Spike from *Degrassi High*.[18] Over the years we make them ours. But not everyone approves of them.

MJM to HARCOURT: When a foreign broadcaster buys a CBC show, they have the right to edit?

HARCOURT: Yes, we all do when we are in partnership – but I don't think we've ever done a different version. Earlier on with *Kids of Degrassi Street*, the BBC chose not to buy two or three of the episodes, and PBS censored out the last frames of an episode on abortion.

WHY DRAMA? WHY NOT JUST DOCUMENTARY?

Writer/producer Jeannine Locke, like Trina McQueen, started in current affairs. She too compared the robust health of news and current affairs with the marginalized status of drama – yet saw in CBC television drama a role which television's eye on "real life," edited or live, could not fulfil.

LOCKE [1990]: The best that news (and to a certain degree current affairs) can do is to present as honestly and as thoroughly as possible what is happening. In other areas we have a different responsibility because we have the possibility for shaping. Any subject is a subject for drama. It's the approach that's different. If I have two hours to deal with a subject, then I have a great opportunity to illuminate that subject. I also have a point of view.

If I were doing a film for current affairs about the United Church and its position on the ordination of homosexuals, I would have an obligation to present both sides, because the function of news and current affairs is to present as accurately and honestly as possible what is happening at this moment, with enough background information and interpretation to make the event understandable. That's harder and harder in this period of revolutionary change. Our audience suffers from what Northrop Frye calls "the panic of change." So it's all the more important to use the dramatic form as a means of dealing with that panic, rather than simply exploiting it.

An example of what I mean is *The Greening of Ian Elliot*, which I wrote and produced with a clear purpose in mind. I wanted to deal with two public concerns: the fate of the environment and the division within the United Church over the ordination of homosexuals to the ministry. I also wanted to demonstrate that a small group of people *can* make a difference – their efforts *can* make their world a little safer – and that the same communal effort can lead to a resolution of the homosexual issue. I know that, stated baldly, this mixture of plots sounds implausible. But by making a gay United Church minister the leader of the environmental cause – a valley threatened by a dam – I create the circumstances in which the characters work their way through their "panic of change."

I'm not advocating missionary work as the sole function of a drama producer. What I'm trying to say is that it is our right and responsibility to tackle subjects that may seem to be exclusively in the province of the news or current affairs. We bring a different approach to those subjects. We have the opportunity to shape a situation so as to shed light on it, instead of simply leaving opinion polarized.

I gave a synopsis of *The Greening of Ian Elliott* in a conversation with a chaplain at the University of Toronto who is homosexual and who has "come out." He said, "This is science fiction. It won't work that way. People will never accept homosexuals in the ministry." I replied, "What is the point of my reinforcing that position? I wouldn't bother doing the film." What we end up with is a congregation that is divided. Some will leave. The people who will leave are treated as sympathetically as the people who are going to stay. One of the characters says: "We will leave the church because our church will have left us." At the end, Ian Elliott stays in the community. This is announced by a delegation from the church who acknowledge that not everyone wants him, and it's made plain that he'll need plenty of courage to stay. But the overall feeling is that he and his congregation will endure. So it's not Disneyland on the prairies.

Given this conversation, I noted with interest that the brief public relations release on this drama did not even mention the second focus of the drama, Elliott's homosexuality and the response of his community. "Elliott will help galvanize opposition to this project, but must also deal with an aspect of his personal life that will also create controversy in the community."[19] This self-conscious, euphemistic approach may have been intended to maintain suspense in the plot, but Elliott's sexual orientation is made evident very early on. In fact, two critics made the plot point clear in their preview/reviews and praised the film. John Haslett Cuff wrote: "This beautifully crafted complex film is one of the best that the CBC has produced in many years. The fact that it has been thrown away to this season of repeats ... 10 months too late to reap the full benefits of its topicality is infuriating."[20] And Antonia Zerbisias gave an overview of Locke's career: "True, *The Greening of Ian Elliott* rambles a bit, much like the landscape. And some viewers won't come back after the blare of the ads. But it's so nice to find something that acknowledges that Canadians aren't all lawyers and detectives – and gets right down to the rich roots of part of this great country, the part outside the city limits of Vancouver, Toronto and Montreal. The part that has nothing to do with international co-production deals or global entertainment issues. Jeannine Locke's brand of television will be missed."[21] Locke resigned in 1991, making plain in a series of interviews with the media that she felt the CBC no longer nurtured her kind of drama.

Years before, director Eric Till had answered the question of why we should do Canadian television drama very straight-forwardly.

TILL [1983]: It is so simple. The reason why there are sometimes some really magic programs is that people have a desire and a passion to do that particular program, and they have a way to do it in their head, and they had a reason to do it.

Another answer could be offered by journalist Sid Adilman. In his column, he quoted the claim of Bernie Zuckerman, executive producer of *Love and Hate*, that this four-hour mini-series about Colin Thatcher first terrorizing, then murdering of his wife Joann "has attracted the largest audience around the world of any Canadian movie. Therefore, *Love and Hate* will air even on the biggest TV networks in Italy, France and Japan."[22] It had already been seen by forty-four million viewers on NBC and twenty million on the BBC, and it had also won awards. My view is that it is a superior thriller which tells us something about the social context, a little about the political context, and very little about Joann Thatcher, despite the acting talents of Kate Nelligan. The trial in the last hour of the mini-series was by far the best part of the drama.

What really troubled me, however, was that it seemed to have set the pattern for four years of CBC adult TV drama (1989–93). Violence, crime, guilt, and the courts occupied a lot of the time and money available to the CBC: the intermittent specials of *Scales of Justice*; *Conspiracy of Silence*, the searching look at the murder of aboriginal teenager Helen Betty Osborne; *Liar, Liar*, about false accusations of sexual abuse; *The Boys of St Vincent*, about the sexual abuse of dozens of young boys by ordained men, the dramatization of multiple murders in the Bruce Curtis story; and *Gross Misconduct*, Atom Egoyan's innovative treatment of a hockey player's violent life and death. The 1994–95 season brought us *Street Legal*'s finale, in which Olivia is tried for murder; *Butterbox Babies* – more murder; *Trial at Fortitude Bay* – conflict between Inuit and the Canadian justice system; and a drama simulcast in the United States about the exploitation of the Dionne quintuplets. Crimes of the week became the American staple "movie of the week" in the same period, until the time between the trial and the movie had almost disappeared. Clearly, the CBC does not indulge in that kind of sensationalism, but, up to 1993, adult as opposed to family docudrama on any other subject was rare. Till's "Magic" programs – quirky, individual, adult dramas that are aimed at the mind and heart – are rare. Dramas that reflect our current agonizing crisis of a failing economy or French/English conflict are missing. Instead, the current answer to "Why do Canadian TV drama" seems to be because we excel at lovable or challenging family drama and good violent thrillers, and both sell at home and abroad.

R.H. Thomson balances the corporate, institutional side of this question with an artist's perspective. He also speaks for many of the people in this book.

THOMSON: The reason for the drama in the first place is "story." At the root of it, the stories are about the journeys of lives. No life is without a journey. So whenever you can put a tiny journey or a middle-sized journey or a little shift or a little transformation in, you should. The business community may have taken over and the big mega corporations may be using the drama as a product to beam by satellite across the world, and the producers may be saving their careers doing it, and the actors may be trying to make mega-bucks and have large successful personalities out of it. But the reason underneath all of that, of why their story is public in the first place, is to try to mirror the journey that we are all on.

8 What Kinds of Programs and Why

There is luck to television as there is in life. There is an art and a passion to it. There is also a science to it. There is a way of maximizing opportunities and minimizing risks. Through studying the past, through watching what the current masters are doing, there are things that are fairly true every time. IVAN FECAN

What kinds of programs and why? Most media specialists focus on markets, trends, changing social contexts, new technologies – all valid factors that shape the choice and aesthetic of television programming. Postmodernist questions about authorship, and the conclusion that such authors do not exist, seem to be particularly relevant to the collectively made "product" of television. Yet this book demonstrates that the answer to questions about what programs and why lies with the individuals who write, direct, produce, act, design, photograph, or crew a television drama. I embrace the paradox that the "death of the author" postmodernists reject. Television drama is a collective art with no single author, yet it can and it often does bear the imprint of one man's or one woman's sensibility.

The best television is a *gestalt* greater than the sum of its individual contributors. The creators should make that happen as often as they can. The decision-makers should provide a time, a place, a set of policies, and a network where the creators can do it. And we, as viewers, should respond in a multiplex way to television drama that transcends the paradoxes that both bedevil and sustain it. The on/off button is still the final element that determines what kinds of programs are available to us.

In April 1992 CBC research officer Philip Savage sent me a copy of *How People Use Television*, a survey of a decade of television research into audience patterns intended to help planners and programmers by providing a profile of viewers and their habits.[1] The terms are defined in the usual way: a "share" is the percentage of the *available* audience watching television over a period of time, and "ratings" indicate the number of Canadians in the actual audience who were watching in a given minute, quarter-hour, or hour. The word "ratings," however, is often used to describe "*all* quantitative measurements of audience size, including shares."[2] Ratings and shares have been around for many years and were based on the diaries kept by a "typical cross-section" of viewers selected by the Nielsen ratings service. Many researchers pointed to the regional and urban skew of the Nielsen figures or of those from the Bureau of Broadcast Measurements. In 1989 the controversial "people meters" were introduced in Canada. These mechanical black boxes did not depend on diaries, and therefore on human memory, but on a meter attached to the television set and triggered by viewers using a remote control. The people meter also measures "zapping" and "channel hunting" – and thus redefines viewing in minutes, not quarter-hours. The controversy arose when the ratings and shares for most programs fell – affecting advertising revenue and causing consternation in the boardrooms of American and Canadian networks.

This quantitative way of measuring does not provide a sponsor or a network with information about what a viewer remembers, which may be affected by whether she was reading the newspaper, combing the cat, or transfixed by the suspense. The people meter does not know whether she liked the program and thus might return next week, stay tuned to the network, think of the network favourably, or buy the product advertised. For those vital reactions, the networks selectively engage in qualitative research outlined in more detail later.[3] The CBC survey concluded that, in the 1980s, "large majorities of Canadians rate television as the 'most entertaining,' 'most informative,' 'most educational' and 'most believable' of all mass media ... Compared with other networks, both CBC and Radio-Canada distinguish themselves in the public's mind for their Canadian programming over all and receive particularly strong support for their information, children's and cultural programming."[4]

In the 1950s and 1960s Canadians with access to one channel, the CBC, demanded that it carry American hits. By the 1980s the context and the expectations had changed. When there are many choices available – after cable and earth dishes have given many more people direct access first to more American networks and stations and then to specialty channels – viewers no longer demand that the CBC supply American programming. They choose the CBC for their own news and current affairs; for commercial-free, non-violent, and carefully crafted children's programming; and for "culture."

Culture can mean high culture – international programs available from PBS or other specialty channels, or the more eclectic and manageable CBC doses found on the Sunday arts magazine or for an hour a week with *Adrienne Clarkson Presents*. Culture may even appear as the rare Shakespeare or Gilbert and Sullivan production, or as a music or dance special. But if cultural is defined more broadly as popular culture, then the video music hits, the variety specials, *Friday Night with Ralph Benmergui, Rita and Friends*, and even segments of *On the Road Again, Man Alive*, or the *fifth estate* provide samples of music, theatre, or dance backgrounds. The drama segment of culture is certainly still alive and in variable degrees still distinctively Canadian, though sixteen arts and science producers lost their jobs in June 1995. Even as the network has lost viewers in absolute numbers, due in part to the audience fragmentation experienced all over the industrial world, the CBC audience is composed for the most part of people who choose to watch it rather than those who didn't get around to turning off the set – the LOP or "least objectionable program" watchers.

Whatever the viewing habits and choices, after forty years of struggle against the size of this country, television signal coverage in the 1990s is 99 per cent of the total population. As Philip Savage, of the Audience Research department, and Ernie Dick, the corporation's archivist, pointed out, the numbers show that there is still a substantial core of support for the CBC among "ordinary people."[5] This core has not declined in numbers and is self-defined as people who look for ideas when they watch television, who expect to be "stirred or moved" – my word would be "engaged" – specifically by the CBC. The CBC "reach" – the percentage of available viewers who sample the network in a week – was 79 per cent in 1981–82 and 79 per cent in 1991–92.[6]

Another way of measuring that core of people who value the CBC, as producers, directors, and writers have argued for forty years, is by the quantity of flak the CBC receives when it does something fails to make people think and feel deeply. Viewers still assert ownership of the programs and the corporation by writing, telephoning, talking to newspapers and MPS, and, as they did in 1990, gathering in thousands when their regional stations were closed.

According to the September 1992 figures, 99 per cent of viewers could get twelve channels, 96 per cent could get nineteen, and a surprising 86 per cent could get more than thirty. By 1 January 1991, 71 per cent of all Canadian households had access to cable. The time spent viewing is also surprisingly stable – about twenty-three hours a week. Young people watch less television, but children and adults over fifty redress the balance. More women watch than men during the day, roughly equal numbers in prime time, children tune in during the morning and late afternoon, and teens are likely to view available programs from 4 to 10 PM. Those over sixty-five watch less before 8 AM and after 11 PM, but the adult viewing audience as a whole tends to be constant throughout the day. For some reason, more francophones watch television at noon than anglophones. As has been the case for many years, the amount of viewing decreases as the level of education increases. In 1992 those who have completed university watched on average seventeen hours a week – still more than two hours a day.[7]

All the shares of viewing audience have shrunk since more choices became available. In 1984–85 the CBC share was 22 per cent, CTV was 29 per cent, U.S. stations were 32 per cent, and pay-TV had a 2 per cent share. The 1991–92 figures were CBC 19 per cent, CTV 24 per cent, U.S. stations 27 per cent, and pay-TV 12 per cent. Yet, in 1989, one-third of total and one-quarter of prime-time English-Canadian TV viewing were Canadian programs. Those numbers may well change as digital compression, fiber optics, direct broadcast satellites, and other technological innovations put us all in the 200 channel universe of interactive television – television that will present itself not like a "channel" or even like that already overused metaphor "the information highway," but like a shelf in a library where we will become our own programmers – if we can afford to pay the fees for the program we select.

One example of the fragmentation of audiences is that most familiar television icon, *Hockey Night in Canada*. In 1972, with not many choices for a Saturday night available, it averaged almost 3.2 million viewers; in 1990 it was 1.5 million. *Front Page Challenge* went down from 2 million to around 600,000, and was cancelled in 1995. *Marketplace* began in 1972 with 500,000 viewers, varied between 1 million to 1.8 million in the next twenty-five years, and retained 1.1 in 1990. Not all audiences shrank, but the trend is overwhelming and not confined to Canadian programming. Disney's Sunday-night hour has gone from 4.5 million to 1.5 million. The industry now accepts that the days of predictably huge shares are gone, except for Quebec, where some téléromans like *Les filles du Caleb* still command vast audiences over many weeks. Neither made-for-TV movie specials nor even the much hyped closing of the *Cheers* bar could match the two-hour special that closed *M*A*S*H** a decade ago. In the 1990s the only time that everyone is likely to gather around the communal television set is in time of war or natural catastrophe or during the opening of the Olympic Games in the host country.[8]

What do Canadians like, according to CBC audience research? "A substantial majority of Canadians – 64 per cent – prefer [entertaining/relaxing and make-you-think/informative] types of programs equally."⁹ That is not what the lowest-common-denominator, passive consumer view of audiences would suggest. If the programmers and planners were guided by this finding, they would try to create two-thirds of their programs to do both – and that would indeed give the CBC a distinctive footprint. Sixty-two per cent of viewers also strongly agree or somewhat agree that "American television programs [have] too great an influence on the Canadian way of life." On this issue, compare the 15 per cent who strongly disagree in 1986 to the 9 per cent in 1991; yet, in the same period, viewers were watching proportionately greater amounts of Canadian programming.

The CBC report suggests that the viewers' attitudes to CBC drama, or what it calls "the 'inferiority' complex concerning domestically produced drama programming, may be diminishing." Many people at the CBC, including Ivan Fecan, who basically decided what drama would be broadcast for several years, expressed deep frustration that viewers can love *Road to Avonlea* or *Street Legal* and never realize that they appear on the CBC. The "if it's good it has to be broadcast by someone else" syndrome is very damaging in these straitened times. This lack of recognition is perhaps the reason why the public is enthusiastic about the way the CBC informs it, but 34 per cent feel that the corporation entertains them fairly poorly or very poorly and that CTV has more entertaining programs [70 per cent] than the CBC.

Overall in 1984–5 from 6 AM to 2 AM, CBC and CTV made up a 50 per cent share of viewing; by 1990–91 that share had declined to 38 per cent. However, time shifters were not counted, even though VCR penetration was estimated to reach 75–80 per cent by the mid-1990s – unexpectedly with no regional variations. I can repeat from a conversaton with one of the twenty-two Inuit who are the permanent residents of Bathurst Inlet, ranging from a matriarch to toddlers, that they have two VCRs and Nintendo, powered by the lodge generator in the summer. The community decided, however, not to have an earth dish for television. They are simply too busy in winter to bother.

Among the detailed findings about who is watching, the most interesting is that the prime-time viewing peak for all choices available is at 9 PM on Sunday night, when 40 per cent of all people over the age of two are watching television. The CBC did not touch this slot in its repositioning, leaving the full 7–10 PM time period intact for its prized movies and mini-series.

In Toronto, fewer people look at CTV or the CBC than the average across the country. Pay and specialty channel viewing is a little higher, but viewing of "other Canadian" independent stations is well above the national average. Viewing of U.S. stations is lower. In Vancouver, CTV does slightly better, thanks to BCTV. The CBC's share is three points lower and the u.s. share is 37 per cent – well above the national average of the 28 per cent.[10]

One question raised by the cbc report whether the cbc should serve a mass audience or see its viewers as a set of pluralist audiences. The research indicates that "the audiences [for] cbc/Radio-Canada are really a collection of many audiences to particular programs that attract, in some cases, extremely different demographic groups."[11] For example, for *Front Page Challenge* 60 per cent of the audience is over fifty years of age. But a surprising 10 per cent of those watching are under eighteen. More men watch hockey, more women watch *Street Legal*, and more children and adolescents watch *Road to Avonlea*. Yet the audience for the "family program" is less than 30 per cent children and adolescents. Since at least the early 1970s the cbc has tried to make family programming that also entertains a significant number of adults. These numbers would suggest that they have succeeded.

Numbers are not everything – at least not to the critic. I have always found the qualitative ratings based on responses by audience panels, survey questions, and by focus groups to be of greater interest than the estimated numbers watching or even the demographic breakdown by age, sex, education, region, economic status, the urban/rural dichotomy. The cbc report indicates that the cbc was one of the first in the world to use the enjoyment indices (or eis), a qualitative indicator.[12] The eis for *Street Legal*, for example, can be broken out by character – Leon, Carrie, Olivia, and Chuck; Chuck and Olivia tied at 78. The questions reveal that 93 per cent agreed that the show was "entertaining," while only 65 per cent opted for "heart-warming"; 17 per cent agreed with "slow-paced," and a mere 7 per cent with "boring." *Dallas* ranked slightly lower than *Street Legal* in the ei stakes.

Audience response is also tested by pressing buttons for the Program Evaluation Analysis Computer. This method may be used with focus groups of eight to twelve people "lead by an experienced discussion leader." Focus groups are also used with programs already on the air to test out new characters or projected changes in plot development. In the Black Art of predicting hits, his method is much in vogue.

It is disheartening to watch the graph on the viewing of cbc television drama crawl ever so slightly upward when audience researchers look at the percentage of programs viewed between 7 and 11 PM. In 1984–85 the percentage of total viewing hours occupied by Canadian movies/drama was 2.4. In 1988–89, when there were more hours of cbc drama available a week, the percentage inched up to 4. Playing the stats game, one could argue that the percentage nearly doubled. But these numbers must be seen in the context that sitcoms, cop and lawyer shows, and movies of the week account for a huge proportion of what is offered on other regular, pay, and specialty channels. Drama is viewed 60 per cent of the time by English-Canadian television viewers. In other words, television drama is still the program of choice for the majority for much of the time – well ahead of sports – as it has been since the 1950s. And, since the 1970s, about 3–4 per cent of the available drama has been Canadian. Is it likely that Canadians would watch a larger percentage of Canadian drama when 96–97 per cent of the choices in drama available come from other cultures? Complicating the answer to that question is another factor besides availability, the fact that many American (and British) shows are "presold" because they are adaptations of movies, novels, characters familiar from detective genres, or spinoffs from other television series. Dramas can even be presold by the news itself in the case of the six-month turnaround in the United States of news stories into "docudramas."[13] Stars can also sell specials and series – not predictably, but often enough.

As an increasing body of contemporary research demonstrates, many viewers are not passive but are interactive with the programs.[14] Certainly, television is widely used as an occasion to relax – as a soporific. But we also use television to fill our need for reassurance, for stimulation, for companionship, and for news about local taxes or the weather on Sunday or the latest political crisis. The same viewer may well look at *Murder She Wrote*, the O.J. Simpson trial live on Newsworld, a rerun of *Street Legal*, *Family Feud*, *Rita and Friends*, *Hockey Night in Canada*, and the City Hall meeting on cable.

MJM to DAVID BARLOW, producer [1988]: Tell me about audience research. Do you find it useful?

BARLOW: Yes. Very, very useful.

MJM: In what way?

BARLOW: It tells you who watched and what they thought of it. It's more impersonal and therefore probably more reliable than your mother.

MJM: And in series television, that can have some influence.

BARLOW: Absolutely. It's really a business. You are creating a product that is meant to be sold, and the way it's sold is that people watch it.

MJM: The good side is that it's an interactive medium.

BARLOW: Absolutely. It's an exchange – the same exchange that would go on if you were manufacturing a line of clothing or a car.

MJM: When you got audience research on *Seeing Things* over several weeks that said, "We find this character dull as dishwater," he was likely to disappear?

BARLOW: Yes, or change radically. You know, audience research is not infallible. It's amorphous and it reflects transient attitudes. Even though it's a broader sample, it's really no different than stopping somebody in the hall and saying, "So, what did you think?" and analysing what they're saying. It never comes totally objectively, but always with baggage.

MJM: In some of the episodes of *Seeing Things*, the things that I would like in terms of irony and ambivalence were not what audience research indicated would work for audiences.

BARLOW: You are an atypical viewer because you have too much education and you know too much about the business. Your age (between thirty and fifty) and the fact that you are female are the only two things that make you a typical viewer.

MJM: But occasionally, presumably for your own sake as writer or producer or for the actors' sake, you want to branch out and hope to take your audience with you.

BARLOW: That's right. You've always got to make that decision: To what extent are we going to go to where the audience wants to go, or where we want to go and hope the audience will follow? Very few things come out in isolation, particularly on TV. With *Seeing Things* we went a little more to the audience. Now Louis Del Grande feels that a lot of that wasn't conscious, it was just a reflection of him doing the show, but we did tend to skew it. We were getting more kids than we ever thought we would get, so we tended to do stuff that would play to that audience. We thought it was crazy not to acknowledge they were there. If you look at the early shows they're far blacker and bleaker and tougher in retrospect.

MJM: They are.

BARLOW: But we saw those statistics that showed those kids were there and we thought: "This is crazy walking around with middle-aged angst. Let's come a little bit to the kids and see what happens." We did, and more of the kids came.

MJM to NADA HARCOURT, creative head of series [1991]: What about audience research?

HARCOURT: We get ratings. We now get "people meter" ratings that tend to favour long-running series as opposed to new series. It's an American system.

MJM: Do you still have audience panels as a research tool?

HARCOURT: Yes we do, at certain times of the year, based on diaries with specific questions. Often the information you get is already known, so you get a reinforcement of your own mistakes. What is most effective for series is focus groups. Early on, we bring in the production teams, including the writer, to meet with a hundred people, carefully chosen to discuss the exploration of character and the premise of the series. The audience research people try to give us the target audience, an appropriate mix of people who often haven't seen the show if it's new. They view one or two episodes simultaneously with the production team, and then react to it. You get some very interesting comments that are "gut" comments. That's very productive.

MJM: These discussions would be less structured than written questions and answers on a panel.

HARCOURT: Then you break up those people and have a group of men talking about it and a group of women, and that's interesting, too.

MJM: That's a relatively new thing, is it not?

HARCOURT: Yes, over the last three years.

IVAN FECAN, director of entertainment programming [1989]: *Degrassi* has become a better show, because it's honest. People can take something out of the show. It's doing something that the Americans cannot do. They would never play it on prime time because their corporate standards people would never let them. As a country we are a lot more open – it means we can talk more honestly to our audience, the people of this country.

Given the emphasis on our own culture, the trends in television drama like the mini-series, the budget cutbacks, and the ever increasing emphasis on "ratings," "share," and "reach," the choices many contemporary makers and decision-makers face have narrowed the range of dramatic forms and content available to us. Are there enough of us "mavericks, smallfrys and saboteurs instead of servants of the status quo" either *making* or *viewing* CBC television to keep it from sliding into the frenetic or the banal?[15]

What kinds of programs should we have? As the years pass, the choices narrow and then broaden out in slow irregular rhythms. Why should we make them? For reasons more diverse than the programs themselves. And for whom? The answer over four decades has been, for Canadians. Whether that diversity of program and that focus on the diverse nature of our viewers will survive into the 1990s was the original question behind the impulse to rewind the record and search for answers – a search now flavoured with elegy or urgency, depending on the context in the crisis that has taken shape in 1995.

In the final analysis, someone has to decide what kinds of programs will be selected for production based on the variables already outlined. The voices of early supervising producers Robert Allen and Mavor Moore, on the one hand, then director of entertainment Ivan Fecan (later vice-president), on the other, stand at either end of the history of CBC drama to date and will help to delineate for the reader the spectrum of reasons, institutions, personal preferences, constraints, and assumptions about the audience which shaped those choices.

THE DRAMA MIX: WHAT AND WHY IN THE 1950S AND EARLY 1960S

In the early days, the CBC concentrated on anthology drama, ninety-minute to three-hour drama specials and original musicals. Series were left to the American networks. But what constituted "drama" (and who did it) was very flexible.

MJM: You had an enormously ambitious first season of drama, doing the ninety-minute and even two-hour dramas as well as *Sunshine Sketches*.

MAVOR MOORE, first supervising producer of drama [1990]: There were several important things about it. We were trying not to categorize the programs; we were trying, for example, to do documentary programs that were part drama and part discussion. The very first dry-run we did was a social play by Len Peterson, followed by a discussion by a couple of psychiatrists and social workers.

MJM: That got on eventually.

MOORE: Yes, *The Landlady*. Then, we were trying to do panel shows that involved drama and news. Everything was mixed up. *Tabloid*, for instance, with Ross McLean, was mixing news and drama long before this even became a contentious policy.

MJM: There was also the special, *The Odds and the Gods*, which was a collage of drama and documentary about Hurricane Hazel.

MOORE: Yes, there were all kinds. We were not doing things that fitted into the pigeon-hole of straight drama. But when we did do straight drama, we used it to develop our audiences. At first we tried to do works which had some immediate appeal, some fame of their own. Everyone knew *Sunshine Sketches*, and we knew there would be an audience for that, just as there is for *Anne of Green Gables*. But because we did it in serial form, this also gave us an opportunity to bring a half-a-dozen writers along. We commissioned the writers to write episodes for *Sunshine Sketches*, hoping that the idea of the series as a whole would be so popular that it would carry the odd weak script. That was how we tried to train our producers and our dramatists – putting them on a platform where, even if they occasionally fell off, it wouldn't be too bad. We did several classical plays for that same reason. We thought people would be interested in the shows as shows.

MJM: In effect there is a recognition factor with melodramas, popular adaptations, and the classics.

MOORE: Yes. Then we found as we went along that the producers began to specialize in various sorts of plays.

MJM: After you left the senior producer's job in those early years, the CBC became very interested in doing indigenous musicals.

MOORE: This had always been an aim of mine. I felt that musical theatre was the theatre of our time. I was also interested in breaking down the pigeon holes. I saw the musical theatre as one way of bridging from music to theatre. From the very beginning, in any of the television that I'd seen in the United States or in Britain, I felt that the attempts to do television versions of orchestra concerts were just disastrous. The idea of a camera roaming around looking at the idiotic expressions on the faces of the musicians while they're playing Tchaikovsky's *Romeo and Juliet*! I saw the musical theatre as a way of involving music and opera in a visual medium. We started doing operas very early on.

MJM: Including the first full-length opera telecast in North America.

MOORE: *Otello*, with the Canadian Opera Company. We had a marvellous musician named Franz Kramer to produce it.

MJM: He seems to have been something of a mentor to people for a while.

MOORE: Yes, indeed. He was European. Kramer had been one of the remarkable group of German orphans who had come to Canada at the beginning of the war. A student of the composer Allen Berg, Kramer had been trained in Vienna. He was a first-class musician. He did bring some European flair to the station.

MJM: But he didn't stay?

MOORE: Perhaps ten years, no more.

MJM: But that was long enough to have a real influence.

MOORE: Indeed.

In these comments Mavor Moore reveals the roots of a television aesthetic that has flourished intermittently in the CBC, the idea that programs need not be pure drama or pure documentary or conform to the norms of a given genre. Examples would include the eclectic mixes found on *Folio* and *Festival*, hard-to-categorize series like *Cariboo Country* and *Seeing Things*, documentaries that contain drama like *The Valour and the Horror*[16] and *The National Dream*, topical "issue-driven" anthologies like *For the Record*, and some of the documentaries of Harry Rasky.[17]

Hugh Gauntlett, head of arts and sciences in 1985, confirms the fact that dramatic forms and dramatization turned up everywhere on the schedule from 1952 to the present.

GAUNTLETT [1985]: Nobody has a prescriptive right to these things. Some departments are defined by subject matter, others by audience (like the Children's Department). Nobody has any exclusive rights to any method or any content, except current political controversy, which has got to be news and current affairs. Even science is not the prerogative of music and science. The Current Affairs Department produced *The Medicine Show* recently. And "arts" has covered a whole range of stuff. It has covered upscale art – Group of Seven, Emily Carr, the programs both internally and externally produced. It has covered Canadian history, as in *The National Dream* and explorers' programs. But it has not covered 100 per cent dramatized history. Biographies are dramatized or not dramatized at all, or they can be done in funny formats. Arts and sciences includes anything Harry Rasky does – which is increasingly, but not exclusively, about artistic personalities. It can include *Hand & Eye*, a mini-series about crafts (glass, pottery, etc.) with an international perspective, a series that treats these crafts as art. Science and music is very undefined, and has tended to be what the producers wanted to do.

As supervising producer, Sydney Newman helped to shape the genres and formulae of the Drama Department in the 1950s.

MJM: In *On Camera* (which were half-hours), there was a strong thrust to be topical.

NEWMAN [1984]: I wouldn't say more for it than for *General Motors Presents*. It was simply me, with my Film Board background, in charge of theatrical films. The best way to capture the imagination of your public is to speak to them about the questions that are on their minds at the time. That is the way to build audiences and give your stuff relevance.

MJM: There was one program by Mac Shoub called *Big League Goalie*. It came out of a newspaper headline. You would be able to respond to headlines much more quickly in the 1950s than anyone could now. In fact, you could do a script and get it on the air in a couple of months, not eighteen.

NEWMAN: Yes, providing I could get the writer to do it. When Russia invaded Hungary, I said, "We must do a play for *GM Theatre* about a family caught up in this." I called my story editor, Nathan Cohen, in and said I wanted a story on the Hungarian invasion by Russia, right away. I had on my staff George Salverson, a very good writer, one of the original *Stage* writers and a story editor for *On Camera*. I called George in and I said, "George, drop everything. Burn the midnight oil." He wrote a one-hour play in about four days. I sent telegrams off to get the newsreel footage from France and Britain of the Russians. We went on the air about four weeks later with a play about the invasion of Hungary. It was very crude, but it had that spark of immediacy. That was not a unique characteristic of *On Camera*. It was just simply me talking to my audiences. "What concerns them today" is what I tried to present, a creative interpretation of reality.

From the 1950s to 1969, *Folio* and then *Festival* was the flagship of the CBC, where the classical, the experimental, jazz, gospel, ballet, poetry, and short films could find a home uninterupted by commercials. Robert Allen was its executive producer.

ALLEN [1981]: First, everything we did was done because some producer wanted to do it. Never was a producer asked to do something he didn't want to do. What do you get, if you do that? You get junk! The producers wanted to do all kinds of things. They were creative, they were alive. My function was mainly to select whatever I thought most appropriate, both for each person and for the series. I was also balancing the year's schedule.

There was a deliberate, conscious effort to do a kind of programming that was not available from the States. There was something similar in the American series *Omnibus*, but it contained a lot of documentaries as well as other programs. I wasn't interested in documentaries, and I didn't think that the CBC drama producers would want to work with documentaries.

We were also reading widely, keeping in touch with the theatre in England and in New York, and we were finding new material. We were always trying to be a little ahead of the others. We did a lot of American, British, and French stage plays, partly because they were a greater source of significant statements than were available at home. This country had not produced many playwrights and certainly not playwrights that had something important to say. But when we found them, we did them, if at all possible.

The only television network or station in the United States which is not privately owned is the loose confederation of stations called PBS. As National Educational Television (NET) in the 1950s, it produced ten hours of broadcasting a week, including news. Although it first became a "national" network in 1967, it has always been a marginal organization.[18]

ALLEN: The people in New York at PBS were working hand-to-mouth. They were trying to get the rights to do a play that was just being done off-Broadway, and they wanted to do it "next week."

It was difficult for us to get rights to a play. We would phone the New York agent, but we would have to explain who the hell we were, and where we were, and what it was all about. In the early days we were told, "We have never heard of Canada." About five years later, however, many agents in New York became aware of Canada as a source of television talent. Some of our actors and directors had gone down. But they also became more aware that there were some interesting programs coming from here. So we could then phone and say, "We are from the CBC," and they would have welcome mats rolling towards us.

I asked story editor Alice Sinclair to elaborate on her sketch of *Festival* as an embattled kind of program.

MJM to SINCLAIR [1988]: Was there a feeling that *Festival* was an outsider, on the leading edge?
SINCLAIR: It's what we thought we had to do at the time. Whatever you're doing at the time is always a battle. There are awful rows. Five years later it's become the "golden years of television." *Ghosts* and Ibsen and Anouilh and Pinter [about whom many battles erupted when his plays were first broadcast on CBC] do not have much connection to the real lives of Canadians.
MJM: No, but what *Festival* did do was educate some of our key young people about the theatre. I'm convinced that without the radio's "theatre of the air" and television theatre from 1945 to 1966, we would not have had a renaissance in Canadian theatre across the country in the early 1970s. It exposed potential directors and actors and writers in small towns to classic and contemporary theatre – the caviar as well as the sturgeon.
SINCLAIR: Do you think the CBC would have done better, without actually saying, "We are now going to educate you folks," to have had a series called "Foreign Theatre"?
MJM: World theatre was what you were doing. Perhaps that's what it should have been called.
SINCLAIR: Instead of a kind of mix.
MJM: A mix that included Canadian scripts was available on *GM Presents, On Camera, Playdate,* and the like.
SINCLAIR: And they were always more popular.
MJM: And a lot of them were written more to formula, based on the tried and true elements of familiar storytelling, which has its own

pleasures for a viewer. One of the things about great theatre is that that's what it is – great theatre. I will argue over and over that minority viewers who prefer challenging drama have rights too.

SINCLAIR: This has always been a contentious issue for the CBC.

MJM: Because all these interests have to fight it out on a single channel?

SINCLAIR: Yes.

In the early days of the CBC, the Drama department offered a mix of programs. Hailey's thriller *Flight into Danger* appeared on the same channel as Sartre's *The Unburied Dead*. The chilling short tales of *The Unforeseen* could be found where the viewers could also see Webster's *The Duchess of Malfi*, one of the best and least familiar of the Renaissance tragedies.

In June 1993, at a banquet honouring the contribution of Paul Almond to those first decades, Paul Rutherford and I had a chance to ask him why so many classic and contemporary "high art" plays appeared on the CBC in the years 1952–68. Rutherford and I see those plays differently. To me they are the seed-bed for much of the flowering of English-Canadian drama.[19] In Paul's opinion, their prestige, consumption of resources, and distance from ordinary viewers meant that a chance for the growth of indigenous television drama was wasted.[20] Almond's succinct reply to Rutherford's question about the early emphasis on the theatre of the world was, "We were a bunch of little shits and that's what we wanted to do."

Perhaps the men with extraordinary talent who came into the CBC in the 1950s and early 1960s did so in large part because they could explore that kind of drama. Where else could they do it? CBC Radio was hospitable, but was dominated by Andrew Allan, Esse Ljunghe, and Rupert Kaplan. The Canadian theatre was struggling to stay alive, theatres opening and often closing within a year or two. Television was attracting superb designers, inventive technicians, and hiring the cream of Canadian actors. And these producer/directors had the chance to do Pinter, Anouilh, Beckett, Exton, Shakespeare, Shaw, Ibsen, and Brecht for thousands of people. Where else could directors in Canada stretch themselves on the best of 2500 years of drama in the West? They may have been "little shits" to insist on doing it, but they learned from it. Moreover, viewers got a unique opportunity to stretch themselves by watching it. I would argue that Canadian television drama as a creative medium grew up when confronted with the formidable challenges of this kind of material, and that many in the audience grew as well. The kitchen-sink realism of American television's "golden age" was continually hampered by the unwritten, advertiser-driven rules of what could or could not be depicted. But *The Duchess of Malfi*, as a "classic," could present class conflict, incestuous love, graphic violence, and superb if demanding dialogue for all concerned. The same people also directed, designed, and acted in the Canadian scripts that were developed for *First Performance* and *GM Presents,* and the audiences also overlapped.

Using an anologous argument, there are those who say that the Stratford Festival hampered the development of Canadian theatre, and those who argue that Stratford and the "alternative" and regional theatres began in opposition and grew into symbiosis. I believe this was also the pattern in the early years of Canadian television. Regrettably, one-half of the creative tension in the partnership that is the experimental, the classical, and the contemporary drama has faded, and Canadian television is the poorer for it.

Director Eric Till summarized very effectively the strengths and weaknesses of the CBC's output in the days of *Folio* and *Festival.*

MJM: I sense, not a contradiction, but a paradox. Producer/directors were allowed to be passionate, idiosyncratic, to do the things they wanted to do, within the budget constraints and *Festival's* overall mandate. There was a fair amount of room for individual imprint. Yet you are saying that this group became so self-enclosed that it lost touch with the place [Canada] and the time [the late 1960s].

TILL [1983]: Absolutely.

MJM: So, *Festival* produced some very good television, but it also produced a kind of élitism. Effectively, what we needed was both consciously populist and more challenging drama, and we didn't have both.

TILL: GM should have supplied the populist, but it didn't. Sydney Newman created some of the greatest television writers that the medium has ever witnessed at the BBC. I don't know why he didn't do it here, but he did it over there! And he did it with immense anger, impatience, and frustration.

MJM: Why didn't the CBC add to its mix the "popular" series formats of sitcoms and copshows?

TILL: The same reason that was often given in regard to comedies on television. "Comedies don't work well on television. There aren't many people around here who will direct comedy, and it is hard to do – so don't do it!" That was a well-known attitude. Norman Campbell did several pieces with Eric Nicol, but in Vancouver, not here (I hate to say it). I was one of the few people in Toronto who enjoyed diving in and tackling a comedy, because I think it is wonderful to make people laugh. I think comedy is the most difficult form of all drama. It is infinitely harder to make someone laugh than cry. It is quite easy to make people cry, actually.

I suspect that if you had given the challenge to somebody like Norman Campbell later on, he probably would have pulled it off. Norman, more than any other director who has ever worked at the CBC, has "the common touch." He has an extraordinary way of reaching out to a big audience.

Norman used to do a lot of original musicals. *Anne of Green Gables* was the first. I worked as a studio director on at least three of his musicals. There was a real clinker, with prehistoric animals or something [*Look Ma, I'm Human*, 1957]. Regardless of what we thought about them, they reached an audience. Whenever Norman did a play, he would do it in a fashion that would irritate the "esoterics" around, but the audience would be immensely entertained. I think that is a true gift. He did all those Gilbert and Sullivans, totally unaware of what D'Oyly Carte, or anyone else, thought about them. He just did them. He did them more like a farce than a musical comedy, but that is what people wanted in those days. He would never do the same thing today, because the audience is much more sophisticated. But Norman was able to reach a big audience, with something I can only phrase as "the common touch" – we needed more of those people.

In his conversations with me, Sydney Newman also identified himself as a person with a feeling for what ordinary viewers, after a hard day, might like. Executive Hugh Gauntlett identified another:

GAUNTLETT: Thom Benson [who became the director of English entertainment programs, the predecessor of Jack Craine and Ivan Fecan] was the antithesis of an artistic, terribly cultured CBC executive. He was like Sidney Newman – a very creative person in television. Under Benson's leadership, some terrific drama work was done in the Features Department – for example, the program about the death of Tom Thomson by Peter Kelly.

MJM: You were talking about him nursing the first year or two of *The Beachcombers*.

GAUNTLETT: Yes. I think that Thom's strength was certainly at the popular end, what I call the "shaggy Canadian" end.

MJM: Which is a balance to what had been perceived as –

GAUNTLETT: – that theatrical, European, Brecht and Strindberg kind of approach. Thom had no sympathy with that, no personal understanding of it. He disliked it and feared it, so unless it was overwhelmingly necessary, he was not going to suffer it. We made a big effort in the late 1960s to Canadianize *that*, to have Canadian originals in *Festival*, such as all that work with Chuck Israel and other writers of that era.

WHAT AND WHY IN THE 1970S

Eric Till's analysis of how these tensions played themselves out during the 1960s suggests another reason for the marked constriction of content and form in CBC television since the 1970s. The next two decades were shaped by a generation unconscious of the corporation's own achievements and tradition as well as by the inevitable adjustments to the changing technology and the changing political context. The amnesia among many of the producers, directors, and writers was not shared by every head of drama, particularly not by John Kennedy, who had come up through the ranks. Nevertheless, it meant discontinuity and a loss of pride and confidence until a new body of work was built up over the ten or fifteen years after, say, 1968.

In the reorganization of the corporation in the late 1960s, Fletcher Markle followed Robert Allen, but he was the first person actually named as head of television drama.

MJM to GAUNTLETT [1985]: Fletcher Markle had a fair amount of background in television.

GAUNTLETT: He had been in Hollywood for ten or fifteen years and had been married to American actor Mercedes McCambridge. He had been a radio writer, a director/producer in the Andrew Allan era. He was a Canadian who had gone to Hollywood relatively early and he appeared to have made the transition to television in Hollywood. He flourished there, but always kept a foot back here, as host of *Telescope* and other things. He didn't appear to have become completely Americanized, and he came back. What he did do was *Jalna*. Other things he talked about (but never did) were inappropriate. It was "Let's do the short stories of F. Scott Fitzgerald" – not a bad idea, but what the hell has that got to do with us? Curiously, that was an idea that would have been quite viable around here in the early 1960s. At that time "nationalism" had not yet been invented as we know it.

MJM: What you do get during his time was the decision to make *To See Ourselves* (1971–74), an anthology of Canadian short stories.

GAUNTLETT: The producer was David Peddie (son of Frank Peddie). It was quite a nice little series.[21]

MJM: At that stage, perhaps for the first time, the CBC seemed to be thinking about certain conventional television forms that were popular in Britain or in the United States. You begin to get formula television in the very early 1970s.

GAUNTLETT: I was asking myself "What happened to *Festival*" in that period. I can well remember Doug Nixon, the executive responsible for the CBC schedule during the 1960s, saying there were certain things that the CBC would always have. We would always have an hour-long prime-time public affairs magazine. We would always have a series of distinguished dramas like *Festival*. We would always have an experimental half-hour. When Nixon no longer made the decisions, it was suddenly as if we had none of those things. I remember it strikingly, because there were two periods where we dropped the prime-time current affairs magazine.

There is a connection between what happened in public affairs and what happened in drama. There were three or four years, 1969–73, in which there was no public affairs magazine. Then Peter Herrndorf, who became head of current affairs, made it the bread and butter of the business. *Festival* disappeared in that same period, and its contribution to the schedule as a place for the arts and for experiment was gone for good. In 1969 *Festival* went off the air, except as a confusing title resurrected occasionally to sell a program with the cachet of former years. In the 1970s it was almost as if *Festival* had broken into fragments: "drama special" fragments and "experimental" fragments, none of them having the energy or the coherence that *Festival* in its better years had. *Festival* had been a place where you sampled a variety of things. You might get ninety-six minutes of Anouilh followed by twenty-four minutes of jazz. The clock took over in the 1970s. Commercials became the norm. There were no non-commercial slots anymore. Whatever went out was sponsored. That was directly caused by the second Fowler Commission of the late 1960s which came up with the instruction "make more money!"

MJM: The hours available for drama start to shrink significantly.

GAUNTLETT: That is also when the complexity of production and the emulation of film really took off.

HOW ADMINISTRATIVE STYLE SHAPES PROGRAMS

John Hirsch replaced Fletcher Markle after a hiatus in which the CBC conducted a major examination of its problem in drama.

MJM: Hirsch is a very controversial figure.

GAUNTLETT: Yes, indeed. Honestly creative and honestly destructive. There is a curiously close marriage of the two. He tended to create and destroy the same people, which is a bit wasteful.

MJM: Some of the drama in his period was very interesting.

GAUNTLETT: It was the last moment in which we were doing "drama," frankly.

MJM: Yes, rather than "stories." Obscure or not, some of it was very good – some of it was awful. But there seems to have been a tremendous amount of energy in Hirsch's era.

GAUNTLETT: There was a good deal of interaction with the Canadian theatre. There was a good deal of "what do you want to do?" and "let's try this," of inventiveness. But *A Gift to Last* and *King of Kensington* came out of it as well as "theatrical" creations. My own view is that if this place were ideally managed, one would try to alternate a John Hirsch and a John Kennedy; one who would stir the department up and stand it on its ear, and another who would sort it out and get it all settled down again. But then you need another one to stir it up again. What has happened to us recently is that such alternating has not happened and, in effect, the whole message is to stir nothing up and get 1.6 million viewers. That is really a very cramping instruction.

Executive producer Maryke McEwen worked for John Hirsch as a story editor:

McEWEN [1984]: John changed over the years. He came in really believing that if two thousand people watched the show, that was more than you would get in a theatre, so that was a good thing. Coming from a theatrical background, he had an elitist kind of view of television. This was a much larger stage than he had ever seen. He liked to take chances. That was a good and a bad thing. Sometimes he took chances on completely bizarre things that died immediately. Other times he took chances on people like Ralph Thomas, and he got *For the Record* out of it.

You just never knew where you stood with John. That was hard to deal with. When he was dealing with an entire department, it was tricky, emotionally. With John Kennedy, you know you have somebody solid there. If he is going to be angry with you, you will have a conversation about it. You don't get sudden blasts from behind. Hirsch wanted excellence. He made you fight for that, but he wasn't clear on what was excellent. When he'd take a personal affront, it didn't matter what you did. You couldn't redeem yourself.

MJM: You mean he was a grudge-holder?

McEWAN: No, he didn't hold grudges. He could hate you one day and forget about it the next. Meanwhile, you thought he still hated you. People really suffered from that.

DON WILLIAMS, director [1985]: I knew John when I first started at Manitoba Theatre Centre. That was really my formal training as a director. I probably learned more from John Hirsch than from any other single person. We had a good relationship for many years, but after he became head of drama for the CBC we didn't get along so well anymore.

MARIO PRIZEK, director [1983]: This was the same time that Canadian theatre was in its rambunctious adolescence. Of course there was theatre before then, but this was the time when nationalism was emphasized, when a great many energetic things were happening. Yet the CBC was out of touch with it almost entirely before John Hirsch's term. There were several reasons for that. A lot of these shows were performed in other parts of the country than Toronto so unless they appeared in print and you could take them to your executive or your supervising producer, all you had was the occasional newspaper clipping with which to convince them. Also, those early types of improvisational theatre, like the Toronto Workshop Productions, were not really transferable to television. They worked because of the direct contact with the audience.

MJM: When there was an attempt to transfer some of them to television, most didn't work very well.

Collectives like Rick Salutin's *1837* and Theatre Passe Muraille's *The Farm Show* were problems. More naturalistic shows like David French's *Leaving Home* worked better. Yet the English television version of Tremblay's highly stylized play *Les Belles Soeurs* was superb.[22] In the early 1980s John Gray's *Billy Bishop Goes to War* and *King of Friday Night*, and Linda Griffith's *Maggie and Pierre*, all presentational theatre pieces, worked very well in the hands of directors who understood both theatre and television. Prizek talked atout those who did not make the transition.

PRIZEK: At the beginning of the John Hirsch period, he let go many of the television producers and brought in his friends from the theatre. They didn't know a thing about a television studio. The people who were doing the shows didn't know how to frame a shot, how to cut from camera to camera, even *when* to take the cut. There were also stage performers who had not appeared in front of a camera before.

RONALD WEYMAN, executive producer [1987]: When Hirsch came

to the Drama Department, he was a man who was determined to make his mark on everything. He worked out of his own compulsion. Literally, six months after a program had been shot, he would say, "I want this changed."

Hirsch was still trying to find his way in a letter he wrote to the *Globe and Mail* in March 1975:

Obviously it is not up to the CBC to go wildly off into avant-garde styles and far out situations and language, but rather to remain just a few steps ahead of the whole viewing public. In recent years [the Canadian Viewer] has become accustomed to a lot of harmless, rather blah material from CBC drama [he is ignoring *Reddick, God's Sparrows, Twelve and a half cents, Vicky,* and a few other very disturbing dramas of 1968–72], pieces rich in mild boredom and fake metaphysical significance. Vigor and challenge came from American programs ... Sitcoms there have tastefully and successfully handled such difficult 'subjects' such as abortion." He goes on to promise readers "crime stories, day-time soaps, gentle comedies, serious classics and you name it. All are needed."

But the aesthetic of programming was irrevocably changing. One segment of that change was a feature film, which Hirsch defined to television critic Jack Miller as "just plain pop, a ratings grabber." It debuted on a Saturday night. The Canadian–American co-production *The Man Inside*, written by Tony Sheer, starred Americans James Franciscus and Stefanie Powers and Canadians Donald Davis and Jacques Godin. The producer, Wilton Schiller, came from the American TV series *Police Story*. The press release described it as a film where "the emphasis is on *action* when an undercover Mountie infiltrates a narcotics ring."[23]

WEYMAN: I can remember Hirsch saying to me on one occasion that one has to reinvent the wheel for oneself. Surely, if you don't understand the wheel, you should be introduced to it, but to reinvent it is an unnecessary task. Hirsch seemed to have to reinvent it again, though he did so with a great deal of input. He had more money and more support than had ever been given. He didn't entirely know what to do with it, but it wasn't entirely his fault. I was around. My opinion was asked a number of times, but I was weary and the people who had been in place had dropped away, one way or another. They had gone to Hollywood or to England, or had simply died in their shoes or got fed up. But there was an additional amount of money to give drama priority. A certain amount of waste went on, but at the end of it another step had been made.

Anyway, he had the money to do whatever he wanted. He didn't ask anybody's opinion. Or if it wasn't in his own experience, he discarded the opinion. For instance, he did two or three splendid studio productions, the kind of thing that Bob Allen had being doing for decades, which I had viewed as great in its time but which were no longer commercially viable. He brought in some British directors, much to the annoyance of all the people who *did* know how to do studio drama! And that took him about a year.

Writer Grahame Woods agreed with the consensus:

WOODS [1989]: Hirsch had passion, but it was directed in the wrong areas. In my opinion this criticism applies to his term at the CBC and at Stratford, too. The minute he got the job, he started paving the way for his experts. When he came to the CBC he wanted to bring in Brits because "they were the ones with experience, we've got to learn from these people." Then he was complaining he couldn't do his job because the corporation didn't give him enough money.

When I asked Ron Weyman about the lively drama special *Get Volopchi!* starring the very fine expatriate Canadian actor John Colicos, his reply gives us another glimpse of Hirsch.

MJM: It could have turned into a series, couldn't it?
WEYMAN: No. I know why – because I made it. When Hirsch arrived, he hated it. He hated it because it wasn't his. It was rerun three or four times and I said: "John, let's do a series!" He said: "We aren't here for that kind of nonsense," or something like that.

Actor/writer Hugh Webster, whose memory stretched over more than four decades of radio and television drama, also had a revealing anecdote about John Hirsch.

WEBSTER [1984]: John Hirsch didn't want to put on *Freedom of The City*.
MJM: Hirsch didn't want this done? [I said, astounded, because Hirsch had given Till *carte blanche* when asking him to do something for the drama department.]
WEBSTER: John Hirsch saw it when it was finished and said, "It's not going on" – and then took off for California. Everybody in the

TV Drama Department got together and sent a telegram to Hirsch, insisting that it be shown. The whole department!

MJM: That says something for the Drama Department at that time.

WEBSTER: Absolutely.

MJM: How could Hirsch miss the quality of it?

WEBSTER: I don't know. Eric was shattered when he first heard the news. Then, of course, the thing was an enormous success. We hit editorial pages across the country with that show because it was about the conflict of Protestants and Catholics in Ireland.

MJM: Very timely.

WEBSTER: Oh, was it ever!

MJM: Also very innovative television in a formal sense.[24]

Thus it is evident that by the mid-1970s, decisions about what kinds of programs would be made depended first on the directive from senior management to make Canadian cop shows and sitcoms, then on the personal taste and sensitivities of one man, John Hirsch. After Hirsch left, John Kennedy, who was experienced in CBC management (in 1990–95, director of television for the Western Region), became head of TV drama for a decade, after which he retired. Ron Weyman saw the job itself changing to fit the evolution of the corporation.

WEYMAN: I didn't take on the job, and Bob Allen also eased back. So you get someone like Kennedy. I don't think there was anybody else at that time who was quite right for the job and about whom the CBC could say: "We've got to have an administrator in here who is one of us, who knows what the structure is, and at the same time a fellow who is creative enough, loose enough and open enough to encourage and to re-build confidence." In the end it was a good move. The nature of the CBC was changing during that time, and it has changed even more since John has been there.

Hugh Gauntlett has been involved with creative people as a CBC administrator for thirty years. His view of the 1970s from the quite different perspective of the mid-1980s was measured but tinged with regret.

GAUNTLETT: The achievement in the 1970s was really to have more success in formula entertainment than we ever had. Sitcoms and *Beachcombers* and even some of the other things, certainly *Gift to Last*.

MJM: *Gift to Last* broke its formula in some episodes, and that was interesting.

GAUNTLETT: But the price of having achieved that was to have lost everything else! And that has partly to do with the restriction of having only seventy hours during the early to mid-1980s and the amount of effort that goes into movies.

MJM: Is it also because memories are too short or people are new?

GAUNTLETT: I think that has something to do with it. I have a sense, as I suppose all aging people do, that there were traditions and standards around a generation ago that aren't there anymore, because there is no continuity. If you go back a generation, it was the only game in town and everybody who played that game was part of this tightly knit family. They were here for a life career, including the writers and the performers. The CBC repertory company was the CBC repertory company. Now all kinds of other things have grown up, including a domestic theatre and bits of a film industry and certainly a lot of television, not much of it very relevant. The tribal identity of the people who work here has deteriorated considerably. And most people are oblivious of the fact that anything has been lost.

Starting next month (1985), I will be taking over as head of arts and science. Since the department is on its knees, I will start by answering the question you were asking me, "What is it for? What is it meant to do?" One of the things I have great difficulty in getting across to the producers (whose average age is fifty-three), is that we now have a network that is no longer the fully balanced service it once was. It is now a service that provides distinctively Canadian popular entertainment. Popular entertainment includes news, current affairs, sports, drama, some variety, and that is about it. And you can get science in because Jim Murray has cleverly turned science into popular entertainment with *The Nature of Things*. But we are no longer the network that had *Festival*, and that's why the people in arts and science have nothing to do. Unless there is a second network, music might never come back.

I leave the reader to judge whether arts and music had made a comeback with Adrienne Clarkson's one-hour arts anthology (scheduled when affiliates, the majority of CBC stations can and do opt out) or the more ambitious three-hour Arts Magazine that appeared for three or four years on Sunday afternoons. Together, they are better than no arts and music. How much better? Using qualitative rather than quantitative measurement, the fact is that a full-length production of a play, opera, ballet, or concert is now unknown. CBC English Canada has not been given the arts coverage Radio-Canada has offered to its much smaller market in the same period.

In June 1995 the arts and science areas were gutted by cutbacks. Gauntlett had retired a few years before and Sunday Arts was cancelled for the 1995–96 season. Tours of live performances have been cut back. The size of Canada and the dispersion of its population has not significantly changed. The arts have matured and grown in the last thirty years, so there is far more talent to choose from. But it will not be seen on the CBC – and music, dance, theatre, and their sisters have never been welcome at CTV and Global.

THE 1980S: ALREADY UNDER SIEGE

GAUNTLETT: Read the government and the CBC documents. They are going to try to increase Canadian content and replace U.S. drama with Canadian drama – which has gotten to be the same kind of drama by definition. They are so obsessed by this goal that they exclude anything else on this network.

MJM: Juneau, in his 1974 CRTC report, said flatly that no CBC audience should be regarded as a mass audience, but should be regarded as a plurality. That definition is just words on paper now, wouldn't you agree?

GAUNTLETT: Absolutely! In my youth you could reconcile the fact that you were out hustling for a buck and trying to introduce people to Bertolt Brecht at the same time. You can't reconcile them anymore. The Janus-faced approach is still there. I know that Juneau lusts after our being a distinguished network, but he is the guy who is setting the audience targets and going along with the commercial targets that make it absolutely out of the question.

Five or six years later, I interviewed the man who had to reconcile the expectations of quality drama, which looked and sounded different from its American counterpart, and ratings, which would spell survival in an era of privatization, hostility to public broadcasting, and fragmented audience.

FECAN [1989]: Excellence is difficult to talk about because it is not an industrial approach to something. It is not as if, when we make a lot more television drama, we are going to do a lot better. I'm not arguing against doing more, I am just saying that the first principles have got to be excellence, and excellence means a series of different things. If you have a half-decent schedule, some promotion that is targeting the people you should be reaching, and the gumption to stick with it long enough, chances are it's going to work. There is luck to television as there is in life. There is an art and a passion to it, as well as a science. There is a way of maximizing opportunities and minimizing risks. Through studying the past, through watching what the current masters are doing, there are things that are fairly true every time.

MJM: Things that are "learnable"?

FECAN: Learnable. Maybe it's not a science, but it is as much of a science as many of the pseudo-sciences are.

MJM: In whatever medium? Tape? Film?

FECAN: Tape or film are both questions of cost and artistic vision. I'll start out in the day and I'll say, "I'd like to have a cop show, I'd like to have a hospital show, I'd like to have this, I'd like to have that." People come back and say, "Well, that's fine, but here's what I'd like to do." Then you decide what you want to work with, what you don't want to work with. You go to development. Some scripts stand out because the people really have something to say. That's what you make.

HARCOURT: *Kids of Degrassi Street*, which was an "after school" program, had a very strong operating principle: that children had true lives, that they did not just participate in lifestyle concerns as in North American television – who to date, how to look, which form to fill out in *Seventeen Magazine* – that superficial, shallow view of the lives of children and adolescents. Being a woman and a mother, nurturing and raising a child, I could understand that children were not spared the effects and the chance to exercise power, the growth of character. *Degrassi Street* was an exploration of the fact that we are concerned about larger issues from a very young age. We are struggling, as we struggle for our own identity, to understand what we are to become and how we view major social issues that affect our lives directly. *Degrassi* went on to look at the lives of children in public school, and then, in its best incarnation, in junior high school and high school. I think that the reason the program was enjoyed in Canada, Britain, and the United States was that people were able to say, "This program is different; this program is honest; these are the true lives of children," and therefore it was on the edge of social change. *Degrassi* entertained them, but it also made them stop and think and engendered discussion after the show. *Avonlea* came out of the success of the style, the look, and the feeling of gentler times, which had been explored in the two mini-series *Anne of Green Gables* and *Anne of Green Gables: The Sequel.*

I asked Harcourt where the ideas about what kinds of series to make came from.

HARCOURT: In spite of the fact that we work very long hours on the production and the execution of the series themselves, we must all be very informed. We must read, go to movies, watch television, and be aware of the other series that are on.

MJM: You said the magic words: "We must watch television."

HARCOURT: That's right. We watch television, we watch all the genres, we watch what is successful in other countries, what's successful in North America. It's very challenging to get all that under your belt.

According to Harcourt, success in series at her level depends on an "intuitive process that occurs in your selection of people."

HARCOURT: It is not simply an assessment of the concepts, it is an assessment of whether the people are up for the long term. If you and the people you work with are diametrically opposed in your view of characters, it's important that you abort the process. As head of series you think you've bought into a specific concept. If it rapidly becomes something else, it's probably a good idea to abort the process before you kill each other. I'm here for the overview and to support creative people, but I'm also here to hold them to the vision of the series they have proposed. Given the myriad things that occur through production, the interaction with other people, and the hand-to-mouth nature of things, the challenge is to say, "This isn't good enough, because remember what we set out to do in episode 3 – I'm holding you to it." That's very difficult when you are shooting in a week. Often excellence gets put on the back-burner and expediency dictates, because you have to deliver.

When you stop a movie and say, "OK, we're going to do re-shoots," you can change the location, you can recast the character. Often you don't have that luxury in series television. So the challenge is to be right the first time with a great number of people. It demands great concentration.

MJM: There's really no down-time either, is there? Even if it does snow in Canada, the production keeps going. The longer the series has become, the less down-time there is and the more constant the pressure. Is there ever a more relaxed time in the rhythm of the year?

HARCOURT: No, there isn't. At this time of year Ivan will be very interested to know what else I have in development. But it's virtually impossible for me to say because I have three new series already scheduled, but whether they work out or not is unknown to decision-makers in November or January.

MJM: You certainly don't want to do three new ones every year. So success is it's own reward. It gives you a little breathing time to go on to develop other things.

THE 1980S: "TIME TO DO MORE HISTORICAL DRAMA"

Martin Kinch was working on period drama when I talked to him in 1984 – a series of drama specials under the title *Some Honourable Gentlemen* and a marked contrast to much of his work as co-founder and artistic director of the Toronto Free Theatre in the early 1970s. His sharp sense of the grotesque and his determination to challenge the audience survived during his four years with the CBC.

KINCH: The joy of doing something in the nineteenth century is that it's far enough away that it allows you certain kinds of liberties, which are wonderful. Still, I've got Prime Minister Thompson's granddaughter calling me up, furious that we had her grandfather land in a fruit bowl when he dies.[25]
MJM: Because he hadn't really?
KINCH: No. He "croaked" in the salad or something.
MJM: When I saw it I thought, "It doesn't matter whether it happened or not, it's exactly right!"
KINCH: But there are people out there to whom it does matter, much as I hate it.
    For example, the script about the assassination of D'Arcy McGee – *A Passion of Patriots* by Ken Gass – obviously relates to the whole FLQ issue. So what one does is take one's concern for government power and justice and dislocate it to the nineteenth century, so one deals with it more easily. The thing about doing *Flush* was not that any of us believed that the Manitoba Schools question was going to blow up in 1984. We wanted to do a show about the level of cynicism that all of us perceived in government. By moving it back into a period we felt nobody was the least bit interested in anyway, we could do things.
MJM: Who could have anticipated that, by the time the program was finally telecast, the whole question of language rights in Manitoba would be a hot issue again?
KINCH: Well, exactly. Now, I'm getting the opposite feeling. Having spent so much time reading a lot of the history for *Some Honourable Gentlemen*, I've become more interested in how various periods are really different; how they are not the same as the period we are in. We live in a country where nobody knows his-

tory anyway. The first time viewers ever know about the history of all those crazy prime ministers is when they see a *Flush of Tories*. If I give them a picture that is totally inaccurate, am I doing any good at all? I wonder. I think I'm making a good play.

We had a lot of trouble defining this series. John Kennedy and I both got involved because he had to sell it to Jack Craine, then director of entertainment, and Denis Harvey, vice-president of English television, so I had to provide him with definitions that made sense. I was trying really hard to get a definition that defined the program; didn't terrify everybody out there; allowed me to do what I wanted to do; and was relatively honest, so that when they came back to me I could say, "Look, it's all there on paper." It's very tricky. To me it's most important to define history in Shakespearean terms (without being pretentious about it) in the sense that history is a story – a fairy story with people who are larger than life, who should be dealt with in that way.

MJM: We should use history as our European ancestors used medieval morality plays?

KINCH: No. What I'm saying is that history is material for drama. It is not drama, and it is not a matter of dramatizing it. It is a matter of using history to point out or to get at those themes that seem to be common to where we are. It is often simply a matter of taking something and dislocating it.

In our two-part show about Sam Hughes, when we got into the problems dramatically it made sense to go back to the history. Quite often that solved our problems. *Hughes* is a really interesting show, because it is more accurate than almost any show we've done – and as a result it is stronger. But it has this real problem. Sam Hughes is a kind of warmongering Tory businessman with few virtues; yet if you take three hours and study anybody, he becomes quite interesting and sympathetic. It is virtually impossible to avoid this outcome when you do history plays.

MJM: Old rascals eventually become lovable.

KINCH: Yes, but we're not talking about old rascals, we're talking about really dangerous people. This is one of the problems of doing historical plays. What I'm doing is sharing with you some doubts and some questions I have.

PERSONAL VISION FOR THE 1980S

Writer/producer Jeannine Locke made her own distinctive kind of programs for other reasons.

LOCKE [1989]: I was much criticized for the ending of *You've Come a Long Way Katie*, when the woman dies. I wanted to demonstrate that you just don't put alcoholics into treatment, file them away, and then the curtain comes down. Institutional solutions are the end. In other words, file alcoholics away, let somebody else deal with them there, and send them back to you clean and problem free. It doesn't work that way, and I felt it was time to make that point.

MJM: Did you have a real battle within the CBC, before you got to the shooting stage, to make that point?

LOCKE: I didn't have a battle with John Kennedy. When I went to the Donwood treatment centre to talk to Dr Bell about allowing us to film there, I told him what I proposed and where it was going, and he said "Good. Families send us their people and we are supposed to send them out cured."

MJM: So he saw Kate's death as realistic.

LOCKE: And, interestingly, so did the audience.

MJM: They didn't write to you saying, "How dare you kill off Katie?"

LOCKE: The only people I heard that from were people in the business, but not a single letter.

MJM: How did the actor, Lally Cadeau, feel about that?

LOCKE: The actors were much involved, because we filmed the treatment episode in the centre. It made an impression on the actors to be surrounded by people in treatment.

MJM: How does the television drama you write and produce differ from the others on the box?

LOCKE: I think that most drama nowadays on television is about power. I remember being at a CBC think-tank, and people were talking about drama as being about power and lust, sex, and a lot of hate.

MJM: Betrayal and greed.

LOCKE: I don't know why – maybe it's coming out of Saskatchewan – but I have always been far more interested in the helpless in the fray than I am in the people in power. I've never been star struck. I like to show how people feeling helpless can find within themselves enough hope to make some improvement to their lives. That sounds really corny. I was asked once on an interview on the *Journal*, "Why do you always deal with ordinary rural people?" and I said, "Because not very many other people do. I might as well set out my territory."

MJM: And yet in *The Other Kingdom* you chose as your protagonist a woman who seems to have it all, including power. She is a media figure, an urban figure, she is very together. The unravelling of her sense of self when she is diagnosed as having breast cancer, and her remaking, is the drama. Effectively, cancer is the leveller. Her encounter with Ruby, a lovely old lady with no pretensions, makes us get inside the illness.

LOCKE: Who is more helpless than the person who enters the kingdom of the sick? The greatest compliment you could get from someone who has endured this illness has always been, "I learned a lot." I don't know whether we are going to get that any more. Maybe it's a sign of the times that sample audiences just have to press a button on a monitor. They don't have to say why they liked anything. Our audience measurements include people who watch for one minute.

I asked Jeannine Locke about her reasons for doing *The Greening of Ian Elliot*, which examines environmental issues and the ordination of practising homosexuals.

LOCKE: The United Church were very interested because they had meetings coming up, including the General Council. They thought they might show this film, so they wanted to see it. When we showed it to them last week, one man stood up and said, "Thank God for the CBC." He said, "This film accomplishes more than the church itself has accomplished in the last three years." I wanted very badly to do this film, because it seems to me that the United Church is one of the few peculiarly Canadian institutions created to meet peculiar Canadian needs. And the environment is also involved. But I doubt that the *Greening of Ian Elliot* stands high in the list of CBC priorities right now. It will probably get short-shrift in this budget in terms of promotion, because it's not the "crime of the week" or a sitcom series or a fairy story.

Locke was absolutely correct. The delay to a June air date insured a relatively small audience in the "off season," and the promotion was only adequate. It has not been rerun.

Jeanine Locke usually worked on dramas with a strong sense of social justice, using a particularized sense of place and well-developed characters. Generally, she had about ninety minutes of a two-hour slot to tell her story. The producers of the topical dramas in *For the Record*, which were often about the need for social justice, had about fifty minutes – a different sort of challenge.

Maryke McEwen began as a producer on *For the Record*, then took her concerns about urban problems into *Street Legal*, which, in its early years, emphasized the cases – both serious and silly – of the lawyers rather than their personal lives. One of her most recent productions was *The Diary of Evelyn Lau,* a drama special about a middle-class Chinese-Canadian girl who runs away to become a street kid, then a prostitute and drug addict, and finally a writer of some distinction. We discussed the problems and strengths of topical dramas in 1984.

MJM: One of the hazards of the *For the Record* kind of material is that it can get too didactic, with too little entertainment and, given its short time period, too much instruction.

McEWEN: Or too much information. It can be too close to reality. Reaching that balance is very hard. You can pick the wrong story, which doesn't translate onto television. Or you're caught up in your research and you want to say everything – and it gets boring. It's a hard form to work in.

MJM: I know that you've had some feedback from the groups whose lives you've reflected. Have you enjoyed that?

McEWEN: One of the most satisfying things about doing *For the Record* is that you get that feedback. People say, "Thank you for the show," or they say, "It really helped me to get out of a bad situation." Sometimes you can use the shows to do work in the area of the topic. Bill Gough's *A Far Cry from Home* has been used quite a lot by women's centres and social workers. It makes you feel good, because you know you're giving people something they can hang onto and make use of. For me, it has always been one of the reasons for doing *For the Record.* We aren't doing the programs just to do a show. We aren't doing them to change things but to open up people's eyes, so they can look at a subject in a new or different way, to see the people instead of the facts.

MJM: In *Ready for Slaughter*[27] you thought about what the urban viewer knows and may not know and you said, "Okay, meat comes out of the hind end of a cow. I will present the birth of a calf in the first few seconds."

McEWEN: A lot of people didn't like that birth. I always thought it was so nice.

MJM: I thought it was an excellent idea, but you really took a risk with it, didn't you?

McEWEN: Yes, but I didn't realize it until after I got the feedback: "What did you do that for? It was revolting." Lots of people don't like that sort of thing, I discovered. I think it's neat. I always get a tear in my eye when I see a birth, so I figure everybody will. They don't.

The rural farmers whose dilemmas were portrayed praised the film at the local previews. I asked Maryke McEwen what sort of show she thought *Street Legal* would be and why?

McEWEN: I'd say it is an ensemble series. I couldn't do set characters or set structures. That would restrict me dramatically. This way I can do characters who can grow and develop, who can change, who can come and go. The other thing from my roots in *For the Record* is that the story can tell itself. The story has to find its own pace, rhythm, structure, all those things. Any story that has to do with the law is going to reflect society in one way or the other. If the character has to change because the story demands it, then the character will change.

MJM: And if none of your regular characters are foregrounded in a particular episode, it's not a disaster?

McEWEN: No, the story becomes more important.

In a later conversation, Maryke McEwen departed from her earlier sense of the importance of story over character. She came to the conclusion that *Street Legal*'s success depended much more on characters (Leon, Carrie, Chuck, and eventually Olivia) than on plots. If "success" is defined as ratings and audience enjoyment, character is more important to series television. Audiences must identify with the "stars" week after week or they won't keep watching. My own view remains that the most satisfying series television regularly steps back from a focus on personalities and their relationships to emphasize issues in the real world.

Nevertheless, *Street Legal*'s ratings rose in direct proportion to the objectification of the women and sometimes of the men. When McEwen left the show, what had been a strongly particularized series about Canadian law and the clients who must live with its limitations became a series that often, not always, emphasized emotional melodrama and formula devices of suspense: Will Leon be mayor? Will Leon be disbarred? Will Chuck be imprisoned for murder? Will Carrie really marry Dillon? Will Olivia marry Chuck? Will Alana divorce Leon? Will Olivia get away with it again? How will the writers deal with the fact that Sonja Smits is leaving the show? There were still many good moments, but the bite and relevance and the sense of the ridiculous that made it different to a considerable degree disappeared.[28]

FORMULA, INFLECTION, OR INNOVATION?

When it comes to the relationship of formula to innovation or even inflection, Sydney Newman, with his experience and his detachment, places the responsibility on the head or director or vice-president in charge.

MJM: What was the role of experiment in the general flow of television drama, the kind of program that would challenge some of the more obvious strictures of the day? That sort of thing was integrated at the CBC in the 1950s, but was split off in *Q for Quest* and *Program X* and then disappeared in the 1970s as a regular element of the mix.

NEWMAN: My own view is that television has never had time for experimentation. If the 1950s were good years, it is only because the advertising agencies were too ignorant (and so were the bosses of broadcasting organizations) to control the output of their people. When original programs came along, it was simply because the person in charge had a personal view he was able to express without the heavy hand of knowledgeable control over him. Usually, one did things on the run, and marvellous things happened. Now, it is so highly controlled that it takes a very rare individual in charge, such as a director general or a controller of programs, to risk losing an audience. They are very few, very rare. Jeremy Isaacs had that opportunity and so did the controllers of the BBC, particularly director-general Hugh Greene, who ran the BBC in the 1960s.[29] Take the Canadian example. The reason the CBC does damn little work of that sort is because the competitive factors against them are so strong that they simply dare not risk anything. That's why it's tepid, pallid stuff. If you go further and make a political statement, governments, regardless of party, are totally oblivious to the value of the creative act and its impact on the consumer. They don't see the role of the arts as having a stimulating effect on people's morale and their capacity to face disasters such as unemployment and depression. It's not that governments have been specifically harsh on the CBC. Where they have been totally delinquent is that they simply allowed the private sector to do whatever it wanted. The CBC, which had a great deal of money, was then forced to compete for audiences. In that competition, the stuff became more and more degraded. The greatest responsibility must accrue to the Canadian Radio and Television Commission, which has been absolutely dreadful in not forcing private television to contribute to Canadian unity, Canadian *esprit de corps*, and so on. Terrible, disgusting, and they helped kill the CBC – Canada's only genuine major voice.

Experiment and sitcom both belong on television, and both can give pleasure to the same person. The range of television's potential is enormous and the ways the viewers use television are just as varied. Why do sitcom? Not because the Americans do it, although some American sitcoms have dominated the international market for four decades. It's often funny. It's usually cheap to buy. Yet the United Kingdom, France, Italy, Norway, Holland, the Philippines, and Hong Kong all do sitcoms of their own because each culture inflects what is funny differently. Moreover, some things are humorous only in the context of a specific culture. That's why we should do our own sitcoms. But there have been seasons (1993–94, 1994–95) without a CBC sitcom.

Producer Joe Partington, who has worked on *King of Kensington*, *Flappers*, and *Hangin' In* as well as the complex tragi-comedy *Sanity Clause*, also values indigenous comedy.

PARTINGTON [1989]: In the summer of 1989 I was asked by Paul Chato to be producer of *Material World*, a half-hour situation comedy on tape with executive producer Katie Ford. She was back from the States, where she had been executive story editor and writer on *Family Ties* [an American sitcom that was a major hit in the 1980s and is still doing well in reruns]. *Material World* was created by Jane Ford, her twin sister, Paul Pogue, and Hilary Shepard. The pilot was written by Jane and Paul.

MJM: How many episodes are in the works already?

PARTINGTON: Part of the deal, which is standard at this time, is that they get a pilot go-ahead. The writer/creators will come up with six outlines, so they'll know where the show is going. All of that is supposed to happen simultaneously, so that if the administrators like the pilot they can give the go-ahead to the block of six and get them on fairly quickly. We did six in the fall of 1989 plus the pilot, so it will be seven episodes ready for February 1990. There was no audience testing on the pilot of *Material World* to my knowledge. It was given the go-ahead on the "gut feel" of the regime.

MJM: It seems that good sitcoms take on resonance and memory. One of the things I remember about *King of Kensington* was the way in which the show recapitulated (in the final episode) the life of the series itself. *King of Kensington* to some degree had a memory, although I recall few references, if any, to Cathy once she was gone. What do you think about memory in sitcom? *M*A*S*H* had it, but lots of successful sitcoms lack that kind of depth.

PARTINGTON: *M*A*S*H* was unique. They had that life and death situation, people could actually die. So the memory is nostalgic, sentimental.

Material World mark I (winter 1990) was a disaster, but it was given another chance the next season. A very much rearranged mark II in the 1991–92 season had voice-over comments from Kitty, memories of her childhood, a few fantasy sequences, more topical material, and better writing – it had some texture. What it did not appear to have is follow-through. Kitty had breast cancer in the 1991–92 season, in a well-written episode that ended with the young star giving her audience a small reassuring talk on the subject. Then the subject was dropped. Plans to marry and other crises and questions arose, but no reference was made to an experience that should alter the life and perspective of the protagonist. Other plot lines have spanned more than one episode, but as far as I know this one simply vanished. The following season, mark III (1992–93) was introduced in which her acerbic, insecure, and charming room-mate's character was developed. The series continued, intermittently, to tackle difficult subjects. For example, it included an episode on the self-image of women. Kitty, her mother, her room-mate, and Lucy, her up-to-date late adolescent musician salesgirl, all try to look like anorexic models for Kitty's fashion show. Although much more interesting than its earlier versions, *Material World* (mark III) was not renewed for 1993–94. Yet, according to the summer 1993 *Media Watch Bulletin*, the episode "Always a Woman" won an award from the organization, which looks for, documents, and reports on negative stereotypes of women and minorities on television.

PARTINGTON: There are a couple of things to avoid in sitcom. I learned them from Jack Humphrey, but I don't know who he learned them from. Avoid self-pity. Audiences do not like self-pity. I used to wonder if it was because Jack had a personal distaste for it, but I think he was right. If King was being self-pitying about Cathy's leaving him, who cares? You couldn't go back to it in a positive way. What could he say? "She was better in bed than the girl that ..." or "she cooked better." So I think it depends very much on the flavour of the series. *M*A*S*H* had the best of all worlds.

You hear all these negative comments around here about *Cosby* and how the spinoff's success is due to its scheduling (after *Cosby*). You see it in the top ten week after week and I think, "Are these people totally out of their minds? Don't they realize that if a huge audience watch *A Different World*, there must be something about it that's attractive?" I watch *Cosby* and I'm not hung up on "Is there really a black family like this" or this "disguised racism" issue. I see things that echo my own experiences with my own kids. It's beautifully done and it's simply written. It's about nothing in particular, and no one else can do it.

MJM: It depends on Bill Cosby's talent and on audience identification. That's one of the problems with something like *Mosquito Lake*. There was nothing a viewer could connect to even if she owns a cottage. *In Opposition* ran on the same joke that *Not My Department* depended on – that all bureaucrats and most politicians are bumbling fools. It doesn't talk about constituency problems in a funny way. I feel sorry for the actors who are stranded in the middle.

I start out always predisposed to like whatever I look at on the CBC. But I am also an academic critic with a long memory rather than a journalist who hasn't watched anything before 1980. As far as I'm concerned, the 1989 sitcoms (*Mosquito Lake*, *In Opposition*, and *Material World*) are up against the others over the years at the CBC and they don't stand up to earlier successes.

PARTINGTON: The show has to succeed, whatever show it is, on it's own terms. The audience has to accept the characters for who they are. I'm astonished at the level of reality in *Roseanne*. They don't resolve anything.

MJM: Resolution, narrative closure, is the norm for sitcom, isn't it?

PARTINGTON: And that's not bad.

The following years produced a better crop: *Material World* (mark II), *Max Glick*, and *Mom PI*, for all of which Nada Harcourt was responsible.

HARCOURT: I was offered a script many years ago that a director of television in Winnipeg actually fought to have done because he believed in it, based on Morley Torgov's *The Outside Chance of Maximilian Glick*. It seemed to me, in those early days, that in an early script incarnation it had some problems. Anyway, the script got done in spite of the fact that I wasn't particularly interested in developing the movie. I'm very grateful that somebody else had a passion for it, because when I went to see the movie (produced by Stephen Foster and written by Phil Savath) at the Festival of Festivals it struck me immediately that here, during Meech Lake controversy, was a very strong operating principle for a series. What could be more specific than a Jewish boy growing up in a small town in Manitoba in Beauséjour, struggling to form his own identity against a loving group, including his grandparents and his parents. They in turn are deeply committed to preserving their identity and making their son Max aware that it was the governing principle of their lives. There's a lot of conflict, but it seemed to me that this family was a metaphor for all Canadian families, whether they be Polish or Ukrainian or Jamaican or Irish. We have all gone through that process.

We wanted to place the series in 1963, because it was an extremely interesting time for Canada. We were beginning to feel that we were, culturally, a separate country. It was the beginning of Vietnam. We accepted draft dodgers from the United States who were not committed to that war. It was the beginning of the Bilingualism and Biculturalism Commission, where we were exploring the two founding nations. Yet you have this specifically Jewish family that somehow encompassed all those issues. I don't think anybody, when it was initially pitched, expected it to be as humorous and as intelligent as it was, and to have its operating principle so easily understood. It has great charm. That was another instance in which we were proactive in suggesting that it should be a series.

The original creators of the movie and now co-producers of the current series are Phil Savath and Stephen Foster. Because they were new to doing a series, which has many other components like financing and distribution, they were partnered with Sunrise Films, which had a lot of experience.

Shooting the series in Vancouver sacrificed the bleakness and the expansiveness of the original prairie setting, which had emphasized the isolation of the small Jewish community. Nevertheless, the series found comic elements in out of the way places. For all its unevenness of tone, it was less a formula sitcom and, like *Material World* and *Mom PI*, more a comedy/drama series.

HARCOURT: I think the thing that attracted me about *Mom PI* was the idea in the 1990s of doing a series about a single mother who was a waitress, a blue-collar woman living and working on the east side of Vancouver, and her growing self-esteem. Her perceptions are so acute as a mother nurturing her children. Also, she is able to do three things at once, a skill that a great many women can respond to. The intuitive aspects of the female are coupled with a cynical gumshoe who had a heart attack and who doesn't really believe in human nature. He suddenly begins to see that he needs her optimism. It's a wonderful relationship. We totally lucked out in being able to get Stuart Margolin and Rosemary Dunsmore, who have incredible chemistry on air.

The other aspect was that we weren't going to do a violent series but, like *Barney Miller*, we attempted to explore human nature humorously. All the secondary characters are slightly off the wall, a bit eccentric. So it is not a typical "buddy" crime series, not at all. That's what makes it quintessentially Canadian but also a program that should have universal appeal.

Keeping a long-running hit going is as much of a challenge as inventing a new series. Yet another kind of program the CBC has prided itself on doing well is the family action/adventure show. I interviewed Don Williams when he was executive producer of *The Beachcombers* in 1985. This interview was conducted before the writing in *The Beachcombers* became stale, the action/violence took over from characterization, and the unfortunate introduction of the new characters Dana and Sam further diluted the distinctive motifs of the series.[30]

MJM: When you became executive producer of *The Beachcombers*, what sort of energy did you bring to it?

WILLIAMS: The first injection of energy came from a fierce loyalty towards the show, based on the proof that something from the regions could be successful using the measurements of success that the "big boys" use – ratings and international sales. Here was a show that was a major international export, a Canadian produced show with a large Canadian audience. Moreover, the series is fairly unsophisticated and doesn't fall into any of the North American traps.

MJM: Such that the violence is directed towards objects, not people?

WILLIAMS: Yes. I was motivated by the fact that it could be sold to thirty-six countries and have an audience of two million in Canada without violence.

MJM: It has also become less sexist as time goes on.

WILLIAMS: We have a loyal audience. I believe that people watch it all the time or never watch it. I thought that was a marvellous opportunity to touch on some issues that were usually thought of as subjects reserved for more serious shows like *For the Record*. The whole excitement for me was having that loyal audience to sneak up on.

MJM: When a producer trusts an audience, a good series will often kick into what I call "anthology mode."

WILLIAMS: I recognized that there was a bit of a tight-rope there and I didn't want to go crazy with it.

MJM: For example, you couldn't suddenly make Nick an unlikeable, horrid man.

WILLIAMS: And you also can't preach to the audience. A lot of people have a hard time resisting that temptation.[31] I thought that there were a lot of areas we could venture into if our characters still behaved as the people the audience knew from the beginning and the landmarks of the show were still there, so people could touch base with them.

MJM: Would you say one landmark is a careful ambivalence towards the belief systems of the Native people interacting with Nick, Relic, Molly, and Constable John? I have found that to be one of the strengths of the show.

WILLIAMS: Yes. From what I can discern, that subject has its greatest success with our European audience, but not with our Canadian audience. Yet, if it's not successful with our Canadian audience, we're doing it wrongly. We should be able to make Canadian audiences interested because it's close enough to home.

MJM: Maybe you do it once in a while for the minority who do care.

ON CRITICS AS VIEWERS AND SURROGATES

MJM to NEWMAN: Were the critics in Britain ever of any use to you other than in drawing audiences to what you were doing? The quality of television criticism in British newspapers is fairly high.

NEWMAN: Yes, it is, very high. I was too pig-headed and single-minded to be influenced by them. I loved the praise that I got, and I sure got tons of it. But I don't think that I learned anything from critics at all.

MJM: So you didn't miss that quality of criticism when you were here?

NEWMAN: Maybe at first, when I was starting, I took the critics somewhat more seriously. The critics in Toronto were mostly ex-sports writers.

DAVID GARDNER, actor/producer [1983]: In the 1960s the Publicity Department would gather together newspaper criticisms from across the country, so you would get a synopsis of all the reviews from Halifax to Vancouver. You would get reviews by Les Wedman in Vancouver and by Pat Pearce in Montreal. That was one kind of audience response – after the fact, but at least you knew about it. In this country it is so important to get that kind of feedback, and very difficult because of the geography.

FECAN: The same episode of *Mosquito Lake* that was attacked in Toronto was praised in the regions. Now it's not that good, it's an average show. It's as good as 80 per cent of the new shows on American television.

MJM: Do critics influence the audience? The *Toronto Star*'s Jim Bawden and the *Globe and Mail*'s John Haslett Cuff?

FECAN: I don't think they influence the audience a great deal, but they contribute to the idea that, as Canadians, we're not very good at doing things. Some reviewers don't like *Street Legal*, which is fine. But what is not fine is when it beats every show in its time period and they don't mention that either. They will not mention that because it goes against their particular thesis. There is one reviewer currently who believes we should be PBS and who writes every review from that perspective, whether the show is any good or not. When we announced *The Adrienne Clarkson Show* as a year-round fixture, that critic did not even mention it in his column, because it went against his thesis.

AUDIENCE/CBC INTERACTION

It doesn't take an expert in reader/response theory to know that the individual sensibility of viewers, counted one by one, does make an imprint on a television drama. Collectively, if few of us watch a program, it will disappear, in part determining what we will be offered next. Our letters and calls shape the plot lines of soaps, the fate of characters, the series themselves, and the inflections of or adherence to formula of whole genres. The "couch potato" is an unhelpful myth. We all have eyes and ears, fingers to zap, and the ability to concentrate if need be, and most of us have opinions about some of what we watch.

Here is what the makers and decision-makers say about the viewers.

ALLEN: I don't know that we learned much about how we were being received generally. In the 1950s and early 1960s the information coming in was spotty. A telephone call, ten telephone calls, a bunch of letters. There was no way of measuring if those letters represented a consensus.

From time to time there were threats about the very existence of the corporation, and there always have been. We had to set those criticisms aside because we had to get on with doing the show. There were other people who had to worry about them.

MJM: *Festival* was a follow-on from *Folio*. Why did you change the title from *Folio* in the 1950s to *Festival* in the 1960s?

ALLEN: That may have been a result of our feeling so good about our increasing audience and their enthusiasm that we decided to celebrate by calling it a Festival. And to get away from the academic implications of *Folio*.

MJM: Why would you have presenters at the top of each show, introducing them briefly? Sometimes yourself, sometimes other people.

ALLEN: That began out of the same impetus which determined that we had to put *Point of Departure* on at 11:30 at night instead of at 9 o'clock. Management requested that we explain what we were doing, to give some indication to viewers what they were in for. The theory was that if you had a perfectly respectable person like Clyde Gilmour as the presenter, people would stay and not run away! I did it a lot of times, because I felt I knew more about the program than any presenter. Sometimes our programs were short of the required time, and there was also a need to fill after the program. We devised something called *Theatre Party* in which I interviewed some of the cast, in a very ad hoc, ad lib, chaotic fashion.

MJM: So that would mean that you wouldn't have to come in right at ninety minutes, which is one of the problems with precise time slots.

ALLEN: The whole presenter business also had its positive value. When we were doing Pinter or Arden's *Sergeant Musgrave's Dance* or a lot of those things, it was helpful to tell people who had no idea who these dramatists were something about them.

MJM: Yes, I can see that. Who had heard of Pinter in the very early 1960s? Yet the reactions Pinter's kind of play would get is astounding. I have come across the correspondence in the files in the library.

ALLEN: You get far more response negatively, from people who don't understand what is going on, than you get appreciation from people who do understand. At least that is the way we justify ourselves.

MJM: No, that is genuinely true. People remember with pleasure those programs, but I doubt that they ever sat down to tell you so.

ALLEN: They certainly didn't write and say, "We really do like to see people who are not married in the same bed." Do you know how many prudes rushed to their fountain pens to tell us that they didn't want to watch that kind of thing again?

Story editor Nathan Cohen also served as surrogate for the viewer when he turned from the craft of story editor and on-air host of a very literate and funny panel show called *Fighting Words* to the role of drama critic for the *Toronto Star*.

TILL, on what Cohen thought of CBC TV drama]: Cohen was a good lad, though, you could phone him. I was putting a film together that was having a lot of trouble, and I didn't realize he was quite ill. I needed an opinion from outside, and I thought, I'll just phone Nathan; he doesn't do film reviews, so he is not going to be uptight about that. I talked to him, and, although he was just a few days away from dying, he was thrilled. I said, "Nathan, I just need someone to come and tell me what is going on with this thing. I am so close to it that I can't find out what's wrong with it." He was that kind of person, he was very dear in that regard. I remember he said when *Kim* came out that it was the very best piece of television that had ever been produced. I said, "A thirty-minute, come on Nathan!" He said, "You shut up." He thought it was highly original. I never thought of that. But that's what we did then. We didn't stop and think, "Oh, yes, I am going to be original," we just did it![32]

When we did *The Offshore Island*, the corporation was very nervous. I was called to account to Michael Sadlier, who said: "Eric, where is your interpreter? How are you going to deal with this? What about the incest in it? What about the anti-Americanism?" And I just kept saying: "Don't worry about it, it is going to be all right." But they were so nervous about it. In the first place, I was asked to write a preamble, which was sent out to all the columnists, a kind of "Warning, don't let your little children watch it!"

MJM: Did you?

TILL: Oh, yes, if I hadn't written it, somebody else would have had to. Then they stationed across the country – in Montreal, Toronto and Vancouver – people to monitor all the phone calls. I didn't know that – I was told about it two days later. And Michael Sadlier was to receive from these people all the information about the response after the program had gone on the air.

MJM: And what was it?

TILL: It was enormously in favour. There were those people, inevitably, who were upset, but you always have them. I have a newspaper clipping from some small town which said that Till obviously has to be a communist, because he did this piece called *Pale Horse, Pale Rider* about a young American who doesn't want to go to war, and everybody knows that all good red-blooded Americans are not afraid to go to war. It is McCarthy, isn't it. A complete, wonderful misinterpretation of it all.

MJM: But at least they let *Offshore Island* go out at the normal time.

TILL: And they repeated it three times! With *Offshore* there was so much press about it, all basically saying, "Thank Christ that the CBC will put on something like this." Then, of course, Michael and all the other fellows were very pleased.

MJM to NEWMAN: The audience research and ratings people tell me that audiences resist the ambivalent or the open-ended.

NEWMAN: They are stupid, unimaginative, and they don't even know their own medium.

MJM: Are you talking about the research and ratings people or the audience?

NEWMAN: I'm talking about the people who are interpreting the audience. The point is that I made my reputation on the single play, the anthology series, where you produce a different play every week. How do you hold an audience? There is no continuity of actors. There is no continuity of writers. The only continuity is the style of the program and the state of mind of your particular audience. You cater to a state of mind. You also cater, to a certain extent, to a cultural background. I would never do a working-class play one week (I was called the king of "kitchen sink dramas") and Ibsen the next week. That is too big a jar. I was able to sustain that audience week after week because I hit that same set of audience expectations. That is the primary function of the producer, a man in charge of a run of shows. Style and content pertinent to the times, elements like that, develop audience loyalty.

MJM: So that the audience will say, "They are going to surprise me again, tonight, but I know that I'm going to understand what I see and I'm going to like it. If I don't, I'm going to come back next week because I'm probably going to like it next week."

NEWMAN: The CBC just doesn't understand that. In Hirsch's era, when they created *For the Record*, which was wonderful, it seemed to be a renaissance. Yet the program schedulers kept interrupting it even though they did only about six episodes a year. They would interrupt it for a hockey game. They couldn't build up a loyal audience for that Sunday night. They did everything to screw up the single play. Of course, a single play is the hardest thing to do, but you need a producer who is single-minded, can express what he wants, and can get a group of people who are like-minded and who stay with it week after week. You need an organization that will go on the air for thirty-nine weeks.

I asked producer Herb Roland, who worked on popular series in the 1970s and 1980s, about calls and letters.

ROLAND [1989]: Yes, I had some interest groups. I had the women down on me from somewhere in Nova Scotia because of one show. And some other really nice ones, but never en masse. But with *Gift to Last*, we came on the first week and they started to write, not sackfuls, but like this: "I sat in here and I just cried," "I'm proud to be Canadian," "My family gathered together, we would never miss it." The letters were unbelievable, so touching, so genuine. There were a lot for Gordon, but also for the whole show, hundreds. I asked the production secretary to type out all the interesting ones and I probably have them somewhere. It wasn't just the ordinary "Oh, he is lovely," but it was from the heart – what it meant to the families gathering after dinner or having dinner early so they could all sit down. It was so genuine, and from right across the country.

MJM: Nobody was worried about its being set in southern Ontario?

ROLAND: Nobody. It was Vancouver, it was Victoria, it was Quebec, it was Newfoundland, it was everywhere. It was sold right across the world. At one time, it was the top everywhere. In Italy, they changed the name to *The Destiny of Lions*, don't ask me why.

MJM: How funny and how very un-Canadian, although Ruth Springford's character, the matriarch Lizzie Sturgess, was a lioness – she really was.

ROLAND: Yes, that was fun.

McEWEN: If you can get both that specialized audience and the broad one – then you've done something. I think you can do both. I don't see that they are mutually exclusive. Look at *Ready for Slaughter*. That was a farm show. Who is going to watch a farm show? A lot of people actually watched it and liked it because they liked the guy. They didn't have to know anything about farming. They liked the story or they liked being against the establishment. If you like that kind of story, it works. I wasn't doing that for farmers. There is a political reason for doing *Ready for Slaughter* to a wider audience, but the other side of me simply wants to do a good show. If nobody is going to watch it, why do it? It's like painting a painting that nobody looks at.

There are times when you get really discouraged. When you do shows that you really believe in, that no one else seems to care about. That is when you run into a fine edge. I don't think you can do a show just for one audience – white, middle-class families. But when you pick something that is so obscure or unlikeable or whatever that the audience doesn't want to see it, then you failed. That is depressing, but you can still try again.

Writer/producer Jeannine Locke was emphatic about the distinction between the need for the CTV or Global networks to deliver audiences to advertisers and the responsibiity of a crown corporation to its audience.

LOCKE: I don't expect a private broadcaster to regard his audience out there as an audience of *citizens*; they are *consumers*. But we can't behave that way.

MJM: No, working within the corporation allows you to make some assumptions about what your audience will stay involved with, their attention span if you like, their interest in issues, their ability to be a bit more complex in their response.

LOCKE: This is why I feel so strongly about television movies. Coming out of current affairs, I've the greatest feeling for that.

MJM: We were talking about *Chautauqua Girl*, and you spoke about defending a sequence that you are obviously very fond of as a producer and I was very fond of as a critic. I wonder if you would be allowed to do that in 1989? That was the long sequence with "Unto the Hills."

LOCKE: Yes, but also the subplot of the United Farmers Of Alberta.

MJM: The politic context of the film.

LOCKE: The director Rob Iscove, who was based in Los Angeles, a wonderful director, said, "It will never sell. No one will understand what this is all about." Of course, it wasn't just about the United Farmers of Alberta, it was about dissent, it was about alienation, it was about feeling remote from centres of power and culture. It turned out that most people in this country felt that way. Not only in this country, because *Chautauqua Girl* has sold widely.

The audience response is the most heartening thing that happens. We were deluged with letters about *Chautauqua Girl*. Without a single exception, there were references to the scene of the old woman, and to the scene out in the field [where the Chautauqua troup's Scottish tenor sang three verses slowly and powerfully of "Unto the Hills."] And similarly with *Island Love Song*, with *The Other Kingdom*, with *You've Come a Long Way, Katie*.

MJM: What did you hear about *Island Love Song*?

LOCKE: *Island Love Song* roused up every Cape Bretoner who was away from home, and that was the start of it. There were letters from every region except Newfoundland. What almost all of them expressed was gratitude for the reassertion of values they thought were gone. Also a way of looking at people in hard times without simply leaving them there in the pit. This was the story of how people with a steady experience of hard times have managed to make life not only tolerable but precious.

MJM: And *Chautauqua* did that as well.

I asked writer/producer Bill Gough and his wife Anna Sandor who they did their work for?

GOUGH and SANDOR [1988]: For yourself.

MJM: Isn't that interesting. I get that response from the creative side every time. "If it's for myself, if I am pleased with it, it is likely to reach an audience."

GOUGH: Yes, it will.

SANDOR: You say for "yourself," but that covers a lot of territory. We all do things for bread and butter. *Danger Bay* is not for myself. Although, when I write a *Danger Bay*, it's got me in it and things that I feel, otherwise I can't do it. But when you do something major, the initial impulse has got to be for yourself. I was going to write *Two Men* even if I had to put money from my own pocket out to do it.[33] It was something I had to say, something Bill wanted to produce.

We are both at a stage in our lives and in our careers where we are secure enough that, even if the critics slaughter us, we look at something, we like it, and we realize that it was the best we could have done at the time. Conversely, we have had wonderful critical response with programs we haven't personally been pleased with it. It's because we know that it could have been better or it just wasn't the way we wanted it.

GOUGH: Television becomes an élitist form if you think there is a mass out there who conform to trends and have beliefs that are predictable and can be responded to simply by analysing them. You don't have a mass audience. You have got individuals watching your show. So you can never figure out what they are going to like. You can't do it that way. It doesn't work that way. But any decision you make is not yours as a specific, isolated individual. It is a collective decision based on what aunts, uncles, cousins, friends, teachers, pets have done when they have responded to you over your life. So it is automatically a collective decision. There are no individual decisions.

This mixture of instinct, experience, and consultation has been replaced because the decision-making is now concentrated in one place – the director of programming. The person who made that change and whose guesses became what we saw from 1988 to 1994 was Ivan Fecan.

FECAN: We are trying to get a *Codco* series going. So we tested it and we also tested *Four on the Floor*, the Frantics' series. Then we tested for a comparison between the two. You look for different indications of testing. A show like *Four on the Floor* tested really high among kids and teens. That tells you something. It tells you that you are probably going to get a small audience, because kids are underreported and teens are fickle viewers. It tells you that it will probably do very well in the unreported audience and that you should play it before eight o'clock.

The under-twenty audience didn't get *Codco* at all. The twenty-to-thirty-year-old audience found it very funny. The over-fifty audience was outraged that public money was spent on such a show. That is a good sign. And, overall, you get a sense of where the strengths of the show might be.[34] This is my theory. For ten or fifteen years we have not kept pace with the kinds of television our public watches. We have not kept pace with the lessons to be learned both here and around the world. I firmly believe that television has changed dramatically over the last five years.[35] I believe it was changed by the people who protested in the late 1960s on Yorkville Avenue and in Gastown and in all those kinds of communities across Canada. Those people, by and large, with the exception of a few things like *All in the Family*, didn't watch television in the 1970s because television didn't relate to them as a generation. The generation that grew up with television, the Baby Boomers, the Yuppies, whatever you want to call them, were a bigger influence in Canada than they ever were in the States. They lasted longer here, proportionately, and they figured into things. That audience single-handedly changed television in America; they are responsible for *Hill Street Blues*, for *St Elsewhere*, for the smart comedies. They are a more discriminating audience, more television literate, though I don't mean they are necessarily intellectually smarter.

MJM: I know what you mean. They know the grammar.

FECAN: Yes, they know the short forms and they are more demanding.

MJM: Their attention span is not eroded?

FECAN: Well, maybe it is. The medium is now capable of saying a lot of things very quickly.

MJM: Do you think their generation has the same expectations about dialogue?

FECAN: They have better expectations. The biggest mistake you can make is underestimating that audience. They are a lot smarter than many of my peers in the business will credit them, and, in the end, they are right. It doesn't mean that the mass rules.

MJM: You have just described programs that have some ambivalence in them. It is a quality that anthology is much more comfortable with than series television. Yet you have identified the American series that are edgy, that don't always have a happy ending.

FECAN: They are honest. They have a lot of the virtues of *Wojeck*. It is talking with an audience and hearing what that audience has to tell you – what people have to say in cabs and in coffee shops and then coming on again the next week and talking to them again. The good shows always have that kind of relationship, because they are about something. They are not only about big issues and moral dilemmas, they are also about people and their struggles – the good versus evil struggles; the right to resist crime struggles; the person with emotional struggles – the delicious and painful moments one goes through. These are the things that good television drama is about. If you don't do that, you are going to have a hundred hours of amorphous stuff, at best.

Much of television's output remains amorphous, including the endless reruns of some specialty channels and the endless videos, obscure sports, or repeated news updates and weather reports of channels designed primarily to be sampled, not watched hour after hour. To be Canadian, to be creative, to be distinctive in presenting the multiple personal visions of talented writers, producers, directors, and actors, to let people savour the best of earlier series and specials is how the CBC won and held audiences. Failure to be those things has resulted in periods of drought for both the corporation and its viewers. In the 500-channel universe fast approaching, amorphous programming will ensure the demise of the CBC. In chapters 9 and 10 we will see how the decision-makers have dealt with the rapidly changing broadcasting context.

9 Policy

CBC HOME DELIGHTFULLY DIFFERENT. The Americans contributed the exterior, the Canadians the interior ... Enclosed within an immense box-like grid, the contents seem to be bursting out from every corner ... The impression is of a series of buildings, some square, others apparently circular. More than anything else, the Broadcast centre is an exercise in manipulating form and volume.[1] CHRISTOPHER HUME

These comments in the *Toronto Star* on the CBC's new English Broadcasting headquarters focus on the building and its impact on the Toronto landscape. As I rewind and search my thinking on the corporate policy and evolving ethos of the CBC, I wondered if the elements of the new "centre," as described, would serve as a metonym for the corporation in the 1990s. Or are they ironically at variance with the current reality of the CBC.

SOME OF THE QUESTIONS

Often the first question I asked in these interviews was how Canadian the interior of CBC drama was during its many phases. "Canadian," as we are discovering more and more in the 1990s, can be defined (or erased) in many ways. So I also asked the creative people and the decision-makers to clarify what was understood by the term. Exactly what can be defined as Canadian becomes a recurring theme as people talk about a variety of issues that are reflected in decisions about policy. It is also one of the basic parameters of the CBC ethos, and the interior as well as the framework of "the immense box-like grid" that is CBC programming.

How did the CBC get from teleplays by Canadians on all kinds of subjects in the 1950s to Denis Harvey's vision of what Canadian should be in the mid-1980s and Ivan Fecan's interpretation of "Canadianization," which was attacked in the print media for being "made-in-Canada Americanization." Is the latter judgment fair? How does the CBC keep its ratings up, its costs down, and the backbenchers (and cabinet) content without turning the Canadian interior into an American space?[2] The 1987 Drama Subcommittee Report, an internal document that tried to address the problem, also asked these now urgent questions and many others.[3]

Whom will we try to reach? What is our target audience? What is the demographic strategy of the Drama Department? Are we going for youth? Are we going for the 40-year old generation? What will the environment of the Nineties be? What will the environment of the television industry be? What will be the character of the Nineties' generation and the themes which will emerge? Are we using all of the research tools available to us to figure out how to successfully reach the target audience? ... to figure out the themes and concerns which are special to this audience? How will we recruit and train the next generation of producers, writers and craftspeople? From these fundamentals of direction and strategy there flow the specifics of regional/network ratio, developing efficient production methods, what should be produced by us and by independents. We have been unable to aggressively and forthrightly seek out the kind of independent production we want, the kind of co-production we want, or to state clear objectives for our own creative people because we don't have a clear agenda. The various key players – from the Head of Drama up to the President – have agendas, or fragments of agendas. But there is no single one.

The question is whether things have changed significantly since the creative thinking that went into the report. Two years later Director of Programming (at that time) Ivan Fecan sketched an overall vision of CBC drama which included some answers to these questions.

IVAN FECAN [1989]: I would mount a strong argument for popular programming. Television is a public art, it's not a private art. If you believe in what you are doing, it has got to be important and central enough to a country so that people care enough to watch. Philosophically I would argue for populism regardless. But if the CBC were completely funded by government revenue I might not make the same kinds of choices about some other things that I do have to make when most of my money comes from the private sector. Unlike CBC radio and unlike (to the same degree) CBC French television, CBC English television depends mainly on revenues from commercials.

MAKING MYTHS

Whether good or bad, during the 1990s or back in the 1950s, Hugh Gauntlett pointed to drama's importance to (though not its priority in) the television mix. "Internally, drama can be the most important thing to do at the CBC" – a fact lost on many politicians, who see news and current affairs as vital mirrors of their times (and faces), but not the vital functions of myth-making and communicating the myths others make.

Myths have been defined many ways. Anthropologist Claude Lévi-Strauss and other structuralists would define myths as the most basic sites of contestation about the values and dreams of humanity. These narratives can serve as strategies for mediating or even transforming the wisdom of the collectivity, the audience as it were. Roland Barthes, however, long ago pointed to the invisible or naturalized ideologies of dominant myths. In common usage, myth connotes "untrue." Thus, a myth can exist as an archetype of the collective unconscious, the site of political or social conflict, as a reinforcer of normative values, and a slow transformer of attitudes, ideas, and desires, or all of the preceding, depending in part on the position of the viewer vis-à-vis the television text.

Every social group creates all of these categories of "myth," including the amorphous and atypical "corporation" which is the CBC. Corporate or individual policy, either stated or assumed, can prevent some subjects from reaching us on television while foregrounding others. Policy-makers can create Newsworld, the channel where breaking news appears, and then can make the decision to carry hours of the Oka crisis live. Newsworld became the place on the channel selector where a variety of fundamental myths were played out in real time with real consequences. Policy can also distance those issues and the resulting agencies by placing them in a fictional setting fifty years in the past. Policy can place the evolving story of Aboriginal rights (and the wrongs they address) live on Newsworld, which was not available to as many Canadians in the 1990s, and put the 1930s fiction about residential schools, *Where the Spirit Lives,* on prime time CBC available to most Canadians. Individual producers at *the fitfh estate* covered residential schools in a searching one-hour documentary, and *Man Alive*'s producers showed the beginning of the healing process undertaken by Native groups who recover and exercise their own spirituality. Where and when the program is broadcast helps to determine the construction of this particular "Canadian issue."

Drama's role in this range is its unique ability to focus, humanize, and provide the context for current events and, most importantly, their subtext. *Where the Spirit Lives* succeeded only in part. Fudging the devastation of physical and psychological abuse with a hopeful ending, and thus alienating some of those who were its subject (while ironically winning awards for it), reveals an ideological process of making myth that will not, however, be the last word on the subject. Yet, *Where the Spirit Lives* (1982 – rebroadcast at least four times) may have helped to create the context of more openness to the racism of our history. The next phase of "policy" on this subject may be Native voices telling their own story through the camera and in the editing room.

GETTING HERE FROM THERE

When I began to write this book in 1988, the survival of the CBC seemed to me in doubt. As I end it in mid-1995, the survival of Canada may be in doubt. How did we get to this place of doubt from the 1960s era of growing and vibrant nationalism? How did we get to the 1990s struggles with "Canadianization" from the nascent but less troubled nationalism of 1952? Not being an expert on the constitution or the economy, I will concentrate on rewinding the cultural record of TV drama and its makers to see what it may tell us.

In 1952, when the CBC belatedly initiated television service in Montreal and Toronto, and CBC television drama under Mavor Moore went into dress rehearsal for its debut, antennae all along the border regions were pointed to the American border stations. Audiences had been tuned to American forms of entertainment through radio since the late 1920s and television since the late 1940s. Some Canadians were ready and anxious to provide attentive audiences to the more serious anthology drama that was reaching the height of its popularity with *Studio One* and *Playhouse 90* and the less serious plays on *Four Star Playhouse* and *Loretta Young Presents*. Others were more enthralled by the Norwegian-American nostalgia of *Mama* or the blue-collar befuddlement of *The Life of Riley*. The kids were fascinated by puppet shows like *Kukla, Fran and Ollie, Howdy Doody*, and heroes like *Hopalong Cassidy* and *The Cisco Kid*.

MJM to MAVOR MOORE [1990]: I sense that people felt that television was *the* place, not with the tradition or the audience, as with CBC Radio, but where the excitement was going to be.

MOORE: It was exciting, partly because we didn't know what we were doing. We didn't know enough to know when we were doing things wrong; we just went ahead and did them. And this applies to the administration as well as the programming. For example, shortly before we went on the air, Stuart Griffiths, Fergus Mutrie, and I realized there was no way we could do it with the small staff we had budgeted for.[4] So we decided we would hire a lot of extra script assistants and floor managers using "artists" contracts, which were allowed because we could have as many casual artists as we needed to put a show on. We made a phone call from Fergus's office to Ernest Bushnell, vice-president in charge of television in Ottawa. Stuart told him, there was a pause, and Bushnell said, "What's that?" Stuart said, "Do you want me to repeat it?" Bushnell said, "No, I never heard it in the first place." That was the end of it, and we went ahead and did it. When Donald Madsen, later the CBC's acting president, found out that this had been going on for some time, he threatened to fire Bushnell, but he didn't.

THE EVOLVING STRUCTURE OF NETWORK DELIVERY OF PROGRAMS

In the early 1950s the Conservatives in particular wanted the CBC to serve only the places where private enterprise would find it uneconomical to have stations. The strongest support for CBC national television came from Quebec, primarily on the grounds of cultural survival. Eventually both Liberals and Conservatives favoured some sort of mixed system, and settled down to argue how such a system should be developed.

The 1957 Fowler Commission on Canada's unique position vis-à-vis the United States addressed the external constraint imposed by our geography: "The central, unique fact about Canadian broadcasting is that we are here in North America, a nation of 16 million people living beside a nation of 168 million which speaks the language of our majority and is rich, inventive, with a highly developed broadcasting system of its own. No other country is similarly helped and embarrassed by the close proximity of the United States."[5] In Canada of the 1990s, only the numbers have changed.

It could be argued that, through the years, the United States has functioned as our laboratory. Thus we have avoided the more inane series about witches or flying nuns, "gong" shows, or "funniest" home videos. Instead, when we are not preoccupied with reproducing the forms and themes of American popular culture, we repeatedly demonstrate that Canadians can do work that is unique simply because the hands and brains doing it belong to specific individuals educated and shaped by the experience of living in this country.

In the 1950s the British responded to the demand for private broadcasting in a different way. They set aside a channel and let production houses make proposals for the use of certain times of day. The winners were to provide distinctive regional programming and to create some prime-time broadcasting under the regulation of the Independent Television (then Broadcast) Authority. Until Thatcher's ideological obsessions put ITV licences up for auction, pushing all private television in the United Kingdom into unpredicted and unproductive turmoil, the situation had been stable. If licence holders did not live up to promise, their licences could be cancelled. Some companies have performed well enough to hold their licences for thirty years.

This system is in marked contrast to Canada's Board of Broadcast Governors and its successor, the CTRC.[6] It took thirty years for regulators to find ways to compel private broadcasters to provide good Canadian drama or children's programs. In tandem with the independents who produced programs for the independent channel, the British government had established BBC-2 in 1964 as an alternative, free-service public channel. Not until 1977 did a president of the CBC, Al Johnson (1975–82), press hard for a CBC-2. In the 1980s Britain established channel 4, a real alternative to the three channels already available on British television. Canada is still waiting for a CBC-2 "to offer distinctive, thoughtful, alternative programming, commercial free on cable," with repeats of successful programs and programs for smaller, specialized audiences.[7] Oddly enough, broadcast consultant Kealy Wilkinson says that, in her opinion, "the time may be coming to revive the CBC-2 proposal."[8] Ironically this "rerun heaven" may only be available to those who choose direct broadcast satellite over cable, since the CBC plans to offer such a channel on satellite primarily for the American market. The CBC has also sold some recent prime-time series (*Wojeck*, *Seeing Things*, and *Street Legal*) to Showcase one of the specialty channels licensed in 1994 as the "fiction" channel.

From the vantage point of the 1990s, a widely available CBC-2 could combine repeats of our excellent broadcast heritage and thoughtful new programs, the best of *Vision*, the educational networks, and well-loved regional programs, and be a place for low-cost experiment. Johnson's blueprint paper fell into the void and, with it, a chance in the 1970s to strengthen our mutual bonds. The vice-president of English television, Ivan Fecan, was still dreaming in 1993 of a CBC-2 and 3 and 4, reflecting each of his new "time zones ... particularly the after 10 PM block." But he had no idea how to pay for it, and "that's all that's stopping us."[9] However, since the survival of the CBC itself is now in question – and many of the dreams old and new are gone – CBC-2 is unlikely to appear among the 500 channels soon to be available.

In 1989, however, the CBC after a very public struggle within the Conservative cabinet, did win approval for an all-news channel. Newsworld began to develop a profile in public consciousness several months later when the Meech Lake crisis was followed in quick succession by Oka and the Middle East War. Newsworld provided Canadians with their own ongoing flow of news, live action, and interpretation, and with a package of news, sports, and weather at 10 PM – a package that attracted many of those who did not choose to watch the repositioned 9 PM–10 PM *Prime Time News*. The 1995–96 season at Newsworld simulcasts *The National* (whose name returns to the main CBC English channel) and adds well-known personalities like Pamela Wallin and Ralph Benmergui to host call-in shows also featuring guests, shows that are stoutly defended as not being *Larry King Live North*.

As far as drama, children's, and arts producton is concerned, in an era of cutbacks and the pursuit of ratings, the CBC English Network has begun to resemble a channel 4 – in terms of being a buyer of programming rather than a maker. But unlike channel 4, experiment, innovation, and oddities can find no regular home on Canadian television. Ivan Fecan points out the key difference:

FECAN [1989]: When you think about channel 4, the British Network, it's very adult. It's adult because a group of businessmen decided that this was something that was necessary to the overall culture of Britain, and the British Parliament agreed. It's run out of an ITV levy and it is financed to get a forced share. It does a whole lot better than a forced share of the audience, but it doesn't have to attract a mass audience.

ITV's channel 4, added in the 1980s to BBC-1 and BBC-2, is shared by several licences. The programming ranges from superb modern films to American football to small independent British films like *My Beautiful Laundrette* and wide-ranging short documentary series like *Testament*.

SYDNEY NEWMAN [1984]: What makes channel 4 on ITV different from the BBC's channel 2 and commercial television is that Jeremy Isaacs and his successor as director general have been trying to do as many offbeat things as they possibly can so as not to be in direct competition with the others. They are not allowed to have any studios or production staff of their own. Everything they do must come from independent producers.

Naturally, they are getting much more diverse material. By trying to be different and coming from no enormous bureaucracy, except that ITV makes the final selection, the channel looks somewhat different. At present it is earning about 8 per cent of the audience.

MJM: It is not really the place, specifically, where innovative or experimental forms of television are produced, but it is a channel where such material regularly appears.

The CBC has been expected to make television in a context without precedent (until recently) elsewhere in the world. Since 1952 the CBC has been underfunded in the project of purchasing stations wholly owned by the corporation, underfunded after 1964 for operating costs to make programs, and has endured endless governmental reviews whose recommendations were usually ignored. Since its inception, it has been unable to do certain kinds of long-range planning because the available money was part of an annual budget and subject to political expediency. The 1991 parliamentary task force recommended a three-year cycle of government funding as a sop to a CBC forbidden by the CRTC to solicit ads in local markets it can no longer afford to serve. Since this recommendation was not adapted, the downward spiral of too little money to fulfil its renewed (1991) mandate continues.[10] As one CBC insider put it, "The Corporation is underfunded and overmandated." I will deal with the most recent parliamentary committee and the latest governmental policy, apparently a rehash of the old, in chapter 12.

In the 1980s and 1990s the CBC is expected to increase its expensive Canadian content and, at the same time, attract more commercial revenue from a small market during a severe and prolonged recession. It is also expected (to paraphrase its mandate in both the 1968 and the 1991 Broadcasting Acts) to reflect our regional identities, serve as patron to the arts, and inform the population about the important issues of the time.

But there are crucial differences between the 1968 mandate and the 1991 rewriting of the CBC's objectives. What the 1968 bill gave the National Broadcasting Service, including the CBC, as a mandate was a directive to "contribute to the development of national unity and provide for an expansion of Canadian identity" (section 2g iv).[11] What the February 1991 Bill C-40 substituted was the phrase reflecting the uncertainties generated by the Meech Lake and Charlottetown efforts to reach a consensus on what Canada is as a nation state: "contribute to shared national consciousness and identity." However, C-40 did add that the system was to "reflect the multicultural and multiracial nature of Canada" and to address the concerns of women, Aboriginals, the disabled and children.[12] In other words, the new mandate added more specific responsibilities to the CBC mandate, while the organization got less and less money. That pattern has continued in 1995.

THE CONTEXT OF DRAMA POLICY, 1952–64

Even without such clear and formal statements of purpose as the 1968 mandate, the CBC was already self-defined by the processes that governed the making of ideology, the telling of stories, and the reflection of its audience during the period 1952 to the mid-1960s. The Drama Department at that time was a closely knit group of producers, designers, camera, lighting and sound men, script assistants, and story editors who looked at each other's programs, and who criticized and encouraged one another in an atmosphere of considerable competition and remarkable support.

MARIO PRIZEK, producer/director [1983]: Robert Allen got the flak at the weekly meetings. When he was head of the Drama Department, almost every week we had a meeting at which we all discussed what we were working on, how it was going, telling one another and telling him. And at the beginning and the end of seasons we'd discuss things that we wanted to do individually and why we wanted to do them. We sold them to the whole department, as well as to Bob. He was very democratic that way. After that time the whole process became much more secretive.

There seems to have been general consensus along these lines during that period: Canadian television drama should entertain, inform, reflect national and regional concerns (intermittently and with significant gaps), experiment with television as a medium, show Canadians what classical and contemporary world theatre looks like, explore the relationship of the documentary and the fictional, inflect some forms of American popular culture (cop shows, mysteries, sitcoms, supernatural anthology, whatever) and ignore others, and continue with the "single" play – whether a light comedy, a theatre adaptation, a docudrama, or an intensely personal vision.

During the first ten years of CBC television, there was no obvious need to take stock of what was happening and where TV drama was going. In the mid to late 1960s, however, with the advent of film, changes in management, the internal evolution of the decision-making process, the steady loss of experienced talent in every area, and repeated studies by the governments of the day, the time had come for management and the creative people to talk, think, and make some decisions. By 1968–69 the need was critical. Yet, from 1969 to 1973, as far as long-range planning and decision-making were concerned, the Drama Department was simply treading deep water while the people in the life-boat seemed to be rowing in circles.

In October 1964 Mavor Moore wrote to Prime Minister Pearson on the 1968 mandate, after Pearson had consulted him repeatedly on the new Broadcasting Act: "Until and unless [someone] with programming ideas and the experience to implement them is appointed to head the CBC it will continue to be a sick body – if for no other reason than that the most experienced of administrators, lacking ... ideas and know how, is at the mercy of those who have them."[13] George Davidson, a good, grey president, to paraphrase Knowlton Nash, was the result.[14]

DRAMA POLICY, 1968–73

HUGH GAUNTLETT [1985]: There was a major reorganization in 1968 or 1969 during which the English Services Division was created, everything was decentralized from Ottawa, and the regions were brought together under Toronto. Eugene Hallman was the vice-president, and the first thing he did was to split the whole thing up the middle and create entertainment programs and information programs with Knowlton Nash, director of information programs. The whole Public Affairs Department was split up into News, Current Affairs, Arts, Sciences and Religion, and Children's programs. So, the information/entertainment division was set up. The first director of entertainment programs was Doug Nixon, who had been the centre of everything. What he did was to take the department heads and put somebody over them. In drama, Bob Allen had been reigning over drama for a dozen years, even longer if you go back to his work with Sidney Newman, and he had it all after Newman left. He was regarded as being overly engaged in *Festival* and the top end of the scale, and not sufficiently creative at the popular end of the scale. Laurel Crosby, one of the founders of the Canadian Players at Stratford, joined us and worked her way up. Nixon gave her a whole new title and put her over Bob Allen. She had not been there six months to a year before Nixon left, to be replaced by Thom Benson. Benson looked around and said, "Laurel is fine, she is a terrific administrator and a tough lady, but we need some creativity in here, and I want my old friend Fletcher Markle." So he made Markle head of drama. There was this coming and going of people at the top. Drama was a crucial area in which each head tried to get his person to produce the result he wanted. Then, if you go forward to the mid-1970s, Don MacPherson was the vice-president, and the bee in his bonnet was to reduce the number of departments, thus reducing the administrative overhead. He also wanted to stop this 50–50 split, because it meant there was nobody running the network. So information programs were reduced to Current Affairs and Arts and Sciences was taken away. John Barnes, who had been head of music, now headed Arts, Music, and Science. At the same time, the department called "Features" was abolished, and what was left of it was dumped in other areas.

I think that much of that reorganization, the creation of the divisions, and the transition in terms of personalities, structure, and purpose that then ensued was bad for drama. The whole period between that reorganization and the arrival of Hirsch in 1974 was a period of disintegration. As the reorganization worked itself out in personal terms, a number of senior people came and went.

Knowlton Nash quotes Denis Harvey, who worked for Don MacPherson, as criticizing his "irresolute management style. 'I had to do every tough thing,' he recalls; 'I got fed up,'" and so eventually Harvey quit – to return later on.

Fletcher Markle was appointed head of TV drama in April 1970, a few months after Laurel Crosby had been appointed "planning and production director of drama." Within three years Crosby was out, Markle was not running drama and preparing to leave, Ron Weyman and Robert Allen were working as executive producers of specific projects, and the hunt was on for a new head of drama. Of the "second wave" producers from the late 1950s and 1960s, Daryl Duke, Paul Almond, George McGowan, and David Gardner were all gone.

No clear policy came out of all this activity until 1973, when three very senior executives, including the vice-president of English television, Peter Hernndorf, prepared a report on the problems of the Drama Department as part of an exhaustive search for a new head of drama. It was tabled in the context of a severe crisis in the morale of the surviving members of the department and the production people, a crisis that by then was quite visible on the nation's television sets. Another 1973 report by Vincent Tovell provided insights into the whole program mix.

What is striking is how many reasons for the malaise in both reports had already been identified by Robert Allen ten years before in a report dated 9 July 1963. This memorandum was addressed to Doug Nixon, director of programming, English Network. Copies went to Michael Sadlier, program director TV Network; Hugh Gauntlett, his assistant; and John Barnes, production manager TV. It was sent for information to executive producers in drama Ed Moser, Daryl Duke, and Ron Weyman; to Hugh Kemp as script supervisor; to radio and television producer Esse Ljungh; to radio's supervisor of *Anthology* Robert Weaver, and to J.W.R. Graham, director of TV operations.

In this memo Robert Allen emphasized that his ten suggestions represented a consensus in the Drama Department. His main points are interwoven with my comments. *Involve the producer/director sooner and more deeply in the search for development of writers and plays.* As we have seen, the producers did eventually assume more control of both. *Give the producer more time to work on scripts.* In drama specials this happened. In series television, then unknown in Canada but now the norm, there is never enough time. *Find and use more producers; new ones should be trained, and experienced producers brought in from the United Kingdom and the United States. Find more script editors for* Quest, Playdate, *and* The Serial. Both points suggest a department with human resources stretched to the limit – in 1963! *Increase the liaison between the producing departments and the National Script Department. Try plays entirely on film. Increase VTR facilities, mobile VTR for location shooting, and more VTR time, so that one can rehearse and record when ready rather than using the live-to-tape technique.* The tug of war between electronic (tape) drama and film was rooted in the fact that the corporation did not have adequate resources to support both. It continued into the mid-1980s. *Put more writers under annual contract, so that the CBC has a stable of full-time professional writers.* Although certain writers became associated with specific series, the development of television writers is still to some degree a haphazard affair at the CBC. Interviews with Nada Harcourt and Ivan Fecan indicate some improvement since the mid-1980s, but gifted writers like Grahame Woods, Bill Gough, Anna Sandor, and Jeannine Locke have left.

Finally, Allen's goal was an *image for each drama series, an image based not only on what we would like a drama series to be but also on the actual capabilities of a group of full-time, professional, properly paid writers.* These sensible suggestions were largely ignored between 1963 and 1973.

Some changes did occur, reflecting not so much policy decisions as the result of individual initiatives. In the early 1960s Ron Weyman succeeded in getting *The Serial* partly on film and *Cariboo Country* completely on film (after 1962) for its six to eight episodes a year. *Wojeck*, a filmed series, followed in 1966. Meanwhile, the producers were stretching the live-to-tape rules of sequential videotaping by forcing more and more editing until technology and evolving studio technique gave videotape some of the advantages of film. *Quentin Durgens, MP* (1969) began that process in series television. But the most fundamental problems of all, that is finding good scripts and developing good producers and directors, intensified as directors and writers migrated into film or emigrated.

A glance at the plans for the fall and winter schedule for 1971–72 show the situation towards the end of this period for the fall: Sunday at 9:00 PM, the prestige slot: four anthology drama films and eight *Quentin Durgens, MP* (repeats; Thursday at 9:00–9:30 PM: seven half-hour episodes of taped drama gathered under the title *Theatre Canada* (adaptations of Canadian short stories) – a total of one-and-a-half hours of drama a week, some of it repeats. On Saturday at 8–9 PM, on the rare occasions when no hockey games were scheduled, there were repeats of old dramas. Thus, the total per week was a maximum of two-and-a-half hours of Canadian drama.

The winter schedule began in January. It listed *Paul Bernard: Psychiatrist*, a half-hour co-production with Michael Spivak called, rather unfairly in the memorandum, "a soap opera," time TBA; Sunday at 9:00 PM: ten film dramas: *The Manipulators* (new episodes) and ten *Overlanders*. Both series came from Vancouver, but *The Overlanders* did not find favour, so only a pilot was made and shown. On Wednesday at 8:30–10:00 PM there were two electronic productions of "classic American drama," and on Thursday at 9:00–9:30 PM *Theatre Canada* continued as an anthology renamed *To See Ourselves*, with thirteen short stories adapted for film. The Thursday slot would be followed by twenty-two taped programs of a more experimental anthology called "Project" (renamed *Program X*). These programs also added up to two-and-a-half hours a week of Canadian drama.

Thin as it looks, there were more drama hours in the 1971–72 season than in the 1984–85 season, and there was an attempt to revive the experimental slot. *To See Ourselves* was a competent, sometimes very good anthology of adaptations of Canadian short stories.[15] For purposes of comparison, in January 1995 the CBC offered from 7–10 PM three hours of adult or family drama, a half-hour of specifically children's drama, three half hours of sketch comedy, plus irregularly scheduled movies and mini-series – much of it made by independents and in the regions.

The regions were restless and Toronto was, for the most part, in a holding pattern in the early 1970s. In 1971 Philip Keatley was asking management whether Vancouver was a specialty house in film, a "change of pace" production group, or a development centre for new projects. I found no record of a reply in the National Archives files on the CBC.

Ten years after Robert Allen's report, Thom Benson, the director of programming Entertainment, English,[16] complained that the cost of hardware (stations, transmitters) robbed the budgets of programming.

We have a package of four or five feature films that we plan to show within the next year. A lot of our little half-hour dramas *To See Ourselves* are very good ... some of them are not so good. Writing in this country is a terrible problem. We just have not got good writers ... We are always under extreme pressure to extend our coverage ... well an awful lot of our budget goes to expansion of our facilities. We are required to build a station ... instead of just a transmitter – studios ... in Calgary, in Yorkton ... you know, serve the north. This is costing a hell of a lot of dough and it cuts down what is available for programming. Now programming people, myself included, are constantly battling ... What goes to programs, I will say categorically, is too small a percentage of our overall budget."[17]

In the same period, Vincent Tovell took a longer view of the whole spectrum of broadcasting and pointed to similar questions in his internal report headed *Further Notes on CBC TV Network program Mix* (January 1973).

Jacob Bronowski [*The Ascent of Man*, BBC] reminded us that it is the function of TV to make "coherent" 20th Century culture. This means, presumably, the adequate combining of reportage with helpful reflections on it – that is, seeing important events and issues and seeing them in perspective.
    CBC Network programs can be divided into the 6 following categories:
1. Public events (political and social occasions, sports, space shots).
2. Newscasts.
3. Current issues (immediate interpretations of topical questions).
4. Amusements (comedies, dramas, variety, music, panels, movies, etc.).
5. Documents (issues put in perspective).
6. Instructions (*Galloping Gourmet* to *Sesame Street*).
    The first three categories have interesting characteristics in common:
A. They are "immediate" programs, and to many people "pure television." They attract audiences because they take you to the action, often as it is happening.
B. They are, in the main, electronic productions requiring an "instamatic" technology.
C. They tend, for a variety of reasons, to preempt other programs. The prestige of one network, as compared with another, is often measured by the speed and fullness [comprehensiveness] of such programming.
    The second trio of categories also have interesting characteristics in common – and are significantly different from the first three:
A. They can be described as "perspective" programs and they attract audiences for a variety of reasons, among them the expectations of recreation, reflection and refreshment.

B. They are, in the main, film programs (or combined tape and film), pre-recorded, and they can be used repeatedly.

C. They tend to yield place in the schedule to more immediate programs and, if scheduled as a series, they are frequently interrupted by programs of a higher priority.

Is the proportion of "immediate" programming in the CBC schedule increasing – bearing in mind our expanded facilities for covering events and a growing enthusiasm for spectator sports within our scheduling offices? Are more CBC time and resources going into the immediate?

This clear national overview is still relevant twenty years later. Within ten years, programs like *The National* and *The Journal* had pre-empted one-third of weeknight prime time at the expense of time and resources that were or might be spent on "perspective" programs, although *The Journal* provided excellent short documentaries providing a background and perspective to the immediacy of the news.[18] To return to Tovell:

What proportion of our national network air-time is now allocated to each of the six categories listed above – in prime-time? Can appropriate proportions for these categories be established? If so, what would be the implications for:

a. program planning (staff recruitment, budget allocations).

b. Regional development.

c. Program unit structure.

d. Consolidation.

e. Further uses?[19]

That very succinct set of questions is still relevant to the 1990s.

Tovell's overview was amplified as far as drama was concerned on 29 June 1973 when a "Report of the Drama Search Committee" by Thom Benson, R.W. McGall, and Peter Hernndorf was sent to Eugene Hallman, vice-president of English television. The report was the result of interviews with "over 100 people across the country [including] writers, performers, directors and producers, newspaper critics, academics, theatrical entrepreneurs, artistic directors of both regional and underground theatres, senior officials associated with public funding organizations, Canadian expatriates working in Britain and the United States, television network executives in the U.S. and key figures in television drama."

John Hirsch, the head of drama appointed to implement these recommendations, characterized the confidential report this way: "This is not a battle of David [presumably himself] and Goliath [senior administrators] because Goliath came out with a very well-written report on CBC Drama. The people who wrote that report are not idiots. I'm simply filling positions created by that report."[20]

What was absent from the screen most of the time in the years 1968–73 was also spelled out in the Drama Search Committee's report. Overall, the committee reported that the Drama Department was not a cohesive unit. It lacked professional pride. There was no long-range vision; no attempt to develop consistently good, young writing talent; and no consistent feedback from producer to producer, from unit to producer or director, or from management to unit or producer.

The corporation had compounded the problem at the management levels by its lack of consistency in drama scheduling and by its refusal to allocate funds for development or to improve facilities. Both management and the national Drama Department were out of touch with the regions and the vibrant new theatre emerging all over the country. What I saw on the screen at the time and what I analysed for the 1973–74 Committee on Television and what I have seen in retrospect – with a few honourable exceptions like the excellent *Twelve and a Half Cents, Vicky, God's Sparrows,* and *Reddick I and II*[21] – confirms the report's conclusion: that by the early 1970s the CBC was "middle brow, middle class, and middle aged in its approach to TV drama."

The cures proposed by the McGall/Benson/Herrndorf triumvirate are more open to debate. "Introspection and preoccupation with technique," which are not at all evident in the journeyman work of the period to this observer, are to be replaced with strong story lines and attractive identifiable characters. They also make the flat statement that "the television medium demands clarity." I doubt that the authors would be so categorical now, but I suspect that their stress on clarity, strong story line, and likable characters expressed a deeply felt frustration after the much publicized and often damned *Jalna* and its failure to tell a well-loved story in a straightforward and more successful way. Obviously, some television forms demand clarity. Others are valuable because they mystify, because they raise, without satisfying, curiosity, or because they challenge the viewers' expectations about genre, story line, stereotypical characters, and what's "right" and what's "wrong" within recognized societal norms. The report also makes a strong case for more material that is accessible and Canadian. Once again the connection is made between the development of talent and television drama. There are clear echoes of Allen's 1963 report.

The recommendations met with mixed success. Producers' responsibilities were formally split off from directors' responsibilities at that time – so the *de facto* situation became *de jure*. The CBC did have a brief fling at training writers and directors, although no formal apprenticeships were organized. No formal national liaison with universities and schools was set up then or later, as the report had suggested. However, a drama script department was developed as well as a centralized casting office. The suggestion that the department try to repatriate successful actors such as John Colicos, William Shatner, Christopher Plummer, Toby Robins, and Donald Sutherland, as well as directors like Arthur Hill, Daryl Duke, Ted Kotcheff, and Paul Almond was implemented at intervals. These stars have returned occasionally for drama specials or mini-series, as have some of the directors, but there has never been enough work to keep them here.

Herrndorf, McGall, and Benson were blunt in 1973 about the need to pick a head of drama and then trust his judgment to choose a creative staff and make good programs. They were critical of the inappropriate delegation of decisions on matters of detail up the line and of the managerial interference back down the line. This basic managerial principle – to trust the creative staff to get on with it – was often ignored by Hirsch, was honoured by Kennedy, and became a source of division and recrimination among some of the talented people who were critical of the "new look" era of drama production under Ivan Fecan. Others found the new era revitalizing. The programming tells the story, as always.

This 1973 report stressed the fact that the Drama Department needs to and must be able to take risks to spend development money on programs and series. It also stressed the need to absorb substantial writeoff costs when something doesn't work, because the opportunity to take risks is necessary for good television and that means there must be some margin for error – a luxury unavailable in 1973 and a goal further out of reach in the 1990s.

The report's most fundamental recommendation finally became a guiding principle in the late 1980s and early 1990s. It pointed out that to achieve more quality drama, the number of drama programs must increase, and it foresaw a drama schedule made up of thirty-nine one-hour dramas in an anthology of classics: Canadian plays that are "indigenous, contemporary, honest, often provocative in theme and content ... strong on story, characterization and dialogue and light on production virtuosity"; two major "high impact commercial drama series"; and a family adventure series. The Collaborators and its successor Side Street (one per season, not two) and The Beachcombers were the result of this last suggestion. The anthology of dramas became a few dramas a year for a few years. The anthology of Canadian plays appeared and disappeared in varying formats over the next two decades. "Two high impact commerical drama series" running at the same time finally occurred in the late 1980s with *Road to Avonlea* (what Fecan called in the 1993 interview a "home run" – a program that was watched by more adults than children and was sold all over the world) and the even longer-running *Street Legal*, and then, overlapping them both, the first two seasons of *North of 60*. Two of the three are co-productions with Telefilm and others.

The report also recognized the need for a development slot for a relatively select audience, suggesting that an anthology be produced across the country in a late prime-time slot with varying goals. *Judge*, *Inside Stories*, *The Way We Were*, and *Family Pictures* fulfilled some of those goals in the 1980s, including the developmental role of a half-hour anthology, but as family entertainment the last three were rarely experimental in form or challenging in content. *Codco* was the closest to this ideal. The blueprint also embraced drama specials which were flexible in form and length and which would include classics, theatre adaptations, and co-productions. From the perspective of the pinched 1980s and the troubled 1990s, this goal sounds wonderful and completely out of reach in the drive for the expensive production values of what Canadians, conditioned by American "slick" production values, have come to expect.

POLICY IN THE HIRSCH ERA

John Hirsch, a theatre director of international reputation, co-founder of the Manitoba Theatre Centre, and co-artistic director at Stratford in the late 1960s, was selected to oversee the "renaissance" of CBC television drama envisioned in this report. He had no direct experience as a television executive.

When in the 1980s he became artistic director of the Stratford Festival for the second time, I tried twice to meet him for an interview, but he found it impossible to keep the appointments. Thereafter, before his death in 1989, his peripatetic life made it difficult to arrange an interview. To provide his own perspective on what he was attempting to do (and noting that these remarks were made for publication in newspapers rather than in sustained private conversation), I have used the extensive clippings available in the Metro Toronto Library and the CBC reference library. Other internal documents are to be found in the National Archives CBC files.

From a *Toronto Star* clipping headlined *"CBC's White-Hot Hope"* by Ron Base:

And what about Hirsch? Would it be better for him to fail than to succeed? He allows himself a hint of a smile. "I think there is as much danger in succeeding as there is in failing. But I swam in the New York waters, if I survived those sharks I can survive this. Again, I am not here for life. I've given myself four years. If nothing else, I can create organized chaos."

The rhetoric in this interview is quickly replaced by reality:

This must be the poorest production centre in the world. There isn't enough money to do *Uncle Tom's Cabin*. Yet everyone pretends the CBC can do *The Second Coming* and *Ben Hur* in one evening. Let me tell you there isn't enough money for the chariot. People who think we can do what others do should have their heads examined ... They don't understand the relationship between money and production, they are ignorant. People have to be educated as to what things cost. Sure, the BBC can produce *The Forsyte Saga* but does anyone ever ask what it costs? I just came back from a meeting with the *Hallmark Hall of Fame* people. The budget for those shows starts at $600,000. We have $40,000 real money and $80,000 funny money [primarily in-house costs] to do the same thing" ... I haven't even got a television set yet.

This latter remark is telling. It is not likely that Hirsch, a theatre director, had ever watched much television – and the VCR had yet to be invented. Hirsch's program plan for the 1975–76 season emphasized his double purpose: to reintroduce high-quality drama programs as alternatives to what was imported and to establish a training program. He noted that it was unhealthy to avoid conflict and stated flatly, "National awareness comes from self-awareness ... It will be necessary to develop 18 dramas to ensure 13 worthy of broadcast. Five may have to be thrown away," a luxury he was shocked to find did not exist. He was also searching for "freshness of vision and individual voices" to fill some late-night or Sunday afternoon slots.

He told his staff that he wanted to "continue the work of 'Festival' ... the only true repertory theatre of this country ... plays from the classical repertory of all nations ... but accessible not esoteric; comedies as well as popular dramas." He also talked of looking for fully mature actors of stature. Of course, he had dozens of such actors, experienced in both electronic and film drama available to him both in the regions and within a few blocks of 790 Bay, but he seemed unaware of that fact.

He envisioned ten sixty-minute films for an anthology that would be "journalistic" and relevant, some commissioned from "the Atwoods of the country," which would also involve young film-makers. From this we can detect early support for what became R.L. Thomas's concept of a topical "journalistic" anthology eventually called *For the*

Record. Thomas and his successors asked directors like Allan King, Don Shebib, Gilles Carle, Claude Jutra, and Robin Spry to direct the hour-long films.

Hirsch was also looking for twenty-six hours of sitcom and twenty-six hours of a family show. *King of Kensington* and *A Gift to Last* fitted into those generic slots in the mix he was developing, though the economies of an hour-long show made a twenty-six week season impossible at that time. He also proposed "immediately to set up one or two development units to create Canadian myths from material just sitting there. These shows should be unashamedly mythological, patriotic, arousing self-awareness of Canadians to our past of which we can be proud."

The result was intended to be five hour-long shows. *Ambush at Iroquois Point* (1979) was the only tangible result. In this plan, Hirsch encouraged the formation of production teams and, by implication, the use of outside people brought in on contract. He also emphasized the importance of the regions, seeing Vancouver as the second production centre and Winnipeg, after a training period, as a source of film anthology. He sharply criticized the situation in Montreal where the CBC facilities were unavailable both to experienced bilingual producers and to new Quebec playwrights.

Overall, his plan was to increase the hours of drama on the CBC from 77 in 1974–75 to 96 in 1975–76, 102 hours in 1976–77, 107 in 1977–78, and 126 in 1978–79 (echoing the 1973 TV Drama Report). Hirsch summarized his directive as "to go where the talent is and the stories are." He admitted that his plan would cost more than the drama study had envisaged, but he expressed no doubts that the money would be forthcoming.

Technological change, budget squeezes, and the advent of the *National/Journal* weekdays in the 10–11 PM slot in 1982 made those numbers of hours for drama a fading dream. John Kennedy pointed out to me in 1984 that his budget of hours available for drama in one year was seventy.[22] "The volume has not changed in ten years. Substantially it has been around 70 hours." It eventually rose to more than 120 hours with the advent of Telefilm, and has continued to rise in the early 1990s.

By the fall of 1974, Hirsch had instituted writer's workshops for professional writers, including some of the new generation of regional playwrights. He then went ahead to present adaptations of all kinds of contemporary Canadian scripts. He authorized adaptations of plays by Carol Bolt, Michael Cook, David French, Michel Tremblay, and Rick Salutin, introducing Canadians in smaller centres without regional theatres to a stimulating new generation of playwrights, directors, and actors. Not all the scripts were successfully adapted to television: *1837* did not work, for example, and *Red Emma* was unrecognizable, but *The Farm Show* and *Leaving Home* made the transition more successfully. Most of the scripts were condensed or even rewritten. Nevertheless, this was a major achievement, the best of which was a brilliant adaptation of Tremblay's *Les Belles Soeurs*.

Hirsch had tapped into the creative energy loose at the beginning of the alternative theatre movement in the late 1960s. He was also the last head of Television Drama to do classical and contemporary European theatre on television, and, caught in the hot winds of nationalism, he was roundly criticized for it in some quarters. Yet he also presided over efforts to get a workable sitcom going and instituted the CBC's "first" made-for-television movie, *The Man Inside*. It was proclaimed in the press release of 31 August 1976 as the "first movie" (typically ignoring David Gardner and Timothy Findley's *The Paper People* in 1967) "produced by the CBC in association with National Telefilm Associates of the U.S. who supplied over 40 percent of the direct co-production cost in return for international distribution rights" – a further extension of Hirsch's efforts "to compete internationally in major league commercial television through co-production cost sharing ... an action packed thriller." The film starred Americans James Franciscus and Stephanie Powers, but was written by a Canadian, Tony Sheer. I have never heard of the producer or director. The executive producer was John T. Ross, and the subject was basically undercover RCMP in pursuit of evil drug lords. The United States partner put up $75,000 of the $300,000 needed.

In essence, the possibility of a profound renewal of television drama was opened up in 1974. Unfortunately, within two years, the budget for drama, far from being expanded over a five-year period, was slashed by $700,000. Equally serious was the fact that Hirsch also lost ten hours in the yearly schedule. *Peepshow*, where new directors and writers learned their craft and tried new techniques, was one of the casualties.[23] After eighteen months on the firing line, echoing the complaints of Weir ten years before, Hirsch told Blaik Kirby that "promotion was recently cut to absolutely nil, with some of the most interesting drama coming up ... How do you expect ratings, if you don't go to the people and tell them what's on ... : This is the only show business organization I've ever worked in where they believe in cloistered virtue." Promotion did improve over the next decade, but until quite recently the CBC promotion has often been too little, too late. Kirby went on to say that Hirsch had no control over the context of American sitcoms and cop shows still bought by the CBC to fill its prime time. "There is a nagging fact that Hirsch gets no help from the CBC's drama imports. All of them – every single one – are popular American pap. He has no say at all in what is bought. So the best foreign shows, which could increase the supply of and appetite for good TV drama, are ignored."[24]

"Hirsch finishes the job as CBC Drama Chief but Dream went Astray" was the *Toronto Star* headline on an article written in 1978 by Jack Miller:

"Everywhere else in the television world, they think we're wonderful," says Hirsch. "*The Dreamspeaker* was the talk of the Prix Italia in Venice last year. The BBC bought it right there and most European TV networks will probably buy it. PBS bought *Sarah* and *Gift To Last* and it wants *Catspaw* and *Ladies in Retirement.*"

Hirsch seemed to be wrenching these boasts out, one by one, after long pauses, almost reluctantly: his years at the CBC were not all happy for him and they fell far short of making all his dreams come true.

He got neither the money nor the Network air time he had expected when he was talked into the job. Other departments' demands resulted in TV drama getting little more of the schedule than it had before. And repeated federal monetary squeezes meant there was no effective budget increase. "We were barely able to keep up with inflation."

"We have some of the best work we've ever done, this season," he said, "*A Gift to Last, Bethune* and *The Tar Sands* – all wonderful. And *Hedda Gabler.* And still to be shown are *Drying Up the Streets*, which has a superb perform-ance by Don Francks, and *Tyler*, which has been chosen to go to Cannes."

"So what, of all his work at the Network, made him proudest?"

The question brings a rare real smile from the long face: "I lasted. When I came here, people said I wouldn't stick it out more than six weeks. But I had a four-year contract and I lasted the whole four years."

"And nobody's mad at me."

In that he was quite wrong. Anecdotes about his destructive man-agerial practices are as plentiful as praise for his daring.

After his death, there were tributes to Hirsch for his work on tele-vision. In an interview with Henry Metkiewicz, Peter Herrndorf said:

He had a high-energy idiosyncratic style, but that is what gave him such tremendous passion and volcanic energy and made him a larger-than-life figure.

It's also what made his work for the CBC important. He created *For the Record* [I would modify that to "facilitated"] and he brought current affairs people into the sphere of drama. He also persuaded French-Canadian directors such as Claude Jutra and Gilles Carle to work their magic for English-speaking audiences.[25]

Al Waxman, the star of *King of Kensington*, said in the same article: "The amazing thing was that he used to come to the set, watch the tapings and actually root for us. He was a tough task master, as is anybody in this business who's any good, but he had a lot of heart and he took personal joy in seeing Canadian talent developed and celebrated."

Yet many of the CBC survivors from that time say that Hirsch's years were characterized by ruthlessness, capriciousness, favouritism, and sound and fury; that he interfered directly with shows, withdrew his support at a late stage from some of the best work, lowered morale in the regions, and created internal chaos whenever he touched down. At the same time, he continued to value and to give opportunities and creative freedom to experienced people like Eric Till, Paul Almond, and Allan King. He had the imagination to put feature film directors to work, and he tried to open up the narrowing range of mainstream North American television drama, which by then virtually excluded experiment, stylistic innovation, and non-formula television. His four-year stint as head of TV drama is still a matter of debate within the CBC itself.

My own view of the Hirsch era is that, like the work of his predecessors and his successors, the results of Hirsch's efforts were uneven. He did a lot of damage internally to what remained of the cohesiveness and continuity of the Drama Department in Toronto and the regions, but he also helped to reconnect the CBC to the country as it was in the 1970s. The 1987 drama report quotes extensively from both the Drama Search Committee Report of 1973 and the final report of John Hirsch in 1978, which in many ways served as commentary on the 1973 report. The 1987 subcommittee members obviously shared his vision and his frustration, whatever they may have remembered or forgotten about his managerial techniques. The last word belongs to someone who did not work under him.

FECAN: The last time somebody had a clear hands-on style in the more exact sense of that term was John Hirsch. He was both energizing and immensely destructive, I think, more in the manner in which he overrode or made decisions than because of his attention to detail.

The key issues of 1974–86 continued to be the number of hours allotted to drama and how they were scheduled, and the working environment for the creative people who had to produce the drama.

Eric Till spoke to director Allan King (*Warrendale, A Married Couple, Who Has Seen the Wind, Ready for Slaughter*), one of the interviewers for The Committee on Television who was examining the CBC's spectrum of broadcasting in preparation for the 1974 CRTC hearings. They discussed a number of aspects of the CBC's structure and policies.

ERIC TILL: The biggest impediment to higher-quality production and the effectiveness of producers is the quality and proliferation of middle management and the way it has of delaying and inhibiting decisions. There are profound problems of priorities, and middle management or senior management is oversensitive to political pressures to multiply the service at the expense of improving its quality.

KING: What are the problems for Thom Benson?

TILL: Immense. In the first place, anyone in that position cannot avoid the complex internal politicking from both above and below. Whatever one's opinion of his record of achievement, the job can't help but be like a single tin can on the fence before a hundred rifles.

There was one story I wanted to do where an individual in a lower echelon of government discovered the power of the rightwing – I mean the U.S. rightwing – in terms of its domination over the money in this country. And at that time I was told, "No, you can't do that kind of subject here. You mustn't touch that sort of subject. It's too political – mustn't touch it." ... Of course we must. We must let our writers write political plays. We can't let them write love stories with sad endings all the time ... the British do it enough. There are some people who write some ferociously political plays."[26]

Those three powerful subjects named in 1974 – the resurgence of right-wing politics and the collapse in Canada of the left, the economic and cultural relationship of Canada and the United States, and the power of globalized big business – are still missing from the CBC roster. Only a handful of exceptions have come close to the genuinely political contemporary drama of the BBC, programs like the six episodes of Alan Bleasdale's *Boys from the Blackstuff* or *A Very British Coup*, both shown in North America in the 1980s. *For the Record* came close in the 1970s with *Tar Sands*, a hard-hitting look at the oil patch which became the subject of a law suit and was never rebroadcast. *Oakmount High*, about an anti-Semitic teacher in an Alberta high school and the community who supported him, was not shown in Alberta until the court trial of James Keegstra was over. *They're Drying Up the Streets* was a fine two-hour docudrama special about drug abuse, and *Turning to Stone* was a searing two-hour drama about the Kingston Women's Prison. The politics of power was a subdued theme in *Love and Hate*, where the political stature of Colin Thatcher was sketched as a factor in Joann Thatcher's unsuccessful search for safety, and a more restricted but deeply felt subject in *The Boys of St Vincent*.

Topical drama does not necessarily mean political drama. We satirize but no longer regularly and seriously explore sensitive issues, notably the painful divisions between the ways Quebec sees Canada and the diverse ways Canada sees Quebec. Are there no sponsors available, no producers interested, no writers? Is the problem unstated CBC policy, evolving corporate ethos or survival instinct? I don't know. I report Ivan Fecan's answers to the questions I have just raised in chapter 11. Meanwhile, I simply draw attention to the gaps.

So did the Subcommittee on Drama in 1987. In suggesting that the CBC undertake a prime-time half-hour serial twice weekly, they argued that:

1. We need a stronger sense of daily life, the workplace, the streets in our drama. The realities we all see in our other lives outside the CBC appear on the screen too rarely. We're still too white, too remote, and concentrated too much in offices; we have a high ratio of period settings. When we treat controversial issues, we often do so in a socially earnest fashion. Too rarely do we recognize ourselves, our neighbours, our neighbourhoods on the screen. Too rarely do we recognize our own fears or our own concerns.
2. We can be topical and relevant to the minute, contemporary to people's lives. A serial, in quick turnaround production, is the next best thing to life. We can refer to the postal strike now, we can make a crack about billion-dollar submarines while it's on our front pages; we can weave in references to AIDS sooner than twelve months after *Time* has had it on the cover. We can exist in the same real time as people's lives. A serial can ride the national moods, reflect the music of the pop charts now (even if it's only a teenager listening in the background in a scene), and run counter to the "canned" feeling of most prime-time fiction.
3. The serial should have an edge, and be close to the edge

Scoop, the Radio-Canada serial that closely reflects life and politics in contemporary Quebec, enjoys huge ratings. That its one season dubbed into English on the CBC did not win a large audience simply argues that the rest of Canada still needs its own urban national serial – with an edge.

DRAMA POLICY AFTER THE 1987 DRAMA REPORT

In the decade after John Hirsch, John Kennedy oversaw many popular and critical successes at the CBC.[27] After Fecan's appointment, Kennedy headed west to look after that region. Kennedy's style was, within clear parameters, to let people get on with their jobs. After the role of head of drama was abolished, many of those decisions landed on Ivan Fecan's desk. I asked him about his own reputation for a hands-on approach to everything from casting to publicity.

FECAN: Every American network is run that way, every studio is run that way, and the British networks are run that way. I'm the director of programming, not the director of scheduling, and I'm held accountable for what goes on the air. That means that you have to make sure that you're taking the best possible shot. I believe in giving the producers and their teams money and confidence, and in developing a programming team that debates things out. But at the end of the day somebody has to make a call on whether you make something or not. When you don't have a lot of money to start with, you can't do that lightly. It's the only way I know of doing the job.

MJM: It seemed clear from everything Denis Harvey said that this was the reason you were wanted for the job.

FECAN: I made it very clear how I felt it should be done.

MJM: Then choosing Ivan Fecan as director of programming was a major policy decision.

FECAN: There's only one way to do the job, in my view. It's the way its done everywhere in the world, with a few exceptions. I'm sure there are always exceptions.

Here Fecan comes close to arguing for one controlling sensibility that would give a network a distinctive sensibility. In fact, Fecan articulated this two years before Gérard Veilleux's epiphany about recognition and repositioning.[28] Fecan's vision meshed with Veilleux's vision of repositioning the CBC to give it a distinctive footprint. When Veilleux fired Denis Harvey and split his job in two, Fecan became vice-president of entertainment et al. (August 1991) and Trina McQueen became vice-president of news and current affairs. When Veilleux "laterally arabesqued" her into vice-president of regions, Fecan became vice-president of English television. Trina McQueen left the CBC to help develop and become vice-president and general manager of Discovery, a specialty pay channel. Veilleux called Fecan "an agent of change."[29] As vice-president for English television, 1992–94, we see the result on our screens in 1994 and 1995. What we see is not, however, the result of any one person's vision, but of the corporate ethos – or lack of ethos (see chapter 10).

FECAN: The other implication is that the network is a place that has a vision – not necessarily a narrow vision. There's a personality, a through-line on which everything in that system is put out. In an environment where you're deluged by forty channels, many of them offering the same programs, its very important to be identifiable. Its very important to have a point of view. Your point of view may allow for many others to be expressed. But there still has to be minimal consistency, whether it's quality, attitude, or whatever. NBC [where Fecan worked for Brandon Tartikoff] allowed for many different people to express themselves.

MJM: But it had a flavour, a texture?

FECAN: It had a texture. If you were going through the dial, you knew the dial was on NBC. You just knew it! You would never see a "jiggles"³⁰ show on NBC, because that was not acceptable.

MJM: "Standards," again; that was your word.

FECAN: Not the American network executives in charge of standards and practices, because they're the censors. We don't have that here, and we don't want to have that here. The kind of excellence you want to strive for, the kind of quality we're capable of, we did consistently twenty years ago, we've done intermittently since, and now we have to start doing it consistently again, as much as we can.

Will BBS allow Fecan as a new vice-president to develop distinctive programs of quality? The answer will not be visible on our screens until 1996–97.

POLICY AS REFLECTED IN THE SCHEDULE
AND THE PERFORMANCE MIX

Once upon a time, in the old days (1952–67) when anthology was the norm on the CBC, programming and scheduling the mix was a relatively simple matter, at least in drama. Program scheduling is much more complicated now. Yet two programming constants determined schedules from 1952 to the mid-1990s. First, the schedules of American networks, and later Baton, and later still Global/CanWest and popular specialty channels were crucial, as the CBC tried to counterprogram to known hits or second guess what would flop. Moreover, for most of that period, the American-originated programming in the CBC schedule were "simulcast" – broadcast at the same time as the program was scheduled in the United States. Second, and more and more disruptively as the years went by, the hemi-demi-semi finals of the hockey season pre-empted much of the prime-time period of late March, April, May, and in 1995 until 14 June.

In Robert Allen's day, only the Stanley Cup series itself was likely to dominate the schedule. Contrast Allen's control of the schedule with what happens now!

ALLEN [1987]: Obviously, I would inform my superiors of what we were intending to do. And I think, often, I would supply them with scripts. Whether they read them or not, I don't know. Certainly I was having to decide not only what was going to be recorded (live to tape) by what director by what day, but also what was going to be transmitted in what order – with occasional changes (interference, if you like) when those on high decided that they were going to buy a special from the United States (or whatever) to put in that spot. But the sequence in which things happened was mine.

By the late 1980s the internal lineup of series episodes was determined by executive producers with their supervisors. The overall schedule, however, was worked out by Ivan Fecan, director of programming, consulting the creative heads of sitcom, series, miniseries, and movies and then approved by the vice-president of English television, Denis Harvey. I asked him whether he decided the details of the overall schedule.

HARVEY [1988]: It's my approval, finally. Traditionally it's always been the director of programming who puts the schedule together and brings it to me. A lot depends on the U.S. buy and what the U.S. networks do with their shows. We try to simulcast, if we can, because it gives us more revenue. If we can't, we don't. The final setting of our schedule depends on when we complete our U.S. buy and find out where the U.S. nets are running those programs. Ivan Fecan will go to Hollywood with Trina McQueen and the head of sales, and they will spend a couple of weeks there doing the buy. Ivan will be talking to me on the phone, every couple of days, during that time.

We are 40 per cent information programming in the CBC. *The National* and *The Journal* are anchored at ten o'clock every night and you cannot touch them. You don't have your full network at seven o'clock because the affiliates aren't there. You're narrowed down to about a two-hour bracket to try and fit in all your Canadian programs, plus the U.S.-originated programs. We wanted to get *Street Legal* away from the mid-1980s U.S. hit *Moonlighting*. The only way we could do it was to switch *Man Alive* and *Market Place* to Tuesday night in front of *the fifth estate*.

The information side was really angry, saying that it killed the shows. But I finally had to say no, that my decision had to be to protect *Street Legal*, because we had to get it in a better position.

I don't often have to get into it. But yes, it's my final decision, absolutely. It also comes down, sometimes, to sales revenue. Sales will say, if you put a program there we're going to lose $500,000 over the season, and I have to say, "Sorry, that's the way it's going to have to be." Or, if I don't think its going to make a difference, I'll go back to Ivan and say, "Does it really make a difference to you? We could lose a half a million dollars. Think about it." And he'll say, "Maybe I can." But if it comes down to it and he says, "No, I really want it there," then I have to make the decision of whether to sacrifice the $500,000. Again, as our advertising revenue becomes more important, that is one of the big decisions you have to weigh.

MJM: I noticed with this season's *Street Legal*, two things happened. One was that there was the lead-in episode immediately followed by the next episode in the same week. It got a running start.

HARVEY: You mean the Sunday/Wednesday bit?

MJM: The other thing that I noticed (I don't recall seeing it before, and it's so simple) was a message to the viewer saying, "We'll be back next season." That tells the viewer, "This series hasn't been cancelled. It's going away after ten or fifteen episodes but it will be back!"

HARVEY: I know. One of the terrible tragedies in the CBC, is that we can't make twenty-two episodes.

In 1991, 1992, and 1993, *Street Legal* ended with the classic American device perfected by *Dallas* a decade before – a cliff-hanger after much longer seasons than earlier series had enjoyed. However, it is worth noting that it was John Kennedy's rooted conviction that "the moment that [the makers'] attention span is diluted by too much volume ... exhaustion sets in, you begin to pay less attention to it ... I also contend that, nobody else in the world except our neighbours to the south do the kind of volume that the North American audience wants to see on television."[31]

I asked Ivan Fecan what factors determined his scheduling practices and how they interacted with his decisions on what programs to produce or to buy.

FECAN: It is different on different nights. On Monday night [1987–88] I consciously made the choice to go for women and for children and teens. We put *Danger Bay* [family/adventure] in at 7:30, left U.S. sitcom *Kate and Allie* where it is, moved *Degrassi Junior High* [family] to 8:30, and picked up a CBS block at 9:00. What we ended up doing was creating a real flow, because the viewers were not the same audience but were a compatible audience. It

has turned into our strongest night. *Danger Bay* last year was doing maybe 700,000. It is now doing 1,200,000; of that, 300,000
is due to its being on the full network, because the affiliates have
to carry it at that time; 200,000–300,000 is due to the night and
the adjacent positions. It flowed into *Kate and Allie*, which is a
simulcast with CBS. So that should gross up to about 1.82 million.

   Degrassi did about 300,000–400,000 on Sunday at 5:30. The idea
was to move it to 7:30, originally. Then I decided that if we were
going to put it in prime time, we should do a double or nothing. I
screened the episodes of the show, I believed in the show, and I
knew the episodes were of an improved quality. We don't call it
"drama," because it doesn't come out of the Drama Department; it
comes out of the Children's Department. We placed it at 8:30
because I decided the ideal audience for it was parents, children,
and teens. If I placed it at 8:30, it would be a "real show." If I
placed something at 5:30 or 4:30 or even at seven o'clock, then the
audience it is intended for, older children and teenagers, would
assume that it was intended for them and, therefore, they wouldn't
watch it. Also, we sold it as *Kate and Allie* and *Degrassi*.

I spoke to Nada Harcourt about program genres, and the interplay
of scheduling and content.

MJM to HARCOURT [1991]: I was interested in the scheduling of
   Mom PI because it's in the "family slot." You focus on a single
   mother and children, but the material has an adult edge to it. [My
   students compared *Mom PI* to *Simon and Simon* and *Scarecrow
   and Mrs. King* and one or two other American comedy/mystery/
   action shows that were an hour long.]
HARCOURT: When you think that children watch prime-time television and they watch *America's Most Wanted*, I'm very pleased that
   we can actually remind the audience that this woman's son and
   daughter are living in the 1990s where they absorb that kind of
   information.
MJM: And, as you say, it's not a series full of punchups and gun
   shots.
HARCOURT: Exactly. But it is also attempting to deal with the
   realities of the 1990s in a way that is slightly darker than simply
   avoiding the issues.
MJM to FECAN: The actors and the audience have both grown up
   with *Degrassi*. From the kids of *Degrassi Street* to the kids of *Degrassi Junior High*, you have really moved into more adult subject
   matter.[32]

FECAN: Our number one show in this country is *Disney*.[33] On the CBC, in terms of share, *Disney* often outperforms *Cosby*, although in hard numbers it doesn't because it airs at a different time, while *Cosby* is a simulcast. If you want to talk about honesty in numbers, first you look at the simulcast, because, on a non-simulcast basis, *Degrassi* outperforms *Kate and Allie. Danger Bay* almost outperforms *Kate and Allie*. It gives you an entirely different perspective on how we reach our audience. We all play the simulcast game and everybody makes a lot of money.[34]

 Disney is something the entire family can sit down and watch. It is also something we should be doing a lot more of for ourselves. But *Disney* provides an enormous lead-in for the children's cartoon series *Raccoons. Raccoons* leaves us with about half the audience. Still, 1.5 million is very substantial for a dramatic show.

 Look at *The Beachcombers* at 7:30. All the main competition is at seven o'clock. At 7:30, 300,000 kids change the channel following the *Raccoons* to another program rather than *The Beachcombers* – kids two to eleven. I have to ask myself why: we know they are up and probably at home. If *Beachcombers* or some other show could get a few hundred thousand more kids watching, so that it had 1.5 million viewers, then "Canadianization" would become so much more real. It would mean that our shows and performers were better than American shows. There is some science to scheduling. I call it science – a pseudo-science. There is a way of maximizing what you have and minimizing your risks. If by adding a couple of new kids to *Beachcombers* and trying to do a lot of things with the stories, we have a few hundred thousand more viewers, we are then in a position where we can talk about whether *Beachcombers* should go on for a lot more years – whether there is growth to it or whether we should really be looking at developing replacements for it. [*Beachcombers* was canceled in 1990, and *Road to Avonlea* fills the 7–8 Sunday slot.]

"Canadianization" here has shifted meaning from a description of what is broadcast to who is watching. Many broadcasters define "Canadian" as "made here and watched here" and stop. Fecan, Harvey, and their immediate predecessors had a more complex view. But as the managers and the "broadcasting environment" change, the concept also continues to shift ground: "As a country we are a lot more open" or "We can talk more honestly to our audience." Fecan and his creative head of drama series, Nada Harcourt, demonstrated that in the one-hour *Degrassi High* opener on Erica's abortion (1990). When PBS again ran the series, it clipped the last ten seconds from the show – the closeup of the tiny fetus "doll" thrust at Erica and her twin Heather by Right-to-Life picketers. Yet in a later episode that focuses on the aftermath of the abortion for both sisters, that doll haunts Heather's dreams. A moment of richness and complexity perfectly acceptable to a Canadian audience was not deemed acceptable by the American Public Broadcasting System.

As in this example, what is Canadian about the program mix should and does change as the society it should reflect changes. However, the mix is also shaped by the CBC's financial picture, which is immensely complex and has been since the 1970s.

HUGH GAUNTLETT [1985]: The CBC is dealing with a set of objectives, a set of priorities, some of a very specific kind; for example, there shall be a business program shown in prime time. It's dealing with a program pattern that is much more complicated and fractured than it used to be. Hardly anything runs for the whole season.

MJM: There are a few two-hour programs now.

GAUNTLETT: That's right. And, in addition to their program job, McQueen and Jack Craine [Fecan's predecessor as director of entertainment programming] are managing an onerous set of business constraints. It is not only the revenue, but the indirect inventory differential and the working capital level. We also have an annual commitment for expenditures to the American Federation of Musicians. We cannot redirect time and money out of entertainment into news and current affairs and easily keep up expenditures on musicians. So every once in a while we have to go to little orgies of music. The relationship between production and telecast in financial terms is exceedingly complex, with about four different ways of measuring any change. Then there is sports and its unpredictability [How many games will be in a Stanley Cup?].

Those constraints remain. But the thinking has shifted radically for drama in one respect: "series" television is now routinely defined as sixteen to twenty episodes.

HARCOURT [1991]: Other producers have something to prove creatively, as in the case of Maryke McEwen or Brenda Greenberg, her replacement as executive producer of Street Legal. David Barlow and Louis Del Grande did eight hours a year of Seeing Things, because they wanted a certain quality or excellence. I'm sure that John Kennedy asked them to do thirteen or enquired, "Could this concept be done in a half-hour?" and they said, "No, it's this, and this is what we want to do." My job is being very respectful of the creative aspect. But Ivan and I have a yearly schedule to fill, and the volume is astronomical.

John Kennedy firmly believed that quality could suffer under the American model:

Having found success, or something that is perceived to be a success, one is always under some pressure to deliver more and more and more of it. And the difficulty there is that a writer can only do so much before a certain automaticity sets in. You lose the integrity that you had which caused the series to be a success in the first place. I'm particularly thinking of the writers and the creative control over the piece. Now whether that is exercised by the writer or by some other member of the unit, is, to me, really neither here nor there. But rigorous attention to why we're doing this in the first place, and what it is about, has to be paid in order to get it done well. The moment that your attention span is diluted by too much volume, too many things to do in one day, exhaustion sets in; you begin to pay less and less attention to it."[35]

There is no doubt that series television, whether the last season of *Street Legal* or *LA Law*, presents stale writing, formula direction, and exhausted actors in episodes that do not meet the standards of the rest of the series. The much more limited runs of BBC imports are more likely to be of uniform quality.

HARCOURT: There's no question that Ivan and I would like to do limited series as the British do. Some subjects should be six half-hours or eight one-hours. But we don't have the luxury of doing as many. Advertising revenue is extremely important to us. The continuity and the likeability of characters that you want to follow for a long time is something that we must have. That is the base, the first tier. Can we do anything beyond the base? It is our hope and dream that we can. With additional funding we could, but we must respect the base. The base is the continuing character series.
MJM: Is there any depth to the front bench? Or is the financial constraint such that there is still nothing to fall back on when, inevitably, some series do not find an audience?
HARCOURT: Development is still cheaper than production. Not everyone can do a series. Certainly, given the amount of money that would be forthcoming from the CBC, Telefilm, and a partner, one has to have a great deal of confidence in the ability of the production team to execute. This is not something that we handle

lightly. The creative concerns are paramount, but financing concerns are paramount as well. There aren't a great many core companies playing in that market-place.

MJM: Atlantis, Alliance, Sunrise, and ...

HARCOURT: Primedia. The hope is that you can bolster a new group with an experienced group. That happened with *Mom PI* and with Atlantis. We hope that the next time out the new regional independents will have their own track record [and indeed that has happened, although CBC and Telefilm funding remain crucial for much of the distinctive material.] We have fewer producers working on staff in-house than we had in the past, so good ideas come proportionately more from the outside.

We will take our risks if a series is improving, if it is growing, if its potential is being explored, if things are being fixed in it. It's very difficult, because they're always on the run and we can't write off things. We can't throw things aside.

MJM: So there is a strong impetus to integrate those improvements.

SCHEDULES, PROGRAM MIX, AND THE AFFILIATES

Trina McQueen, then the director of network television, helped me sort out the problematic relationship between the CBC, which has never had the money to buy key stations in every region and thus to completely cover the country independently, and the privately owned affiliates who are free to stay within the CBC and accept their schedules – or with CRTC approval disaffiliate and find programming elsewhere.

McQUEEN [1988]: There is a category called reserve time, which affiliates must take, and a category called "available time," which they may or may not take. If they do take a program, they may play it at their own scheduling convenience. From seven and eight in the evening is also affiliate time. There are about twenty hours of time reserved for CBC-based programs in prime time, generally between the hours of eight and eleven each night. The only prime-time hours that are currently not reserved are 8–10 PM Thursday night. There are often drama presentations and arts presentations on Thursday night.

Some affiliates will take the Thursday night arts program and schedule it for a Sunday afternoon. The problem is that they are choosing an "off time," when audiences are traditionally small. In

1990–93 the CBC carried *Adrienne Clarkson Presents, Codco*, and *Kids in the Hall* in that Thursday night slot, which only the CBC-owned stations must carry. Affiliates can choose to sell Thursday prime time to advertisers who want American series. For example, one Thursday in March 1992 the CBC scheduled a ninety-minute comedy special called *The National Doubt*, starring Greg Malone and Tommy Sexton of *Codco*. It was, regrettably, a hit-and-miss satirical look at Canada's endless constitutional committees, intermingled with pleasant singers from across the country and framed as a [k]nightly quest, a parody of Bergman's early masterwork *The Seventh Seal*. That evening, one of the affiliates in southern Ontario (Barrie) chose to substitute an odd mix: *Cousteau's Rediscovery of the World* and *Run Away with the Rich and Famous.*

By 1994 the arrangements seemed to be more flexible – but not necessarily more favourable to the cash-strapped CBC. *TV Guide* for 12–18 November 1994, for example, shows that as always on Sunday, the CBC and its Barrie affiliate carry the same prime-time drama special at 8–10:00 PM (and not surprisingly *Road to Avonlea* at 7 PM). On Monday, both carry two American sitcoms between 8 and 9 PM, but then Barrie chooses *Market Place* and *The Royal Canadian Air Farce* while the CBC carries the hard-edged comedy *Kids in the Hall* and the daughter of *Codco, This Hour Has 22 Minutes*. On Tuesday both carry *the fifth estate*, but Barrie chooses a version of *Magnum PI* over the CBC's more challenging documentary series *Witness*. On Wednesday there is an hour of American sitcoms, followed in Barrie with a *Remington Steele* (mystery show) rerun and on the CBC with a TBA. In January that became a half-hour American sitcom followed on the CBC by *Liberty Street* and another American sitcom, while Barrie stayed with *Remington Steele*. On Thursday, Barrie reruns *Hawaii Five-O* against the CBC's *Nature of Things*, but both broadcast *North of 60*. On Friday both run the new music program *Rita and Friends* and the new drama series *Side Effects*. Saturday, during the hockey strike, is irrelevant to this sample. On Sunday afternoon, 1:30–3:00 PM, when the CBC offers regular arts programming, Barrie offers *Real Fishing* and *Whiz Kids*, but rejoins the network for CFL football or another sportscast.

MCQUEEN: Obviously their position is that they want to use those prime-time hours to make as much money as they can, so they tend to schedule American programming. The CBC-owned network stations, however, exceed Canadian content regulations. The fundamental debate that's going now between the affiliates and the CBC is over those hours. It is a very strong debate and it is not over [it is still not over in 1995]. We have had two solid years of trying to get the affiliates to sign a new contract with us, and the dispute has been over half an hour of extra reserve time, which they have been carrying very reluctantly. We will have another major dispute with them, which will mean some of them disaffiliating, or going to some sort of twin-stick arrangement. A "twin-stick" would be where the affiliate decides to own two television stations. The first station will be entirely CBC and will carry the entire output of CBC. The second station will be almost entirely a commercial station. So while he won't make much money on the CBC station, he'll be able to amortize some of his costs and he'll make a good deal of money on the commercial station. ·

MJM: And the CRTC will love him because he's also providing full CBC coverage in the area. So they'll allow him to get away with less Canadian content on the other.

For example, CKNX-Wingham, Ontario, runs identical prime-time schedules with CFPL-London. Both run almost exclusively American material in prime time. Both are twinned with a CBC repeater station that transmits Toronto's CBC-owned station CBLT to southwestern Ontario on three UHF channels. Because it is owned by the CBC, it carries the full complement of CBC Toronto programs, including regional and local newscasts. Viewers without cable can now watch the full network offerings – but may well look at the twin-stick stations of London or Wingham when Toronto-oriented news hours at 6 PM and 11 PM are broadcast.[36]

FECAN: We force affiliates to carry a certain number of shows as part of the reserve network. The other shows, I have to seduce them into carrying. This year the affiliates are carrying more of our dramas. When I say dramas I mean movies, serial drama, and comedies. I don't mean sketch comedy, but I do mean situation comedy. They are carrying more than they have ever carried before, because when they previewed the shows they felt that these shows are as good as whatever they could buy in the United States. So why should they spend their own money buying American shows when they can run the Canadian ones which are going to do as well?

The first empirical sense I had that things were working was that our audience went up. But the first visceral sense was when the affiliates gave us a standing ovation in 1989–90 and said that this was "the best schedule they ever had." They want to carry these shows. It's the toughest audience in the country, with vocal private broadcasters like Doug Bassett, who owns CFTO, the CTV station in Toronto, Dr Allard, and Allen Waters.

All of them also own rival stations for Global CanWest, CTV, or independent stations. What puzzles me is how the CBC can function when some of the key stations in their coverage are owned by voting members of rival boards at CTV, CanWest, or Global. Yet the CBC has to keep the affiliates happy to ensure a CBC presence in every region. The conflicts of interest multiply as the years go by. Moreover, the small independents like London and Wingham are being bought by the larger players. After nearly thirty years of internal civil war, CTV has been reorganized so that major shareholders can more easily set policy, in return for providing $20 million, a fresh infusion to make new programs. But since 1993, CTV stations like Kitchener's CKOC have been up against CTV stations like CFTO Toronto, which often schedules programs from Douglas Bassett's rival Ontario Network/ BBS. The "network" arrangements in Canada, both public and private, are in flux – just as they are the world over.

Fecan's comments about the way the CBC operated in the 1980s and early 90s make the contrast between commercial-free CBC Radio and CBC Television services obvious.

FECAN: The majority of the money that comes to English television networks is commercial money – is advertising money.[37] There is really very little Treasury Board money in the CBC. As long as that is so, your decisions have been made for you because there are options that you can't consider, whether you want to or not.

The double pressures from affiliates and the absolute need for sponsors have increased the emphasis on ratings, ratchet by ratchet, over the years. This means that the publicity needed to hook viewers for a given series or special is even more vital.

HARCOURT [1991]: We are also under the gun to produce revenue. So those prime-time spots are taken by commercials with their five-second clips and their fifteen-second clips. That revenue supports all the other programming, including information and drama programming. We have very little free time for promotion. We don't have large publicity budgets, yet publicity is tremendously important in letting the viewer know that a new series is on the air. It's very difficult.

"On-air" promotion is the most critical, followed by weekly supplements. They are what get you audiences. We used to be able to

do one half page in the weekly supplements to launch new programs twice in a season, but we can't afford to do that now. It's
difficult at all times of the year, because every season depends on
the new shows. All the Canadian press gets hype and brochures
from American shows. People are people, and if they have a pile
of colourful stuff, they write it up. Do they have the concurrent
package from the Canadian producer? No.

MJM to FECAN: Even if you get nothing but great sitcom scripts,
you can't do a whole season of sitcoms.

FECAN: If I had great sitcom scripts, I would put more sitcoms on
the air and probably change the people who are doing series
drama for us.

MJM: If you got a year when there were no scripts in a particular
area, wouldn't you still have to try for a little bit of variety in the
program mix? To put it another way, suppose you got no comedy
that you really thought was worth doing ...

FECAN: Then I probably wouldn't do any [as in 1993–94 and 1994–
95 when no new sitcoms appeared]. As part of Canadianization we
have been given money to do remedial development. We haven't
done development for years. We have many shows on the air that
are expected to die in full view of everyone, and it is not a pleasant
thought. But that is how we kill our shows here. We just let them
atrophy on the air.

MJM: Too often because there is not something in the wings?

FECAN: It is a scandal, because there is no need to do that. You can
take a show off and bring it back in specials; you can keep it alive
in a lot of ways; or you can simply take it off in a dignified manner. But you should not keep it on the air and have the people you
live with as characters die in front of your eyes out of neglect.[38]

MJM: Things like *M*A*S*H* pass into the mythology of popular
culture partly because they got out while the getting was good, and
they got out in a superb way.

FECAN: They got out like a class act.

Our system is called a "mixed system" of public and private broadcasters. The results are also very mixed indeed.

Sam Levene started out in current affairs in the 1960s, eventually
became executive producer of *For the Record* for several years, and
produced some fine Shakespearean adaptations, *Vanderberg*, and other
drama series. He has a long memory for the history of the CBC and
points out that the emphasis on ratings is not new. What may be new
is how that drive for ratings narrowed the choices of programs being
made during the late 1980s.

LEVENE [1988]: We always wanted big audiences. The emphasis on ratings has grown over the ten years I have been in drama, certainly since the big cutback of 1984. It has been an increasing obsession. I think Denis Harvey's view is that we can't survive otherwise – we *must* get bigger audiences, and therefore, we must do more mass-audience appeal shows. It has increased, and increased, and increased. The only way you can do issue-oriented drama now is if you make an issue part of a dramatic series like *Street Legal*, for example [in part because the topical anthology *For the Record*, which varied in audience numbers between 700,000 and 1.2 or 3 million, vanished in the late 1980s].

MJM: In its early years, *Street Legal* did tackle topics like the rights of the mentally challenged,[39] or the fear of Latin American oppression that can haunt recent immigrants, as in the episode "Tango Bellarosa."

LEVENE: Yes, but it has to be done in a dramatic series with a continuing character. For years, now, it has been believed that there is not a big enough audience for anthology drama. Anthology drama may be dead in Canada.

Too often I see four-hour mini-series that should be two hours long, and two-hour specials that should be ninety minutes, so I asked Ivan Fecan about the apparent death of the hour-and-a-half slot:

FECAN: I don't think that I would ever not do something that is ninety minutes just because it is ninety minutes. I have a preference for two hours because the other half hour is hard to find and to match. You can find a half-hour very easily. Open the door and twenty "half-hours" will run in. But they may not match in terms of flow. It doesn't mean you don't do it, but you want to be very sure that ninety minutes is the right length. When you think about it, a two-hour program with commercials is close to ninety minutes running time.

MJM: Yes, I know. I asked purely as a critic, because there are a lot of two-hour movies on our own networks and on others that should have been fifteen minutes shorter.

FECAN: That is a different matter, because you can fill the last ten minutes very easily. If you have a strong picture and you are seven or eight minutes light, you can easily order up, in a day or two, a seven or eight minute trailer about the next five pictures coming down. We started doing that this year, and we are doing that more and more. Obviously you want to go for the time slot that makes sense. I think a picture or two came in short this year or we asked for things to be shortened, and we ended up just ordering a trailer or two of the next three or four movies.[40]

CREATIVE CONTROL

Fecan says that the department that originates a show is irrelevant to when it is scheduled or how it is promoted, and that includes the CBC Children's or Arts and Sciences Departments or independent production companies like Playing for Time [the *Degrassi* series] or Sunrise [*Danger Bay* and *Max Glick*]. The relationship between the creative people and the network seems to be no more vexed for independents than it is for "in-house" programs. I asked him how that relationship worked when it came down to the thorny issue of "creative control."

FECAN [1989]: On a show that already exists, like *Degrassi*, you have the episodes, the story lines, the writers, plus whatever editorial assessment eventually gets put in there.

MJM: From whom?

FECAN: From the CBC development executive, who is the member of the programming team that tracks the show.

MJM: How does it work for producers like Anne Wheeler or Kevin Sullivan, people who make the two-hour movies and the miniseries?

FECAN: We make some "in-house" [very little by 1994], we make some independently, and some are even more complicated co-productions where we make them and somebody else puts up the money.

MJM: Are those the most difficult decisions to make?

FECAN: The decision is based on the script, more than on the industrial policy. We go for the best script. If it turns out in the year that most of the shows are done outside because that is where the scripts came from, then so be it.

   We make "two-and-a-half" kinds of movies now. We make family movies for 7–9 PM on Sunday. *Where the Spirit Lives* falls into that category. We make movies with a point of view and a hard edge for Sunday, 8–10 PM. An example of that is *Love and Hate*, a two-part mini-series which I think is the best work we have done "in-house" in years. Bernie Zuckerman produced it, and Francis Mankiewicz directed Kate Nelligan and Kenny Welsh. Great cast.

MJM: Yes, that's a powerful team. [The same team, which included writer Suzette Couture, made *Conspiracy of Silence*, broadcast 1–2 December 1991.[41]]

FECAN: Suzette Couture came up from her comedy act as a writer in sketch comedy. It's that "farm team" system. You don't expect Wayne Gretzky to score every goal, but even less would you expect someone who has never been on skates to score every time. You have to have the development, you have to have that process. If you don't have it, you're dooming yourself.

We also decided that we wanted to get into low-budget independent "theatricals" [films made for cinema, not television], not as financiers but as an "after market." I don't want to go through a thousand scripts and be part of the production financing of the hundred that get financed. If a movie gets financed, something smaller like *Vacant Lot* out of Halifax or *The Last Winter* out of Winnipeg or *First Season* out in Vancouver, I'll put up a smaller amount of money to have the rights to it after pay TV. But those films are essentially lower-budget theatricals. [Instead of scattering them through the schedule on an ad hoc basis, "repositioning" opened up the Thursday 10–12 PM "arts slot" in 1992–94 for Canadian cinema, which included, as well as well-known films like *Jesus of Montreal*, neglected films like *Crosscut* and *South of Wawa* – decidedly adult films for the "adult" slot. This slot disappeared in 1994–95 when the news was moved back to 10 PM.]

THE PRESTIGE SLOT AND HOW TO FILL IT

Since the 1950s Sunday 9–11 or 8–10 PM has been the night when the flagship dramas – the expensive specials, the mini-series, the controversial docudramas – have been launched. The 1987 drama report also recognized that tradition and the new economic realities.

"The Main Event" is the keystone night of Drama production, and it's seen to be a success. It is steadily increasing its audiences, and yields a rich mix of films, TV movies and mini-series. Mini-series are clearly a successful form, and are efficiently launched from this Sunday night slot. It is attractive to independents and to CBC producers. It has attracted writers and directors of distinction as well as introduced new, individual voices. It is an attractive vehicle for co-production with other broadcasters and the National Film Board. We should confirm this direction, and stay on course. This is working. This production stream holds the promise of assembling, over time, an impressive record of some of the best television fiction on North American television."[42]

MJM to FECAN: What about Sunday night eight o'clock to ten? This has always been the premier slot on the CBC.

FECAN: There I'll take a risk on a script that might not be commercial but might be artistically interesting. Louis Del Grande did a movie for us this year.

MJM: I've seen the script of *Sanity Clause*.

FECAN: Yes, a crazy script. I thought Louis could pull it off and he did. I hope to get it on this year if finances allow for it. So I'll take the occasional risk for something that isn't straight ahead commercial. [It was broadcast on April Fool's Day, 1990.]

Unlike virtually every other movie shown in that season except *The Greening of Ian Elliott*, it has not been rebroadcast. It was not a family show or a ratings booster like *Love and Hate* – just superbly quirky television. It was a hit with my third-year students.[43]

FECAN: An average movie of the week takes twenty-four days to shoot. Costs may run to $2 million. Probably the script gets kicked around for development longer than an episodic script – not a pilot script but an episodic script. You would think that, since there is more attention put into it strictly in terms of very cold business programming terms, a movie or a special ought to do better for audience numbers than the series in the time period. Otherwise, you'd be far wiser to do the series, because you have to sell each movie individually to the audience.

What has not happened is the drama report recommendation that "We should be presenting at least one Shaw and one Stratford per year and probably at least one or two regional productions."[44]

Economics, intuition, internal and external politics, the talent of the people pitching outlines and ideas, and their creative teams all mould the season we, as viewers, take or leave every year. Denis Harvey, who made the final decisions in the 1980s, provides an example of a hunch that paid off in ratings.

HARVEY: I pushed *Street Legal*. First I was excited about *Shell Game*, the two-hour pilot, and I gave the go-ahead for the series. I think we made eight the first year. I said, "Can't you make at least twelve or thirteen?" They just couldn't. I said, "If you get through the season with good ratings, I want to go full season next year." My director of programming said, "You're crazy; this is a shitty series." I push things at times, like that. But when I'm in Ottawa, I can't be a programmer. In fact, I got into programming too deeply before Ivan came and I found myself expressing opinions with not enough information – and that's dangerous. You've got to leave it to the creative people.

MJM: Has the vice-president of the English network always been in Toronto? You're the last person in the hierarchy who's on the deck where the programs are actually made.

HARVEY: It's bad enough with me meddling without someone in Ottawa meddling who's got no experience in the business.

"Prophetic words," as a badly written soap opera script might say, given what happened to repositioning, the radical strategy for CBC survival put forward by civil servant and then president Gérard Veilleux. But what drove Veilleux to resign was not the problems in programming or even in the personalities around him – it was the CBC budget. Trina McQueen did not leave the corporation soley because of conflict with Veilleux. Knowlton Nash quotes her as saying she was "bone-numbingly" weary at the prospect of more budget cuts.[45]

INTERNAL FINANCES: CBC TELEVISION DRAMA

CBC financing has never been completely straightforward in the sense of knowing the precise cost of script development and the immense resources needed to put the program on. With annual funding from Parliament, subject to whatever arctic winds are blowing in a given year, genuine long-term planning with its attendant economies has been a dream, not a reality.

CBC television finances have been a labyrinth with no minotaur as an excuse and no Theseus to the rescue. Ministers like Conservative Flora MacDonald and Liberal Michel Dupuy who hope to provide a clue, a way out, have no clout in cabinet or are in the post only briefly. Robert Allen remembers how it was, even in the "golden age" of television drama.

ALLEN [1981]: What I remember most clearly was that it was not possible to refuse to transmit a program that was made. Where were you going to enter it in the accounts, when it wasn't on the air?

We could develop a script and decide that it was not going to work and save a lot of money by not spending the money on producing it. Every year I would have a long session with somebody about monies that had to be written off. My answer was that the script was not good enough. Often I would think "this is not a good show" – we did our best, but something is not good enough. There was no "writing off," to use a technical term. The shows that were produced [prepared in advance and taped or put on kinescope] had to go on.

It is interesting to speculate to what extent that inhibited experiment. I remember being very conscious about not wanting to put into production something I was not confident would be worth seeing. I didn't want to experiment and fail, even though I accepted failure as part of the process of creation.

GAUNTLETT: One of the reasons why there was so much more drama in those days was because it was very simply manufactured. The escalation of cost is partly inflation, partly changing standards of production. But we also make more ambitious programs, as everybody does. Consider the CBC's escalation from the days of the large studio dramas to the period mini-series *Empire Inc.* In the case of *Empire Inc.*, we are well within sight of American costs on a one-on-one basis.

ALICE SINCLAIR, story editor [1988]: We had five productions cancelled.

MJM: After the $10 million budget cut in 1980?

SINCLAIR: Yes. I went away in August and came back to find out that four were gone.

GAUNTLETT: There are procedures to write off programs, but it is very rare for a completed program not to be telecast. That is not the result of any rule. There's moral pressure from the auditor general not to waste the public's money. You do not have to justify a program you telecast, even if it was a bomb. If you write off a program, you've got to have a good reason. Usually the reasons are that, in the middle of production, it was pre-empted by a news special in the studio, or the mobile unit broke down, or somebody died, so that they couldn't complete it – but not because it was not very good. Even pilot programs that are not successful are usually telecast in some obscure slot.

MJM: So there has never been a situation where somebody could do it and ...

GAUNTLETT: ... just throw it away, no. [HG in 1989 on rereading the transcripts: "But there is more of it now, with Fecan's emphasis on 'development.'" However, the episodes of the dreadful sitcom *Mosquito Lake*, which were still on the shelf after it was cancelled, were all eventually shown in the summer of 1992.]

MJM to SINCLAIR: Does anyone shelve a program already "in the can" for reasons of controversy or budget?

SINCLAIR: If you want to see a real dog, watch on Christmas Eve or New Year's Eve.[46] Those are the ones that we can't afford not to schedule, yet we don't really want anybody to see them. Unfortunately, even before this very tight situation, we could afford to write off scripts, but we could not afford not to air a production. Also, we have to be on the air so many hours a day, seven days a week, and you have to put something on.

MJM: In the 1970s and 1980s the accounting system was very odd.
SINCLAIR: We have another anomaly. In the fourth quarter we have shows that have been produced. All the writers have been paid, the performers have been paid, the musicians have been paid. Everybody's been paid, but we can't afford to put the show on because we don't actually put it down on paper until it goes on air. It boggles the mind. We haven't got the budget and we can't afford it. We guarantee ACTRA and the Musician's Union a quota of so many dollars. ACTRA we never have any problems with, but in the fourth quarter everyone is coming around saying: "Listen, you've got to have live musicians."

Sanity Clause was broadcast on the first day of a new budget year, April Fool's Day, 1990. The date may have been prophetic, since it was the last television drama to take major risks with the forms of television or be self-reflexive of the medium itself until Atom Egoyan's *Gross Misconduct* in 1993.

Canadianization in the fragmenting market of the 1980s was not an easy task, as John Kennedy knew. A sense of ongoing change and ever increasing constraint is apparent as early as this excerpt from his notes for an internal CBC review of priorities and objectives as they affected regional broadcasting and drama.

"When I took over this job, I thought that virtually anything was possible. All it took was money and some encouragement. Today, I read again that drama is a priority and that is an encouraging sign. I am still waiting for the money. While the CBC's planning process was a major factor in the way in which those ideas were approved and budgets allocated, that planning process was not the driving force behind what we did in the 1970s. That is not the case today. Today, Network planning runs me, at both the practical and philosophical levels."[47]

It cannot be said that the situation has changed in the last twelve years.

I would add a curious sidelight on the issues of finances and artistic standards. *Wojeck: Out of the Fire* went into production in February 1990, then stopped with thirty minutes of film shot due to "problems with the script." Antonia Zerbisias reported that a CBC spokesperson confirmed at the new season's launch on 27 May 1991 that the film would be broadcast in the spring 1991–92 season. Her version was that the half-hour of film already shot would be incorporated into whatever script was finally used.[48] It would seem to me that "waste not want not" was carried to extraordinary lengths in this instance.

However, some of the press coverage of *Wojeck: Out of the Fire*, on 15 March 1992, suggested that they had begun all over again. Other critics stressed the false start eighteen months before. In any case, the two-hour special incorporated both the strengths of the early series and the radically changed sensibilities of a 1990s audience. Indeed, those very changes over two decades, both the gains and the losses, were its theme. Whatever its troubled history, *Wojeck: Out of the Fire* demonstrates that what happens off camera is not always visible on the screen.

It has been very difficult to fathom how the corporation's finances work. Here, drafted by six people very much involved with getting programs on the air, is recorded their frustrations in the 1987 drama report:

A dollar is not a dollar, it is either a manpower dollar or an overhead dollar – and in the end there is a black market. Everyone soon learns that a good drama producer is part chartered accountant, part lawyer, and most of all, part alley cat, scrounging resources, begging Film departments to provide this or that, cajoling production. A certain amount of this skill is essential to being a good producer, but in Drama, the logistics are choking creative endeavour.

Ex-chair of the Board of Governors, experienced producer/broad-caster Patrick Watson, had this to say about CBC finances: "This is a Corporation where it's very difficult to wrench the numbers out. It's so intricate ... layered and with a reporting system that has been so unclear, confused and wallowing in cheating and lying – often for very good reasons because the managers felt the only way they could do what they had to do was to cheat and lie – that getting the numbers in was terrifically difficult."[49] He laid this problem directly at the door of the Juneau regime, during which "all of the TV decisions of consequence were taken at head office." In chapter 11, Fecan outlines a new "all cash" way of financing introduced to the corporation in 1992. But the CBC after sixty years still does not have stable financing.

FINANCIAL SYSTEMS AND MORALE

How the financial administration (and confusion of the 1970s and 1980s) directly affected the makers of programs is addressed by writer Anna Sandor and producer/writer Bill Gough.

SANDOR [1988]: It's really hard. So often we've had something and we've talked about who would be the ideal director. Obviously, when you've got Mr or Ms Ideal in your head, they are likely to be busy. So what have you got?

GOUGH: You've got someone who got the go-ahead only two months ahead of the shoot.

SANDOR: With *Two Men* we were so lucky to get Gordon Pinsent as the antagonist. It was just a total fluke.

GOUGH: And I managed to get the right crew together. John Vernon, the protagonist, also happened to be available.

MJM: There is not much lead time for designers or anyone else, is there?

GOUGH: Nothing. We had a brilliant designer, Arthur Harriot, so it was possible. But the show cost 30 per cent more than it should have because of the loss of lead time. Not only that, *Two Men* was turned down two years ago and it took me two years to get it going again from outside.

MJM: Is the problem that the budget is decided in Parliament from year to year? That the CBC never knows how much money it will have? Or is it people not making decisions?

GOUGH: That's where it occurs. I don't think it is a question of annual budget, because you know there is a base that you aren't going to drop under [not so in 1995]. So it's a question of who gets what to do in advance. But you cannot do it the way it is now done. As for ratings and what audiences may like, the only blanket statement you can make is that you can't make blanket statements. Who knows what is going to happen? Who knows what people are going to like? I don't know that. I know what I like doing and it seems to coincide, but that is no guarantee.

In other words, television drama is an art, not a product, and it cannot be produced under the controlled conditions widget-makers enjoy in their factories. As John Hirsch said in 1987 in "A Personal Report" on his four years as head of CBC television drama, (1974–78):

The separation of the Drama Department from the Service Departments as it existed prior to 1974 still continues to a great extent. There exists a lack of CREATIVE co-operation between the Plant and TV Drama. This will persist as long as the personnel in these departments continue to consider their departments as separate entities. It is necessary to establish a really creative unit which would obliterate the difference between the so-called creative people, and the technicians and designers.

[The committee preparing the 1987 report compared the units that work with those that struggle].

At the subcommittee's one plenary meeting, the theme of dedicated production units was a subject of immediate consensus. *Chasing Rainbows* and *Street Legal* operate as independent companies, as far as possible. They are off premises [which seems to be another pattern connected to artistic success, as with Weyman and *Wojeck,* Keatley and *Cariboo Country,* Roland and *Gift to Last*]. The producer is in charge of a fully integrated unit and crew, and the spirit of a team, as well as the efficiencies of a team which has worked together for some time, begin to come into play.

Setting up the team in the first place is a nightmare, and it occurs each and every time a producer is about to produce a show. Teamwork is helped by maintaining the integrity of the team and continuity of its members. That is difficult and frequently impossible at CBC. It is hard to be proud of your work when no one else is. Producers work hard to interject pride into the teams, but all that hard work is destroyed when the team returns to the "plant." A crack drama props person should always do drama – it is both a reward and a recognition of excellence. Do not also use this person as a moving man.

Similarly, a drama gaffer and his or her assistants should be experts. Do not also treat them as truck drivers. A dolly pusher is a specialized job, dedicated to camera. At CBC, that same person hauls cable, sets up and strikes sets, drives trucks, and off-loads equipment. A director of production works long and hard. He or she is a highly specialized creative person on a drama team. At CBC, to fill a gap, a D.O.P. might be doing "streeters" between dramas. CBC appears by its actions to have no respect for the jobs. How, then, does it expect the worker to have any pride for himself or herself.

[The logical solution follows.]

Keep a team together, dedicate it to drama production, give production responsibility and accountability, teach our people the new expectations now required of them, and efficiency will increase, morale will improve, and creativity will be freed to create rather than to waste its energy and will fighting conflicting systems. The basis for an approach to drama production is series. Series can build teams, generate product in quantity, amortize costs and maximize resources.[50]

The report's emphasis on the working conditions of series appeared to be received doctrine under Fecan, but the dedicated teams approach is more difficult to achieve (see chapter 11).

DOLLARS AND CANADIAN CONTENT

Despite the continuing financial squeeze, the numbers of scheduled hours of drama – and other Canadian content – continue to rise. In the 1960s Canadian content as a whole reached 52 per cent, in the early to mid-1970s, 74 per cent, in the 1980s, Juneau managed to get it up to 80 per cent.[51]

Executives can take two kinds of risk – qualitative and quantitative. Quantitatively, there is no question about the fact that CBC management in the 1980s took risks.

HARVEY: We are heading into a very good first year [1988–89]. The question is whether we can hold that up, whether the money will be there in the second and third years because the government is not promising it to us. We are headed into the biggest development year in the CBC's history and the best year we have had in five years.

MJM: At least you have been discussing a long-range plan for the development of more TV drama, despite the fact that the financing has always been ad hoc from the government.

HARVEY: Frankly, some of our bureaucrats from head office have said they don't think we should start it. I said, "I have got the money now. Let me, at least, get the first year and we'll worry about the second and third years a year from now." It may all collapse a year from now.

In response to this success, the Conservative government made further cuts in the CBC budget in the fall of 1989 and again in 1990. In 1991 they gave the CBC a one-time grant to cushion the costs of "downsizing" the corporation, but slashed the budget further in 1993. The Liberals had started the squeeze in the 1970s and early 1980s, and in 1995 continue the pattern. "Over-mandated and under-budgeted" is no longer a joke.

Writing several years later, I can assess the value of Harvey's three-year gamble. Looking at the "third year," 1990–91, and judging by the number of new programs,' *Max Glick, Mom PI,* and *Material World* (mark II) were three moderately successful dramatic comedies; *Urban Angel* presented six gritty hour-long episodes of a new series set in Montreal; *Street Legal* returned; *Degrassi High* finished on a roll; *Beachcombers* endured a much less propitious conclusion; a half-hour teen soap, *Northwood High,* started up; *Road to Avonlea* anchored the Sunday family hour; and *Family Pictures* (which disappeared thereafter) presented a half-hour drama anthology, independently produced in the regions. From the point of view of series development, the gamble paid off. Also from that point of view, the decision to go with the same shows in 1991–92 allowed the CBC to build audiences and did not drain the budget for further immediate start-up costs, which made good sense. Predictably, the decision to stay with what had been successfully developed provoked a new round of media criticism about "Americanization masquerading as Canadianization." "Canadian" in the writing of media critics is seldom defined, even in negative terms, and depends on which series is under discussion – sometimes on which episode. When *Urban Angel* was later replaced by twenty plus episodes of *Les Filles du Caleb* (a dubbed téléroman renamed *Emilie* that had attracted record audiences in Quebec), it made an interesting shift in the mix and helped to mask the effects of the 1991 budget cuts, which would otherwise have been more visible by 1992–93. By 1994–95 *Street Legal* had been replaced by *Side Effects*, and *Degrassi High* by the very different but successful adolescent fantasy *The Odyssey*; the eighteen to thirty crowd had *Liberty Street*, and the traditional CBC audience for drama, augmented by viewers among the First Nations and in the North, watched the third season of the hour-long *North of 60*. No anthologies and no sitcoms were scheduled, but there were three series of sketch comedy, *The Royal Canadian Air Farce*, *This Hour Has 22 Minutes*, and *Kids in the Hall*. There are no national or regional anthologies, and fewer mini-series and drama specials.

Much of this increased quantity in series TV has been made possible by Telefilm, which subsidizes independent television movies and series.[52]

HARVEY: I don't think you can underestimate what has happened in the last couple of years in the private sector. The private sector didn't exist four years ago. They have done some amazing things in four years. Ivan's argument is always that you can't learn except by doing. The only training ground is to team them up with people who are good and put them on shows, to work under the people who write the shows.

MJM: Is there now the luxury of not showing something that is disastrous?

HARVEY: No. *Not My Department* was the first time in CBC history that we ever cancelled a show.[53] What Ivan will do is spend a lot of money on the scripts. He won't take anything to pilot unless he is fairly confident.

MJM: Sometimes, though, the pilot doesn't work, but the series does, if it's allowed to settle in.

HARVEY: *King of Kensington*.

MJM: Yes, exactly, or *Shell Game* [the pilot for *Street Legal*]. *Shell Game* was mediocre as a mini-movie, but *Street Legal* has settled into being a good series.

HARVEY: If we get approval for the new headquarters [and they did], it means that we've got a future; without that, we haven't got a future. We won't have a network in ten years if we don't have a building. So that will be positive. The other positive thing we've been hearing for some months now is that they may be giving English and French television a special grant, not a lot of money, for drama programming. We're talking $10 million in English and $20 million in French.[54] What they should do is go back to Caplan-Sauvageau's early report.

MJM: Amen! And do it.

HARVEY: Juneau always says, "There are no new answers, the only answer is money." Caplan-Sauvageau's report is wonderful. You'll never get a better report on broadcasting in this country.

Regrettably, the 1986 Caplan-Sauvageau report was shelved.[55] Flora MacDonald, the minister responsible, lost her seat (she became an effective host on a specialty channel, Vision's *North/South/North*).[56] Marcel Masse could never in his undistinguished stints as minister responsible for cultural policy be accused of real interest in or knowledge of the national project that is Canadian broadcasting. Unsurprisingly, he simply ordered another set of studies.[57] The broadcasting legislation in draft for three years was finally enacted in 1991 under yet another minister, Perrin Beattie. Beattie's short and undistinguished tenure in the ministry was rewarded by the new Liberal government with the once-prized job of president of the CBC in 1995. The appointment astonished the experts – and fuelled suspicions that the government has no commitment whatever to the survival of national public broadcasting. Beattie, like most of his predecessors, has no experience in broadcasting. Nor does he have any administrative experience, in either the public or the private sector.

INTERNATIONAL SALES

MJM: I'm getting the message that international sales don't help the revenue situation much.

HARVEY: That's correct. I think we make between $1 million and $2 million a year back to CBC on English television sales because most of the money goes in "residuals" to writers, actors, etc. That's peanuts to us. It will never get above $10 million. Never.

MJM: So you can argue to politicians that CBC drama presents Canadians in our TV drama around the world, but you can't argue that it helps the corporation financially.

HARVEY: No one makes money on foreign sales, except the Americans and the BBC.

Until the 1980s the CBC did not market its very fine specials, mini-series, and anthologies aggressively. Since 1955 there have been sales of scripts, tapes, and films to major markets overseas, but intermittently and not as part of an organized, consistent sales effort. Only recently has the corporation negotiated practical, flexible contracts with any of the unions for such sales.

Fecan confirmed this situation several years later to Andrew Borkowski: "The money we make from International Sales of our programming is just gravy. We don't factor it into our decision-making when we develop a project."[58]

Another factor in the financial picture is that, in Canada, there are not large numbers of independent producers with the capital to make the ninety or one hundred pilots from which the American networks may choose six or seven. Of those which are chosen for a new season on an American network, two or three would survive. During a season, one or two might become a solid hit. The world-wide ratings-buster that ensures worldwide sales of series like *Dallas* or *The Cosby Show* comes along once every few years. Even more rare is the 1990s "jiggle" show *Baywatch*, which did not do well in North America but is the biggest international ratings hit to date.

The complex world of deals, sales syndication, and "in-house" and independent sales, as well as the market itself, helps to determine what viewers see and what they don't in the television drama we buy from other broadcasting systems. According to CBC management, marketability does not influence what they produce.[59] If a series is to be profitable, it must be "stripable" – it must have enough episodes to run five days a week during the day or late evening hours. No Hollywood independent production house makes back its costs on the first sale – the first prime-time run on an American network or a first run in syndication. Without ratings, public identification with the leading actors, or a track record of hits, it is *always* a gamble when producers enter the market with a new product. Residuals from sales abroad and stripping to individual stations make the profits. To make any money – which is not supposed to be the function of the CBC, but has been the subtext of various government commissions and task forces since 1961 – a CBC series must have about fifty episodes available for syndication. One hundred is the target for most series, roughly five seasons of twenty new episodes each. Until 1988, however, most CBC series averaged eight or ten episodes a year. *Side Street, Beachcombers, King of Kensington, Hangin' In, Seeing Things, Street Legal, Danger Bay, Degrassi Street, Degrassi Junior High,* and *Degrassi High* are the only series in the 1970s and 1980s that survived long enough to be sold on a weekly basis for a full forty-two week season. The wonderful *Gift to Last* had twenty episodes. It was not stripable, though it was widely sold to other government-owned networks around the world which do not follow the American scheduling model. Such residuals do not cover the costs.

CBC Enterprises was established in 1981 and reorganized in 1989. An interview with Dennis O'Neill on 23 February 1983 provided some interesting insights into how and what the CBC sold abroad in the increasingly difficult broadcast climate of the 1980s. No one in the CBC ever countenances the suggestion that programs are made with an eye to the foreign market, as were CTV's failed imitations *Police Surgeon, Trouble with Tracy, Snow Job,* and *Check it Out!* or the completely international *Littlest Hobo. Night Heat* became CTV's first breakthrough to American (summer) prime time – largely by toning down the scripts and featuring familiar American stars in the episodes. CTV's *ENG,* a more complex show of higher quality, is selling briskly abroad (including some American pay channels) – and it does not pretend to be set in an anonymous city. Its format is more distinctive than that of a cop show and its cultural context is clearly Toronto, Canada. It would seem that in the 1990s international distributors and buyers are more interested in Canadian material from Canada, not our versions of brilliant scripts from world theatre or imitations of other cultures' successful programs.

With a hundred channels on satellite and cable and an increasing emphasis on costs, other sales, though not envisioned as a break-even proposition, are not irrelevant; for example, the 1990 sale of *Love and Hate* opened up the U.S. networks as potential prime-time markets for *Liar, Liar, Conspiracy of Silence,* and *Million Dollar Babies.* There are also several prime-time Canadian content co-productions, such as *Alfred Hitchcock Presents, Sweating Bullets,* or Sonny Grosso's violent, exploitive update of *Dragnet, Top Cops.* (To this viewer, it really is very odd to see fine actors like Chapelle Jaffe mouthing wooden dialogue in a southwestern Oklahoma accent.)

No one can predict who will buy what. For example, conventional wisdom says that anglophones can't sell humour to Latin America – but the CBC had real success with *Wayne and Shuster* specials. A German station also bought lots of dubbed *Wayne and Shuster.* In this case, Johnny Wayne and Frank Shuster supervised the editing of the material made and broadcast since 1967 into eighty half-hour-long programs, with new openings and closings.[60] The result was good sales abroad. Not unexpectedly, the lavish Gilbert and Sullivan Stratford productions do not sell to non-English-speaking countries because it is easier to sell programs that don't have to be dubbed. Therefore, skating specials like Toller Cranston's *Strawberry Ice,* which is all visuals and music, were easier to sell than other specials. In the Caribbean it was presented as a Christmas special. The CBC followed this success with other skating specials for Cranston, and later Kurt Browning, Eisler and Brassard, Elvis Stoyko, Brian Orser, and Elizabeth Manley, and CTV has followed suit.

Surprisingly, CBC Enterprises could not sell Eric Till's excellent drama *Bethune* to the Chinese – yet the CBC did, a decade later, co-produce *Bethune* the movie, which was also shot and edited as a mini-series. Even in the 1990s ABC, NBS, and CBS show almost no foreign television, although several of the cable networks depend heavily on the BBC, CTV, and increasingly on CBC series. However, Canadians also purchase far less foreign programming than most advanced countries. The Europeans, British, and Australians, our best customers, ask us why we don't buy and broadcast more than the handful now on display. Perhaps, like the Americans, our buyers don't give their audiences credit, although Global, outbid in the mid-1980s on the expensive American programming by CBC and CTV, had some success with lighter British fare before it returned to American reruns and Canadian content co-productions like *Diamonds* or *Top Cops*. Another reason may be that BBC programs are no longer counted as partial Canadian content.

In the 1990s, Newsworld has opened up a space for international sixty-minute documentaries on *World's Best* and other perspectives on news and current affairs from abroad. Multicultural stations show us Brazilian soap-operas and Chinese newscasts. But until 1993 the best foreign TV drama was most likely to appear on provincial educational TV networks or PBS, not on the CBC. The reshuffling of the schedule to create an adult 10–12 PM slot changed that briefly. In 1992–93, for example, Alan Bleasdale's *GBH* ran for several weeks at 11 PM, having been first introduced with a two-hour opening segment in the adult 10–12 slot. In 1994–95, with the return of *Prime Time*, followed by local news at 10:00–11:30 PM, the CBC is still supplying the wakeful or the addicted with the outrageous BBC comedy *Absolutely Fabulous*.

The CBC rarely gets feedback from countries where a program is sold, either in the form of reviews or letters from viewers. There are some exceptions. Louis Del Grande, star of *Seeing Things*, was greeted warmly by Spanish tourists in Toronto, much to his astonishment. Australians wrote letters praising Lally Cadeau in the hard-hitting three-part drama special *You've Come a Long Way, Katie*. The streets emptied in South Africa during the weekly broadcasts of Gordon Pinsent's gentle series, *A Gift to Last*, about life in turn-of-the-century small-town Ontario, yet it is not one of the CBC's bestsellers elsewhere.

Everyone seemed to like the spectacular scenery and amiable characters of *Beachcombers*. Dennis O'Neill also remarked in the early 1980s that "the sales department is built on *The Nature of Things* and, more recently, on *Wayne and Shuster*, *Empire Inc.*, and now *Seeing Things*." The price is variable, basically what the market will bear. The same program can be sold for a few hundred dollars in a small Third World country, and for more than $100,000, depending on the size of the buyer.[61]

Almost every country in the world has legislated quotas on "foreign" content. Canada is the only industrialized nation with a television and film quota *not* for foreign material but for our own. The United States does not have such a quota, but its privately owned networks form the tightest monopoly in the world. Cable specialty channels and direct broadcast satellites may open cracks in the electronic ceiling, but in Asia DBS broadcasts are new and continue to be dominated by worldwide Hollywood product.

Not unexpectedly, international awards send up the price, as Academy Awards did for the documentary *Just Another Missing Kid* and for "Boys and Girls," from the anthology *Sons and Daughters*, produced by Atlantis films and first shown on the CBC. An Emmy, the Golden Rose of Montreaux, the Prix Italia, and the Academy Award are all particularly valued, with the Golden Rose the prize of prizes in Europe. The Rockies, awarded for excellence in various television programs at the Banff Festival, are increasingly valued by the profession after only a decade. In the 1980s I sensed an ambivalence in some levels of the corporation to entering a competition, perhaps rooted as far back as the embarrassment of controversial dramas like *Offshore Island* (1962), which made the corporation very nervous at the time and brought director Eric Till and the CBC many awards. Or the 1964 *Open Grave*, which caused an uproar in Parliament, made headlines across the land, and won the City of Genoa prize the next year. The CBC seems more willing to enter its programs at festivals in the 1990s.

Video cassette sales are a burgeoning market for some nations. In countries like Sweden, where, until quite recently, there have been very few choices on the available channels, VCRS are common and sales promising. Direct broadcast satellites and cable may well affect the sale of cassettes in those countries in the 1990s. In India during the 1980s and 1990s, in small villages, people get together to buy VCRS in such numbers that the movie houses are threatened and, with them, India's flourishing film industry.

In the early 1980s CBC Enterprises cleared ten dramas with a commercial distributor to be sold all over the world for home video –

chiefly "those with a little action." An episode of the *Phoenix Team* (not one of the most distinctive or distinguished programs made by the CBC) was one of the ten. Home video purchasers in the United States, like their network counterparts, are reputed to want guns, detectives, and spies, but ten programs of that kind were difficult to find in the CBC inventory of the mid-1980s. However, Home Video did take *Crossbar, Bethune, War Brides, Coming Out Alive,* and *Spring Hill.* In a conversation in October 1991 with the much reduced office at CBC involved with sales of broadcast materials to the public, I discovered that those were no longer being marketed and had been sold off at fire-sale prices. More recently, *Anne of Green Gables,* an independent production made with the CBC, has been available everywhere on video. However few CBC dramas are available for rent or sale on video in Canada. Astral Communications is releasing one or two every month for sale for private viewing in 1993 – a major step forward for individual accessibility – but the new CBC boutique has no catalogue for people who are at a distance from headquarters. These limited releases do not, however, address access for use in the classroom.

There can also be some re-editing when a program is sold elsewhere. When I mentioned that I didn't think the highly acclaimed three-part drama special *You've Come a Long Way, Katie* should have been three hours long, I was told that many buyers agreed. A buyer-distributor thought of editing it to ninety minutes or two hours. When I asked whether anyone in the corporation had protested, O'Neil said, "by and large we don't tell them, but it hasn't actually happened. It's a proposal." Publicity helps, of course. *Jalna* had one of the biggest publicity buildups for a drama in CBC history. When it was re-edited into a more linear narrative for foreign sales, O'Neill reported that "the BBC is still mad at us." The mini-series is said to have recovered its costs.[62]

Another CBC blockbuster, *Riel* (1979), is a different but also interesting case history on the constraints on selling CBC drama abroad. Here the co-producer owned the resale rights but he did not try to sell it. A shortened version showed up in 1991 on several local stations, and the full-length version was marketed on cassette by Astral in 1993. Sales of *Seeing Things* were blocked for two years after the show finished, also because of contract disputes.

Perhaps the last word on the sales potential of clones of formula American programming comes from Peter Lord, who sold CBC programs in London: "The attraction of *Empire Inc.* in the United Kingdom was that it's not *Dallas* but has a real *Canadian* flavour." The italics on the word "Canadian" are Sid Adilman's – and therein lies the dilemma.[63]

IN HOUSE AND CO-PRODUCTIONS

Empire Inc. was an expensive, beautifully made in-house mini-series. Joan Irwin, an experienced newspaper critic who wrote a series of thoughtful articles on the state of Canadian television in the mid-1980s predicted the death of all "in-house" drama at the CBC unless some of the financial constraints were removed – yet in-house drama can be made more cheaply and should be more innovative than independent television.[64] But purely in-house drama has become the exception, an increasingly rare commodity at the CBC. By 1991 more than 50 per cent of CBC drama series were made as co-productions or independently: *Road to Avonlea, Northwood, Urban Angel, Mom PI,* and *Max Glick,* compared with the in-house productions *Material World* and *Street Legal.* The series *Liberty Street* and *North of 60* are co-productions.

Co-productions are not a new thing. The CBC co-produced the 1960s series *Seaway* and *The Forest Rangers,* as well as drama specials in the 1960s, 1970s, and the 1980s. And if I am sardonic about the all-American *Top Cops,* then I should also remind the viewer that certain things have not changed since 1968, when Ron Weyman had his star, his writer, and half his production team on *Wojeck* bought out from under him by Hollywood. *Top Cops* at least keeps Canadian actors, directors, writers, and crews in Canada. Co-productions are another way of doing that. See chapter 12 for a longer discussion of current practices in co-production.

Some things do change, however. In the 1960s the CBC was not enthusiastic about co-producing series. Ron Weyman takes up the story:

WEYMAN [1987]: Halfway through the 1967 season, some friends of mine came over from England, from ABC, to see about putting some money into a series. It didn't work out. So here they were on this side of the Atlantic with nothing much to do. I invited them out to the set of *Hatch's Mill,* set in 1830s.[65] They saw all the crazy stuff going on. They hung around there for three days, after which time they said: "Look, we have got a lot of money, and we are looking for somewhere to put it. For our book, this is it! A co-production." They were willing to put out an amount of money that was the equivalent of our total budget! All I knew was that we were making something that was interesting enough that people in England were willing to co-finance and co-produce it, providing we improved the scripts. I didn't have enough writers. They also wanted us to have an English editor attached to it, and to make it a little more "classic." The financial returns were astonishing; it was too good to be true. But I got a note back from Doug Nixon saying that it was finished – forget it – we weren't going to do it!

Circumstances alter attitudes. The CBC is now very interested in co-productions. Every country in the world is pursuing co-productions, and many production companies seek foreign partners. Many of television drama's forms – action-adventure shows, historical dramas – have become too expensive even for the BBC or the American independents. The day of the lavish mini-series may be gone unless new arrangements are worked out.[66] A fairly recent example (1990–91) would be the expensive period mini-series about a former Russian czarina, *Young Catharine*. It was broadcast on American cable station TSN (unavailable at that time in Canada) and then on Canadian private TV. Several countries, including Canada, France, and the United States, invested in the mini-series, which was shot in Russia and starred French, Canadian, and American actors.

HARVEY: A lot of the production will be independent. The Liberal government and then culture minister Francis Fox started to press us to go outside some years ago. We brought out a paper in which we committed ourselves to 50 per cent of our entertainment production being independent by 1990. What we have been saying, for years, to our international producers, our unions, and the external, independent producers is that, as we remove the U.S. programs, the independent sector will fill those hours. In other words, we will continue to do our basic product within the CBC, but the independent sector will get all the incremental production. There are five-and-a-half hours of U.S. prime time left. So it really is Canadianization we are talking about. We'll continue to do some programs inside. But what we hope to do, even when an independent producer is involved, is to use our own facilities. This will keep our unions working. We don't have big drama staffs in this country anyway.

I asked Denis Harvey about the process, who did what, and about the ever present problem of "creative control." He told me how the relationship with Canadian independents like Sunrise Films, Playing for Time, or Atlantis worked.

HARVEY: We assign a producer to every production. We have veto rights over casting, director veto rights, and script approval rights. It's in the contract, and they don't get to shoot until the final approval of the script. Obviously, the outside creator still has the final word, but we watch it very closely.

MJM: What about foreign production partners? I notice Disney's hand in *Danger Bay*.

HARVEY: Get Nada Harcourt, head of drama series, to tell you the story of the first meeting ever with Disney on *Danger Bay* [a successful family adventure series shot in Vancouver]. They wanted to call the Vancouver Aquarium "Sea World," after the U.S. one. They wanted the name "Stanley Park" removed. They wanted more American leads. But we held firm and won our points. There is another funny story. One of the episodes was based on the birth of a live killer whale. The kids on the show were all excited and there were to be some birth problems. Disney would not show the birth. Yet it was really moving to see this whale being born under the water.

MJM: Of course!

HARVEY: It was beautiful. They fought us and fought us. I think the compromise was that we saw part of the birth on television.[67] There was another funny one when Doc's girlfriend (in this very platonic relationship) put her purse down in the house. One Disney producer said that it looked like she was going to stay overnight ... if you can believe it.

MJM: Yes, I believe it.

HARVEY: We finally went over her head. It was "Walt ... Walt ..."

MJM: "Walt wouldn't"?

HARVEY: Yes, really. They used to say that, evidently. "Walt wouldn't have allowed this." Every time you have a co-producer it affects the product. There is no question about it. The only thing is that Disney is a natural partner for us. As a public broadcaster we can get along fairly well with Disney. We have difficulty getting along with some other people.

MJM to HARCOURT: You're describing the CBC as a facilitator and a grandmother or godmother to a series rather than the birth mother. When you join Disney or another very strong partner, the question becomes, How do these relationships work? How Canadian is a co-production allowed to be? This must be a very difficult bargaining process.

HARCOURT: It is a very difficult bargaining process. I should let the audience be the judge. It's difficult for the press to be the judge because they don't understand the financial concerns, but I would say, on balance, that the battles we've fought we've won.

When it comes to a series set at the turn of the century like *Avonlea*, the demands and expectations of other partners are not a big consideration because you're really not exploring social issues, you're exploring human nature. A series like that makes a wonderful international co-production.

MJM: I have a lot of trouble with CTV's *Bordertown*. It's a Canada/France co-production ...

HARCOURT: And it looks like a "deal" being shot.

MJM: It also looks like something that is intended for one of the pay channels in the States.

HARCOURT: There are creative ways to make co-productions intrinsically Canadian and to make them palatable to the rest of the world. But that is always the challenge and that's really where the CBC executives are very protective of that cultural mandate. That's where your stamina and your ability to fight for those things really counts for a great deal in the equation.

The 1987 drama report was more blunt about logical partners for the CBC:

We have, of course, been involved in many co-production arrangements with other broadcasters indirectly – through projects with Canadian independent producers. It is useful to list some of these:
Disney: *Raccoons, Edison Twins, Danger Bay*
PBS: *Anne of Green Gables, Owl TV, Kids of Degrassi*
HBO: *Canadian Conspiracy*
BBC-TV: *Heaven on Earth, Going Home*
Thames TV: *Glory Enough for All, Thalidomide*
China: *Bethune, Journey of Tears*
Central TV: *Democracy*
Channel 4: *Anne of Green Gables, American Century*
We have had considerable success in producing arts and children's television programs with TVO involvement. TVO is a minor partner in several of our children's series, e.g. *Kids of Degrassi, Owl TV*, etc. where they take second window [that is broadcast the episodes or series after their first run on the CBC]. TVO is now interested in participating in such projects as Stratford and Shaw Festival productions. These projects are on our drama agenda; we can retain all creative and production controls; and the secondary use on TVO does not affect us. This is a good possibility to get additional moneys for these productions. Similarly, we can develop low-cost drama for children and family viewing – projects that respond to the mandates of both agencies.[68]

McQUEEN: Independents have charges, completion guarantees, interest costs, and overhead. The CBC can amortize, but the independent producer has to cover costs. Telefilm, to a certain extent, has helped overcome that situation, but if Telefilm continues in it's present state of crisis or if it isn't expanded, then I don't know what is going to happen to the independent production industry. I think it's teetering on the edge of disaster. Of all the things in the 1980s, independent production is one of the most exciting and one that's challenged a lot of our myths about how drama can be done and how it should be done. We've learned at lot from independent producers like Kevin Sullivan [*Anne of Green Gables*], for instance. Paul Saltzman [*Danger Bay*] created a successful series outside on his own.

The funding for Telefilm was expanded, then contracted as the 1990 recession hit. Telefilm and the NFB (a very important co-production partner with the CBC – *The Boys of St Vincent*) will undergo a review of their mandates by a special committee composed of Pierre Juneau, Peter Herrndorf (now president of TVO), and Catherine Murray (a professor at Simon Fraser University, as well as WTN and *Owl TV* board member). If Telefilm and/or the NFB are killed off, the CBC will have lost its most important co-production partners. If the CBC is killed, the NFB loses a crucial window to its audience, and Telefilm its most significant partner.

On 20 November 1994 two dramas were broadcast in prime time which illustrates the two roads co-production can take. Greg Quill in the *Sunday Star* points out the differences: "There are shows that are made in Canada by Canadians for international audiences. *Million Dollar Babies* is one. Its big concession to its American partner was casting a well-known American TV star, Beau Bridges, in one of the leading roles." Since he had already praised the mini-series in his *Saturday Star* review, he cut to *Avalanche*: "*Avalanche*, produced by Toronto's Atlantis Films for CTV and the U.S. Fox network, and starring Americans Michael Gross and David Hasselhoff, is something else altogether – a cheap, formula-based psycho-thriller that has no redeeming value at all, other than that it's a watchable nail-biter whose every plot twist is predictable, and whose only attraction is a goody-goody (*Baywatch*'s Hasselhoff) playing against type."

As the TV universe fragments and international co-productions become more necessary and abundant, we should worry that TV dramas such as *Avalanche* may be cheaper and easier to make than stories such as *Million Dollar Babies* and *Conspiracy of Silence*, original pieces that reflect, for international audiences, something of our own experience. Those projects were co-produced in part with independents, but the CBC retained fundamental approval on the elements and worked closely with their partners thoughout.

Producer Philip Keatley summarizes the problems that can bedevil both independent producers and the public broadcasters they work with.

KEATLEY [1985]: Bill Armstrong [then executive vice-president] and I were talking about standards of excellence and the problems we have at the present time when there is no more money and the outlook is for less. If you don't sell programs to the United States, there is no way your investors can make money back. But if we sell a concept in the United States, they want it to be an American show. Why should we use Canadian money to make American programs? That's not what the CBC should do. Then he said, "Therefore our hope is through Telefilm, that somehow, with the help of independent producers, we can find a new way of making Canadian programs. That's our future in the key field of drama, which we all agree is the place where the CBC must grow and not weaken. Somehow we have to draw from the regions all the things that we need." He also talked about the problem, not of "critical mass," but about the fact that there were so few opportunities for people because the restrictions were constantly increasing.
    I feel violently that in 1985 we're not talking about a network. We're talking about preserving at all costs Toronto and Montreal – that is, two super stations. With the satellite technology, that's all we need. But that's not a network, that's two super stations. Network, to me, means drama in Regina and drama in Windsor. [Ironically in the early 1990s, Max Glick, Northwood, and Mom PI were all shot in Vancouver, Urban Angel in Montreal, and North of 60 just outside Calgary. Toronto had Street Legal, Material World, Side Effects, and most of the Road to Avonlea. However, Keatley's prophesy may be the CBC's response to the $350 million cuts of 1995–98.]

Three years later, Trina McQueen did not agree with Keatley that the network was being turned into two superstations, but she did say the roles of in-house production and co-production were changing with the shifts of viewer taste and evolving technology.

MJM: Most creative people – writers, directors, producers, and so forth – are on contract now, aren't they? They're not staff any more.
McQUEEN: I'm not sure what the figures are, but I would say it's probably been a 180-degree turn since the 1950s and 1960s, when nearly everybody was staff. Now nearly everybody is not on staff.

There's still a core of staff producers and they tend to get a lot of the best opportunities. These people have wonderful opportunities, as well they should. I remember when I was at Banff that a British producer sat with me through a demonstration of how you get an independent production done, with all the dealmaking and the tax problems and putting the various government bureaucracies together. He turned to me and said: "After I've been through that, I wouldn't have the energy to produce the program." That's so true. There must be room for staff producers. People who are creative talents, but who may not necessarily be business talents, or administrative talents ...

MJM: Or deal makers.

McQUEEN: Deal makers, yes. The art of the deal is not the only art. God bless those who can do everything. One of the things that has happened this year is that, for the first time, we are putting substantial amounts of money into project development. This may be, along with Telefilm, one of those changes in Canadian drama about which you look back and say: "Oh, of course." Somebody said once that everybody has got a programming strategy, everybody's got a distribution strategy, but nobody's got a strategy for getting the stuff actually produced – for bringing together the money and the people and the resources, and doing it. Telefilm is one of the few things that's actually a production strategy. The other is development. This year we put in $6 million, because development really demanded money.

You've got to build the machine. One of the things you can look at is how we've done news and current affairs, which has always been organized along the lines that our entertainment or drama programming should have been organized. It's always had development, pilots, cooperative experiments, and room for challenge. One of the reasons is that there's so much of it – it's churned out day after day, week after week. When you have that mass, you can have all kinds of experiment. You were talking about English-French cooperation, and I was thinking of how the news department has recently signed on a lot of bilingual correspondents who will report in English and French for both Radio-Canada and the CBC. But maybe current affairs is saying to us, here's a model for how drama can do it.

After Ivan Fecan's arrival, the Drama Department was reorganized into separate units: series, comedy, movies, and mini-series. One of the arguments made for the restructuring was that it would free both contract and staff producers from having to spend time on a daily basis with the costs of production and that it would free their energy for what they did best – write and make programs.

As Fecan pointed out, the distinctions, between "in-house" productions free of the constraints we have just explored, and "co-productions" is rapidly disappearing.

FECAN: I'm not sure what "in-house" is anymore. I'm not sure co-production is a bad thing. Our crews have never been more busy, our design department is bursting at the seams. The issue of whether we own the copyright is not so big an issue to me. The issue is whether I can do the number and the quality of dramas I want to do. If, by bringing money in from outside, I can get more on the screen, more quality or more episodes, co-production makes sense to me.

MJM: I suppose we should clarify the terms for the record. There are two kinds of co-productions; the co-productions that are with Canadians outside CBC, and international co-productions with the Disney Channel, France, Germany, or whatever.

FECAN: It gets really messy. The pure definition of "in-house" is a show that we make totally. We own the copyright.

MJM: *Street Legal* would be an "in-house" production.

FECAN: *Street Legal* is not completely "in-house," in that we don't have a studio and we have to rent one. We don't have a full-time film crew, so most of the crew is freelance. The writers are all freelance and the producer is on contract and not permanent with the CBC. So, is it "in-house" or not? I don't know. But, technically, according to the definition I just used, it is an "in-house" show. Then there are shows produced independently for which we have creative approvals. Technically those are co-productions, but we approve every stage of the script. We approve the cast, the director, the writers, we screen the dailies, and we have all the same editorial controls that we would have for something we own.

MJM: These shows would be?

FECAN: They would include *Danger Bay* or *Degrassi*, many of the Kevin Sullivan projects, *Raccoons*, *Babar*, and all the Atlantis material. In those cases, there may also be non-Canadian money or there may not be. Some are financed completely with public money, by a little bit of Telefilm, a little bit of provincial money, a little bit of tax shelter money. But the point is that we don't own the show in any way. We only own a licence to broadcast. We rent the show. [Telefilm's approval of a project is conditional on the independent producer finding a Canadian network willing to broadcast the programs.]

MJM: But you have creative approval of it.

FECAN: We have all the creative approvals we want. But in those shows there may be more compromises because, if a partner who puts in half the money has a viewpoint, you listen. So far I don't think we've ever been in a situation that has been detrimental on anything of importance to us. I'm not sure that's true on the other networks, but we've been very careful about the partners, the kinds of projects, and the parameters of those projects. The projects all tend to be very culturally specific to begin with. You don't really have a disagreement over where the city is, as you might if you were doing *Night Heat*. We are very careful about that.

It gets very hazy. There are more and more co-productions these days where we own some part of the title, but not all of it, because we bring somebody in or somebody wants to join us in making something we want to do, but relieves us of the entire financial burden. There are all kinds of variations. [The implication is that the CBC's control over a project is proportional to its capital and that it does not "own" the rebroadcast or sales rights to any but "in-house" productions.]

MJM: The overseas sales are not so important to the financing or the decision-making, are they? Or is that changing?

FECAN: For "in-house" it is not important to us for very selfish reasons, because we don't realize any of the money that comes from those sales. My concern is not to make programs for South Africa. Apparently we sell programs to them occasionally.

MJM: *Gift to Last.*

FECAN: I'm not interested in making programs for other countries, I'm interested in making programs for this country.

MJM: But with the co-productions it may be otherwise. The foreign sale there may be important.

FECAN: In co-productions, yes. The foreign sale is obviously more important when somebody has to try to get their money back.

MJM: But those sales wouldn't be made through the CBC, would they?

FECAN: Some are and some aren't. Sometimes CBC Enterprises has decided to bid on the right to sell an independent program in some part of the world. They sell *Danger Bay* in Europe, even though it is an independent show. Elsewhere in the world it is controlled by Disney.

MJM: I'm trying to unravel the factors in making the decisions. It seems that overseas sales are not really an essential part of the thinking, at least not for now.

FECAN: Not for now.

MJM: What you are describing is a slow but steady evolution towards more and more independent material, where the CBC is primarily a buyer. But is the CBC an initiator?

FECAN: There is no difference in the development of a Canadian "independent" show and a Canadian Broadcasting Corporation "in-house" show. They are developed in the same ways by the same people. The only difference is the financing. The movement is a conceptual movement from the notion that to maintain and develop Canadian drama television you needed to do it all at 790 Bay Street to the notion of the larger community that may or may not be employed full time by the CBC. You have to have the core group in existence in the community, not necessarily at 790 Bay.

MJM: Is that concept yours? Or does that come from Denis Harvey?

FECAN: It comes from the reality in the industry.

MJM: Has somebody sat down and said, "OK, we are going to do it this way?"

FECAN: To be precise about it, for at least a decade it's been government policy.

MJM: Because of Telefilm?

FECAN: With Telefilm and by the manner in which the CBC has been treated financially by governments. But it is also the choice of many of the creative people outside the CBC who have a lot of opportunities available to them and who feel that they don't have to go to the United States or Britain or France. They feel they can make a go of it here and do better by hanging out their own shingle than by working within a larger structure. From my point of view, as long as there is enough work in the community at large and the core is there, it's fine with me. I don't feel there is any advantage necessarily in doing it all in-house. I think it is good to have the skills in-house, but my interest is the network, not the network as production house. I don't see the CBC as a production house as our first order of business. Our priority is to be a network.

MJM: That is a major change, although a slow one. It's a different way of thinking about making programs.

FECAN: It's not for me.

MJM: It wouldn't be for you. I'm thinking back over twenty years.

FECAN: Twenty years ago there was not the opportunity to get a lot of independent work. The CBC was pretty well it. Now there is so much opportunity that if you are good and if you want to bet on your own talent, you probably would do better on the outside because you own your negatives.

In my mind I run two businesses. My first business is a network business and my second business is a production company that supplies things that the network needs and can't get, or that are impossible to get from the outside world.

MJM: "Can't get," "Aren't possible": What are those factors?

FECAN: The more Canadian, the more difficult it is to finance with foreign money. *Street Legal* would be impossible to finance today with foreign money without tax shelters. So it is necessary to be able to produce some shows in-house. It doesn't mean that *Street Legal* won't make money for us now that it has dramatically improved its quality. It is a show that has a life outside Canada, without compromising the cultural identity of where it was made and the stories and the characters.

MJM: I have a question about the relationships between people. When they were all on one floor where they could talk to each other, cross paths, look at each other's stuff, there was a kind of ferment. Now the various people we have named are at various locations, although many of them are in Toronto. Do they ever interact?

FECAN: They interact through industry groups, through industry functions, they interact socially. They don't interact at a coffee machine or at a watercooler, but that doesn't hold anymore for the in-house producers.

MJM: Will the new CBC building make a difference? Will it at least concentrate the facilities?

FECAN: We apparently don't move in until 1995 or 1996. That is half the way into the decade. [They started to move in the fall of 1992 and phased in production through 1995. The drama studios were up and running in 1993, and by 1994 much of the English-language radio and television operation was in place.] Not only the in-house producers but also the co-producers will all be working under one roof. That will be very exciting. There are those who have been here for two decades and there are in-house producers who have been here for two weeks and are attached to a particular project. There will always be a bit of both, but there are more and more people that are brought in to do a particular project.

Producer Joe Partington has seen the evolution from predominantly in-house productions to the range of inside/outside productions now going on. Many of the writers and in-house producers for sitcom are new to the CBC.

MJM to PARTINGTON [1989]: You were talking about a real tension between the Canadianization of the network and the Americanization of the comedy side of the network.

PARTINGTON: Yes, but there are very specific orders from Ivan Fecan that the American references be cut out and Canadian ones be implemented. That is happening and that's great. Yet *Seeing Things* probably had more foreign sales than any other show. There are a couple of ironies; first, Louis Del Grande, star and co-producer of *Seeing Things*, was born in the States, as was Martha Gibson, Louis's wife and co-star. In effect, their personas do appear as New Jersey American. Yet there are more Canadian references in *Seeing Things* than all other shows combined. Any one episode has more, and it hasn't hurt the foreign sales.

Of the projects made by the new group of writers and producers brought in to create *Mosquito Lake*, *In Opposition*, and *Material World* (mark 1), the trio of 1989–90 sitcoms, two of them sank and the third, *Material World*, was revamped in subject, content, characterization, and tone.

PARTINGTON: They are very talented, very intelligent, and very focused, and they resist input from anyone outside their little group. [Like their mentor, Fecan, they were said to dismiss all CBC sitcoms before their arrival in 1988.] The executive producer of *Material World* and the two co-creators, who are also the writers of this series, all have dual citizenship. *Material World* is still their show, but it made a big difference having an experienced Canadian director, Alan Erlich, direct the pilot – a big, big difference. Alan also directed four of the six following episodes. So I don't think the show looks more American as such. It looks professional, and that is often equated with being American.

MJM: That's nonsense, of course, for both makers and audiences. I wrote four hundred pages of *Turn Up the Contrast* trying to demonstrate what nonsense it was.

PARTINGTON: Yes. Canadians want to see a show that is a little slower, a little more amateur, less slick.

MJM: I don't know whether "slower" equates with "amateur." R.H. Thomson talked to me about working on American television with American actors and how the writing and even the editing were so extroverted. In *Material World*, which is about the clothing or 'sh'mata trade, are they not going to make any Spadina jokes?

PARTINGTON: No, none whatsoever. It doesn't occur on Spadina. The family may be Jewish, they may not be. So it isn't rooted.

MJM: It isn't culture specific at all?

PARTINGTON: No, not at all.

MJM: It's not Toronto specific?

PARTINGTON: No.

MJM: It's not even Canada specific?

PARTINGTON: Yes it is, and the network is insisting that the references be Canadian rather than American.

Joe Partington was describing the first short season of *Material World* and unwittingly providing a diagnosis of what ailed it. To return to our opening metaphor of an American building and a Canadian interior, in its first season, *Material World* (mark I) had not only an American exterior but an American interior. In *Material World* (mark II), the key characters of Kitty's mother and the treasurer of the company, Bernice, remained drearily two-dimensional, and Jayne Eastwood's formidable dramatic and comic talents were wasted. Mark III, when the wise-cracking Bernice was written out and Kitty's mother found new independence and a more credible persona, was more culturally specific and much less broadly farcical. It still had no roots in Spadina or the "rag trade," which is a rich part of Toronto's industrial and cultural history. Nevertheless, the writers and producers presented much more credible, less clichéd situations and extended the show's appeal by concentrating on Kitty's individual personal reactions to those situations. It was still an electronic sitcom in format, inflected towards more complex dramatic situations at irregular intervals, yet it was firmly centred on its young star. There was no mark IV. *Material World*, like most sitcoms everywhere, did not end. It simply disappeared. In 1993–94 and 1994–95 the CBC rebroadcast *Max Glick* at 7:30 and *Mom PI*, at 10:30 but did not produce or buy a new Canadian sitcom for prime time.

DEVELOPMENT OF DIRECTORS, PRODUCERS, AND WRITERS

If there was one clear message in every report to the corporation since Robert Allen's in 1963, it was that the development of directors, producers, and in particular writers has been/is/will be the CBC's greatest need. The report of the drama search committee in 1973 stated: "We would recommend that the CBC and the Drama Department embark on a major program of training and recruitment for its producers and directors. While our neglect of training and recruitment has been generally detrimental to all of the program departments, it has created particular problems for television drama." Therefore, "We would recommend that the CBC and the Television Drama Department embark on a major program of writer development ... because writer development is a long and difficult process ... and because we will be trying to make up for lost time."[69] John Hirsch commented on the inplementation of this report:

"While the CBC Drama Department solicited work from more than 230 Canadian authors, it also would have been useful to conduct specific workshops in writing for television ... The recommendation to "begin to devote time and effort to individual writers who show promise" (Drama Search Committee report) was not adhered to ... The promise that the CBC would "begin to develop writer workshops and regional writing seminars to provide ongoing assistance to promising writers" was not fulfilled. The recommended provision of 'seed' money to allow special kinds of assistance to writers did not materialize."[70]

The Drama Subcommittee report concluded:

There is a sorry record of at least fourteen years of evidence that the CBC English Network never embarked on an even mildly serious effort to redress a problem which would cripple the increased production of Canadian television drama in its infancy. Throughout the interviews conducted for this sub-committee report – interviews with producers, writers, administrators – one recurring theme came up: There aren't the writers to deliver what we do now, much less more ... there aren't enough competent, never mind good directors ... assistant directors ... directors of photography ... Does that mean there aren't enough talented people? we would ask. No, the inevitable reply was, there's a wealth of talented people. There's a poverty in trained, developed and experienced people.

It's an extraordinary experience hearing this time and time again from producers, directors, and writers themselves. This is not a case of administrators giving excuses, blaming the subordinates. This is endemic and, to all appearances, absolutely true. There is no other discipline of production within the CBC which so uniformly declares that it does not have the fundamental base on which to build.

There were single attempts, here and there, by individuals within the Drama Department. But never were the funds made available to the Area Head to even begin the level of development work required, despite the fact that this need was underlined by every exterior examination over the past 15 years, and underlined by the Area Heads themselves.

The capacity of the English Network to effect Canadianization through drama programming is dependent entirely on its success in first expanding – substantially – that pool of skill and experience. Consequently: A development period must precede any significant increase in output. This development period, which would take probably two years (and which should remain at constant level after those two years) should be characterized by:

- recruiting new, young writers and producers and directors, and cinematographers, both through our in-house programs, and also through the independent companies we encourage on the outside,

- designing the workshops, environments and training vehicles to bring them to a level of skill to take on the challenge,
- developing a system of pilots, and more pilots and more pilots to simultaneously develop the younger newcomers, give margin for experiment and error to our current staff, and encouraging new ideas and formats.

...

We all know we have to bring in a sense of the streets, and a sense of a generation about which we have no direct experience except through our children; of races and ethnic groups which are unfamiliar to our daily experience. We all sense the gap between what we see at the Warden subway station and what we see on our own screen. All this talk of workshops and development and training boils down to opening the doors, and letting those unfamiliar people, the next generation, in. And once in, let's show them the shortest distance between the door and the levers of production. Then, the air will begin to crackle with new ideas, and a sense of contemporary relevance.[71]

Except for "pilots and more pilots," these recommendations have been partially implemented through the "Collective Visions" program (see chapter 3). New development money was found from the reorganization of the structure of drama production and from new accounting procedures. That development money should bear fruit on screen in the 1990s.

PROGRAM DEVELOPMENT

FECAN: We try to weed out most of the weak projects in the script stage. The ones that are close go to pilot. I try to do five or six episodes to see whether the problems of the pilot can be worked out. I use this episode run to compensate for not having the volume that other countries have.

There is no shame in failure. In other countries, ninety-nine out of a hundred fail, and nobody is upset about the ninety-nine. That's just the way it is. What you're upset about is if you don't learn from those errors. But if in the ninety-nine you discover a handful of writers and stars or develop them in ways that were not possible before, you've got something for reference. You keep backing the creative people and, sooner or later, they will produce a hit. In our country we are young, yet we have this idea that if one out of three pilots doesn't work, that is a tragedy. This is so ill-informed.

MJM: Our culture has a many-faceted sense of inferiority. One of the ways we show this is panic about failure.

FECAN: You have to be prepared to go through it. One mediocre

show leads you to one "OK" show, and that one may lead you to
one "not bad" show. There is no short-cut. You have to do the
homework. I think one of the surprises I've had is how little
confidence we have in ourselves and in our creative people, as a
country. I'm really surprised by that, because the rest of the world
does not lack confidence in our people. It is so unnecessary. It's
negative, and it drives people out of the country.

MJM: It has since 1952.

FECAN: It has and it continues to. Our creative people deserve
better, frankly.

THE IMPACT OF POLICY CHANGE

Inevitably there are those who see the new systems in place and the
new people differently from the way those people see themselves.
Producer Bill Gough is one.

GOUGH [1988]: Fecan represents an incredibly distressing turn in a
public network. This isn't a network that is funded by entrepreneurs or by people for commercial gain. It is funded by taxpayers.
As such, they have got to expect a certain return for their money.
There is no point in asking taxpayers to support an incredibly
expensive network unless it is doing something very special. It is
required to do something very special. I see a diluting of what it is
required to do. It's a thrust that began at the time of Juneau and
Harvey, and I think it's most distressing.

   The emphasis is on series, ratings, and a greater involvement of
people in research to support what they believe are the trends and
then to program for them. That is a totally incorrect way of programming. It's done adequately by all sorts of other networks and
studios, so I don't see why the CBC should be floundering around.
Quality is the only measuring device that exists for drama quality.
Quantity is a by-product. It is not what you aim for. It will naturally occur if something is done well. You don't have to think
about it.

   Wojeck worked in its time and *The King of Kensington* worked as
a series. To a certain extent *Seeing Things* worked as a series –
though that is such an eccentric series that it was very much like a
series of one-hour dramas. *A Gift to Last* was an absolute success
in terms of audience and provided an interesting set of stories that
dealt with many factors (certainly designed to get ratings) but that
coincided with beliefs and feelings. It was a wonderful series that
probably would have continued if they had been able to deal with

Gordon Pinsent in the way that Gordon Pinsent should be dealt with. The CBC should simply ask him what he would like to do and then let him do it. That's what I do with Gordon Pinsent. But there is no room in the system for something like that. [For Fecan's reply, see chapter 12.]

Views differ markedly about what kinds of programs are being used to implement Canadianization, but all at least agree that there is more Canadian programming to be seen. Where did the commitment to trying to fill up more hours with Canadian drama with ever shrinking budgets come from? Denis Harvey painted a word picture of the way it evolved.

HARVEY: About a year ago we took around one hundred people to Deerhurst to look to the future and decide how we were going to survive. It was forced on us by the fact that we are in the middle of the first budget from Michael Wilson. Three more years of "no inflation" and continued staff cuts at 1 per cent a year. A couple of us had been arguing with our senior management in Ottawa that if we continued the across-the-board cutting, which is the way it was done in the first two years (1985–86), with no attention to priorities or anything else, at the end of five years we would be in sad shape. So we took one hundred people from coast to coast, network and regional people, and presented them with this terrible picture: "You are going to lose these shows, this staff, and you are going to have a very watered down corporation. What can we do to make sure we do the best we can with the money we will have left at the end of five years?" What started to generate through it all was this old theme that we must Canadianize, we must get rid of the U.S. material – something we have been promising now for fifteen years in every speech, in every annual report, and everything else.

It just swept us to the point that on the final morning it was really incredible. People's voices were shaking and they had tears in their eyes. It was the closest thing to a religious revival I have ever been near.[72] So we went away from that saying, "This is impossible. Not only are we being squeezed, but to Canadianize is very expensive. How can we deal with this?" We set up a task force of six people in the spring, and they produced the 1987 drama report. They worked all summer on it. We in senior management gave them five basic objectives. One was that there had to be a better reflection of the entire country on the network. We just could not go on much longer without more reflection of the regions. It was partly for political reasons, but partly because we just weren't doing it. Out of that came decisions whereby regions end up with more money than they had. But they would have to make network programs, not regional programs. In other words, something had to be sacrificed.

MJM: So a regional drama program like *Tales from Pigeon Inlet* or *Lies from Lotus Land* would disappear. Everything that is made in the regions must go on the network, except the supper-hour shows.

HARVEY: Yes. I don't want to say everything, but by the end of three years, yes. They will make no more local drama. They have got to make drama that is good enough for the network, and their budgets will be increased to do that [which came to pass by 1990].

What Harvey could not have foreseen was that the logic of the directive to the regions to concentrate on making national programs was one of the factors which appeared to lead to the choice to cut local programs and to close local stations when the axe fell in 1990. No one seems to have foreseen the perceptions of people who lived outside Toronto/Ottawa. One person told the CRTC in the spring of 1991 that the "CBC had decided Calgary is worth less than ten episodes of *Street Legal*."[73] Harvey, who according to the public announcements had been in ill health, resigned as vice-president of English television in the early months of 1991.[74] The job was left vacant for two years before being given to Fecan.

There are people who saw these developments coming in the mid-1980s and who didn't like them. This is what actor/writer Hugh Webster and drama producer Martin Kinch had to say in separate interviews in 1984:

MJM: I'm shocked by the number of producers who say they don't watch television.

WEBSTER: But it's true. They don't watch very much television because there's nothing to watch. If I had to watch the kind of stuff that my kids watch all the time, I'd spend my time crying. I see a great dream going right down the drain. There's nothing I can do about it to change it.

Martin Kinch had a sixth sense about the result of the coming shift in emphasis to independents, quantity, and ratings.

KINCH: What terrifies me is that they will decide to make the CBC a commercial network. The Drama Department as a whole – this collection of eccentrics of one sort or another – are not the people who put together a commercial network. They're people who put together quite extraordinary shows.

This may well be why so many of a particular generation had stopped writing, directing, or producing drama by 1992. Several retired or changed careers, others went into or back to the Arts or Current Affairs Departments. Moreover, it is difficult to judge the degree of self-censorship that goes on in the 1990s. Was Jeannine Locke's drama about the Alameda-Rafferty Dam, *The Greening of Ian Elliott*, postponed for nearly a year because this kind of low-key, low-cost, in-house drama is now the exception not the rule? Or because it would disturb the flow of family drama in the high season (September–February) programming? That question has arisen before in our broadcast history.

In 1985, while talking to Philip Keatley in Vancouver, I defined CBC television's functions as "The defence of our border. Theatre doesn't defend our border; television does."

KEATLEY: How are you going to cause that to happen in the 1980s?
MJM: First of all, you have to get people to notice that it isn't happening or is happening a little less each year.
KEATLEY: I think they've noticed and they don't care. Maybe we have to invent new mechanisms that will subvert some of the technology. What I and others have in mind is, if we have to create independent producers, independent writing companies, and ways whereby new projects will come into existence when the CBC is not going to be here to commission them, we'll have to do that. Maybe we aren't going to have public broadcasting in this country for a while. I don't know.

From 1988 to 1992 I took the fact that CBC series drama and drama specials did not get under the skin of audiences as a sign of ill-health in the network; particularly that drama was not a merciless mirror regularly held up to our folly and our error, outside of the sharp sketches of *Codco* and one or two mini-series a year like *Love and Hate* and *Conspiracy of Silence*. But in 1992–93 the situation improved with *The Boys of St. Vincent* [I saw it on cassette because it was banned in Ontario], *The Valour and the Horror, Liar, Liar*, and *Gross Misconduct*. Several episodes of *North of 60* signalled the return of more serious drama made for adult audiences. More than three million people watched *Butterbox Babies*, a chilling exploration of evil, in January 1995.

It is also worth noting that *The Boys of St Vincent* (like *The Valour and the Horror)* eluded efforts at censorship because the NFB (part-nered with an independent company, Les Productions Téléaction) had the conviction and the resources to put these programs on cassette for sale or loan so they were not completely subject to external (or internal) censorship once completed. No such "State" institutions exist in the United States. More important is the fact that the commercial constraints on the independent television film-makers and the Ame-rican networks would have ensured that such programs not be made.

In my experience, American television seldom looks at the ques-tion of human evil with any seriousness. The cartoon evil of melo-drama, which appears in every action/adventure, every soap and Saturday morning cartoon, and too often on the "news," is easy to enjoy and then dismiss. The societal evil that can be addressed and redressed is more comfortable for viewers to deal with and will occa-sionally appear on American television. But having explored the in-stitutional and explicable evils of church and state, *The Boys of St Vincent* placed the fundamental evil of sexual predators of children precisely where it belongs – in the inexplicable and terrifying parts of human experience we call tragedy. Tragedy is a rare commodity on television anywhere, but it has appeared occasionally on the CBC since the 1950s.

What *was* American, and unforgivable, was the insertion of the commercial breaks for Air Canada airline travel to faroff escape resorts. If ever, in its forty-plus-year history, CBC television required a program to be "sustaining" (without commercials, as with most controversial programming until the late 1980s), it was *the Boys of St Vincent.* Yet CBC executives would not or felt they could not afford to broadcast three hours of prime-time drama of this kind without commercials, a damning indictment of the system that can still create and disseminate such magnificent programs, only to dangerously weaken their impact. Even so, as Magder points out in more detail regarding other series and specials, without the tax dollars of the CBC, the NFB, and Telefilm, the independent company could not have made the film. Since the mid-1980s the CBC has either commissioned or bought, rather than made, television dramas of all types, but our distinctive voice still depends on public institutions.[75]

TRINA McQUEEN [1988]: Certainly, one of the roles of CBC pro-gramming is to challenge people, to provoke and even to offend them. That's the way a society grows, through anger and debate, and the resolution of that debate, and perhaps understanding what hasn't been thought about, both the light and the dark. CBC drama programming should reflect both of those aspects. What does get people mad nowadays, that's the thing? You can touch people more easily than you can make them angry and offended.

Part of the program schedule of the public broadcaster should be saying things that are unfashionable, that are unwelcome. A lot of these issues have been trivialized by American television movies. They take the most sensitive subject, cast beautiful people, and have some sort of resolution at the end. Every taboo subject has been touched on, but touched as you would touch a hot stove, very carefully.

John Kennedy speculated that audiences are less likely to be upset because, with the choices available, they can simply choose to watch something that isn't going to upset them. In the 1960s the CBC was often the only TV available.

MCQUEEN: Still, Canadian viewers are willing to be upset and to be challenged. I think of *Planet for the Taking*, which really challenged the whole idea of progress, growth, and human comfort to a certain extent and which drew audiences of two million people up against programs like *Dynasty* and *Hockey Night*. One thing that says as much for or about the country as about the CBC is our willingness to watch difficult programs. Look at our Tuesday night and you see a very large audience share, 25 to 30 per cent of the audience, watching *the fifth estate*, *Marketplace*, *Man Alive*, and *The National* and *The Journal*, apparently enjoying them and accepting that they will be given new or different ideas. They choose that over other kinds of programming. In the same way many of our dramas, the toughest dramas like *Turning to Stone*, achieved good substantial audiences with very difficult subjects. Why would anyone sitting at home in the evening, presumably tired from work, choose to watch *Turning to Stone*? Because people do have minds, and they do want to use them.

The drama report expressed this point rather coolly.

What we have been less successful in is relevance and contemporary flavour. The American series are remarkably quick to deal with AIDS, Contragate and events in the news. *Miami Vice* wove in the French sabotage of the Rainbow Warrior in New Zealand with breathtaking speed. *Seeing Things* has often achieved such immediacy, and *Street Legal* aims for it. We believe our hour-long series must be above all completely contemporary; we cannot afford, in this particular stream, costume dramas or heartwarming evocations of a rural pre-war past none of us ever had. We have to fight *Miami Vice* and *LA Law* and *Moonlighting* for the attention of our 16 to 40 audience, and we should fight aggressively, dealing with all the themes of sex, love, mixed families, race, political corruption, and this generation's search for security. We must address the same mix of themes that the popular music addresses, because we are fighting for the same audience.[76]

My question is how? How often? At what point does "relevance" resemble a tabloid headline used to titillate, not to probe. Actor R.H. Thomson was asking the same question as early as the summer of 1989, before "reality" television dramatized the "shock of the week" on every network – Amy Fisher on three networks, Harding-Kerrigan (the skating duo), Lorena and John Bobbitt, and, most notoriously of all, the media obsession with O.J. Simpson's flight, arrest, pre-trial, trial, and acquittal for the murder of his estranged wife.

R.H. THOMSON [1989]: The CBC has stopped leading the audience and its expectations. We imply that a public body cannot lead, that it has to respond to the public. That implies that public bodies like the CBC are followers, and that is what the major U.S. networks have become – followers. They don't dare lead anywhere lest they leave out some audience. It robs them of initiative, of the exciting things that come with leadership and perception.
MJM: It also robs them of audiences.

Sydney Newman summarized the issues at stake in the debate about what should be put on the air and how as a society we should accomplish it. His overview of Canadian broadcasting today is an inside/outside perspective of some value. At the time of this interview he was working on a project for Britain's channel 4.

MJM: Canada is my major focus, but I'm interested in distinctions and differences. The most obvious difference between the U.K. system and ours is the fact that IT [Independent Television] gives the BBC a run for its money, because it is regulated and financed differently. In Britain there is also a different broadcasting tradition and context.
NEWMAN: The British are the cleverest people in the world at protecting themselves. Their broadcast system is simply a marvel to behold. In the 1950s there was a monolithic BBC and it was becoming fat and lazy. Pressure creates commercial television. Since the BBC is a national service with hardly any attention paid to regionalism, the ITA was created to govern a series of fourteen regional stations whose first concern is regions. They are allowed to band together to form a network only in the evenings. So they

have one national network focused on national concerns, and another network with regional concerns. Then the competition of commercial television with the BBC was such that the BBC reduced standards and went to the government and said, "We cannot compete because these people are just allowed to do anything." In fact, my dramas at ABC in the United Kingdom were beating the BBC. The BBC were able to say, "We must cater to all kinds of people with all kinds of cultural backgrounds and, therefore, we need a second channel." The government allowed the BBC to create BBC-2, which is designed not to be popular, but to cater to the individual tastes of the minorities – not regional minorities, but cultural minorities.

MJM: As with BBC Radio's old *Third Program* [now Radio–3].

NEWMAN: Exactly. Twenty years or so later, a fourth network was given to the Independent Broadcasting Authority, again different from the other three. But channel 4 is not allowed to make its own progams. They must go to the private sector and buy them.

Relate all that to Canada, and per se the utter stupidity of our country. We have a national service in the CBC. We allow the commercial guys, who are regional, to compete nationally, degrading the CBC. The CBC, in its befuddlement, starts to go regional, dispensing money and wasting it away in the regions, money they really need to make mammoth programs. Now, with the new media coming in on cassettes, satellite, and cable, the CBC is nothing. See how clever the Brits are, having four networks, each defined to perform in a different way to satisfy their British audiences. These four networks provide more varieties of TV than we get on Toronto's twenty-two channels.

Ivan Fecan's answer to that kind of argument is very straightforward.

FECAN: There is talk in Ottawa that they will do a channel primarily for what they call "minority programming" – arts and documentaries.[77] I think this is a mistake, because if it turns out to be government policy that we should be channel 4, then it's here now. It's really simple. Just get us off advertising. If arts is done well in television, it will get an audience, as we have been able to demonstrate.

MJM: I think another channel should be a place to put alternative kinds of broadcasting, as well as retrospective broadcasting. It's partly a matter of confidence and pride. American audiences and American scholars are in seventh heaven because they can look at their own TV history in rerun. They've got that huge volume of stuff to look at. But we have a fair amount of volume, too, even though for years we did not take care of it in any kind of appropriate archive. In Britain they have formal ideas about retrospectives, but they've got the arrogance, the pride, the accomplishments, and the channel, to do that. Here we sit with an inventory of wonderful programming that we never see again. When I beat the drum for another channel, it's not for the élitist taste. It's because I think we should get some of it back, the good, the bad, and the indifferent, especially the stuff that people loved.

FECAN: You make a good case, but I wouldn't underestimate the issue of pride. We have to take much more pride in what we do as a country. We sell ourselves shorter than anybody in the world sells us.

MJM: It's amazing the number of people who do come back from countries abroad and say, "I missed what I had." Yet my students are still in the mind set: "If it's good, it wasn't made here." Often it has been made here; they just don't recognize it. Their ignorance about Canadian programming still catches me by surprise.

FECAN: I see it in two ways. I did a pilot with the *Kids in the Hall* last year, but I couldn't get arrested for it here. When the pilot played in the States, it got positive reviews and we got a series out of it, financed in part by American money. It's running now on HBO, a pay-TV channel in the United States. I got unbelievable reviews from *Newsweek* to *People* to John O'Connor, the best American television critic, very well informed. I can still barely get arrested for it, but I have a better chance with the show here now, because it's got the American seal of approval. Yet the show hasn't changed.

I see shows of ours that are not among the top group of shows we have ever made but are average – no better or worse than 80 per cent of the new shows on American television this year. But in our case it's a headline, "CBC screws up." In the case of American television, it's just an American show and we might like watching it or not, but there is no attention paid to it.

What is most striking as an apparently unchanging fact of corporate policy is Eric Till's 1974 summary of the priorities of the institution: "The structure of the corporation is upside down. The tip of the pyramid is sticking in the ground." John Kennedy used exactly that metaphor to me in his account of a "powerful discussion" he had with upper-level management in the mid-1980s. I see no clear evidence that the pyramid has righted itself with the downsizing of the

1990s. The slow drain of some of the best and most experienced talent from the CBC on and off screen suggests otherwise.

Still, the growth of independents and co-productions could work towards more flexible and creative working conditions. Trina McQueen did say that "the question of drama has troubled the CBC from day one and it's a particularly Canadian obsession. We have this belief that we can grow and flourish as a nation state if we have a new constitution and a popular sitcom."[78] Nevertheless, the questions remain. Do Canadian broadcasters give up on sitcoms and concentrate instead on shows we easily recognize as "ours" like *Road to Avonlea, Street Legal, North of 60, Northwood, The Odyssey,* CTV's *ENG,* or Global's *Madison?* Or do they make clones of American action/adventure series like Global's *Destiny Ridge, Tekwars,* and CTV's *Counterstrike, Matrix,* and the quintessentially American *Lonesome Dove?* These are all co-productions with Germany, the United States, or France, and most use public money from Telefilm.[79] The distinction between public and private begins to dissolve. The question is whether the CBC can reinvent its policy and ethos to survive as a maker, and not merely a buyer, of dramatic programming. And there are many who would say that the point of origin – in-house, co-production, or simply buyer – is irrelevant. I don't agree.

Located in Toronto, the new CBC English Broadcasting Headquarters concentrates, at last, the production facilities scattered since 1952 over a dozen buildings. But to return to our opening metaphor, can the CBC continue to exist "within [this] immense boxlike grid"? Will it continue to be a "series of buildings," some departments circular, some square? Will it have an American exterior? Most important of all the questions, will it be Canadian in its vital working spaces? Will there be places where the imagination can thrive, and different voices be heard? As we shall see in chapter 10, that depends not only on policies arrived at in the upper levels of management but also on the ethos to which makers and decision-makers both subscribe.

10 Ethos

Ethos: "The prevalent tone of sentiment of a people or community; the genius of an institution or system"[1]

The Shorter Oxford English Dictionary gives the first modern usage of the term as 1851. Thus, "ethos" is a word not only associated with Aristotle and Western traditional thought, but also a term adapted to the industrial revolution 150 years ago. It is worth stressing that it is not a synonym for "corporate culture."

Let us begin with a quick sketch of the context within which an identifiable CBC ethos took root, flourished, changed, and ...? How that sentence ends depends on who is talking. Some say it has died, others that it has changed but still flourishes. Still others claim that it never was: those are more likely to be the young who were not there, and who disbelieve or devalue what they are told. Many were not born when the CBC television ethos, which was rooted in CBC Radio's sense of itself as a "National Theatre of the Air," shaped the first golden age of Canadian television drama.

THE CONTEXT OF CBC TELEVISION ETHOS

The foundations for the CBC ethos in television drama were laid in 1950, when all kinds of people were gathered together and sent to the United States for training. They returned to a collection of scattered buildings and hastily adapted spaces (most of them still in use forty years later) and were told to get on the air and on the job. I would summarize the ambiance at that time as "Get drama of all kinds – Canadian, classical, contemporary, original, and adaptations – on the air in quantity and continue with CBC Radio's unwritten mandate as a National Theatre."

Mavor Moore was the first chief producer in CBC television in 1950, and, in 1953, assistant program director.[2]

MJM: There are so many conflicting stories of what happened over the years.

MOORE [1990]: This is why I'm doing my memoirs now. But I've got to research it, I don't trust my memory. I don't trust anyone else's, so I don't know why I should trust mine.

MJM: I remember your telling me once that the CBC started out training television people by offering them to the other networks?

MOORE: Not quite. The Massey Report, when it came out, recommended that Canada go into television (this, of course, had to go through Parliament), but the CBC, which had been chomping at the bit to get into television, went ahead anyway. We were in operation, actually, before Parliament changed the "CBC Act."

MJM: "Over the dead body" of the NFB?

MOORE: No, I don't think so. There was never any suggestion that the NFB would run television. In fact, there was quite close cooperation with the NFB. One of the senior NFB producers came down to join us, Sidney Newman. The CBC was really into it, making plans and buying equipment, before the act had been passed.

MJM: There is a CBC ethos that carries itself through to the mid-1960s – at least. Paul Rutherford would say it ends there.[3] I would say it takes on a new form, but that it continues. I would also say it's in peril now, but that it had a very long run. Perhaps it had to do, in part, with creative people at the CBC forming a community of sorts as rivals, but also as a community with an understood purpose.[4]

MOORE: Yes, absolutely.

MJM: People were coming and going, new and old, but there was continuity.

MOORE: And all through this we were fighting union battles, too. The whole administrative structure was being formed, we were making that up as we went along.

MJM: But there were not the levels of bureaucracy that there came to be?

MOORE: Almost weekly, we had to change the graph of who reported to whom.

MJM: You were the chief producer. Between you and Stuart Griffiths, you made the program mix?

MOORE: Yes. The two of us did. When I became assistant program director in 1953, that really only recognized a situation that already existed; there was no one in that job before. The job I had held as chief producer disappeared and we divided the operation into – roughly speaking – four departments.

MJM: It's never been clear to me whether Robert Allen was ever actually designated as a head of drama or if he was designated as head of unsponsored drama, or what?

MOORE: I think he was head of drama after network programmer Peter McDonald left; Peter was there for only two or three years.

MJM: By the mid-1950s Sidney Newman seems to have taken over responsibility for the commercial side of drama and Allen the un-sponsored drama.

Sydney Newman articulates the "under thirty-five policy" that the CBC implemented in its formative years.

NEWMAN [1984]: When television began in Toronto, they would not allow anyone over the age of thirty-five to join the television pro-duction services. I was the oldest person hired in television. I was thirty-five exactly.

The CBC started out in television marvellously: they imposed that thirty-five-year-old rule, which I think was generally sensible and they took all the creative staff on one-year contracts. They wanted to get away from this tenure which people in a big organization get to have. Andrew Allan, who should have been head of drama in CBC television, would have had to leave the staff of the CBC, to give up all his seniority, his pensions and everything, to accept a one-year contract. Allan was the most talented, brilliant guy our country had in the area of drama, but he stayed in radio because he didn't want to give up his security. Peter McDonald, one of the junior ra-dio directors under Andrew Allan, and Arthur Hiller, Bob Allen, and a few others gave up their permanent status to get into television.

MJM: One of the things I have argued is that there is a real conti-nuity between the radio tradition of seeing itself as a "National Theatre of the Air" and television.[5] Since we had no national theatre in Canada, radio and then television are where Canadians found an ongoing fictional, dramatized portrait of themselves. The CBC also tackled social issues and tried to push back the lines of what was acceptable in drama to society and what was not.

NEWMAN: You're rather ennobling the situation. Television drama in Canada didn't achieve one-quarter of what Andrew Allan did in his own series.

MJM: The *Stage* series?

NEWMAN: *Stage*, absolutely. That related to a lot of factors. Andrew Allan's show was never commercial. Our stuff was commercial, it was brand new, and the independent stations were growing up, though not yet a network. CBC television drama just never had a chance. I really wish that Andrew Allan had moved sideways to see what he could have done; he was young enough and he was certainly at the height of his powers in 1952.

As Mavor Moore pointed out, Robert Allen, who did risk the jump to television, quickly became a supervising producer of much of the early television drama.

MJM to ALLEN [1981]: It seems to me that *Folio* and then *Festival* were functioning as a window on the world for people. They were contemporary world drama, a way of looking at what was going on, a combination of whatever classic and contemporary drama was adaptable for television.
ALLEN: We didn't do as much Shakespeare as you might have expected, because Stratford had begun the year after we started television. It seemed to me that Stratford was able to do Shakespeare far better than we could. It was also a very expensive undertaking and, as long as we were in black and white, there wasn't the excitement you could achieve with costumes and sets. By the time we got into colour in 1967, there were so many theatres in Canada.
MJM: Yet, effectively, you were functioning as a place where actors could stretch themselves in classical roles that they couldn't get in the theatre of the 1950s and 1960s.
ALLEN: We were also trying to support a large number of actors.

I asked executive Hugh Gauntlett how much money was available to *Folio* or *Festival*? And whether producers had a lot of freedom to do whatever they wished?

GAUNTLETT [1983]: In the 1960s you were dealing with a very simple administrative structure. There was Ottawa, with an executive vice-president responsible for the vice-president of the network; in Toronto there was a guy on the spot who ran the network, a boss of programming, a program director, and what we now call "area heads." And that was really it. There weren't large numbers of supporting troops: it was a very simple conceptual framework. Everybody assumed that they knew what we were for and what we were meant to be doing. It wasn't written down anywhere. There weren't program goals. There wasn't much discussion of audience measurements, because audience was not a problem.[6] We survived and so did CTV. For most of the 1960s Doug Nixon took all the important decisions. He would do that with advice or suggestions from the program departments and using his own evaluations. It might involve looking at figures, talking to people, but broadcasting instinct had a lot to do with it. He was relatively untrammelled by helpful advice from above, by money, or by physical production. He was like an artist with an easel, painting a picture that was the network programming.

On the whole, he was not involved in decisions about individual programs. Take *Festival* as an example. As an act of faith, we believed we would always have an anthology of that kind which would mingle the best from everywhere, which would be quality without inhibition. He made that statement with some emphasis, because *Ford Startime*, the transitional anthology between *Folio* and *Festival*, had been sold down the river, slightly adulterated, as a result of a deal made in a men's washroom in the Royal York Hotel. He had an understanding with Bob Allen as to what the mix would be. Allen came out with his list of things to do, having had the producers, the story editors, and others make their suggestions. Story editors were very important in that department. He would run over that with Nixon. Nixon would not be concerned, unless there was going to be potential controversy. Of course, in the early 1960s there was much more controversy about the content of that kind of programming than there was about our journalism. "Taste" was the dominant problem, which came from the fact that the CBC as a whole was consciously trying to keep up with the "avant-garde." The CBC also regarded itself as the sole channel by which most Canadians could have any idea of what was going on in the world and the community. Therefore, they had a duty to get the "latest and the best." It was at that point that it started to get a little rough.

MJM: Yes. The community standards of Canada at the time were not what I would usually describe as "avant garde."

GAUNTLETT: So when the programs were being made, nobody except Bob Allen would be involved. He wouldn't go near Nixon unless he had a problem, usually a problem of language [scatological or blasphemous language].

MJM: And Allen would identify something that was a little dicey?

GAUNTLETT: Absolutely. It is a well-known rule of thumb that an area head is responsible for detecting what might be potentially troublesome or controversial and for alerting people to that up the line. By the late 1960s, even though the system was still expanding, there were advertising revenue problems. What had to be decided in that context were the elements of the mix – the new program initiatives the CBC might or might not take and how well the existing enterprises were going.

Story editor Alice Sinclair remembers the slow transformation of the ethos as reflected in programming itself.

SINCLAIR [1982]: The mandate was not so much to develop our own indigenous drama as to present world drama. How that has changed!

MJM: Indeed, it has.

SINCLAIR: I haven't heard anyone suggesting doing an Ibsen or anything like it for years.

MJM: Or even a contemporary playwright. No more classic Pinter, no more contemporary Pinter [or Trevor Griffiths or David Mamet et al.]. Yet the CBC did all the early Pinter just after they had been produced for the first time.

SINCLAIR: Pinter was not really one of our successes. He was too difficult to deal with. The audience hated it. "What was that about?" They didn't understand it. His peculiar sort of circular dialogue was unusual. It was long before they made the movies of the plays. I'm not saying we shouldn't have done it, but I don't think it was a popular choice. [They were beautifully done, though, and most of them were very suitable for television as a medium.]

THE CBC AND THE NFB

When talking to producer Ron Weyman, I had named CBC Radio as grandmother to the ethos of service and leadership and the occasional off-the-cuff experiment that developed among CBC television producers. Weyman reminded me that the NFB was grandfather.

WEYMAN [1987]: Most people at the Film Board were there, not because they were going to make a lot of money or that it was a stepping stone to Hollywood, but because they were concerned. They were public servants in a way, but without the stuffiness. They were artists serving the public. This was a gift of John Grierson, but Tom Daley and others were not interested in making money or in a world reputation. They were not interested in using Canada as a stepping stone to Hollywood. Such an idea never crossed one's mind; one was here, being paid to have this incredible opportunity to go and make films.

I discovered the same sort of people in the CBC. The John Barneses, all the original people, were non-commercial. At their worst, they were stuffy, old-maidish, but in the same person you would also find the extraordinary desire to serve, to be of use to the country. The whole question of making money, or making your name, or going to Hollywood, or using the CBC as a facility to learn the tricks so you could go some place else and perform those tricks for money was something that was really rare. Maybe that idea today sounds strange, because today we all know that the CBC is one of the best routes there is for an actor or a writer or anyone to determine how far he can go locally, and to see whether he is ready for the next leap, which is L.A. There is a perceptible shift in motivation today.

In the 1960s, anthology drama died in the United States and westerns and cop shows flourished, because film became the norm. New York gave way to Hollywood as the production centre for American television. Meanwhile, in Canada, the CBC was not making series and, officially at least, not making drama on film.

MJM to HUGH GAUNTLETT [1983]: Was there a formal "deal" between the CBC and the NFB that the CBC would not do film drama?
GAUNTLETT: No, it was a corporate understanding, and it was more than the NFB, it was the whole film industry. That was in the days of Alphonse Ouimet, the very early days of television. Without particular reference to the Film Board, it was constantly quoted to us: "We regret the fact that the film industry must be maintained and supported."

Yet there was a clear contradiction in terms of mandates, for both were agents of national culture.

NEWMAN: First, the Film Board did not do any fictional films until the early 1960s. Fiction was never part of its tradition, but I don't recall any such agreement. I had argued very forcibly while at the Film Board that we should provide the news to the CBC to prevent them from ever having to buy a movie camera. I recall no discussion whatsoever regarding fiction.
     Certainly, the CBC had a very anti-Film Board bias, but I wouldn't call it competitive. NFB commissioner Ross Maclean had felt that, at the Film Board, we were visually oriented and that radio was aurally oriented; consequently, the Film Board should be running the CBC-television service. The Film Board was a reputable and marvellous place. He simply lost the battle. The government went

to the CBC, as all governments have gone everywhere. The radio people broadcast through Hertzian waves sounds, and television is Hertzian woven pictures.

Mavor Moore recalled instances of cooperation with the NFB in the early days, but others got caught in the rivalries that developed between the two.

WEYMAN: It was so stupid. The Film Board said: "We'll look after news. We'll give you one hour a week." The CBC said, "No, we need one hour every day." NFB: "But we don't have the cameramen." CBC: "Get the cameramen. There's a guy who runs a drug store somewhere out west, and he has got a little camera; if something happens on his doorstep he goes out and shoots it!" NFB: "It won't be good quality." CBC: "It will exist." You had these extraordinary discussions with the CBC over who had the responsibility to translate this country day after day, hour after hour, in visual terms. You also had the official film agency with the Film Board sitting there saying, "We can't do that." I was really troubled by this. There seemed to be two camps. And I can remember saying, "I have got to work for CBC for a year and act as a liaison, so that we can at least talk to one another in the same language." Donald Mulholland, a good friend of mine, said to me, "Well, Ronnie, you are either for us or for the CBC!" I said, "Mul, come on! This is the greatest opportunity that the Film Board has ever had to be seen, to be used in a much more effective way!"

Sometimes they found ways to work together. The centennial year encouraged the NFB and the CBC to collaborate formally on doing drama specials for broadcast in the *Festival* time slot.

ERIC TILL, director [1983]: *Waiting for Caroline* and *The Ernie Game* had their problems; there were supposed to have been three films, but those two used up all the money. I know that because I was supposed to do the third one. There was this peculiar notion that the people here, at the CBC Drama Department, knew how to direct actors but didn't know a thing about directing a film! The Film Board knew everything there was to know about film, but didn't know a thing about directing actors! That is no way to make a film. I remember there were extraordinary hassles (I wasn't a part of it), mostly because one party didn't understand the other one's attitude, dilemmas, needs, or whatever, so it was a mess.[7]

FILMED DRAMA

Despite years of filming *Cariboo Country*, the growth of *The Serial*, and the success of *Wojeck*, film drama still struggled to find a place at the CBC. Ron Weyman takes up the story.

MJM to RONALD WEYMAN: *Wojeck* ended up with enormous ratings and tremendous feedback.

WEYMAN: It was the dawn of a new time in Canadian TV, but we didn't have the ability to follow through. We worked our way through to demonstrate that we could do filmed series, and we were told, thank you very much, but we have lost half our people. I got no feedback from my bosses on it. I read that Thom Benson had suggested that it would be a good idea to do the filmed series *The Manipulators* from the West Coast.

MJM: You read this, but you hadn't in fact been told?

WEYMAN: That's right! In the newspaper! Well, what does this do to the resources we have got in Toronto? Thom said, "Don't worry about that. This year *Manipulators*, next year we are back in Toronto." I said, "But Thom, we can't run things this way." I finally demanded a meeting with Benson and with two other guys, his bosses, who shortly after that vanished; Bob Allen was there – everybody was there. There were a few passing jokes made, but the fact was, there was no policy!

So Fletcher Markle, head of TV drama, arrived, and we got into *Jalna*, a film serial of the novels. It seemed to me that I could become involved, if I wanted, or not, if I didn't feel inclined to do it. And then I had lunch with John Trent, the production director, who very much wanted to do it, and I said, "Well, good luck!" But once again we were going back to square one! By this time there were two good teams of film people as opposed to simply studio people.

MJM: *Jalna* is the expensive, extensively and elaborately publicized period piece that used up all kinds of resources. *The Manipulators* is filmed on the west coast, fifteen shows only, over two seasons, then recycled on *Sunday at 9*. Next thing is *The Collaborators*, the CBC's first real cop show. There is no through-line of policy at all.

WEYMAN: And presently, you got a bit tired, a bit weary with all of this. But out of it, a number of people got the idea of writing film and shooting film. Today, there are a lot of people in Toronto who are very good at shooting film that sells around the world. I think that has been part of the payoff.

MJM: The journalistic dramas of the late 1970s and 1980s are also a heritage of the 1960s, specifically *Wojeck*, which proved you could do a TV drama on film with a topical thrust and a sense of social conscience.

There were frustrations and missed opportunities at every stage of the CBC drama's history. The tension between old ways and new, between the CBC's relative freedom of opportunity in the first fifteen years, the desire for star treatment or sometimes simply the respect one had earned as an actor, writer or director, and the offers of much more money, came together in the late 1960s with predictable and temporarily debilitating results.

WEYMAN: I have just described to you a situation where on day one, they are telling me that we are *not* in the film business; day two, six months later, they are telling me, my God, we *are* in the film business: "Can you give us a whole season of film next year?" Philip Hersch had been kicking around for about three years. Well, he caught fire with me and David Peddie, who was a story editor at that time. Hersch wrote the first ten episodes of *Wojeck*. It was incredible.

By year two, we were into a different film stock and we went to colour. The result was that an agent turned up in Toronto and picked up half the cast and directors like McGowan. We had already lost Phil, who had written himself out and was now in Hollywood. They wanted me to go there. They wanted to transfer the whole thing to LA, and I had no option on these people.

So, we had a different team by the end of the second season. Not only writers but actors. We had to invent something new, so we invented a doctor, *Corwin*. Sandy Stern, who *was* a doctor, wrote it. He said, "What are we going to do next year?" I said I didn't know; all I knew was that we had good ratings and I could guarantee six episodes. He said, "Well, the question is whether I am going to stay here, whether I have a future in this country or in L.A.?" And I said, "Nothing has essentially changed here."[8] I put this question to his agent from LA, who by then had also signed John Vernon. He said, "When Canada is as attractive to your talent as Hollywood, that's when you get them back. But as long as Hollywood can give them more work, that's where they are going to go. There is no way you can hold them here. If you give them the same opportunity and the same money, they'll be back here." I said, "So I get back to point zero again." And he said, "That's the way it goes!"

Director Eric Till has worked on projects both for independent producers and for the CBC.

MJM to ERIC TILL [1983]: One thing *Festival* did do was provide a view of the world for people who had no other access to contemporary drama and gave them a look at the classics, whether they had to be crunched into ninety minutes or not. It performed an important function for an isolated and fragmented culture, in a much more theatrical sense than radio. Radio had been doing this, too, but this was a chance for people to see what the world's best drama could look like and sound like at a time when they could see none of it in the theatre. Now we have a different generation who don't know these playwrights and their successes because of the narrowed focus of the CBC. There must have been some interplay between the Canadian content and the world's drama, particularly as it reflects contemporary concerns.

TILL: It is mandatory at the moment that one just does Canadian stories, set in Canada, about Canadians. I don't agree with that aspect. I miss the broader range of subject. I am still immensely saddened that organizations such as CTV and CFTO never lived up to their mandate.

MJM: When, as it did in the mid-1980s, the Supreme Court itself has to force CTV to produce even one hour a week of television drama, it is bad for the country.

CTV: FOR TWENTY-FIVE YEARS MANY PROMISES BUT NO PERFORMANCE

At CTV, the story of television drama is a tragedy or a farce, depending on your perspective. Before the first licence was granted in 1961, the backers had promised the Board of Broadcast Governors programs featuring the National Ballet, the Toronto Symphony Orchestra, the Canadian Opera Company, and Stratford – a feast to surpass the music, ballet, and opera offered on the CBC's *Festival* – as well as programs reflecting farm interests, women's concerns, and sports. Of the eighty-six half-hour slots available in prime time, forty-two would be live productions. Of its budget, 27 per cent would go to live talent. CFTO had told the BBG that, "we are making long-term plans for the building and development of a drama department that will bring to our viewers fine theatrical fare. We look forward to establishing our station as a foremost Canadian stage for the telecasting of the entertainment arts."[9] By 1964, a brief from ACTRA (Association of Canadian Television and Radio Artists) to the second Fowler Commission complained that "despite their promises, not one of the private television stations in Canada has produced a single drama since they began programming more than three years ago."[10]

In the beginning, CTV did try to live up to its promises. However, it floundered financially until fresh capital and a winning formula of cheaply bought U.S. programming and cheaply produced games, quiz, and interview shows took the stations out of the red.

With the advent of CTV in October 1961 in the lucrative city markets, the commercial revenues of the CBC were reduced: in 1961–62 by 12.5 per cent, in 1962–63 by 6.3 per cent. This reduction coincided with a period of government austerity. The result, says Frank Peers, was that "the CBC's own productions, especially those not offered for sponsorship, tended to be reduced, or to be pushed out of prime time ... private broadcasting was becoming the dominant element" in the mixed system we had now adopted.[11] Paul Rutherford remarks about this period: "The CBC was the main source of made in Canada programming" as opposed to "the American invaders and 'their' local network, CTV, both crucial to the quality of Canadian television in English Canada."[12]

In 1965, of the seventeen to twenty hours of optional network production available, CBC affiliates took an average of only four hours. In Weir's view, by the mid-1960s, Canadian programming was being squeezed by "an inexorable pressure of [advertising] agencies for choice time, sometimes to match time with American program schedules – and above all for funds to keep the vast organization [of the CBC] going."[13]

In 1963, Ken Soble, owner of the only unaffiliated station in the rich Toronto market (CHCH, Hamilton), said in an interview with Dennis Braithwaite: "It seems to me that I or any other broadcaster should be encouraged to produce a small number of good Canadian programs instead of a large number of mediocre ones."[14] Exactly the same points were made by Bill McAdam of Norfolk productions in a talk at Brock University in March 1984. Exactly the same arguments were being made by the Canadian Association of Broadcasters to the CRTC in 1990 and 1991 and at the Television Summit called by culture minister Perrin Beatty on 9–10 December 1991. By 1993 the argument had shifted. CAB members now argued that they should be released from all obligations of Canadian content in return for set amounts of money (a tax? a fine? a donation?) given to a Canadian drama and children's production fund. Presumably these programs would be broadcast on the CBC – if it survives.

For thirty years, CTV still had eight shareholders, each with an equal vote despite the concentration of ownership in the hands of three conglomerates: Baton (the Eaton family and Doug Bassett, with ten CTV stations in 1991 and seven CBC stations) and Western International Communications, with three independent, two CBC, and two CTV stations in Vancouver and Victoria. The third major owner of CTV stations is Canwest Global Communications Corporation (controlled by Izzy Asper). Some CTV stations are locally owned by one person. Most have large capital investments in transmission services and little willingness to invest their profits in making programs for the network. Yet every station, no matter what size, has had one vote. Thus, CTV itself has always been short of funds because the stations, not the network, reap the profits. The attempts to reorganize the cash-starved network continued through 1992 and arrived at last at a surprising, last-minute compromise that concentrated voting power in proportion to holdings. However, BBS – a Baton mini-network in Ontario – has already been in conflict with its extended CTV family. Nevertheless, no one disputes that the "ethos" of CTV and Global CanWest has been both defined and driven by the profits to be made. Public service looks out of an upper window occasionally, but the doors are guarded by accountants.

On 14 December 1990, Denis Harvey, vice-president of English Network Television, Izzy Asper, and Linda Schuyler, an independent co-producer of the various Degrassi series with Playing for Time, appeared on a CBC Morningside panel. The subject was the $108 million CBC cutback that resulted in the CBC closing down all specifically regional programs except for a few supper-hour shows. Asper argued repeatedly for the CBC as PBS North, financed by the return of licence fees (a scheme tried and abandoned in the mid-1930s before the CBC was reorganized) and donations, while Global (or even his rival CTV) would continue to expand into local as well as regional broadcasting.

He also said that the private networks would need international partners to make programs economically viable. When Denis Harvey and Kealy Wilkinson, a media consultant for public broadcasters, pointed out that in Canada private broadcasters put U.S. programs into 90 per cent of available prime time, and made few children's shows and very little distinctive drama, the response was that the CBC made U.S. programs more expensive for private broadcasters in bidding for the four-and-a-half hours of U.S. prime-time product then left on the CBC schedule. Linda Schuyler was quite clear in her own mind that her high-quality programs would not have been made without the CBC. Asper admitted that co-producing Degrassi High would have cost him far more than the $60,000 an hour he could pay for an American show. Kealy Wilkinson pleaded for some discussion between the

Canadian public and the CBC before the $50–75 million cut projected for 1991–92, a discussion which did not happen.

Instead, in May 1991 the government chose as co-chair of its federal task force Roy Peters, former president and CEO of Western International Communications, a powerful private broadcasting group. Not surprisingly, the committee recommended that the CBC raise its advertising rates for "premium" shows, cut the number of commercials from twelve minutes an hour to eight, and reduce staff. The CRTC's examination of the CBC decision to close local stations ended with an agreement to allow expansion of the private networks and thus to cut the CBC out of those advertising markets where it no longer had a station. The CRTC has often seemed torn between the ethos of public broadcasting for the public good and the imperatives of the businesses it regulates to "break even" – in fact, to make very handsome profits. I will discuss this at greater length in chapter 12.

MAKERS AND MANAGEMENT

The first major crisis in English-language television was the *This Hour Has Seven Days* flap.[15] The CBC suffered its second major crisis in morale (perhaps in a delayed reaction to the first) in 1968–73. With the exception of *Reddick I and II, Twelve and a Half Cents, Vicky,* the competent half-hour anthology *To See Ourselves,* and *The Manipulators,* that five-year period represented a slide in inventiveness and energy. My sense of that period, based on viewing the programs and on the interviews, is that much of the talent burned out or left without being replaced. Drift is the word that comes to mind, although the administration of the department itself was in constant flux. As I have pointed out elsewhere, the centre suffered although the regions flourished.[16]

As early as 1961 the Glassco Commission had complained about a general lack of understanding between the people making the programs and management: "the existing organizational structure has been developed with the deliberate objective of ensuring that, as far as possible, policies are formulated and decisions taken by groups rather than individuals ... Not one of [the president's] subordinates can ever be held answerable for any particular aspect of policy or operations."[17] This perception was still widely held within and without the corporation on many matters of long-range policy up to the mid-1990s, despite the reorganizing of the Drama Department and the "hands-on" management style of Ivan Fecan. In the late 1960s and early 1970s this kind of structure meant long delays in decision-making – a pattern some argue appeared again in the late 1980s. Certainly, the

1968–73 period was characterized by contradictory responses, refusals to make crucial decisions, and, above all, lack of accountability within the organization to its chief officers and to the public.

Yet, I wonder. Because the managers/taxpayers/newspaper critics/CRTC who are the bosses may not like what the "employees" are thinking, "accountability" can be an excuse to avoid taking difficult decisions or a tempation to shift the responsibility elsewhere. If the CBC had functioned as an efficient, cost-effective, industrial model of management during the 1960s, within a more standardized "corporate culture" rather than within a loosely defined but widely understood "CBC ethos," could CBC drama have taken the risks it did, raised the dust that it did, or created a milieu in which Phil Keatley could make excellent film drama far away in the Chilcotin plateau of British Columbia? Could Ron Weyman have pulled together *Wojeck* at a psychological distance from management in an obscure corner of downtown Toronto, if a rigidly hierarchical structure had been more firmly in place?

KEATLEY: The end of the 1960s were good days for us because in 1966 it was decided that we would have a drama department in Vancouver, which was a major undertaking. The only kind of specialties that were fully recognized at that point were drama, variety, sports, news, and current affairs. At that time, producers were getting separated from the decisions about why we did programs, decisions that were made in levels above the Drama Department or the Sports Department, or whatever.

In Vancouver, there had been a de facto department. Now there was a name for it, a budget set aside, and there was money to develop ideas for which there were no places in the schedule yet. [There were many more American programs in CBC prime time then.] We were getting to the point where people were being assigned to all kinds of projects. The setting-up of the department here really did create more freedom, which, in my experience, is odd. You might ask the other producers and find they say, "Bullshit, all that happened was that Keatley was in charge and he liked that." I don't know. Drama had been too much *my* territory. Various people who had been the senior boys when I first came had moved on. We said: "We have to build this up. It can't be a one-man band. If Keatley's busy doing *Cariboo Country*, what is everybody else doing? Nothing is happening and nobody else gets a look-in. So use other writers, use other people." We started out quite intentionally saying, "In what other directions (that Keatley doesn't like) could people go."

MJM: You had somebody like Len Lauk coming along?

KEATLEY: Lauk had been there all along. He's another graduate of the UBC Player's Club. When *Cariboo Country* went into production, Len was a production assistant bucking to become a producer, and he directed five of the thirteen studio episodes. Then he went off into other things. But he had always wanted to do drama. He wrote and directed one called "The Clubman." It embarrasses him now, but he wrote it with enormous love.[18]

MJM: So there were suddenly a lot of people doing projects that attracted them specifically. In 1966–67 there was also a lot more money around for the Centennial, so you got a real upsurge of energy that carried you into the early 1970s.

KEATLEY: One person who was influential here was Ray Whitehouse. He had twenty years in radio, and then went to Toronto in television. He became the regional program director in television. He really was totally devoted to drama. If you wanted to do drama, he'd cancel the news and give you the money. I think he came back about 1966. It was he who made the Vancouver Drama Department happen. It carried us right through into *The Clients* [1970], which was a very bad show [as well as being the pilot for *The Manipulators*].

MJM: It was full of real experimentation, using film with all kinds of flashbacks, wavy effects, and reverse negatives.

KEATLEY: That was produced by Don Eccleston.

MJM: It was a pretty good script, too. It's not as bad as you say it was. I can see why you made the changes you did with *The Manipulators*, but it's interesting to watch the evolution. *The Manipulators* belongs more to the issue-oriented, documentary-flavoured professionals genre, like *Wojeck* and *Quentin Durgens*, than to the cop-show format.

KEATLEY: That's right. We were after something that almost worked there. It came close. I would do a half-hour documentary for a month and then I'd do some variety, which I did very badly. I'd do some drama, and then I'd do the news for a while. Then I would do "Time Out for Sports."

MJM: Change like that would keep you fresh?

KEATLEY: It really did, and that was one of the great things about working in the regions. We would move everywhere. We were good at a lot of things.

MJM: You were saying that, being from Vancouver, you were able to get to the people who were in Toronto who made the decisions much more easily than the people who were located in Toronto. Ironically, those layers of bureaucracy were not quite the problem for you that they were to drama producers in closer proximity to management.

KEATLEY: No, they were not. Back in Ira Dilworth's day there was the joke: there was the CBC and then there was the DBC. When you got past the Rockies it was Dilworth's Broadcasting Corporation. There has been a kind of unity here.

THE 1970S: THE ETHOS FADES BUT DOES NOT DIE

The early 1970s was a demanding time in our cultural history. The October Crisis had jolted us into a new sense of who we were becoming, both in Quebec and the rest of Canada. Nationalism was wearing a new face, the arts in Canada were in ferment, we had young talented American immigrants fleeing the war in Vietnam, and the "60s" as an era were coming to an abrupt and tragic conclusion. Yet the Drama Department, which should have used our most popular medium of communication to pull these events into the perspective only fiction can give us, was adrift.

In 1973 director Allan King, Patrick Watson (producer, writer, interviewer, and in the early 1990s chair of the CBC Board of Directors), Robert Fulford (columnist and for many years the editor of *Saturday Night*), economist and academic Abraham Rotstein, media critic Morris Wolfe, and several others, plus a team of volunteer researchers, felt strongly enough about the state of CBC television that they formed a Committee on Television. It presented a 187-page intervention that called on the CRTC to rewrite the CBC licence to create a dramatic reorganization of the corporation or to cancel it. Among those who co-signed the introduction and recommendations were Lloyd Axworthy, Margaret Atwood, June Callwood, René Bonnière (CBC), Ed Broadbent, Harry Bruce, Dalton Camp, George Grant, Greg Curnoe, Michael Cross, Donald Creighton, Mel Hurtig, Elsa Franklin, Avrom Isaacs, Pauline Jewett, Douglas Leiterman (CBC), Richard Leiterman, Hugh MacLennan, Douglas Marshall, Marshall McLuhan, John Meisel (the next chairman of the CRTC), W.O. Mitchell, Farley Mowat, Christina McCall, Sidney Newman, Peter Pearson, J.C. Polanyi, Gerald Pratley, Michael Snow, Judy Steed, Miriam Waddington, Joyce Wieland, Budge Crawley, George Woodcock, and Al Purdy – a remarkable cross-section of artistic, academic, and communications expertise covering a wide political spectrum. As a latecomer I did some research on drama for them, and have retained a copy of the intervention. The letters in the appendix are truly damning. All address what they see as the loss of the CBC ethos. I will quote just one from Stan Fox, a senior producer who sent his letter of resignation to George F. Davidson, secretary to the Treasury Board.

I've been with the Corporation for over ten years operating on many levels and in a great variety of activities. I can remember when I joined the Corporation, I came into it with a feeling of awe. At that time the CBC seemed to stand for courage, independence and experimentation in broadcasting. However, it was not popular. Its radio service never attracted as many listeners as the private stations and I quickly learned after I was inside the Corporation that this lack of popular appeal was something which had to be hidden, especially from the politicians in Ottawa. The Corporation had to maintain several illusions in fact. First of all, that it was efficient in an area in which efficiency was impossible in the business sense of the word; that it was similar to a "free enterprise" institution, although, in fact, it was an instrument of socialism. This kind of deception has continued to exist to the present day. The highest level of Corporation executives are still trying to give the outside world and particularly the business community the impression that the CBC is as "good" as General Motors in the sense that it is operating in similar ways and to similar ends. That we are completely unlike the larger private corporations of Canada, and should be, is something that we are still quite ashamed to admit. We spend thousands of dollars on fees to management consultants to investigate us, to "improve us," to make us as much like General Motors as possible, quite forgetting the fact that we are in no way engaged in making a profit in the way that General Motors does and that the kind of people we have working for us, especially in the production area, are just simply not found at General Motors. [It is chilling to note that the CBC's response to its most serious crisis to date (1995) is to spend hundreds of thousands of scarce dollars on yet another management consulting firm.][19]

The existence of the Committee on Television intervention was an affirmation from those who cared about public broadcasting *outside* the CBC that the organization was perceived to have lost its way. Drama came in for a particularly scathing analysis.

The 1974 CRTC report titled "Radio Frequencies Are Public Property"[20] contained many of the recommendations of the Committee on Television, which may have been coincidence – an indication that the commissioners were already thinking along the same lines – or not. The central recommendation that the CBC be disbanded and restarted as two independently run, adequately financed parts (one devoted to transmission and the other to production) was ignored, to no one's surprise.

During the waves of reorganization through the 1970s and 1980s the CBC has had, as one might expect, a variable record in management. Individuals speak of others up the ladder warmly, and have throughout this book. On the other hand, there have been several waves of talented people who left the CBC because their talents are underestimated or simply dismissed. Grahame Woods is one of Canada's most talented and sensitive writers of television drama. He has stopped writing after twenty-two years and taken up social work. In essence he identifies the shadow side of the CBC ethos, which one finds alluded to (particularly by writers and actors) from the days when radio was drama's home right up to the present.

WOODS [1989]: The CBC have a thing – I think it's a mentality that runs right through the corporation – that they'd like to hold people down. "If they get a sense of their own importance what will it do to the system?"

MJM: There are to be no star actors, no star cinematographers, no star writers.

WOODS: Yes, exactly.

MJM: No star directors or producers for that matter.

An aside from Richard Collins is apt here: "The CBC's refusal to develop a star system is probably the most important instance of the pervasive and damaging Canadian "snootiness" about popular entertainment ... The contrast between the single contribution Sydney Newman made to television drama in the U.K. and his lack of impact in Canada [at the NFB] after his return is another case in point."[21]

I asked Woods about the "reformation" period (following the CRTC report and an internal review of CBC drama) that is John Hirsch's era.[22]

WOODS: I have a theory that Hirsch changed CBC drama, but not in the way that he was expected to. He swept out all the people with experience and brought in many neophytes. They have created a system that exists today, and they don't know any better because that's the way they were brought up. Hirsch is well known for this. He'd pick up the script for that day's shooting and read a scene that he didn't like, so he'd rewrite it, send it down to the set, and have them shoot his version of the scene.

MJM: Kennedy was "hands-off" in that respect.

WOODS: Yes, Kennedy was more of a technocrat. He was a product of the CBC system, but he gave a great response to Anne's Story [about the effects of child abuse on an adult]. He was probably a little hamstrung by the people about him. The heads of drama have never been given the kind of autonomy I think they should have, the kind of trust they should have. Or, as director Eric Till said to film documentary and television drama director Alan King, who interviewed him for the Committee on Television report: "If you hire John Hirsch for the qualities he will bring to the position, then give him the autonomy he needs to use them. In other words, don't behave like the average television production, where emphasis is placed on hiring highly skilled performers, and then ask them to limit their skills to mere technique in order to get the programs on the air."

WOODS: I have got two or three good ideas sitting on my agent's desk right now, but one of the sad things is that after twenty years of writing you still have to go out and sell yourself every time.

MJM: Do you have the sense that the risk-taking is diminishing?

WOODS: I don't think they've ever taken risks at the CBC.

MJM: Wouldn't you call *Vicky* and *Twelve and a Half Cents* very risky at that time?

WOODS: No, because they came after *Wojeck*.

MJM: I know they did, but they were still very much tougher than most of *Wojeck*.

WOODS: I guess it is naiveté on my part. I just had a feeling that that's what we did. I'd given a lot of thought to the Vicky character, what happens to her after she murdered her children in *Twelve and a Half Cents*. So I put her into Queen Street Mental Hospital. What happens to her when she wants to get out? In those days I was very new. I went to David Peddie and said, "What do you think of this? Why don't we do a sequel?" And he got on the phone and said to Ron Weyman, "Do you want to come in and listen to this?" The conversation lasted ten minutes. "OK, go ahead." I went off and I wrote it in four-and-a-half days. I just sat down and it really came. I've never done that since. In those days you could go in there with an idea. You might not always get the idea done, but at least you'd get good feedback and good discussion on it. You can't do that now.

MJM: Too many layers of people making decisions?

WOODS: Yes, and just not enough air time available. They've allowed the anthology to disappear.

Not quite. In the early 1990s the CBC co-produced or bought from independents in the regions *Inside Stories* and *Family Pictures*, half-hour multicultural or family-oriented anthologies. The important missing element now is an anthology or series made for or by the CBC where viewers can consistently find drama that presents more intellectual as well as more emotional complexity. Early *Street Legal* had it. *North of 60* has it. As Woods said about the 1970s and others would say about the 1980s, "I just had a feeling that that's what we did."

THE ETHOS IN THE LATE 1980S?

MJM: As I understand it, if you came into 790 Bay with a superb story idea or a superb script now, a producer would still have to want to do it. It seems that if it's not a producer's own idea, he or she will be less interested. These days producers prefer to generate their ideas and then find the writer to write the script.

WOODS: I have a good example of this trend. I keep in touch with what's going on, I know actors, what they're doing, I'm a jack-of-all-trades. Director Francis Manciewicz was in talking to Bernie Zuckerman [the executive producer and one-third of the team with writer Suzette Couture that brought to life *Love and Hate* and *Conspiracy of Silence*] and he said, "I just read this fantastic script," and Zuckerman said, "Who is Grahame Woods?" This sums up the attitudes that now prevail. So I went in and it was basically, "Okay, I'd like you to work for my series, which is two-hour movies. Now, come up with some ideas." Eventually I came up with an idea he loved, one I'd always wanted to do. But as we progressed from stage to stage, it became Bernie's story. Bernie said, "Well, why don't you change this slice" or "This happens and this happens." I felt, "You don't want my ideas, you just want somebody to be able to paint by number."

MJM: That doesn't encourage the craft, it doesn't make good scripts, and therefore it doesn't usually make good television.

WOODS: It's like governments changing in Moscow. You come back into favour again.

A case can be made that supervising producers Robert Allen and Ron Weyman, though they fought battles as did their directors, had a fair amount of autonomy. In producer Bill Gough's view, a recognizable CBC ethos as defined in part by the mandate and in part by the internal culture of the organization is disappearing.

GOUGH [1988]: There are some people who are brilliant at spotting ideas, at analysing things, but those people are generally doing it. In the corporation at the moment, the basic ethic is only with the "workers." Things that once were valuable, things that were taken for granted, are no longer the working ethic. There are individuals who are still connected with that drive, that dream, and those ethics. But when former president Al Johnson left in 1982, for the corporation itself, that vanished at the top level. The way people were dismissed, the way people were let go, the total acceptance of budget cuts indicated an altered corporation.

Gérard Veilleux (president 1990–94) vigorously defended the corporation against MP's attacks on CBC personnel at the Commons' Committee on Culture. Yet as Veilleux himself admitted later, the fast and ruthless firing of people in the 1990 regional cuts was very badly handled even using the standards of ordinary late twentieth-century management practice. Moreover, the CBC is not just a business. Not letting people make a final program to wrap up and say goodbye to their faithful audiences badly hurt those who made the programs and those who watched them. No closure, no dignified departure was permitted. As the president of the Association of Television Producers and Directors, Arnold Amber, wrote in 1991, "One day a treasured employee, the next a potential enemy ... years of loyalty and service paid off with stupid and painful indignities."[23]

Ivan Fecan explained to Andrew Borkowski in 1993 that, "on the arts and entertainment side there's been quite a lot of change going on for the past five years so there was probably a lot more openess to change." He accepts responsibility for the abysmal mistake in the News division in 1992–93 in which various distinct units were telescoped within a few months. "We really badly underestimated the pain of the change. We really didn't manage it well."[24]

MANDATE WORK AND THE ETHOS

The 1968 Broadcasting Act, which defined the CBC "mandate" and reflected praxis, was in place until 1991. I asked program director Trina McQueen about "mandate work":

MJM: I've had different answers in the last few weeks when I asked about "mandate work." At least you're familiar with the phrase.
McQUEEN [1988]: A balanced service of information, enlightenment, and entertainment, appealing to the whole range of interests and tastes in fair proportion, and contributing to the development of the national unity.
MJM: And diversity – including the development of regional diversity.
McQUEEN: If I were sitting down to write a mandate for a public broadcasting organization in this country, I don't think I could do it any better, and I hope people don't try. It may be a goal or a whole bunch of goals.

MJM: I have called it impossible.[25]
McQUEEN: I don't think it is impossible. To me, it neatly says what
we should be doing, and many of those goals can be achieved in
one program. What could you possibly take out of that mandate
and yet still retain a Canadian public broadcasting service? All
those things are essential to reflecting the complexity of this very
complex country.

THE MANDATE OF THE 1960s

Ivan Fecan has a different but parallel interpretation of "mandate
work." It is that the CBC itself should produce or commission from
independent producers a kind of program that no private station or
network would touch. The implicit parameters for this definition
seemed in 1989–92 to be that most of the programs were not too
commercial or too controversial in content, not too innovative in
format or perhaps too distinctively Canadian in focus. In 1992–94
formal innovation and adult content returned to some degree with the
10–12 PM slot created by repositioning. Fecan put it this way in 1989:

FECAN: My point is that these shows are not starting out to get
enormous audiences, but they are going to serve a core audience
that no one else will serve in this country. We are doing them for
core audience reasons, for counter-programming reasons, for
positioning reasons, and because somebody has got to do it.
MJM: What they used to call "mandate work"?
FECAN: Yes, but the thing is that we have slipped on so much of
our mandate, for money reasons largely, that I don't know it is
"mandate work" anymore. I am actually choosing to do it. That is
what I am saying. Nobody is telling me to do it. I am actually
choosing to do these kinds of programs because I think it makes
sense for us to do it.
    A lot of people, for whatever reasons, think that I am typically
very commercial. When I want to be very commercial I certainly
can be. I don't think I sell anything short in the process of being
commercial. I don't think reaching an audience is negative or bad.
I think that's the business we're in. But what they forget is that *I
Am a Hotel* [1984, a wonderfully poetic film fantasy based on the
songs of Leonard Cohen starring Cohen as singer/narrator and
protagonist] is a show I brought to the CBC. I did *The King of
Friday Night* [also 1984, the highly stylized, innovative version of
John Gray's stage hit *Rock and Roll*]. What they forget is that I was
involved in the Robin Phillips thing [a TV adaptation of John Mur-

rell's *Waiting for the Parade*]. What they forget is that I do two kinds of shows, shows that get audiences and shows that are good for art and meet other kinds of standards.

As vice-president in charge of entertainment program development at Baton, Fecan "seems poised to take over the in-house entertainment production mandate that CBC TV is apparently ready to abandon."[26] Co-productions and Baton-originated productions "all ... expected to be sold to American and other foreign broadcasters" include *The Silken Laumann Story*; *Wild Geese*; a six-part adaptation of Robertson Davies's *What's Bred in the Bone*; the Rick Hansen story; and *Proof Positive*. The writers include Suzette Couture, Anna Sandor, Nancy Isaac, and George Jonas. Two co-produced movies with American subjects are already sold.

CRTC regulations require a certain amount of Canadian content on prime time. Nevertheless, Fecan is quoted as saying, "We're not developing these programs out of obligation, but out of a desire to keep building a genuinely Canadian TV repertoire."

ETHOS ERODED BY CORPORATE AMNESIA

The ethos whose shape is detectable in many of the interviews in this book has been under pressure from successive government inquiries and commissions, budget cuts, and CTV and CAB sniping. But it is truly threatened, truly eroded most by corporate amnesia. Producer Herb Roland retired shortly after he pointed out to me a few of the consequences of the corporate "forgettery":

ROLAND [1989]: They did the pilots for the three new sitcoms nearly a year ago and they brought in a Hollywood director. Because they brought this guy in from the States, every freelancer refused to work for the CBC unless they had already signed their contract. Management thought that nobody here knew how to work four cameras.

MJM: I know an actor who has recently returned to Toronto. Her sense is that nobody has ever heard of her and nobody will give her any job to do, ever again. The fact that she has been an experienced television actress in a well-loved series, made a name, and so forth, is lost.

ROLAND: Tell me about it. You only have to go through the lobby of 790 Bay, where the Drama Department is located, to see people who are well established and who nobody knows. They are sitting there, they are auditioning, and nobody knows them.

Producer Sam Levene has not forgotten the CBC traditions.

MJM: There is a generation that is completely unaware of what the CBC did before they themselves walked in the doors. I observe that there is very little sense of tradition or building on a past right now.

LEVENE [1988]: I agree. I don't think anybody remembers what we did before. I don't think anybody really cares, because there has been a generational change in the network leadership. The heads of network themselves don't know what we did twenty years ago. They couldn't care less about it. Therefore, nobody is around to encourage us to have tradition, to remember what we did. At this point I can hardly remember *For the Record*, much less *The Open Grave*.

Levene also defined several aspects of the ethos past and present.

LEVENE: I guess *For the Record* was mandate programming in the best sense of the word. It was done not grudgingly, but with the strong feeling that "We are the CBC, and if we don't do it, nobody will, and we should be doing it!" You have got to be careful when you start remembering. But I used to think that there was a sense of history down here, when I came to the CBC. When I started to produce documentary, the first generation of the television people were still active.[27] When you worked with them you knew what they had done. There is stuff you write about in *Turn Up the Contrast* that I haven't seen, but I know about it. I did see *The Open Grave*. A lot of the things I didn't see, but I somehow feel as if I know them. So, in a certain sense, it is part of my consciousness and part of my tradition.

Television deals with the here and now. Television network executives are under pressure to get audiences. This year's programs will either make it or they'll be dead. Next year they don't want to remember any dead program from this year. That is the business, and it has always been that way in the States, and it is increasingly that way in Canada.

Sam Levene, who began with *This Hour Has Seven Days*, is now producing for various programs including *Man Alive*, one of the very few programs free of commercials. It was twenty-five years old in February 1992, unique in its focus in human ethics and religion, and is sold all over the world. Pure "mandate work," I'd call it, and one of the places where the CBC ethos is still alive, behind as well as in front of the camera.

Sam Levene and the producers on *For the Record* often approached their topical dramas with both passion for the issues and great care for the lives affected by those issues. This combination of producers' and writers' ethos is part of a tradition stretching back to the beginning. I tried to verify my sense of the ethos and tradition of the CBC in the 1960s as contrasted to the early 1980s with Hugh Gauntlett, who was a decision-maker rather than a maker.

GAUNTLETT: Your description of the internal culture of the Drama Department in those two periods is absolutely true. It is connected with the other question we were talking about – the fact that people functioned as producer/directors. There were in effect three drama departments: specials, electronic, film. But each of those groups had a kind of internal cohesion, given the fact that everybody was on staff, or on a continuing contract relationship and very rarely worked anywhere else. Freelances didn't come in and out very much, although Paul Almond, Mario Prizek, and later Eric Till worked freelance. Many of them were forced to work together. On *GM Presents* perhaps four or five people would produce twenty or thirty hour-long programs in the course of a year, whereas now *For the Record* has one executive producer with perhaps a couple of producers who are involved in managing the individual episodes, and in come several freelance directors. There isn't even a *For the Record* unit with any cohesion, yet it is an exactly similar kind of operation – although *For the Record* costs more than *GM Presents* did.

Up to the mid-1960s, everybody who worked here was quite clear as to *why*. There was nowhere else to work. They were all engaged in this common enterprise. Although there were, naturally, personal jealousies and all those things, the people working in TV drama were subordinated to a larger unity, which I don't want to exaggerate or glamourize, but which existed. From the mid-1960s on, even in our part of the industry, people were coming and going to Hollywood, freelancing. The CBC itself was more confused about its role. It's the fruit, I suppose, of the 1968 Broadcasting Act. *The Seven Days* crisis was also a critical event in the middle of that.

MJM: People do tend to put a finger on that.

GAUNTLETT: It was a huge turning-point, not that it caused anything, but it neatly symbolized the state of the corporation at that time.

MJM: It seems to have changed people's perception of television.

GAUNTLETT: Exactly. When you look at that crisis in the political way, there were very few people involved who were part of that long-standing CBC ethos. They were all perfect examples of people who had come in from hither and yon, enormously skilled, all very keen on the idea of public broadcasting – but dyed-in-wool CBC?

And yet *Seven Days* did use several people who had roots at the CBC. Mavor Moore wrote some of the lyrics for the satirical songs that were a popular feature of *Seven Days*. Patrick Watson was a freelancer for the CBC. Richard Leiterman, who came from *Close-up*, was also a freelancer who "argued that both the dictates of journalism and the bias of television made outmoded 'the old myths of objectivity' and 'studious neutrality' still enshrined in CBC live." Others like Donald Brittain, Allan King, and Daryl Duke wrote for the *Document* series and then went on to do interesting CBC television drama.[28] Myths live on. Yet CBC ethos in the years 1952-68 was not simply a myth, nor was the burst of energy following the appointment of John Hirsch.

Hugh Gauntlett, two years later, again reminisced on the changing ethos of the 1980s.

GAUNTLETT [1985]: John Kennedy is probably the most sane, humane, likable, decent head of drama the place has ever had. And yet, there is no doubt that he presides over the most fractured department, simply because the whole structure of program planning, production, and telecasting forces it to be fractured. And there is no payoff for him in trying to transcend that. He is presiding over a shifting pool of people who come in and out, some of whom are there permanently, more of whom are there quasi-permanently. Half of them just come and go.

I think it would be wrong to see John as the nice guy who is the passive servant of the system. That is not so at all. He is a nationalist; he responds to a set of circumstances; and he has a sense of personal limitations. Even if he thought it was right for the CBC to be doing obscure, Hungarian playwrights, he would not get himself in that position. What I am suggesting is that for him to survive as a head of drama, he has got to do the kind of drama he does because that is what he can do [usually a contemporary original script or rarely an adaptation of an original Canadian play].

MJM: I see your point.

GAUNTLETT: We can't have self-indulgence unless we have a critical mass. Once we get the critical mass, we can start to play games. Yet it is obvious to me that we'll never get the critical mass. The latest version of getting the critical mass via co-productions on the outside is an even bigger fantasy than the Hirsch fantasy, which proclaimed that Hirsch could "double our internal production in the next five years." The critical mass is in fact what we already have. That's what produces a drama department that is rather conservative and tenacious.

MJM: Conservative and tenacious are two very good words for it because there is a sense of not giving up, but not taking many risks.

GAUNTLETT: Not taking many risks, absolutely.

MJM: I see fewer risks in 1985 than I did four years ago.

GAUNTLETT: You may be right, simply because the general pressure on the time and money gets more and more acute. I am the guy who hired John Kennedy over a lunch in Quebec City to do this for two years, to stabilize things after the creative fury created by Hirsch. Five years is a long time to do one of those jobs, because they are extremely taxing. [In fact, John Kennedy was head of drama for nearly ten years before becoming head of arts and sciences for two years and then retiring as regional director of the Western Region.]

THE FRENCH, THE ENGLISH, AND THE ETHOS

Corporate ethos was at stake in 1959 when the francophone producers in Montreal were engaged in a long and bitter strike that divided the English producers (who did not join their brothers in the strike) and the French producers on the picket lines. The strike politicized the Radio-Canada personnel (particularly René Lévesque) in ways that foreshadowed the separatist ferment to come. The ensuing bitter division may also have contributed to the deepening of the two solitudes of French and English drama. After the cancellation of *Les Plouffes*, there was never again a consistent, coherent attempt on a regular basis to show one culture to the other in series, serials, sitcoms, téléromans, or the other forms of popular television that both the CBC and Radio-Canada were developing. I use the plural form of the verb, since in many ways the two "sub" groups functioned independently, more and more so as the Quiet Revolution took hold. To cite just one example, more than two decades have passed since the October Crisis, one of the most dramatic moments in our history. No anglophone writer or producer in television drama has ever tackled that subject. This reverberating silence of ours on the tensions between Quebec and the rest of Canada means we have not been given a chance to assimilate through our imaginations the facts and the myths that have brought us to where we stand in the 1990s.

Symptomatic of the changes within the corporation and in the country at large is the fact that the mandate, as phrased in 1968, promoted national unity. The CBC was to "contribute to the development of national unity and provide for a continuing expression of Canadian identity" (2, g, iv; The Broadcasting Act, 7 March 1968). In 1991 the new Broadcast Act substituted for that sentence the phrase "to contribute to shared national consciousness and identity" (Bill C 40, 3 m. vi, Feb. 1991). Yet in both cases the notion that the two cultures should communicate using more than the headlines of *The National* and *Le Point* seems to be a fundamental component of the CBC ethos. Between crises, however, particularly in our fictions, the silence widens the gap. Yet as Trina McQueen pointed out, *He Shoots, He Scores* was shot in two languages. Sitcoms and soaps can help, but so would major drama specials written for English Canada on the rise and fall of René Lévesque, or a francophone family split between Saskatchewan and Quebec or between the Reform Party and the Parti Québécois. *Urban Angel*, a series set in a Montreal newspaper in 1990 and 1991, managed to be completely apolitical. In the fall of 1992 it was replaced by a dubbed version of the hit Téléroman *Les Filles du Caleb*, retitled *Émilie*, a period piece set in Quebec seventy-five years ago. In 1993–94 *Scoop*, another resounding success, was dubbed and shown in English Canada at 10 PM. Its second season, reflecting its ratings, was broadcast at 11:30 PM. The CBC did better thirty years ago than it does now in this area.[29]

In the 1960s a few francophone scripts were translated and performed in English. In the mid-1970s Tremblay's *Les Belles Soeurs* was successfully produced in English. In the 1980s there was nothing. In 1991 Tremblay's *La Maison suspendue* was produced by Primedia for telecast by some independent stations as one of several television adaptations of English-Canadian theatrical productions. An adaptation of one of Carbone 14's Image Theatre Productions, *Le Dortoir*, appeared on *Adrienne Clarkson Presents*.

Dubbed or subtitled versions of some English mini-series have appeared on Radio-Canada, and a few of the French mini-series (*Laurier, Mills of Power, The Dream Begins, Shehaweh*, and *Duplessis*) have been broadcast on the CBC. According to Collins, however, "the English run of *Duplessis* omitted the last three episodes in which the negative elements of Quebec nationalism ... are made most explicit."[30]

MJM to TRINA McQUEEN [1988]: Something that's also missing is the translation into English of scripts that have worked on francophone television.

McQUEEN: Yes. I'd love to see *Dames des Coeurs* [a popular Radio-Canada téléroman].

MJM: I'm thinking of Dubé and a few others from the past who were prolific, and whose work *was* presented occasionally. But there isn't a sense of that now; *Laurier, The Mills of Power,* and *Duplessis* were dubbed into English, but where is the drama translated from French to English?

McQUEEN: Well, what's *He Shoots, He Scores?*

MJM: You don't want me to tell you.

McQUEEN: I happen to like it.

MJM: *He Shoots, He Scores* is entertaining, but there's so much macho "me big hockey star" going on, it turns me off. But that's largely a matter of taste. Yet I know that there weren't enough people in English Canada watching to keep the English production of it going for a third season.

McQUEEN: But this was a program that was shown in two languages.

MJM: I was thinking of serious TV films looking at relations between the two cultures. *Don't Forget: Je me souviens* (1980) was the last time when the CBC looked thoughtfully at this subject in drama. I was also wondering about programs that worked well simply because they were good television, but which we can't see because they were in the other language.

McQUEEN: I agree with you, but I have to come back to the fundamental fact about CBC drama, which is that there isn't very much of it and there are all sorts of goals, just as the mandate expresses. In order to serve the mandate, you have to have a large quantity of material. That is a starting point. Before you even think about quality or the variety, you have to have the number of hours, the people, the resources which will eventually translate into programs that people want to watch with which to express the mandate. But if you're trying to do it on seventy-six hours a year, that's a recipe for almost certain failure in every area.

We have come a long way since "the CRBC's insistence that programs produced then use both languages set off howls of protest against French 'polluting the air'" from across the country in the 1930s.[31] Indeed, looking for Canadian content for his adult prime slot, Veilleux increased significantly the amount of dubbed material from Radio-Canada. However, in the long walk up to the referendum on separatism, such efforts were seen not as contributing to national understanding but to further alienation.

The Quebec view of more recent CBC history was conveyed to the producers of the CBC by *La Presse* reporter Daniel Lemay, who wrote in "The Veilleux Years": "According to Mr. Veilleux, 'cross-cultural programming would give Canadians "the best of both worlds" ... [and] cooperation which would increase the "distinctive nature"' of the CBC's programming while reducing expenses." Lemay acknowledges that "since 1992, the CBC's stations have shared some 130 hours of drama: *Scoop, Shehaweh, Émilie, Blanche,* among others, have been translated into English, while francophones were able to see French versions of *Road to Avonlea, North of 60,* and *The Boys of St. Vincent.* The sharing also extends to TV news, sports and music." But, he concludes, with a Quebecker's viewpoint, "these internetwork, exchanges were designed more to support efforts to Canadianize the English network, which was in a bad way."

The increase in cross-cultural programming of the early 1990s also came about because of the CBC's effort to increase the number of prime-time hours that were Canadian in origin. Lemay does admit that there is one advantage of pooling resources with the English network: "The French networks, traditionally strong in 'big' news stories, have developed a capacity to react to breaking stories which they did not have," and he cites Oka and the Gulf War as examples.

Nevertheless, the perception in Quebec of the internetwork exchanges, according to Lemay, was that "twice as strong in terms of market, the French network could very well have survived without cross-culture. The concept has caused a good deal of concern among certain groups in Quebec favouring Quebec sovereignty who saw it as a subtle way of promoting Canadian unity."[32] Their message says we don't need it, and it may be a federalist plot. It is quite probable that anglophones may soon react to similar efforts in much the same way. Bridges are hard to build when there are armed check-points at either end.[33] If Quebec should separate, it probably would not affect English-language television as it is, at all.

TELEVISION GENRES AND ETHOS

The ethos of any large organization is, in part, organically rooted in the ability and vision of the people who work for it and their responses to outside pressures and, in part, defined by its history and its original goals. At the CBC, as everywhere else, the two often collide. This is made more visible by questions about typology – the genres of programs to be made; genres change, inflect, disappear. Periods of flux in drama series are usually followed by longer periods of predictable drama "formats." Story editor Alice Sinclair remembers.

SINCLAIR [1988]: What is obvious is that people like series and serials better than they like anthology. They like the familiar.

MJM: The Americans recognized that by 1960 and abandoned anthology. Some very good television can come out of single episodes of series and serials, but it's a different kind of television –

"long form." One of the reasons people don't like anthologies is because, on the whole, anthology demands that you pay attention to it.

SINCLAIR: And you have to pay attention to it right off the top.

MJM: You can't just listen to it while making cabbage rolls or fixing a lamp. You actually have to look at it.

SINCLAIR: Yes, you do. One of the reasons why I enjoy commercial drama is that during a commercial you can get up and get yourself another drink or you can go to the bathroom or you can put the dogs out. If there are going to be distractions, you can often channel them into the commercials.

GAUNTLETT [1985]: In the 1960s, arts and sciences were part of the Public Affairs Department, which did two things essentially. It dealt with current controversy, what we now call "current affairs," and it was also adult education. It had a whole subdivision called, in the early 1960s, "adult education." They would do Canadian history using Jack Saywell or another historian.

MJM: There was some drama in those programs [Horizon, for example]. Drama popped up in the stangest places. But there were also many small documentaries on artists and musicians.

GAUNTLETT: That's right. Public affairs did pure drama as a matter of policy, once a year or thereabouts, usually by Allan King. Allan King's dramatic flair was nourished by public affairs. It was curious, because he was always the kind of documentarian who appeared to be manipulating things, so he was always merging towards fiction. He did a couple of very strange pieces of fantasy on film as public affairs specials, long before he ever did what you call a straight drama.

MJM: Yes, he came very close to "straight drama" with something called "Dreams" [for Q for Quest in 1962]. It was a fictional film based on a crisis in these people's real lives, but people played themselves. Still, they had lines to say; it was not improvised. It was very much betwixt and between documentary and drama.

In the 1980s and 1990s, drama, as a way of getting at a point of view or recreating something the cameras missed, is still used by news and current affairs on rare occasions – always with a clear statement preceding it and often with an element of stylization that distinguishes the recreation from "news footage." Otherwise, the walls between drama and news and current affairs seem impenetrable. When they are momentarily breached, dismay and confused thinking among audiences and critics can result, as in the responses to The Valour and the Horror. In that case, some viewers who were used to fact and fiction carefully separated into different genres did not pick up on cues for fictional flashbacks, such as a ruined airstrip or a broken control tower cross-faded into an airstrip full of planes and a tower with windows intact. "Real" pilots in the film wore blazers and were in their sixties. The boys in uniform, recreated or fictional characters, were around twenty. Whatever long-term judgments are made about the films' thesis – and the controversy continues, then chairman Patrick Watson and CBC ombudsman Bill Morgan notwith-standing – the dramatized segments were clearly distinguished from the documentary sequences.[34]

FROM "HIGH" CULTURE TO SOAPS

By the 1980s arts and sciences, now a separate department, was another haven for the occasional experiment or the documentary flavoured with dramatization, but it was in sharp decline. Under Hugh Gauntlett and then John Kennedy, arts and science made something of a comeback in the late 1980s, and then took a different direction under Ivan Fecan when he took over from Jack Craine.

MJM: You said you were going to build up arts and science pro-gramming.

FECAN: One of the things I feel I've been able to achieve is the first prime-time, year-round, arts magazine show ever, starting six months from now. That is something we have been trying to do for twenty or thirty years. Over two seasons of on-air development, we were able to get the *Adrienne Clarkson Show* to the point where we were comfortable to take the next jump. It's amazing because, in one fell swoop, we will have an extraordinary amount of arts, documentary, and performance on the air. We're generating a lot of material, not necessarily "in-house" again. If you see yourself primarily as a drama producer or a variety producer and you're in development for a movie or series, development can last a long time. You're going to want to do things just to keep your hand in. One of the things that our producers are finding is that they are able to do a small documentary for Adrienne Clarkson. It has also turned into a wonderful thing for us because we are using a high standard of professionalism. We are using it in a different way. Also, there are lots of opportunities for independent producers to produce specific things for that show. I'm really proud of that.

MJM: You are describing an "arts magazine" in effect.

FECAN: It will be an hour long and each week there will be a small arts/newscast. There will be a main feature, probably forty minutes in length, and there will be a short subject. So it will not be a traditional magazine in the sense of a minimum of fifteen stories.

The one-and-a-half to three-hour show on Sunday afternoons ran throughout the fall and winter seasons when not pre-empted by sports. It was cancelled for 1995–96. Although it was not carried by all CBC affiliates, it strongly reminded me of a combination of *Q for Quest*, *Festival*, and *Take 30* in the early 1960s. It was a welcome return of "arts" to the mix. The differences were primarily due to advances in technology. Nevertheless, the fact is that straight drama has no home. The other arts appeared in excerpts there as well as on *Adrienne Clarkson Presents*. The profiles of artists and craftsmen, musicians, architects and dancers, and glimpses of their work are welcome. What we do not see is full length works of music, dance, or drama.

Specifically, there has been no effort to adapt to a studio environment Canadian plays at the cutting edge – those of George Walker, Morris Panych, Judith Thompson – or main stage hits by writers like Anne Chislett or David French. As a matter of economics, electronic studio drama is still cheaper than film. On the basis of both the economics of television and the mandate, it's a notable absence. Our theatre is where we talk to ourselves. But the symbiosis of theatre and television found on the BBC or on PBS is missing (and missed) on the CBC.

Soaps are a long way from opera, ballet, and poetry, but they also have their place in a broadcasting mix intended to serve a wide public. Global and overseas partners did co-produce a hundred episodes of *Foreign Affair*, an "international" soap that I find difficult even to sample, and CTV tried a half-hour soap in 1994 (exotic cars manufactured by exotic men who love and betray their exotic women), a co-production called *Family Passions*. There has never been a CBC-originated soap for the national network.[35]

FECAN: I'd love to do a soap. I just don't know how to pay for it, that's my problem.
MJM: Because of the startup costs and the fact that they're so slow to gain audiences?
FECAN: The startup cost is not the problem. It is the cost of doing it every day and having the quality and variety involved in it, so it isn't thin. By nature, soap operas have to be competitive. Particularly in daytime television, people don't sit down to watch; they watch as a secondary activity. They don't necessarily watch every day, but they tend to be drawn to the set when something happens that they are interested in. So, by nature, there's a repetitive qual-

ity to the structure of the soap. The costs are such that the only way we could think of doing one is to partner with an American, and we're not interested in doing that because it would make the program into something we don't want to do.

MJM: So it could be a long-range milk-cow for the CBC, but you can't get it started.

FECAN: It would be not only a long-range milk-cow, but it would mean long-range development for writers and actors.

The subcommittee on drama in 1987 looked at serials (the soaps are listed as serials in TV guides), the family hour, mysteries, mini-series, and specials. Their rationale for each form is fascinating.

The serial should be the primary development vehicle for young writers. The serial will serve as an excellent development ground for directors, assistant directors and all other roles in drama production. The dynamics of any department are improved when there is a floor where the lights are on late and expedience rules. It's invigorating, particularly in an environment when the gap between conception to execution can be two years. Mistakes are more easily retreated from and the costs are low. Consistent characters, same central set, controlled environment, tape production, allow laying off the costs over a long period. Once the core set and production team are in place, a sense of team emerges; energy is not constantly expended assembling new units. Familiarity masks a lot of inadequacies. Fine tuning is possible more in a serial than in any other drama form.

...

Various studies have shown that contrary to what one would expect, television is a relatively group medium. Families will, given the appropriate programming opportunity, watch a program as a group, something that is scarce in radio, and impossible with any form of reading (except children's stories). Television is not per se an individual medium. This is critical when formulating our strategy for the living rooms of the country.

When is the last time we remember looking forward to gathering around the TV set, in a family, to watch a regular program together? We should design a stream of production which aims precisely at this objective. In effect, we propose a Canadian "Disney." This would eventually be a series of 22 episodes, with very high production values, rich exteriors, and a current of adventure and quest and triumph. We will eschew endings in which the main character commits suicide, develops cancer, or copes with Alzheimer's. We are in the myth building business here, and our tales should be heroic, triumph over adversity, full of adventure. Here, unlike the hour-long series, we could indulge also in nostalgia, childhood past, adolescence. The highest rated programs in recent memory have included such settings – *Chautauqua*

Girl, Anne of Green Gables, My American Cousin, Hockey Night. A sense that everything is still possible.

Finally, a note about audience strategy and the Nineties. We believe that "family" themes will be a central strategy to adopt for the upcoming decade. The society is increasingly urbanizing, and family units are scattered. The yearning for family values, and a sense of place, a sense of things being possible for a generation which is worried if it will ever have a job, or ever own a house, or, since both partners work, if they will ever be able to have more than one kid. These will be dominant themes of the next decade. Let's plan to deal with the themes of tomorrow, and address the audience's needs.[36]

Sorting out what kinds of programs to produce and producing them is one of the most important indicators of a CBC ethos. A less vital but oddly revealing one is the way CBC drama presents itself. Self-promotion has been very spotty over the years, although the question of whether Dillon and Carrie would marry (*Street Legal*, fall 1991) confronted people all over Toronto from billboards to bus shelters as well as on rival television stations and stations. It suggests a pride and confidence too often lacking in the past among the makers as much as the decision-makers. Unlike Radio-Canada, the CBC has not been particularly good at self-promotion until very recently. Francophone culture in Quebec enjoys having audiences for a range of artists, from known pop stars to serious novelists and playwrights. In Quebec's culture these people are on talk shows, in tabloids, and even on page one of the newspapers. *Il Lance, Il Compte* was featured on mugs, posters, and T-shirts. The diverse but familiar world of Quebec "culture" is much more a part of everyone's ambiance. Fecan sees the connection between this atmosphere (or the less-integrated but powerfully popular culture of the United States and Britain) as necessary to the growth and celebration of what we do in English Canada.

FECAN: We are also developing an entertainment magazine show. Again it is part of the overall strategy. I'm very concerned that in this country the only stars that exist are politicians, bureaucrats, sports figures, and businessmen, and now a new mythology of business stars.

MJM: And the CBC has played right into that, with *Venture* among other programs.

FECAN: When you think of it, it makes sense because many of the major journalistic publications in the country have a lot of business coverage, cover Ottawa in a big way, cover local politics in a big way, and have very big sports sections. Our own journalistic organizations bend over backwards so as not to appear to give bias or precedence to any CBC production or any independent production on the CBC. Therefore you are more likely to find a review of a show being done for another network, or coverage of an American star, than you will with Kate Nelligan when she does *Love and Hate*. So it became clear to me that it is necessary to introduce a non-journalistic entertainment magazine show that is basically there to build stars and to build name recognition.[37]

That magazine did not appear. But "events" like the special on the Dionne quints, *Million Dollar Babies*, do find their way onto *Midday*, *Morningside*, and other CBC radio and television magazine shows. Perhaps more important is the fact that the CBC buys advertisements on privately owned stations in large markets.

CENSORSHIP AND ETHOS

One of the primary questions raised by an attempt to define a CBC ethos is censorship. Visible attempts at censorship often create hostility or laughter rather than happy audiences, a lesson never fully learned by large organizations of any kind.

MJM to ALLEN: The *Festival* series, in particular, took up radio's function of pushing certain subject matter into the more acceptable range – that is, pushing the boundaries of censorship back inch by inch as time went on.

ALLEN: That was intentional.

MJM: It seemed to me that in your schedule there was a judicious mix of something that might stir things up and then something that would be less of a problem. Was there ever anything ready for production that was shelved specifically because it was too controversial?

ALLEN: Of course. We had an absolutely fabulous production of Anouilh's *Point of Departure*, which Paul Almond directed with William Shatner – a Rudy Dorn set – it was gorgeous.[38]

MJM: Yes, I have seen it.

ALLEN: It finally went on the air at 11:30 at night. I don't remember why now. I don't remember anything about it that would seem questionable.

MJM: They were lovers in bed together and they weren't married! And it was 1960!

ALLEN: A few years later the decision was made to cancel Mario Prizek's opening episode of *Eyeopener* on the afternoon of the day it was being transmitted. I remember people saying at a meeting:

"Well, what have we got to broadcast in it's place?" It turned out that we had a BBC production of a dance program about Isadora Duncan. I hadn't seen this and I don't know who had seen it. But when it came on, it turned out that most of the dancers were bare-breasted! I sat there that night when it went on the air wondering what had gone on at that meeting!

Mario Prizek's memories of struggles with censorship in the 1960s were still vivid in 1983.

PRIZEK: I was executive producer of a series called *Eyeopener* in 1965 as well as producer-director of some of the shows within the series. Before all this happened I had given a full report to an earlier group of CBC brass about the series, in terms of what the series was going to do, the audience it was trying to reach, and individual items within the series. As I got each item developed, with authors and researchers and so on, I sent all this stuff to the "Kremlin." But just as I finished taping and editing the last show and the first show was to go on the air, the old administrators were thrown out, and a new bunch came in. The first thing they did was to view each of the shows that were already in the can, approved by the first bunch. I said: "Gentlemen, I cannot predict the vagaries of the CBC when I'm planning far enough ahead to do a thirteen-week series."

The first program scheduled to go on the air was one of the shows I had directed. That night I returned to my office to pick up some papers before going home to watch the program on the air. I bumped into one of our publicity people coming out of the office building, which was then on Yonge Street. He said, "Mario, what are you substituting for the *Eyeopener* tonight?" I replied, "What do you mean, 'substituting'? It's scheduled to go on the air." "Oh no, it's been banned." I got to the phone to the Kremlin [1290 Bay, where the directors and vice-president then were] and raised absolute hell. I demanded an immediate meeting. I said, "Do you realize what you've done? This is right on top of the nationwide scandal you've had with *This Hour Has Seven Days*!" The papers were eager to get anything else they could on the CBC. I said, "As you know, the series is almost all in the can. All publicity has gone out to the press and when they don't see the program on the air tonight, what do you think they're going to do? They're going to say, "Why?" And even if I don't tell them, they'll find out that you banned it and then you've made fools of yourselves and the whole corporation."

The first program was called *A Borderline Case* with the early Second City troupe [their successors developed the sharply satirical television hit of the early 1980s *SCTV*]. This was before separatism was being talked about except among the very young Québécois. I got wind of it and I thought it would make an interesting satirical review. We improvised it as a mock-documentary report, conjecturing that French Canada had already separated from English Canada, called itself "Laurentia," and had a seat in the United Nations. The skit started in the United Nations with a great uproar going on between the Big Powers, each accusing the other of having made a new nuclear test. In a quiet moment, the member from Laurentia stands up and says: "We did it." Then all hell breaks loose. We copied the *Doctor Strangelove* set in Studio 7. There's a scene where a bilingual reporter stands with one foot in Hull and one foot in Ottawa, talking to the audience of potential violent confrontation between Laurentia and English Canada. The CBC brass regarded this as dangerous political propaganda and they banned it.

As a result, I resigned for seven years as executive producer from the CBC. I still directed shows for them and I said, "I'll complete all the projects I have in-house," but I also said, "I don't want anything more to do with the League of Frightened Men."

I talked to Hugh Gauntlett about the *Eyeopener* case because he, too, was involved.

GAUNTLETT [1983]: I was partly the cause of the dustup! The *Second City Review* had satirized the queen. The program had been screened in the old Kremlin and it was decided we would not put it on. Bob Allen, who was head of the department, was part of this decision. I was assistant program director, and I was told to inform Mario Prizek, who was the producer. He was at Sumac Street, where the props, costumes, and sets are made, and I didn't get to him. He was walking home, past the building where our PR people work, and one of them walked out and said, "Say, Mario, what do you say about them killing your show?" The next thing we had was union grievances and all that stuff. Now we have what is known as Prizek's law: "You must not screen a producer's program without him being present," which on the whole is a sensible rule.

As writer/adapter Hugh Webster recalls, Eric Till also ran into pressure from the CBC management.

WEBSTER [1984]: In the case of *Offshore Island*, Michael Sadlier refused to okay the script because of its implication that, with only four people surviving a nuclear holocaust, there must inevitably be incest.[39] But it was clear in Marghanita Laski's script, in a conversation between the brother and the sister. The sister wanted to have a child, and the only person she could have a child by was her brother. The brother was at his wit's end because of the guilt. He didn't quite know how to handle it, but he really wanted to lay the sister too because the biological impulse was there. "Nix on that," says Sadlier. Then Eric Till got in touch with Laski and she said, without the incest, which is an integral part of the play, there's no point in doing it. She wouldn't let us do it without it. So Eric and I were faced with how to do it. We knew it was a blockbuster of a piece. Then I got an idea. Why don't we have the two men, the older man and the brother, discuss it using the pig as a means of getting it across. The older man points to the pig and he says, "You see, it doesn't make any difference to her if it's one of her sons or anything."[40] That scene was sent to Laski and she okayed it. That's how it got on the air. It wasn't an idea that came flick like that. I had wrestled with it for a long time.

The drama was way over in time. It was overwritten because we didn't have the time to work on the script in the fall and make our cuts, as we should have done. I remember Irene Worth, the star of the piece, was absolutely incensed at the fact that it was overwritten. She said, "Oh, you did the adaptation? You should write it to time," and she did the "grand lady of the theatre" routine on me. I said, "Miss Worth, you are lucky it's on at all." And it's true, because if we hadn't found a way out of the incest dilemma that show would never have gone on the air.

Other instances of censorship in the mid-1960s included refusals to air Ron Kelly's drama for *Explorations* on teenage violence, "Cuba Si" for *Intertel*, a *Closeup* on McCarthyism, and "City of Night" for *Q for Quest*.[41] The CBC did, however, air "Ciaou Maria" on *Camera Canada* over the protests of the Italian community.

Censorship is still with us in the 1990s. Alice Sinclair and I talked about viewers' attitudes to television characters.

SINCLAIR [1988]: Part of the fun of *Barney Miller* is getting to know the characters, so they should act in character every time.
MJM: They are perceived by the audience as friends who have dropped in.
SINCLAIR: Yes, that is such a strong thing. "How dare you pipe

this filth into my living room." That became a cliché among us for an objecting letter, followed by, "Why don't you go back to where you came from?" There is no question that people do regard a television program as something like a friend they have invited into the living-room, and if the friend is offensive they don't like it. Just last week we were discussing whether we could use the word "arsehole," and we decided to leave it in and see whether it got pulled out. Although I'm making fun of this imaginary letter of offense, there's no question that you do watch those things differently at home.

MJM to actor R.H. THOMSON [1989]: With the 1970s adaptation of *Of fhe Fields Lately*, there was some censorship of the language from the theatre to the television camera. I remember looking at it with the play in my lap and seeing the softening of the language, phrase by phrase.

THOMSON: That's always been the case. I did a little film in Vancouver last fall [*The First Season*, broadcast after theatrical release on the CBC in 1990]. We'd just done some looping for it and for lines like "That's the first fucking thing I tried." I did three versions; "That's the first f'ing thing I tried," "That's the first freaking thing that I tried," and "That's the first friggin' thing that I tried." I thought, "Does the CBC not want 'fucking thing that I tried'"? and the editor said, "It depends who's getting it, it depends on the mood at the moment." Sometimes they will let that stuff go by and other times they want "friggin."

MJM: And yet they've shown the Bob White documentary [where expletives pepper nearly every scene].

THOMSON: It wasn't thicker language than *Tyler*.[42] That's never been rerun.

MJM: Has it not been repeated at all?

THOMSON: Whether because of language or not, I don't know. It went to PBS, though, because some friends said they saw it in Boston.

The most insidious form of censorship is self-censorship, and that can happen to any actor, writer, director, or producer, and to any decision-maker in management.

MJM to producer MARYKE McEWEN [1984]: You have been working in the Drama Department, in the territory that is least likely to be self-censored.

McEWEN: I've never felt censored by ... well, yes I have. There are times when "the powers that be" get nervous. It's not that one hasn't done a show, or at least that I haven't, because of that, but ...

MJM: What do they do, send vibes down to you that the subject is a bit dicey?

McEWEN: After *Tar Sands*, you know if you do anything with a politician you're probbly going to get into trouble.[43] It's bullshit censorship, really, because you can do anything you want to some poor guy on the street who doesn't have a voice in Ottawa. Since the politicians don't watch TV, the only time they ever notice is when somebody goes after them. I haven't felt it, really. But you do ask yourself, "Did you do that drama right?" I don't think you can sit there and say, "I'm God. I'm going to say what I like." You have to respect the audience.

MARTIN KINCH, producer [1984]: There is some degree of self-censorship. It's hard not to realize that you are making a show for a certain kind of slot. You want people to see it and you want to make your point, whatever that may be. Therefore, you tend to be self-censoring. That is a mistake, given that your ideas are not completely aberrant.

I also think that self-censorship affects writers. Writers will come in to me quite often, handing me stuff that is half as good or interesting or powerful as what they can write. It has to do with what they believe is possible within the CBC. You have to kick people and say, "I'm not interested in this stuff." I don't know how other producers feel about that. I'm just aware that this kind of impulse simply leads to bland. I've gone through this in theatre. There are two ways of getting people into the theatre. One is to do really extraordinary work, which as an artist and a human being you can do only in certain conditions and in a certain amount of time. The other is to do work that is as bland as you can possibly make it. And you'll probably get the same size of audience, though not the same audience.

Ivan Fecan said to Andrew Borkowski, editor of *SCAN* in 1993: "I wanted programs to be more focused as to whether they were popular or alternative. I was disturbed by what I saw as a lack of clarity of purpose in some cases. If we were going to do a *Street Legal* I felt it should be popular. On the other hand, if a program was going to be alternative – like *Adrienne Clarkson Presents* or *Codco* – it shouldn't try to be popular."[44]

All very well, but both of those cited were not carried by the affiliates, so their reach was limited to CBC-owned and -operated stations. Nevertheless, in a few memorable instances, *Love and Hate, Conspir-*

acy of Silence, Liar, Liar, and in programs co-produced with the NFB and independent companies, such as *Justice Denied, The Valour and the Horror,* and *The Boys of St Vincent,* the CBC has recovered some of its bite, its relevance.

Finally, let us hear from Fecan's successor, director of entertainment Phyllis Platt talking to Jeannine Locke.[45] When asked if her style of management would continue what Locke called "management-driven programming," Platt replied that although she learned a great deal from Fecan, "I probably give [producers] more time than Ivan did to make their decisions as to what to recommend for development ... We hold two major retreats a year in which my management group discusses a very wide range of things within which there is always a significant element of philosophical debate." When asked about the increase in numbers and kinds of program no longer guaranteed full network exposure, Platt cited the lateness of the decision to drop the repositioning strategy and ongoing concerns about revenue to explain the situation for 1994-95. She does seem to recognize that programming for the thoughtful adult viewer should be part of the ethos of the CBC. She cites *The Boys of St Vincent* and *Conspiracy of Silence* as "seminal event programming ... that illuminates who we are as a people, but I don't think we do enough. And I don't think we do it in a form that has enough impact ... I'd like to examine a limited series form that allows us not to jam a story into a two-hour format or a one-hour format or into a 13-week or a 26-week format. Obviously that represents a scheduling head-ache, but I'd like to experiment." "Experiment" implies a new concept, but that statement to me describes much of the programming of the 1950s and 1960s.[46] It also reminds me of John Kennedy's view that some subjects and genres that were given a limited number of hours would lose their quality and freshness if they were expanded to standard runs of thirteen or twenty-six weeks.

CULTURAL APPROPRIATION

Some readers are likely to have thought about the ethical problems of telling other people's stories, whether wholly fictional or based on fact, to millions of people here and abroad. So have producers at the CBC, long before the issue of cultural appropriation made it to the cultural agenda. For instance, in 1966 producer Philip Keatley was trying to tell the story of a culture clash between a coastal Native group and one from the interior without violating the sensibilities of the Spirit Dancers he and writer Paul St Pierre were portraying.

MJM: I noticed with a *Cariboo Country* episode called "All Indian" that you stated clearly (to the complete confusion of most people east of the Rockies, I'm sure) that these were not real dances owned by the Salish people. It must have been quite mystifying.

KEATLEY: Tough! The people who understood it got the formal notification. The people who didn't understand it thought it was strange. But that was the way to do that show. For a lot of drama we say, "The audience isn't really going to understand this," yet that is what drama is about.

That such issues are complex is evident from the fact that in February 1992, Canadian Press reported that an Aboriginal man who had been abducted by the Spirit Dancers at the request of his wife had then charged the secret society with assault. When Native and white cultures clash in the courts, many Aboriginal people are caught in the middle.

In an article in the *Canadian Journal of Law and Society,* I described the unorthodox procedures and outcome of a trial in *How to Break a Quarterhorse* (1967, writer Paul St Pierre and producer/director Philip Keatley).[47] One anonymous referee, a judge, commented that he/she was unfamiliar with the show, but "amazed to learn it was done in 1967 ... contemporary in style and content – extraordinary writing. Now in remote communities our white, justice system is struggling to replicate forms of traditional dispute resolution mechanisms." On 5 December 1994 the CBC returned to the subject with *Trial at Fortitude Bay,* a production considerably less complex in its characterization, dialogue, plot, and dénouement.

Treating Native cultures as if they were one monolithic structure is one of the worst mistakes much of dominant Canadian culture (French and English) has made over the years. The CBC record on the subject is mixed. It also appears to be a touchstone for culturally specific differences between anglophone and francophone television drama.[45]

Producer Don S. Williams faced similar ethical problems in the early 1980s with *Beachcombers.* By then the countrywide public discourse on the issue was becoming more complex.

WILLIAMS [1985]: I'm worried about authenticity, and it's very hard to find. Before I became executive producer of *Beachcombers*, while I was a director, I was painfully aware that there were a lot of "Indian" shows that lacked authenticity and there were strong upsets in the cast because they said a given scene wasn't true.

MJM: It wasn't true in feeling or in detail?

WILLIAMS: It was not true in that it was false information. They would say, "No, that's not the way our religion is."

MJM: What about "The Soul Catcher" episode, for example?

WILLIAMS: A little touchy.

MJM: Well, shamanism can be a touchy subject.

WILLIAMS: The thing that I've since learned is that I don't know if our sources are being truthful. Sometimes I think they are doing exactly what I would do if I were them – leading me on and you and everyone else, as often as possible, having great sport doing it.

For example, when I directed *Death of a Nobody* (1967) and *Horse for Running Buffalo*, I found that only slowly could I start to trust the information I was getting from Native people, because only slowly did they accept that I wasn't trying to bugger them around with the product I was doing, that I was trying to do it right. Through the ballet version for television of *The Ecstasy of Rita Joe* (1974) and other work, I got to the point where I had a pretty good relationship in the Manitoba Native community.

We've had trouble on *Beachcomber* scripts because the writers would promise me that they had properly researched a script, and then there would be reactions. Marianne Jones, who plays Laurel, Jesse's wife, has really devoted a lot of her energy over the past eight or nine years to Native concerns, in the sense of retrieving some of the old religion and some of the old culture. She is involved with Margo Kane, who played Salmon Woman in the "Salmon Woman" show.[49] Margo started a Native theatre company, *Spirit Song*, in Vancouver, and Marianne is one of the principle performers in it. They do pieces that they think are important for young Indian audiences.

So Marianne is both very conscious and conscientious. She'll say, "Don, I've got to talk to you," and I say, "What's wrong, Marianne?" "Well, it's not like that." And I say, "But Marianne, Barbara talked to one of the Native people at the UBC Museum of Anthropology. I got all the information from them and they told me that this is the way it is!" And she'd say, "Well, I'm afraid that it isn't." George Clutesi, who is from time to time on the series, says the same thing, but his attitude is, "Well, that's not right, but if you want to do it that way, then OK." He plays right along with it, but he makes sure he points out to you that it's not quite right. I have a lot of problems because I guess I have a conscience about it. I don't want to do the old storybook Indian. I don't want to do anything that's a white man's notion about how romantic the Indian culture is.

MJM: In *Beachcombers* this theme is a way of perceiving people's relationships to their environment, their past, and to each other – the sense of Native religion, cultural identity, and belief. What *Beachcombers* scripts offer are situations for which, to a rationalist, there must be a rational explanation. But the series repeatedly says "Maybe. But maybe not!" It presents Native spirituality and Native versions of what may have happened as "fact," without apology and without explanation. This approach seems to be a very authentic thing to do, and distinctive to the series.

WILLIAMS: If a mask is involved, I like it to be right, but that's not what worries me so much as the much more serious cultural statements.

MJM: And that's where the difficulty comes? People saying, "You are not telling the story the way we understand it?"

WILLIAMS: That's right, or "You got the wrong message" or "the wrong philosophy." My great problem is trying to open doors and not break this trust. I'm wrestling with it.

After Don Williams went on to other things in the late 1980s, *Beachcombers* virtually abandoned that motif, losing one of the series most distinctive, valuable, and topical elements. This is just one of the many kinds of ethical dilemmas that can face producers, directors, writers, actors, and senior management.

IN WHAT WAYS DOES THE CBC "ETHOS" INCLUDE WOMEN?

We all know that 52 per cent of Canada's population are women. It is also a commonplace of critics, on the rare occasions when the issue is recognized, that "screened women" are far less visible and too rarely heard when they do speak. And many of us know that change, though visible in the media, is too slow. Who is represented on the box is more fully addressed in the conclusion of *Turn Up the Contrast*. As a feminist, I will probably write some day about women as subject and object in CBC television drama, though I'll be delighted if someone else does it first. Meanwhile, the organization Toronto Women in Film and Television have documented what it is like to be a woman off-camera in *Changing Focus: The Future for Women in the Canadian Film and Television Industry*. In "Breaking the Frame," Margaret Visser says:

If women's traditional skills are what women are allowed and generally prefer to practise, for example, why are women so under-represented in television programming for children? Producers of films for children in English, funded by Telefilm – admittedly the overall sample is not large – are 76 per cent men and only 8 per cent women (the rest are a combination of men and women); directors, 77 per cent men and 23 per cent women; scriptwriters, 78 per cent men and 22 per cent women.

Men are even preponderantly represented as *performers* in what is created on the television screen as typically a child's world (55 per cent men, 41 per cent women, the rest unknown in English; 60 per cent men, 30 per cent women, 10 per cent unknown in French).[50]

There are women in the 1990s who have escaped the old shelter of the Children's Department while staying with drama, rather than going over to the more fertile ground of news and current affairs. They include Brenda Greenberg, executive producer of *Street Legal* and *Side Effects*, with previous experience in American soaps, and Katie Ford, who returned to Canada from her success with the American sitcom *Family Ties* to work on *Material World*. A careful search of the most recently available 1991–92 *Who's Who in Television* turns up a few names of women drama producers with CBC credits in the last decade – Nancy Shapelle, Louise Clark, Elsa Franklin, Vivienne Leebosh, Heather Marshall, Deepa Mehta Saltzman, Carole Moore-Ede – who also work as producers on independent productions that appear on CTV and Global, for example, *ENG*, *Sweating Bullets*, and *Bordertown*.

Cultural critic and labour historian Susan Crean, writing in *Changing Focus,* sketches the attempts at employment equity made in a formal way in the mid-1970s.

In 1975 , the CBC head office set up an office of equal opportunity (OEO) to ensure that corporate hiring practices were corrected to prevent further injustice. The OEO was very active in the first five years of its existence, but found all its efforts (policy, reviews, awareness seminars for women, "sensitization" sessions with managers and staff) had little impact. The results were so poor that the executive vice-president was persuaded to include an equal opportunity objective in his 1980 annual operating statement. Had this been implemented all hirings, transfers, and promotions would have had to take the goal of ending job segregation into account. But with the arrival of a new president, a change in government, and continuing rounds of budget cuts, it was soon forgotten. In any case, in 1983 a royal commission on employment equity was convened under Judge Rosalie Abella. Although Abella concluded, as the OEO had, that employment equity has to be mandatory, the Conservative government passed legislation in 1986 following the letter of her recommendation but rejecting her advice to accompany any program with

tough enforcement mechanisms. The law, in fact, does not require companies or crown corporations to enforce employment equity, only to have a
program and to report employment statistics to Ottawa annually. So the CBC
was relieved of the obligation to enforce its own policy or heed its own
experience, and the movement for reform was permanently stalled. In 1985
the OEO was closed and its director laid off."[51]

For this book, I asked an actor (Kate Trotter), a producer (Maryke
McEwen), and two successful women in the upper and middle
management of the corporation (Trina McQueen and Nada Harcourt)
to talk to me about being a woman in "the business." I asked each of
these four women what it was like to work for an organization that,
in upper management and in many technical areas, is more than
three-quarters male. Perhaps that fact, or the fear of change, produced
the legendary announcer's spoonerism, "This is the Canadian Broad-
corping Castration." This wry joke points directly to the overwhelmingly male ethos and corporate culture that has been the CBC for most
of its history. The statistics available in *Changing Focus* are quite
damning. The study also adds voices to the faceless numbers by
liberally quoting women from senior managers to grips and sound
editors, all of them anonymously. The same fears and frustrations
which kept those women anonymous mean that some of the verbatim
portions of the transcripts of my interviews, now deposited at the
National Archives, are not available to scholars until the year 2020.

MCQUEEN: I am responsible for the planning department, the
   group of people who puts together an operating plan for all departments of the CBC. I'm responsible for cost management – the
   budget of each program – the commercial sales department, the
   business affairs department ... basically the non-progamming side
   of CBC English television. It's a fascinating change for somebody
   who spent most of her life in programming.
      Something that is often quoted from the Fowler Report of the
   late 1950s is the statement: "The only thing that matters in broadcasting is program content. All the rest is housekeeping." I regard
   that as a male chauvinist statement because it is dismissive and
   contemptuous of the role of housekeeping. Since I've been in this
   job, I have seen how bad housekeeping can defeat the best of programmers. When you look at Canadian drama and the problems it
   has had (setting aside the successes, which have been enormous),
   the failures have often been not creative failures, not distribution
   failures, but housekeeping failures. In other words, the failure to
   provide an environment in which an activity could take place

smoothly, with continuity and with some kind of health, which is a rough definition of housekeeping.

To me, news and current affairs have always been a house that has been very well kept, and people who live inside that house have flourished and have been allowed to be creative. The other side of the CBC, through inattention or other preoccupations, has been a badly kept house, a house where objectives vary from year to year, where the furniture is always in different places, and where things don't work smoothly. I see that, when I look at the CBC by decades. The first, 1952–62, was the period in which people started, the era of the brilliant amateur, so to speak, when everybody was having a great time and stuff was getting on the air with almost no supervision. The decade 1962-72 was an era when people built: they built buildings all across the country and they built a management structure. Then 1972-82 was the decade of news and current affairs, and all the housekeeping, the resources, and the attention went into making sure that we had an excellent department, culminating in the introduction of *The National* and *The Journal* at 10 PM. During that time, the program director, Jack Craine, had an exhausting job to maintain and to extend drama. And he would fight for more drama. He used to say, "We are producing our facts and importing our fantasies, and that is not good for a country." But because of him the climate has changed and improved. I hope that 1985–95 will be the era of drama and that we will see the kind of attention, the kind of housekeeping that news and current affairs has had also given to drama.

TROTTER [1989]: There are a lot of very powerful male producers, and one can't waste a lot of time railing against them. You know why people can maintain power over actors? Ultimately, all actors who are worth their salt fear that they are not good actors. The minute someone looks at you sideways, you think, "Well, I am not good enough to be actually complaining." It's only directors of real talent who will let actors feel their own power. Directors who have not got a lot of talent will undermine you all the time. It is very easy to undermine an actor because you will believe that you are bad at the drop of a hat. That curious vulnerability always baffles me. I think this tendency is very female.

MJM: That feeling of vulnerability could be the result of a very hierarchial, very male-socialized way of thinking, couldn't it?

TROTTER: I was auditioning once. In walked an actor I knew and she had on the tightest, shortest, lowest cut, black dress I had ever seen! I thought, "What part could she be auditioning for? It can't be the part I'm auditioning for because that dress is dead wrong!"

Let me tell you she got the role. She said to me, "Kate, you got to get yourself a black dress!" She was laughing, but she was right in a way.[52] What do you do? Get the little black dress? Or try to hang on to your integrity and work at a deli counter? There are wonderful non-sexist directors and producers, but you are in trouble if you don't identify the ones who are chauvinistic and not so wonderful.

Listen to how the messages are mixed in the following conversation. Like many women I talked to for the record or off the record, Maryke McEwen began by saying "no problem" and then, as the conversation progressed the picture changed somewhat.

McEWEN: For me, personally, I have not had much problem being a woman in the CBC. That has less to do with the CBC itself than with working with the right people. It can hold you back in some ways when you run into male bosses who really do like you but who don't want you to get any further because they like you where you are. That happens in all kinds of business and it has happened to me a few times.

I also ran into problems with the CBC middle management, many years ago. I was applying for a staff, not a contract job. I found out later, from someone who was on the Board, that those guys really hated me because I was ambitious. They could feel it, even though I didn't say anything. I knew at that moment that there was no way I was ever going to get anywhere on staff at the CBC, and I quit. The minute I started freelancing everything was fine, more or less.[53]

I've probably been paid less than the guys, all the way through. I have no proof, but I can almost guarantee that one. It's very useful to have a woman who has risen from the ranks [in Maryke's case from production secretary to story editor, to associate producer, to producer and executive producer] and takes 10 per cent less every year, so you never do get ahead. Women work harder than men, and that's very good for the men they work for, so they're not going to hold you back.

I haven't really run into problems with the guys I work with. You have to handle it yourself. Having a woman's strengths are quite useful for producing. Being a mother is very useful training. That's what you are most of the time – a mother. I don't mind.

MJM: Mediating, comforting, sometimes manipulating and making the decisions without ...

McEWEN: ... the ego conflict. It's also much easier on the creative people. The guys like it, actually. They would just as soon give up these ego conflicts when they get a chance.

You still have control over them, but they don't feel they are being stifled and you get more out of them. Now I can fight on my own turf, by my own rules. I'm not easily threatened. It was hard on those ladies who preceded me [there were one or two in adult drama before 1980, notably Maxine Samuels who was the independent producer of *Seaway*, the early 1960s action series].
It's not so hard for me. It's not easy, but it's kind of funny sometimes. You get a sneaking pleasure when people say, "Is that really the producer?"

MJM: When everyone assumes that you are your own secretary.

McEWEN: Yes, it's great. The guys [the technicians] get pleasure out of it, too. They love pointing me out on the set because they think it's a riot.

MJM: As a woman you are still a rarity. There is Anne Frank ...

McEWEN: ... and Bonnie Siegal and Jeannine Locke. We are it [as "in-house" drama producers around the CBC] in an essentially male environment. There are still not many women.

MJM to HARCOURT [1990]: Can I ask you about being a woman at the CBC?

HARCOURT: This is the third time I've been asked this question in the last three interviews I've had – two of them have concentrated mostly on the fact that I am a woman because occasionally somebody will want to do something on the women executives at the CBC and whether their particular sensibility as women influences program content.

The more fundamental question is, How do women network executives respond to the challenges we are facing? They are no different from the male executives. It is a shared problem: the cutbacks at the CBC have been devastating, and the CBC's cultural mandate is constantly under review. Our successes have been extraordinary, I think, in a very difficult environment. The challenges I face have less to do with my being a woman than being a skilled guerrilla fighter, trying to make sense out of the environment and trying to keep my priorities on what really matters – the program content.

What is very clear, though, is that the more women there are in management, in the board room, the more there is an articulation of views, a much livelier discussion, and a much more supportive point of view. I think had there not been a Trina McQueen working for Jack Craine in the early years, my career would not have taken off. The anthology *Sons and Daughters* came out of a Children's Department that wasn't supposed to do drama. When Trina started to cry in a viewing room at the end of the first show of *Sons and Daughters* [based on an Alice Munro short story that examines sexism] and said to Jack, "Give her whatever she wants – I've never seen anything like this," you begin to understand how important it is to have another woman as part of the decision-making process. It's that cross-fertilization that is terribly important.

It was more difficult for others in the early years. Dodi Robb was the first female head of the Children's Department, and I was second. It must have been much more difficult for Dodi. There hadn't been a concurrent listening point of view in the boardroom then. In the past the discussion would be prioritized more in terms of male concerns – news/sports or sports/news.

Joan Donaldson [head of *Newsworld* until a tragic accident] and Trina have said yes to all those famous things like *If You Love This Planet* and abortion stories. "Would you air them?" "No, they're not journalistically balanced," a man might say – and a woman might not.

I'm a woman executive who deals with many more male writers and male producers just because of the nature of the industry at this time. I would hire a writer who is male, who writes a three-dimensional woman character well, before I would hire a woman who writes a two-dimensional woman character badly. However, I am likely to take a risk on women directors or women writers because I think it is important from a developmental point of view. It's hard to have male critics and male producers who often suggest that the reason we are not doing great cop shows instead of a *Degrassi* or an *Avonlea* is because I'm a woman executive. *Au contraire,* it is not because I'm a woman executive; it is because I am a smart woman who knows that the audience wants that. Until they put a woman in that job, nobody developed those kinds of ideas. I don't have to articulate that point of view, it is simply a fact. It is simply a fact that my concerns in the early years were concerns that the audience accepted. As Ivan Fecan says, people are chosen as "filters" because of their track record, not because they're women.

In my case it wasn't John Kennedy [head of TV drama for a decade], it was Denis Harvey who brought me into drama. Before Telefilm went on to be a fully formed organization – bringing new players into the marketplace of ideas – the imperative was already there at CBC to "bring in people in their twenties who have a feeling for kids." [The "youth equated with new ideas" motif recurs throughout the CBC history.]

Independent production was a big pill to swallow; it challenged the way we did business in those years. It was a double whammy in that I was supportive of it. The fact that I was a woman was not really the thing that made some people nervous, but the fact that independent production was becoming a reality. If there was anything draining in my early years, it was that I was a woman in a boardroom with a lot of men, and also that there were changes. I was challenging the status quo of mostly in-house production – that was the difficult part.

Trina McQueen has the last word among the women I interviewed.

MJM: Things have changed for women at the CBC, but they've changed relatively recently.

McQUEEN: John Kennedy is the major factor. He is an example of a man who is a better feminist than most women. He gave women the opportunity. In fact, in many cases he forced the opportunity down their throats while they kicked and screamed against it. He's an extraordinary man.

MJM: Is it unlikely that there will be backsliding? Will women in the upper echelons of broadcasting become a fact of life rather than having to fight to make their way?

McQUEEN: Definitely not. I think for the next century it's going to be a fight. One man made the difference, but one man could also make a difference the other way. As much as John did, CBC drama is still a male-dominated activity and more changes have to happen. More has to be built on the very good foundation that John laid, but there's no guarantee that will happen, no guarantee at all.

Trina made that prophetic remark in 1988. And what has happened to these women? Kate Trotter continues her distinguished career as a stage actress, occasionally working in television primarily as a character actress, usually in secondary roles. Leading roles in serious drama are hard to find for women in their late thirties and early forties. Maryke McEwen found that the 1989–92 emphasis on family programming made it more difficult for her to get adult projects on air, but she managed to get the very disturbing *The Diary of Evelyn Lau* dramatised and on air in 1993. In June 1995 she was one of sixteen in-house producers laid off. Nada Harcourt had been head of development for creative series with a reasonable track record of new and ongoing successes, the latest being *North of 60*. In the spring of 1993 she became executive producer of the last season of *Street Legal*. Like Harcourt, the new head of creative series is also a woman drawn from the Children's Department. Harcourt succinctly pointed to a problem bedevilling all creative heads in the "hands-on" mode.

HARCOURT: I wonder how long anybody can do a job like this. It is a real burnout job simply because, in order to be cogent in terms of the philosophy, you have to have time to read, to think, to be involved in other media – you just simply must. So there's no weekend, there's never a weekend. [Nada Harcourt retired in 1994–95.]

The continual "battle readiness" state that both makers and decision-makers experience in the 1990s will create more casualties before the picture clears. Add to those pressures those of being a woman in a pervasively all-male environment, and it is little wonder that people step out of those situations if they can.

Trina McQueen's story is the most enigmatic. In 1992 the very few senior women in CBC English network management, both in radio and television, were laterally arabesqued into less important positions. Trina was reassigned from the powerful position of vice-president of news and current affairs to the less influential position of vice-president of the regions, where staff attrition accompanied station closing and "downsizing." In July 1993 it was announced that she was leaving the CBC to be vice-president and general manager of Discovery, the most successful of the specialty channels licensed in 1994. She was replaced by Donna Logan, who had been sidetracked a year before from her position as vice-president of English radio. McQueen left, in part, because of conflicts with Gérard Veilleux and because she did not wish to implement further damaging cuts to the programming side.[54]

In response to Veilleux's corporate shuffle, begun not long after his own appointment, more than one thousand women and some men signed a petition within the corporation protesting the reorganization and pointing out that only 19 per cent of the senior management at the CBC were women. The chairman of the board, broadcaster Patrick Watson, seemed to have nothing to say about the issue. Veilleux, who had no experience in broadcasting but plenty of bureaucratic expertise acquired at the Treasury Board, seems not to have responded formally to this petition. None of the women producers and executives I interviewed for this book are with the CBC in mid-1995.

Regrettably, the record of the private sector is worse. Kealy Wilkinson, who has worked in broacasting on air and as a producer and manager for thirty years, writes in *Changing Focus*:

In private radio and television broadcasting operations, women account for only 1 per cent of senior management and 16 per cent of middle management, while their representation in professional and semi-professional categories is somewhat better, 25 and 22 per cent, respectively. Comparable figures for the public broadcasting sector are slightly more encouraging, with 14 per cent of senior and 19 per cent of middle management identified as female, as are 34 per cent and 27 per cent of those in professional and semi-professional job categories.

...

Gender balance in both the decision-making and creative components of Canada's media is of particular importance to the making of our myths and messages, to the shaping of our society, and the choices we make about our collective future. The images presented by the electronic media are critical to these processes. At a time when we are engaged in serious efforts to reconfigure our national, economic, and political structures, it is particularly important that action be taken to ensure balanced gender representation in television and film. At a time when most jurisdictions and many industries are addressing the same fair-employment issues, there can be no justification for exempting Canada's film and television industries."[55]

Finally, Annette Cohen, a television producer, sums up some of the questions raised by these interviews:

It is common practice to observe that when the voice of women is denied access through the system, the experience of 52 per cent of the nation's population is denied. In fact, given the power of mass communications, this denial does not affect 52 per cent of the population, it affects 100 per cent. Every one of us, male and female alike.[56]

After I published an article on this topic in *Frequénce/Frequency* in 1994, I received a letter from Monique Coupla, director of Equitable Portrayal in Programming, pointing out that she had not experienced or observed any discrimination at the CBC based on gender. In a report prepared for Status of Women Canada by Liss Jeffrey, "Progress in Canada toward Women's Equality and the Media: Access to Expression and Decision Making, 1980–94," released in February 1995, Jeffrey concludes: "Talented women have made and will continue to make their distinctive mark on Canadian media. Equitable participation has not yet been achieved but progress is substantial." Yet McQueen, Harcourt, McEwen, Locke, and several others have all retired, left in despair, or been "fired." It would appear that the CBC can afford equity – and certain kinds of talent – only when money is plentiful. The CBC gave me the following table.

Table 1
Representation of Women in the CBC (per cent)

	1976	1982	1988	1991	1994
Producers	16.7	19.6	36.2	42.2	46.3
Announcers-hosts	11.4	18.1	28.9	35.9	39.5
Journalists and other program presentation	18.2	26.1	39.0	40.6	43.4
Technological	2.1	3.5	4.3	6.8	8.2
Production, design, and staging	28.8	31.2	36.5	39.2	47.7

ETHOS AND THE REGIONS

Part of the mandate of the CBC, and intermittently of the ethos, has been to show each of the regions to the others. Distinctive regional voices spoke within series like *The Serial, The Manipulators, Beachcombers, Ritter's Cove* and *Danger Bay*, and the twice-weekly evening soap *House of Pride*. In the late 1980s and 1990s Vancouver reappeared in several series: *Max Glick, Mom PI, The Odyssey*, and *Northwood*. There were also anthologies like *Studio Pacific, Shoestring Theatre, Tales from Pigeon Inlet*, and *Lies from Lotus Land*, and contributions to anthology appeared in *For the Record, The Way We Are*, and *Family Pictures* (1990–91) and in the specifically ethnic *Inside Stories* (1989–91).

In many ways the factors of distance and a small population, concentrated in a thin ribbon along a 5000-mile border with the United States, have worked against the development of indigenous broadcasting. But in some respects, Canada's deeply felt regional divisions and the distance from Ottawa or Toronto to Winnipeg, Vancouver, or the Northwest Territories have worked to the advantage of creative people who simply improvised with what they could scrounge, then went ahead and made programs. Sometimes these improvizations created a fresh look at some parts of our country, as in *Tales of Pigeon Inlet* or *Cariboo Country*. It took well over a decade, but local programs in Newfoundland such as *Up at Ours* and *Wonderful Grand Band*, which appeared in other regions intermittently, produced performers experienced enough in television to give us the intensely regional yet intensely Canadian satire *Codco*.

Philip Keatley explained why the West Coast had always managed to have some sort of presence in the CBC drama mix.

KEATLEY: Theatre belongs to Britain: with the concentration, size of the population, and tradition, it is uniquely theirs. Film belongs uniquely to the United States; it's right for its size and space and the way it fits together. Television is the medium for Canada, because we've got those five-and-a-half time zones and that string of people. You can't tour the repertory company and can't afford the number of prints you need for films.

Hugh Gauntlett looks at Vancouver from the point of view of middle-management based in Toronto.

GAUNTLETT [1983]: Vancouver was a pioneer in film of every kind. For the first few years on air, CBC staff there were not connected to the network programming and, therefore, they inferred that they didn't have the capacity to produce drama electronically [in the live-to-tape days] so had to use film.[57] They were a long way away, and it was a period of decentralization. They did just what they wanted to do.

MJM: Keatley and the rest had the sense that they could get away with it because they were on the other side of the mountains.

GAUNTLETT: And who was going to bother them? Because it was nobody's business in Toronto, in those days, to inquire what they were doing on the local scene. And in Ottawa, nobody cared. Charles Jennings presided over all that, a very gentle man in many ways. He was a patrician figure and, above all, a most patriotic man, the kind that the CBC had in those days, although a little more worldly than some.[58]

There are a number of cycles, and every time there is decentralization, as there is now [1983], we have a renaissance of regional drama. So having been brutally decentralized this year, everybody is talking about regional drama next year. That is one cycle, which ended five or six years later. Another cycle is between economy and efficiency: here you look at the resources in the region and decide what you can do with them to satisfy that community. In most cases, you'll decide that drama is the last thing for you to do. But if you are looking internally and subjectively, rather than objectively, you'll feel that drama is the most impressive thing you can do. There are times when you can get away with that and there are times when those in central authority (whether it is Ottawa or Toronto) will not, for example, let somebody develop regional journalism, just because they feel like it. But what their regional director will let an individual do is just as important as anything that belongs to rational management.

"Creative accidents" are another factor. You can have the most skilled managers deciding what we ought to do, setting up development on it, and launching it with massive support. It's a complete flip-of-the-coin whether the result is *90 Minutes Live* [the CBC effort to do a late-night talk show hosted by Peter Gzowski, which did not find its feet] or *The Journal*. Conversely, you can decide that there is no way we are going to do any more drama in Vancouver, and then Paul St Pierre will walk in with a script and it will be irresistible. One thing will lead to another and, before you know it, you have done regional drama. The point I am making is that the Hollywood factory theory of how programming is made is of limited application. Conversely, some programs happen simply because someone has invented the program to serve some useful social purpose. It goes on being broadcast even though the planners and the managers had never conceived it that way.

Even the select few trying to reach consensus on regional drama for the 1987 drama report could not agree on whether to fund drama in the regions in the 1990s.

This sub-committee believes that most locations should not produce network drama. We fear a situation where every Director of Television starts using the Telefilm fund, first for local drama, but then inevitably developing hopes for network release, increasingly deflecting scarce regional resources towards a goal which we, as a system, cannot afford to have so dispersed.

Furthermore, this sub-committee is divided on the issue of regional drama production for the network; Marc Blandford, who made network drama work in a region with *Empire*, is deeply suspicious of frittering away the inadequate quartermaster's store hours before a major engagement with the American networks; Maryke McEwen feels strongly that the crisis is overriding: The issue is to produce hours upon hours of new and good Canadian drama, and to cloud the issue with considerations of where to produce it is irresponsible – produce it where you have the infrastructure: [that is] Toronto and Vancouver. Both argue from passion to produce good Canadian drama, and a fear that if we blow it this time, we'll be in fatal circumstances. In other words, their arguments are Canadianization arguments, and not centralist, arrogant or anti-regional.

Steve Scainie points out there is nascent talent in regional centres such as his (ironically, Toronto – one can be isolated even at the "centre") and it cannot find development ground, or access to training, and network exposure.

Bernie Zukerman, a recent addition to the Drama Department, stresses how complicated the production process is, how advocates of regionalization fail to understand the extraordinary support network required, and the scarcity of craft skills. He can see the possibility of producing network drama outside Toronto and Vancouver, but only if the proper groundwork is laid and the base of talent is developed, and craft and technical skills assembled, and also fears indiscriminate and naive regionalization. He is skeptical such serious work would be done by the CBC, and shares the fear that this would deflect critical funds at the time of the Canadianization push.

No one is opposed to regional drama production for the network per se; no one disputes there is a great deal of talent to be developed. None of this is an ideological issue of the regions versus the centre. All arguments pivot on funds, and their allocation. [Rather ingenuously, too, the report equates production values with network standards and then, circle complete, with centralized facilities.]

In the end, the most compelling argument against de-centralizing Drama in the next three years is Canadianization. In and of itself, a sober, calculated, decentralization is possible if it is done by putting in the right supports, and going through the right development process. Emotional exhortations, regional nationalism, or force of will are not enough.[59]

The report ignores the ongoing success of Vancouver and the cost, in terms of our ability to understand each other, when regular drama production in Montreal closed down and the notion of good television coming from places other than Toronto and Vancouver disappeared. Amnesia again.

Producer Philip Keatley directed and produced nearly all of Paul St Pierre's *Cariboo Country* on location in the Chilcotin. It was one of the best CBC anthologies in its more than forty-year history, and its "production values" – resonant black and white cinematography – stand up to any 1990s definition of quality.

KEATLEY: We did the first episodes of the series in the studio. Then we did a show called "The One Man Crowd," which we filmed for the first time in a little riding academy out in Burnaby that was trying desperately to look like a western homestead. As soon as we got outside, things started to happen that were much better, much more true to the ideas and the themes of the story. The pace got tight. We agreed at that point that we would develop more scripts to be filmed in the future, maybe up in the Cariboo itself.

ROBERT ALLEN [1987]: *The Education of Phyllistine* and a couple of the other long ones were done by cooperation between Phil Keatley in Vancouver and me in Toronto. He was getting things written and I was getting the money to produce it. *Phyllistine* was marvellous, beautiful. These pieces weren't commissioned by me. West Coast writers at that time would have been developed by Philip and his people. It would have been ridiculous to do it any other way.

Ron Weyman made room for the series to have national exposure by clearing time on *The Serial*.

WEYMAN: I may have asked Keatley to give me material. That's quite possible. I was under the naive impression that it was a single CBC and it was interesting to have things produced outside Toronto. As far as I remember, there wasn't as yet what developed later, a very positive schedule of regional material fed to a network. There wasn't the exchange between the regions that now happens [a policy that was replaced in 1990 by the decision that regions must produce drama only for the network].

As we have seen, from Hugh Gauntlett's point of view there weren't layers of bureaucracy between the people who made the shows and the people who made the decisions back in the 1950s and 1960s. Keatley, sitting in Vancouver, saw it rather differently.

KEATLEY: At that time, we had a peculiar setup in which we had a regional program director and a local program director. The regional program director was Doug Nixon, who later went on to run the network. The local program director was Marce Monroe, who also later ran the whole network.
MJM: I'm trying to get a sense of whether there were many layers of decision-making.
KEATLEY: Yes, there were. In the 1950s and early 1960s the regions were much more separate. When we got our own budgets at the beginning of the year, producers asked for the money, time periods, various things. We were not a connected network. When you had to schedule everything and you couldn't get the national programs, except kinescopes delivered in a can, the whole attitude towards programming ideas was different. Even so, there were certain programs which simply had to be shown to the rest of Canada because they were too expensive to be done just for a local audience.
MJM: Did *Cariboo Country* come under that heading because it was film?
KEATLEY: It did, yes. Also, there was a policy change. We had a visitation from the network program directors who came to Vancouver and said, "Things are changing in television. The days of studio drama are over." *Playhouse 90* [1956–60] had moved to Hollywood and started on film. *Festival* was beginning to talk about doing some films. The *Serial* was just beginning. Ron Weyman had come from the Film Board and was trying very hard to sell a series on film, which was really unusual because television didn't do those things. So these gentlemen in Toronto said, "You guys are out of drama because you haven't got a studio and the

facilities to come up to network standards. So, you'll have to do something else."

MJM: Yet Vancouver had been feeding programs to *Playdate* and other anthologies as a studio production centre for four or five years. Those programs were up to network standards. Suddenly it was decided that your studio drama wasn't good enough?

KEATLEY: Right. I think that at the same time the same thing happened in Montreal.[60]

MJM: By this time there were also other drama producers/directors.

KEATLEY: Yes. There was Mike Rothery, Alan King, Ron Kelly, Jack Thorne, Len Lauk. Anyway, the reaction was violent. My local bosses said, "Vancouver not doing drama! There is a long history in storytelling here, attempts at films, a strong tradition in radio, and a strong little theatre tradition as well as a professional theatre tradition. It's a blow against the heart to think of being chucked out as not being up to network standards." Marce Monroe said to our visitors, "You're crazy! You can't just do that." And they said, "Film is the future and you can't do film. You don't have a film unit." He said, "Don't be so stupid. We can do it." They said, "We have to have film for this fall," thinking that would stop him. He replied, "Phil Keatley has a series ready to go – new scripts written by Paul St Pierre for *Cariboo Country*." They asked, "How many have you got?" "Well," says Marce, "I think he has thirteen." They said, "Okay. You'll have to submit them to the network and we'll have to see if they are indeed up to network standards."

MJM: Hadn't *Cariboo Country* already run on network?

KEATLEY: Yes, but it had been buried. It had been run as a summer replacement, so it had not drawn much attention. Marce phoned me and said to get those scripts and get them in the mail. I said, "What scripts? I have first drafts, two pages each scrawled on two sides of a piece of foolscap." "What! You told me you had ..." "No, I didn't." So he said, "We're going to do this."

What happened was a typical thing in the CBC. The scripts were submitted to Bob Allen, who wasn't in theory head of drama, but who had to decide whether they were up to network standards. Now Bob had never done a foot of film in his life, but he had Ron Weyman snapping at his heels and he finally concluded that they should do a short film serial called *The Road*. He was busy getting the scripts written and put together. Bob said to Ron, "If these *Cariboo Country* scripts go, they'll have to be in the same time slot as yours" – that is, "they will pre-empt your shows." He then said to Ron, "Will you please look after this and, when Keatley sends the scripts, say whether they are up to network standards?"

I had never met Ron, but I had known Bob all my life. He had been out to Vancouver and he was the first person who ever hired me as an actor. We sent two or three scripts down and got an answer back that they weren't up to network standards. Munroe was expecting that. He said, "We're sending Phil Keatley down to Toronto to work with whomever is necessary to bring these up to network standards." Marce said to me, "Go to Toronto and don't come back until they say yes."

MJM: So you did.

KEATLEY: Yes. He said, "When you run out of money, send for more." I went and literally sat outside Bob Allen's office for six weeks. The big complaint was that Paul's stage directions didn't make sense and you couldn't divide up these scripts into shootable sections. They just didn't read as film. That is where they were unprofessional. Until they looked right and could be treated by actors and crew as professional pieces, they were not up to standards. What it really came down to was having to put stage directions in caps and dialogue in lower case. We had to put it on a sheet of paper so that it read like a script. So we sat down and did that. People didn't understand things, so we changed them. In my own head I was saying, "Okay, I know it's going to look different and it's going to sound different, but when I get back home I'll just put a line through this." I also knew that this was going to make Paul St Pierre crazy, because he doesn't like things explained.

MJM: But the changes demanded by the network wouldn't mean the finished script would necessarily resemble anything that appeared on the screen.

KEATLEY: Of course not. But I knew that Paul wouldn't know that and I knew I was going to have a problem when I got back. I was prepared to compromise anything to get it to go. At a certain point they broke down and said, "All right, do six episodes." Ron Weyman, to his everlasting credit, was the one to say, "Okay, good luck with it." He was just starting The Road. He even shared new microphone technology with me. Vancouver didn't get back into studio drama until we moved into this building in 1976.

MJM: You lived under the umbrella title of The Serial until the end of Cariboo Country? Neither Weyman nor management seem to have tried to impose eastern stereotypes on this program in the artistic or conceptual sense, as in "This is how to represent 'an Indian' or 'a cowboy.'"

KEATLEY: They asked questions that annoyed Paul more than they annoyed me. They kept saying, "But that isn't dramatic."

MJM: His dramatic structures are very interesting because they are anecdotal, they meander, there is time and space.

KEATLEY: There are also absolutely arbitrary jumps.

Eric Till comments on the success of *Cariboo Country*;

TILL: The earliest success I can remember shaking up this department was Phil Keatley's *Cariboo Country*. It was a lovely program, and it quite surprised everybody here with their lofty ideas of what drama ought to be. Suddenly, in came this simple, gentle, very human, very real, utterly charming piece of film from the "boondocks." One began to wonder, "What the hell is going on in Vancouver?" You discover that at that point there were people out there in Vancouver who said, "To hell with Toronto, we are going to make our own films!" And they did! Among them, *Cariboo Country*. Sadly, that freedom vanished.

Cariboo Country ended with three one-hour specials by Paul St Pierre on *Festival*, ending with *Sister Balonika* in 1969. By 1971, however, Keatley had a new hour-long series about a parole officer up and running.

KEATLEY: When we did *The Manipulators* (1971–73), we really needed to be cold-blooded in planning how to get a series, because it was getting expensive. These big film dramas were costing a lot. Yet we had to have those, if we were going to have the amount of production to make it possible to do other things as well.

When we got into *The Manipulators*, we wanted to do another film series, because these genres run in a cycle of about five years. Most of the series will last about a year and a half. We were still under Fletcher Markle when we started *The Beachcombers* in 1972. The atmosphere of the network had changed by that time. Ray Whitehouse and I sat down and said, "The hour-long shows are not going to hold up and they certainly aren't going to be offered to Vancouver or places outside Toronto. Toronto has a unit that's up and running and they have to keep feeding it."

We couldn't be the centre of the economy or of the politics, yet we had all these pretensions. I suppose the network commitment was there in 1973–74, when the studio was built. This signified that Vancouver was to produce major studio drama. Who was pulling the strings at the other end? Well, they changed all the time; some of the people you've been interviewing, John Kennedy among them. Kennedy had been a unit manager in the Drama Department back in the 1960s when I did *Cariboo Country*. We had been friendly in a reserved way over the years.

MJM: Montreal as a drama production centre was dead by 1971, so it was basically Vancouver and Toronto.

KEATLEY ... with Don Williams doing a one-man act in Winnipeg and coming out and directing for us. All of our script commissioning was centralized. There wasn't a pot of money for commissioning in Vancouver and another one in Toronto. But we kept running into the fact that writers were writing for the two places and not getting the same kind of treatment. Ideas were coming up that were so close together that they should either have been combined or not done. So we decided to go back to where our roots were, that we should be doing regional drama, and it should be happening whenever anybody, like Don Williams, was around and wanted to do it.

MJM: What you were trying to get within a unified administrative situation were opportunities for a regional structure – a confederation.

KEATLEY: Yes. Canadian drama from everywhere. In Vancouver the morale has been bad because in 1978 the whole apparatus was intentionally dismembered. When I went off to train people in Toronto, there were four staff producers, two other people who directed full time, two story editors, and a casting and contracting department of three people. There were the hour and ninety-minute programs being done out of the studio, and *The Beachcombers* was still running. When I came back at the beginning of 1981, there was one story editor under contract to *The Beachcombers*, two producers who were committed full time to the CBC, and everything was on the basis of ...

MJM: ... the "pick-up" contract?

KEATLEY: Yes.

Regional drama in the 1970s took a very different form after *Cariboo Country* and *The Manipulators* ended. As sometimes happens, the CBC was slightly ahead of the trends. The decision was to try a twice-weekly night-time soap – a new concept at the time, shot in several locations across the country.

HERB ROLAND: *House of Pride* was a nightmare. Jack Nixon-Browne and I were working on the same floor and we were talking about the idea of doing an "evening soap." I think it was he who suggested we go across the country.

MJM: That was part of the hook, wasn't it – that it would be in various production centres?

ROLAND: It was a wonderful idea and completely impractical, which we found out. It was a logistics nightmare. *House of Pride* was originally meant to be two taped half-hours a week, so the audience didn't have to wait long between episodes. But they liked the first three episodes so much that the network decided two a week was wasted. That was part of the reason that it was too disjointed.

MJM: Granada's decades-old success, the daytime soap *Coronation Street*, is twice a week, and so is the BBC 1980s hit *East Enders*.

ROLAND: This is the English way, and no one wants to know about that. But we didn't link the stories enough. Initially it was wonderful, the whole family from across the country gathered in Toronto to celebrate the eightieth birthday of the patriarch, who dies on you before you even get there. The funeral, the will, the whole thing about the farm: Is it going to be sold to make everybody a fortune or do we want to stay on the land? But then the family dispersed back to Vancouver, to Winnipeg, to Halifax, and Montreal.

MJM: Four production centres besides Toronto were involved?

ROLAND: With a little bit in Edmonton.

MJM: And Halifax had done no national drama up to that point?

ROLAND: To be frank, in Halifax it was wonderful. They welcomed you with open arms and said, "Show us!" I'll tell you what worked. The actors were wonderful. We had the finest actors in Quebec; they were so professional. It turned out that one or two of them were really strong separatists at the time, but they were professionals. They spoke good English, they thoroughly enjoyed it, and we got along famously. But we had to redo a lot of it here.

MJM: Was there a director in each location?

ROLAND: Yes. But then the word came down from Hirsch (he never really wanted the whole thing) that I was to direct everything but three or four in Winnipeg and a few in Halifax – twenty-six episodes across the country, except Jack did three or four in Winnipeg. Eventually we cut out Vancouver and Montreal. We did three or four in Halifax and three or four in Winnipeg. I did all the Halifax and all the Toronto ones. What an experience, though! It was just a nightmare. We spent a lot of money the first year, but by the second year we were exactly on budget. What a lesson!

MJM: What kind of audience response did you get?

ROLAND: Not bad, nice nucleus, but it was on at 7:30.

MJM: I didn't ask you for numbers.

ROLAND: We got a very high enjoyment index when we stayed in Toronto for a while. In other words, when the story became a really good continuous story. But when we started nipping backwards and forwards ...

MJM: You lost viewers and they said so?

ROLAND: And you could see it in the ratings as well as the enjoyment index. When we stayed for about three, four weeks on one story line in Toronto, it would climb.

It took determined men (there were no women producer/directors for adult regional television whom I have discovered) to find the resources for regional drama made strictly for the regions.

MJM to WILLIAMS [1985]: Were you the primary person in regional drama in Winnipeg in the late 1960s and early 1970s?

WILLIAMS: I will be totally unabashed and say "I was it" – there wasn't any room for anybody else in terms of budget and facilities. A couple of other people made attempts to stick with it, but I didn't give up easily when nothing was happening. Also, I got in on the ground floor. The Winnipeg station had done studio live dramas in the very early days, and they did a fair bit of drama through the school telecasts. It was strictly the top man, the regional director, who had the notion that the network could and should do drama and that we shouldn't. But we managed to do the first film drama in Winnipeg, *A Bucket of Tears for a Pound of Jam* by Betty Reed.

MJM: Was that because the Centennial was generating a fair bit of money and energy?

WILLIAMS: I don't think it had anything to do with the Centennial. It had to do with the stubbornness of Don Williams and the courage and faith of Jack Phillips.

Alan Kroeker, who did Winnipeg's CKND's independently produced dramas in the 1980s, was once the assistant cameraman in our film drama crew. Some of the members of that crew had more film-making experience than I did, but I had the drama and theatre experience and the experience of working with text and with actors. Altogether, we didn't know very much. We stumbled through that first show together, quietly trusting. One of the reasons it worked was because we were all at the same level, and we really had to rely on each other. It wasn't very good but it showed that, although we didn't know what we were doing, at least we knew a little bit more than we thought in terms of the process of film-making as a dramatic form, and the differences between that and documentary film-making.

Then we made *Death of a Nobody* in 1967 [an unsparing half-hour docudrama about the casual and unpunished murder of a young Native] and we were quite pleased with it, as was Jack Phillips. We had sent it to the network for screening and they sent it back with the usual response, "It's all very nice. Hope you

enjoyed yourselves doing it, but it's not up to network standards."
But we entered it in the internal CBC Wilderness Awards, not
really expecting anything to happen. We didn't think anything
from the Prairies was going to win. In the spring of 1968 I got a
message to come to Jack Phillips's office and he said we had won
the Wilderness Award. I said, "What did we win? Best Photography? Best Lighting?" He said, "No, we won the whole damn
thing, don't you understand?"

The network had a bit of an embarrassment because they had a
deal with the awards committee. Whichever film won the "Best
Film of the Year" would be aired in prime time. *Death of a Nobody*
changed the attitude of the regional director.

MJM: Working with authors would come fairly naturally to you as
an actor and a writer?

WILLIAMS: It all helps. As a director I've had many actors who
have told me they can sense that I know what it is like to be
where they are.

MJM: Did scripts come in to you or did you go out and find them?

WILLIAMS: I went out and found them, except in the later years,
because by then there was a momentum there. I was established
and people started coming to me with scripts, like *Puptent*.[61]

MJM: Did you have any money for script development?

WILLIAMS: One of the problems was there was no money to throw
away. The tendency was that as soon as the CBC invested money,
that project was going to be produced come hell or high water.

MJM: Were they sponsored or sustained?

WILLIAMS: Sustained, except in the later years. In the earlier years,
the CBC was more used to doing sustained drama. By the time we
got into the late 1970s, we had to put in commercials. Often, they
were half-hours at 7:00 or 7:30 PM. That time slot was really
tough.

MJM: Was the 7:00–7:30 time slot a constraint on your subject
matter?

WILLIAMS: Yes. *Puptent* went to a later time, which was appropriate, because there was nothing in it for kids. The whole structure
of time slots, and what was local and network, changed from year
to year.

MJM: Did any of these get on the network?

WILLIAMS: None of the projects that were purely local. For example, when the network had the anthology series, *To See Ourselves*, I did a production for that out of Winnipeg. The executive
producer of the series said, "Here's a script and I think you should
do it." There were also a couple of projects that were done specifi-

cally for the network. I did *Almonds and Raisins,* which was done here because it's a prairie story.

But Don Williams, who had done Winnipeg dramas in Winnipeg, dramas specific to Vancouver in Vancouver, had an idea that could have spanned the country yet be shown in each region to advantage.

WILLIAMS: *Red Serge Wives* is primarily my project. I fought for it for eight years. I thought it would make a good series, based on the book, because it contains first-person accounts by women who were wives of Mounties at different periods. Here are wonderful true stories about women who were forced into roles they didn't want, or walked into them totally unsuspecting. I couldn't get anybody interested in the project – local or network. I put it on the shelf and each year I would pull it down and try again.

In the end, *Red Serge* was redesigned in Toronto to fit within a standard family/adventure format and focused on an American rum-runner and his three marriageable daughters (by three wives). The dramatic conflict arose when Abe's quasi-legal activities attract the attention of a northwest Montreal police contingent. Meanwhile, his daughters attract three eligible Mounties. The sense of period was recreated well enough. The basis of the project as Williams saw it, however, as an anthology of stories about the wives of these mythic figures, vanished. *Red Serge* did find a place on the network for two short seasons before it was cancelled.

WILLIAMS: My idea was that it should always be anthology with a hook. Each one is a separate story about another woman who married a Mountie. But the swing is away from the anthology, with a hook towards series with constant characters. I know why the decision was made to go towards a series format. Carelessness is the big factor. You work so hard at getting things done that you get careless about how you do it.

   This whole regional anthology project [*The Way We Are* ran in the late 1980s] is about a year behind. They got to a point where they didn't know if the project was on or off, because we couldn't find enough material. One of my original questions was, "Does a regional anthology mean that the network is going to put up a certain number of dollars, and is each region going to get its slice?" The answer I received created a lot of concerns. The regions weren't going to "do their thing" – the network was going to tell them what to do. What we promptly got was a syllabus that described to us what the criteria were for doing regional television. There could be no swearing and it had to have a sense of place. The really bad news was that there was going to be an executive producer in Toronto to run the series, and everyone who produced the show, from whatever region, would be working for him. There are two problems with this: first, when the executive producer is from Toronto he is right down the hall from network and is therefore getting his orders directly from them. The executive producer should have been from the regions, so he had some of the fervour and passion of regionalism and anti-network feelings.

It's the old thing that I used to fight years ago. You propose something to the network and they say, "We'll buy it! We love it!" Then they change this and that. What did they buy? What did they love? There's nothing left. This whole regional anthology represented a real regression back to another day at the CBC. [It produced some good half-hour stories, though.]

HARCOURT: Over the last couple of years almost 50 per cent of the Telefilm allotment had been spent in the regions. Crews in Vancouver don't really care whether Paul Saltzman [*Danger Bay*] is paying their bills. The writers are very happy to be working and creating. The reality is that those independent productions have spent their money in the regions. They're also very labour intensive. The budgets are about 65–70 per cent for labour.

The East Coast and Newfoundland have never been a regular supplier of drama or of variety and arts programming to the network. Seven episodes culled from two seasons of *Up at Ours* were shown on CBC-owned stations in 1980, and there was a variety show called *Wonderful Grand Band* for a short while. The popularity of *This Hour Has 22 Minutes* (1994–), daughter of *Codco*, ensures that it is a happy exception. People down east, however, still remember what happened to *Don Messer's Jubilee*, which is a well-known instance of the CBC replacing regional Canadian music (which had a devoted audience on radio and television for thirty years) with a clone of American 1960s folk pop called *Hullabaloo*. The CBC's reason? The audience for Don Messer was not young and groovy – that is, desirable demographically. *Hullabaloo* faded rapidly. Ironically, more than twenty-five years later, repackaged episodes of *Don Messer's Jubilee* have been a surprise early evening success on the network and Rita MacNeil's pure Cape Breton voice heads the first successful weekly popular music program in many years.

But the East Coast has never been as well equipped as Vancouver to make its presence felt in the national network. One idea that would have enriched the parched reality of the late 1970s did not, regrettably, come to pass, as told in a summary of a discussion between John Hirsch and Doris Gauntlett, one of the key story editors in the mid-1970s, dated 29 May 1974.

HIRSCH: The Maritimes' drama is very much one of a "narrative" tradition. This, for them, is "drama." Regions should be encouraged to videotape these narratives against authentic backgrounds lasting from one minute to fifteen minutes. These could be used regularly in one minute or minute-and-a-half segments after the news; or be part of a show which is one of those "catch-all" shows, before the weather, or whatever. This could be the basis of activity which could be developed ... to embrace the whole of the Maritimes ... and to be Networked. We can pepper National broadcasting with fillers, jokes. These can concern history, mythology etc. ... It is the tradition of yarn-spinning that we must start with in the Maritimes. It has certain advantages; it's cheap and easy to record ... The Drama department should then be able to cull the best and put them on the Network. Also important, that the CBC should be able to have a mobile film unit that can do dramas across the country. The object must be flexibility in order to be governed by what is going on and where.[62]

In 1987 the drama report specifically rejected the idea of a mobile "swat team" for dramatic production, partly because regional producers would fiercely resent the idea. On the other hand, with videocams in the hands of viewers (a $1600 super 8 camera produces broadcast quality), the idea of local anecdotes for and by local people could now find a home. Wouldn't such a series of shorts be enjoyed across the country? Wouldn't it make the CBC look/sound different from the rest on the box?

In December 1994, journalist Harvey Enchin credited "an experiment combining digital technology, training and consensus management" to the CBC Windsor station after drastic cuts in 1990.[63] "Camera operators were taught to be reporters. Reporters learned to shoot with videocams." What possibilities does this open up for drama? Flexibility? Lower costs and cooperation between unions and management? Videocams might bring the return of regional drama for local audiences. Could people walk off the streets into the studio with twenty-two minutes of a good watchable piece of fiction?

Since the demise of Montreal as a regular supplier of drama in 1971, Vancouver is, as it has always been, the main counterweight on the network to the centralized vision.

KEATLEY: The CBC in Vancouver, going right back to its beginnings, has always had pretensions as far as drama is concerned. I think it is geography as much as anything else. We are not the media centre of the world, nor are we the economic centre of Canada. So, in carving out some kind of character of our own among the arts, drama has been the art most favoured by radio people, and it moved straight over into television.

MJM: There have always been drama producers, directors, writers, and actors in Vancouver.

KEATLEY: Again, there was a long tradition of people coming out here to try their wings. I think it went back to the most important regional director, Ira Dilworth.

MJM: Yet the ambiance here at that time, as in most other centres in the country, was that the professional theatre was a very fragile creature indeed. Although the CBC was setting down roots in drama, an actor really couldn't earn a living in the theatre here because there wasn't enough work.

KEATLEY: That's right, not at that time. I don't altogether agree with critical mass as a concept. However, it's true that only a certain number of people make a living in one place. What happened in radio was very specific. Andrew Allan was sent out here to start a drama idea he had. He used a bunch of local actors, including Lister Sinclair and Lister's wife Alice, Fletcher Markle ...

MJM: ... who also wrote a *Baker's Dozen* [an early anthology of successful radio dramas from the West Coast].

KEATLEY: And writer Eric Nicol. The development went very well. They moved it to Toronto to became a prestigious radio drama anthology, *Stage*. *Stage* took all of those people, because it was an opportunity no one could miss. Then Fletcher took the *Stage* idea down to the States and it became *Playhouse 90*.

MJM: I see a pattern repeated over and over again in Toronto. A unit comes together, which is working superbly with a writer, a director, and actors, and suddenly there's a raid from the United States, the entire thing gets swept away, and you have to start again. Is Vancouver to Toronto as Toronto is to Los Angeles? You also have people like Daryl Duke and Mario Prizek going east from here in the 1950s.

KEATLEY: And they also came out of exactly the same kind of Canadian system. Mario was in the Player's Club, and a painter and a writer. From here, he went into the CBC and then east. Norman Campbell and Daryl Duke went to the Film Board first, then the CBC, then to Toronto, and then south.

MJM: You stayed here.

KEATLEY: Yes, because I really had a physical attachment to the landscape in this part of the world. Also, I like beginnings more than big times.

MJM: There is also a group of actors and writers who work for the network from here. They are not moving to the centre either.

KEATLEY: You get the "centre stories" from many of them – Michael Mercer and Anne Cameron. They came back because they find that it's better for them to write here.

MJM: You were telling me about your sense that so many CBC people are displaced from their point of origin. This sort of person sees things from "away," as you put it.

KEATLEY: To me, that is the real glory of Paul St Pierre, whose childhood was spent in the East Coast. It's not that he is from away, he completely belongs here. But he has the cynical eye of a good writer and he always has a story.

But the advantages of distance have diminished in recent years. *Max Glick, Mom PI,* and *Northwood,* on the 1990–94 schedules, were all shot on the West Coast.

HARCOURT: I look at all of the dailies of the shows that I'm responsible for, because the changes occur in the dailies. I will often see the dailies before the producer who was on the set does.

MJM: How do you do that located in Toronto, when they're shooting so much in Vancouver these days?

HARCOURT: Tapes are couriered. It's easier if something is shot in Toronto, because I get them instantaneously. The dailies are where you get your chance to "speak now or forever hold your peace."

MJM: Can you get back to the producer on site in time to get a change implemented?

HARCOURT: Yes. With Vancouver, the time difference plays in our favour because I'm always here at seven o'clock and it's only four o'clock there, so it's towards the end of their shooting day. Everybody has cellular phones; I can talk to anybody at any time.

MJM: In that sense it's a very "hands-on" process for you.

HARCOURT: Absolutely. I was executive in charge of *Mom PI* and on *Max Glick,* because they are new series. They are being settled in first season, so I will do it myself and then delegate somebody to take over when it's up and running. That's how it works.

The tensions between the centre and the regions were always present, overt or subtextual. Sociologists John Jackson and Greg Nielson have looked at this dialectic in "Broadcasting: Centralization, Regionalization and Canadian Identity."[64] Tensions were evident behind the cameras even in small but telling details like a title theme, as music consultant Ed Vincent comments.

VINCENT [1989]: In 1972 I was asked to assist in setting up the music tracks for *The Beachcombers*. At that time, there was no one out there who had experience in providing a music track from records, so they asked if we could send someone out. After having settled with them that I was there because I was a CBC employee and that I had no feelings about regional television, I did six shows in six weeks out there.

That the debate is unsolved is apparent from the lack of consensus in the 1987 drama report:

Nothing is new in the debate. John Hirsch fought decentralization passionately, and excerpts from his parting memo give a flavour: "A policy of 'let all flowers bloom' was announced. In light of the Corporation's recognition that we were desperately short of expertise in the area of drama, and that all resources needed to be pulled together in order to produce programs of quality, I could never understand this attitude, as there are no regional points in Canada where drama can be produced without massive infusion of outside help" (July 1978). *Beachcombers* belied some of his arguments, as did the emergence of Vancouver as a secondary production centre; Mike Daigneault cites the battles which led to the production of *Empire* out of Montreal, as an example of how it can be done if the will is there; Marc Blandford confirms this view, but points out that the talent base assembled in Montreal either scattered or moved to Toronto in the end.

There are two rigid schools on the regional questions, and intermediate variants. One school asserts that drama is so expensive, and requires such a critical mass of manpower, facilities, support departments and capital equipment, that the country can barely afford one centre, and even that one centre is inadequate. The second school argues that dramatic production has become Toronto-centric, disconnected from the country, self-indulgent, and arrogant, which accounts for our inability to gain wider followings for our productions; this group argues that there should be a devolution of funds and facilities to the "base," where the people are, where we know their concerns, and where, through decentralizing Toronto, a new, relevant Drama department will emerge, along with a new generation of writers.

We cannot even agree among ourselves in this network on what a "regional" production is. A lot of producers believe that any drama shot in a regional environment is ipso facto a regional drama. This has the virtue of classifying everything we do as a regional drama, since everything is shot somewhere in the country. This "backdrop" theory of drama, however, does not address the real grievances expressed in the regional locations, and need not delay us here.

There is a bureaucratic model which surfaces periodically, which envisions turning over the national drama budget to the regional directors, a theory which boils down to "give us the money and we'll send you the tape" – a sort of theatrical Meech Lake. It shouldn't be necessary to have to argue against this model, which became unfashionable with the introduction of national standards.[65]

The last word on the place of the regions in the mandate and ethos of the CBC goes to the upper-level management of the 1980s to the mid-1990s – Trina McQueen, Ivan Fecan, and Denis Harvey.

MJM: If there's going to be a CBC, some television drama has to come from the regions.

McQUEEN [1988]: To me, this is one of the fundamental problems of the CBC, especially in entertainment. Once again, news and current affairs has to a certain extent solved that problem, not to the liking of everyone, but at least it's done its best so that news and current affairs is produced in every location from Charlottetown to Vancouver.

There is still a lot of doubt among people about whether it's possible to have an entertainment industry with many production locations, but I think we have to take the leap of faith and say, "Yes, it is possible." It is possible if we want it, if we manage it, and if we resource it. There have to be four or five major centres where good drama can be done in this country, or the CBC will fail in many respects.

MJM: The East Coast has never been a major producer of region-to-network programs, although they do local stuff.

McQUEEN: The regions have been focusing their efforts on comedy and children's programming. That seems somehow to have taken root.

MJM: Newfoundland has been doing some Newfoundland drama, for and about Newfoundland. I haven't had a chance to go out and look at it.

McQUEEN: *Up at Ours* or *Wonderful Grand Band* [both seen in other regions].

MJM to IVAN FECAN: What regional development is being attempted?

FECAN [1989]: The producers that we develop in *Family Pictures* are now developing movie-of-the-week scripts or theatricals because they've learned some of their craft. With some of them we have been trying to support their movies, so they could learn that next step. Maybe two years from now they may be accomplished enough to try a series for us. You have to have a progression. You don't jump into doing a series.

There are a lot of independents. There are great film crews in Vancouver and great crews in Edmonton. Saskatchewan does not have the independent crews yet. There is one terrific crew in Manitoba. There are plenty in Ontario, plenty in Quebec, and there are a few crews in the Atlantic provinces, "pick-up" crews that different film-makers use. We don't own these crews, but we don't own most of our "in-house" crews either. Most of them are freelances. These people are terrific. Many of them have been trained by the CBC, and many others have been trained by the American productions in this country.

MJM to DENIS HARVEY [1988]: I have noticed that things are more constricted than they used to be, as far as regional visibility is concerned. I'm talking about the sense of our own landscapes.

HARVEY: That was something I said over and over again four years ago: Please show me more country. I think of things like *Striker's Mountain*. It shot only a pilot and fell through as a series, but it was outdoors and it showed our mountains. I certainly think that *Chatauqua Girl*, produced by Jeannine Locke, showed our country.

MJM: It did.

HARVEY: I think *Island Love Song*, also produced by Jeannine Locke and set in Cape Breton, did.

MJM: I suppose my sense of a lack of regional visibility is because the movies are shown infrequently.

HARVEY: Well, one a week. Fifteen nights during the winter in 1988. In *Seeing Things* you saw Toronto. *Street Legal?* Come on!

MJM: Very Toronto.

HARVEY: The one thing I said to Maryke McEwen, when we finally approved *Street Legal*, was not to lose Toronto. I wanted to see Toronto every night of *Street Legal*. A couple of times she has got away from it and I complained about it. I think we have become used to seeing the beauties of a San Francisco or a Los Angeles or a New York. Damn it! Toronto is one of the great cities in the world. Let people see it.

We were being pressed politically by the financial constraints of our own government, by Telefilm, by our own people, by provincial governments, to do more in the regions. With the 1980 and 1985 cutbacks, the CBC had to stop doing something. One of the answers was to do less regional programming and to have the regions do network programs. I think if you took a schedule now, about 26 per cent of the material on any one day originates in the regions. It should jump to about 41 per cent at the end of three years. Now it is not all drama. There will be a network garden show and so forth.

MJM: When I was in Vancouver in 1985 the morale was on the

floor because of the across-the-board cuts you were speaking of. The plant was still there, but the people were missing. Are they being brought back?

HARVEY: Not yet. In fact, probably never. The biggest loss there was the design department, set building, and so forth. We'll farm that out instead of having fifty people come back on staff. We'll just contract out when we need sets for shows.

What is currently at stake in the regions versus the centre question is the survival of the regions as distinctive entities.[66] Philip Keatley points out wryly that Vancouver had a core of talented people who stayed because they could find work there, and another group who went up to the majors from the "farm team." Ivan Fecan stresses the importance of the apprenticeship system to the success of expensive mini-series. Trina McQueen sees the importance of regional stories, not just as fulfilling the mandate, but as integral to the national soul.

Months before the 1995 budget or the report of the House of Commons Committee on Broadcasting, David Kaufman of the editorial board of *SCAN*, the magazine for CBC producers, wrote that "the rapid turnabout of the espoused philosophy of Canadian Liberals can only mean one thing for the public-sector economy in Canada: a period of rapid deflation and shrinkage ... CBC management and employees have been reluctant to face a difficult truth: many Canadians are indifferent about the CBC's survival and some would like to see it go down. In fact the odds of the CBC surviving in its present form are just about nil. The lesson for management is very simple: 'It's about program production, stupid!' The only way the CBC can hope to fulfil even part of its mandate is to cut out everything that doesn't contribute to program production."[67] Kaufman goes on to quote the old professorial warning to first-year students: "Look at the person on your left and on your right. At least one of you will not graduate." This is a sobering note as the CBC and its unions head into the most important round of bargaining in years.

It is also a sobering note for those friends of the CBC who do remember what the corporation has accomplished over the years and would like to see it survive in some recognizable form. The key question amid these tensions and contradictions is about to take centre-stage. Will the CBC pull out of all the centres except Toronto and Vancouver, and provide political coverage only for Ottawa? Or will it back into fortress Toronto and fortress Montreal? If the CBC becomes two super stations in order to "save the national network," my own view from the centre (Ontario) and the periphery (St Catharines) is that the CBC will quietly flicker, sputter, and go out.

11 Interview with Ivan Fecan

Television is about the artist. If television is driven by technology or
deals, then it won't have the passion. It's very easy to be seduced by the
technology.[1] IVAN FECAN

In July 1993 I had a third interview with Ivan Fecan, at his suggestion. Both the broadcasting context and the political/social agenda are
changing rapidly, so much so that the survival of the CBC, indeed of
public broadcasting worldwide, is now in question. In a sense, the
continuity and coherence of this narrative is also under pressure from
the rapidly changing broadcasting context. Thus it seemed sensible to
keep this last interview as a separate chapter and to bring the technological, regulatory, and co-production updates together, along with my
summary, in a concluding chapter. The previous ten chapters could
be read as a rewind and search, while the last two chapters look forward a short distance into an uncertain but, on a good day, a potentially exciting future.

In *Turn Up the Contrast*, I reserved one chapter for an interview
with John Kennedy, head of drama in the late 1970s and 1980s, and
essentially gate-keeper for the Drama Department. In 1989, the
department was completely reorganized, with program-making dispersed and decision-making concentrated in the hands of Ivan Fecan.
The losses and some of the gains of that radical shift have been
running motifs, particularly through chapters 1 to 4. I will offer my
own assessment of the results in "Wrap-up." Here is Ivan Fecan answering some of the questions that arose from the previous chapters.

This interview is supplemented with quotations from a wide-
ranging interview Andrew Borkowski had with Fecan in the May/June
1993 issue of *SCAN*. Fecan asked me to read it before I came to talk
to him, presumably because he thought it a useful account of his
current thinking. Knowlton Nash's *Microphone Wars* also supplies

some of the context to this interview, which occurred at a time when "repostitioning" was in process and Fecan was responsible for all of English-language television, including news and current affairs.[2]

FECAN: 1989: it's hard to believe I've been here so long.
MJM: It has been meteoric.
FECAN: It's been an incredible ride. Meteoric is not the word; "roller coaster" is what I'd choose.

TECHNOLOGY

FECAN: We now shoot 16-mm film at thirty frames a second, so there can never really be a print. This allows us to edit on non-linear systems with multiple screens, and it cuts our editing time down by half. Just about all the equipment in this new CBC head-quarters building in Toronto is now digital. I'm not sure, but I suspect we'll probably be editing on a digital system and the tape will be digital tape. In this building I don't think we have a single analog piece of video or audio; its all digital.
MJM: It's sounds as if you've got the equipment to go with the building. That was a question at one point.
FECAN: We haven't bought all our equipment, we're buying it at the last possible moment to take advantage of what's happening in the equipment world. I had a meeting with the president of Sony Canada and he was telling me that in his field what he thought would take ten years is taking a year or two. We were not supposed to have production in this building until this year. We ended up making a studio and having it operational last year, all with digital equipment that wasn't supposed to be available for many years and at a cost much less than we anticipated. Not only has the speed of development telescoped, but the price has been compressed. Our editing in film like *Street Legal* and *North of 60* tends to be digital editing now.

In the 1990s the issues of cultural appropriation (see Williams in chapter 10) have risen for museums, university instructors, theatre companies, and the CBC, to name a few of the traditional, self-defined guardians of cultural heritage. In the area of representation of Aboriginal peoples on TV, the picture is changing after forty years.

FECAN: There is *North of 60*, there's the Native anthology series that will be starting, and two movies of the week that we've approved – one that will start shooting this fall. As soon as Telefilm gives it a green light, we'll start shooting the other [*Spirit Rider, Medicine River*].

MJM: What is the Aboriginal involvement on those projects?

FECAN: It depends. On *North of 60*, there's a lot of apprenticeship, the majority of the cast, and a lot of consultants who come down from their villages and consult with the producers and the writers about whether the scripts achieve the right tone. It's shot in a working village. Some of that village was built by Aboriginal crafts-people who came down from the north. Some of the writers are Native now, and one of the directors. It's very much thought of as a mainstream series. But the additional benefit is that Aboriginal writers and directors have been given experience. On the Native anthology, the writers are Native and the actors are largely Native. Novelist Thomas King is the story editor. We're looking hard for Native directors. There's not as many as we'd like and they need more opportunity to work.

MJM: How about producers?

FECAN: We have a Native producer on it, but she's not the lead producer. I'm not sure how many Native producers there are and what their level of expertise is yet.[3]

CROSS-FERTILIZATION

MJM: One of the things that was said is that this building would finally make it possible for people to cross-fertilize more easily. Yet the independents are now working all over the city and all over the country. Does anybody ever meet anybody in the corridors any-more? Would that be still an advantage?

FECAN: It's not like it would have been if we had housed all the creative people in the country in one place, because directors are shooting, people are writing, and producers are creating every-where in the country. It's a much more open kind of system, and we're buying from a much wider range of people.

   Getting back to your point, there used to be some thirty build-ings. I can honestly tell you it was easier to do a co-production with the BBC or with NBC than to do a co-production between News and Entertainment at the CBC, because everybody has built up defences. That's changing now. This building is making that quite different. News has not moved in totally, and they won't be able to function until February 1994. Of the people who have moved in, the barriers are softening much faster than we had hoped and it's great. I don't think we'll fully feel it for about a year, when just about everybody is in. There should be cross-fertilization. The accounting department is next to the *Street Legal* sets. The accountants coming into work see scenery stacked in the hallways and the makeup crash-carts – they see what we do.

Fecan has a point. In many large institutions, physical geography and psychic territory reinforce each other, even if the barrier is only a staircase to a different floor. At least an accountant tripping over a flat knows first hand where the set budget went. A line entry now has a physical reality.

PRODUCTION TEAMS AS REQUESTED IN THE DRAMA DEPARTMENT

MJM: The 1987 drama report was very passionate about dedicated teams, the idea of being able to count on the same designers, the same crew people, and so on. I heard the same need expressed in interviews with producers in the four or five years before. People also voiced concerns about everybody, from the director of photography to the makeup person, being treated with "respect." This seemed to translate into "some turnaround time" and appreciation for the craftsmen they were. Teams of this kind are a motif from the 1950s on. They did exist, then they got broken up, then they seemed to exist informally. Then you get something like *Seeing Things*, where there is a certain amount of scratching and fighting to get and to hold together what became a winning team. Are teams of key people now policy or is it still an ad hoc thing?

FECAN: It depends totally on the producer. Most producers want a consistent team on a project and, in just about every case that I can think of, that is what happens. But nobody shoots twelve months a year. We reserve the right to assign people to other things during the four or five months that a production isn't in progress. By and large that is the only way it can work. Our resource base in real dollar terms keeps shrinking. Yet we're trying very hard not to shrink our output and, in fact, to increase our output in different ways. It becomes really important that we can use the resource that we have as creatively as possible. By and large the director of photography, art director, and the "keys" [key grip and so on] are assigned to a production and stay with a production. Some of the help that department heads have is more transitory than others, but the "keys" are the ones that we really are concerned about.

FINANCING "ALL CASH"

FECAN: It's taken us a long time, but this year we have a new financial system up and running alongside the old financing system. It's a transition year. I call the new system "all cash." The accountants call it something else. Basically, if the all-cash budget of *Street Legal* is three-quarters of a million dollars an hour, then that's what we should think of it as, not $300,000 an hour because somebody pays for all the other stuff. In other words, hidden costs are now visible. I don't know of a single producer, or any other person charged with dealing with resources, who doesn't want to know what it costs. They want to know, because they want to get the most for what they have. I think the Hugh Gauntletts of the world, as living historians of this place, probably understand better than I do what happened in the 1970s.

MJM: Gauntlett basically thought the system of the 1970s and 1980s was crazy, and he said so.

FECAN: They brought in a system that dictated a few years in advance what day the Toronto Maple Leafs would play, what time and what day Anne Murray would come to sing in our studios, and when the next drama would be. It penalized anything that didn't take place a year or two years in advance. I'm not sure whether it made us more efficient or not. I don't see any evidence.

MJM: People who were working under it didn't seem to think so.

FECAN: What I do know is that it totally destroyed any initiative for being current or topical, or sensing an issue on the street and reacting to it in terms of drama. You could do it in terms of news, because news was blockbooked for facilities, people, and equipment. You knew every day at six in the evening there would be a one-hour local newscast. Within that context you could blockbook and still react to something going on in the street. Anything else you couldn't.

MJM: You're used to long lead times.

FECAN: Not anymore, that's one of the things that we've changed.

MJM: Can you be really responsive? How does that work?

FECAN: Last January we committed to making the mini-series *Dieppe*. It will be on the air on the first weekend of this January.

MJM: And it's huge.

FECAN: True, the script was sitting there and we did just a little polish on it. It was one of the scripts we had developed and were waiting for the right time. But that moved very quickly. We spend our time now on scripts and a lot less time on executing them;

because we have got that so finely tuned we can execute much quicker now. Our turnaround time is a lot less, so we can get a topical subject to our audience more quickly. That's something we've conciously been trying to do. [The topical dramas of *For the Record* rarely took less than a year from concept to broadcast.]

CREATIVE EXECUTIVES ARE WOMEN

Bearing in mind the substance of *Changing Focus*, published by the Toronto Women in Film and Television organization, I asked Ivan Fecan why he had been honoured by TWIFT for advancing women in the industry.

FECAN: Theoretically it is for people who benefit the cause of advancing women in television. Most of my senior creative executives over time have turned out to be women. I didn't just come in one day and get rid of everybody and hire women, but that's how it worked out over time. The majority of my executive producers have been women, and most of their lead characters have been women. I don't feel that by doing that I've done anything particularly deserving of an award, it just made sense. The women who were promoted at the time are still the most talented people for those jobs, so why not? But apparently this is an anomaly in terms of broadcasting, and it shouldn't be. Now I am responsible for a lot of other areas, and we have a lot of progress to make in those other areas.

REPOSITIONING

As Fecan said at the Michener Symposium in 1993, specialty channels like CNN, Arts and Entertainment, and Nashville have doubled and tripled their audiences in recent years. But, as he also pointed out, government policies based on addressing the questions of not enough Canadian content or Canadian channels will have to change because of the increased capacity from new technologies. Fragmentation does attack the traditional economic base of Canadian broadcasting, but some of the second round of specialty channels (YTV, Vision, TSN) have created new Canadian programs. Nevertheless, in the early 1990s, fear, anticipation, and antipathy have greeted the imminent prospect of the 200-channel universe. The third round of specialty channels introduced in January 1995 are struggling.[4] The CBC's response has been to join a consortium to broadcast CBC programs by direct broadcast satellite – beginning to reach out to Fecan's "extra quarter billion" viewers. At home, the CBC also tried to reposition the network in the widening broadcasting spectrum by programming three mini-networks on weeknights: a "family" slot from 7 to 9 PM, "prime-time" news and current affairs from 9 to 10 PM, and "adult" programming from 10 to 12 PM.

FECAN to BORKOWSKI: I guess the obvious is that we're alternative driven, that we're not there to do the things that the private sector already does, that we have more range, that it's a place for artists, that it's a place where you can see the country – all of the obvious things that any of us working here believe in.

SCAN: So does that mean that we'll be looking for different formats, different approaches?

FECAN: After ten o'clock is the closest we come to a public broadcasting schedule. That's not to demean the shows we do before nine, but we need them to earn larger audiences and therefore revenue, because that's the flawed way we support ourselves.

After ten I can choose solely based on quality and mandate and range and diversity. And audience matters to the extent that, if no one's watching, then you have to ask yourself if you're doing it right. But it doesn't matter to the extent that we need three rating points of women eighteen to forty-nine or else we're in deep trouble.

To be number one in Canada is very simple. You've just got to have more money than the next guy so you can go to Hollywood, buy the top-rated shows of the season and you too can be number one.

I have some very radical ideas about private broadcasting. I don't think they should have any Canadian content requirements whatsoever. I think they should be allowed to do whatever they want to do to make money – if we get totally funded so that we can get out of commercials and do our job the way all of us want to do it. Right now you've got a mixed system where the privates aren't as private as they want to be, and the public sector is nowhere near as public as it wants to be.

The fundamental thing was not the news at 9:00 but the ability to not care after 10:00 [about] whether we made money or not. And that gives us freedom to be a lot more experimental. Last year, because the decision was taken so late to try this, we were basically moving in pieces we already had and just arranging them in that order. This year I think we've done a slightly better job but it's nowhere near as interesting as I'd like it to be. Next year I think it will be.

I tried to clarify this distinction further, using *Street Legal* as my example.

MJM: I'll quote you shall I? "I was disturbed by a lack of clarity of purpose in some cases. If we were going to do a *Street Legal* I felt it should be popular. On the other hand, if a program was going to be alternative like *Adrienne Clarkson Presents* or *Codco*, it shouldn't try to be popular." The implication or the inference is that popular equals audiences?

FECAN: I'm not against a program being popular. I'm against it having as it's primary *raison d'être* audience or commerciality. If nobody watches it, then on any scale it's a failure, but I wanted it to be driven by artistic merit and vision rather than some sort of cost-per-thousand efficiency. We're trying to go a lot more on a BBC-2 analogy with what's happening after 10 PM.

I don't think *Street Legal* has had a set formula over the six years. The formula has varied with each producer, and even within the run of the three producers it's varied a little.

MJM: It concentrates more on the relationships that it used to.

FECAN: In the second full season [the third year of the run], we introduced the Olivia Novak character. The main reason for that was because we felt that all the characters were the same.

MJM: They were all good guys or variations on how to be a good guy?

FECAN: If everyone agrees, if everyone is entirely moral without any lapses, if everyone has the same point of view, I don't know where the drama is. Drama comes from conflict. That conflict and the characters in conflict provide a platform for interesting entertainment about relationships, and act as vehicles to debate various issues.

MJM: The topical issue was a strong element in the first two or three seasons and is still a running element, but the emphasis has changed.

FECAN: It's still a running theme. My only criticism of the first few years is that it was very topical but it was preaching to the converted, because there was no real disagreement about the issues.[5] Where was the drama? Showing *Street Legal* in the 7–9 time period means you get an audience. It's not there to be narrow casting, it's there to be broadcasting.

MJM: What you're talking about is the concept of the pluralities of audience and not a mass, which has been an issue since the CRTC replaced the Board of Broadcast Governors.[6] And I take your point that an audience caught in a pattern is very easy to break, but very hard to make. The CBC sent me ten years of audience research, which was very helpful.

In the *SCAN* interview you were clearly defining the CBC as a place that had more range – a place for artists, a place where you can see the country doing things that the private sector doesn't show.

CANADA/QUEBEC AND OTHER SENSITIVE SUBJECTS

I asked Ivan Fecan about my perception of some specific and puzzling gaps in subjects chosen for drama presentations and about some subjects new to the network.

MJM: What we don't have is an English "take" on Quebec.

FECAN: We tried that with *Urban Angel* and it didn't work out very well. I'd like to try that again.

MJM: It didn't work out partly because it conveyed the emotions and interactions of big city newspaper drama but not the specifics of English/Quebec tensions. I look from 1970 to 1975 and I see that nothing appears on the October Crisis on the CBC until 1975. I look through the dramas, the specials, the series, and so forth. *Don't Forget, Je me souviens* (1980) is the only one to address this specific topic. There is lots about the topic on news and current affairs, but I wouldn't be doing this kind of research if I didn't think that drama had a different way of reaching an audience. An example is *Where the Spirit Lives*. Through electronic mail I've been put in touch with a young Navajo girl. She had seen *Where the Spirit Lives* on PBS and she wrote a college paper that so affected people in her class that they wept. This is in a college that is two-thirds Navajo in New Mexico. Her sense of it was, "My God, this happened to somebody else?" Later e-mail and NATIVE-L put me in touch with another adult man, also in the United States, who said esentially the same thing. To me, that's what drama does, it personalizes abstract issues and makes them concrete. That's what I'm not finding, not hearing, not seeing about something that's so close to us all – Quebec.

FECAN: I think your observation is dead-on, the whole subject of English/French relations in Canada is a fascinating one. We have a mini-series in development about the Plains of Abraham with Dick Nielson writing, where we get at, in a historical context, some of the foundations. It's a subject for me like (this will probably sound very bad in print) *Conspiracy of Silence* (racism) or *Boys of St Vincent* (sexual abuse). It's a controversial subject that you better be sure is done well, because nothing else is acceptable. Everything must be done so well that it is above reproach.

MJM: I think anybody would understand that.

FECAN: A lot of people wanted to do different things about what happened in Newfoundland, but we waited until we got the one we thought would be best. We didn't decide to make *The Boys of St Vincent* until we were comfortable with the quality of the script and the quality of the approach that director John Smith is going to take. We were waiting for those kind of scripts on French/English relations. Whether it's because people don't feel there is a network appetite or whether it's because it is not something that writers are dying to tell stories about, I have to say we are not inundated with proposals for such things. There are very few I can think of.

One of the problems in not being faceless and in owning up to responsiblity is that people then think you make all the decisions. I have a very good development team, and they make most of the decisions. With all the decisions we make, the one thing we never do is create a program or movie. We don't write it. The idea has to come from somebody, over a lunch or dinner or a drink. Somebody might have an idea about something, but unless a creator – and usually that means a writer and not a producer – has a burning passion to tell a story, it just doesn't happen.[7] We don't order stories into existence. Somebody has to want to say it, to tell it, and have something fresh to tell about it, something compelling.

MJM: Particularly on something that is as sensitive as the way Quebec relates to Canada.

FECAN: Because of the sensitive nature of these subjects, the only additional input we might have is no different from that in *Conspiracy of Silence* or *The Boys of St Vincent* or *Dieppe*. We want to make sure that when it is done (and it ought to be done) it's done really well. Our purpose in doing it is not to start an argument or start a fight, but to break walls down and say some things that might lead to more understanding.

Knowlton Nash has this to say about Fecan's role in *The Valour and the Horror* controversy: "Fecan's basic criticism of the blunder was in how it was platformed [advertised to create audience expectations]. 'It was platformed as an objective piece of work. It was never platformed as an essay or a point of view piece. There has to be room for all different points of view but when you are doing something controversial you have to work twice as hard to make sure your facts are correct and you have to platform it correctly.'"[8] Nash says Trina

McQueen, who did have script control over the series, "says she 'would have so labelled [it] if she had realized how controversial it was going to be.'" When channel 4 in Britain (where "Bomber" Harris is still a controversial figure to historians – but not to the surviving aircrews) broadcast the series in 1994, discussion panels on the "facts" followed each film.

Since the rise of the series and the demise of anthologies, which in Canada dates from 1966 with *Wojeck*, series drama has often been the vehicle for the explanation of topical subjects. However, critics like John Haslett Cuff have complained that the handful of topical movies-of-the-week in the 1990s have followed the American trend of "crime-of-the-week," as in the ABC, NBC, and SCBS movies on Amy Fisher, the film on the WACO cult, which was broadcast before the ashes were cooled, and the film on O.J. Simpson and Nicole Brown, which Fox originally intended to broadcast before Simpson's trial had begun.

FECAN: In all the issue programs we've done, we've scrupulously avoided the gutter approach. We've had all kinds of scripts pitched to us about movies for the-crime-of-the-week and whatever. Every single time we have resisted the temptation to make those things. We've only made them when they're about issues, and when they have some sort of higher purpose. I didn't want to get into the run of the mill, crime-movie-of-the-week kind of thing.

If we did *Conspiracy of Silence*, it would not be merely about a crime. The crime is not what the movie is about. The movie is about racism. We used the crime to give us the springboard to get into the subject. People couldn't deny that it happened, they couldn't deny the circumstances. It gave us the opportunity in that context and in a not-too-distant time to talk about how much racism is a fabric of this country. I don't think we've shied away from any big issues, but we've always been very careful to do them very well. We were also very careful not to take them out of their Canadian context. I believe that the characters and the issues only make sense within a particular context, not within a generalized context.

MJM: Canada is not always the peaceable kingdom – that's demonstrable.

ON AMERICAN REACTIONS TO THESE DRAMAS AS EXPORTS

FECAN: Oddly enough by making some of these programs culturally specfic, *Conspiracy of Silence*, *Boys of St Vincent*, *Love and Hate*, and *Liar, Liar* have become our most successful television exports.

MJM: The audience figures are formidable.

FECAN: And the figures keep increasing. *Liar, Liar* [about a child's false accusation of child abuse lodged against her father] was on CBS at the end of June 1993. It was number 1 for the night, it was number 4 for the week, and, with great respect to the cast, the cast is not what Americans consider a "star cast."

MJM: No, but they were very good.

FECAN: It did not get promoted and it was the highest-rated Tuesday night they had had in eighteen weeks. They scratched their heads about it and said, "Well, you've broken all the rules. You tell a story that's a lot blunter than we'd ever tell it, you don't have (aside from Kate Nelligan) anybody who is known to an American audience in it, in the court scenes your lawyers wear "costumes"; this violates every single development rule we have and yet you've done better than we have for four months. What's going on here?"

When we did it with *Love and Hate*, they said, "Well, it was a fluke." When we did it with the next one, *The Bruce Curtis Story*, they said, "Well, you're lucky." When *Conspiracy of Silence* did it, they said, "Well, maybe Bernie Zukerman, the producer, Frances Mankiewicz, the director and Suzette Couture, the writer, are magic." Then *Liar, Liar* did it and it was not Bernie, Frances, and Suzette, it was Nancy Isaac, who has written only episodic before, and it was Angela Bruce and not Jim Burt, creative head of movies and mini-series, who developed it. The producer is somebody we hired after the script was written. So what this string of successful exports to the United States is pointing to is that there is now a development system that works, that has a life of its own now, and it draws on people from across the country, not just in any one place or any one group.[9] We've really worked very hard to try to draw from people across the country, and that's how you get more voices.

FECAN to BORKOWSKI: Where we've strayed is because of the compromising position that having commercial revenues puts you in. The money we make from international sales of our programs is just gravy. We don't factor it into our decision-making when we develop a project. The money we make from commercials, on the other hand, is already there in the budget. We have to consider that.[10]

FECAN: From the beginning there were always one or two people who decided ultimately whether something would be made or not – that hasn't changed. There is still someone who decides ultimately. My guess is that I have a lot less to say about it now because there are a group of people in development that shortlists it and makes the decisions for me at this point.

Mjm: Who are they? You've mentioned them several times.

FECAN: Phyllis Platt is now the program director and Jim Burt looks after movies, with two people in particular who are pretty amazing, both women. Debbie Bernstein looks after series drama and she also has a very strong second. There is a new head of children's who hasn't started yet, but I think he'll be very strong.

MJM: So the creative heads make up this development team you're talking about?

FECAN: This is the development team with the program director.

THE BASIC REORGANIZATION OF DRAMA DEFENDED

I value the many accomplishments of CBC drama over four decades. When Fecan's executive assistant asked me what I wanted to discuss, I quoted from the *SCAN* interview: "I wanted to bring the network's arts and entertainment programming into the twentieth century. I wanted to bring the quality up." I defined that quotation as symptomatic of cultural, and specifically corporate, amnesia and said I would challenge it. Forewarned, Fecan had time to give a reasoned response to my question and to defend his reorganization of the Drama Department. Readers of the first half of this book have heard a good deal about the impact of that reorganization, as well as details about earlier difficulties and successes. It is therefore appropriate to present Fecan's own articulation about the changes in ethos and policy during his time as a key decision-maker.

FECAN: The last time you talked to me I was in the middle of yet another controversial changeover because the departments, per se, were disappearing. It was not unlike what the BBC is trying to do. We're now, on the entertainment side, doing it successfully. These people in the development team are buyers and developers, and their job is to develop material and see it through production regardless of where it comes from.

MJM: You're describing radical change, and radical change it was. It's been long enough to see that you've had some major successes from that radical change. By now you've been here long enough [five years] to be directly responsible for a history.

FECAN: And it's very much what I set out to do.

MJM: That was one of the things that struck me: what you told me in 1989 is what I see on my TV set in 1993. As far as I'm concerned, there are two linked questions. One rises directly from the interview in *SCAN*, where you said you "brought arts and entertainment into the twentieth century"; and the other is my sense that a generation has either moved on or retired. Are those two things linked?

FECAN: What we were doing in the 1970s and early 1980s was good and appropriate for the context of those times. I found myself in a different time where, as a "boomer," I didn't see myself or any of my colleagues (attitudinal colleagues I mean) reflected anywhere on the screen in Canada.

MJM: So you felt it was a generational issue.

FECAN: I felt there needed to be room for other kinds of things to happen – which is not to say that the other generation shouldn't and didn't have room to do its thing, too. But I felt it should not be one to the exclusion of everything else. At the same time, we were into a situation (which is very boring) where we were short of money over one of the annual government cutbacks. We had a system where we had departments. The Drama Department had producers assigned to it and had budget and air time assigned to it. The head of drama would feel a very human obligation to make sure that the people assigned to him would have something to do. Because these people were camped outside of the office of the head of drama, he would pass these people on the way to the office and pass them on the way to the elevator, and he would have a very human kind of feeling of obligation to these people. I don't mean to personalize it with the head of drama, because it was true in every department.

MJM: Yet personalities are a part of it.

FECAN: So every department had producers who seemed to get preference because they were there, as opposed to producers who were working on their own or in Vancouver, Calgary, Halifax, or Winnipeg. They had money, cash and resources, and air time dedicated to them. What happens in any bureaucracy in that situation is that you never do anything except use everything you have. Most budgets in bureaucracies are not built on a zero base; they're built on some variation of what you did last year.

One of the things I did, which was very controversial and has really only worked in the last year or two, was that I took away all the money and all the air time and assigned the producers to the head of in-house production. So producers from arts and science, music, children's, drama, variety, and comedy all worked for heads of production. I restructured the development department so that their job is to develop material and to see it through production from the point of view of a creative person, without any concern for where the material comes from. If there is an in-house producer who hasn't done anything for a year, that is not his or her problem. It's the problem of the head of production.

It freed up an enormous amount of money because, all of a sudden, the hidden money wasn't hidden and we were able to redirect that money to actual projects rather than to things that maintained bureaucracies. That money became the money we used to fuel whatever growth we had. But it was a major cultural shift for a lot of the in-house producers.

Many of them took it very hard because in the past the deal was that they made what they wanted, they developed what they wanted to develop, and they produced it. They felt that the CBC's obligation to them was not just to pay their salaries as a development cost but to let them make what they wanted to make. I don't view it as a generational thing. I just view it as a "this is the way business had been done here" attitude – but it was not the way I wanted to do it. I felt my obligation was to give them a home, to pay their salaries, to fund their development costs, to give them the freedom to develop pretty much what they wanted to develop. I did not feel that I owed each and every one of them a million dollars a year to make something. Instead, the best idea would get the production money. My obligation to them was to give them that kind of shelter. But my right, with the creative team, was to look over all the different things that had been developed and to put our money in the ones we believed in most.

That was unacceptable to some people, and I think that's unfortunate because this is an entirely appropriate way for a network to behave. What has happened is that we've ended up putting the money into a much wider range of people than before.

MJM: That's what you were forecasting at the time and that's what has happened – it's visible in the credits.

FECAN: I feel that the goal of more voices is important.

MJM: You're saying this is the way you had to accomplish that.

FECAN: That had to happen, and some producers, such as Bernie Zukerman and Alan Burke, had no problem with that. Bob Sherrin isn't doing as much drama, but he's doing a lot more arts. A lot of people have found that this works for them.

MJM: They find other niches, like Sam Levene?

FECAN: Sam's doing *Man Alive*. A lot of producers have found that this is a reasonable way of working. Some producers felt it was inappropriate, that it was not how they want to work, and I respect that, but they made their choices. There were people who didn't feel that this was how they wanted to live their professional lives at the CBC.

MJM: This is at the producer level, largely, because when you come to writers and so forth, the whole perspective is different?

FECAN: The writers are all freelance and have always been.

MJM: From 1963 to 1993 there has been an ongoing problem at the CBC about writers. There hasn't been enough money to develop them, there hasn't been enough to pay them, to keep them home, to give them things to do. Talk to writers and they say there's no respect, because scripts are often changed entirely and they contrast their situation to that of writers for the BBC or the many writer-producers in the United States. Are there any glimmers of sunlight over a dark and confused picture that does seem to have gone on a long time?

FECAN: It's hard to generalize. I would hope that writers who work with us at the CBC feel that there is a lot more respect in the last few years than there was before. But, as in any situation, those who found their material made might feel more positive than those who found their material not made.

MJM: I've been talking only to people who have had their scripts made. I'm echoing report after report from producers who say, "We need writers and we need investment" in them. I know you did some master classes and workshops in the last few years.

FECAN: We've done a lot of training over the last few years. But the other part of the equation is, in order for us to find the Nancy Isaacs [*Liar, Liar*] of the world, we need to have series on the air whether it's *North of 60* or *Street Legal*. That's one of the things that people often forget.

And so the relationship between the "populist" and the "demanding" forms of television reappears, not as a polarity but, as the cultural materialists have always argued, as a symbiosis. Producers, directors, designers, "keys," and crews move among the demanding "one-off" drama specials like *Sanity Clause*, the different and equally tough demands of series like *North of 60*, and a twelve-minute profile of a ball-player for *Midday*. Drama is part of the continuum of the network's output – and that output is, as it has always been, designed to win the loyalty of the taxpayer/viewers.

12 Wrap-up: Or, This Disruption Is Not Temporary

The days when the Government would instruct people what to watch are gone. PERRIN BEATTY[1]

Perrin Beatty was one of the youngest ministers in the Conservative government of 1984–93. Unlike more senior ministers born in the 1940s, he is a member of the television generation. During his lifetime, most Canadians have used television as a way to spend some of their time every day of the week – and most have taken for granted that it should be a medium controlled in Canada by "arm's-length" boards and commissions. Yet Beatty, in his remarks as reported, predicted that the CRTC will eventually become irrelevant as new modes of delivery make it impossible to control viewer choices. With the July 1995 agreement of cabinet and the CRTC, Expressvu will begin direct broadcast satellite (DBS) signals to pizza-sized dishes that cost $1000. Signals are decoded by black boxes that Expressvu rents for $30 a month – or less than most full cable services. Including local Canadian stations, 100 channels will be available. A competitor will be up and running a short time later, both licensed by the CRTC.

However, only signals delivered by fiber optic cables or digital compression on existing cable channels will in future be governed by the CRTC's control over the cable and telephone monopolies. Since Beatty spoke in Vancouver in 1992 at what was billed as "a media summit with all the players," the papers and magazines in North America have been filled with brave new visions of what the "electronic highway" will offer and how it will change our lives.[2] Those digital interactive "black boxes" will also replace today's analogue television receivers with computers. They will, in theory, provide shopping, video games, access to worldwide information nets, and even newspapers tailor-made to a viewer's interests. One of the odder things about the "great cable consumer revolt" of January 1995 was that subscribers assumed that this technology was already widely available, so they couldn't see why they could not "pick and pay for" whatever services they liked. Hence their outrage when they were told they had to pay for the seven new licensed specialty services in order to receive "old" favourites like A&E and TSN. In a very few years they will be able to pick and pay; hence the rush to launch new services now when viewers can still be corralled into buying the new in order to receive the old – a marketing strategy that infuriated cable viewers and caused the mighty Rogers cable company and its imitators to apologize and restore its old pay tiers. It did not mean, however, that the new Canadian channels were given the lower numbers on the dial where older sets could receive them. The CRTC refuses to regulate where a cable channel puts most of its stations, so those lower numbers are still devoted to shopping and real estate networks owned by the cable companies.

Moreover, "unbundling" the new services may well mean that most of them will disappear in the consumer backlash. Liam Lacey reported in the *Globe and Mail* in July 1995 that the six new channels had been bought by 60 per cent (about 4 million) of the cable subscribers, instead of the projected 90 per cent (7.2 million). This shortfall has meant that some services may request that the CRTC ease the Canadian content regulations governing their licences. This would mean fewer new Canadian productions commissioned from the flood of proposals on the desks of the presidents. Trina McQueen of Discovery commented: "Lead us not into temptation. If our purpose is to get Canadian voices heard, that is not the way to go." According to Lacey, Discovery has 4.4 audience share; Bravo and the Women's Network, 0.5 each, and Showcase, 0.8, based on the first half of 1995.

Whether Showcase, Bravo and The Women's Network (the three that show TV drama) survive or not, the same old problems of where all this material will come from persist. Largely ignored by the media that sketch out this glowing future are the two questions: How the programs will arrive, and how they will be paid for. In these areas, technology and regulation remain intertwined.

Harvey Enchin in a front-page newspaper article headed "TV control no longer so remote" quotes CRTC chairman Keith Spicer: "We're seeing a massive change in how Canadians interact with television, as they move from being passive viewers to being discriminating TV consumers demanding more control."[3] It is discouraging that the outdated idea of viewers being passive, with its connotations of helpless victims, still appears in the pronouncements of the chair of the CRTC.

In the 1990s CRTC decisions mean that the monopoly cable companies will lose their guaranteed profits of 23 per cent of net assets as well as the automatic increases tied to the consumer price index. Moreover, the customers will not have to cover the full costs of "digital video compression" or of "addressibility" – of more channels and the box that makes the television set interactive. The CRTC has even directed the cable companies to pay rebates to their customers, or to contribute over five years to a $300 million fund for Canadian production. This sum amounts to $60 million a year. Since one episode of an hour-long American prime-time drama costs well over $1 million, this fund would cover about one hour per week of that form of programming – or many more hours of cheaper fare.

Ian Morrison, speaking for the special interest group Friends of Canadian Broadcasting, was more pessimistic about the CRTC ruling. He called the new regulations a licence to print money for the cable companies, and pointed out that the production fund would pay realistically for only one thirty-minute drama a week. As Enchin also wryly noted, the "administration of the fund has not been sorted out."

And where would those programs appear? According to the CRTC, on the new Canadian specialty services that must be developed to match the new American specialty services. Cable's response through its spokesperson was that the 1:1 ratio would mean that cable would have to dump three existing U.S. channels in 1993. In the future, viewers forced to subscribe to Canadian cable companies could be denied such toothsome new American specialty channels as a channel with twenty-four hours a day of five- to ten-minute commercials, a crime channel, a romance classics network, a game channel with interactive games using touch-tone telephones, a "golden American" network for those over fifty, a global village network of international business and lifestyle programming, and Talk TV, which would provide sixteen hours a day of interviews and viewer call-in. The 1:1 ratio aside, if a viewer did have access to such choices, there are still the two key questions: first, whether advertising revenue would drop because the audience would fragment further when viewers flicked to a crime channel or a channel featuring an hour of ten-minute infomercials; second, whether viewers would willingly pay for them on their monthly cable bill. Even if viewers choose instead to pull such channels off direct broadcast satellites (DBS) through rented decoders, the most important questions still remain. What will the demographic profile be of those who choose to watch a given channel – or program – among the two hundred channels on offer? How many viewers will sample the flood of programs, and then return to the big hits on the easily available (and free) channels?

Viewers in Canada already pay for decoders for their satellite dishes because there are no over-the-air channels available and/or they cannot get cable. Then they complain that no satellite carries local or regional news.[4] Thus, cable could still have a real function in delivering the highly rated local news/weather and sports programs, but the viewer dependent on satellite feed only will never see local stations, which cannot afford to use satellites. Moreover, access to decoders for satellite feed is no guarantee that favourite services will not be scrambled.

"CBC climbs aboard 'death star,'" proclaimed the *Globe and Mail*.[5] Cable and network competitors were said to be reeling in shock. The corporation with a private partner is not only repositioning itself for the Canadian viewer in the 1990s, it is going out to meet the world by running programs on a direct broadcast satellite. The CBC has not shown that kind of self-confidence, whether born of desparation or not, since the early 1960s.

A glimpse of the future, which will also include much more pay-per-view, is offered by the "first bulk television system in North America." The newspaper reporter continued: "the 150 channel Time-Warner Quantum System in Queens, New York, offers choices on the screen in general categories such as new hit movies, children's shows, special events and adult movies. When a viewer 'clicks' on choices, more and more specific menus are displayed."[6] But she quoted the reservations of David Ellis, "we're not suddenly going to be scanning 385 channels every evening," and media consultant Paul Audley, who says that "techno-fetishists are buying into fantasies" if they think that more viewing will be better viewing. "There are a finite number of viewing hours and a finite number of viewers and a finite number of dollars."[7]

On 29 March 1993, the *Globe and Mail* in an editorial headlined "Navigating in a 500-channel universe" predictably weighed in for a much reduced role for regulation: "We go back to the book analogy ... there is space on the shelf for books that have not found an audience as yet, but may in time. It is here, in expanding artistic choices beyond what consumers themselves might demand, that the state still has its uses ... through direct subsidy to producers, through independent granting agencies such as the Telefilm fund – and of course through the CBC." Of course. This is a position oddly inconsistent with this newspaper's regular editorial stance, which assumes that the CBC is an inefficient and nefarious boondoggle foisted on taxpayers. Mind you, it also has had little good to say about the cable companies or the whole industry. "The industry may choose to call [DBS satellites] death stars but the death they bring, we should not mourn. It is the death of poverty of choice and of state control on free expression. Best of all, it is the death of a corrupt and contented racket where success depended more on the ability to fawn upon the regulators than to deliver quality programs to consumers. The age of consumer freedom is now two years away. Tick, tick, tick."[8] The timing was out, but not by much.

Keith Spicer took up the challenge of the 29 March editorial in a later article on the Commentary page. "Broadcasting regulation: Is it obsolete?" read the headline. He began with the premise that "countless interactive cable channels will leave the lab and enter most living rooms in only four to seven years." After citing the success stories of Canadian content regulations – a whole Canadian music industry and millions of dollars of independent television production – he described both industries as "mature" now and able to "thrive on their own." Again as a representative voice for the CRTC, he pictures the viewer in the past forty years as incapable of oppositional (here defined as within the dominant discourse) much less resistant readings. It is only in this new technological world through which he volunteers to guide us that "Canadian consumers [will have] unprecedented control of programming that, for 40 years, they swallowed passively." Clearly he has not talked to the CBC audience research department, which has documented the outspoken reactions of Canadians to a variety of shows, especially documentaries and dramas over those same decades.[9] He continues, "The CRTC welcomes this as a deeply democratic evolution. It also believes that, with a little nudging, these forces can enrich and anchor Canadian Society ... With the CRTC's happy connivance, consumers will be 'regulating' the market far more than today ... We think the market – that is, the consumer, will gradually be able to replace the CRTC in many areas." The $300 million levy on the cable companies, who after all never make the product they sell, is to "boost Canadian programming at home as well as exports ... Already the commercial success of Canadian programs is eclipsing the old Cancon [Canadian content] obsession."[10]

As defined in his article, the role of the CRTC continues to be to push for more equitable representation by Canadian broadcasters of women, children, and multicultural and aboriginal communities, to reduce the amount of violence depicted, and to control cable rates. Spicer then goes on to identify "a final area where we may need to help: managing the accelerating convergence of telecommunications [a reminder to the reader that the 'T' in CRTC stands for both television and telecommunications] ... As the titans clash, somebody, amid all the chaos, may need to stick up for consumers and artists in case the all-wise market doesn't." The irony is noted. Otherwise, he reminds us, if the CRTC disappears we could have "a private interest with few scruples, for example, about invading your private interests with its new technological toys; that is what ideology-driven rather than needs-driven deregulation could bring." Yet there is a growing unease about the CRTC's apparently "business-driven" decision-making in recent years. Roger's takeover of other cable services, and acceptance of negative marketing techniques, are only two examples. Technological convergence may end the CRTC's ability to regulate content or to control common means of transmission early in the twenty-first century.

Other cautionary words appear in this discussion. Reuters news agency report by David Morgan, headlined "Interactive TV needs fine-tuning," begins with the statement that the much heralded information highway, discussed in the media, depends on technology not yet in place. In fact, "much of the technology does not exist." Several rival consortia to pioneer the technology and software, manufacture it, and market it do exist, but if they do not manufacture their technology to a common industry standard, viewers will be unable to take their black boxes from region to region and no one in this mobile society will buy one. If, as some people think, the cost to the consumer of these services could be $1000 a year, who will want them? Morgan addresses another key issue: "'Also in doubt is just what will be available in the way of programming at the outset. What the industry promises is that viewers will be able to watch what they want when they want and have the convenience of banking, shopping, ordering takeout food, and playing games on TV. But I'm not sure they'll be able to deliver much more than a kind of high-tech TV Guide and video games,' said a sceptical TV industry executive."[11] Morgan does not point out that the VCR permits people to watch what they want when they want to right now and that the other services listed are already available by phone – at least in Canada. Nor does he point out that the sceptical TV industry executive may work for one of the networks and thus may be speaking wishfully, since one of the effects of the new technologies seldom discussed in these articles is the possible demise of *all* existing networks.

The three articles by Enchin, Spicer, and Morgan appeared in the *Globe and Mail* within twelve days of one another. Taken together, they illustrate the debate, confusion, and overstatement that surround the hydra-headed snake of technology/consumer choice/regulation in the 1990s and the fact that no magic sword has yet been found to prevent the heads, when lopped off by governments, regulatory bodies, cable companies, or satellite owners – those desiring to shape the future in one particular direction – from growing right back again.

Antonia Zerbisias, who has covered the media beat for some years for the *Toronto Star*, has written one of the most coherent analyses for non-experts about the selling of interactive television.[12] She too points out that much of this technology is still on the drawing board and that efficient technologies already exist for doing things like ordering pizza. In addition, she identifies other issues that are seldom addressed in the 1990s flood of "hyperactive hard sell." There are privacy issues – using interactive television means that the viewer's tastes, purchases, and bank balance are all on record. There are the viewers' preferences for interaction with live objects like ripe fruit or live people like bank tellers. Zerbisias draws pointed analogies with computers that are never used and vcrs that defeat their owners. Although the issue of good programming is glossed over in the article, she does look at costs, with quotations from Florian Sauvageau to back her point: "I fear that information will become just a commodity for which we will have to pay more and more."[13] She also quotes the chairman of the still largely ineffective Federal Communications Commission (fcc) in the United States as saying that pay-per-view must not replace 'Free tv' because it is "essential to a well-informed citizenry and electorate in a democracy." Zerbisias herself asks, "And then what? Do better-off citizens subsidize 'lower income groups' cable bills just so we're all on an equal democratic footing?"

The article raises very real questions. Newsworld, Vision, ytv, and other basic services could disappear into the more expensive "pay" as opposed to "basic" tiers of cable. But democracy also depends on libraries with searchable databases and actual books that can be taken home and read forwards, backwards, and reread with ease; affordable newspapers with the same hardcopy advantages; broad-interest radio stations and television channels; and all kinds of activities undertaken by citizens daily in the community. None of these appear to be threatened by the new technology and what it may or may not offer.

When the computer and the television set merge into one device as predicted, the flow of information, entertainment, and education will increase. Academics and businesses already pay for online searches of specialized databases. That sort of knowledge is costly and is used primarily by researchers. Many no-charge databases are also available, through electronic mail and its more sophisticated offshoots, Internet and Web sites. Freenets – public access points to Internet – are springing up all over North America. They are available to anyone with a pc or Mac and a modem, and do not involve long-distance charges if a Freenet is available locally. The average subscriber donation to these no-profit local Freenets is $10 per year. Once on the network, all sorts of discussion groups and databases are available. Databases may be searched and the Internet navigated via software packages delighting in names such as Gopher, Veronica, Archie, and www (World Wide Web). Subscribers may have a chat or post to a bulletin board, contact a long-lost friend in New Zealand, or send graphics images, fully formatted text programs, and even short animations. Users can look up the book catalogue in their local or university library, and online catalogues in libraries around the world. Online conferences are being held in this hyperspace, with the advantage that new participants can read the discussion of the previous days or months before jumping in, or simply "lurk" – listen in. They can search the discussion archive using a keyword of their choice. This seems to be "democracy" fighting back on the information front – and having a lot of fun in the process.

In the more immediate future, the two-hundred channel universe is the context for those who have to plan for the next decade of broadcasting. Mark Starowicz, the influential maker of documentaries and the progenitor of CBC radio's *As It Happens* and CBC television's *The Journal*, fears that specialty channels that might or might not appear on the basic tier of cable could be used in dangerous ways. In extracts from a speech called "The Gutenberg Revolution of Television," he said:

In fact we may see a blend of general service and commercial interest. Take any industrial lobby that already produces a considerable amount of public propaganda – the nuclear industry, for example ... It produces documentaries and magazines and educational material. Why would it not find common interest with other like-minded industrial interests and see merit in joint ownership of a technology/science/environment channel, which is not overt advocacy or advertising but which is a visually rich general interest channel, which nevertheless commissions programs and works more fitting with its technological perspective – a sort of 'technology is good' channel.

He also imagines shopping channels that specialize in cosmetics or home repair, channels devoted to horoscopes and spiritualists, "the ultraconservative channel, the local and national gay service," fragmented music channels, "the computer buff" channel. He concludes, "Stand back, look at the news and magazine stand of today and you see the future."[14] The shift in metaphor from the *Globe and Mail*'s bookshelf to that of a news-stand suggests different expectations about the capacity of the program to engage and the capacity of the viewer to concentrate and connect.

The danger implied here is not visible but invisible propaganda. American fundamentalist Christian channels already mix the old and the new in just the way Starowicz describes, but the point of view is quite visible even to the "naive" eye (if such can be found in the 1990s). The viewer who regularly chooses to watch the televangelists, the "news" as reported by Pat Roberts, and "clean" sitcoms of the 1950s knows what is being marketed. Televisually literate people also see the encomia to the weapons and tactics of the Second World War and the Gulf War on the Arts and Entertainment channel as the products of the u.s. military. They may be cheap for A&E to program, but the price-tag on the viewer's time and pocket-book is quite visible. To get a look at all that exciting, often very beautiful combat footage, a viewer either listens to the jingoistic sound track or switches on the mute button. Both Spicer and Starowicz seem to agree that viewers will passively soak up the message, but is this necessarily true?[15]

The emerging technologies we have been discussing allow viewers to be instantly interactive. Many people have sent e-mail to John Pannikar, program director at Discovery, who invited viewers to critique the pilots of five different potential series, each one exploring cyberspace. Viewers could also fax or write letters, but the e-mail is central to the fact that people take time to comment and Pannikar has time to reply on an individual basis to e-mail. The Discovery website also gives hypertext about the programs, providing another way for viewers to connect to the service. The most interesting thing about this interchange – an approach that has the active support of president Trina McQueen[16] – is that any viewers who comment intelligently on the organization, accessibility, and accuracy of the information these five different approaches to the highway take will directly influence which one is developed into a series. Knowledgable criticism comes from those who know and those who want to learn for the price of a Freenet and a modem. If this is not an information programmer's dream, it should be.

Meanwhile, another player enters in the set itself – high definition television. Japan's decade-old analogue HDTV has not been adopted by the rest of the world. American and European breakthroughs in digitizing and compressing images has made the analogue process obsolete. Nevertheless, the high-definition image that could also offer a much larger image than those currently available requires new technology to record, process, transmit, and receive the programs. If all the stations and networks switched to HDTV, there are two possibilities: one is that digitally compressed images may still be broadcast over the existing bandwidths; the other is that, if HDTV prevails, cable will be necessary to receive the signals. Which one it will be is fundamentally a made-in-America political choice. What we may see in the shorter term is cheaper sets, with the same companies making the sets and high-definition video discs to go with them – just as the Marconi company bought stations and broadcast programs in the 1920s to sell radio sets.

"HERE" IS WHERE TECHNOLOGIES CONVERGE

Where is "here?" is an old question for Canada. "'Here' is where technologies converge" is one of the new answers supplied by the 1990s. It is implicit in geographer Paul Adams's discussion of "Television as Gathering Place."[17] Geographers are asking themselves "Where is here?" and concluding that "mass-media conveniently provide simplified and selective identities for places beyond the realm of immediate experience of the audience and hence tend to fabricate a pseudo-world of pseudo-places." These pseudo-places lead people to experience actual places in terms of these stereotypes.[18] Others accuse the "politics of distraction," which impose a social structure, rather than the media themselves for a pervasive sense of placelessness. But Adams argues that television *is* a "place" by pointing out "the decreasing importance of location in the structuring of social life and the construction of meaningful human experience." Television, he argues, serves various social and symbolic functions (like monuments or more abstract symbolic spaces) previously served by places: sensory communion, social congregation, the attribution of value to persons and objects, and the definitions of an "us" and "them." He also points out, "the very characteristics of modern architecture, 'fiction, fragmentation, eclecticism, all suffused with a sense of ephemerality and chaos'[19] ... are eminently typical of television." "Where technologies converge," then, may be the first postmodern nationless state.

What is particularly apposite in this closely argued paper is the accelerated identification of the convergence of time and space (first noted in 1975) which electronic mail and interactive television/computers create. A sense of community is one of the pleasures of e-mail right now. One can listen in to conversations that intercut from Canberra to Vancouver to a small college in New Mexico, which have "flares" of emotion like real conversations, as well as a new shorthand of symbols conveying emotions. The technology permits "real-time" conversations among many parties, or formal e-mail conferences prearranged and fully as challenging as "live conferences" can be – if less serendipitous in contacts and casual exchange. Hypertext is yet another new technology that gives a reader access to many levels of information in many combinations. The volume of discourse is much greater. No wonder the mildly contemptuous designation "snail-mail" now signifies any mail that does not travel at the speed of light. The newly affordable technology around the corner will mean that images captured from a televison program or from the VCR, or sounds from a CD player, will also form part of the data being collectively analysed. When time and space converge in this fashion, *all* the media interact. Of course, the meanings signified are also transformed as the context changes, sometimes in ways so fleeting it is impossible to analyse them.[20]

CO-PRODUCTIONS: "SOFTWARE" OR PROGRAMS

What is not in the language is not in the mind. As a vice-president of CanWest Global Communications Corp. in charge of programming said, "Co-production is a burgeoning area, driven by economics ... We have all these channels and everybody is looking for product or software."[21] Does the language betray the way that Canadian decision-makers in the private sector think? It is true that actors (most of them have no stake in equating the theatre, radio, television, or film with the respectable and stable world of finance) have called what they do and where they do it "the business" for a long time. This seeming paradox exists because, historically, acting has been seen as a disreputable way to earn a living. Since that remains true, the term has never lost its ironic edge. Television executives who focus on the profits and losses call programs "products" with "shelf life." The function of living metaphors is to call attention not only to likeness but difference. Unfortunately, the terms "products" and "shelf life" have long since lost their metaphorical bite. But "software" as a metaphor for programs, by further analogy, casts the network as "the hardware" and the viewer as the "work station" on the network, the passive receiver of the electronic signal.

Are co-productions or any productions "software"? The *Globe and Mail* announced through one of its television critics, Liam Lacey, that "U.S.T.V. focuses on Canada: Americans want to focus on co-production expertise."[22] The body of the article, however, warns that when what one television executive called the "product or software" is co-produced by Americans, it will increasingly be under American control. And the market may narrow again because the recent changes in American laws allow the networks to make their programs "in-house." Ivan Fecan, in his last interview with me in July 1993, suggested that the failure of *Urban Angel* (a series set in Montreal) to address the English/French tensions in any sustained way was because it had been co-produced with a U.S. network.

In Canada, many co-productions are deals between a variety of Canadian producers and buyers. Pat Ferns, president of Primemedia Productions, has a long history of success in television drama documentary and children's shows, including the anthology *The Newcomers*, the mini-series *Glory Enough For All*, and the made-for-television films *Heaven on Earth, Going Home*, and the remarkable co-production with BBC Scotland, *Billy Bishop Goes to War*. In 1992 he described to Andrew Borkowski how he managed to get a handful of remarkably challenging Canadian plays adapted and broadcast for television using funds from a consortium of independent stations. "If you are talking to a station that spends $5,000 an hour on drama you will have your work cut out for you. If you ask them to put $250,000 into a two hour piece of drama, they'll say you are out of your cotton-picking mind [though an hour for a series might well cost the producers three or four times that]. But then, if you say, but I will give you eight of these for the price of one, then you'll have 16 hours not 2 and it's 150% Canadian content so you have 24 hours credit with the CRTC and we'll give you three plays, that makes seventy-two hours. Then all they have to do is do the math and they realize they're paying under $5,000."[23] It must be said that this is not 72 hours for the viewer, but seventy-two hours of Canadian content as the CRTC counts.

A year later, also in *SCAN*, Ferns is paraphrased by David Ellis as saying that the industry could go in one of two directions: "less expensive ways of producing domestic programming, driven less by high production values and more by characters and stories," or "more costly, high production value international programming that requires more partners and possibly more diffuse story lines to interest those partners."[24] Ellis himself foresees that "local programming would then become cheaper while international programming would become bigger and more 'event-oriented.'" He continues, "This segmentation of production values and budgets could help Canadian producers reduce the risks in the development of new projects."

Borkowski points out that the new channels on direct broadcast satellite means that long-lost programs will have new shelf life for the independents and the CBC, "bargain-basement windows [may] open to simple fare like poetry readings or one-man dramatic pieces or public affairs chat that is both cheap *and* intelligent." Might the CBC at last reduce costs by reusing old programs or recycling the idea of *Shoestring Theatre, Program X*, or *Peepshow*, seeing itself as a place for inexpensive experimentation?[25]

In a different key, Borkowski quotes Trina McQueen, "I look to technology as the great unexplored frontier." Finally, what he calls "outside observers" are paraphrased as saying that "the CBC has a jump on the other broadcasters. With English, French and all-news channels on offer, it has a head start on becoming the kind of multi-signal operator that most networks will have to become just to stay visible." If Ellis's unnamed source is right, CTV and Global might be released from any Cancon obligations so that all expectations and resources – perhaps through subsidy by the private sector – would allow us to concentrate our resources and expectations on the CBC.

Indeed, if CTV is allowed by the CRTC to do as it wishes, we had better count on the CBC and we had better ensure that there exists a CBC to count on. In March 1993 CTV proposed to mount four new specialty channels, but would not say what they would look like except that they would be "for higher-quality, low-cost programming." In order to achieve *a 12 per cent return* on revenue, CTV said it "cannot spend more than 60,000 dollars an hour on Canadian drama," because they claim that they do not break even on any Canadian programming. Gord Haines, chief operating officer of Alliance Communications Corporation, our largest television production company, pointed out that in "Britain the private sector would pay up to 1 million dollars for an hour of indigenous prime-time drama."[26] On 18 August 1993 newspapers ran an article by Jim Bronskill of CP, who reported that CTV was asking the CRTC to reduce the amount of dollars it had to spend on Canadian programming. The CRTC had made it a condition of licence renewal that CTV spend $93 million a year. In a new submission, the network is proposing a cut to $58.5 million for 1994–95, with a rise to $70.4 million by the year 2000. The CRTC has been reasonably consistent in recent years. The licence for the Global network was renewed for four years only because of a "concern that the licensee may not have contibuted to the Canadian broadcasting system as fully as it should have given the resources available to it" and that the CTRC had ordered Global to invest $9.7 million in new Canadian drama and to program three hours a week of Canadian drama in the 8–11 PM slot in the 1993–95 seasons.[27]

Participants at the 1993 Banff Festival were told that Canada was a hot location for co-productions, according to Lindsay Meredith: "the world is interested in us because of our environment."[28] Two articles appearing in the *Globe and Mail* and the *Toronto Star* pointed to two different directions which co-productions might take.[29] One picked up the environmental or "Canada is about great scenery and the repository of wilderness values" version of why others want to make programs here. Lacey again reports on the filming of *Destiny Ridge*, a series about a group of park wardens near Jasper in the Rockies. It is co-produced by CanWest/Global network, Atlantis, and Great North production companies and Germany's public network ARD-Webung, who together put up the $10 million for thirteen episodes. Thus in the first season German actress Elke Sommer played a local lodge owner. The town of Jasper, which "has a special place in German hearts, [because it is] a more wild and rugged environment, the essence of ... the Germanic [version] of the 'sublime,'" played Jasper. "Set design by God" says the headline – or as writer/producer Larry Raskin says, "[the scenery] is a character in everything we do." That may be so, but when the German money left the series the next season, the park setting and Elke Sommer were both dropped and the producers added new characters and a good many sexual encounters – inflecting the series away from action-adventure towards soap opera.[30]

The other article points to a Canada/France co-production, called *Scene of the Crime*, produced by Stephen J. Cannell who wrote scripts for *Barretta* and *The Rockford Files*, and who wrote and produced *The A-Team* and *Wiseguy*. CBS has already run the series on late-night television. As with several other co-productions, Canada's "window" comes later, and in prime-time. This twenty-two episode hour-long action/adventure series, filmed half in Vancouver and half in Paris, is made relatively inexpensively and features that old/new idea of repertory companies: a mix of ten Canadian and French actors, rotating lead parts with bits. Cannell told Jim Bawden that this deal, his first international deal, is the wave of the future, because the 500-channel universe creates increased opportunities to make a sale.

In the fall of 1994 entertainment sections of Canadian newspapers headlined the new phenomenon, *Due South*, a co-production running on CBS and CTV simultaneously. It is shot in Canada, set in Chicago, and stars a Canadian as the upright RCMP, his deaf lip-reading wolf Diefenbaker, and a hip, weary Chicago detective. The combination of plenty of action and deft satire on both the United States *and* Canada added up to a fresh approach to the cop show. The writing is usually funny, the improbable plots swiftly proceed and the whole thing is quite entertaining. Someone interested in reception theory could have a fine time sorting out the variant readings north and south of the border.

However, thanks in part to its place in the schedule, American ratings sagged and CBS did not renew the show. Intense discussion in the newspapers followed. Would a hit show in Canada be killed because American buyers could not be found? Australians and the British had enjoyed the show. CTV's first reaction, together with Alliance, the production company, was to kill the show because it would cost them significantly more to make it without an American sale. When it became clear that such a decision would be a public relations disaster, they changed their minds. As one producer pointed out to me recently, distinctive programming like *North of 60*, or even the goofy but endearing *Due South*, serve as loss leaders for independent producers, a way of keeping or establishing a relationship with CTV or the CBC. There is no Telefilm money unless a Canadian network will show the program.

But this kind of co-production is the exception. For example, Atlantis co-produced for the private broadcasters *Neon Rider* and *Maniac Mansions*, both with a distinctive Canadian flavour. It also co-produced for them *The Ray Bradbury Theatre, African Skies, White Fang, Tekwars,* and *Destiny Ridge*. As Ted Magder points out, "In the period between 1990 and 1993, close to 68% of the license fee revenue received by Atlantis came from broadcasting and distributors outside Canada. It is little wonder that audiences in Canada have trouble distinguishing Atlantis productions as 'Canadian.'"[31]

As one might expect, academics take a longer view of the potential benefits and drawbacks of contemporary co-productions. Colin Hoskins and Stuart McFadyen of the University of Alberta list under "potential benefits": pooling of financial resources; access to foreign government's incentives and subsidies; access to partner[s] and third-country markets (for example, in free-trade areas); learning from partners who may be more experienced; risk reduction "through product portfolio diversification"; cheaper foreign means of production; and desired foreign locations. The "drawbacks" identified are the costs associated with putting it all together; "loss of control and cultural specificity"; "exploitation or cheating by the foreign partner"; and the very real possibility of creating a more formidable competitor. They then give specific examples of how co-production with Canada can mean cheaper input costs, can augment financial resources, and even "circumvent quota barriers," including access to the European Community. They also chart the growth of this strategy especially for large-budget projects. In their view, the variation called "Twinning," where each partner retains control over one of two projects, lessens the problems of a Canadian version of "Europudding." The authors see International Joint Ventures as the way to go when large budget specials aimed at international audiences are involved, but argue that in the case of "relatively low budget productions aimed at domestic audiences ... purely domestic production is appropriate."[32] It is also worth noting that, like *The Valour and the Horror* made with the CBC, *The Boys of St Vincent* eluded efforts at censorship because the NFB (partnered with an independent company, Les Productions Téléaction) had the conviction and the resources to put these programs on cassette for sale or loan so that they were not completely subject to external (or internal) censorship once completed. No such "state" institutions exist in the United States. More important is the fact that the commercial constraints on the independent television film-makers and the American networks would have ensured that such programs were not made.

In my experience, American television seldom looks at the question of human evil with any seriousness. The cartoon evil of melodrama that appears in every action/adventure, every soap and Saturday morning cartoon and too often on the "news" is easy to enjoy and then dismiss. The societal evil that can be addressed and redressed is more comfortable for viewers to deal with and will occasionally appear on American television. But having explored the institutional and explicable evils of church and state, *The Boys of St Vincent* placed the fundamental evil of sexual predators on children precisely where it belongs – in the inexplicable and terrifying parts of human experience we call tragedy. Tragedy is a rare commodity on television anywhere, but it has appeared occasionally on the CBC since the 1950s.

What *was* American, and unforgivable, was the insertion of the commercial breaks for Air Canada airline travel to far-off escape resorts. If ever in its forty-year history CBC television required a program to be "sustaining" (that is, without commercials, as with most controversial programming until the late 1980s) it was *The Boys of St Vincent*. And yet CBC executives would not, or felt they could not, afford to broadcast three hours of prime-time drama of this kind without commercials – a damning indictment of the system can still create and disseminate such magnificent programs – only to dangerously weaken their impact.

Nevertheless the program was made and aired on prime time on the CBC. In the United States the mini-series has been shown in art cinemas and given awards – but its February 1995 television debut was not on a major network, but on the Arts and Entertainment pay channel. As Magder points out in more detail regarding other series and specials, without the tax dollars of the CBC, the NFB, and Telefilm, the independent company could not have made the film. Since the mid-1980s the CBC either commissions or buys, rather than makes, television dramas of all types, but our distinctive voice still depends on public institutions. From a different sensibility, then, as well as different systems of making and delivering programs, comes different practices – and in the case of *The Boys of St Vincent*, a difficult to endure and a memorable television drama.

Setting aside the agonizing of those inside the industry for a moment, from a viewer's perspective I wonder whether, when our skies are open to 200 or 500 channels, we will learn to be as cosmopolitan as the Europeans, through careful selection or even by sampling the sheer diversity of choices? Would we then stop teaching ourselves that to be different-looking or -sounding is bad?

The extent of CBC co-production with independent and overseas production is one of the reasons critics give for recommending the closure of the CBC itself. In the 1990s, not for the first time, ex-CBCers were calling for the CBC to be executed swiftly and buried discreetly for failing to live up to their expectations. Stanley Burke, a well-thought-of news anchor of the 1960s and early 1970s wrote a polemic in *the Globe and Mail* calling for the "respectful burial" of the CBC, because it has failed to unify the country and "has little power to create something that almost doesn't exist" – namely a distinctive national culture. "It was a noble experiment but conditions have changed and more money won't solve the problem."[33] This jeremiad was bracketed by a donnybrook in the *Canadian Forum* between Daryl Duke and Adrienne Clarkson. The *Forum* also provided Duke with a chance to reply to Clarkson's response, and published a difficult-to-read reproduction of Ivan Fecan's letter to the editor, which compared the schedules of 1969–70, not long after Duke left the network, with the 1992–93 evening schedule. Fecan also contrasted the twelve hours of American programming on the CBC schedule then with the two-and-a-half hours now. Basically, Duke claimed that the CBC cannot be distinguished from an American network, and listed all kinds of voices that are missing. Clarkson pointed out all the diversity Duke had missed.

The *Forum* later asked Duke to review Knowlton Nash's *Microphone Wars*. In keeping with his passionate responses to what he perceives as the make or break crisis now confronting the CBC, he writes:

The battle for the future is not over 'revenue streams' or 'strategic alliances' with the Power Corporation [a reference to the CBC/Power corporation DBS]. The battle is over content and over meaning. Meaning requires the return of public affairs programming, as distinct from the emptiness of news ... Meaning requires etablishing culture as a regular and admired part of the CBC schedule ... Meaning also requires that regional production be restored ... Nor can a country as complex as Canada be programmed from the Toronto-Ottawa-Montreal triangle ... Meaning requires addressing the fact of race. Canada is now an ethnically diverse and rich country.

In the end it is not businessmen or politicians who are a threat to the CBC but the belief of the Corporation's leaders that they can somehow protect themselves by appeasing these interests.The CBC cannot please business. Nor can it ever win over politicians . Business is interested in profits, politics in power. Public broadcasting inhabits the world of values."[34]

BACK TO SCHOOL FOR MAKERS AND
DECISION-MAKERS

Whether it be *Maclean's*, large circulation Toronto, Vancouver, and Montreal newspapers, the small but venerable left-wing *Canadian Forum*, or the feisty *This Magazine*, the debate about the CBC goes on in English Canada. Collins's assertion that the CBC is divorced from the intelligentsia of English Canada is accurate as far as the overall broadcasting picture goes, aside from the Newsworld/CBC News department's Rolodex of academics. Nevertheless, the programming as well as the economics and politics of the CBC does receive serious attention in academe, in the Canadian Communications Association and in the Association for the Study of Canadian Radio and Television/AERTC, among others. The problem is that what is said in the academic journals and books is seldom read by the makers and decision-makers of the corporation.

In its cover story "Prime Time Wars: The CBC Struggles to Survive in a 200 Channel Universe," *Maclean's* (30 August 1993) had reduced the threat from 500 to 200. The numbers are meaningless, of course. The fact of many more channels is the issue. The story by Ray Corelli is a counterpoint of several anonymous complaints about demoralization and on-the-record statements of confidence from people like newsanchors Pamela Wallin and Peter Mansbridge, the new vice-president of news and current affairs Ted Kotcheff (who had gone by 1994), vice-president of English television Ivan Fecan (who had gone by 1994), the chair of the board, Patrick Watson (who had gone by 1994), and Peter Herrndorf, chair of TVO and one of the three CBC executives in the early 1970s to write the report already cited in chapter 9 that reorganized the Drama Department.

HERRNDORF [on the CBC past and present]: The internal battles at a broadcasting company matter so much because the consequences show up on the television screen. The differences in these battles are not just differences of personality; they are frequently differences of emphasis and differences of philosophy, and they are very important. The CBC started as a movement, a movement that rolled across the country with people demanding a broadcast service that somehow reflected their reality, and the CBC is going to have to go back to that, back to a time when it was essential in every major community in the country. It's more than just a television program or a radio program. It is a set of ideas and a lifestyle and an involvement with the country.[36]

As is so often the case in public discourse about the CBC, what is missing from the overall portrayal of the CBC in *Maclean's* as "middle-aged," with "shrinking budgets, dwindling hopes and discordant voices," is any sustained attention to the actual programs on air, and yet the CBC, like all networks, will live or die on what it broadcasts, not on who is speaking to whom off-camera. The two are interdependent, of course, as this book demonstrates. Nevertheless, both academics and periodical and newspaper reporters still tend to concentrate on the internal and external politics of the CBC – not on the programs.[37]

There is one exception – the fixation on the *Prime Time News*. As Peter C. Newman put it: "I sort of gave up on the CBC when they cancelled *The Journal*."[38] The uproar and the drop in ratings suggest to me that Canadians in a curious act of metonymy make the CBC News on the main network stand for the CBC itself. Other programs are enjoyed and watched in great numbers, but at present viewers seem to feel that news and current affairs *is* the CBC. Critics of the move to 9 PM, on the other hand, point out that the change in time was supposed to increase the audience for the news hour.[39]

FECAN: Those critics wouldn't be saying that if they'd listened to what we were saying last May. We never said (the move to 9 PM) was there to increase the audience. We said we wanted to be an alternative to private broadcasting. We said we wanted to rely less on commercials for part of our schedule. We have, by the way, increased audience sustantially on Newsworld (the 10 PM half-hour of national news, weather, and sports), which the critics seem to forget is a related move.

But levelling that charge at us is like saying we've lost a race we've never been in. Last May, the message that we wanted to send was that, maybe, over time, we have drifted into that race and it wasn't appropriate for us to be in it. We wanted to state that everything we're going to be doing, as much as finances will allow us, will be geared to moving us out of it.

With the move back to 10 PM and the departure of those who were the architects of repositioning and of *Prime Time News*, the CBC appears to have rejoined the ratings race for the 9–10 PM week-night slot.

Despite Trina McQueen's sardonic remark: "The question of drama has troubled the CBC from day one and it's a particularly Canadian obsession. We have this belief that we can grow and flourish as a nation state if we have a new constitution and a popular sitcom,"[40] the questions remain. Do Canadian broadcasters give up altogether on sitcoms and concentrate instead on shows we easily recognize as "ours," like *Road to Avonlea, Street Legal, North of 60, Northwood, The Odyssey,* CTV's *ENG,* or Global's *Madison*? Or do they make clones of American action/adventure series like Global's *Destiny Ridge, Tekwars,* and CTV's *Counterstrike, Matrix,* and the quintessentially American *Lonesome Dove*? These are all 1994–95 co-productions with Germany, the United States, or France.[41] In fact, the distinction between public and private begins to dissolve.

THE WORLDWIDE THREAT TO PUBLIC BROADCASTING

There are also external factors that have changed irrevocably the context of the debate about the CBC. Perhaps the most serious is the decline of the commitment to public broadcasting worldwide. In the late 1980s the Mother of them all, the BBC, under Thatcher was facing the possibility of placing advertisements on one or both of BBC–1 and BBC–2 – a paradigm shift that seems (after major changes in practices) to have been averted for now. Recently, Henry Porter in the British Sunday paper *The Guardian* (19 June 1995) reported that the morale at the BBC was at a record low. Program-makers were micro-managed "loaded with targets and goals, none of which is ever satisfactorily achieved." He quotes a "well-known producer" who has left the BBC: "No one can tell you if they have the money for your program next year – you don't know who to ask, how to get a deci-sion." After outlining both the history of the BBC and many current interviews, Porter lays the situation directly at the door of the director general, John Birt. In an uncanny echo of fears shared with me in recent months, Porter concludes: "[Birt] did after all bring some sense of order to the BBC's finances. But his administration has become absorbed in ... the mechanics of change rather than its effects. It is a classic case of the triumph of management over leadership." Manage-ment without leadership would badly damage the relatively robust BBC. It could destroy the CBC.

ITV is also in difficulty. After a scathing dissection of then Prime Minister Thatcher's broadcasting policies and the 1990 act culminat-ing in an ill-advised auction of Independent Television company licences, Richard Dunn (CEO of Thames Television and chair of the ITV Association, 1988–90) concludes: "In the circumstances [the auc-tion, defined elsewhere in the article as a 'blind crapshoot'] who can honestly blame the ITV companies if, after being forced by the Act to put the Treasury Board first, they tend to put the share-holders second and the viewers third." What he describes is, of course, the North American norm.

Dennis Passa of CP reported in 1991 on the budget woes of the Australian Broadcasting Commission: "Critics say the network is too fat, supporters say it hasn't got the resources to do its job."[42] Six weeks later Stephen Godfrey of the *Globe and Mail* began a detailed analysis of television in France with the words "They were all set to have the state funeral for French public television this Spring," pointing to the transformation of TF1 as "once the largest and most successful public network in Continental Europe [which] became a commercial network in 1987, and its success has destabilized the entire French system." He did document the joint venture of France and Germany to create La Sept, a cultural channel, but he concluded that "the battle of 'citizens versus clients' in the new Europe is far from over."[43] In the opinion of Eli Noam, professor of economics at Columbia School of Business:

Neither governments nor public broadcasters will become obsolete. The latter will continue to have important functions, in particular producing or distributing programs that are not adequately provided otherwise ... governments ... will have to seek new approaches ... since an outright ban is easier to enforce than a partial regulation in a complex environment. On the one hand, television program networks are becoming global, reducing control; on the other, local and regional broadcasting is emerging [local broadcasting is a relatively new phenomenon for much of Europe]. The notion of the state as the appropriate territorial and regulatory unit comes into question, both from Brussels and the provinces. And from the citizenry, as the notion of the freedom of videospeech grows familiar, government interference is challenged.[44]

By the mid-1990s it is not clear whether the battle for a new Europe as a coherent political entity is being won – never mind the survival of broadcasting systems that might help forge a Euro-identity. The problem is clearly recognized, however. The challenge is to avoid programs that look like and taste like "Europudding," the code word for programming that resembles blancmange.

Pierre Juneau, the former CRTC chairman and president of the CBC for seven years, in a keynote address in June 1993 shared with ASCRT/AERTC his sense of the ebbing of public broadcasting as an instrument of political and social culture – and his efforts, along with those of many others around the world, to rally support for this key contributor to the national and regional identity. In brief, his remarks were a blend of fear and hope and a determination to turn the tide. He spoke at length about supranational efforts, as the skies fill, to renew and reposition those agents of public broadcasting that exist in the older and the newer democracies. Two years later Bill Roberts, a TVO executive, wrote: "The Swedes have had their ... budget clawed back by 10 per cent," the Germans are looking at nationalizing ARD and 2DF, "RAI in Italiy is a mess," Spain's RTE "is reduced to running U.S. game shows, "and there is a similar mood in Singapore and Mexico. However, he saw hope because he thinks PBS may survive, other governments are having second thoughts, Juneau's World Council for Radio and TV now exists as do Input and Public Broadcasting International – all launched or managed by Canadians. As he said: "Public Television is an essential producer of domestic content."[45]

In the early 1990s, sales to major American networks were building self-confidence at the CBC in those who define the ultimate success as a sale to NBC, but worrying those who think that anything we export to the United States must be a clone of American programming. NBC did buy the mini-series *Love and Hate*, about the Colin Thatcher murder. Audience figures for the program at NBC were 44 million, for the BBC, 20 million, and there were also sales to Italy, France, and Japan.[46]

These sales signify that carefully crafted psychological studies of brutal murders, all of them very violent in places, seem to fit into the American trend of "murders of the week" – literally by the dozen.[47] The four or five drama specials a year included irregular but annual appearance of *Scales of Justice* (with over three million viewers, a record in English Canada), the 1992–94 seasons *Gross Misconduct* (hockey/murder), *The Boys of St Vincent* (boys sexually and physically abused/corrupt government), *Liar, Liar* (daughter's false accusation of sexual abuse against her father), the justifiable homicide of a wife beater in *Living with Billy*, the 1994–95 mini-series *Million Dollar Babies* (the history of the Quints extravaganza), *Trial at Fortitude Bay* (rape, suicide, and culture clash), and *Butterbox Babies* (a docudrama about the serial killing of dozens of babies in the 1930s). The CBC resources for adult drama seem to have been devoted to the disproportionately criminal and the bizarre. Yet each one is carefully contextualised, well written, with first-class production values.

Perceiving this spate of programs, both friends and foes of the CBC fear when they point to the "Americanization" of the network that the corporation will follow rather than inflect (or ignore) a Made in America trend – fears that have been expressed over the years by many of the makers of the programs interviewed in this book. In 1990 Peter Trueman predicted a downward slide in the *Toronto Star* in an article headlined "The network isn't in the poorhouse yet," which contrasted what TVO would do with the money spent on the CBC.[48] *Globe and Mail* critic John Haslett Cuff has preached against what he sees as a pattern for some years. Yet as Denis Harvey wrote in an article for the *Globe and Mail* a few weeks before the launch of that season, "How can the *Degrassi* shows be considered vapid imitations of u.s. television? ... *Street Legal* is not a copy of *LA Law* ... the cbc has the only consumer show on prime-time television in North America – *Marketplace*."[49] To update his argument, *Northwood* was not *Beverly Hills 90210* , *Liberty Street* is not *Melrose Place*, and *North of 60* is most emphatically not *Northern Exposure*. Most cbc genres remain distinctive influences on their genres or, with *The Odyssey*, major departures from standard children's adventure programs.

LAST WORD

As the reader will have discovered, this book is not a history of cbc drama, not an overview of its social and artistic development, and not a reference work on programs. It may be deconstructive, because some of the interviews I have gathered in *Rewind and Search* explore the gaps and fissures in the program texts themselves as well as in the patterns of the cbc drama mix. I have not used the semantics of semiotics, although there are many descriptions of the working processes and therefore of the codes of television drama and how they evolved as the technology, personnel, and policies of the cbc changed. The book is, among other things, an oral history . Yet it is focused not so much on what verifiably "happened" – since events often left no trace of their passage, not even a kinescope or tape for the archives – but rather on an attempt to record, with the active editorial involvement of the people interviewed, what they thought and felt about what they perceived to be happening. These interviews supply fragments of both the context and the intertextuality of the programs that finally made it to air. Since those fragments are often contradictory, this is a book requiring an active reader who may, from the evidence presented, draw very different conclusions from the ones I draw.

The fact that broadcasting in Canada is in a state of rapid flux involving often unforeseen changes makes it difficult to extrapolate with any certainty new patterns from the old. The major survival move by the cbc new policy of "Repositioning" has now been abandoned, and those who implemented it are gone. One result of the cbc retreat and the additional cuts might be the Americanization of our television drama as the cbc churns out action/adventure series and sitcoms intended specifically to emulate American prime time. To offer some balance, the cbc could also continue to commission (with the help of multinational deals) the expensive *Road to Avonlea* kind of family fare for which there is a broad international market. In an attempt to generate advertising revenue, the cbc could cut back on content and simply buy cheaper American product – or it could, like CTV, find international partners and make formula crime shows like CTV's *Counterstrike*, with lots of sex and perhaps a little less violence. The problem is money. Slick TV drama is expensive. Imitations rather than reflections of American programming are a waste of taxpayers' dollars when most Canadians can get "the real thing" with a flick of the dial. The CBC could also make our own brand of trash TV, the cheaper "reality shows" that feature endless gossip, glimpses into the houses of the rich and famous, raids on crack houses, and rescues from every form of accident and mayhem – or whatever the next American trend may be.

All of these directions have been suggested by political parties and the Canadian Association of Broadcasters private television – in the past. Few would go that far now, although CTV and CAB still insistently demand that the CBC abandon income generators like sports and only make or carry programs that have less appeal to advertisers. The government may even rewrite the mandate to reduce expectations of the CBC.

In the expensive and difficult area of CBC drama that is my focus, let us look at what the CBC in this most unstable time can do. *North of 60*, though it has many of the elements of the family/adventure genre – kids, strong heroic figures, a bush setting, and worthy (in this case often complex) messages – provides a brand new inflection of the genre.[50] Most of the characters, all but one of the leads, and most of the guest stars are members of the First Nations. It also focuses on the intractable problems of isolation, a way of life under pressure, unemployment, kids without fathers, the erosion of language, alcohol abuse and self-hatred, and the threat of AIDS. Many of the situations presented are not resolved. By its third season the focus moved completely to Michelle Kennide, the Mountie/recovering alcoholic/ single mother who was born in Lynx River – and on all her family and friends and adversaries. Thus *North of 60*, despite its 9 PM time slot, is not standard family/adventure fare. Together with the very adult fare of the CBC's current event programming, *the fifth estate*, and *The Nature of Things*, this series would suggest that, despite the failure of repositioning, the CBC will not interpret its 7–10 slot as a home for safe programming.

The 1994–95 season also brought us the broad comedy of *Royal Canadian Air Farce* back to back with the sharp satire of *This Hour Has 22 Minutes* (stepdaughter of *Codco*), a shaky mini-series, *Side Effects*, with various doctors (probably too many) in a clinic, and *Witness*, a regular slot for documentaries. Regrettably, many affiliates opt out of or reschedule to less favourable times all of these programs but *Side Effects*. Moreover, there are persistent rumours that at least three of the most distinctive CBC programs – *Man Alive, Marketplace,* and *The Nature of Things* – will be casualties of the next round of cuts in early 1996.

If CBC television executives raided their own archives for some ideas, we might see short one-act plays as places for writers and directors to develop on a shoestring, or panel shows that made people both laugh and think along with the panel. They could try a half-hour a week devoted to labour or women's issues to match the business and consumer emphasis on *Venture* and *Marketplace,* using skits and satire, as well as interviews and panels, remotes and archival footage. They could look to the Vision network for some new ideas on how to reflect our diversity of cultures and beliefs, with more concentration on limited series as a complement to *Man Alive.* They could decide that culture could come out of the Sunday afternoon ghetto, bring back the dance, readings or dramatized adaptations of poems, short stories, and serialized fiction, or adapt hit plays by people like George Walker, Morris Panych, or Judith Thompson. They do move the "best of *Midday*" over to Newsworld once a week. They have launched a very successful eclectic music show, *Rita and Friends.* They could rerun forgotten treasures like *Tyler, Turning to Stone, Sanity Clause,* or series that do not date like *A Gift to Last.* In other words, they could create niches where those whose talents lie fallow and who are alienated from the CBC could entertain and inform us again – or they could abdicate these functions to Bravo, Showcase (partly CBC owned), the Women's Network, or Discovery – if these specialty channels survive.

Trina McQueen was quoted in *Maclean's* on the reasons for her departure from the CBC. "I left the corporation because of the diminishing budget. I had come to the end of my ability to put people out of work, to shut down programs, to overload the people who were left. If the corporation takes another hit of $150 to $200 million, it will be the end of the CBC as we know it. But that's not the central issue anyway. What we need to do is rethink the role of public broadcasting in Canada."[51] Harold Redekopp, currently vice-president CBC Radio and in the 1990 round of cuts vice-president, regions, was quoted saying: "I've been through this crucible before, but this is worse, because what we are seeing today is just a down-payment. [In three years] you won't recognize the CBC."[52] Firing "in-house" personnel does not necessarily save money. As one person who has chosen to work both in-house and freelance pointed out to me, it is more costly to obtain his services on a per project basis, as well as paying managers to administer the huge load of paperwork, than to retain him on contract. Will the million-dollar management consultants notice? Or will they, as would be natural, talk mostly to those who speak the same language – the managers? That would pose no serious problem, except that many of those who remain as decision-makers either have shallow roots in the CBC or have expunged what memories they had about the CBC ethos or the evolution of policy – and too often they have little experience in making programs.

It is taken as a hopeful sign that President Beatty embraced the July 1995 auditor general's report. I have never spoken to anyone at the CBC who did not have concrete ideas about how to eliminate waste, who did not wish to rationalize accounting procedures – but $350 million cannot be found that way.

It does not matter whether the period being discussed is the mid-1950s, the mid-1970s, or the mid-1990s. The makers of television drama, at every level from cameraman to executive producer, have to engage in the enterprise with creative solutions to specific artistic and technical problems presented by a series or a special, and to an idea of what sort of program distinguishes the CBC broadcasting mix from that of every other channel. Throughout this book, it is apparent that the inevitable arguments and conflicts between makers and decision-makers can be either creative or they can be immensely destructive. It remains to be seen which pattern will prevail in the next few years.

What then can be said? There is no doubt that there has been waste at the CBC. There is also no doubt that members of parliament on both sides of the House hold the CBC in contempt. Indeed, some see the corporation primarily as the disloyal opposition which was not pro-federalist in Quebec in the 1980 referendum[54] and which subverts patriotic values with programs like *The Valour and the Horror*. The casualties from cutbacks, drastic internal changes, and weariness at the inevitable inertia and inefficiency of a large corporation are many and well-recorded, both in the academic confines of this book and in the entertainment and gossip columns of the newspapers. A few of the voices in this book are stilled: Alice Sinclair and Hugh Webster. Almost all the others have left the CBC: Philip Keatley, Mario Prizek, Ed Vincent, Robert Allen, Ron Weyman, Jeannine Locke, Nada Harcourt, Sidney Newman, Martin Kinch, Bill Gough, Anna Sandor, and Grahame Woods. Denis Harvey and John Kennedy have retired. Sam Levene produces for *Man Alive*. David Barlow works for the CBC as an independent producer/story editor/writer. Joe Partington and Maryke McEwen were cut in the latest but not last round, as were Harry Raskey and Norman Campbell, both giants in the arts, and Flora MacDonald, a new producer whose *Small Gifts* was shelved, then aired to excellent reviews and a CBC Anik award. Ivan Fecan and Trina McQueen have joined the private sector.

In the Middle Ages, people all over the world believed that the health of the kingdom depended on the health of the king. There is no doubt that lack of leadership from the decision-makers can make it difficult, even at times impossible, to create good television drama, as Trina McQueen reminded us in her comments on the importance of the "housekeeping." The new "king" of the CBC, Perrin Beatty, has no qualifications for the job. It is well known, however, that the prime minister was turned down by other candidates. Perhaps Beatty deserves credit for courage, at least.

Does the health of the CBC depend on the mental and emotional health and courage of its directors and vice-presidents? Does the health of our kingdom depend in part on the survival of a publicly owned and regulated CBC? If it disappears, as well it may, we will find out.

Early drafts of the report of John Godfrey's Heritage Committee on the role of the Canadian Broadcasting Corporation in the multi-channel universe sparked a lot of debate in the newspapers in the spring of 1995.[55] The TV Guide, in "Shows at Risk," reports that Phyllis Platt, director of entretainment, is looking ahead to producing more children's shows and more short-run series. These would be relatively cheap and would not commit the CBC to vast spending unless they were a success" – a tactic that the writer does not mention the CBC used for most of its history.[56] Even TV Guide, short on memory though long on nostalgia, goes on the record to say that "it's ironic that more cuts seem likely to come ... just when it's producing more of the high-quality shows you want to watch." The article perpetuates the myth that most of the CBC history consisted of programs described as "more a pill you had to swallow than dessert you wanted," and concludes: "Though we may not cry for the network, we will miss the shows." Jim Bawden, who has a much longer and more accurate memory, pointed out in Starweek that, although the CBC had bungled the application of the $44 million cut for 1995 in getting rid of Harry Rasky, Norman Campbell, and "dozens of productive lesser lights," the cuts themselves are continuous and serious. He sketches the programs that have disappeared over the years: Emmy winning ballet and opera; "crafted features like Chautauqua Girl" and others by Jeannine Locke; productions of the Shaw Festival; and prestigious mini-series as diverse as The Tenth Decade, Democracy, "or even Jalna." He notes that Small Gifts was the only film of its kind in 1994–95, and that Hymn Sing will now depend on repeats. "Each cut is another wound against public broadcasting," he says. "We are all diminished by the prospect of a CBC unable to make vital programming decisions."[57]

Antonia Zerbisias and others got a head start on the "fix the CBC" game. In "If I ran the CBC ..." Zerbisias says she would force all delivery systems (cable, satellite, and the phone companies, if they converge) to contribute to a TV production fund because "cable only puts 5% of its net income into Canadian programming – i.e., into community cable channels." "Do more programming from regional production centres," she advises. Concentrate on more programs with "shelf life" that can be exported; keep sports; shut down the Ottawa head office; trim the public relations staff and some of the in-house operations like drama suites for editing. "To my mind," she concludes "government has essentially sentenced the CBC to die a long slow death."[58] Conservative columnist Dalton Camp had exactly the same conclusion after the Heritage Committee report came out.[59] Not if the CBC adopts "the magic bullet" defined as narrowcasting, digital compression of signal and satellite delivery," according to the experts interviewed by Mary Gooderham.[60] Robert Mason Lee's viewpoint in his column "The West" rewrites CBC history as having as its *primary* mandate to reflect the regions. He has his doubts about both the Heritage Committee and the three experts Pierre Juneau, Peter Herrndorf, and Catharine Murray, a professor at Simon Fraser University, board member of the Women's Network and OWL TV, and a former vice-president of Decima Research. This triumvirate was asked by the Liberal government in the spring of 1995 to study (again) the mandates of the NFB, Telefilm, and the CBC. Lee praises Newsworld and CBC Radio as "modest, honest enterprises – much like the country they reflect," but he damns the "slick enterprise like the television network which reflects the country it envies." His suggestion is that they take seriously "a much humbler, much more important role of making the country real for the people who live here ... it would make Rex Murphy a star from Newfoundland, not from Toronto."[61]

The neoconservative thinkers of the Fraser Institute and similar organizations also had their say to the *Globe and Mail*'s most right-wing columnist, Andrew Coyne, before the Heritage Committee report was tabled.[62] Basically, their dilemma was to reconcile the impulse to privatize with the indisputable reluctance of private enterprise to pay for and air the sort of program the CBC mandate has required.[63] Arthur Gelber suggests that the CBC merge with TVO, not a popular idea with the other nine provinces, I would think.[64] There were many other suggestions. Put news only on a public channel; put out to competitive tender the rights to show a block of Canadian programming; split the CBC into several pay channels; and the oddest of all: subsidize the viewer for watching "Canadian or otherwise favoured programming" – which logically suggests that the only audience for such programs would be found in our jails.

When the Heritage Committee, or at least the Liberal members of it, tabled a report in June 1995, the *St Catharines Standard* informed its readers that the recommendations included the following: The CBC should develop a "full-scale corporate re-engineering plan; look to new technology but make sure that its main service remains free; continue to sell advertising but look also for corporate sponsors and foreign sales; have access to at least half of the programming fund from the distributors of TV signals; audit the costs and benefits of pro sports but continue to broadcast them; consult unions about savings that could be used by contracting out; and do a better job of producing quality Canadian programming." Beatty is quoted in response in the *Globe and Mail*: "The CBC will become smaller and more focused – we have no choice."[65]

"Everything that can go wrong in the writing of a government document went wrong with this one," says Robert Fulford,[66] whose knowledgable critiques of the CBC go back to the early 1970s when he was editor of *Saturday Night* and one of the chief instigators of the detailed critique of the CBC in the intervention of the Committee on Television to the CRTC. He points out that "its timidity" cannot be blamed on the need for consensus because the Bloc and the Reform Party did not sign but issued their own "entirely predictable reports" (recognize the uniqueness of Quebec, says the BQ; privatize, says Reform). "The main report ... might be summed up in six words: 'The CBC should probably do better.'" As Fulford points out, most difficult questions were referred to the auditor general, whose report a month later did document the still vexed questions of accountability and transparency in the CBC accounting systems – a report Beatty welcomed. But Fulford was right when he said there was not much new in the report in response to what the committee itself identified as inevitable major change. If anything, he understates the banality and basic futility of the report. Rob Carrick, in the CP story, said that John Godfrey thought the report offered solid suggestions to the CBC, while defending its existing grant.

The *Globe and Mail* supplied extracts of the recommendations taken from the final Heritage Committee report. They advised that the CBC should buy all its drama programs from independents; move to cable; put advertisements on CBC radio for the first time since the early 1970s (at a time when many private radio stations are struggling); cut most sports coverage; and reconsider any commitment to regional programs.[67] Private broadcasters have lobbied for the last two recommendations for years.

Despite the ongoing public discussion, the only consensus that appears to exist is that $350 million out of the CBC budget will force either the CBC or the government to redefine its mandate. Prime Minister Chrétien explained to Peter Gzowski on *Morningside* on 1 March 1995, following Paul Martin's budget: "When you cut farmers and transfer payments and 40,000 (civil servants), we cannot spare anybody, including the CBC. We don't do it out of joy. We had to do it. You cannot privilege the CBC. It is not cut more than others, yet some will say it is one of the easiest to cut ... It's a cultural institution. The masses are not very upset if you cut them." These words have the clear implication that the CBC was lucky the cuts were not worse, because no ordinary viewer cares. He may be right.

As I try to assess the future of the CBC, as so many people have felt constrained to do in 1995, I find that my own hopes and fears for the CBC have undergone a sobering metamorphosis. I began writing this book with the hope that the CBC could recover its heart in spite of (or perhaps because of) the ongoing crisis that has plagued it from within and without since the mid-1980s. After all, in 1987, when faced with yet more substantial cutbacks, those who make programs and decisions about them went to Deerhurst and returned with new determination to make less go farther and more creatively. But revelations and tongues of fire cannot be summoned repeatedly at will. Instead, since 1987, too many of the best have given up, retired, gone to the independent sector or to private networks, been laid off without dignity or recognition of their contributions, and in some cases needlessly humiliated. It has been said repeatedly in defence of the CBC that if the governments of the last decade had cut their budgets to the degree that the CBC had to before 1994, the federal government would be running a significant surplus.

It is also easy to play with figures. But the indisputable fact is that the CBC has been in a steadily escalating financial crisis since 1985 and that the stable funding which should have been in place since the 1930s is still not forthcoming. I have never spoken to anyone at the CBC who does not agree that there are misplaced priorities and that programming suffers from a structure which is still an inverted pyramid. The point of the whole enterprise now seems mired in quicksand. Expensive management studies have not corrected that and are unlikely to do so. Meanwhile, morale has sunk inevitably to new lows and the results will eventually be visible on our television screens.

Over the years of research and writing this book, I find that the tone of the last four chapters in particular has changed. *Rewind and Search* could now be read as an epitaph – either for the CBC as it was or, it may be, for CBC English television itself. It is television (both English and French) – together with Radio International and the in-

valuable Northern services which are at risk from the broken promises, indifference, and cultural amnesia without, and from the lack of
vision and leadership within.[68]

Many people, myself among them, think that CBC Radio may survive in a recognizable form because it still has a faithful, vocal, and
influential audience. Moreover, radio is much less expensive than
most forms of television, and, despite satellites, more easily responsive to breaking news, current affairs, and new programming ideas, if
it has a cadre of talented and experienced people. Peter Gzowski is a
Canadian icon with a million friends, who provides one of the few
thoughtful places where English Canadians debate political and
cultural affairs. If the next *Morningside* season were cut in late June of
any year, we would miss it three months later. Contrast television
drama or a major documentary series. The eighteen-month development and production time makes cuts less visible.

Unfortunately, even before the evidence is in from the Juneau/
Herrndorf/Murray committee report and there is any government
response to it or to the Heritage Committee report, it is possible that
the CBC television network will already have been doomed. Let me add
my best guesses to the dozens already in play in the form of five
possible scenarios.

SCENARIO 1 The CBC sells all its stations and transmission facilities
and becomes a production company that provides the children's programs and the arts and drama programs not broadcast by the private
sector. The CRTC compels the private networks, as rent for their
licensed use of our airwaves, to carry the children's programs in a
weekday morning children's hour, with the remaining programs scattered through the prime-time schedule.

But the CBC has already laid-off, retired, or fired many of its directors, producers, and editors, and its ability to produce programs is
attenuated. Further budget cuts will accelerate the decline. Many of
the wonderful facilities that came to Toronto thirty years too late are
not fully used. Yet if the CBC decides to earn revenue by renting its
unused production facilities to independent producers, private broadcasters will argue that it presents unfair competition to the private
sector's production plants. However, if the CBC does not continue to
produce programs, the new CBC headquarters is likely to become just
another piece of 1980s real estate looking for a buyer in the cash-
strapped 1990s.

SCENARIO 2 The CBC could continue to act on our behalf as a patron,
a channel 4 without a channel, commissioning works in the public

interest that no private broadcaster would agree to put on air and then broadcasting them on "the CBC night" on CTV and CanWest Global. The CBC would be a network for a night, but would make no "in-house" programs.

But without any other role, the CBC would be duplicating Telefilm's role. Despite the cuts it has already suffered, Telefilm will probably survive the budget and mandate review under way because, without it, no Canadian arts, science, and music programming would get made. The independent production companies would also stop making distinctive drama for the remaining networks – all of which depend on Telefilm subsidy for their more distinctive series. For any challenging or unusual content to make it to air, the CRTC would still have to require regular hours in prime time to be ceded by the private interests to such programming – if the CRTC itself survives into the next century.

SCENARIO 3 The CRTC could set up a channel like Britain's channel 4. Ivan Fecan, probably facetiously, said he would be glad to run such a channel – subsidizing and buying such programming – if he had the money and if the CBC did not depend on advertising.

I do not see any public demand for such a channel, but that could change if three things happen: If the rest of the cash-strapped provincial governments follow Alberta's example and sell off their educational networks;[69] if Bravo, the new specialty pay service devoted to the arts, gives up its struggle to stay afloat and sinks; and if PBS is effectively killed by the American Congress. In those circumstances, all of which are distinct possibilities in the next two years, the desire for a channel that commissions and schedules this kind of alternative programming might grow.

The first three options assume a functional CRTC in the next decade or two. But in the coming world of technological convergence and apparent lack of political will, the existence of an effective regulatory body is no longer a given.

SCENARIO 4 The CBC could put what slender resources it was given into Newsworld and move that service onto channel 6. That would mean retaining some of the plant, as well as its transmission capability. This outcome would acknowledge that the arm's-length relationship which makes it possible for a crown corporation to cover stories that privately owned networks have been unwilling to spend money on (loss-leaders like the national news or *W5 with Eric Malling*) is worth preserving in some form. Equally important, Canadian viewers still care passionately about their news reports, documentaries, and current affairs.

Politicians and high-ranking civil servants seldom watch television. Like many academics, they genuinely do not know about most of the programs that have been discussed here and in *Turn Up the Contrast*, and they have no knowledge of what is currently being broadcast. The indifference of much of the political and cultural élite is not shared by the general public, who consistently prefer television drama to all other kinds of programming. Regrettably for all networks, those viewers have lost track of who makes what. I often hear comments like "Good program, *Street Legal*. Must be CTV." For some years now, helped by the zapper that reduces the impulse simply to watch whatever is on the channel next, viewer loyalty has been to the programs, not the networks.

The exception for politicians and ordinary viewers alike is the news. Despite the conviction shared by all governments in Canada since the 1930s that the CBC is "out to get them," no government is likely to destroy altogether the place where ministers are so often seen and heard, which carries their news conferences live, and which daily covers national crises live for extended periods.

The proposal cut from the July 1995 report of the parliamentary committee but still in play – that the CBC get rid of its costly transmission facilities and its affiliates, and move to cable – has been justified because of cable's penetration and because direct broadcast satellites are about to go into service. Of course, those services have to be paid for directly by the viewer. Thus, without "free" television, our poorest citizens could not get the national television service even if it did survive. Retaining Newsworld on the accessible channel already reserved for the CBC would partially answer that problem. Moreover, since Newsworld now depends on the other service for repeat programming, perhaps a handful of the compatible existing CBC programs would survive – *the fifth estate*, *Marketplace*, *Midday*. Perhaps not. Purchased programs like *Fashion File* and *The Antique Roadshow* are cheaper.

The proposal that the CBC close its headquarters in Ottawa has been made for years. The retrenchment to a French and English Newsworld would make that inevitable. The savings in dollars and the boost to both efficiency and morale make the proposal attractive in any case – but it would be too little too late to make a significant difference.

SCENARIO 5 The CBC could shut down all television services in both languages. Except for the special case of the United States – which fills not only four networks with programs, but much of the world's television schedule, and may cut loose what little government subsidy there is for the anomalous PBS – Canada would then be the only in-dustrialized nation not to have its own publicly owned national tele-vision network. It would be the only nation in the First World with direct over-the-air access to the cornucopia of wax fruit that is much of American programming.

The October 1995 referendum crisis, which remains unresolved, may affect the thinking of the Liberal cabinet for the straightforward reason that the CBC and Newsworld were the only places where citizens could find consistent, detailed analysis during the day and, more usefully, in prime time. CTV, the only other network with complete national coverage, broadcast the World Series and its regular commercial programming instead. Yet, given the short attention span and cultural amnesia of both the Liberal and the Conservative govern-ments, or should a Reform government be elected, with great regret I think scenario 5 is a real possibility in the next four years.

I do not think that the CBC should continue as it has been for the past decade. Money aside, changes have to be made. I do believe, however, in the necessity of a publicly owned network. In my hopeful moments I think that, even if the CBC is doomed to an ignominious slide and eventual shut down, we as a society will probably try to reinvent such a network some ten years into the next century. But often I wonder if Canadian viewers first have to lose not only indivi-dual programs and series but the network itself – and discover that they miss it.

Rewind and Search was never intended to be an epitaph. I would never say that the CBC is incapable of new ideas, careful planning, and a coherent sense of what can still be accomplished. I believe that it can survive these times and rebuild – but only if creative people with both justifiable pride and the memory to supply the context missing from the picture are all allowed to help write the new rules – and then to work within them. My evidence quoted in previous chapters is thirty years of internal reports that not only diagnosed the problems, but also proposed concrete and practical solutions. Put simply, the question must be: How can the CBC – specifically its decision-makers – create a working environment for the people who make the pro-grams, because those people and the programs they make are the point. How can the decision-makers keep and nurture, find and train the "makers" they need to keep the operation running? Trina Mc-Queen called it "good housekeeping." It is the only way to keep the house.

Notes

INTRODUCTION

1 The earliest such book is the one most like *Rewind and Search* in form. Eric Sherman wrote *Directing the Film: Film Directors on Their Art* for the American Film Institute (Los Angeles: Acrobat Books 1976). It interweaves conversations and commentary by topic. In this book each "voice" is distinguished simply by headings and extra spaces. Undesignated blocks of text contain the "editorial" voice. Horace Newcomb and Robert S. Alley's *The Producer's Medium: Conversations with Creators of American TV* (New York: Oxford University Press 1983) presents a set of interviews with leading American producers which is interlaced with detailed editorial commentary. Richard Levinson and William Link's *Off Camera: Conversations with the Makers of Prime-time Television* (New York and Scarborough, Ont.: New American Library 1986) includes producers, directors, an actor, writers, an agent, program suppliers, and a vice-president of a network, also with substantial interpretive comment. In Jack Kuney's *Take One: Television Directors on Directing* (New York: Praeger 1990), Kuney interviews ten directors and amplifies their answers to his questions so that a student or an inexperienced reader can understand the answers or be aware that there are other ways of approaching the topic explored.

2 For example, political analyst Stevie Cameron. See her articles, including "CBC staffers' fear of people in high places," *Globe and Mail* 5 October 1992.

3 I outlined my interview protocols to both my university's Committee on Research on Human Subjects and to the SSHRC grants' committee.

4 I don't think this book is the place to make a canon of tips and statements for trainees in the various creative fields, but I hope that students
in community colleges and universities who already use *Contrast* for a
variety of purposes will find this book even more useful.

5 Many of which are deposited in the National Archives of Canada in
Ottawa.

CHAPTER 1: DIRECTING

1 "Live to tape" meant putting an uninterrupted performance on tape.
"Stop tape" meant a few stops to change costumes or sets. Early tape
was very difficult to edit, so taping a performance in sequence was still
the rule.

2 Janet Edsforth, *Paul Almond: The Flame Within* (Ottawa: Canadian Film
Institute 1972). The filmography (page 36) records that this repeat
production was 27 March 1959. The Canadian production won the 1957
Ohio Award and was repeated 15 April 1960.

3 Mary Jane Miller, *Turn Up the Contrast: CBC Television Drama since 1952*
(Vancouver: UBC Press and the CBC 1987), illustration 2 between pages
214 and 215. See also Sandy Stuart's account of this kind of equipment
in *Here's Looking at Us: A History of Television in Canada* (Toronto: CBC
Enterprises 1986).

4 T. Benson, R.W. McGall, and P. Herrndorf, "Report of the Drama
Committee," 29 June 1973. The authors were three senior executives in
the CBC. I have seen a private copy.

5 See also Miller, *Turn Up the Contrast*, 165–6.

6 Richard Levison and William Link, *Off Camera: Conversations with
Makers of Prime-Time Television* (New York and Scarborough, Ont.: New
American Library 1986), 179–80.

7 See Graham Murdock's "Radical Drama, Radical Theatre," *Media, Culture and Society* 2,2 (1980); 151–678, and Paul Kerr's "F for Fake? Fric-
tion over Fiction," in A. Goodwin and G. Whannel, eds., *Understanding
Television* (London: Routledge 1990), 77–83,

8 The effect was an evocation of shadows burned on to walls by the flash
at Hiroshima. Shadows since have become a conventional signifier of
nuclear holocaust. In the early 1960s, however, it was not a visual cliché
but a resonant dramatic effect.

9 *Playdate*, a sixty-minute anthology that presented comedian Red Skelton
once a month, and in the other three weeks plays like Pinter's *The Lover*
(27 January 1964). Len Peterson wrote *With His Head Tucked underneath His Arm* (28 October 1964). Quite possibly viewers had more
eclectic tastes in those days, or perhaps *Playdate*'s audience members
suffered from the monthly interruption.

10 Edsforth, Paul Almond; "All Aboard for Candy Land" and "Pick a Time, Any Time," both in 1966.

11 Based on Pierre Berton's books *The National Dream* and *The Last Spike*. *The National Dream* and Donald Brittain's *Canada's Sweetheart: The Saga of Hal Banks* had both used documentary and dramatized segments without difficulty. Despite allegations to the contrary, the controversial CBS trilogy on the Second World War, *The Valour and the Horror,* did not invent or exploit the juxtaposition of both kinds of material.

12 And yet Gardner directed one of the most interesting drama films ever produced at the CBC: *The Paper People* in 1967. See also Mary Jane Miller, "Timothy Findley's *The Paper People*," *Canadian Drama*, spring 1983, 49–60.

13 Levison and Link, *Off Camera*, 188.

14 A series' bible is a set of guidelines that also provides backstory for writers on a series, outlining the essence of the series, background on the characters, possible directions for storylines, and technical points (for example, in *Street Legal*'s bible, how Canadian law differs from American law).

CHAPTER 2: PRODUCING

1 Paul Rutherford, *When Television Was Young: Primetime Canada 1952–67* (Toronto: University of Toronto Press 1990), 281.

2 E.A. Weir, *The Struggle for National Broadcasting in Canada* (Toronto: McClelland & Stewart 1965), 403, 407.

3 See Mary Jane Miller, *Turn Up the Contrast: CBC Television Drama since 1952,* (Vancouver: UBC Press and the CBC 1987), 213.

4 Leslie Halliwell, with Philip Purser, *Halliwell's Television Companion* (Grenada: 1982).

5 Although Louis Del Grande appeared in a pilot for a sitcom that wasn't picked up in 1993.

6 See his memoirs, *Reinventing Myself: Memoirs* (Toronto: Stoddart 1994), for a more complete account of television drama's earliest years.

7 Ron Base, "CBC's White-Hot Hope," *Toronto Star*, date not known. When Hirsch described the CBC as a colony, he was the man in charge. The way he saw it determined how he ran the Drama Department, which may be one of the reasons his leadership was creative but also demoralizing.

8 Recent books from Wayne Skene, *Fade to Black : A Requiem for the CBC* (Toronto and Vancouver: Douglas and MacIntyre 1993), and Knowlton Nash, *The Microphone Wars: A History of Triumph and Betrayal at the CBC* (Toronto: McClelland & Stewart 1994), both hands-on producers who took on vital management responsibilities, confirm that this is an ongoing problem.

9 See also Miller *Turn Up the Contrast*, 256–99. Sam Levene was responsible for much of the anthology's reputation for probity and relevance.

10 Given the amnesia that has characterized the CBC for much of its history, it is not surprising that the autumn 1991 drama *Conspiracy of Silence* on the unacknowledged and largely unpunished death of Helen Betty Osborne was treated by publicists and critics alike as the first time such a subject had been presented on Canadian television.

11 Miller, *Turn Up the Contrast*, chapter 11.

12 See below, chapter 11.

13 Compare the situation of the writer/producer in the United States as described in Horace Newcomb and Robert S. Alley, *The Producer's Medium: Conversations with Creators of American TV* (New York: Oxford University Press 1983), passim.

14 Gordon Pinsent wrote this episode. In fact, he wrote fifteen of the twenty-one "chapters"; Peter Wildeblood wrote the other six.

15 Their first child dies hours after it is born; Miller, *Turn up the Contrast*, 177.

16 Ibid., 121.

CHAPTER 3: WRITING

1 *Globe and Mail*, 13 November 1978, in an open letter to writers.

2 E.A. Weir, *The Struggle for National Broadcasting in Canada* (Toronto: McClelland & Stewart 1965).

3 See also chapter 9.

4 Richard Collins, *Culture, Communciation and National Identity: The Case of Canadian Television* (Toronto: University of Toronto Press 1990).

5 Paul Rutherford, *Primetime: When Television Was Young* (Toronto: University of Toronto Press 1990), 294.

6 Mavor Moore, *Reinventing Myself: Memoirs* (Toronto; Stoddart 1994).

7 And eighteen years after *Brothers in the Black Art* on *The Play's the Thing*, 1974. His one-act script *Overlaid* was produced many times over the years.

8 *Theatre History in Canada* 5 (spring 1984): 51–71.

9 Rutherford, *Primetime*, 287.

10 See N. Alice Frick, *Image in the Mind: CBC Radio Drama, 1944–1954* (Toronto: Canadian Stage & Arts Publiations 1987), and Howard Fink and John Jackson, eds, *All the Bright Company: Radio Drama Produced by Andrew Allan* (Kingston: Quarry Press 1987).

11 See Gardner, chapter 1.

12 "Who Was the Lone Ranger?" 23 October 1967, "Amnesty," 4 November 1968, "Gunfighter," 17 February 1969, and two more in 1970.

13 For example, *Les Belles Soeurs, Hosanna,* and *Albertine in Five Times.*

14 For example, *Leaving Home* and *Salt Water Moon*.

15 Canadian academics had not yet published the dozens of books and articles demonstrating that this widely held belief was wrong. See two decades of *Canadian Drama*, now in *Essays in Theatre, Canadian Theatre Review*, and *Theatre History in Canada*, and the dozens of plays that used the forms of popular drama, from satires on Confederation to *1837* and Reaney's *The Donnelly Trilogy*.

16 *Globe and Mail*, 13 November 1978. Hirsch's opinion was shared by Ivan Fecan. See chapter 10.

17 However, popular culture critics like Geoff Pevere and Gary Michael Dault (on CTV National News, 28 December 1991), and others in print, identified 1991 as the year in North America where "reality programming" and live broadcasts (the Gulf War, the Thomas/Hill hearings) became the entertainment of choice, and often indistinguishable from the forms and uses of television fiction. The gap has now closed to the extent that dramatic images of a two-year-old child taken from her adoptive parents in July 1993 were replicated in a movie of the week by late September, three months later. There do appear to be "limits" of a sort, however. Fox network delayed its instant movie on O.J. Simpson until after the trial got under way. But then volumes had already been written about the smallest detail of that case, each presented as a mini-movie. In 1994–95 there was no perceptible difference in editorial judgment or in dramatic presentation between *ABC Nightly News* and *Hard Copy*, and very little in format between *A Current Affair* and an act or scene of a movie of the week.

18 Richard Levison and William Link, *Off Camera: Conversations with Makers of Prime-Time Television* (New York and Scarborough, Ont.: New American Library 1986), 13, 25.

19 Mary Jane Miller, *Turn Up the Contrast: CBC Television Drama since 1952* (Vancouver UBC Press and the CBC 1987), 94–100.

20 Quoted in Levison and Link, *Off Camera*, 44–5.

21 For another point of view, see Miller, *Turn Up the Contrast*, 85–9.

22 The records in the CBC Archives state that Goodship directed this episode for *Vancouver Playbill* (12 December 1958). See also the records in the CBUT collection at British Columbia Archives and Record Service. However, several *Cariboo Country* episodes were retaped for broadcast later – and the records could well be wrong. They are quite sketchy for early regional drama. The British Columbia Archives of Sound and Moving Images and the National Archives of Canada both hold episodes of the series, but I have not been able to view this one to check the credits.

23 The first complex, less formula-driven series picked up by CTV. Grigsby and Samuels are the creators and executive producers of the CBC's successful and 1990s series *North of 60*.

24 *Globe and Mail*, 13 November 1974.

25 Probably the most famous instance is in an episode of *M*A*S*H*. In the last minute of the episode or "tag," Radar, in obvious shock, tells Hawkeye that Colonel MacLean, who had been written out of the show in this episode by the simple expedient of completing his tour of duty, has been shot down. In being true to the basic context of war as well as their own willingness to change the conventions of sitcom, the show's writers and producers broke the most sacred rule of all up to that time: "Thou shalt not kill a major character or introduce real tragedy into this form of comedy." Many years later, that tag is still cut in some reruns.

26 *The Bells of Hell* (recorded 1973), which was the subject of scathing criticism from the Jewish community before its broadcast. It was then cancelled. However, the script was printed in *Toronto Life* and the play was rescheduled for January 1974. As a piece of television it did not deserve the notoriety – it simply wasn't very good. Richler's earlier work for the CBC was quite good, but not, in my view, this self-indulgent, tired piece of satire.

27 Or as Mark Starowicz said at Banff in May 1990, "Drama and news were born joined at the hip" (my hand-written notes). The idea that everything has been dramatized has become a critical commonplace among communications studies specialists from Raymond Williams to John Fiske. See Raymond Williams, *Drama in a Dramatized Society* (Cambridge: Cambridge University Press 1975), John Fiske, *Television Culture* (London: Methuen 1987), and Elayne Rapping, *The Looking-Glass World of Non-Fiction Television* (Boston: South End Press 1987), specifically chapter 8 on made-for-TV movies and mini-series.

CHAPTER 4: ACTING

1 Kate Reid, who died in March 1993, was considered one of the best classical and contemporary actors in Canadian theatre.

2 Paul Almond also shared an anecdote about Earle Grey, one of the first professionals in Canada who brought Shakespeare into Ontario high schools in the 1950s with his Earle Grey Players and who had a prize named after him by ACTRA. "He came over from the U.K. when he was probably eighty-five or ninety years old to present the first prize, and it happened to be won by my wife of the time, Geneviève Bujold (who starred in several of Almond's early films as well as in Hollywood movies). He squinted down at the envelope and announced the winner, 'Miss Guinivere Booge.'"

3 Eric Sherman, *Directing the Film: Film Directors on Art* for the American Film Institute (Los Angeles: Acrobat Books 1976), 162.

4 Quoted in Richard Levison and William Link, *Off Camera: Conversations*

with Makers of Prime-Time Television (New York and Scarborough, Ont.: New American Library 1986), 54.

5 Laura Mulvey, *Visual and Other Pleasures* (Bloomington: Indiana University Press 1989), chapters 2 and 3. Mulvey makes the point that women in Hollywood films are objects of a male gaze, not subjects, and that the films are structured to wake and then satisfy this relationship of spectator to actor. For Mulvey, classic Hollywood film presents the female as always powerless and always available.

6 In this context it is perhaps not accidental that R.H. Thomson's television appearances in the early 1990s are chiefly as the awkward, shy (and much loved by the young audiences) Jasper Dale in *Road to Avonlea*.

7 Quoted in Levison and Link, *Off Camera*, 94.

8 Again see Mulvey, *Visual and Other Pleasures*, particularly the chapter "Woman as Image, Man as the Bearer of the Look," 19.

9 See Diane Mew, ed., *Life before Stratford: The Memoirs of Amelia Hall* (Toronto: Dundurn Press 1989). In a picture of former Canadian Repertory Theatre actors then at Stratford – William Shatner, Donald Davis, William Hutt, Ted Follows, David Gardner, and Eric House – all appeared in early CBC television drama. But Hall, when approached by Mavor Moore in 1952 to be the first woman director of CBC television, writes, "I never gave this proposal any serious thought. I had to finish the job I was on at the CRT" (223). If Hall had accepted, would the history of women's absence from the ranks of producer/director in adult drama been different?

10 *Wojeck* doesn't rate an entry in *Halliwell's Television Companion*, perhaps because, as my research among the clippings at the British Film Institute showed, the British were unsettled by the non-standard look of John Vernon. On the whole, they liked the dramas, but, with the exception of the communist *Morning Star*, they found the casting of the protagonist odd. He didn't look like anyone else on British television at that time and they said so; as in "the closeups of ugly faces coupled with the message that the world is made up of acned predators or gooey do-gooders with strong jaws and steely eyes had me cringing in my shoes. But before then I had succumbed to the gloomy impact," W. Marshall, *Daily Mirror*, 27 June 1969. *The Times*, 22 August 1969, chided *Wojeck* for having "set off from fairly reasonable premises and then going rather further than we hoped, a little way beyond credence, but always with the best of social intentions." Canadians, of course, were excited by the series in part because it was an accurate reflection of their lives.

11 Trotter is a former student of mine from Brock Univeristy. She is also a graduate of the National Theatre School.

12 See also Mary Jane Miller, *Turn Up the Contrast* (Vancouver: UBC Press and the CBC 1987), 265–6, for a more detailed analysis of the problems.

13 Richard Collins, *Culture, Communication and National Identity* (Toronto: University of Toronto Press 1990), 35.

14 Who got into trouble with the bishop for supporting a performance of *Tartuffe* in Quebec.

CHAPTER 5: OTHER ROLES

1 "Drama Subcommittee to the Program Study Team: English Television, 25 June 1987," 3. The status of this report is that of a working document and a *cri du coeur* after the renewed resolve at Deerhurst to "Canadianize," specifically in drama. Although conflicting schedules meant that the full subcommittee met only once, all participants worked on the report. The members were Markye McEwen (*Street Legal*); Marc Blandford (*Empire Inc., Chasing Rainbows*), and Bernie Zukerman (*Love and Hate, Conspiracy of Silence*), all producers or executive producers; Steven Scaini, director of several episodes of *Street Legal, Northwood, Max Glick* and *Adderley*, as well as writer and produceer of short films; Roman Melynk, middle management, then working with independents; and Mark Starowicz, who had been midwife to *The National* and *The Journal* and was still its executive producer. Starowicz ends his introduction with this comment, "This is a rough sketch work in an early, even hasty report from scouts surveying the terrain."

2 Just as the fact that Shakespeare's leading player was Richard Burbage, not Edward Alleyne, shaped his characters, and the fact that his stage was a thrust, open to the daylight with a trapdoor and an "above," shaped his dialogue and even his plots.

3 Mary Jane Miller, *Turn Up the Contrast: CBC Television Drama since 1952* (Vancouver: UBC Press and the CBC 1987), 228.

4 From notes on a conversations with producer Maryke McEwen, story editor Peter Lower, and director Peter Yalden-Thomas during a sound mix of the film.

5 Notable exceptions are David Thorbun's seminal "Television as Melodrama" in R. Adler and D. Cater, eds., *Television as a Cultural Force* (London: Praeger 1976) and Rick Altman's "Television/Sound" in Tania Modleski, ed., *Studies in Entertainment* (Bloomington: Indiana University Press 1986).

6 *The Devil's Instrument* by W.O. Mitchell revolved around a harmonica. A young Hutterite boy is separated from his community by his love of music when he learns to play a harmonica.

7 By the late 1960s and early 1970s the sound, dialogue, effects, and even music were often thin, without resonance, and full of pops and scratches. For a while, CBC sound was often the subject of comment by

critics and viewers alike, because it sounded as if the equipment was not up to the needs of drama.

8 The convergence in post-production of film and tape was completed when the equipment was fully digitized.

9 Richard Levison and William Link, *Off Camera: Conversations with Makers of Prime-Time Television* (New York and Scarborough, Ont.: New American Library 1986), 25.

10 Miller, *Turn Up the Contrast*, 276–7.

11 Rick Altman, "Television/Sound," in Tanya Modleski, ed., *Studies in Entertainment: Critical Approaches to Mass Culture* (Bloomington: Indiana University Press 1986), 39–54.

12 I interviewed Schreibman during the early years of the show, but the tape of our conversation was defective. This paraphrase is based on my notes taken at the time from that tape.

13 In a mystery show, punches do land occasionally. An odd sidenote is that the viewer has been conditioned by decades of Hollywood fights to expect a certain sound, a heavy wet thud, to a punch. Since punches don't sound like that in real life, the CBC has had to "borrow" the sound from the sound track of an old movie to mix into fight sequences.

14 Levison and Link, *Off Camera*, 24.

15 The 1991–92 *Who's Who in Canadian Film and Television* tells us that Hebb did nine episodes of *Street Legal* for McEwen, the feature films *Cowboys Don't Cry* and *Termini Station*, and since 1988 has been working in television in the United States.

16 From conversations at breaks on the set of *Seeing Things*.

17 Miller, *Turn Up the Contrast*, 55–6.

18 In the last fifteen years, designers have rarely used tape imaginatively to explore the possibilities of chroma-key or collage. Contrast the multiple visual styles used in the 1982 ITV Scottish production of the popular Canadian play *Billy Bishop Goes to War*, or even some of the CBC experiments with different conventions in the 1970s (*1837* and *Les Belles Soeurs*). Where is the old gift for studio expressionism, the tape equivalent to the Brechtian counterpoint of visible lights, stylized sound, epigraphs, narrators, film clips, slides, and stills? Realism or heightened realism was still the rule for most tape productions in the 1980s, with the brave exceptions of CBC's *King of Friday Night* and the independent *I Am a Hotel*, both telecast in 1984. Atom Egoyan's 1992 *Gross Misconduct* was the next major experiment in the conventions of television.

19 Toronto's mix of architecture, waterfront, ravines, and neon strips make it ideal for film-makers from Canada and the United States, looking for a variety of periods and settings. During the 1980s it became a major centre for American film and television, and a home for several inter-

nationally successful Canadian independent producers: Alliance, Atlantis, Nelvana, etc.

20 For another version of the interview, plus the full script of *Sanity Clause*, one of the best of recent CBC dramas, see *Canadian Theatre Reveiw* (winter 1994): 56–8 and 60–85.

21 Toronto Women in Film and Television, *The Future for Women in the Canadian Film and Television Industry* (Toronto: Toronto Women in Film and Television 1991), "Understanding the Numbers," 11.

22 Ibid., "Breaking the Frame," 43.

23 "Drama Subcommittee" report, 28–30.

24 Ibid., 30.

CHAPTER 6: TECHNOLOGY

1 See Asa Briggs, *The History of Broadcasting in the United Kingdom*, vol. 1: *The Birth of Broadcasting* (London: Oxford University Press 1961), particularly "Writtle and Its Rivals," 68–89.

2 See also Mavor Moore, *Reinventing Myself: Memoirs* (Toronto: Stoddart 1994), 199–201.

3 Many communities across Canada's north, the interior of British Columbia, and parts of the east coast received no television signals even after the communication satellite was launched. About 20 per cent of Canada is without cable, and most of that area is dependent on the CBC for television. Yet the June 1995 report of the parliamentary committee charged with trying to make useful suggestions to the government about the CBC's future suggested that the CBC be moved to cable – notwithstanding the fees or the coverage restrictions such a change would entail.

4 Webster is central to every university course in English Renaissance drama. He was a brilliant writer of memorable dialogue and his plots are full of suspense, psychological terrorism, violence, and charged eroticism. The duchess's twin brother, whose incestuous emotions towards his sister are strongly implied, imprisons, tortures, and murders her for daring to marry again and marrying below her station.

5 Lloyd Bochner, Michael Learned, John Drainie, and Frances Hyland.

6 See also Mary Jane Miller, *Turn Up the Contrast: CBC Television Drama since 1952* (Vancouver: UBC Press and the CBC 1987), 195.

7 There are no commercials on CBC radio in the 1990s.

8 Miller, *Turn Up the Contrast*, 212, 272–3.

9 Lally Cadeau played an experienced social worker, David Eisenberg her young co-worker, and veteran actor Ruth Springford the sardonic secretary.

10 Mark 1 – that is, the first season. There were two substantive revisions of the sitcom in the next two seasons.

11 A three-part pilot about a rookie policeman which did not become a series.

12 This was the case until fully digitized post-production was available.

13 Jack Kuney, *Take One: Television Directors on Directing* (New York: Praeger 1990).

14 See the mid-1980s CBC adaptation of John Gray's musical *Rock and Roll*, called *King of Friday Night*, for imaginative use of 1980s chromakey technology.

15 These observations are based on a day's taping of *Backstretch*.

16 Miller, *Turn Up the Contrast*, 372.

17 From his notes for a presentation at a "think tank" of top executives, 5 October 1983.

18 The information on the future of digital HDTV and television technology was researched by J.M. Miller, who was for three years chair of computer science at Brock University.

19 It was a huge hit in Britain in 1967, and quite successful on PBS in the early 1970s.

20 See also television adaptations of *Maggie and Pierre* and *Billy Bishop Goes to War*. Both programs are taped studio adaptations of highly stylized one-person stage productions. *Maggie and Pierre* was remarkably and aptly self-reflexive, given its focus on media myth-making. See Miller, "*Billy Bishop Goes to War* and *Maggie and Pierre:* A matched set," in *Theatre History in Canada* 10 (fall 1989): 188–99.

21 The early 1990s sitcom *Max Glick* did play with television's "fourth wall" conventions. Atom Egoyan's *Gross Misconduct* had a fevered look and an intricate structure of flashbacks and flash forwards.

22 H.G. Kirchoff, "CBC Facing Massive Changes," 18 February 1992

23 The full implications of an additional $350 million cut are addressed in chapters 9, 10, and 12.

14 I selected this quotation online from World Wide Web copyright 1993–4. *Wired* magazine hard copy excels in full-colour graphics, interplay of textual formats, and incisive looks at the convergence of technologies and their content.

CHAPTER 7: WHY MAKE CANADIAN TELEVISION DRAMA?

1 Richard Collins, *Culture, Communication and National Identity: The Case of Canadian Television* (Toronto: University of Toronto Press 1990).

2 See chapter 9 for an explanation of this odd, but perpetual, fact of CBC budgeting.

3 Canadian academic critics Seth Feldman and Paul Rutherford and British scholar Richard Collins would agree. For a varied set of views on the subject, see Frank Manning and David Flaherty, eds., *The Beaver*

Bites Back: American Popular Culture in Canada (Montreal and Kingston: McGill-Queen's University Press 1993).

4 Gerry Gross, "A Palpable Hit: A Study of the Impact of Reuben Ship's *The Investigator,*" *Theatre History in Canada* 10 (fall 1989): 152–66.

5 Canada's own hunt for hidden "reds" found its way into our popular culture thirty years later with the CBC's docudrama *Grierson and Gouzenko.* See also Mavor Moore, *Reinventing Myself: Memoirs* (Toronto: Stoddart 1994), chapter 10.

6 N. Alice Frick, *Image in the Mind: CBC Radio Drama, 1944–54* (Toronto: Canadian Stage and Arts Publications 1987), 140–3.

7 The Reuben Ship story was not chosen for development. Perhaps the subject was too expensive to mount or too obscure, or perhaps the mirror image came too close to the perceived political reality in Canada in the late 1980s?

8 On audience research, see also chapter 8.

9 Rick Salutin reported that Disney participates financially in *Road to Avonlea* and "claims they are about family values. Some Canadians in the east are dubious. 'They aren't about family values at all,' said one. 'They are about community values.'" Salutin goes on to point out that Canadians are more likely to find their values in the community, not the isolated and individual family. This focus "may be one matter on which our two nations have not, or not yet, harmonized." *Maclean's,* 1 July 1995, 43.

10 *Rearview Mirror* was scheduled on Sunday afternoons when viewing audiences are small. However, there were no retrospectives – prime-time series reruns of anything older than 1989–90 – in the 1990–91 or 1991–92 season. In 1992–93 *Don Messer and His Islanders* and *Jubilee* were repackaged in early prime time, with guests commenting on the clips chosen. The good ratings for this revival surprised the CBC and delighted CBC archivist Ernie Dick, who reported on the success of this vintage series to the Association of Canadian Radio and Television (ASCRT) in June 1993. In 1994–95 *Max Glick* and *Degrassi High* were rerun in the 7:00–7:30 slot on some CBC stations. Now the corporation is reported to be burrowing in the archives for other resources among its drama programs. What may reappear in day-time or evening hours may be a surprise. Meanwhile, for the first time ever, there are reruns of vintage CBC programming available every night on the new Fiction channel Showcase. It features old favourites like *Wojeck* and *King of Kensington,* as well as newer series from the CBC and from CTV.

11 See Mary Jane Miller, "Inflecting the Formula: The First Seasons of *Street Legal* and *LA Law,*" Manning and Flaherty, eds., *The Beaver Bites Back,* 104–22.

12 Compare the late 1980s independent comedy special *The Canadian*

Conspiracy, still rerun in 1994 as Canadian content by individual stations, which posited a company of well-known expatriate Canadians
playing themselves who infiltrate and corrupt the soul of American network televisiona.

13 Richard Levison and William Link, *Off Camera: Conversations with
Makers of Primetime Television* (New York and Scarborough, Ont.: New
American Library 1986), 253.

14 Knowlton Nash, *Microphone Wars: A History of Triumph and Betrayal at
the CBC* (Toronto: McClelland & Stewart 1994), 540

15 Another Christmas program had built-in expectations of the season.
Tearful daughter and no-good father finally meet in the last scene, but
then we discover that Sally, the "Mom PI," had to bribe the father to
meet with the kid. No sentimental reconciliation is achieved.

16 John Ellis would agree. See his influential *Visible Fictions: Cinema,
Television and Video* (London: Routlege 1982), 158.

17 The reader may observe that, depending on the context, MJM either
favours myth-making or disparages it – a very Canadian ambivalence to
one of the activities usually deemed essential to the "nation-state."

18 Caring and committed lawyers like Carrie and Leon, vamps like Olivia,
handsome but fallible Mountie Eric, and band chief Peter (but not, I
think, complex and troubled Michelle) may also have created a few new
myths.

19 Public relations release, no. 126, 7 May 1991.

20 *Globe and Mail,* 1 June 1991.

21 *Toronto Star,* 2 June 1991.

22 Ibid., 5 October 1991.

CHAPTER 8: WHAT KINDS OF PROGRAMS AND WHY

1 *How People Use Television: A Review of TV Viewing Habits* (Toronto: CBC
Audience Research 1991).

2 Ross Eaman's *Channels of Influence: CBC Audience Research and the
Canadian Public* (Toronto: University of Toronto Press 1994) is a history
of ratings and other audience measurements in Canada, specifically of
audience research at the CBC, and an eloquent attack on the way they
are currently used. See especially chapter 9, "Audience Power versus
Public Needs: Five Arguments against Ratings."

3 Marxist, structuralist, and ethnographic studies have multiplied in
recent years to give a much better profile of the audiences and the way
they use television. A few among the many that I have found useful are
Tamar Liebes, "Cultural Differences in the Retelling of Television
Fiction," *Critical Studies in Mass Communication* 5 (1988): 277–92;
Robert C. Allen, "Audience-Oriented Criticism," in Robert C. Allen, ed.,

Channels of Discourse Reassembled: Television and Contemporary Criticism (Chapel Hill: University of North Carolina 1992); John Fiske, *Television and Culture* (London: Methuen 1987); Ien Ang, *Desperately Seeking the Audience* (London: Routledge 1990); Helen Baehr and Gillian Dyer, eds., *Boxed In: Woman and Television* (London: Pandora Press 1987); and John Tulloch, *Television Drama: Agency, Audience and Myth* (London: Routledge 1990).

4 *How People Use Television*, ii.

5 In a joint presentation to ASCRT/AERTC, 1 June 1993.

6 All U.S. channels combined are sampled by 75 per cent of the population.

7 *How People Use Television*, iii, 35.

8 Nielson figures for CBC, CTV, Newsworld (excluding Radio-Canada et al.) on referendum night were nearly six million. *Maclean's*, 13 November 1995, 11.

9 *How People Use Television*, 10.

10 Ibid., 62

11 Ibid., 64

12 Mary Jane Miller, *Turn Up the Contrast: CBC Television Drama since 1952* (Vancouver: UBC Press and the CBC 1987), 25.

13 Four months in the case of skaters Tonya Harding and Nancy Kerrigan.

14 See Ang, *Desperately Seeking the Audience*, specifically chapter 10, "Revolt of the Viewer: The Elusive Audience," and the "Conclusion: Understanding Television Audiencehood."

15 Richard Levison and William Link, *Off Camera: Conversations with Makers of Prime-Time Television* (New York and Scarborough, Ont.: New American Library 1986), 270. This American book laments the triumphs of formula television while recording and celebrating the exceptions.

16 The *Valour and the Horror* dramatizations were very controversial, even though for viewers fictitious segments were clearly encoded as fictitious; for example, through scenes using no sets and few props, or by prefacing the re-enactments of the briefings before a bombing raid with shots of weedy, crumbling runways. The aging faces of surviving pilots were contrasted to the youthful actors. The veterans who are outraged by these programs say they would have few problems with the past series if it were labelled drama or even docudrama. In this controversy both sides agree that the designation "documentary" connotes a claim to a particular kind of "factual truth." When the *Valour and the Horror* was broadcast by channel 4 in Britain in 1994, a panel discussion was added.

17 In June 1995 Harry Rasky's contract was not renewed, along with that of Norman Campbell. The distinguished arts producer Arthur Miller wrote a letter expressing pained astonishment at this decision to the

Globe and Mail, 24 June 1995. "Mr. Rasky demonstrated a very high level of artistic ability, rare in any country. It is a pity CBC have decided, mistakenly I believe, that he and what he has stood for in this much abused art are irrelevant to their current purposes. I assure you that there are others who will share my reaction on hearing of this decision to in effect excise the spirit from the body of CBC."

18 Sydney W. Head, *Broadcasting in America: A Survey of Television and Radio,* 2nd ed. (Boston: Houghton/Mifflin 1972), 213.

19 Miller, *Turn Up the Contrast,* chapters 6 and 7.

20 Paul Rutherford, *Primetime: When Television Was Young* (Toronto: University of Toronto Press 1990).

21 Note the frequent use by a whole generation of CBC makers and decision-makers of the depreciating adjective "little" when something is praised.

22 "John Hirsch and the Critical Mass: Alternative Theatre on CBC Television in the 1970s," *Theatre Research in Canada* 15 (spring 1994): 75–95. See the "Catalogue of Canadian Stage Plays on English-Canadian Television, 1952–1987," ibid., 96–108.

23 This movie is currently available on video, while most good CBC television drama is unavailable.

24 See my analysis in Miller, *Turn Up the Contrast,* 241–3.

25 Alan Stratton's successful play *Rexy* (about Mackenzie King, also adapted for television) and his farce *Nurse Jane Goes to Hawaii,* a very funny parody of Harlequin romances, were in the same tragic-comic vein. Stratton provokes the viewer into laughter at his macabre scenes, even in his television script for *A Flush of Tories.*

26 So, too, Soames in *The Forsyte Saga,* Sir James in *Empire Inc.,* JR in *Dallas,* Erica in *All My Children,* and Relic in *The Beachcombers.*

27 Analysed in Miller, *Turn Up the Contrast,* 278–81.

28 Mary Jane Miller, "Inflecting the Formula: The First Seasons of *Street Legal* and *LA Law* in David H. Flaherty and Frank E. Manning, eds., *The Beaver Bites Back? American Popular Culture* (Montreal and Kingston: McGill-Queen's University Press 1993), 104–22.

29 Rutherford, *When Television Was Young,* 129. Rutherford accurately, if rather sardonically, comments on Greene's personal finesse. "[He] was the first to nurture and later to kill 'This Was The Week That Was' without provoking any explosion comparable to the 'Seven Days Affair.'"

30 For a discussion of the early evolution of *The Beachcombers* and an analysis of its more distinctive characteristics, see Miller, *Turn Up the Contrast,* 95–110.

31 Preaching is not usually a Canadian vice. American series and movies of the week often preach to their audiences, spelling out in the dialogue the moral of the story.

32 See also Miller, *Turn Up the Contrast*, 310.

33 *Two Men* is about a wealthy old man who was a Nazi during the Second World War and a Jewish old man, his victim, who confronts him. Both have made new lives in Canada, but their earlier lives still haunt them.

34 It found a new, more dedicated audience when it was rescheduled in 1992–93 at 11 PM. The letters of praise continued. Those who hated it were, presumably, in bed, as were the children whose virtue they were trying to defend. The later time slot allowed them to broadcast skits that had been censored during the 9 PM slot. The CBC kept *Codco* going despite low ratings for four years. As Fecan said, "The show was outrageous and touching, often tasteless, very funny, and sometimes incomprehensible all in twenty-two minutes."With Tommy Sexton's illness, *Codco* left the air in 1993 after a good run. Its stepdaughter, the completely topical *This Hour Has 22 Minutes*, uses Mary Walsh, Greg Malone, and Cathy Jones from *Codco* – and enjoys higher ratings.

35 Fecan was consistent. In 1993 he reiterated that view in *SCAN* See chapter 11.

CHAPTER 9: POLICY

1 Christopher Hume, architecture columnist for the *Toronto Star*, 23 November 1991.

2 For a selection of full-scale rants by backbenchers from the 1930s (about radio dramas, features, talks, and news) to the 1990s see Knowlton Nash, *Microphone Wars: A History of Triumph and Betrayal at the CBC* (Toronto: McClelland & Stewart 1994). Suspicions of "high culture" vie with convictions that CBC producers and executives are "Commie pinkos" or, later, that they are tainted with separatism – views often shared by letter writers and newspaper critics.

3 See chapter 5.

4 Griffiths was programmer at CBLT, one of the first two stations on the air, and Mutrie was CBC's director of programming for Toronto – titles ebbed and flowed at the time. A propos of this anecdote is Rutherford's quote from Mutrie in 1950: "The trouble with television is that it's hard to lie about it fast enough to keep up with the truth." Paul Rutherford, *When Television Was Young: Primetime Canada, 1952–67* (Toronto: University of Toronto Press 1990), 10.

5 Quoted in Frank Peers, *The Public Eye: Television and the Politics of Canadian Broadcasting, 1952–1968* (Toronto: University of Toronto Press 1979), 94.

6 Herschel Hardin, *Closed Circuits: The Sellout of Canadian Television* (Vancouver: Douglas and McIntyre 1985); Marc Raboy, *Missed Opportunities: The Story of Canada's Broadcasting Policy* (Montreal: McGill-

Queen's University Press 1990); and Nash, *Microphone Wars*. Nash's detailed portraits of each CBC president emphasizes the importance of the interplay of personalities within the corporations and among CBC personnel and government and the CRTC.

7 *Touchstone for the CBC*, 14 June 1977, quoted by Raboy, *Missed Opportunities*, 250.

8 Andrew Borkowski, *SCAN*, January/February 1992, in "The Attack of the 100 Channel Universe."

9 *SCAN*, May/June 1993, 13.

10 Raboy, *Missed Opportunities*, chapter entitled "The Eclipse of Public Broadcasting."

11 See ibid., chapter entitled "Commerce and Crisis," 176, for the debate that followed.

12 Bill C-40 from chapter 11 of *The Statutes of Canada 1991*, section 3 (i), "Broadcasting Policy for Canada," subsections (m. v and viii). Nash appears to agree with the Conservative government (a rare occurrence) that the old provision permitted interference with the freedom of the CBC. He quotes CBC president Gérard Veilleux: "National unity is a political objective ... the CBC is not a political justification, nor should it be." *Microphone Wars*, 486.

13 Mavor Moore, *Reinventing Myself: Memoirs* (Toronto: Stoddart 1994), 331.

14 See Nash, "A Good, Grey Presidency," *Microphone Wars*, 376–403, on the reorganization of the CBC under George Davidson. Nash sees Davidson as more in tune with the creative people than his predecessor, Alphonse Ouimet.

15 Some programs were redone ten years later by Atlantis for Global's monthly *Bell Canada Playhouse* – a rare excursion for Global into expensive Canadian drama.

16 Nash describes Benson as "an iconoclastic enthusiast with a strong streak of Canadian Nationalism"; *Microphone Wars*, 390. Regrettably, Nash has little to say about CBC TV drama, perhaps unsurprising given his background in news and current affairs on and off camera. In other respects, his book is an exhaustive look at CBC politics and policy.

17 *The Committee on Television Intervention to CRTC*, 18 February 1974.

18 In 1991–92 the CBC added another nightly half-hour of information programming on CBC-owned stations in the 7:00–7:30 pm weeknight slot which has since been replaced by a mix of American sitcoms and Canadian programs. With the apparent failure of "repositioning" (see chapter 12), the CBC has returned the 11:00–11:30 slot for local and regional news. The old/new *National* has continued to appear on Newsworld at 10 PM weeknights, as it will continue to do, whenever the playoffs disrupt the regular schedule – in March, April, and May.

19 The CBC euphemism for sales. We still await a definition of "further

use," which would include "fair use" in the educational or research sense.

20 Hirsch to Ron Base, *Star Television Guide*, nd.

21 Mary Jane Miller, *Turn Up the Contrast: CBC Television Drama since 1952* (Vancouver: UBC Press and the CBC 1987), 227.

22 Miller, *Turn Up the Contrast*, 365.

23 George Bloomfield, the producer, noted the contrast between *Peepshow* and the 1950s experimental dramas: "We were all into politics and some of us had to have our shows defended in Ottawa at the highest levels. [The politics were often existential, leftist, and 'European.'] But what this group [of writers and producers] is into is exposing intimate personal relationships, a very narrow introspective world." Quoted by Sid Adilman, *Toronto Star*, 11 August 1975.

24 *Globe and Mail*, 2 July 1976.

25 *Toronto Star*, 8 March 1989. Peter Herrndorf was then publisher of *Toronto Life* and ex-CBC vice-president of news and current affairs, English Network, and in 1992 he became president of TVO. See Knowlton Nash, *Microphone Wars*, 455, for an appraisal of his career, which I would suggest may not yet be finished with the CBC.

26 *The Committee on Television Intervention to CRTC*, 18 February 1974.

27 See Miller, *Turn Up the Contrast*, 357–73.

28 Nash dates this policy to November 1991; *Microphone Wars*, 509. For a full account of the theory and politics behind the strategy, see Nash's chapter entitled "A Repositioned CBC."

29 Ibid., 513. Nash also speculates that "Fecan got along swimmingly with him" because he was enthusiastic about the changes and was "used to having tough hands-on bosses" (517).

30 More vulgarly known as "T and A" for "Tits and Ass" – as in the 1970s sitcom *Three's Company* or the late 1980s sitcom *Babes*, or almost any comedy produced by Aaron Spelling. See also the full interview with Brandon Tartikoff in "The Network," in Richard Levison and William Link, eds., *Off Camera: Conversations with Makers of Prime-Time Television* (New York and Scarborough, Ont.: New American Library 1986), 245–65.

31 Miller, *Turn Up the Contrast*, 363.

32 It then evolved into *Degrassi High*, a late-teen/adult drama, ending with the two-hour movie special *School's Out* in January 1992 and the six documentary specials called *Degrassi Talks* in February and March 1992. Its successor, *Liberty Street*, also from Lynda Schuyler, arrived as a two-hour pilot that was justly panned. A much revamped half-hour drama intended to appeal to the so-called Generation X opened in January 1995 and looks promising. It has been renewed for 1995–96.

33 Quite unlike the United States. Although our favourite American programs are often different from those south of the border, that doesn't

make our choices "better." *America's Funniest Home Videos*, for example, did much better in the overall 1990–91 Canadian ratings than it does in the United States.

34 Except American advertisers who are, by law, blacked out on cable by Canadian advertisers when a show is simulcast. Thus the vast majority of viewers who get their signals on cable get the Canadian broadcast, even if our sets are tuned to CBS or NBC, not CBC or CTV. Direct broadcast satellites might change that.

35 Miller, *Turn Up the Contrast*, 362–3.

36 The CBC tried to compensate for the closure of eleven local stations in 1991–92 by a devising "regional" weekday supper-hour shows and starting up a few purely local shows at 5:30 PM. After a year, the local half-hour was cancelled across the country, and the supper-hour shows were to be rethought. Speculation in mid-1995 is that both 6–7 PM and 11:00–11:30 PM local programming will be early casualties of the budget cuts. Already the cuts that forced the CBC out of many localities have cost the corporation badly needed viewer support. The only bright spot is their successful bid in 1993 for their first CBC-owned station in New Brunswick.

37 Despite a decade of Thatcher and John Major, BBC–1 and BBC–2 still do not have commercials, but depend on licences paid for each set in use.

38 I would argue that the CBC did that with *Beachcombers*, the one-hour "special" closing episode not withstanding.

39 The program used an actor with Down's syndrome, David MacFarlane in "Romeo and Carol," well before American networks found that acceptable.

40 *Grand Larceny*, for example, a two-hour sequel in August 1991 to *Love and Larceny* (1985), came "in a few minutes light," thus affording an opportunity for other upcoming programming to enjoy some additional advertising. There is much more coverage of upcoming CBC drama specials and documentaries on Newsworld and on *Midday*, the news, information, and entertainment mix offered weekdays at noon. The CBC has even bought ads on the private radio and television stations.

41 Mankiewicz died tragically in 1993, breaking up the Zukerman, Couture, Mankiewicz team.

42 "Drama Subcommittee to the Program Study Team: English Television, 25 June 1987," 15.

43 The script by Louis Del Grande and Neil Ross appears in *Canadian Theatre Review* 81 (winter 1994): 60–85, with an interview with David Barlow by M.J. Miller, "Re: Some Technical Requirements of 'Sanity Clause,'" ibid., 56–8.

44 "Drama Subcommittee" report, 68.

45 Nash, *Microphone Wars*, 540. For the whole story of the conflict between

Veilleux and several of his most senior executives, see chapter 20, "Watson and Veilleux," and chapter 21, "A Repositioned CBC," 477–543.

46 The programs on Christmas Day are not always "dogs." A portrait of Northrop Frye, Canada's most famous literary critic and thinker, by Harry Rasky – without commercials – was broadcast on Christmas Day in the late 1980s.

47 Kennedy, 15 October 1983, 2, used with his permission.

48 *Toronto Star*, 29 May 1991.

49 *Canadian Forum*, June/July 1991, 12.

50 Quoted in "Drama Subcommittee" report, 28–9

51 Nash, *Microphone Wars*, 475.

52 Telefilm, the growth of the independents, and CRTC threats mean that there are other perceptibly Canadian drama series broadcast by other networks in the same period: *Neon Rider, Destiny Ridge, Madison*, and *Bordertown*, all much improved in their later seasons, action adventure clones like *Counterstrike* and *Tekwars* and the most succesful of the series, *ENG* and *Due South*.

53 It was cancelled without showing all the episodes made. *9-B* was cancelled after five episodes, and *In Opposition* and *Mosquito Lake* were shelved. By American standards, the CBC spends very little on development pilots and trial runs. As Fecan pointed out in 1993 (see chapter 11), however, under his management more money has been targeted to the development phases of scripts and to pre-production then was available in the 1980s.

54 The Conservative bill he talked about that was not passed by the Liberal Senate before Parliament was dissolved, C-136, would have allocated $20 million more for English television, $15 million for French television, and $18 million for Telefilm.

55 *Report from the Task Force on Broadcasting Policy* (Ottawa: Ministry of Supplies and Services 1986).

56 She is quoted extensively in Miller, *Turn Up the Contrast*, 380–1, but, as so often, the gap between good intentions and governmental action never closed.

57 See Raboy's "Conclusion" in *Missed Opportunities*.

58 *SCAN*, May/June 1993.

59 For a thorough examination of the economic and political factors that shaped television aesthetics in Canada in the 1970s and early 1980s, see Paul Audley, *Canada's Cultural Industries: Broadcasting, Publishing, Records and Film* (Toronto: Lorimer 1983). See also a prophetic article by Joyce Nelson aptly called "Dumping Ground," *Saturday Night*, May 1981.

60 In 1994–95 Shuster is re-editing the material again for a series to be featured on CBC prime time. In part, it will be a tribute to the passing of Johnny Wayne.

61 See also the one-hour special on broadcasting in an international market, *Distress Signals*, an NFB/CBC co-production in 1991. Little has changed or will change until the new technological revolution arrives.

62 Oddly, Mazo de la Roche's *Jalna*, that internationally successful series of novels written in Oakville, Ontario, which were also a stereotypical product of the British Empire, was reshot as a serial for a French television network, then sold back to us in French in 1995.

63 *Toronto Star*, 30 September 1983.

64 Ibid., 18 January 1986.

65 Miller, *Turn Up the Contrast*, 182–3.

66 *Scarlett*, November 1994, an eight-hour sequel to *Gone with the Wind*, cost $40 million – it was universally panned and rightfully so. It was aired in the "sweeps" month, when ad revenues are established for the winter, and CBS, running third in the overall network ratings, soared to number one. Critics be damned!

67 Ironically, in 1990 and 1991, Marineland in Niagara Falls, Ontario, showed the birth of their baby whale over and over in their television commercials. Context is all.

68 "Drama Subcommittee" report, 42–3.

69 "Report of the Drama Search Committee," 1973, 24, 26.

70 "A Report by John S. Hirsch" on his four years as head of CBC Television Drama, 1974–78.

71 "Drama Subcommittee" report, 6–8, 10–11.

72 I've been told by several people that John Kennedy, then head of drama, was one of the catalysts for this vision. For another point of view see "Drinking Kool-Aid in the Deerhurst Jungle," chapter 7 of Wayne Skene, *Fade to Black: Requiem for the CBC* (Vancouver and Toronto: Douglas & MacIntyre 1993), 122–41.

73 From my notes made off air from CBC Radio *Media File*, 7 July 1991.

74 Nash details the clash between Veilleux and Harvey which lead to Harvey's being "fired." His exit preceded that of other key personnel by only a year or two; *Microphone Wars*, 506–8.

75 Ted Magder, "Making Canada in the 1990s: Film, Culture, and Industry," in K. McRoberts, ed., *Beyond Quebec: Taking Stock of Canada* (Montreal and Kingston: McGill-Queen's University Press 1995), 163–81.

76 "Drama Subcommittee" report, 59.

77 Five years later the CRTC split such a combination channel by licensing several pay channels – two to do arts, Bravo and Showcase, turning down the consortium in which the CBC was a partner in the process – and Discovery, linked to Discovery in the United States, to do science and other documentaries. Will any of them survive into the late 1990s? Stay tuned.

78 *SCAN*, May/June 1994, 25.

79 Other CanWest/Global co-productions are listed by Paul W. Taylor in "Third Service, Third Network: The CanWest Global System," *Canadian Journal of Communication* 18 (autumn 1993): 469–77. Taylor sees no problem in making uninflected and undistinguished action/adventure formats and others. He does, however, remind us that this network gave a new lease on life to the solidly written family/adventure program *Neon Rider*.

CHAPTER 10: ETHOS

1 *The Shorter Oxford English Dictionary*, 3rd ed. (Oxford: Clarendon Press 1959).

2 CBC titles were then and are now remarkably uninformative regarding what the person designated actually does. Moore reports that his superior, program director Stuart Griffiths, asked him to be his chief producer and blackmailed him into acceptance. Moore, "Into Television," in *Reinventing Myself: Memoirs* (Toronto: Stoddart 1994), 188.

3 See Paul Rutherford, "Expectations," in *When Television Was Young: Primetime Canada, 1952–67* (Toronto: University of Toronto Press 1990), 1–38 for another account of a recognizable CBC ethos, which he perceives as characteristic of television's youth.

4 Knowlton Nash confirms this sense of shared purpose and excitement, quoting famed producer/director Harry Rasky, "None of us had a TV set except Ross [MacLean] but we thought we were going to change the world"; *Microphone Wars: A History of Triumph and Betrayal at the CBC* (Toronto: McClelland & Stewart 1994), 235. Eight years later, New Brunswick conservative MP, J.C. Van Home, echoing the sentiments of a vocal and politically influential minority, wanted the government to sell the CBC. "Quebec MP, Louis-Joseph Pigeon demanded 'let the CBC do away with smutty stories and daring costumes ... a clean up job in necessary'" (266). Nash assumes, like many others, that the CBC cancelled *Point of Departure* (1960) because of pressures like this. Instead, the drama was broadcast (I have seen the kinescope) at 11:30 at night. Nash, repeating CBC folklore, perpetuates a characteristic attitude which rewrites a compromise as a defeat. It would be more accurate to say that if the CBC couldn't change the world, it could and often did master the art of using the arts subversively.

5 "Canadian Television Drama, 1952–70: Canada's National Theatre of the Air," in *Theatre History in Canada* 5 (spring 1984): 51–71.

6 For a full history and analysis of CBC audience research, see Ross A. Eaman, *Channels of Influence: CBC Audience Research and the Canadian Public* (Toronto: University of Toronto Press 1994).

7 The NFB, like other independent sources in the late 1980s and 1990s, now supplies the CBC with programming, including drama; for example,

the quartet of films on Native and Métis women, *Daughters of the Country*, *The Boys of St Vincent* and co-productions of drama specials like *Justice for All*, (the Donald Marshall case). The director, producer, executive producer, and director of photography who appear in the credits are often, but not always, associated with the NFB. The production credits come from both organizations.

8 The credits selected by Sandor Stern to represent him in the 1991–92 *Who's Who in Canadian Film and Television*, (Waterloo: Academy of Canadian Cinema and Television, Wilfred Laurier Press 1991) are all American. Most of them are movies of the week or specials.

9 E.A. Weir, *The Struggle for National Brroadcasting in Canada* (Toronto: McClelland & Stewart 1965), 377.

10 Ibid., 403.

11 Frank Peers, *The Public Eye: Television and the Politics of Canadian Broadcasting, 1952–1968* (Toronto: University of Toronto Press 1979), 247.

12 Rutherford, *When Television Was Young*, 8. A London film critic, during a *Midday* piece on the London Film Festival, 18 December 1991, pointed to the exodus to Hollywood as the biggest difficulty Canadian cinema still faced. Again, "plus la même chose."

13 Weir, *Struggle*, 325–6.

14 *Globe and Mail*, 25 February 1963.

15 See also Eric Koch, *Inside Seven Days: The Show That Shook the Nation* (Scarborough: Prentice Hall 1986), which documents how and why *This Hour Has Seven Days* came to life and how, after much public and backroom struggle, it died. Also see Nash, "The Glory and the Hell of 'Seven Days,'" in *Microphone Wars*, 328–56.

16 Mary Jane Miller, *Turn Up the Contrast: CBC Television Drama since 1952* (Vancouver: UBC Press and the CBC 1987), chapter 10, "Regional, or What Toronto Doesn't Know."

17 Weir, *Struggle*, 435.

18 In fact, it's quite good. See Miller, *Turn Up the Contrast*, 335.

19 Committee on Television Intervention (CRTC, released 18 February 1974), appendix 2, 148–9. See also Marc Raboy, *Missed Opportunities: The Story of Canada's Broadcasting Policy* (Montreal: McGill-Queen's University Press 1990), 228–32, and the government publications attached to the CRTC hearings for the complete brief submitted, February 1974. Stan Fox went on to teach film at York University until 1981, and then returned to the industry at TVO. He is now a "semi-retired" consultant in Victoria.

20 Usually abbreviated RF, which covers long, short, and microwave and includes the television bands.

21 Richard Collins, *Culture, Communication and National Identity: The Case of Canadian Television* (Toronto: University of Toronto Press 1990), 212.

22 See also Richard Bruce Kirkley, "John Hirsch and the Critical Mass: Alternative Theatre on CBC Television in the 1970s," *Theatre Research in Canada* 15 (spring 1994): 75–95.

23 *SCAN*, January/February 1991, 2. *SCAN* was a publication of ATPD and CTPD and is now a publication of the Wire Guild. See also Wayne Skene, *Fade to Black: A Requiem for the CBC* (Vancouver: Douglas & McIntyre 1993).

24 "Repositioning: Year 1," ibid., May/June 1993. For a detailed insiders' report, see Nash, *Microphone Wars*, chapter 20, "Patrick Watson and Gérard Veilleux: The Icon and the Enigma," and chapter 21, "A Repositioned CBC," 477–544.

25 Miller, *Turn Up the Contrast*, 15, 211.

26 Greg Quill in *Toronto Star*, 14 June 1995.

27 Levene produced documentary for *This Hour Has Seven Days*, 1964–65; see *Who's Who in Television, 1991–92*.

28 Rutherford, *When Television Was Young*, 408–9. He also provides an interesting, sceptical analysis of both the program's rise and fall and a detailed account of a single program. Leiterman said the same thing in almost the same words in a Newsworld panel about *Seven Days* in May 1993, when he challenged Watson, then chair of the CBC board, and Trina McQueen, then vice-president of regions, to make once again a place for contentious, freewheeling current affairs programming. McQueen pointed out that times had changed: the innocent 1960s had become the cynical and pragmatic 1990s, but that the current affairs producers were still provoking controversy.

29 See a more detailed discussion of the relationship in Miller, "Will English-Language Television Remain Distinctive? Probably," in Kenneth McRoberts, ed., *Beyond Quebec: Taking Stock of Canada* (Montreal and Kingston: McGill-Queen's 1995) 194–6. I argue that the separation of the two cultures as far as television fiction is concerned is already a fact – and has been for decades.

30 See Collins, *Culture, Communication and National Identity*, "The Miniseries," 318–25.

31 Nash, *Microphone Wars*, 99–100. It was perceived as a conspiracy to make the country bilingual. The reorganized CBC is seen as making a contribution to understanding between anglophone and francophone, East and West (141, 147).

32 *SCAN*, January/February 1994, 16, 17.

33 See my response to the question, "Will English-Language Television Remain Distinctive? Probably," in McRoberts, ed., *Beyond Quebec*, 182–201.

34 Nash quotes Watson as saying the McKennas were "fearfully inept" in their dramatic sequences; that, he says, "was the major single source of the problem in the goddamn thing ... they didn't know how to do it";

Microphone Wars, 533. Attacks on *The Valour and the Horror* should focus on the interpretation or the selection of facts, not on the docudrama elements. The BBC's channel 4 showed the series in 1994, to the consternatoin of RAF veterans of Bomber Command.

35 Miller, *Turn Up the Contrast*, 113.

36 "Drama Subcommittee to the Program Study Team: English Television, 25 June 1987," 52–, 61–3.

37 What we got, instead, in the winter of 1991–92, was a weekday half-hour, 7:00–7:30, of "reality" programming called *Newsmagazine*. In 1992–93 the commitment to build Canadian talent into stars in prime time began with *Friday Night with Ralph Benmergui*, a showcase of Canadian talent which had started a rocky first year at 10 PM, was then switched to 11 PM, but was cancelled after a short second season. Toronto-based urban hip failed. *Rita and Friends*, an eclectic mix of musical styles anchored by the much loved Cape Breton singer Rita MacNeil, fared much better.

38 I have seen the kinescope, which confirms Allen's memory. The lighting also contributed much to the expressionist style of the design.

39 "A network program director [who] had the biggest say in the selection of shows for the English Network"; Rutherford, *When Television Was Young*, 73. Rutherford goes on to deconstruct the myth of the all-powerful and eccentric programmer, and outlines the multiple factors that predetermined schedules. Nevertheless, here, as in any individual case, Sadlier could simply have refused to allow *Offshore Island* to air.

40 Later on we learn through a mordant joke that the pig has two heads. Miller, *Turn Up the Contrast*, 220.

41 *Toronto Star*, 28 March 1964.

42 *Tyler* was a memorable ninety-minute special on the problems young farmers had in inheriting land that is also the only capital investment available to their parents in old age. It was broadcast on 30 September 1978 and is still, regrettably, very topical. The ability of "language" on television to shock also has not diminished. In April 1993 a third-year student reported to her communications studies class her shock at hearing "fuck" on television from *Kids in the Hall*. The class in general expressed surprise that such a word would be said on a comedy show on television, although some of them use the expletive everywhere but in class. "The word" is bleeped out in American television. Even in the 1980s the CBC was more comfortable with the word when it was used in a documentary such as the portrait of CAW president Bob White. A serious drama like Fennario's *Balconville* was broadcast late at night in the early 1980s. By 1994, however, *The Diary of Evelyn Lau*, a docudrama based on the diary of a young prostitute from a middle-class home, was laced with many "fucks." Meanwhile, what used to be thought

of as blasphemy is very common – indeed, the concept itself has fallen out of use. As far as street language is concerned, the CBC has always been behind public usage and ahead of American network standards.

43 See Seth Feldman on the *Tar Sands*, "The Electric Table: Aspects of the Docudrama in Canada," in *Canadian Drama* 1 (1983).

44 *SCAN*, May/June, 1993, 7. See also "Wrap-Up" below.

45 *SCAN*, November/December 1994, "Parley with Platt," 9–13.

46 This particular amnesia may be explained by the fact that Platt grew up in the United States and did not become a television producer until 1985. She had been an editor of *Cinema Canada* and *Take One*, but her broadcasting experience was in news and current events. Her current responsibility is for arts and entertainment. This short summary is drawn from *SCAN*, November/December 1994, "The Phyllis file," 13.

47 *Canadian Journal of Law and Society* 10, 2, 1995.

48 It will be the subject of a full-length collaboration between Miller and well-known Québecoise scholar Renée Legris.

49 Margo Kane starred as the Indian woman who is not allowed to exercise her new right to come home to the reserve in *Where the Heart Is*, 24 February 1985, and in CBC Radio's 1991 production of *The Ecstasy of Rita Joe*. On 1 July 1991 she was introduced as an outstanding Canadian at the telecast Canada Day Celebration for her work with theatre and young Native people.

50 *Changing Focus: The Future for Women in the Canadian Film and Television Industry* (Toronto: Toronto Women in Film and Television 1991), 41.

51 Ibid., 52.

52 As Armande Saint-Jean, radio and television journalist and broadcaster for Radio-Canada and Radio-Québec for twenty-five years and now professor at Université de Québec à Montréal, says: "Another factor contributes to what we might call an optical illusion. This illusion stems from the fact that women are widely used in advertising for televised, visual, and audio messages. In other words, we could say that it is easy to believe that the media are a woman's world, where there are "definitely many women," because we see them everywhere"; "Women and the Media, the Real Picture," *Changing Focus*, 119–20.

53 Armande Saint-Jean continues:

> We still tend to evaluate women's capabilities on the traditional models and the values associated with female roles, such as compassion, cooperation, service, and devotion. In this highly competitive industry, the woman who has mastered the rules of the game of confrontation or who appears to be a better player at the poker game of competition is viewed with a degree of suspicion.

In production companies, women in non-union executive positions earn 97 per cent of the salary their male colleagues earn. For non-unionized technical staff, this ratio drops to 67 per cent. Even at the CBC, which falls under the Employment Equity Act, male producers earned 10 percent more than female producers in 1989. Women therefore earn less than men. The same types of differences are also true for government investment in production.
Changing Focus, 121.

54 Nash, *Microphone Wars*, 540.

55 *Changing Focus*, "Finetuning the Picture," 77, 88.

56 Ibid., viii.

57 "Network" programs were recorded from monitors onto kinescopes, and the cans of film were then "bicycled" across the country to stations. As I pointed out in *Turn Up the Contrast*, some of our best early television drama survived because the station in Flin Flon seems to have had a broom-closet where some anonymous Good Samaritan stashed the kines. Unfortunately, as of January 1995, the expensive instrument that transfers imges from kinescopes to tape has broken down at the National Archive, and in the present climate it may well not be replaced. Meanwhile, the kines not yet transferred continue to deteriorate and may well be lost to us. Moreover, in June 1995, responding to budget cuts and a change in librarians, York University refused to house the drama script department any longer. CBC Archives has taken them back, but with shrinking resources, what is their future? Scholars will no longer have easy access to them.

58 See Rutherford's comments on early conflicts in the CBC when Jennings was controller of broadcasting; *When Television Was Young*, 56. See also Nash, *Microphone Wars*, 327, who outlines "the mistrust among CBC senior management," specifically between those, like Jennings, with their roots in programming and those who had always been administrators.

59 "Drama Subcommittee" report, 14–15. Debates over the regional question are a permanent fixture in the CBC. See John Jackson, "Contradictions, Cultural produciton, the State and Electronic Media," *Fréquence/Frequency* 3–4 (1995): 39–54.

60 Not really. *Shoestring Theatre* (1959–67) and its sucessor *Teleplay* (1967–71) kept regional anthology going for another decade.

61 See Miller, *Turn Up the Contrast*, 325–54, for more detail on the regional output.

62 CBC files at National Archives.

63 *Globe and Mail*, 6 December 1994.

64 In Benjamin Singer, ed., *Communications in Canadian Society* (Toronto: Nelson 1991).

65 "Drama Subcommittee" report, 12–13.
66 For an in-depth discussion of the regions' contribution see Miller, *Turn Up the Contrast*, 325–54, and for a different view, Collins, "Dependency Theory and Canadian Television" in Singer, *Communications in Canadian Society*, 160–89.
67 "*OVERSCAN*," in *SCAN*, November/December 1994, 2.

CHAPTER II: INTERVIEW WITH IVAN FECAN

1 From my notes, Wendy Michener Symposium, "Changing Channels: Public Broadcasting in the Ages of New TV Technologies," York University, 24 March 1993. Note that Peter Herrndorf, chair of TVO, who was the other guest, offered the opinion that "the CBC is no longer afraid of talent."
2 Knowlton Nash, *Microphone Wars: A History of Triumph and Betrayal at the CBC* (Toronto: McClelland & Stewart 1994), 509–43. Note also that Ted Kotcheff, vice-president of news and current affairs, unlike his predecessor Trina McQueen, reported to Fecan. After two years and the departure of Fecan for BBS, Kotcheff left.
3 While some of the best scripts for *North of 60* have been written by Native writers like Drew Hayden Taylor, Thomas King, and writer and senior story editor Jordan Wheeler, some of those involved are ambivalent or disillusioned. Although Gil Cuthand directed in 1995–96, *The Rez*, six half-hour episodes, was directed by Bruce McDonald based on the film *Dance Me Outside*. It will appear in 1995–96.
4 In the early 1980s C Channel (c for culture) failed after only a few months. The various monopolies offering regions of the country movie channels made money, and these channels have multiplied on some cable networks. However, Bravo, Moses Znaimer's new and interesting arts channel, is reported to be in trouble along with the other five. *Globe and Mail*, 6 July 1995.
5 Although viewers of the first two seasons will remember that Chuck was the self-made corporate lawyer, the yuppie on the upward track, interested in fast cars and a home in the postmodern style – a distinct contast to leftist Leon and nice but often naive criminal lawyer Carrie.
6 See Nash, *Microphone Wars*, 509–43, for an insider account of the reasons for the accelerated rate of repositioning and the rocky implementation of the strategy.
7 Bill Gough and Anna Sandor might be surprised to find that Ivan Fecan agrees with their passionately held view that the essential creative spark rests with the writer, not the producer.
8 Nash, *Microphone Wars*, 532. The responsibility was Trina McQueen's,

as vice-president of news and current affairs. Nash implies that her vigorous defence of the program against internal attacks was one of the reasons Veilleux replaced her with Ted Kotcheff.

9 *Million Dollar Babies* (1994) was the first of these topical and docudrama movies to be simulcast on the CBC and on an American network. In other words, American network executives had confidence in the CBC's ability to create movies that win ratings, without their first seeing the finished product.

10 *SCAN*, May/June 1993.

CHAPTER 12: WRAP-UP

1 *Globe and Mail*, 10 December 1995.

2 *Newsweek* cover story, *Time*, and *Maclean's*, May and June 1993.

3 *Globe and Mail*, 4 June 1993.

4 On the CBC southern Ontario phone-in *Radio Noon*, 17 September 1993.

5 *Globe and Mail*, Report on Business, 28 May 1993.

6 Mary Gooderham, "ZAP to the Future," ibid., 6 March 1993.

7 David Ellis, *Split Screen: Home Entertainment and the New Technologies* (Toronto: Lorimer 1993). See also Evan I. Schwartz, "People Are Supposed to Pay for This Stuff?" *Wired*, July 1995.

8 *Globe and Mail*, 18 November 1991.

9 See also Ross Eaman, *Channels of Influence: CBC Audience Research and the Canadian Public* (Toronto: University of Toronto Press 1994).

10 *Globe and Mail*, 8 June 1993.

11 Ibid., 16 June 1993.

12 *Toronto Star*, 26 June 1993.

13 One-half of the Caplan-Sauvageau federal task force, now professor at Laval, in a speech to CBC journalists, 19 June 1993.

14 In a short article condensed from the Canadian Embassy's Distinguished Lecture Series, *Toronto Star*, 10 April 1993.

15 See, for example, Tamar Liebes and Elihu Katz, "On the Critical Abilities of Television Viewers," in *Remote Control: Television, Audiences and Cultural Power* (London: Routledge 1991), 204–22, who argue that viewers readily exercise critical abilities when watching all kinds of television.

16 McQueen was quoted as saying to her science quiz's executive producer after the two teams of scientists argued about the correct atomic number of carbon, in prime time: "Can you believe this is on television? Can you believe this is on commercial television? Can you believe this is on commercial television owned by a *beer company*?" Christopher Harris, *Globe and Mail*, 28 January 1995. McQueen also says *@discovery.ca* is the only daily science program in the world.

17 *Annals of the American Geographers* 82, 1 (1992): 117–35.
18 Adams is quoting Edward Relph's *Place and Placelessness* (London: Pion Ltd 1976). Presumably Relph would not be surprised at the Main Street "themed" Mall opened in Los Angeles in 1993. This "place" allows people to shop in a careful recreation of what a city street *should* look like according to our memories or our popular culture, not what a real street in LA actually looks like in the 1990s.
19 Quoted in Harvey, *The Conditions of Postmodernity: An Enquiry into the Origins of Cultural Change* (Cambridge: Blackwell 1989), 98.
20 The word processor used to write this book has the capability of voice annotation and the inclusion of small video clips, something not possible on the printed page. Still, even the knowledgeable writers of the Web site HOTWIRED agree that nothing on screen is as accessible as a book. You can't "visit" a book or get it to talk back to you like an Internet conference, but you can talk to a book, and carry it with you into a bathtub.
21 Harvey Enchin, "Stock Market Proves Attractive," *Globe and Mail*, 17 August 1993.
22 *Globe and Mail*, 9 June 1993.
23 SCAN, May/June 1992, in "The Attack of the 100-Channel Universe III: Canadian Production: More (?) or Less(?)," 6–10.
24 SCAN, March/April 1993, in his chapter "Canadian Producers, Canadian Content," in David Ellis, *Split Screen: Home Entertainment and the New Technologies*, 7.
25 Elaborated in Mary Jane Miller, *Turn Up the Contrast: CBC Television Drama since 1952* (Vancouver: UBC Pess and the CBC 1987), 386.
26 Harvey Enchin, *Globe and Mail*, 23 March 1993.
27 *Globe and Mail*, 9 April 1992.
28 *Sunday Star*, 26 May 1993.
29 Both of 26 June 1993.
30 "Lustiny Ridge," subheaded "all the hot and heavy action's *indoors* this season on Destiny Ridge," by Jim Bawden, *Sunday Star*, 29 January 1995. Bawden reports that the ratings have gone down this season, which certainly proves that viewers are unpredictable. See the apparent correlation of bedroom scenes with increased ratings on *Street Legal*. Maybe the decline demonstrates that the characters have to click with the viewers, who can find steam rising at any time of day somewhere on television.
31 "Making Canada in the 1990s: Film, Culture, and Industry," in Kenneth McRoberts, ed., *Beyond Quebec: Taking Stock of Canada* (Montreal and Kingston: McGill-Queen's University Press 1995), 173–4. Many things have changed since the new and small Atlantis company won an Academy Award for "Sons and Daughters," one half-hour of a six-part anthology called *Boys and Girls* for the CBC.

32 "Canadian participation in International Co-productions and Co-ventures in Television Programming," *Canadian Journal of Communication* 18 (spring 1993): 219–36. For an update on current profits, losses, alliances, and where they may lead in Canada, see Magder, "Making Canada in the 1990s." For a variant on the theme of deals, see *TV Guide*, 28 January 28, 1995, "Blowing Smoke," which reports that the new CBC series for the twenty-somethings, *Liberty Street*, has a character who is struggling to quit smoking because Health Canada has given the production company a hefty grant. The initiative came from producer Linda Schuyler.

33 *Globe and Mail*, 18 April 1993.

34 Duke was producer/director of *Q for Quest* and other interesting CBC television drama and documentary experiments in the 1960s and, later, of mini-series like *The Thornbirds* for American TV. Clarkson is the presenter and producer of an eclectic prime-time arts program bearing her name. See *Canadian Forum*, March and May 1993, and "A Dream of the CBC," ibid., January/February 1995, 37. His review begins and ends with Graham Spry and Arthur Plaunt as young men. Their dream of public ownership of broadcasting gathered support from people all over the country into a Radio League, which pushed successfully for public broadcasting made and regulated in Canada.

35 Richard Collins, *Culture, Communication and National Identity: The Case of Canadian Television* (Toronto: University of Toronto Press 1990), chapter 7.

36 Anticipating governmental cuts before the exit of the NDP and the entrance of the "commonsense" Tories, Herrndorf in 1995 supervised a cutback of his own TVO of 20 per cent, or 130 jobs. Premier Harris had mused aloud about privatizing TVO, as Premier Klein has done with a similar station in Alberta. But as Alberta found with Access, the problem is that not much money is saved unless the Ministry of Education no longer requires television programs for the classroom. These programs must still be purchased from the local experts who are to be found at the educational television stations. The tasks and the costs remain.

37 Elly Alboim, CBC Ottawa bureau chief, was roundly criticized by ex–CRTC chair John Meisel for bias in the CBC coverage, a charge since debated in academic circles. See David Taras, "The Mass Media and Political Crisis: Reporting Canada's Constitutional Struggles," *Canadian Journal of Communications* (1993): 131–48. The CBC defended him publicly after an internal investigation, but is said to have rebuked him privately, and in June 1993 he left the corporation and broadcasting.

38 In "A Matter of Communication," Suzanne Kelman, *SCAN*, May/June 1993, 3–5.

39 *SCAN*, May/June 1993.

40 *SCAN*, May/June 1994, 25.

41 Other CanWest/Global co-productions are listed by Paul W. Taylor in "Third Service, Third Network: The CanWest Global System," *Canadian Journal of Communication* (autumn 1993): 469–77. Taylor sees no problem in making uninflected and undistinguished action-adventure formats and others. He does, however, remind us that this network gave a new lease on life to the solidly written family/adventure programme *Neon Rider*.

42 *Globe and Mail*, 22 June 1991.

43 Ibid., 3 August 1991.

44 *Television in Europe* (Oxford: Oxford University Press 1991), 8–9.

45 *Globe and Mail*, 27 February 1995.

46 Sid Adilman, *Toronto Star*, 5 October 1991.

47 The best-known example, much discussed in the papers and on television itself in 1992–93, was the case of Amy Fisher. In that television season viewers could watch three movies of the week, one each by ABC, NBC, and CBS. All three "docudramas" were filmed and broadcast within a year of the events depicted. Many of my year 3 communications students watched one of them, but only one student, in the spirit of critical inquiry, watched all three. If this was typical, such a surfeit may not happen again. On the other hand, O.J. Simpson coverage specials range from tabloid TV to the headlines of CBC News, with many miniseries to come. Fox network ran an O.J.Simpson docudrama on 31 January 1995 – after the lawyers' opening statements, but before any evidence had been presented in his trial. The CBC's Newsworld offered two fifteen-minute summaries of the trial a day and live afternoon coverage – and received complaints about even that much time being spent on a foreign story like this on "our" news service.

48 *Toronto Star*, 8 December 1990.

49 *Globe and Mail*, 31 August 1989.

50 See Miller, *Turn Up the Contrast*, chapter 3.

51 *Maclean's*, 30 August 1993.

52 *Globe and Mail*, 15 June 1995.

53 Most American programming is cheaper to buy than making our own, but I share Greg Quill's surprise (*Toronto Star*, 2 June 1995) that the director of entertainment, at this crucial time, "cancelled 90 minutes a week of original, inexpensive, popular Canadian, CBC-produced material and [replaced] it with 90 minutes of untested, expensive, American network fodder." The programs cancelled were indeed modest: *Ear to the Ground, Front Page Challenge,* and *Sunday Arts Entertainment.* None of them were broadcast in the 8–10 PM prime-time slot), but it is hard to justify in this climate the purchase of an Aaron Spelling (*Charlie's*

Angels, Beverley Hills 90210) night-time soap called *Central Park West* and an American sitcom for prime time. The 1995–96 season at the CBC includes the second seasons of *Side Effects* and *Liberty Street*, the fourth season of *North of 60*, and the last season of *Road to Avonlea*, all co-productions, as well as four or five movies, including Bernie Zukerman's *Net Worth* about the early efforts of the NHL players to organize, and Anne Wheeler's *The War Between Us*. There are few in-house mini-series and movies – indeed, any drama specials.

54 Conversation, August 1993, with Sheila Feinstone, MP from Montreal, then Liberal critic for cultural matters, and staunch but not uncritical supporter of the CBC as public broadcaster.

55 Three months earlier the *Globe and Mail*, 16 March 1995, reported that Radio-Canada had to lose 750 jobs as its share of the budget cuts and that savings could not come from the regions, so would have to come directly from programming. Michele Fortin, vice-president of Radio-Canada, said: "We will do less drama, we will cut costly shows that don't bring in revenue and we won't be able to do quality cultural shows." She also said that "to leave French television in Quebec to a single private network is cultural suicide."

56 Nicholas Hirst, researched by *SCAN*'s editor Andrew Borkowski, 25 February 1995, 20–4.

57 *Starweek*, 17 June 1995.

58 *Toronto Star*, 18 March 1995.

59 Ibid., 12 July 1995.

60 *Globe and Mail*, 12 April 1995.

61 Ibid., 6 May 1995.

62 Ibid., 13 April 1995.

63 The headline "Global, CHCH-TV short on new Canadian content" tells it all. Greg Quill reports that Global, a powerful independent station in Hamilton, Ontario, will have a co-production reviving the old radio and television favourite from the 1940s to the 1960s: *Jake and the Kid*, *Traders* (about the high-pressure world of commodity futures at the TSE), and twenty-four more episodes of their very good drama for young teens, *Ready or Not*, as well as *The New Red Green Show*, a gentle satire – two-and-a-half hours worth, as well as eight American shows. CHCH had picked up reruns of *Counterstike*, the inexpensive *Comedy Club*, and a U.S. co-produced sitcom *Boogie's Diner* – two hours worth plus ten American shows.

64 *Globe and Mail*, 15 April 1995.

65 *St Catharines Standard* and *Globe and Mail*, 22 June 1995.

66 *Globe and Mail*, 5 July 1995.

67 Ibid., 11 July 1995.

68 See Marina Devine, "Connecting the North," *Aboriginal Voices: The Magazine of Evolving Native American Arts* 2, 2 (1995): 41–3, which outlines the history of the CBC and IBC (Inuit Broadcasting Corporation) in the North and argues persuasively for the interdependence of indigenous broadcasting and cultural survival.
69 "TVO Braces for Privatization Push," *Globe and Mail*, 23 June 1995.

Biographies

ROBERT ALLEN   Producer/director of early CBC dramas such as *Sunshine Sketches*. Allen became program director of CBLT, but returned to producing and became the supervising producer in charge of *Folio*, *Ford Startime*, *First Performance*, and the CBC flagship anthology *Festival*. He was executive producer of several anthologies in the 1970s and 1980s, and is now retired.

PAUL ALMOND   Producer/director of more than one hundred television dramas in Toronto, London, and Los Angeles between 1954 and 1967. Almond has produced and directed dramas for CBC's *On Camera*, *Folio*, *General Motors Theatre*, *Television Theatre*, *General Motors Presents*, *The Unforeseen*, *Play of the Week*, *First Person*, *Festival*, *Q for Quest*, *Playdate*, *Telescope*, and *Wojeck*. His award-winning films include *Isabel* (1967), *The Act of the Heart* (1969), *Journey* (1971), *Final Assignment* (1979), *Every Person is Guilty* (1980), *Ups and Downs* (1981), and *Captive Hearts* (1987).

DAVID BARLOW   Producer/writer and director who started out at the CBC as a unit manager and before that was a stage manager in Canadian theatre. He worked first as associate producer on the *King of Kensington* series in the 1970s and as co-producer, co-creator, and writer of the successful series *Seeing Things*, 1980–86. He co-produced and co-directed *Breaking All the Rules* in 1987 and *Sanity Clause* in 1989, and wrote the script for the feature film *The Prom*, released in 1990. He was supervising story editor and one of the writers on the first season of *North of 60* and producer on *Side Effects*.

IVAN FECAN Director of programming and head of variety at the CBC before heading to Los Angeles as a vice-president at NBC and assistant to Brandon Tarkitoff. He returned to the CBC in 1987, where he became the director of programming. In 1991 he was appointed vice-president of arts and entertainment, English television, and in 1993 he became the vice-president of English television. In 1994 he moved to the Baton Broadcasting System as vice-president of programming.

DAVID GARDNER Actor/producer/director. Gardner produced many televised play adaptations for anthology series such as *Folio*, *Festival*, and *The Unforeseen* in the 1960s, including *Jake and the Kid*, *Mr Member of Parliament*, *Quentin Durgens MP*, and *Yesterday the Children Were Dancing*. He also directed the controversial and brilliant film *The Paper People*. Originally an actor, Gardner returned to acting and directing for the theatre and spent several seasons as a character on *Home Fires* as well as appearing in other CBC dramas. Although he continues to appear in commercials and in series television, he says he is retired.

HUGH GAUNTLETT Middle manager in a variety of capacities from the mid-1960s on. He was the head of arts and science programming in the early 1980s, then went on to be head of TV program development for Eastern Canada. He is retired.

BILL GOUGH Producer/director/writer who started out in radio and then moved to television, where he directed 300 short films for *Here and Now: The Supper Hour Show* before producing many television drama specials including *The Accident* (1983), *Anne's Story* (1984), *Charlie Grant's War* (1984), *The Suicide Murders* (1985), *The Marriage Bed* (1986), *Mama's Gonna Buy You a Mockingbird* (1988), and *Two Men* (1988). He has also produced and written episodes for series such as *Seeing Things* and *The Campbells*. He now works in the United States.

NADA HARCOURT Stage actor turned television writer Harcourt became interested in current affairs and children's drama, went on to become head of children's drama, and helped to develop *The Kids of Degrassi*. She was the head of development for dramatic series for several years, and executive producer of the hit series *Street Legal*.

DENIS HARVEY A newspaper journalist at the start of his career, Harvey became the executive editor of the *Montreal Gazette*, which he left in 1973 to join the CBC in Toronto. There he became chief TV News editor and, later, the assistant general manager of CBC English Service until 1978. Between 1978 and 1981 Harvey was editorial director, editor-in-chief, and vice-president of the *Toronto Star*. In 1982 he became the head of TV Sports at the CBC, and in 1983 was appointed vice-president of the CBC English Television Network. He retired in 1990 to become a special adviser to Gérard Veilleux, president of the CBC. He is retired.

PHILIP KEATLEY   Producer/director Philip Keatley worked on many projects with the CBC, including the award-winning drama special *The Education of the Phyllistine* (1965) and *How to Break a Quarter Horse* (1968). He developed and produced many series for the CBC, including *Cariboo Country* (1963–67), *The Beachcombers* (1971–77), *The Magic Lie* (1975–78), and *Ritters Cove* (1978). Keatley headed the Vancouver Drama Department from 1968 to 1978, and then headed the CBC training program for a few years. He went on to become the western development head of drama from 1987 to 1990. He is retired.

MARTIN KINCH   A director in the early days of Theatre Passe Muraille, Kinch spent a decade as artistic director of Toronto Free Theatre. He joined the CBC in the early 1980s and produced the series of historical drama specials *Some Honourable Gentlemen*. Kinch left the CBC to become the artistic director at Theatre Calgary. He is currently returning to another love – writing plays.

SAM LEVENE   Producer/director/writer who worked on many early CBC series, including *This Hour Has Seven Days*, *Telescope*, and *Gallery*. He was the executive producer of *For the Record* (1978–82) and the series *Vanderberg*. He has been the executive producer on many CBC films, including *Joshua Then and Now* (1984), *Twelfth Night* (1985), *One For the Pot* (1985), and *Murder Sees the Light* (1986). Since 1987 Levene has been working as producer/director/writer on music and dance specials and on the long-running *Man Alive*.

JEANNINE LOCKE   Editorial writer and journalist who wrote and produced all her own film scripts for the CBC, including projects for the anthology *People of Our Time* (1973, 1974), *The Family Prince* (1975), *The Woodsworth Phenomenon* (1976). *The Canadian Monarchy* (1977), and *The Quieter Revolution* (1978). She turned to drama with the three-part docudrama *You've Come a Long Way Katie* (1979–80), *Chautauqua Girl* (1982), *All the Days of My Life* (1981–82), *The Other*

Kingdom (1984), *Island Love Song* (1986), *The Private Capitol* (1988) and *the Greening of Ian Elliot* (1991). She is retired.

MARYKE MCEWEN   Producer of several films for the *For the Record* series, including *Rough Justice, Ready for Slaughter,* and *Blind Faith,* as well as the drama special *Kate Morris, VP* and *Shellgame,* the pilot for *Street Legal.* McEwen then developed, produced, and became executive producer of the hit series *Street Legal* (1986–88) and producer of *Diary of a Street Kid* (1992) and *The Diary of Evelyn Lau.*

TRINA MCQUEEN   A journalist who co-hosted the first season of CTV's *W5,* McQueen then worked as a reporter for national news events covering political conventions and eventually became the executive producer of *The National* in 1978. From 1980 to 1984 she served as program director for the English Television Network, and in 1991 was appointed the vice-president of news and current affairs and Newsworld for the CBC English Network. In 1993 she left the CBC to become president of the innovative specialty channel Discovery.

MAVOR MOORE   Director/writer/actor who has had a long, varied, and productive career in theatre, radio, and television and has chaired the Canada Council. An esteemed playwright, Moore has written more than one hundred plays, musicals, and operas and also writes for radio. He was the first chief producer for CBC English language, and his credits include television adaptations of *Yesterday the Children Were Dancing* and *The Puppet Caravan* (1967), the script for *Inside Out* (1970), six plays for *Program X* (1971–72), and *the Roncarelli Affair* for *The Play's the Thing* (1974). Since then he has taught for a decade and chaired the theatre department at York University, written more plays, acted on television, headed the Canada Council, and written a memoir. He is unlikely to retire.

SIDNEY NEWMAN   Director and editor who joined the National Film Board in 1941. He came to the CBC in 1952, became supervising producer in the Drama Department in 1954, and was responsible for producing *General Motors Theatre* (later *General Motors Presents*), including the first production of *Flight into Danger* as well as the anthologies *On Camera* and *Here and Now.* In 1957 Newman went on to shake up television drama in Great Britain as drama head first of ABC and then of the BBC. In 1970 he returned to be the commissioner of the National Film Board (1970–75), governor of the Canadian Conference on the Arts (1978–82), and then creative consultant to the Canadian Film Development Centre (1982–84). More recently he has also worked on film projects for Britain's channel 4 and other clients.

JOE PARTINGTON He began at the CBC as a unit manager and worked his way up through the ranks until becoming a producer in 1977. Partington's work includes the last two seasons of *King of Kensington, Flappers, Hangin' In*, of which he was also co-creator, and the first season of *Material World*, as well as co-producing the CBC film *Sanity Clause*.

MARIO PRIZEK Producer/director who has produced every type of radio and television program from news and public affairs to documentary, variety shows, drama, opera, ballet, and children's programs. Prizek joined the CBC in 1951 and produced many dramas for anthologies, such as *Folio, Festival, Q for Quest, Ford Startime, General Motors Presents, Program X*, and *Eye Opener*, producing noted dramas such as *The Unburied Dead, Queen after Death, Galileo*, and *Lady Windermere's Fan*. He has spent thirty-five years working for the CBC, and also worked for Granada TV and the BBC in England, NET in the United States, and Classart Films in West Germany. He is retired.

HERB ROLAND Producer/director who has spent forty years producing, directing, writing, and acting for theatre, television, and film. He has produced more than 150 television dramas for the CBC on film and tape, including *House of Pride, A Gift to Last, Judge*, and *To Serve and Protect*, as well as many television stage adaptations for drama anthologies. He is retired.

ANNA SANDOR Stage and television actor turned writer who has written many episodes for CBC series, including *For the Record, King of Kensington, Hangin' In, Seeing Things*, and *Danger Bay*. Sandor has also written many successful film scripts, such as *A Population of One* (1979), *Charlie Grant's War* (1985), *The Marriage Bed* (1986), *Martha, Ruth and Edie* (1987), *Mama's Going to Buy You a Mockingbird* (1987), and *Two Men* (1988). Sandor now works in the United States.

ALICE SINCLAIR Story editor who joined the CBC in 1959. Sinclair has developed many scripts with writers and producers. She eventually became the supervisor of the Story Department at CBC Drama, evaluating scripts and heading up all administrative duties connected with writers. Her more recent credits include the series *Backstretch*, and drama specials *Gentle Sinners, A Nest of Singing Birds*, and *Getting Married in Buffalo Jump*. She is deceased.

ERIC TILL Director/producer who has been with the CBC since 1957 directing many successful dramas, including *Pale Horse, Pale Rider, Kim, Freedom of the City* (1974), *Bethune* (1977), *If You Could See What*

I Hear (1982), *Gentle Sinners* (1983), *Turning to Stone* (1985), *Glory Enough for All* (1989), and *Getting Married in Buffalo Jump* (1990). Till has also directed dramatic segments of *the National Dream* and episodes of *Home Fires* and other series.

R.H. THOMSON   Actor/director who has been making his mark on the Canadian stage since the mid-1970s, primarily in Toronto, in starring roles that stretch from experimental theatre to Hamlet. His work for the CBC includes *Tyler, Hal Banks: Canada's Sweetheart, Escape from Iran, Charlies Grant's War, Glory Enough for All,* and *The First Season.* He also has a continuing role as Jasper Dale on the CBC's hit series *Road to Avonlea.*

KATE TROTTER   Actor who has had starring roles in the Canadian theatre since the 1970s doing everything from the Tarragon Theatre and the Blyth Festival to the Stratford and Shaw festivals. Her television career includes guest appearances on *Judge, For the Record, Street Legal,* and *The Campbells,* as well as several films such as *Joshua Then and Now, Glory Enough for All,* and *The First Season.*

ED VINCENT   Sound effects technician and music consultant who has worked on many drama projets with the CBC since 1954, including *The Great Detective* and *The Beachcombers* in the 1970s. He is retired.

HUGH WEBSTER   Actor/writer who wrote, adapted, and acted in many of the early dramas for anthologies such as *Folio* and *General Motors Presents.* Teaming up with producer/director Eric Till, he adapted dramas like *Offshore Island* and wrote *Kim,* while acting in drama specials such as *Galileo, The Black Bonspiel of Wullie MacCrimmon, The Odds and the Gods,* and revues such as *Oh Canada.* He is deceased.

RON WEYMAN   Executive producer of film drama who has had a varied career. In the 1950s Weyman spent seven years with the National Film Board, where he produced, directed, wrote, and edited more than twenty films. He travelled extensively and learned the trade of shooting film on location, a skill he eventually brought back to the CBC. He was responsible for such programs as *The Serial,* the hit series *Wojeck, Quentin Durgens MP, Hatch's Mill,* and *McQueen: The Actioneer,* as well as producing several drama specials in the 1970s. He is retired.

DON S. WILLIAMS Director, producer, and executive producer who directed drama series such as *Ritter's Cove* and *The Beachcombers*, as well as drama specials such as the award-winning *Death of a Nobody*, a ballet based on *The Ecstacy of Rita Joe*, an adaptation of the post-nuclear cabaret *Last Call*, and the docudrama *Chung Chuck*.

GRAHAME WOOD Cameraman turned writer who has written many scripts for CBC drama. His scripts include "After All, Who's Art Morrison?" in the *Wojeck* series, the drama special *Twelve and a Half Cents* (1970) and its sequel *Vicky* (1973), *Strike!* (1971), ten episodes of *The Collaborators* (1973–74), *War Brides* (1979), various *For the Record* dramas, *Anne's Story* (1981), *Glory Enough for All* (1987), and *The Courage of the Early Morning* (1991).

Index